Stargirl

BY GEOFF JOHNS

GEOFF JOHNS
JAMES ROBINSON
DAVID S. GOYER
Writers

Stargirl
BY GEOFF JOHNS

LEE MODER
SCOTT KOLINS
DAN DAVIS
CHRIS WESTON
JOHN STOKES
MIKE McKONE
WAYNE FAUCHER
Artists

TOM McCRAW
CARLA FEENY
JOHN KALISZ
Colorists

BILL OAKLEY
KURT HATHAWAY
Letterers

LEE MODER and DAN DAVIS
with RICHARD & TANYA HORIE
JOHN CASSADAY and MARK LEWIS
with DAVID BARON
Original Series Covers

COURTNEY WHITMORE
created by
GEOFF JOHNS
and LEE MODER

SUPERMAN created by JERRY SIEGEL and JOE SHUSTER
SUPERBOY created by JERRY SIEGEL
SUPERGIRL based on characters created by JERRY SIEGEL
By special arrangement with the Jerry Siegel family

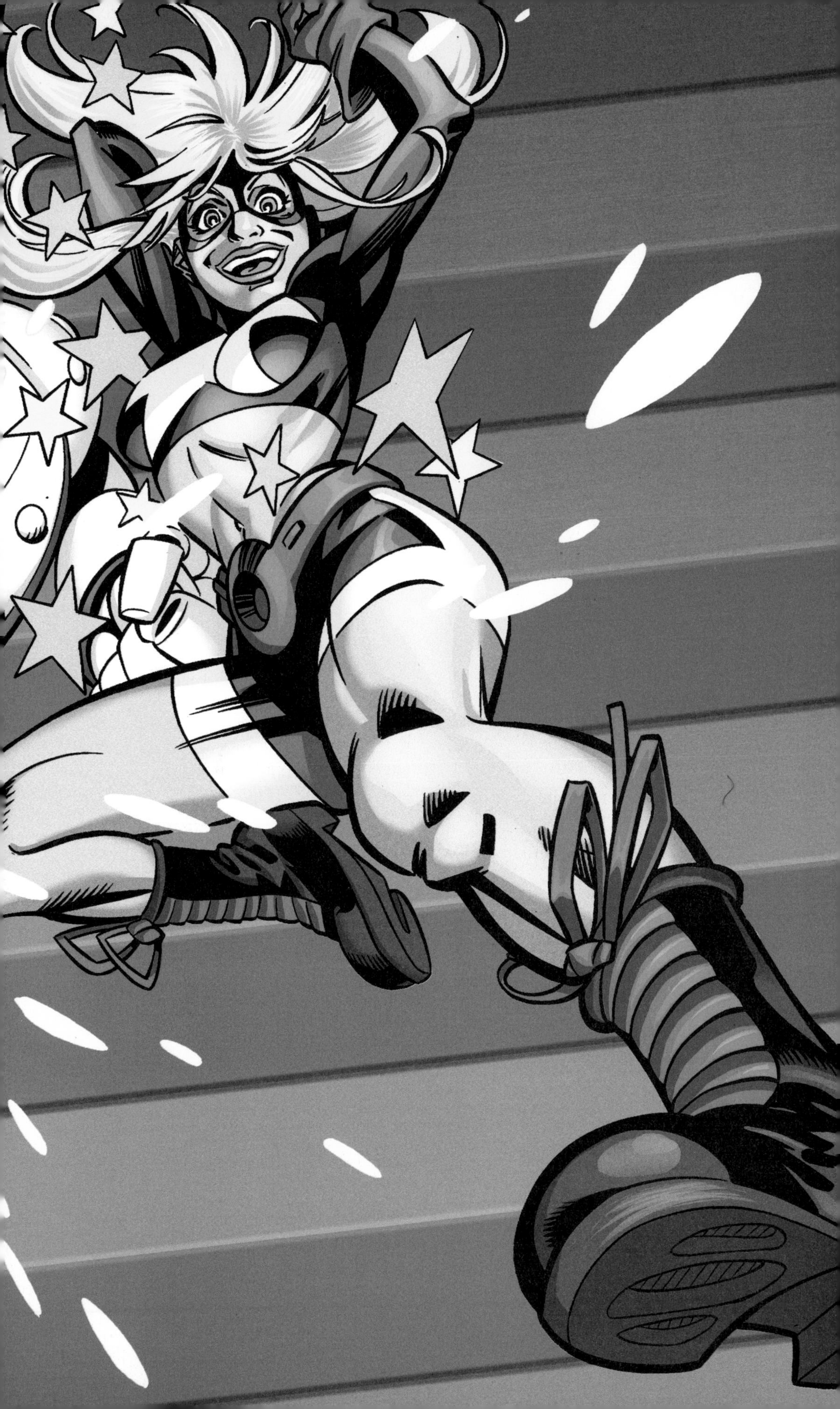

MIKE CARLIN, CHUCK KIM, PETER J. TOMASI Editors - Original Series
STEPHEN WACKER Associate Editor - Original Series
L.A. WILLIAMS Assistant Editor - Original Series
JEB WOODARD Group Editor - Collected Editions
REZA LOKMAN Editor - Collected Edition
STEVE COOK Design Director - Books
AMIE BROCKWAY-METCALF Publication Design
CHRISTY SAWYER Publication Production

BOB HARRAS Senior VP - Editor-in-Chief, DC Comics

DAN DiDIO Publisher
JIM LEE Publisher & Chief Creative Officer
BOBBIE CHASE VP - New Publishing Initiatives
DON FALLETTI VP - Manufacturing Operations & Workflow Management
LAWRENCE GANEM VP - Talent Services
ALISON GILL Senior VP - Manufacturing & Operations
HANK KANALZ Senior VP - Publishing Strategy & Support Services
DAN MIRON VP - Publishing Operations
NICK J. NAPOLITANO VP - Manufacturing Administration & Design
NANCY SPEARS VP - Sales
JONAH WEILAND VP - Marketing & Creative Services
MICHELE R. WELLS VP & Executive Editor, Young Reader

STARGIRL BY GEOFF JOHNS

Published by DC Comics. Compilation, cover, and all new material Copyright © 2020 DC Comics. All Rights
Reserved. Originally published in single magazine form in *Stars and S.T.R.I.P.E.* 0, 1-14, and *JSA All Stars* 4.
Copyright © 1999, 2000, 2003 DC Comics. All Rights Reserved. All characters, their distinctive
likenesses, and related elements featured in this publication are trademarks of DC Comics. The stories,
characters, and incidents featured in this publication are entirely fictional. DC Comics does not read or
accept unsolicited submissions of ideas, stories, or artwork.
DC - a WarnerMedia Company.

DC Comics
2900 West Alameda Ave.
Burbank, CA 91505
Printed by LSC Communications, Owensville, MO, USA. 4/10/20.
First Printing.
ISBN: 978-1-4012-9712-1
Library of Congress Cataloging-in-Publication Data is available.

INTRODUCTION

I've written more than 500 comics, but *Stars and S.T.R.I.P.E.* represents the very first. So before you delve into the adventures of a young girl who discovers her stepfather was once a super-hero sidekick, let me tell you quickly how this all came about...

I fell in love with comic books on a Sunday afternoon when my brother and I discovered my uncle's box of Silver Age books in my grandmother's attic. From there I found the comics of the late 1980s. My imagination was captured by Keith Giffen's *Justice League*, Grant Morrison's *Animal Man*, Peter David's *Hulk*, Neil Gaiman's *The Sandman*, Peter Milligan's *Shade, The Changing Man*, Roger Stern's *Avengers* and John Ostrander's *Suicide Squad*, to name several.

I always thought about drawing and writing comics, but I ended up gravitating toward film-making in college. I graduated from Michigan State University and moved out to Los Angeles to pursue screenwriting. I got my apartment off the Internet. I had a few thousand dollars saved up. And I owned a Grand Am. After weeks of eating Jeno's Pizzas and Pringles every day to save some cash, I ended up with an unpaid internship at Richard Donner's production company. He had directed my favorite film of all time: *Superman: The Movie.*

I remembered something Stan Lee once said about his first job. He ran everywhere. He did it to get things done and to let people know they could rely on him. I did the same thing. And a few months after I was interning, I was hired by Dick Donner as his assistant.

That fall, I was in New York City shooting *Conspiracy Theory.* I met some people from DC Comics, specifically an editor named Chuck Kim. Chuck and I talked for hours about film and comics, and before I left town he asked me if I'd ever thought about writing. I was working over 90 hours a week and writing whenever I could. It took more than a year for me to get a pitch together, but thankfully he was still interested.

At first, we were going to call it *Star-Spangled Kid*, and even at one point *My Greatest Adventure*, but we eventually settled on *Stars and S.T.R.I.P.E.* I wanted to create a super-hero for teenage girls—someone who wasn't a sidekick and who would actually grow over time. I used my sister as the inspiration for it all.

Lee Moder, the artist of this book and co-creator, signed on and started doing some amazing sketches. I'll never forget the day the fax machine in the trailer started spitting them out, on that ultra-thin rolled fax paper. I still have those early designs, and you can see a bunch of them at the back of this volume.

Now for the other half of the *Stars and S.T.R.I.P.E.* equation. Next to the Star-Spangled Kid (Courtney Whitmore) was her stepfather, Pat Dugan. Formerly a sidekick named Stripesy, it was planned that Pat would build a robot that he could control to follow his stepdaughter whenever she went into action. For the longest time, Pat was going to be based back at the basement while the Star-Spangled Kid was out fighting crime. But a month before we turned in the proposal, Chuck called me and said there was a book coming out called *Trouble Magnet* with a girl and a robot. The robot had to go! So we brainstormed, and it turned out to be the best thing that could have happened—it forced us to rethink the entire project, and Pat ended up wearing the robotic S.T.R.I.P.E. suit rather than remotely controlling it. In hindsight, without Pat side by side with Court, this patriotic duo would've lost a lot.

Stars and S.T.R.I.P.E. got approved as a monthly book. I loved working on it. Every second. Even if most of it was on the weekends and nights between my assistant job hours.

Courtney went on to become a mainstay in the Justice Society of America as Stargirl, and my greatest hero in all of this, Chuck Kim, went on to join the writing staff of *Heroes* on NBC. I was fortunate enough to keep writing comics.

I owe so many people thanks for what was my start in this wonderful world: Mike Carlin, Lee Moder, Dan Davis, Tom McCraw, Ivan Cohen, Tommy Zellers, Dick Donner, Lauren Shuler-Donner, Paul Levitz, James Robinson, Phil Jimenez, Peter Tomasi, my parents and my brother and my sister.

This book's a little green, but I think you'll have a lot of fun with it. Thanks for picking it up!

—Geoff Johns
2007

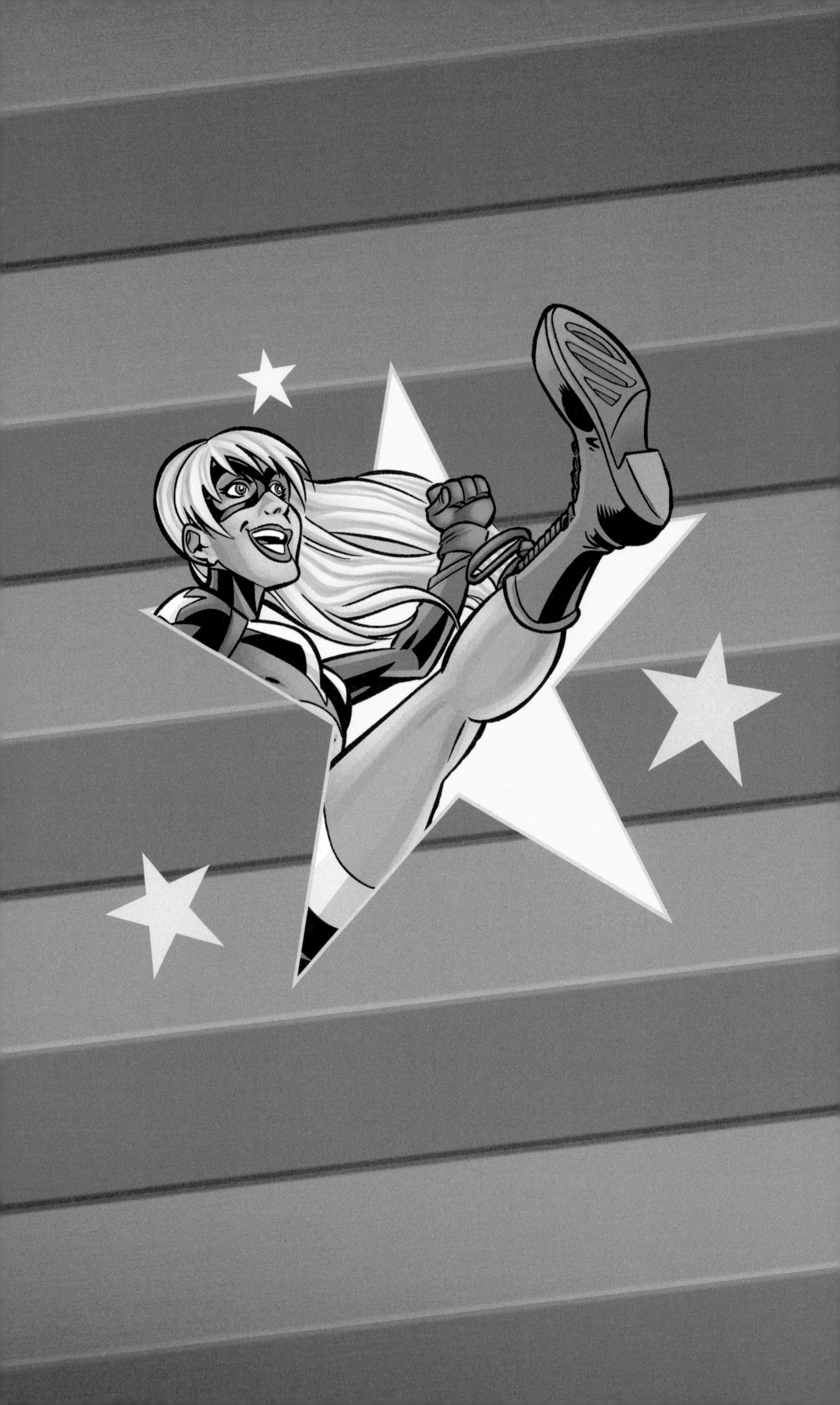

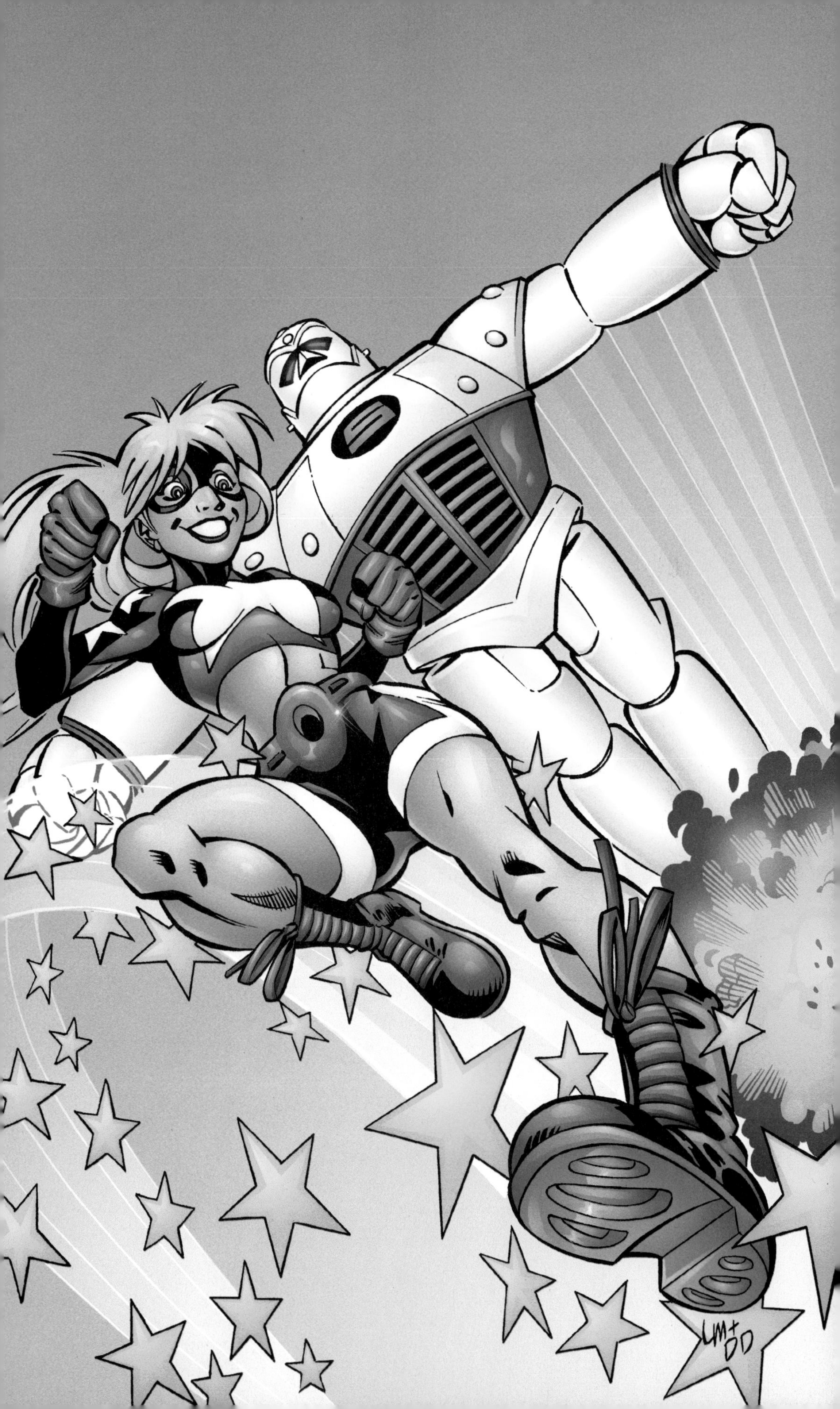

STARS AND S.T.R.I.P.E. #1

Written by GEOFF JOHNS
Pencils by LEE MODER
Inks by DAN DAVIS
Colors by TOM McCRAW
Letters by BILL OAKLEY
Cover art by LEE MODER and DAN DAVIS
Cover color by RICHARD & TANYA HORIE

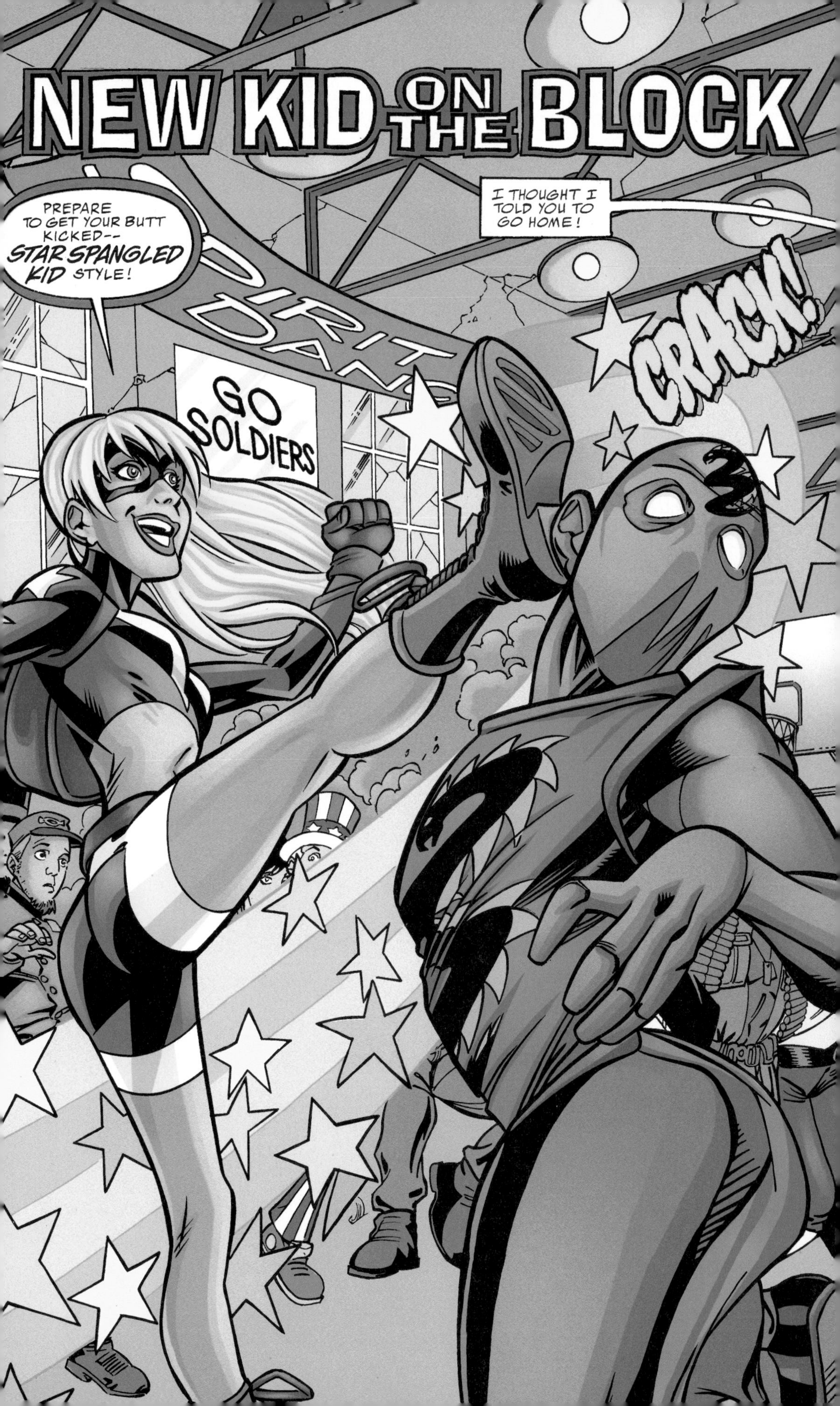

NEW KID ON THE BLOCK
PREPARE TO GET YOUR BUTT KICKED-- STAR SPANGLED KID STYLE!
I THOUGHT I TOLD YOU TO GO HOME!
GO SOLDIERS
CRACK!

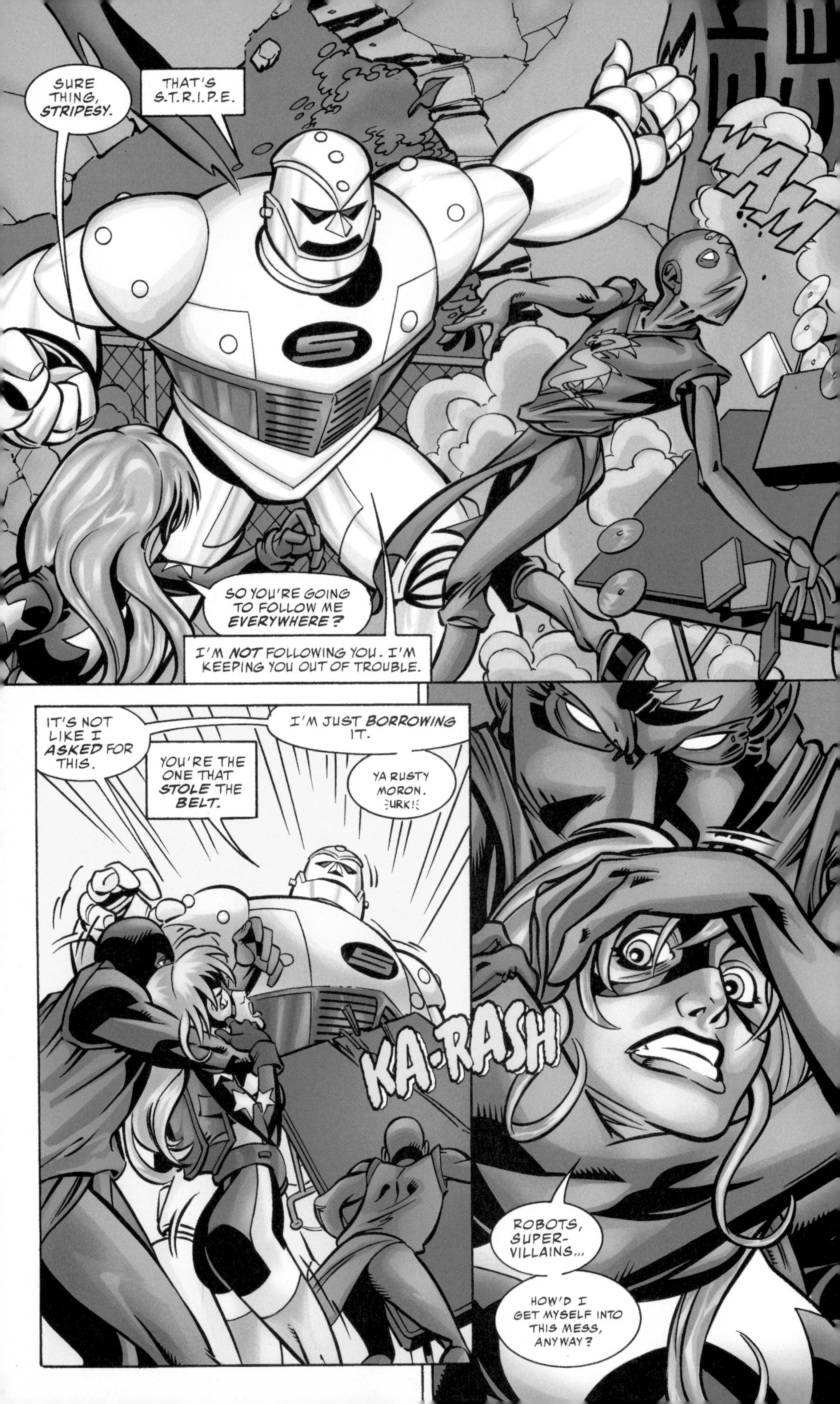

SURE THING, STRIPESY.
THAT'S S.T.R.I.P.E.
WAM
SO YOU'RE GOING TO FOLLOW ME EVERYWHERE?
I'M NOT FOLLOWING YOU. I'M KEEPING YOU OUT OF TROUBLE.
IT'S NOT LIKE I ASKED FOR THIS.
YOU'RE THE ONE THAT STOLE THE BELT.
I'M JUST BORROWING IT.
YA RUSTY MORON. URK!
KA-RASH
ROBOTS, SUPER-VILLAINS...
HOW'D I GET MYSELF INTO THIS MESS, ANYWAY?

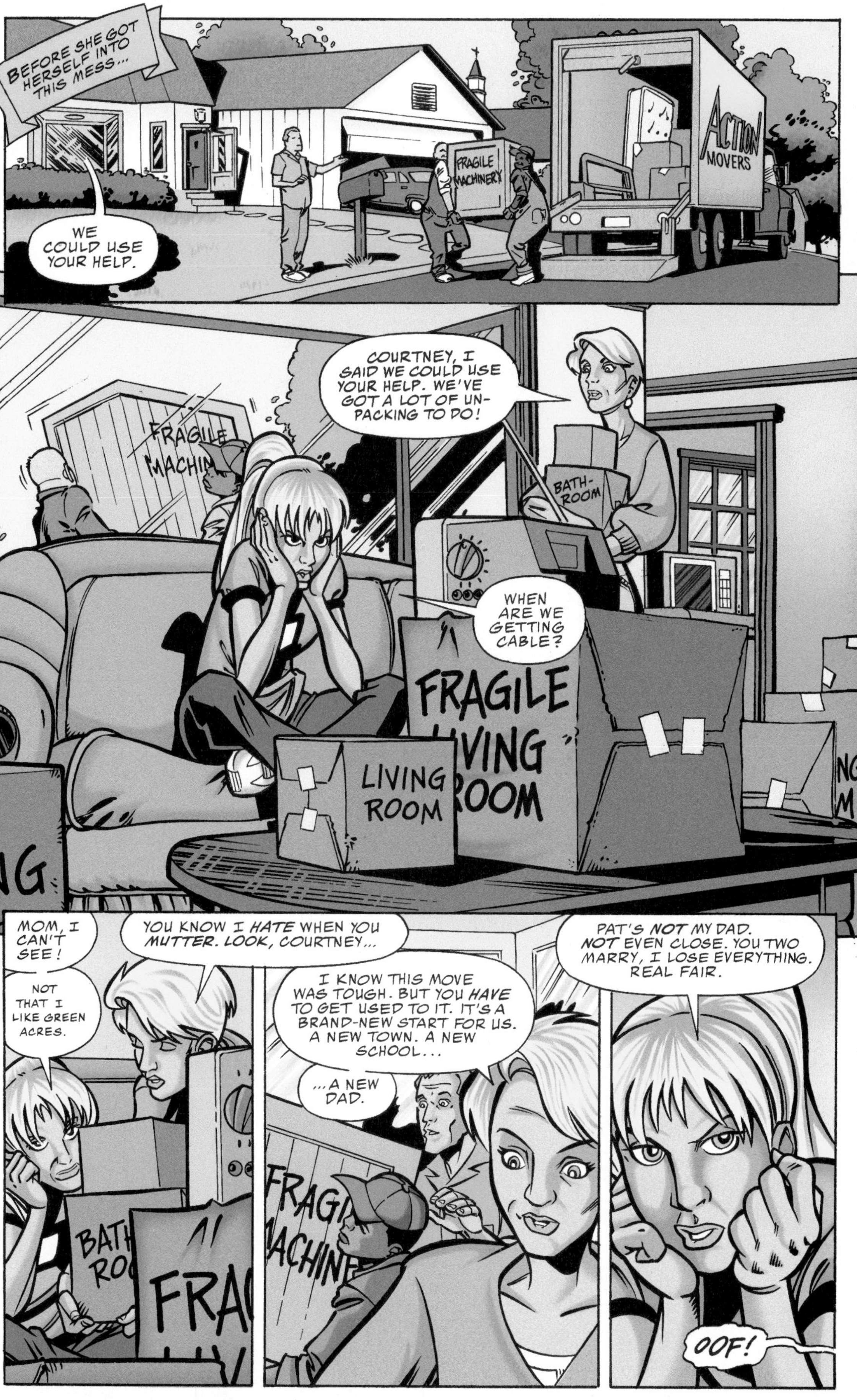
BEFORE SHE GOT HERSELF INTO THIS MESS...
WE COULD USE YOUR HELP.
FRAGILE MACHINERY
ACTION MOVERS
COURTNEY, I SAID WE COULD USE YOUR HELP. WE'VE GOT A LOT OF UN-PACKING TO DO!
WHEN ARE WE GETTING CABLE?
FRAGILE LIVING ROOM
LIVING ROOM
BATH-ROOM
MOM, I CAN'T SEE!
NOT THAT I LIKE GREEN ACRES.
YOU KNOW I HATE WHEN YOU MUTTER. LOOK, COURTNEY...
I KNOW THIS MOVE WAS TOUGH. BUT YOU HAVE TO GET USED TO IT. IT'S A BRAND-NEW START FOR US. A NEW TOWN. A NEW SCHOOL...
...A NEW DAD.
PAT'S NOT MY DAD. NOT EVEN CLOSE. YOU TWO MARRY, I LOSE EVERYTHING. REAL FAIR.
OOF!

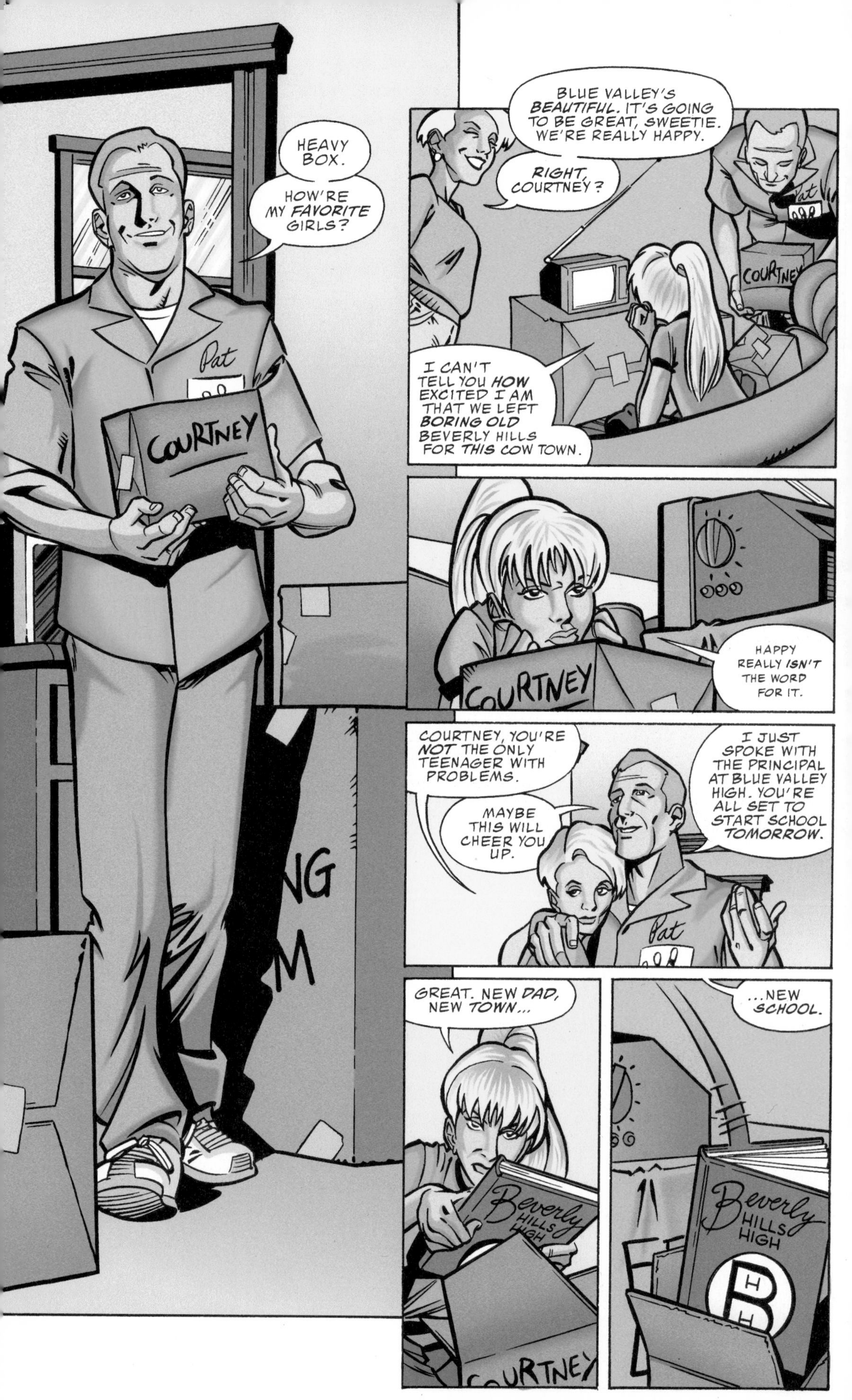
HEAVY BOX.
HOW'RE MY FAVORITE GIRLS?
BLUE VALLEY'S BEAUTIFUL. IT'S GOING TO BE GREAT, SWEETIE. WE'RE REALLY HAPPY.
RIGHT, COURTNEY?
I CAN'T TELL YOU HOW EXCITED I AM THAT WE LEFT BORING OLD BEVERLY HILLS FOR THIS COW TOWN.
COURTNEY
HAPPY REALLY ISN'T THE WORD FOR IT.
COURTNEY
COURTNEY, YOU'RE NOT THE ONLY TEENAGER WITH PROBLEMS.
I JUST SPOKE WITH THE PRINCIPAL AT BLUE VALLEY HIGH. YOU'RE ALL SET TO START SCHOOL TOMORROW.
MAYBE THIS WILL CHEER YOU UP.
GREAT. NEW DAD, NEW TOWN...
Beverly HILLS HIGH
...NEW SCHOOL.
Beverly HILLS HIGH

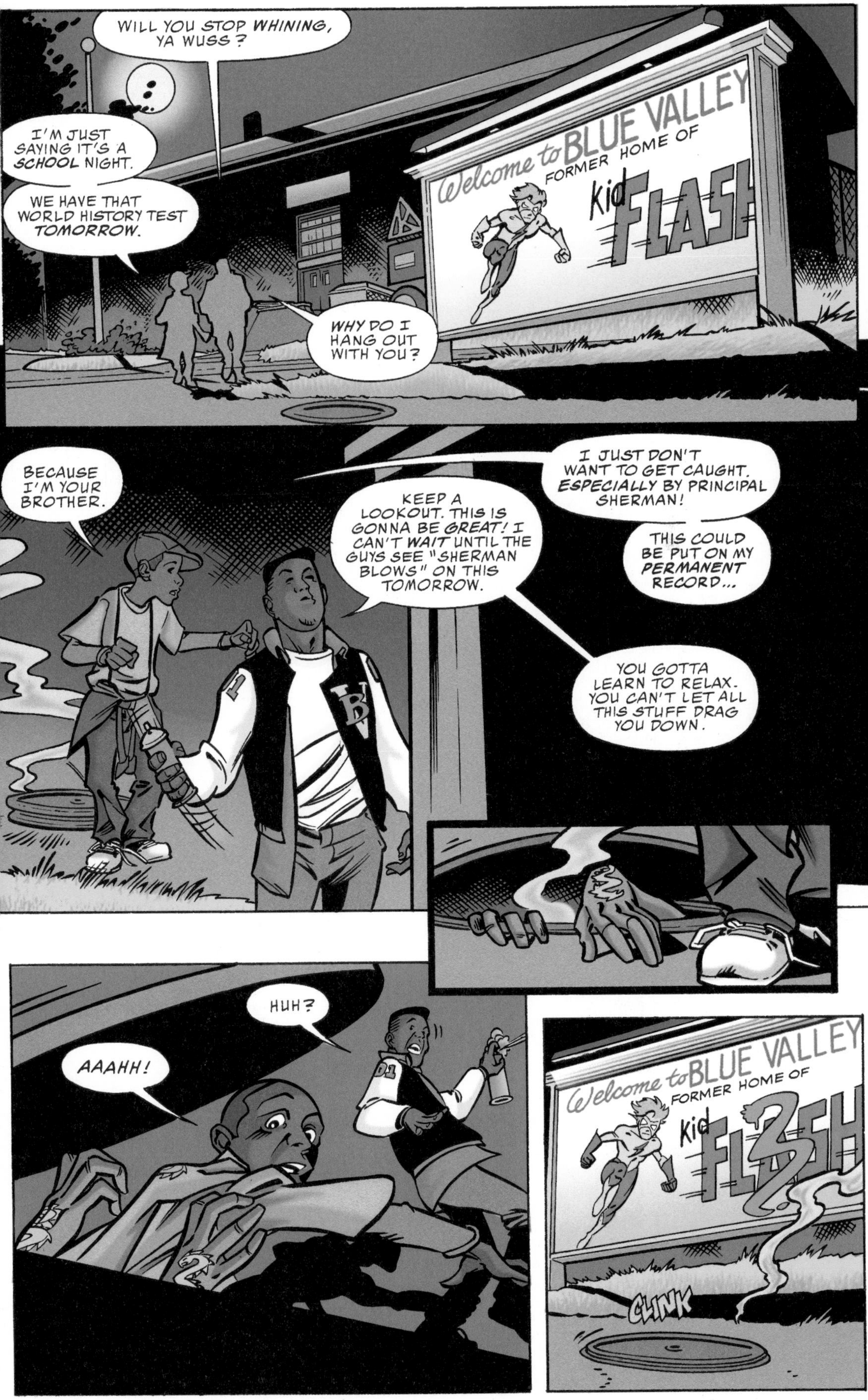
WILL YOU STOP WHINING, YA WUSS?
I'M JUST SAYING IT'S A SCHOOL NIGHT.
WE HAVE THAT WORLD HISTORY TEST TOMORROW.
Welcome to BLUE VALLEY FORMER HOME OF kid FLASH
WHY DO I HANG OUT WITH YOU?
BECAUSE I'M YOUR BROTHER.
I JUST DON'T WANT TO GET CAUGHT. ESPECIALLY BY PRINCIPAL SHERMAN!
THIS COULD BE PUT ON MY PERMANENT RECORD...
KEEP A LOOKOUT. THIS IS GONNA BE GREAT! I CAN'T WAIT UNTIL THE GUYS SEE "SHERMAN BLOWS" ON THIS TOMORROW.
YOU GOTTA LEARN TO RELAX. YOU CAN'T LET ALL THIS STUFF DRAG YOU DOWN.
HUH?
AAAHH!
Welcome to BLUE VALLEY FORMER HOME OF Kid
CLINK

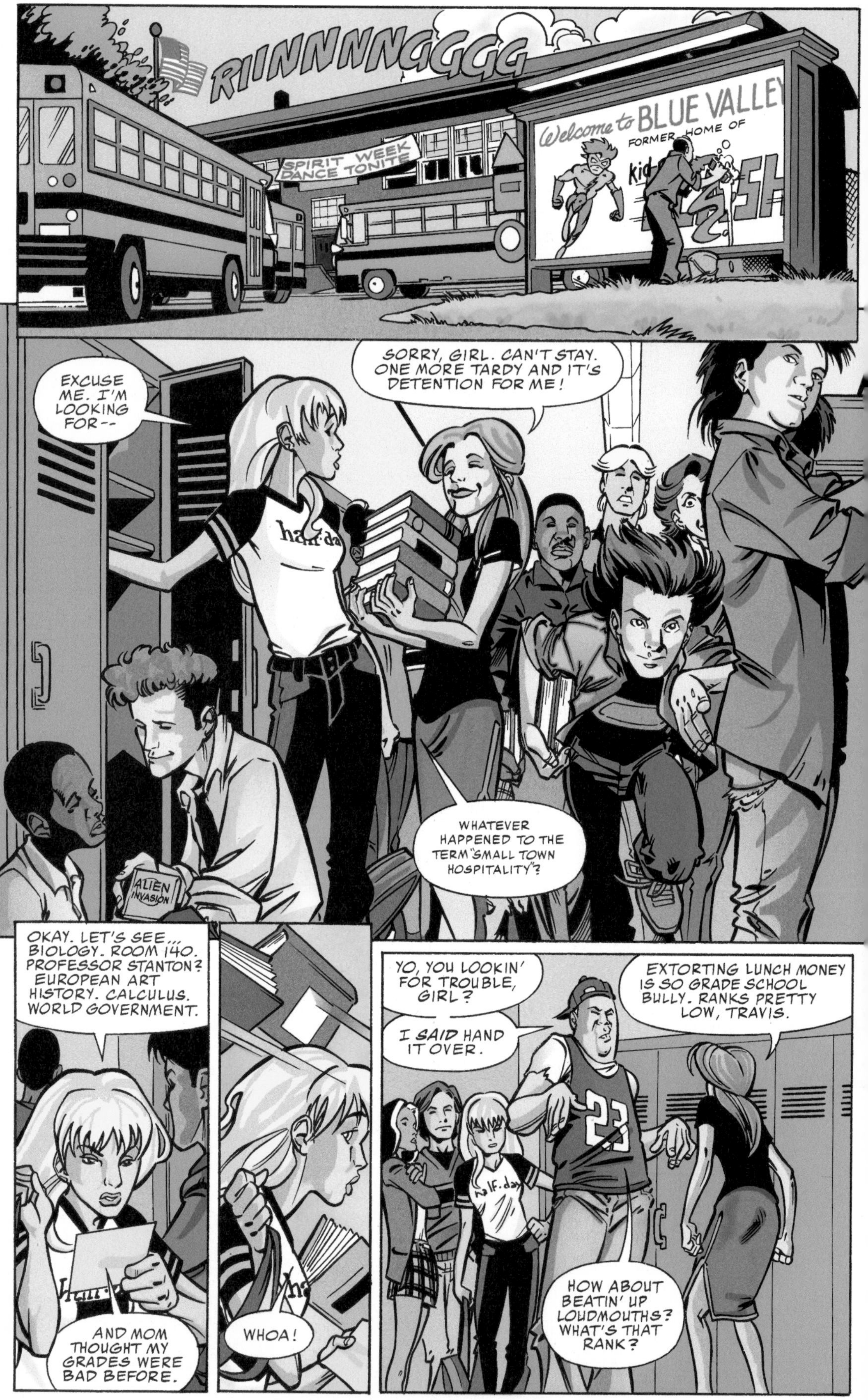
RIINNNNGGGG
SPIRIT WEEK DANCE TONITE
Welcome to BLUE VALLEY
FORMER HOME OF
EXCUSE ME. I'M LOOKING FOR--
SORRY, GIRL. CAN'T STAY. ONE MORE TARDY AND IT'S DETENTION FOR ME!
WHATEVER HAPPENED TO THE TERM "SMALL TOWN HOSPITALITY"?
ALIEN INVASION
OKAY. LET'S SEE... BIOLOGY. ROOM 140. PROFESSOR STANTON? EUROPEAN ART HISTORY. CALCULUS. WORLD GOVERNMENT.
AND MOM THOUGHT MY GRADES WERE BAD BEFORE.
WHOA!
YO, YOU LOOKIN' FOR TROUBLE, GIRL?
I SAID HAND IT OVER.
EXTORTING LUNCH MONEY IS SO GRADE SCHOOL BULLY. RANKS PRETTY LOW, TRAVIS.
HOW ABOUT BEATIN' UP LOUDMOUTHS? WHAT'S THAT RANK?

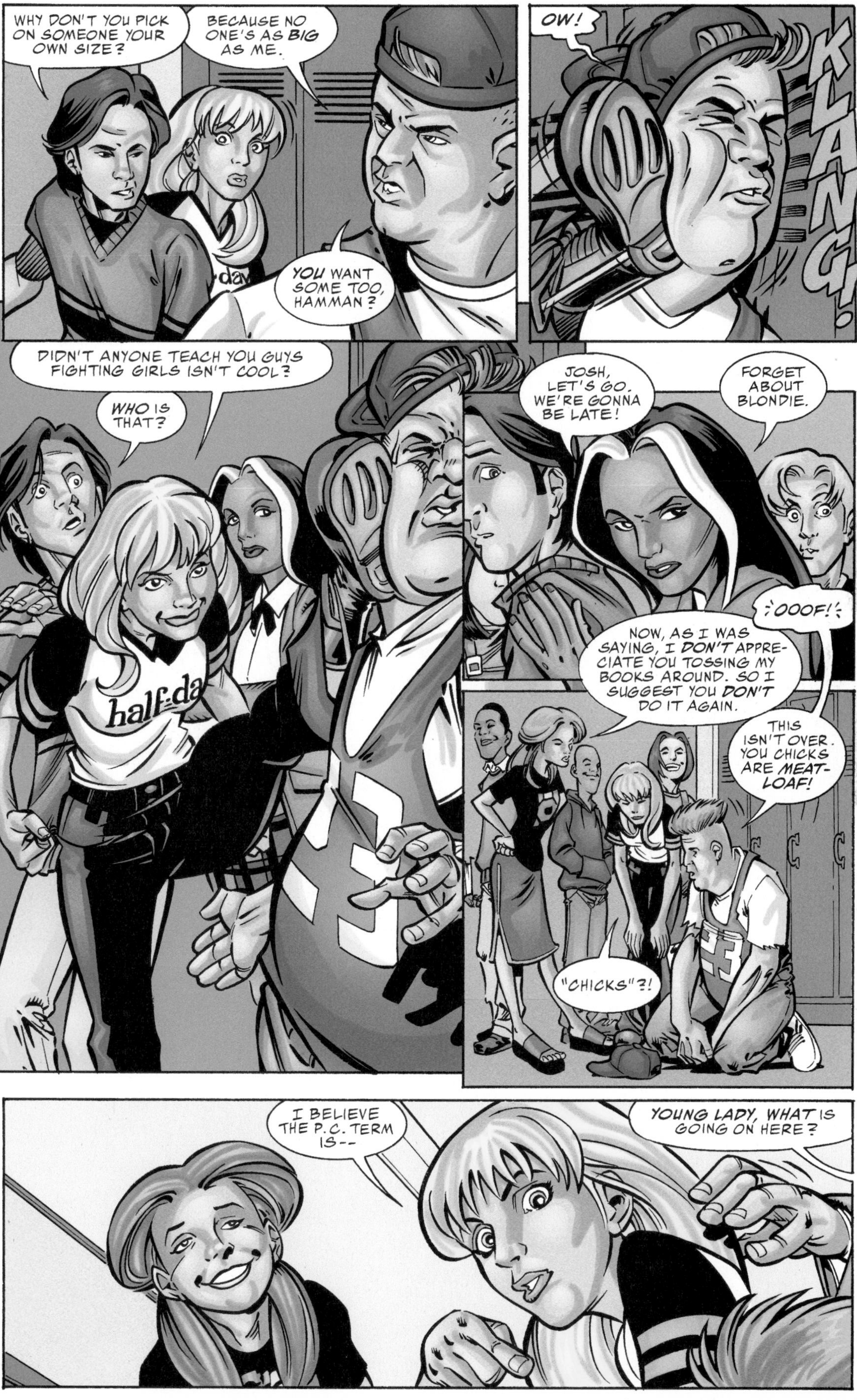

WHY DON'T YOU PICK ON SOMEONE YOUR OWN SIZE?
BECAUSE NO ONE'S AS BIG AS ME.
YOU WANT SOME TOO, HAMMAN?
OW!
KLANG!
DIDN'T ANYONE TEACH YOU GUYS FIGHTING GIRLS ISN'T COOL?
WHO IS THAT?
half-da
JOSH, LET'S GO. WE'RE GONNA BE LATE!
FORGET ABOUT BLONDIE.
OOOF!
NOW, AS I WAS SAYING, I DON'T APPRECIATE YOU TOSSING MY BOOKS AROUND. SO I SUGGEST YOU DON'T DO IT AGAIN.
THIS ISN'T OVER. YOU CHICKS ARE MEAT-LOAF!
"CHICKS"?!
I BELIEVE THE P.C. TERM IS--
YOUNG LADY, WHAT IS GOING ON HERE?

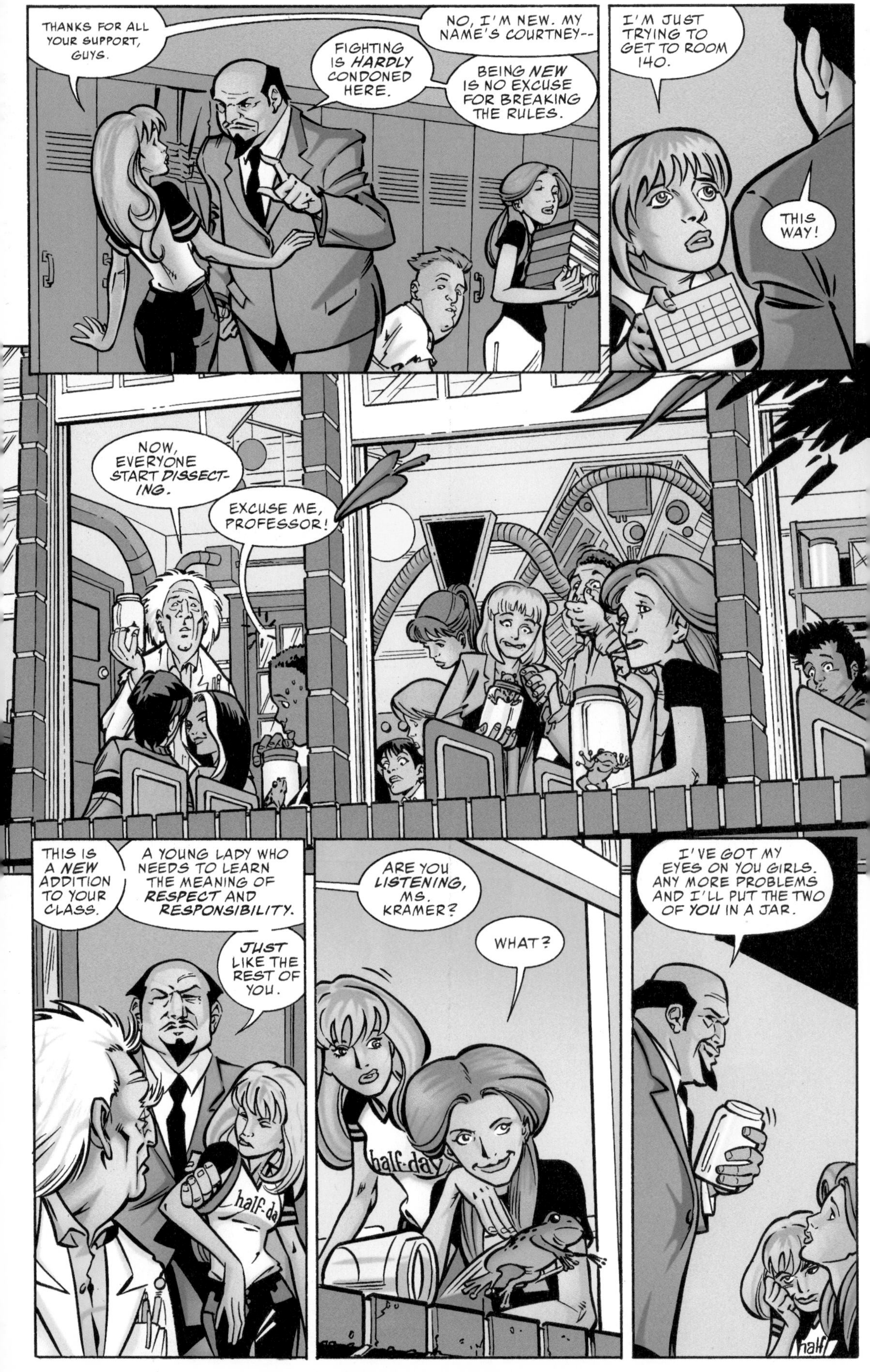
THANKS FOR ALL YOUR SUPPORT, GUYS.
NO, I'M NEW. MY NAME'S COURTNEY--
FIGHTING IS HARDLY CONDONED HERE.
BEING NEW IS NO EXCUSE FOR BREAKING THE RULES.
I'M JUST TRYING TO GET TO ROOM 140.
THIS WAY!
NOW, EVERYONE START DISSECT-ING.
EXCUSE ME, PROFESSOR!
THIS IS A NEW ADDITION TO YOUR CLASS.
A YOUNG LADY WHO NEEDS TO LEARN THE MEANING OF RESPECT AND RESPONSIBILITY.
JUST LIKE THE REST OF YOU.
ARE YOU LISTENING, MS. KRAMER?
WHAT?
I'VE GOT MY EYES ON YOU GIRLS. ANY MORE PROBLEMS AND I'LL PUT THE TWO OF YOU IN A JAR.

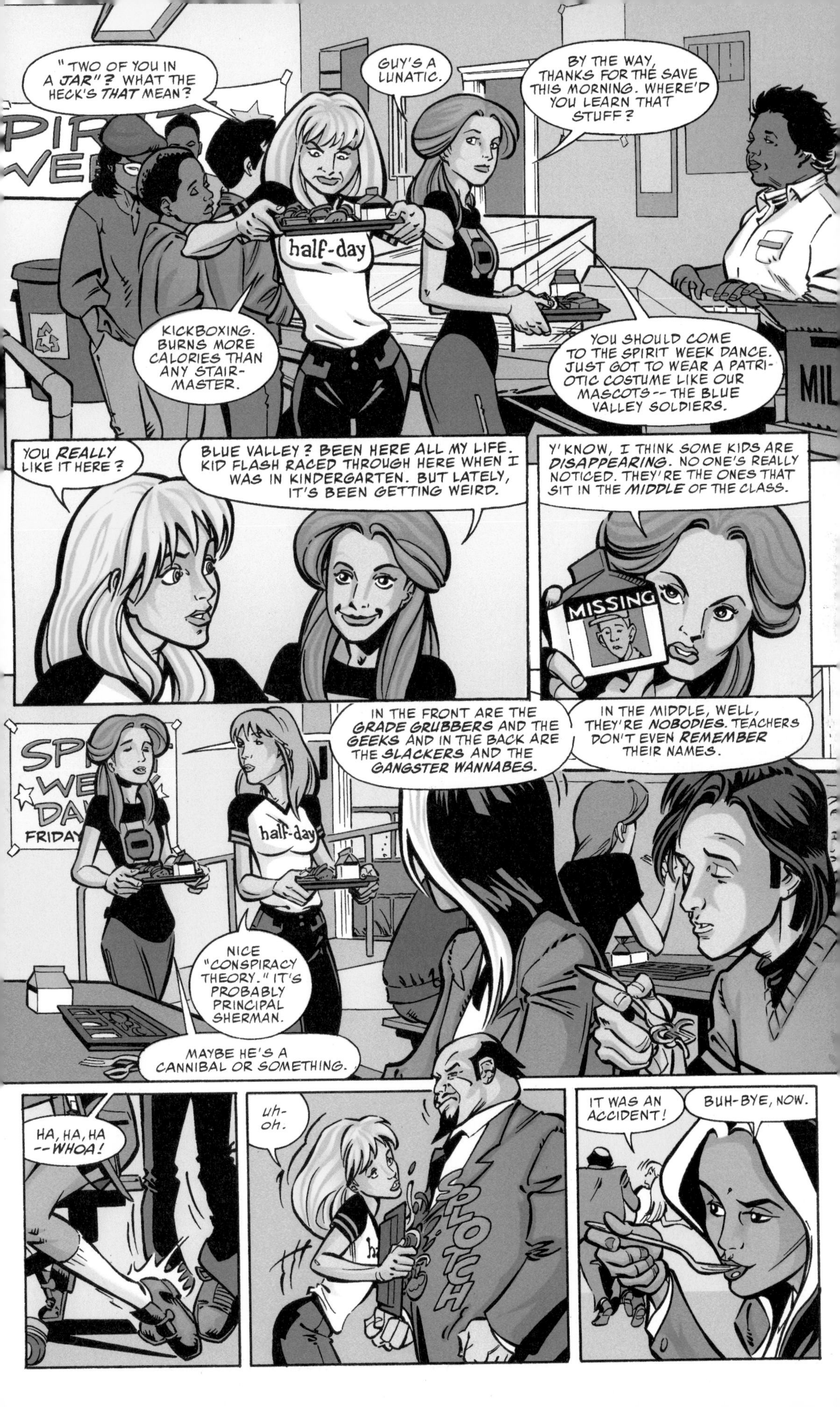
"TWO OF YOU IN A JAR"? WHAT THE HECK'S THAT MEAN?
GUY'S A LUNATIC.
BY THE WAY, THANKS FOR THE SAVE THIS MORNING. WHERE'D YOU LEARN THAT STUFF?
KICKBOXING. BURNS MORE CALORIES THAN ANY STAIR-MASTER.
YOU SHOULD COME TO THE SPIRIT WEEK DANCE. JUST GOT TO WEAR A PATRIOTIC COSTUME LIKE OUR MASCOTS -- THE BLUE VALLEY SOLDIERS.
half-day
YOU REALLY LIKE IT HERE?
BLUE VALLEY? BEEN HERE ALL MY LIFE. KID FLASH RACED THROUGH HERE WHEN I WAS IN KINDERGARTEN. BUT LATELY, IT'S BEEN GETTING WEIRD.
Y'KNOW, I THINK SOME KIDS ARE DISAPPEARING. NO ONE'S REALLY NOTICED. THEY'RE THE ONES THAT SIT IN THE MIDDLE OF THE CLASS.
MISSING
IN THE FRONT ARE THE GRADE GRUBBERS AND THE GEEKS AND IN THE BACK ARE THE SLACKERS AND THE GANGSTER WANNABES.
IN THE MIDDLE, WELL, THEY'RE NOBODIES. TEACHERS DON'T EVEN REMEMBER THEIR NAMES.
FRIDAY
NICE "CONSPIRACY THEORY." IT'S PROBABLY PRINCIPAL SHERMAN.
MAYBE HE'S A CANNIBAL OR SOMETHING.
HA, HA, HA --WHOA!
uh-oh.
SPLOTCH
IT WAS AN ACCIDENT!
BUH-BYE, NOW.

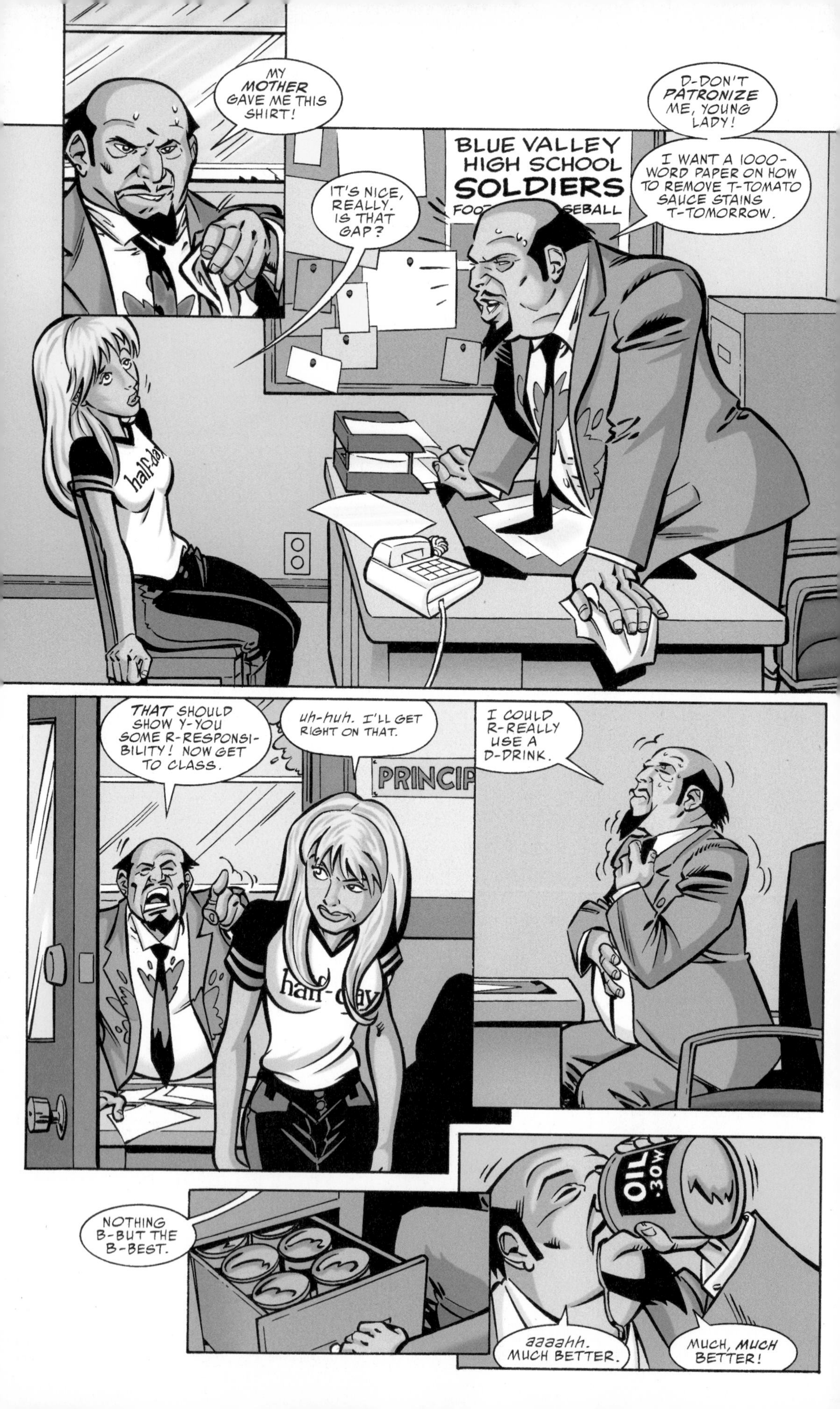

MY MOTHER GAVE ME THIS SHIRT!
IT'S NICE, REALLY. IS THAT GAP?
D-DON'T PATRONIZE ME, YOUNG LADY!
I WANT A 1000-WORD PAPER ON HOW TO REMOVE T-TOMATO SAUCE STAINS T-TOMORROW.
BLUE VALLEY HIGH SCHOOL SOLDIERS
half-day
THAT SHOULD SHOW Y-YOU SOME R-RESPONSIBILITY! NOW GET TO CLASS.
uh-huh. I'LL GET RIGHT ON THAT.
PRINCIP
I COULD R-REALLY USE A D-DRINK.
NOTHING B-BUT THE B-BEST.
OIL 30W
aaaahh. MUCH BETTER.
MUCH, MUCH BETTER!

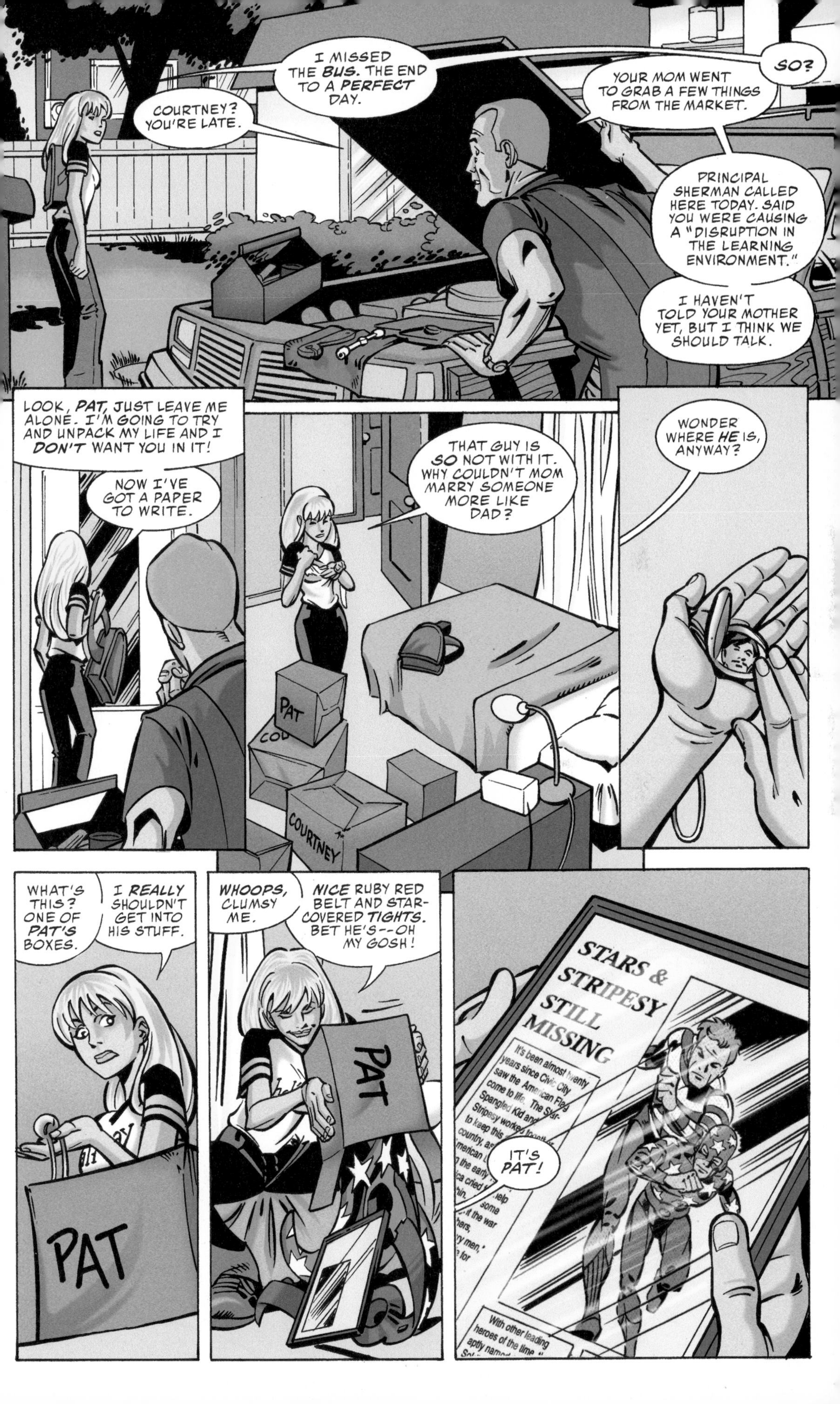
COURTNEY? YOU'RE LATE.
I MISSED THE BUS. THE END TO A PERFECT DAY.
SO?
YOUR MOM WENT TO GRAB A FEW THINGS FROM THE MARKET.
PRINCIPAL SHERMAN CALLED HERE TODAY. SAID YOU WERE CAUSING A "DISRUPTION IN THE LEARNING ENVIRONMENT."
I HAVEN'T TOLD YOUR MOTHER YET, BUT I THINK WE SHOULD TALK.
LOOK, PAT, JUST LEAVE ME ALONE. I'M GOING TO TRY AND UNPACK MY LIFE AND I DON'T WANT YOU IN IT!
NOW I'VE GOT A PAPER TO WRITE.
THAT GUY IS SO NOT WITH IT. WHY COULDN'T MOM MARRY SOMEONE MORE LIKE DAD?
PAT
COURTNEY
WONDER WHERE HE IS, ANYWAY?
WHAT'S THIS? ONE OF PAT'S BOXES.
I REALLY SHOULDN'T GET INTO HIS STUFF.
PAT
WHOOPS, CLUMSY ME.
NICE RUBY RED BELT AND STAR-COVERED TIGHTS. BET HE'S--OH MY GOSH!
PAT
STARS & STRIPESY STILL MISSING
IT'S PAT!

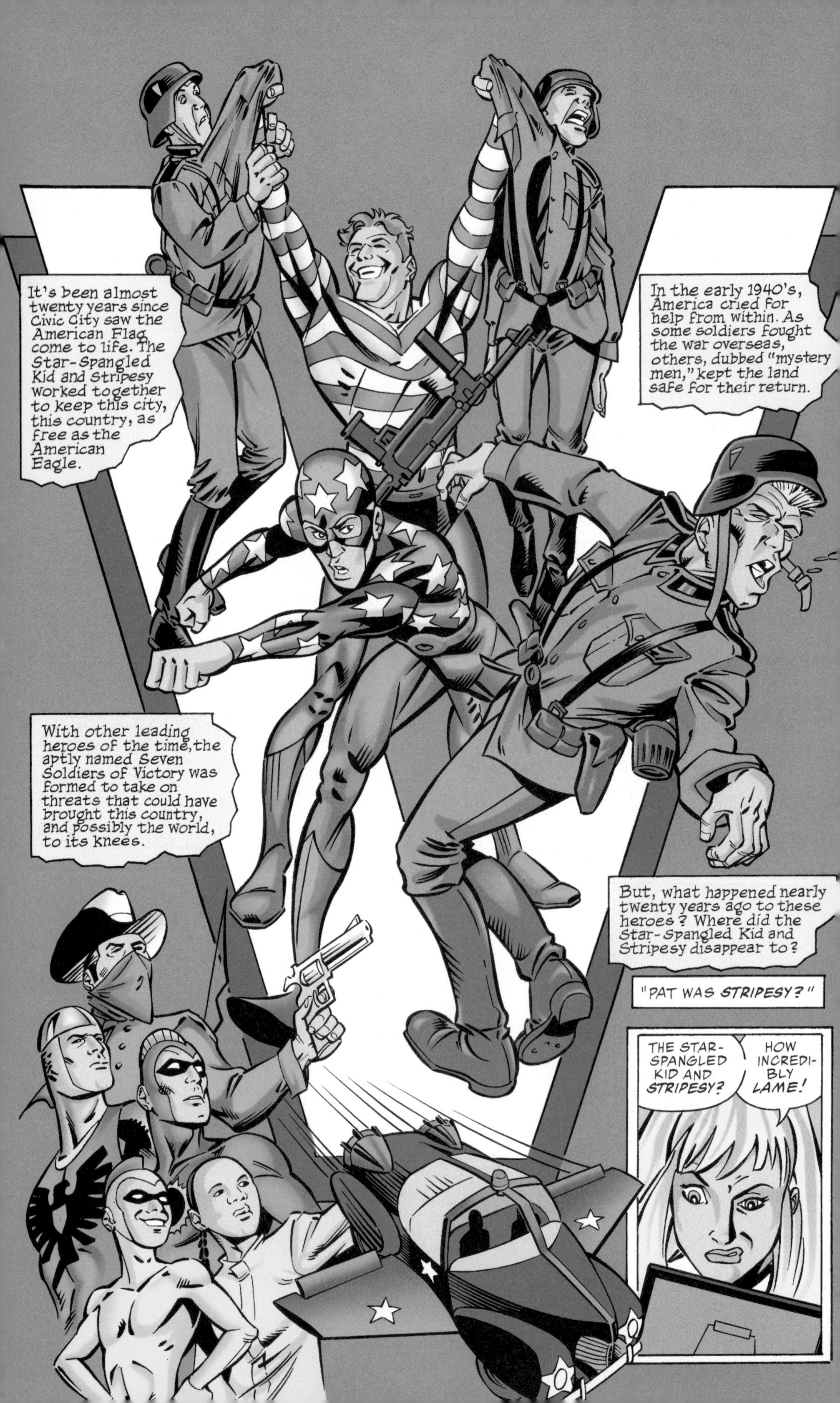
It's been almost twenty years since Civic City saw the American Flag come to life. The Star-Spangled Kid and Stripesy worked together to keep this city, this country, as free as the American Eagle.
In the early 1940's, America cried for help from within. As some soldiers fought the war overseas, others, dubbed "mystery men," kept the land safe for their return.
With other leading heroes of the time, the aptly named Seven Soldiers of Victory was formed to take on threats that could have brought this country, and possibly the world, to its knees.
But, what happened nearly twenty years ago to these heroes? Where did the Star-Spangled Kid and Stripesy disappear to?
"PAT WAS STRIPESY?"
THE STAR-SPANGLED KID AND STRIPESY?
HOW INCREDIBLY LAME!

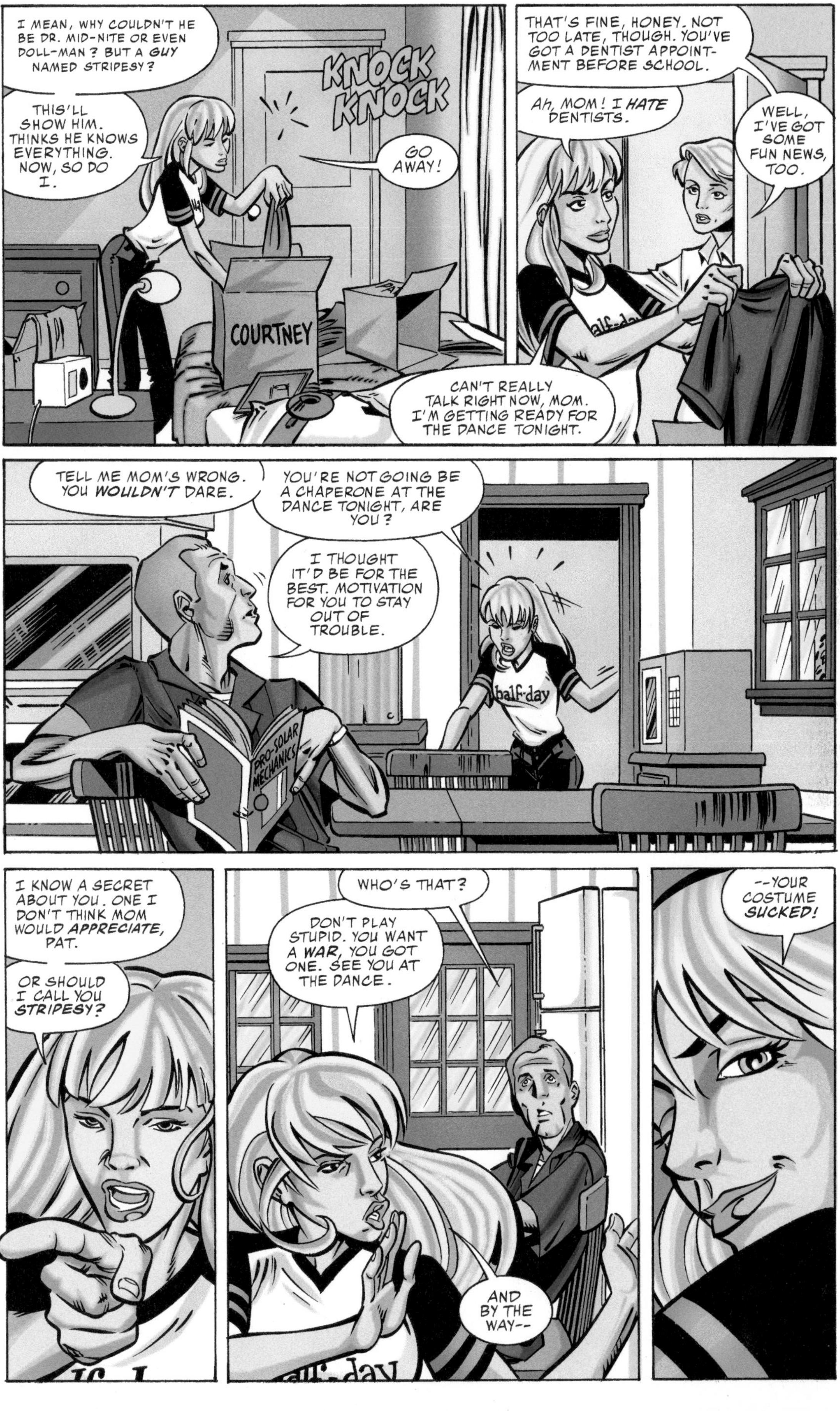
I MEAN, WHY COULDN'T HE BE DR. MID-NITE OR EVEN DOLL-MAN? BUT A GUY NAMED STRIPESY?
THIS'LL SHOW HIM. THINKS HE KNOWS EVERYTHING. NOW, SO DO I.
KNOCK KNOCK
GO AWAY!
COURTNEY
THAT'S FINE, HONEY. NOT TOO LATE, THOUGH. YOU'VE GOT A DENTIST APPOINTMENT BEFORE SCHOOL.
AH, MOM! I HATE DENTISTS.
WELL, I'VE GOT SOME FUN NEWS, TOO.
CAN'T REALLY TALK RIGHT NOW, MOM. I'M GETTING READY FOR THE DANCE TONIGHT.
TELL ME MOM'S WRONG. YOU WOULDN'T DARE.
YOU'RE NOT GOING BE A CHAPERONE AT THE DANCE TONIGHT, ARE YOU?
I THOUGHT IT'D BE FOR THE BEST. MOTIVATION FOR YOU TO STAY OUT OF TROUBLE.
half-day
PRO-SOLAR MECHANICS
I KNOW A SECRET ABOUT YOU. ONE I DON'T THINK MOM WOULD APPRECIATE, PAT.
OR SHOULD I CALL YOU STRIPESY?
WHO'S THAT?
DON'T PLAY STUPID. YOU WANT A WAR, YOU GOT ONE. SEE YOU AT THE DANCE.
AND BY THE WAY--
--YOUR COSTUME SUCKED!

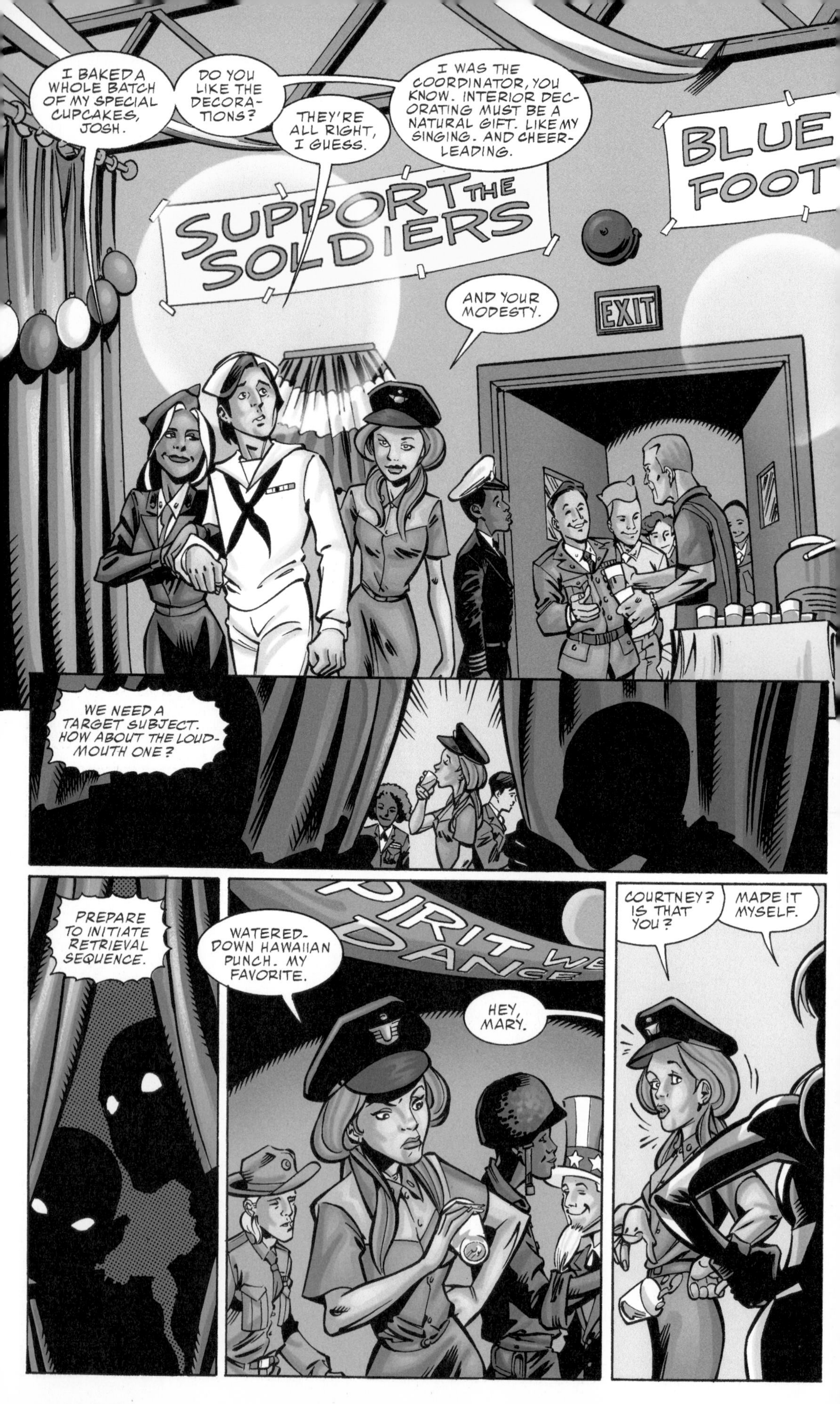
I BAKED A WHOLE BATCH OF MY SPECIAL CUPCAKES, JOSH.
DO YOU LIKE THE DECORATIONS?
THEY'RE ALL RIGHT, I GUESS.
I WAS THE COORDINATOR, YOU KNOW. INTERIOR DECORATING MUST BE A NATURAL GIFT. LIKE MY SINGING. AND CHEERLEADING.
BLUE FOOT
SUPPORT THE SOLDIERS
AND YOUR MODESTY.
EXIT
WE NEED A TARGET SUBJECT. HOW ABOUT THE LOUDMOUTH ONE?
PREPARE TO INITIATE RETRIEVAL SEQUENCE.
PIRIT WE DANCE
WATERED-DOWN HAWAIIAN PUNCH. MY FAVORITE.
HEY, MARY.
COURTNEY? IS THAT YOU?
MADE IT MYSELF.

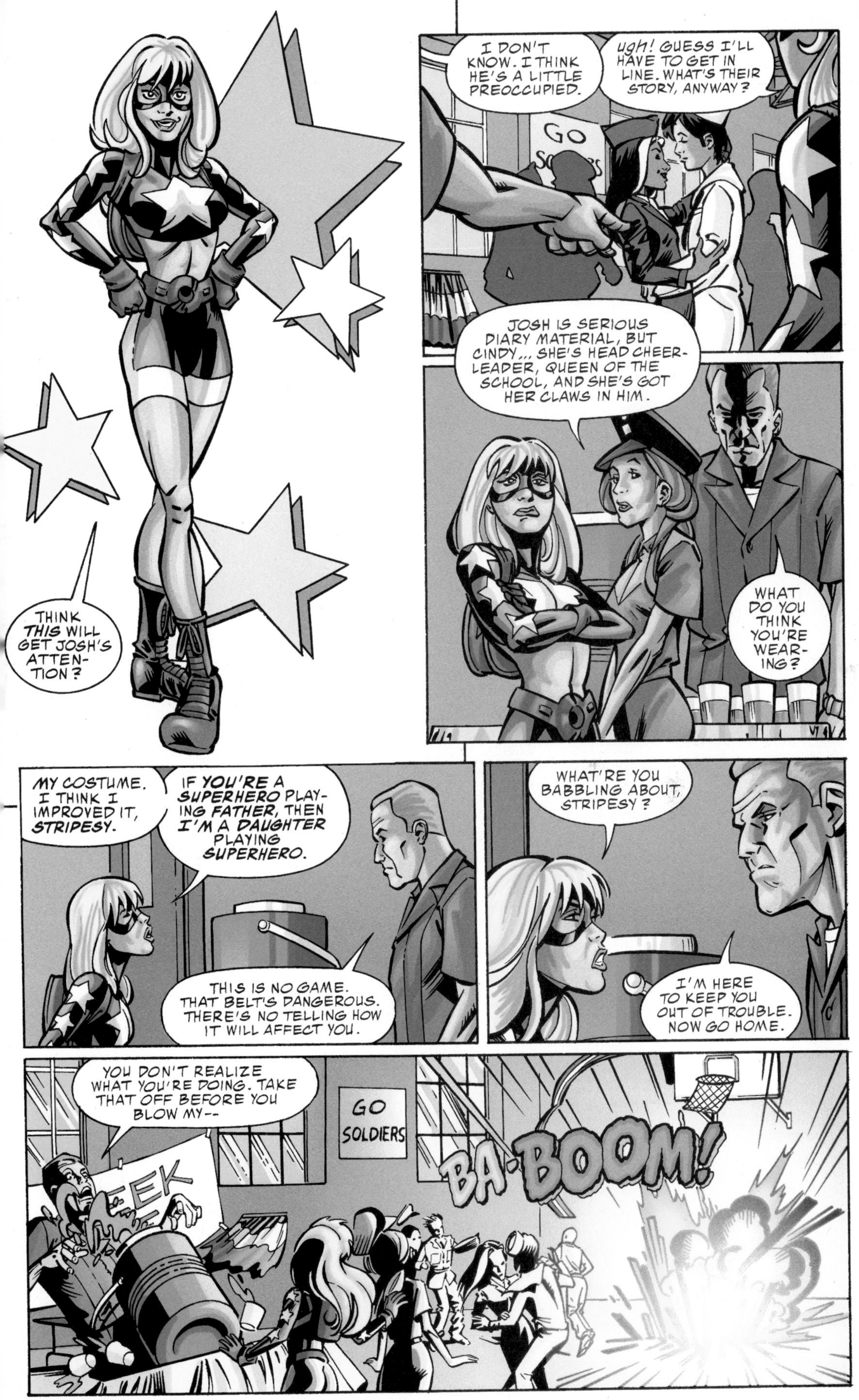
THINK THIS WILL GET JOSH'S ATTEN-TION?
I DON'T KNOW. I THINK HE'S A LITTLE PREOCCUPIED.
UGH! GUESS I'LL HAVE TO GET IN LINE. WHAT'S THEIR STORY, ANYWAY?
GO SOLDIERS
JOSH IS SERIOUS DIARY MATERIAL, BUT CINDY... SHE'S HEAD CHEER-LEADER, QUEEN OF THE SCHOOL, AND SHE'S GOT HER CLAWS IN HIM.
WHAT DO YOU THINK YOU'RE WEAR-ING?
MY COSTUME. I THINK I IMPROVED IT, STRIPESY.
IF YOU'RE A SUPERHERO PLAY-ING FATHER, THEN I'M A DAUGHTER PLAYING SUPERHERO.
THIS IS NO GAME. THAT BELT'S DANGEROUS. THERE'S NO TELLING HOW IT WILL AFFECT YOU.
WHAT'RE YOU BABBLING ABOUT, STRIPESY?
I'M HERE TO KEEP YOU OUT OF TROUBLE. NOW GO HOME.
YOU DON'T REALIZE WHAT YOU'RE DOING. TAKE THAT OFF BEFORE YOU BLOW MY--
GO SOLDIERS
EEK
BA-BOOM!

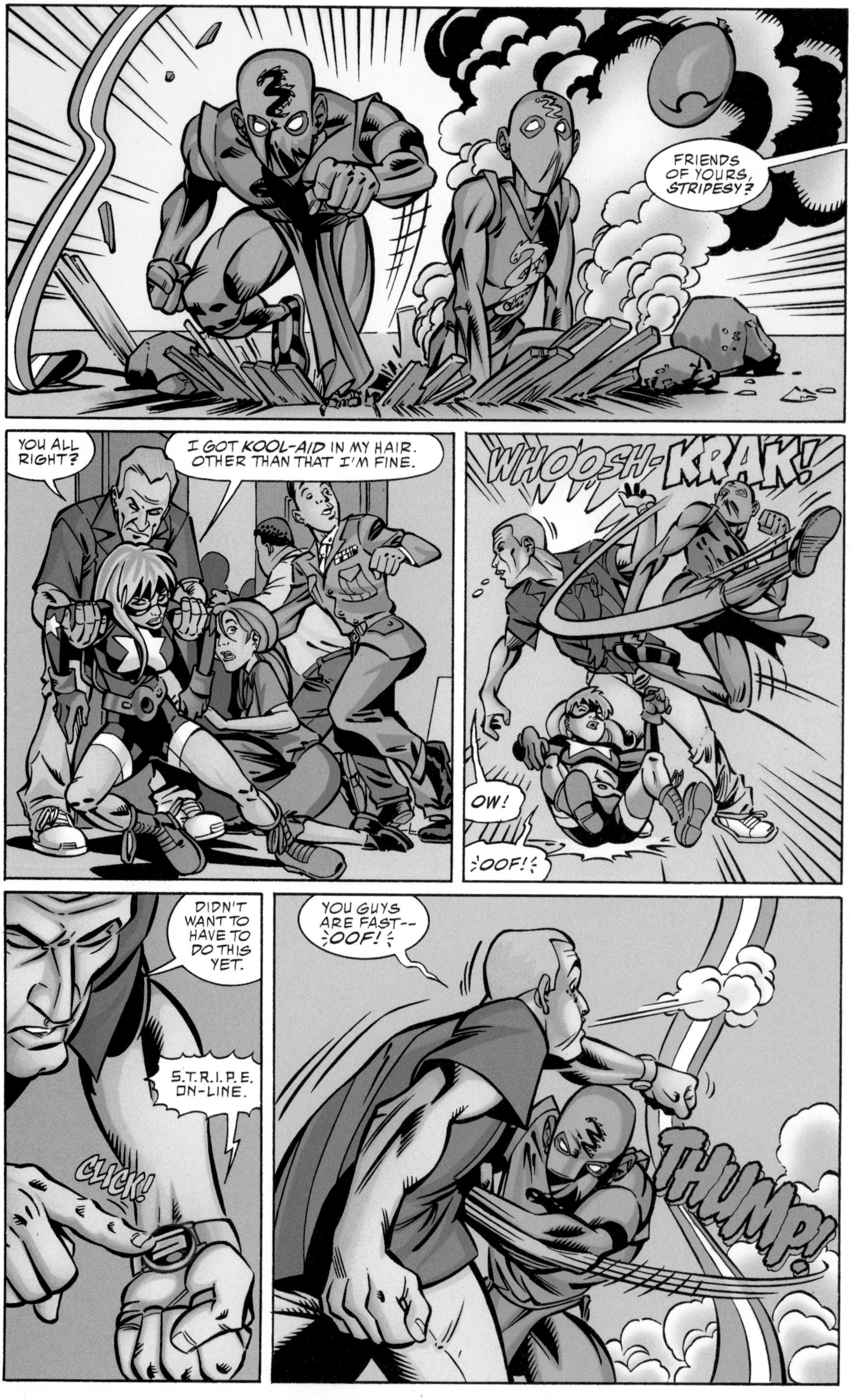
FRIENDS OF YOURS, STRIPESY?
YOU ALL RIGHT?
I GOT KOOL-AID IN MY HAIR. OTHER THAN THAT I'M FINE.
WHOOSH-KRAK!
OW!
OOF!
DIDN'T WANT TO HAVE TO DO THIS YET.
S.T.R.I.P.E. ON-LINE.
CLICK!
YOU GUYS ARE FAST-- OOF!
THUMP!

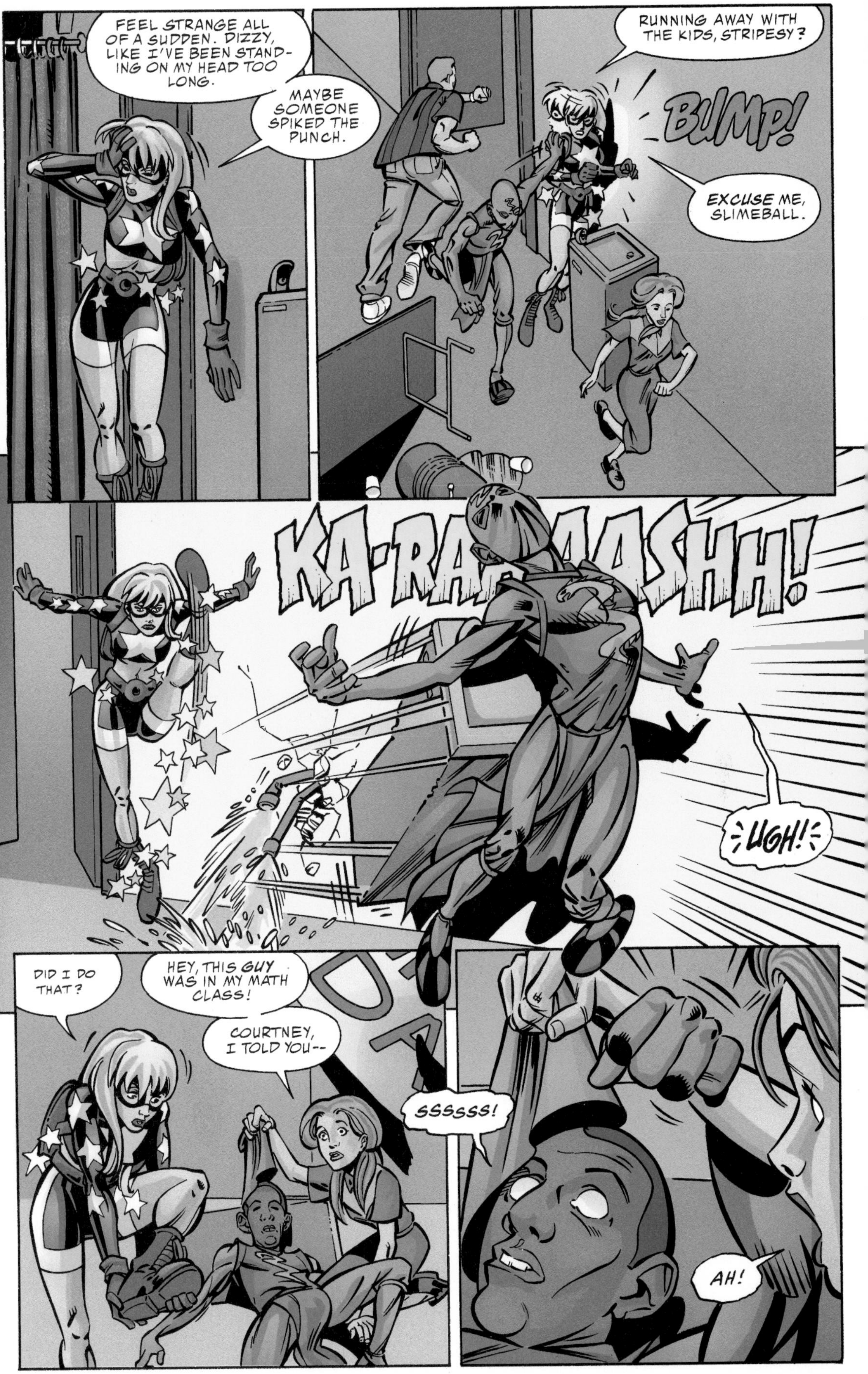
FEEL STRANGE ALL OF A SUDDEN. DIZZY, LIKE I'VE BEEN STANDING ON MY HEAD TOO LONG.
MAYBE SOMEONE SPIKED THE PUNCH.
RUNNING AWAY WITH THE KIDS, STRIPESY?
BUMP!
EXCUSE ME, SLIMEBALL.
KA-RA
ASHH!
UGH!
DID I DO THAT?
HEY, THIS GUY WAS IN MY MATH CLASS!
COURTNEY, I TOLD YOU--
SSSSSS!
AH!

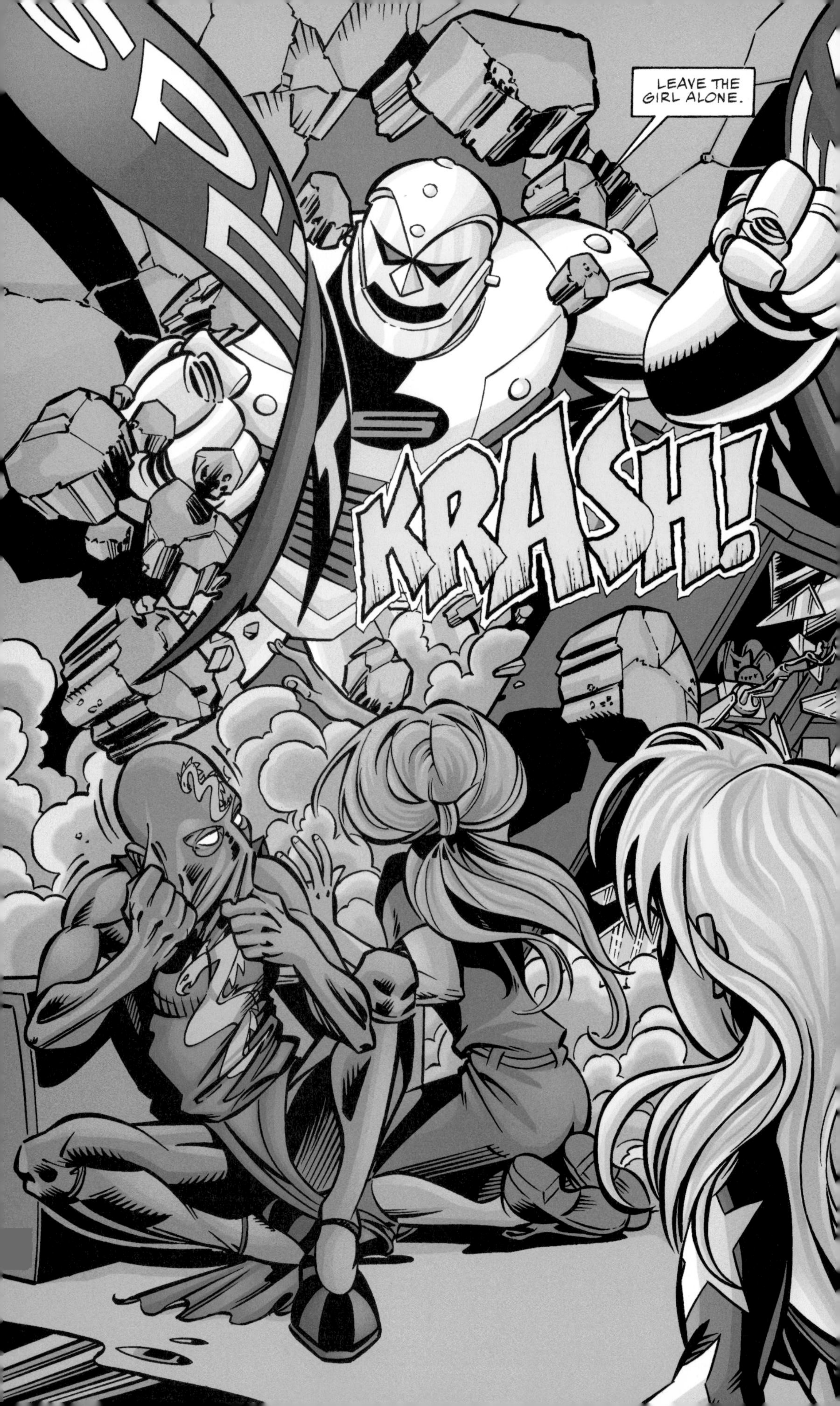
LEAVE THE GIRL ALONE.
KRASH!

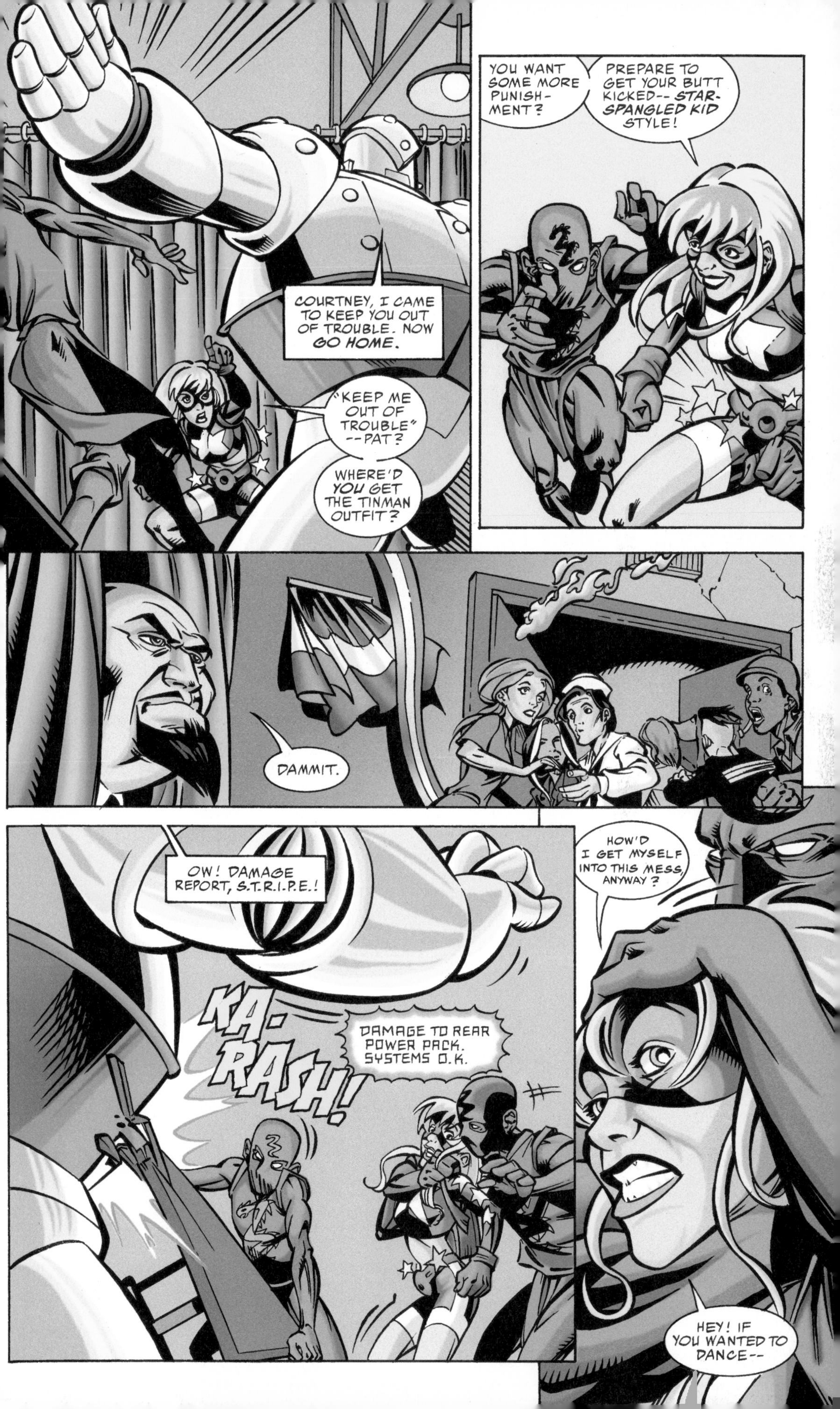
COURTNEY, I CAME TO KEEP YOU OUT OF TROUBLE. NOW GO HOME.
"KEEP ME OUT OF TROUBLE" --PAT?
WHERE'D YOU GET THE TINMAN OUTFIT?
YOU WANT SOME MORE PUNISH-MENT?
PREPARE TO GET YOUR BUTT KICKED-- STAR-SPANGLED KID STYLE!
DAMMIT.
OW! DAMAGE REPORT, S.T.R.I.P.E.!
KA-RASH!
DAMAGE TO REAR POWER PACK. SYSTEMS O.K.
HOW'D I GET MYSELF INTO THIS MESS, ANYWAY?
HEY! IF YOU WANTED TO DANCE--

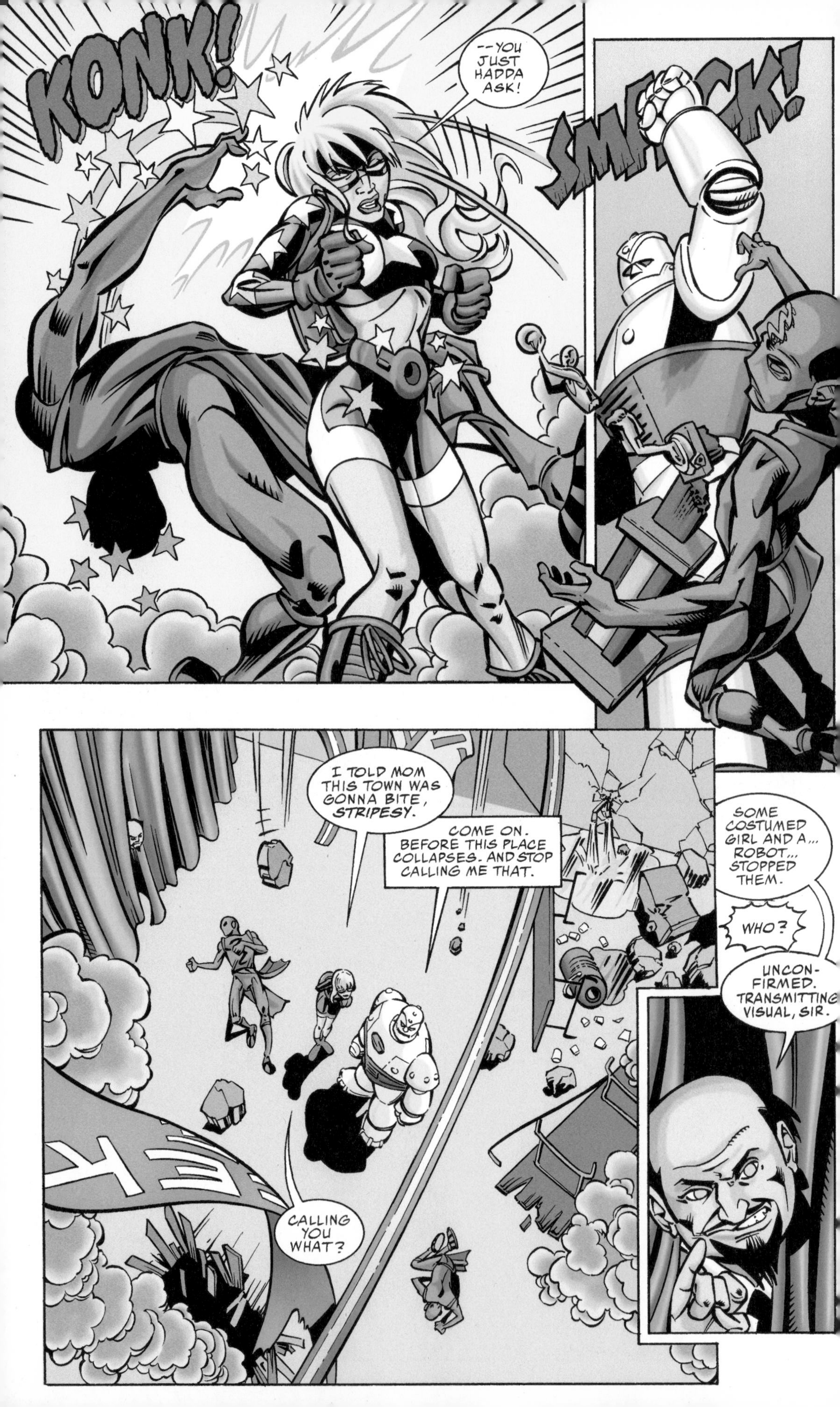

KONK!
--YOU JUST HADDA ASK!
SMACK!
I TOLD MOM THIS TOWN WAS GONNA BITE, STRIPESY.
COME ON. BEFORE THIS PLACE COLLAPSES. AND STOP CALLING ME THAT.
CALLING YOU WHAT?
SOME COSTUMED GIRL AND A... ROBOT... STOPPED THEM.
WHO?
UNCON-FIRMED. TRANSMITTING VISUAL, SIR.

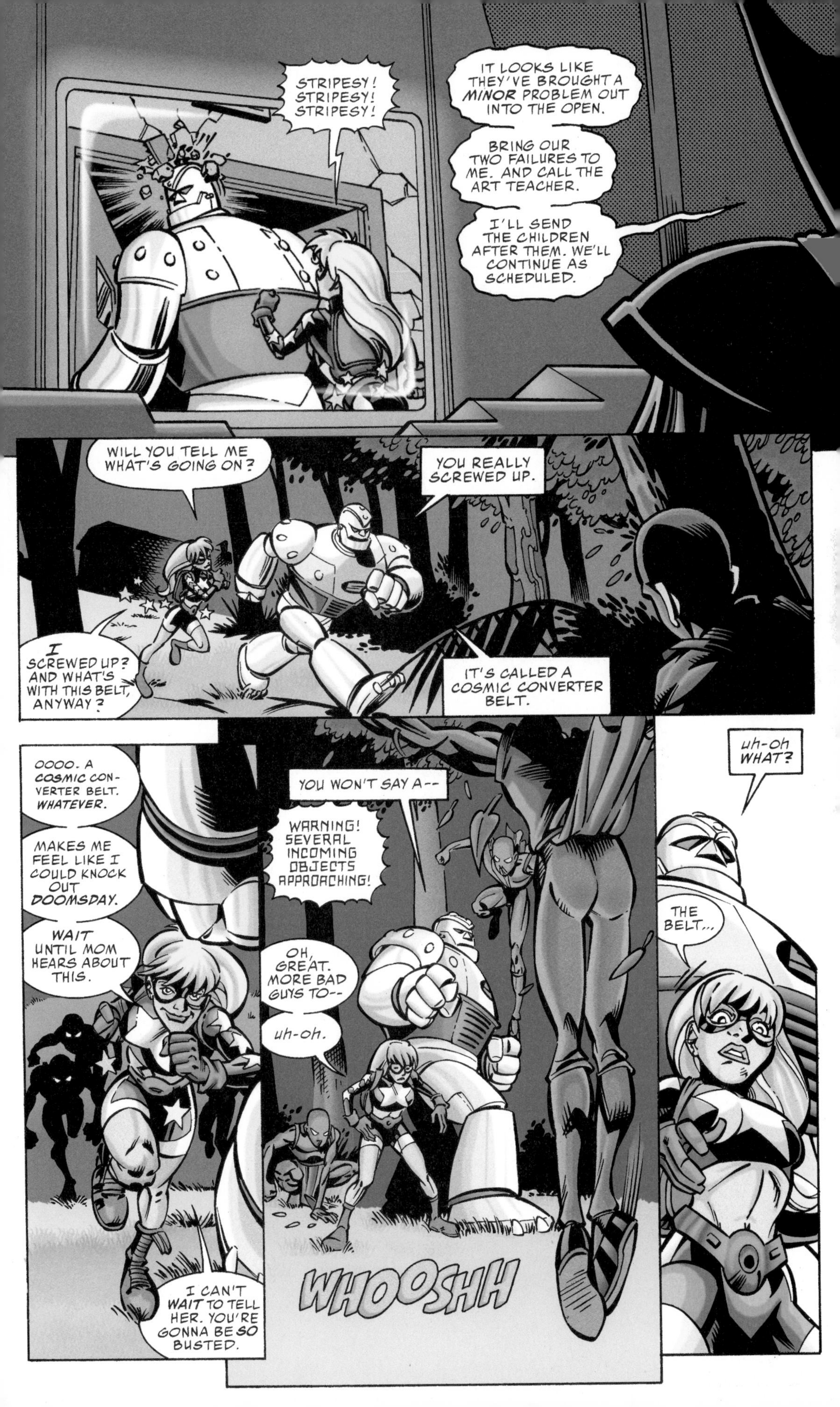
STRIPESY! STRIPESY! STRIPESY!
IT LOOKS LIKE THEY'VE BROUGHT A MINOR PROBLEM OUT INTO THE OPEN.
BRING OUR TWO FAILURES TO ME. AND CALL THE ART TEACHER.
I'LL SEND THE CHILDREN AFTER THEM. WE'LL CONTINUE AS SCHEDULED.
WILL YOU TELL ME WHAT'S GOING ON?
YOU REALLY SCREWED UP.
I SCREWED UP? AND WHAT'S WITH THIS BELT, ANYWAY?
IT'S CALLED A COSMIC CONVERTER BELT.
OOOO. A COSMIC CONVERTER BELT. WHATEVER.
MAKES ME FEEL LIKE I COULD KNOCK OUT DOOMSDAY.
WAIT UNTIL MOM HEARS ABOUT THIS.
I CAN'T WAIT TO TELL HER. YOU'RE GONNA BE SO BUSTED.
YOU WON'T SAY A--
WARNING! SEVERAL INCOMING OBJECTS APPROACHING!
OH, GREAT. MORE BAD GUYS TO--
uh-oh.
WHOOSHH
uh-oh WHAT?
THE BELT...

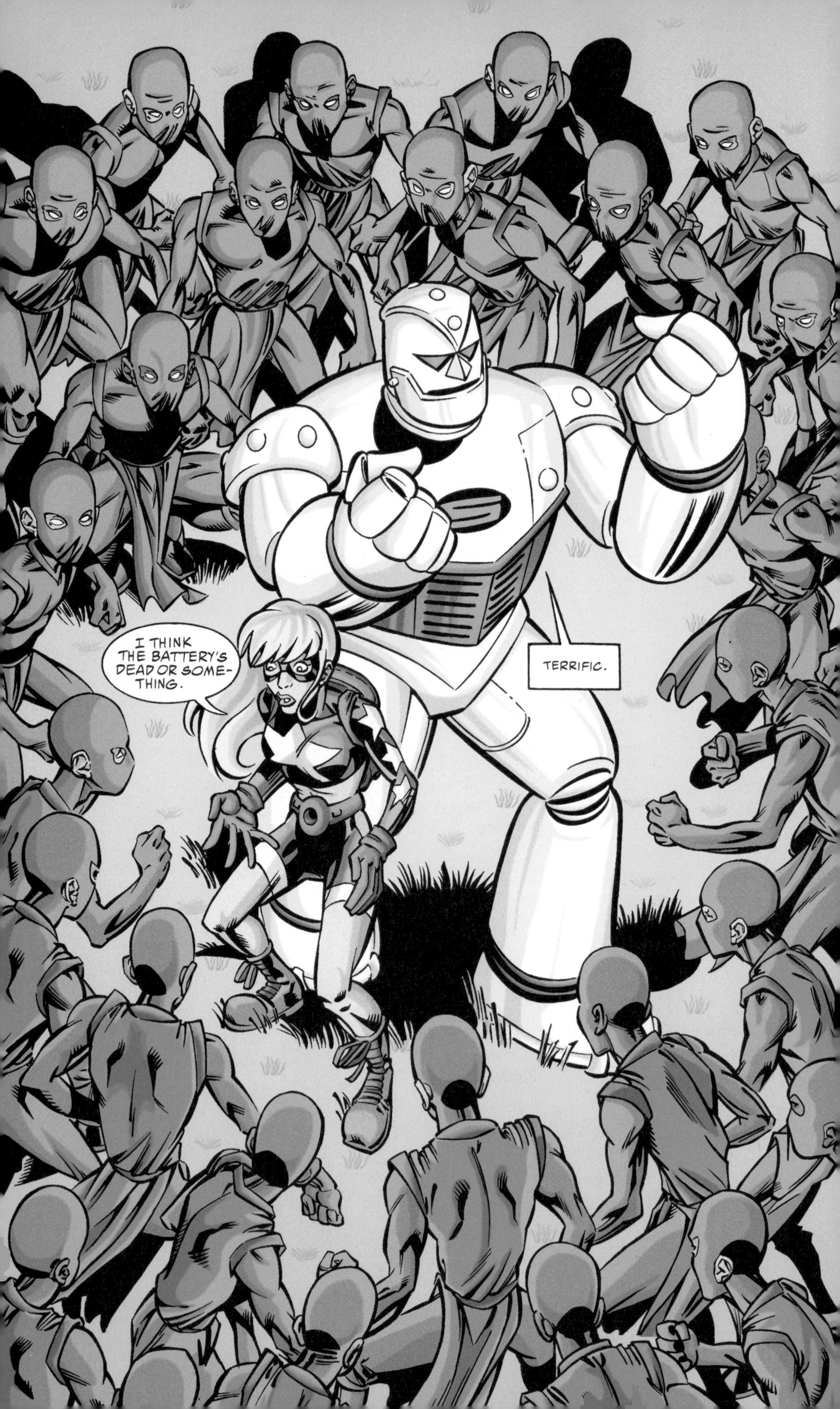
I THINK THE BATTERY'S DEAD OR SOME-THING.
TERRIFIC.

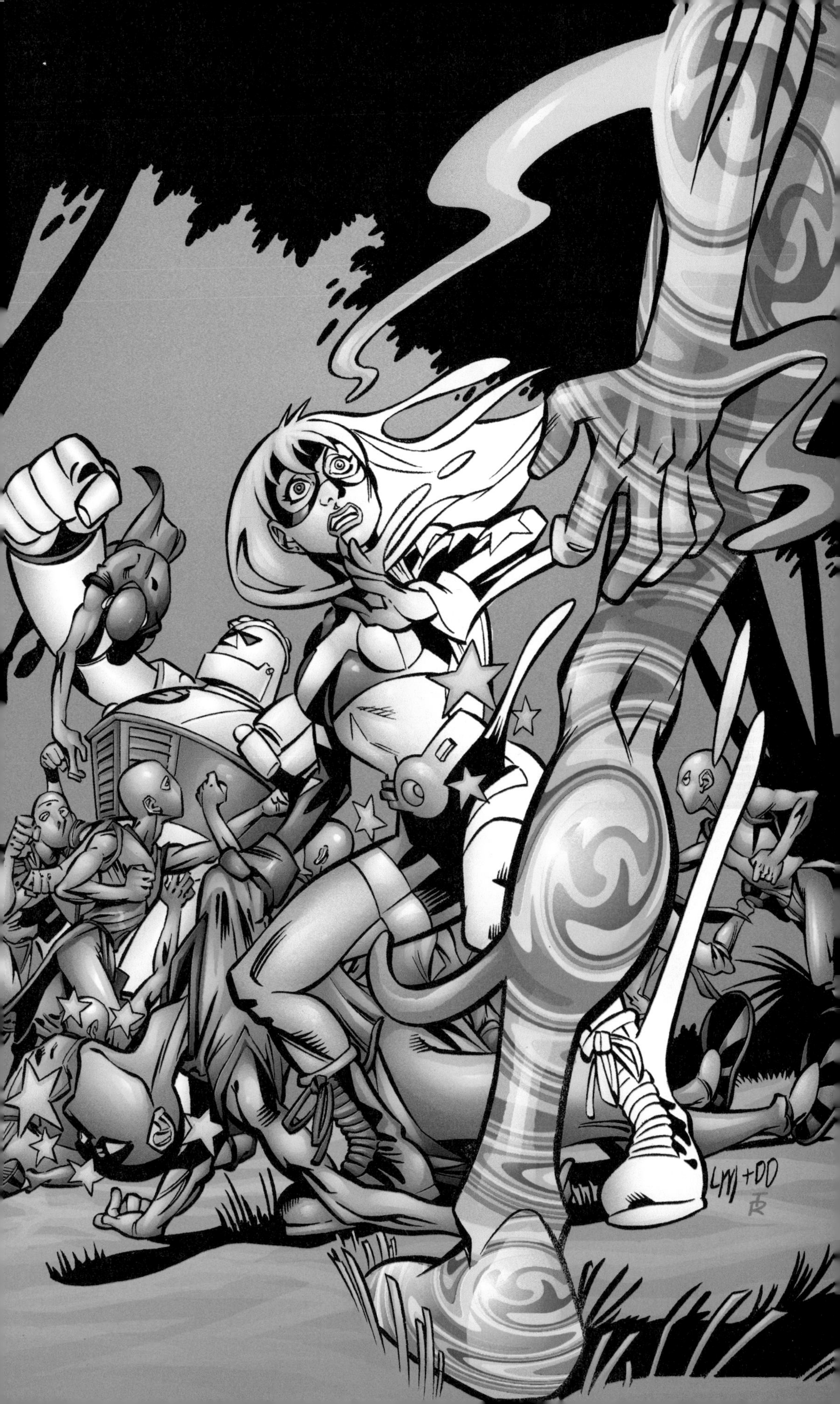

STARS AND S.T.R.I.P.E. #2

Written by GEOFF JOHNS
Pencils by LEE MODER
Inks by DAN DAVIS
Colors by TOM McCRAW
Letters by BILL OAKLEY
Cover art by LEE MODER and DAN DAVIS
Cover color by RICHARD & TANYA HORIE

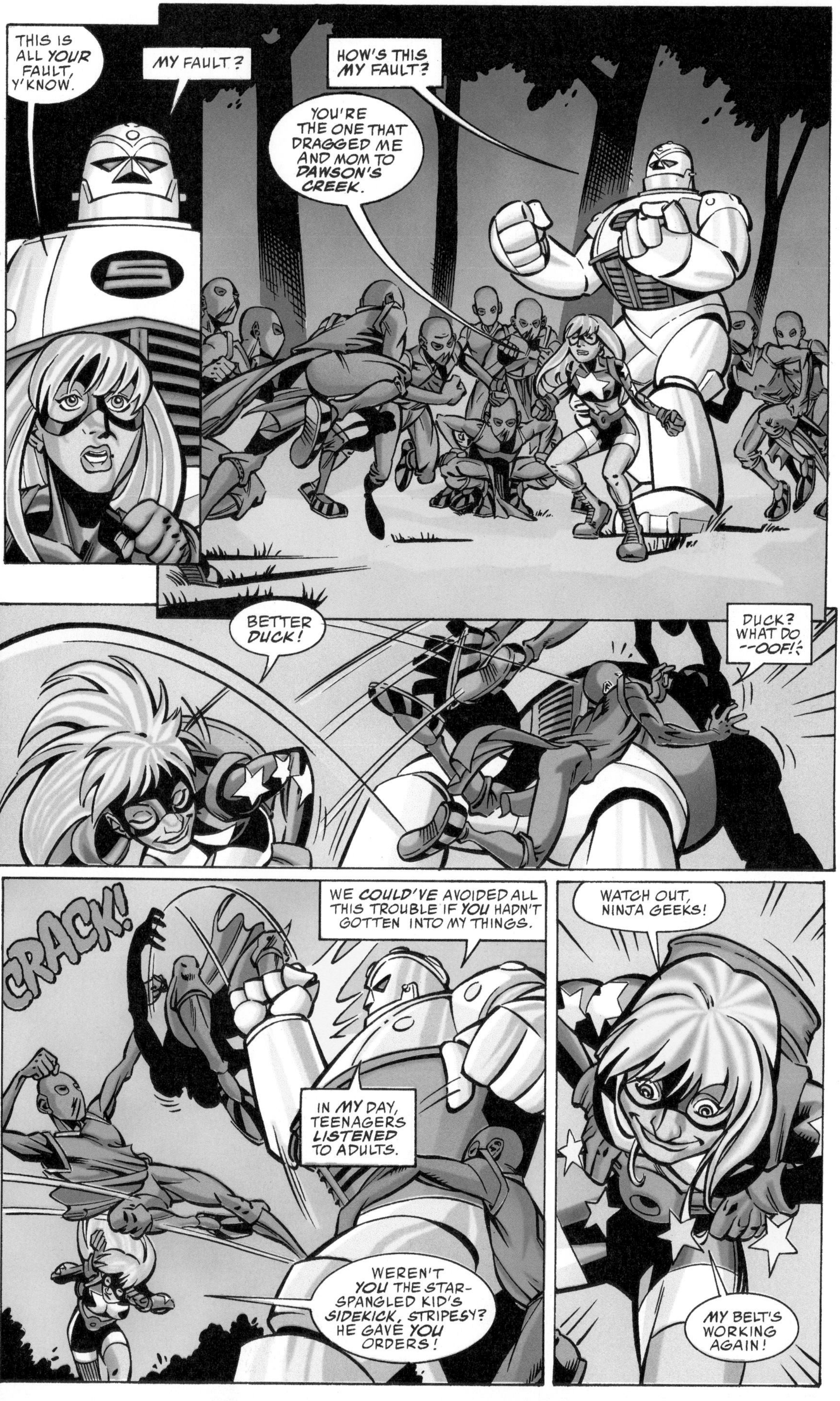
THIS IS ALL YOUR FAULT, Y'KNOW.
MY FAULT?
HOW'S THIS MY FAULT?
YOU'RE THE ONE THAT DRAGGED ME AND MOM TO DAWSON'S CREEK.
BETTER DUCK!
DUCK? WHAT DO --OOF!
CRACK!
WE COULD'VE AVOIDED ALL THIS TROUBLE IF YOU HADN'T GOTTEN INTO MY THINGS.
IN MY DAY, TEENAGERS LISTENED TO ADULTS.
WEREN'T YOU THE STAR-SPANGLED KID'S SIDEKICK, STRIPESY? HE GAVE YOU ORDERS!
WATCH OUT, NINJA GEEKS!
MY BELT'S WORKING AGAIN!

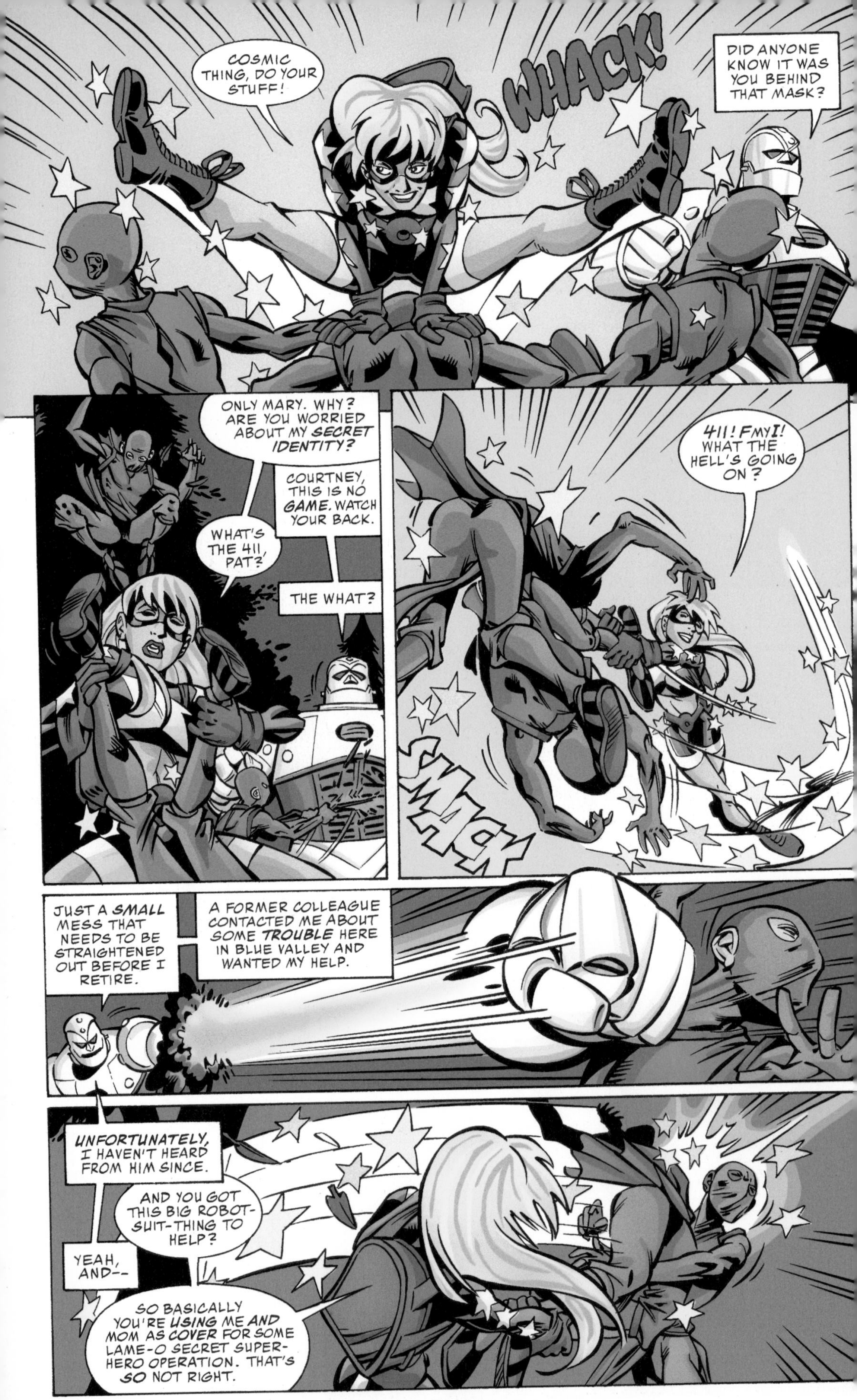
COSMIC THING, DO YOUR STUFF!
WHACK!
DID ANYONE KNOW IT WAS YOU BEHIND THAT MASK?
ONLY MARY. WHY? ARE YOU WORRIED ABOUT MY SECRET IDENTITY?
COURTNEY, THIS IS NO GAME. WATCH YOUR BACK.
WHAT'S THE 411, PAT?
THE WHAT?
411! FmyI! WHAT THE HELL'S GOING ON?
SMACK
JUST A SMALL MESS THAT NEEDS TO BE STRAIGHTENED OUT BEFORE I RETIRE.
A FORMER COLLEAGUE CONTACTED ME ABOUT SOME TROUBLE HERE IN BLUE VALLEY AND WANTED MY HELP.
UNFORTUNATELY, I HAVEN'T HEARD FROM HIM SINCE.
AND YOU GOT THIS BIG ROBOT-SUIT-THING TO HELP?
YEAH, AND--
SO BASICALLY YOU'RE USING ME AND MOM AS COVER FOR SOME LAME-O SECRET SUPER-HERO OPERATION. THAT'S SO NOT RIGHT.

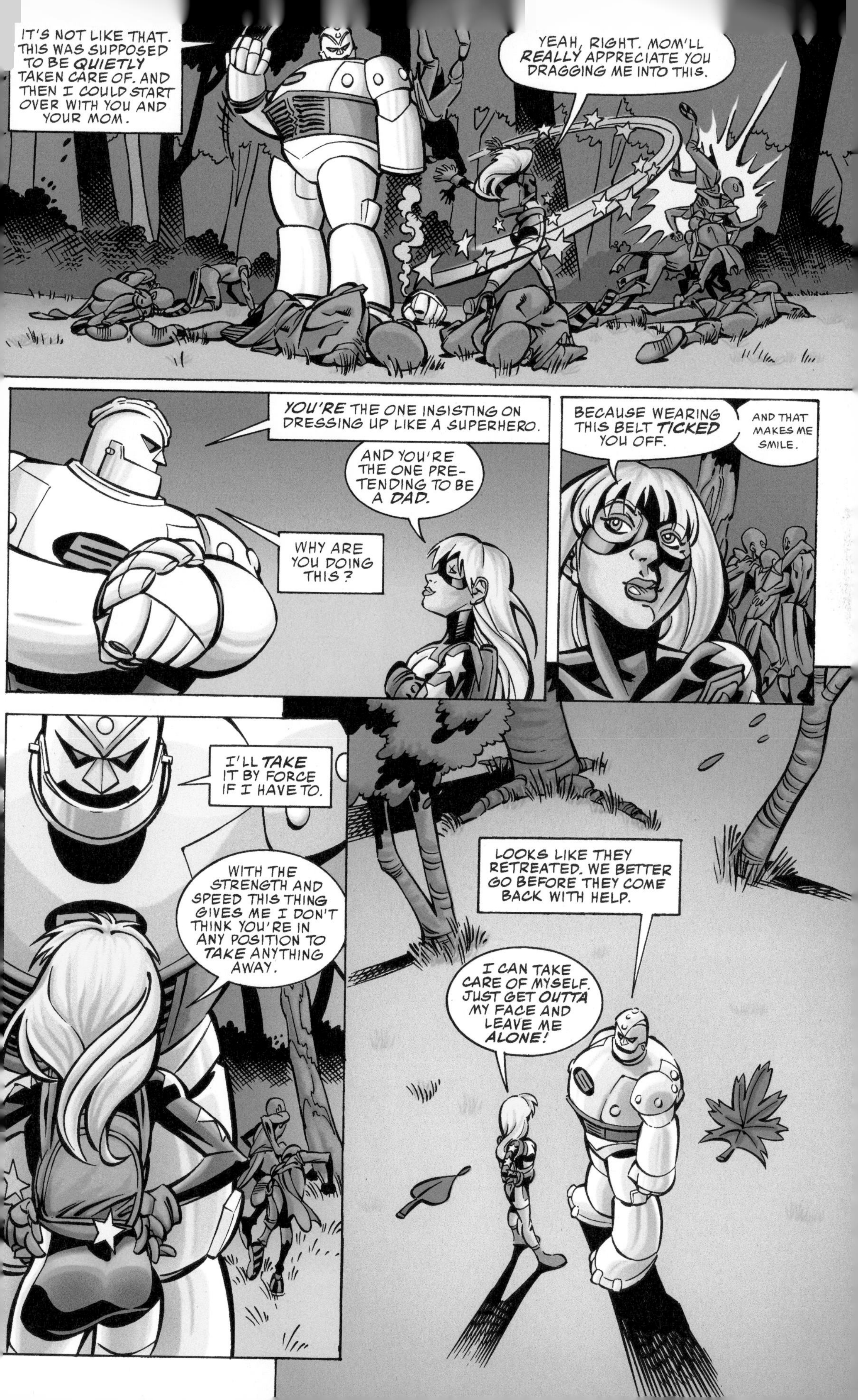
IT'S NOT LIKE THAT. THIS WAS SUPPOSED TO BE QUIETLY TAKEN CARE OF. AND THEN I COULD START OVER WITH YOU AND YOUR MOM.
YEAH, RIGHT. MOM'LL REALLY APPRECIATE YOU DRAGGING ME INTO THIS.
YOU'RE THE ONE INSISTING ON DRESSING UP LIKE A SUPERHERO.
AND YOU'RE THE ONE PRETENDING TO BE A DAD.
WHY ARE YOU DOING THIS?
BECAUSE WEARING THIS BELT TICKED YOU OFF.
AND THAT MAKES ME SMILE.
I'LL TAKE IT BY FORCE IF I HAVE TO.
WITH THE STRENGTH AND SPEED THIS THING GIVES ME I DON'T THINK YOU'RE IN ANY POSITION TO TAKE ANYTHING AWAY.
LOOKS LIKE THEY RETREATED. WE BETTER GO BEFORE THEY COME BACK WITH HELP.
I CAN TAKE CARE OF MYSELF. JUST GET OUTTA MY FACE AND LEAVE ME ALONE!

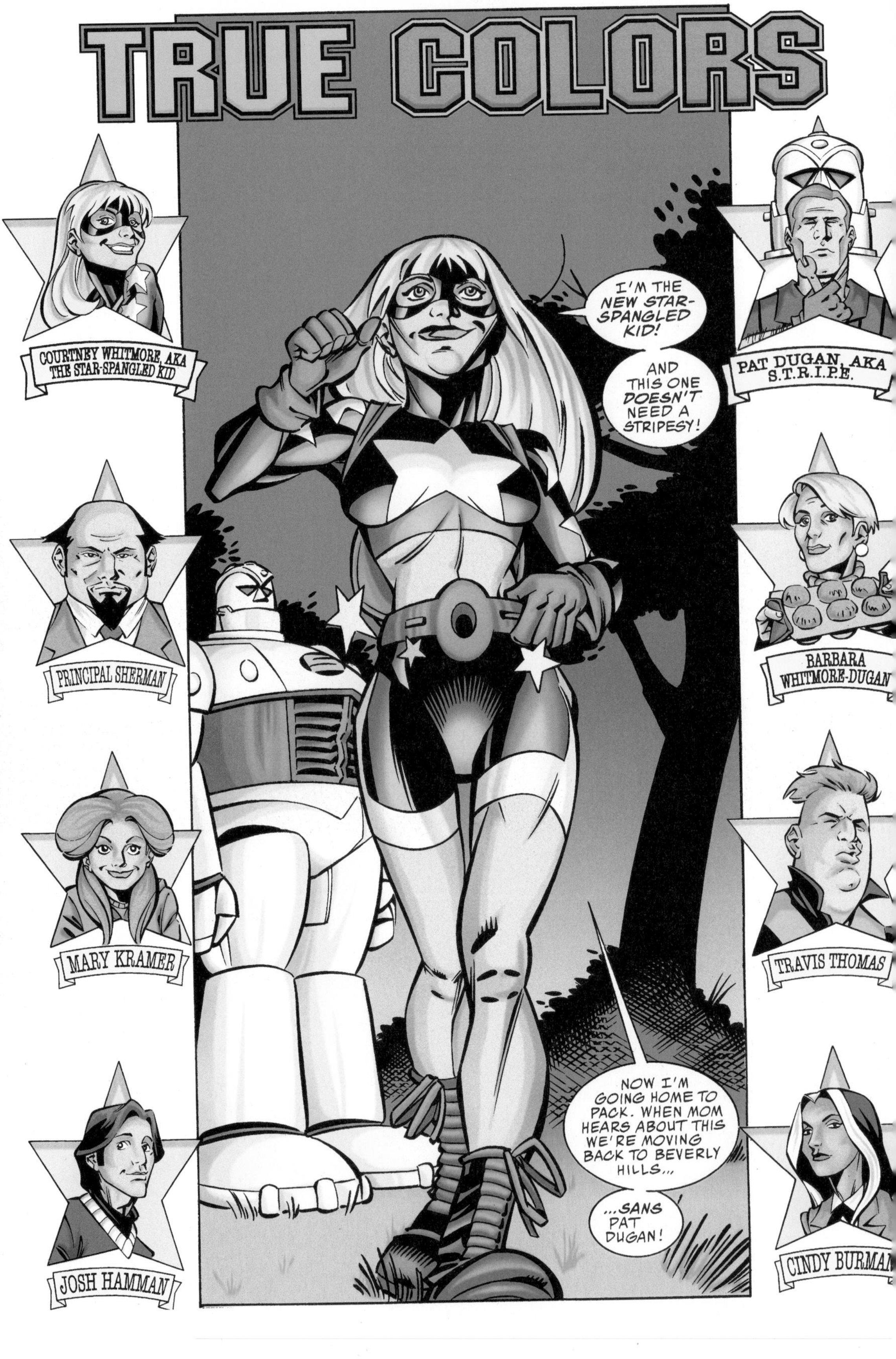
TRUE COLORS
COURTNEY WHITMORE, AKA THE STAR-SPANGLED KID
PAT DUGAN, AKA S.T.R.I.P.E.
I'M THE NEW STAR-SPANGLED KID!
AND THIS ONE DOESN'T NEED A STRIPESY!
PRINCIPAL SHERMAN
BARBARA WHITMORE-DUGAN
MARY KRAMER
TRAVIS THOMAS
NOW I'M GOING HOME TO PACK. WHEN MOM HEARS ABOUT THIS WE'RE MOVING BACK TO BEVERLY HILLS...
...SANS PAT DUGAN!
JOSH HAMMAN
CINDY BURMAN

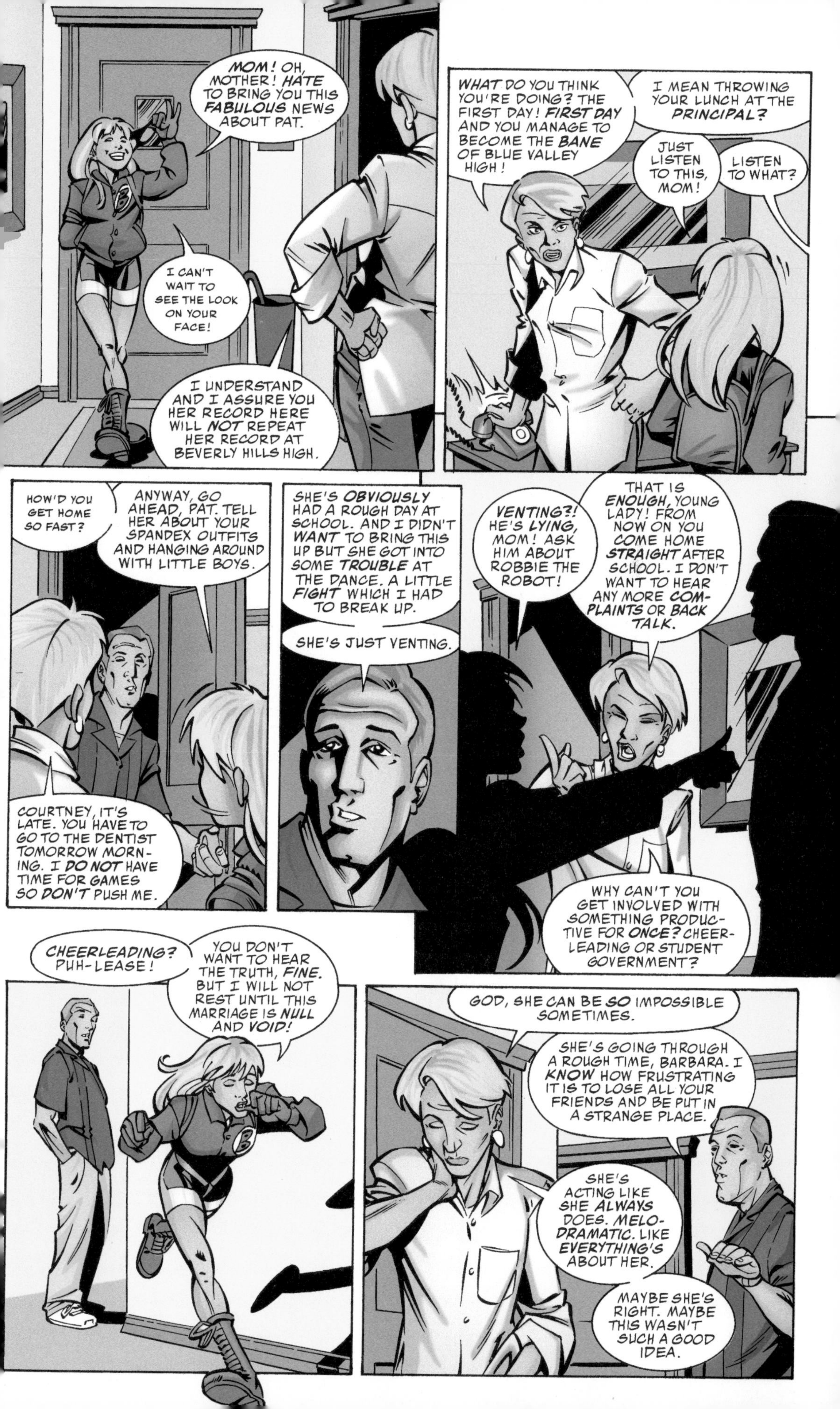
MOM! OH, MOTHER! HATE TO BRING YOU THIS FABULOUS NEWS ABOUT PAT.
I CAN'T WAIT TO SEE THE LOOK ON YOUR FACE!
I UNDERSTAND AND I ASSURE YOU HER RECORD HERE WILL NOT REPEAT HER RECORD AT BEVERLY HILLS HIGH.
WHAT DO YOU THINK YOU'RE DOING? THE FIRST DAY! FIRST DAY AND YOU MANAGE TO BECOME THE BANE OF BLUE VALLEY HIGH!
I MEAN THROWING YOUR LUNCH AT THE PRINCIPAL?
JUST LISTEN TO THIS, MOM!
LISTEN TO WHAT?
HOW'D YOU GET HOME SO FAST?
ANYWAY, GO AHEAD, PAT. TELL HER ABOUT YOUR SPANDEX OUTFITS AND HANGING AROUND WITH LITTLE BOYS.
COURTNEY, IT'S LATE. YOU HAVE TO GO TO THE DENTIST TOMORROW MORNING. I DO NOT HAVE TIME FOR GAMES SO DON'T PUSH ME.
SHE'S OBVIOUSLY HAD A ROUGH DAY AT SCHOOL. AND I DIDN'T WANT TO BRING THIS UP BUT SHE GOT INTO SOME TROUBLE AT THE DANCE. A LITTLE FIGHT WHICH I HAD TO BREAK UP.
SHE'S JUST VENTING.
VENTING?! HE'S LYING, MOM! ASK HIM ABOUT ROBBIE THE ROBOT!
THAT IS ENOUGH, YOUNG LADY! FROM NOW ON YOU COME HOME STRAIGHT AFTER SCHOOL. I DON'T WANT TO HEAR ANY MORE COMPLAINTS OR BACK TALK.
WHY CAN'T YOU GET INVOLVED WITH SOMETHING PRODUCTIVE FOR ONCE? CHEERLEADING OR STUDENT GOVERNMENT?
CHEERLEADING? PUH-LEASE!
YOU DON'T WANT TO HEAR THE TRUTH, FINE. BUT I WILL NOT REST UNTIL THIS MARRIAGE IS NULL AND VOID!
GOD, SHE CAN BE SO IMPOSSIBLE SOMETIMES.
SHE'S GOING THROUGH A ROUGH TIME, BARBARA. I KNOW HOW FRUSTRATING IT IS TO LOSE ALL YOUR FRIENDS AND BE PUT IN A STRANGE PLACE.
SHE'S ACTING LIKE SHE ALWAYS DOES. MELODRAMATIC. LIKE EVERYTHING'S ABOUT HER.
MAYBE SHE'S RIGHT. MAYBE THIS WASN'T SUCH A GOOD IDEA.

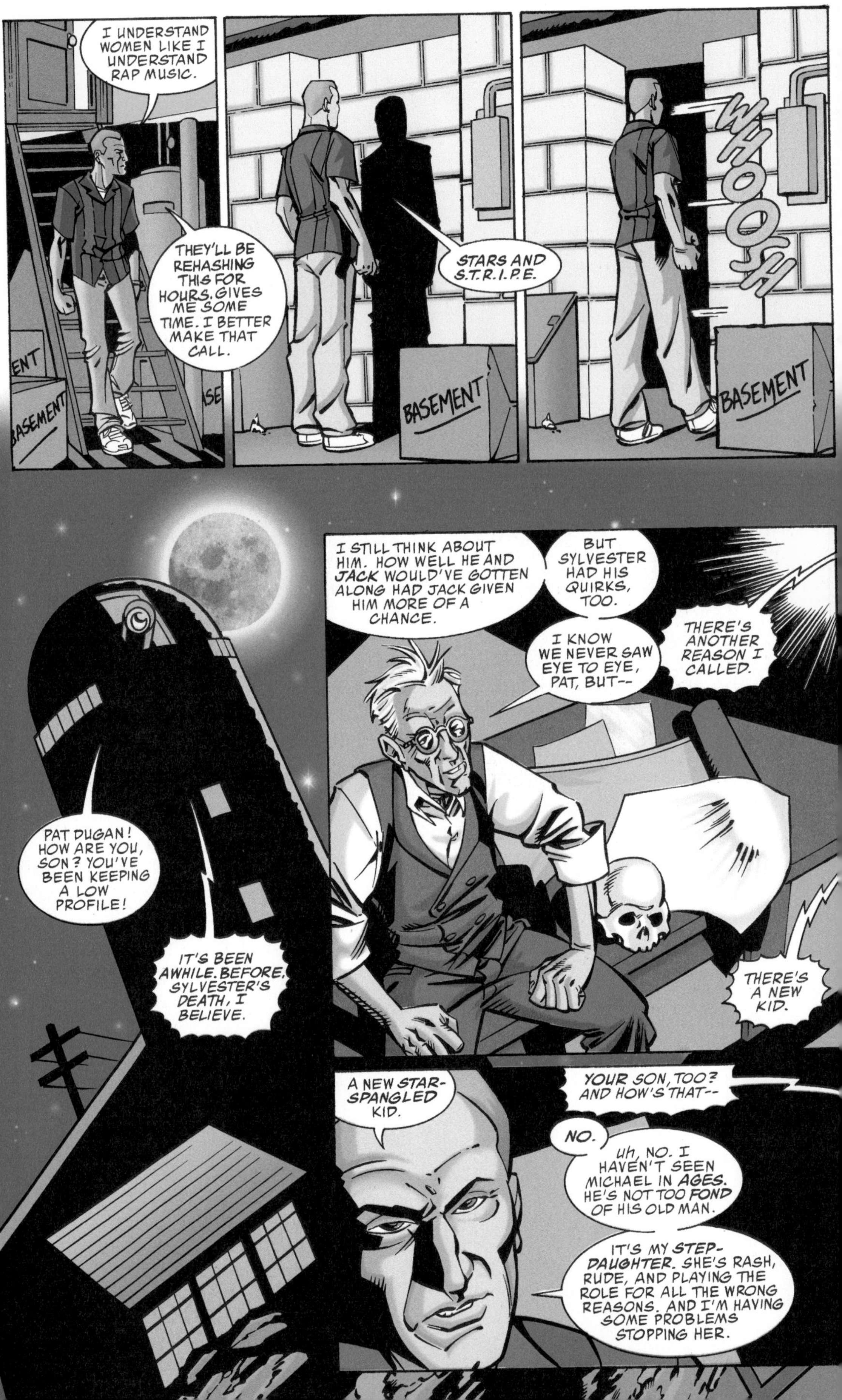
I UNDERSTAND WOMEN LIKE I UNDERSTAND RAP MUSIC.
THEY'LL BE REHASHING THIS FOR HOURS. GIVES ME SOME TIME. I BETTER MAKE THAT CALL.
BASEMENT
STARS AND S.T.R.I.P.E.
BASEMENT
WHOOSH
BASEMENT
PAT DUGAN! HOW ARE YOU, SON? YOU'VE BEEN KEEPING A LOW PROFILE!
IT'S BEEN AWHILE. BEFORE SYLVESTER'S DEATH, I BELIEVE.
I STILL THINK ABOUT HIM. HOW WELL HE AND JACK WOULD'VE GOTTEN ALONG HAD JACK GIVEN HIM MORE OF A CHANCE.
BUT SYLVESTER HAD HIS QUIRKS, TOO.
I KNOW WE NEVER SAW EYE TO EYE, PAT, BUT--
THERE'S ANOTHER REASON I CALLED.
THERE'S A NEW KID.
A NEW STAR-SPANGLED KID.
YOUR SON, TOO? AND HOW'S THAT--
NO.
uh, NO. I HAVEN'T SEEN MICHAEL IN AGES. HE'S NOT TOO FOND OF HIS OLD MAN.
IT'S MY STEP-DAUGHTER. SHE'S RASH, RUDE, AND PLAYING THE ROLE FOR ALL THE WRONG REASONS. AND I'M HAVING SOME PROBLEMS STOPPING HER.

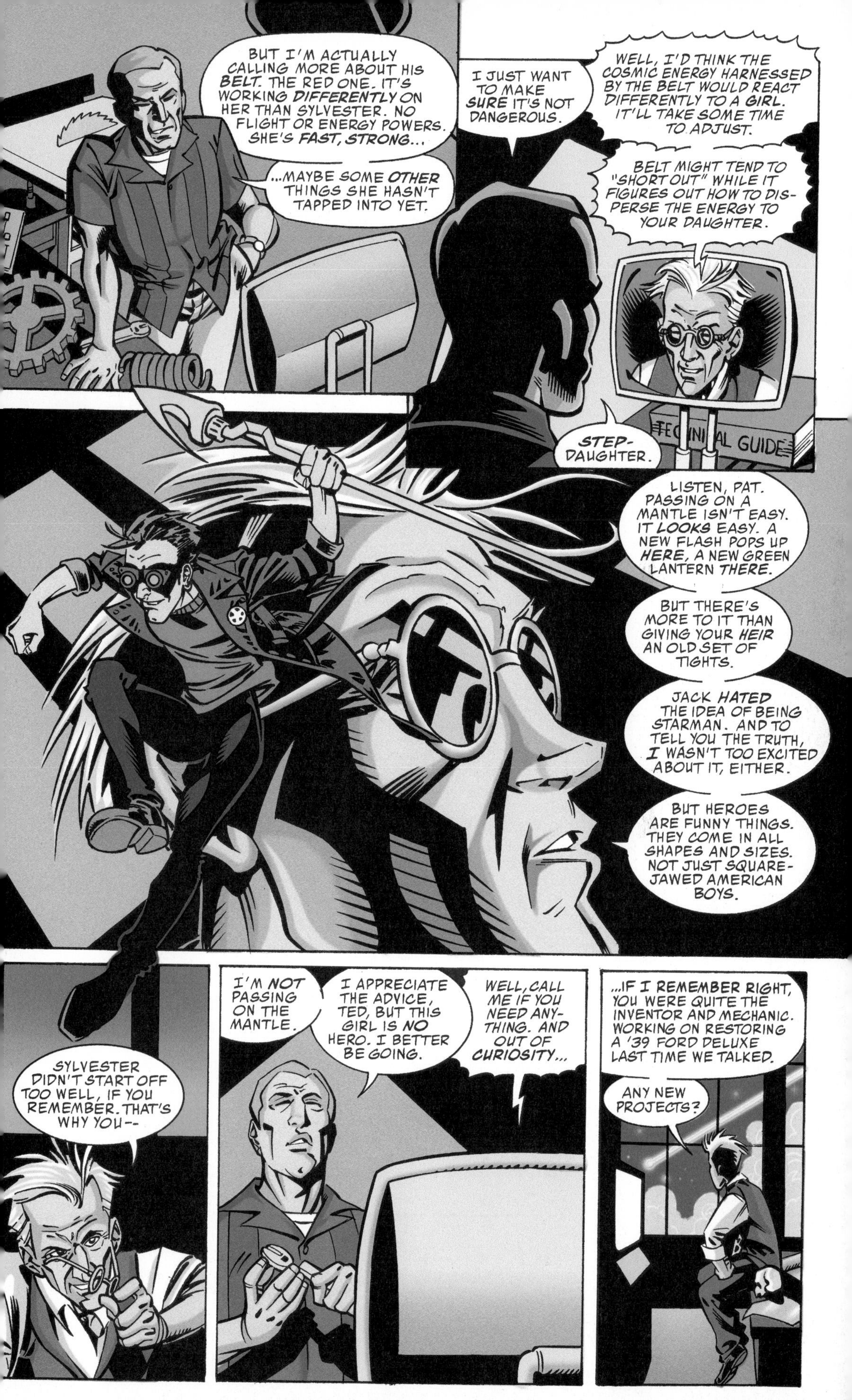

BUT I'M ACTUALLY CALLING MORE ABOUT HIS BELT. THE RED ONE. IT'S WORKING DIFFERENTLY ON HER THAN SYLVESTER. NO FLIGHT OR ENERGY POWERS. SHE'S FAST, STRONG...
...MAYBE SOME OTHER THINGS SHE HASN'T TAPPED INTO YET.
I JUST WANT TO MAKE SURE IT'S NOT DANGEROUS.
WELL, I'D THINK THE COSMIC ENERGY HARNESSED BY THE BELT WOULD REACT DIFFERENTLY TO A GIRL. IT'LL TAKE SOME TIME TO ADJUST.
BELT MIGHT TEND TO "SHORT OUT" WHILE IT FIGURES OUT HOW TO DISPERSE THE ENERGY TO YOUR DAUGHTER.
STEP-DAUGHTER.
TECHNICAL GUIDE
LISTEN, PAT. PASSING ON A MANTLE ISN'T EASY. IT LOOKS EASY. A NEW FLASH POPS UP HERE, A NEW GREEN LANTERN THERE.
BUT THERE'S MORE TO IT THAN GIVING YOUR HEIR AN OLD SET OF TIGHTS.
JACK HATED THE IDEA OF BEING STARMAN. AND TO TELL YOU THE TRUTH, I WASN'T TOO EXCITED ABOUT IT, EITHER.
BUT HEROES ARE FUNNY THINGS. THEY COME IN ALL SHAPES AND SIZES. NOT JUST SQUARE-JAWED AMERICAN BOYS.
SYLVESTER DIDN'T START OFF TOO WELL, IF YOU REMEMBER. THAT'S WHY YOU--
I'M NOT PASSING ON THE MANTLE.
I APPRECIATE THE ADVICE, TED, BUT THIS GIRL IS NO HERO. I BETTER BE GOING.
WELL, CALL ME IF YOU NEED ANYTHING. AND OUT OF CURIOSITY...
...IF I REMEMBER RIGHT, YOU WERE QUITE THE INVENTOR AND MECHANIC. WORKING ON RESTORING A '39 FORD DELUXE LAST TIME WE TALKED.
ANY NEW PROJECTS?

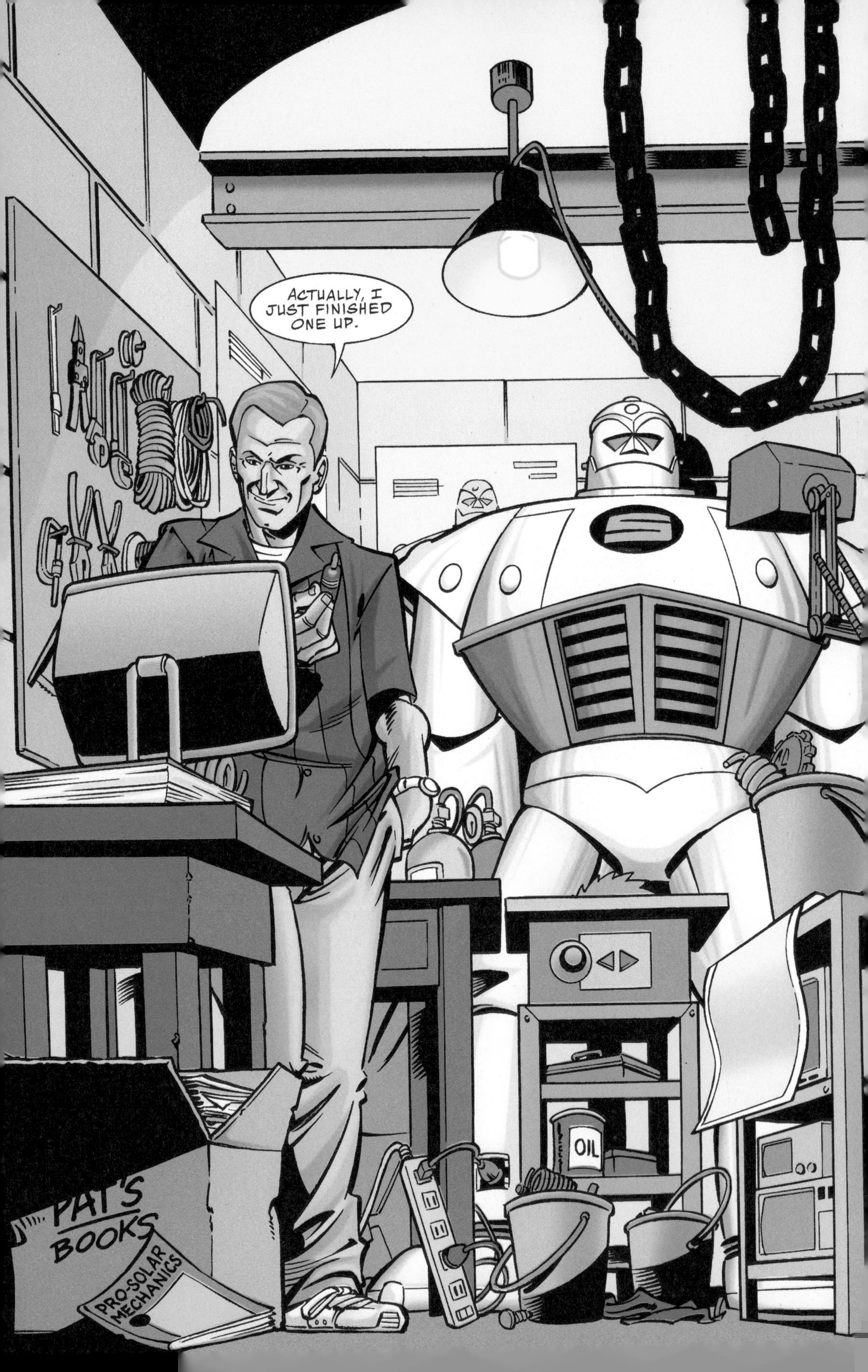
ACTUALLY, I JUST FINISHED ONE UP.
OIL
PAT'S BOOKS
PRO-SOLAR MECHANICS

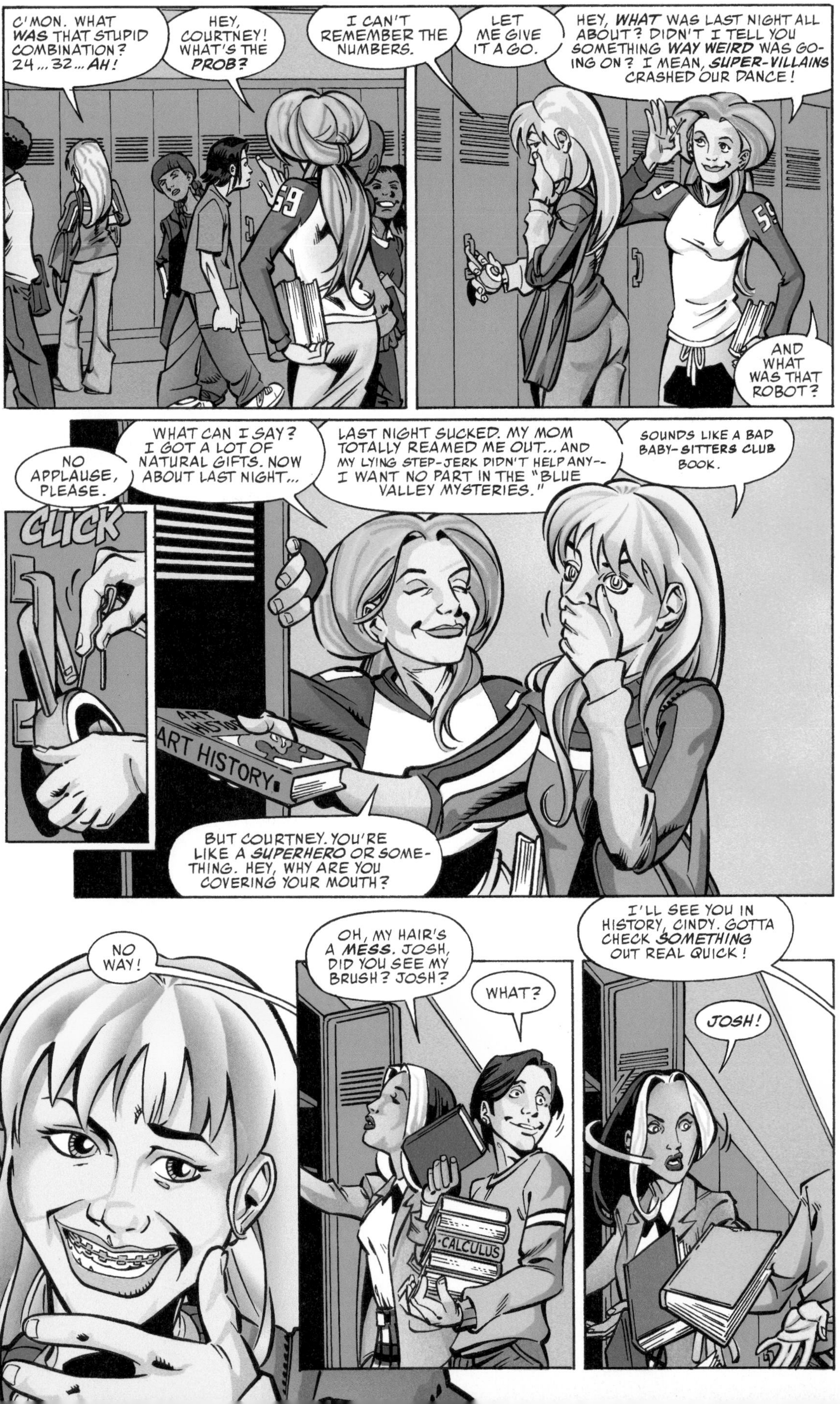
C'MON. WHAT WAS THAT STUPID COMBINATION? 24...32...AH!
HEY, COURTNEY! WHAT'S THE PROB?
I CAN'T REMEMBER THE NUMBERS.
LET ME GIVE IT A GO.
HEY, WHAT WAS LAST NIGHT ALL ABOUT? DIDN'T I TELL YOU SOMETHING WAY WEIRD WAS GOING ON? I MEAN, SUPER-VILLAINS CRASHED OUR DANCE!
AND WHAT WAS THAT ROBOT?
CLICK
NO APPLAUSE, PLEASE.
WHAT CAN I SAY? I GOT A LOT OF NATURAL GIFTS. NOW ABOUT LAST NIGHT...
LAST NIGHT SUCKED. MY MOM TOTALLY REAMED ME OUT... AND MY LYING STEP-JERK DIDN'T HELP ANY-- I WANT NO PART IN THE "BLUE VALLEY MYSTERIES."
SOUNDS LIKE A BAD BABY-SITTERS CLUB BOOK.
ART HISTORY
BUT COURTNEY. YOU'RE LIKE A SUPERHERO OR SOMETHING. HEY, WHY ARE YOU COVERING YOUR MOUTH?
NO WAY!
OH, MY HAIR'S A MESS. JOSH, DID YOU SEE MY BRUSH? JOSH?
WHAT?
CALCULUS
I'LL SEE YOU IN HISTORY, CINDY. GOTTA CHECK SOMETHING OUT REAL QUICK!
JOSH!

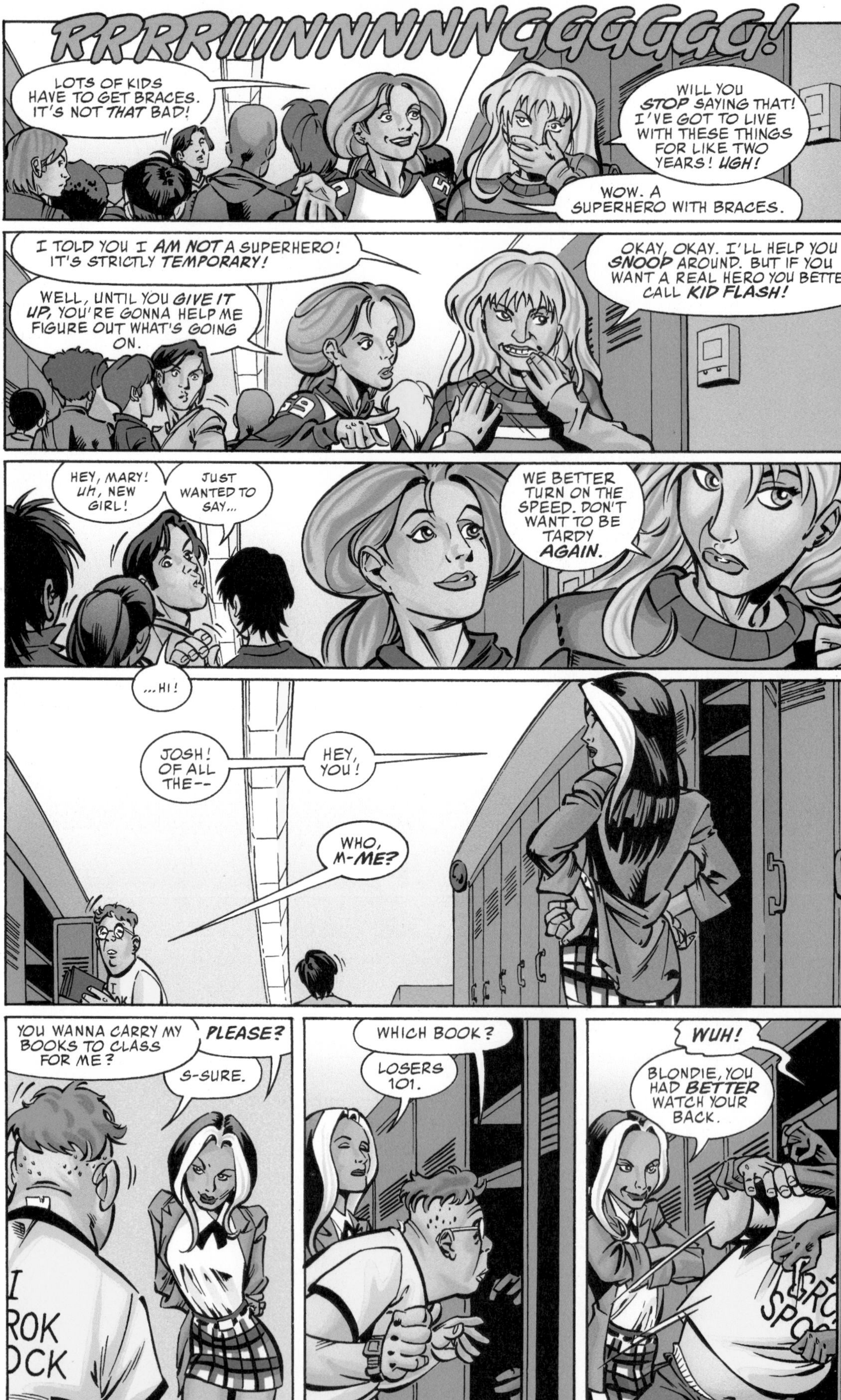

RRRRIIINNNNNNGGGGGGG!
LOTS OF KIDS HAVE TO GET BRACES. IT'S NOT THAT BAD!
WILL YOU STOP SAYING THAT! I'VE GOT TO LIVE WITH THESE THINGS FOR LIKE TWO YEARS! UGH!
WOW. A SUPERHERO WITH BRACES.
I TOLD YOU I AM NOT A SUPERHERO! IT'S STRICTLY TEMPORARY!
WELL, UNTIL YOU GIVE IT UP, YOU'RE GONNA HELP ME FIGURE OUT WHAT'S GOING ON.
OKAY, OKAY. I'LL HELP YOU SNOOP AROUND. BUT IF YOU WANT A REAL HERO YOU BETTER CALL KID FLASH!
HEY, MARY! UH, NEW GIRL!
JUST WANTED TO SAY...
WE BETTER TURN ON THE SPEED. DON'T WANT TO BE TARDY AGAIN.
...HI!
JOSH! OF ALL THE--
HEY, YOU!
WHO, M-ME?
YOU WANNA CARRY MY BOOKS TO CLASS FOR ME?
PLEASE?
S-SURE.
WHICH BOOK?
LOSERS 101.
WUH!
BLONDIE, YOU HAD BETTER WATCH YOUR BACK.

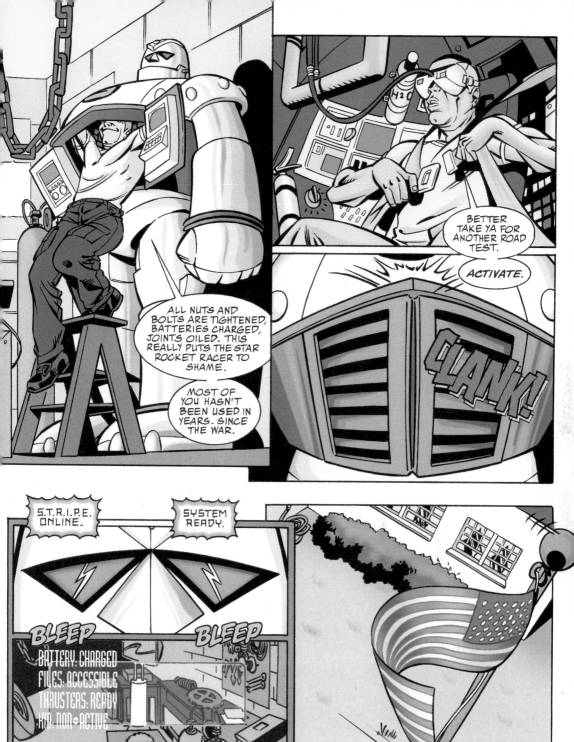

BETTER TAKE YA FOR ANOTHER ROAD TEST.

ALL NUTS AND BOLTS ARE TIGHTENED, BATTERIES CHARGED, JOINTS OILED. THIS REALLY PUTS THE STAR ROCKET RACER TO SHAME.

MOST OF YOU HASN'T BEEN USED IN YEARS. SINCE THE WAR.

ACTIVATE.

CLANK!

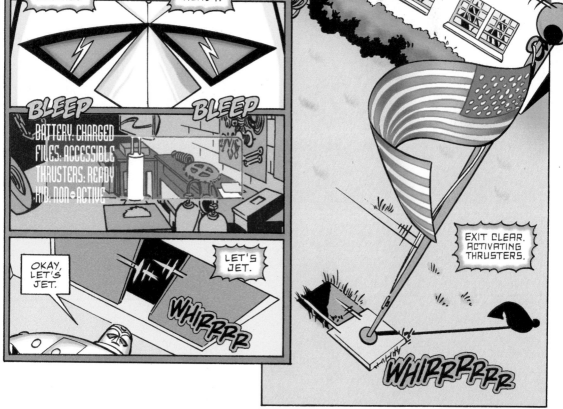

S.T.R.I.P.E. ONLINE.

SYSTEM READY.

BLEEP

BLEEP

BATTERY: CHARGED
FILES: ACCESSIBLE
THRUSTERS: READY
KID: NON-ACTIVE

OKAY, LET'S JET.

LET'S JET.

WHIRRRR

EXIT CLEAR. ACTIVATING THRUSTERS.

WHIRRRRR

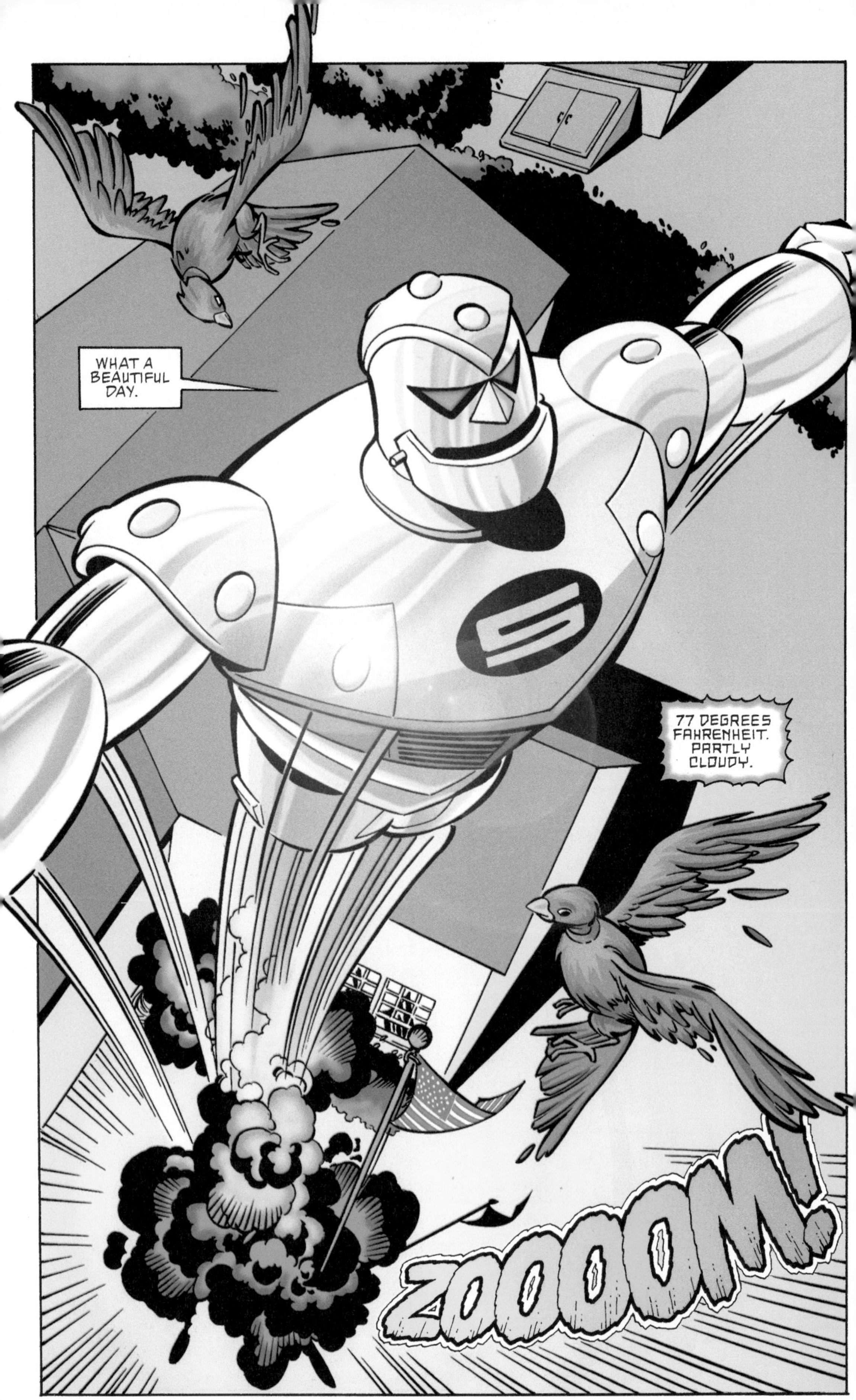
WHAT A BEAUTIFUL DAY.
77 DEGREES FAHRENHEIT. PARTLY CLOUDY.
ZOOOOM!

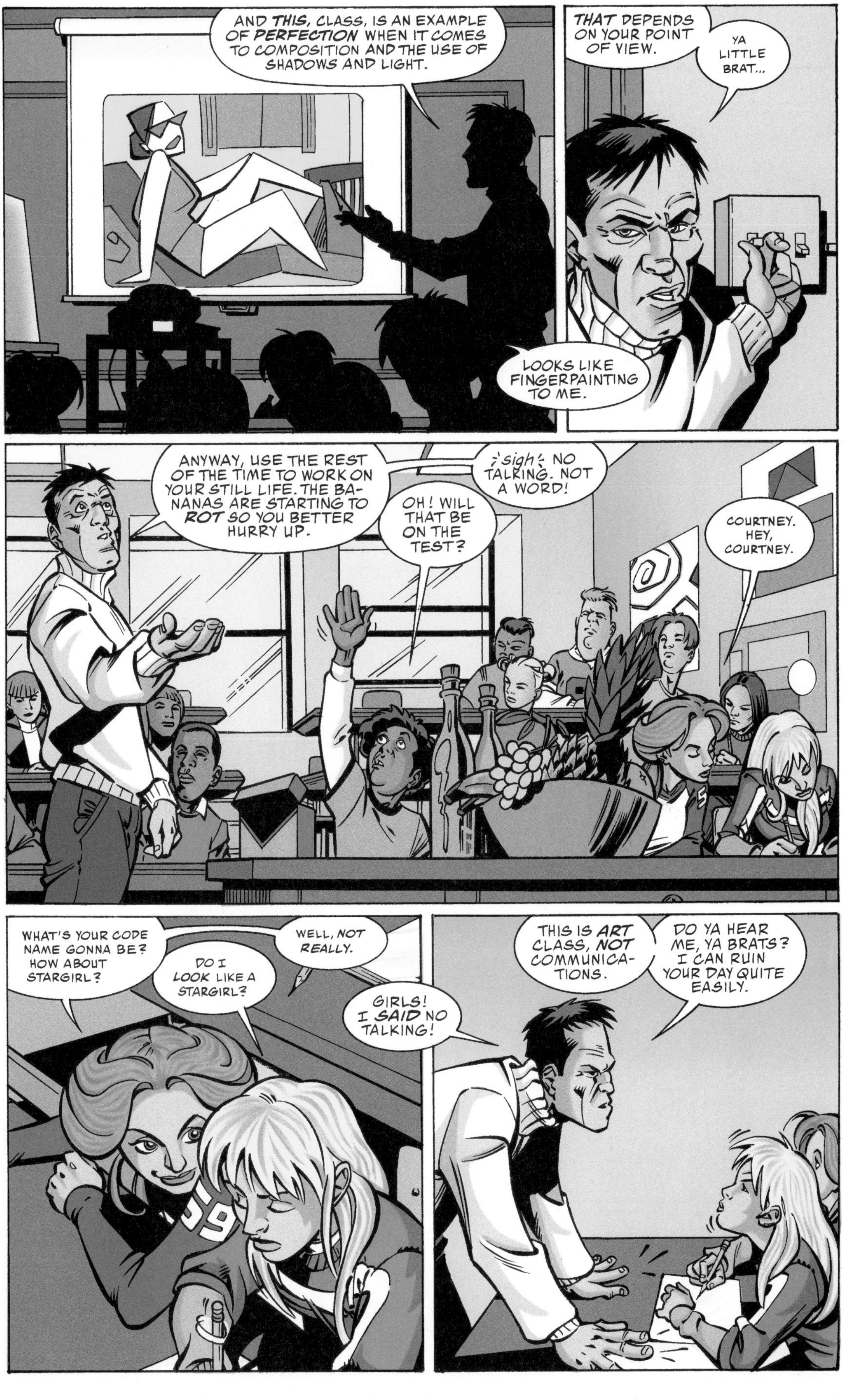
AND THIS, CLASS, IS AN EXAMPLE OF PERFECTION WHEN IT COMES TO COMPOSITION AND THE USE OF SHADOWS AND LIGHT.
THAT DEPENDS ON YOUR POINT OF VIEW.
YA LITTLE BRAT...
LOOKS LIKE FINGERPAINTING TO ME.
ANYWAY, USE THE REST OF THE TIME TO WORK ON YOUR STILL LIFE. THE BANANAS ARE STARTING TO ROT SO YOU BETTER HURRY UP.
OH! WILL THAT BE ON THE TEST?
sigh NO TALKING. NOT A WORD!
COURTNEY. HEY, COURTNEY.
WHAT'S YOUR CODE NAME GONNA BE? HOW ABOUT STARGIRL?
DO I LOOK LIKE A STARGIRL?
WELL, NOT REALLY.
GIRLS! I SAID NO TALKING!
THIS IS ART CLASS, NOT COMMUNICATIONS.
DO YA HEAR ME, YA BRATS? I CAN RUIN YOUR DAY QUITE EASILY.

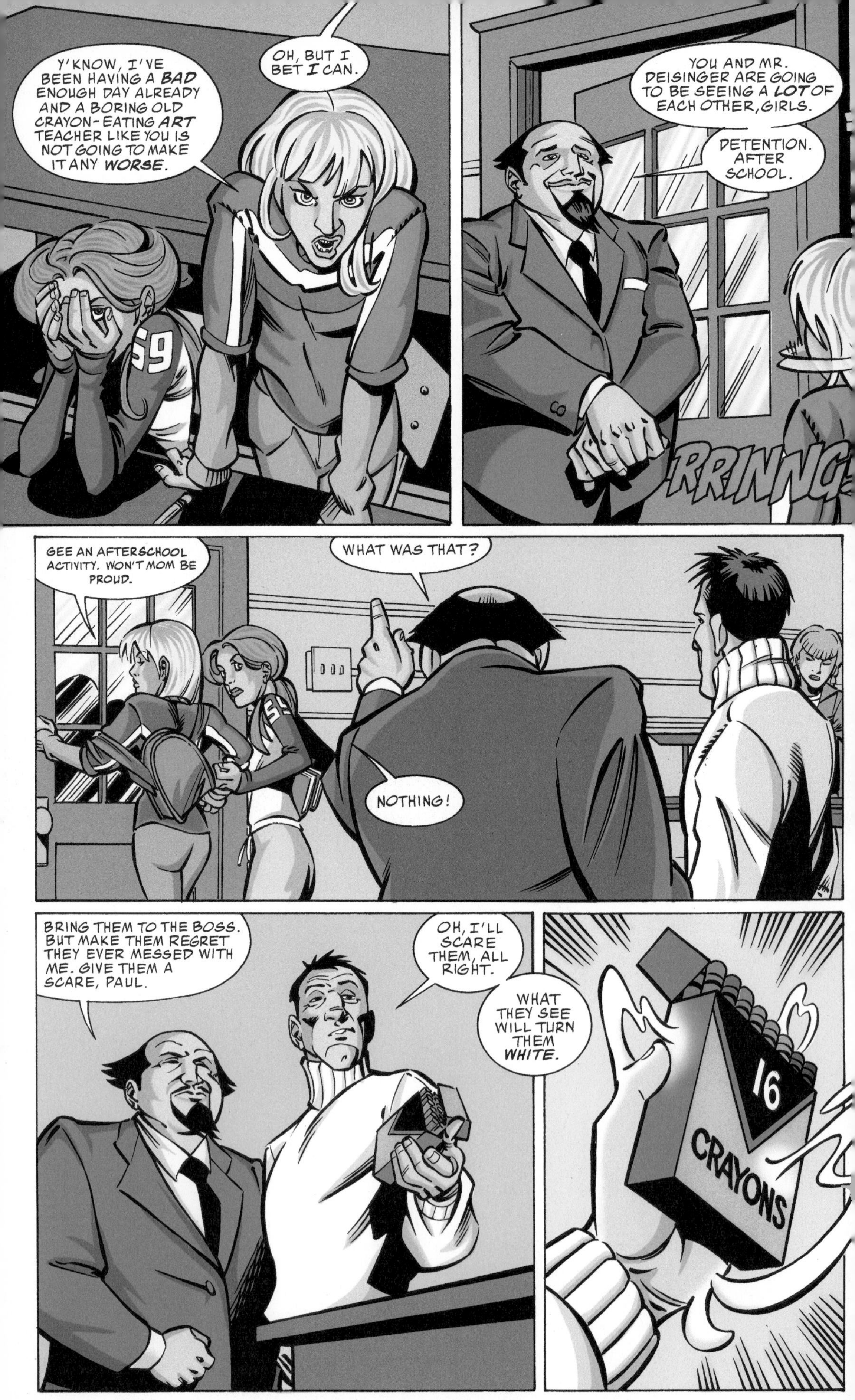

Y'KNOW, I'VE BEEN HAVING A BAD ENOUGH DAY ALREADY AND A BORING OLD CRAYON-EATING ART TEACHER LIKE YOU IS NOT GOING TO MAKE IT ANY WORSE.
OH, BUT I BET I CAN.
YOU AND MR. DEISINGER ARE GOING TO BE SEEING A LOT OF EACH OTHER, GIRLS.
DETENTION. AFTER SCHOOL.
RRINNG
GEE AN AFTERSCHOOL ACTIVITY. WON'T MOM BE PROUD.
WHAT WAS THAT?
NOTHING!
BRING THEM TO THE BOSS. BUT MAKE THEM REGRET THEY EVER MESSED WITH ME. GIVE THEM A SCARE, PAUL.
OH, I'LL SCARE THEM, ALL RIGHT.
WHAT THEY SEE WILL TURN THEM WHITE.
16
CRAYONS

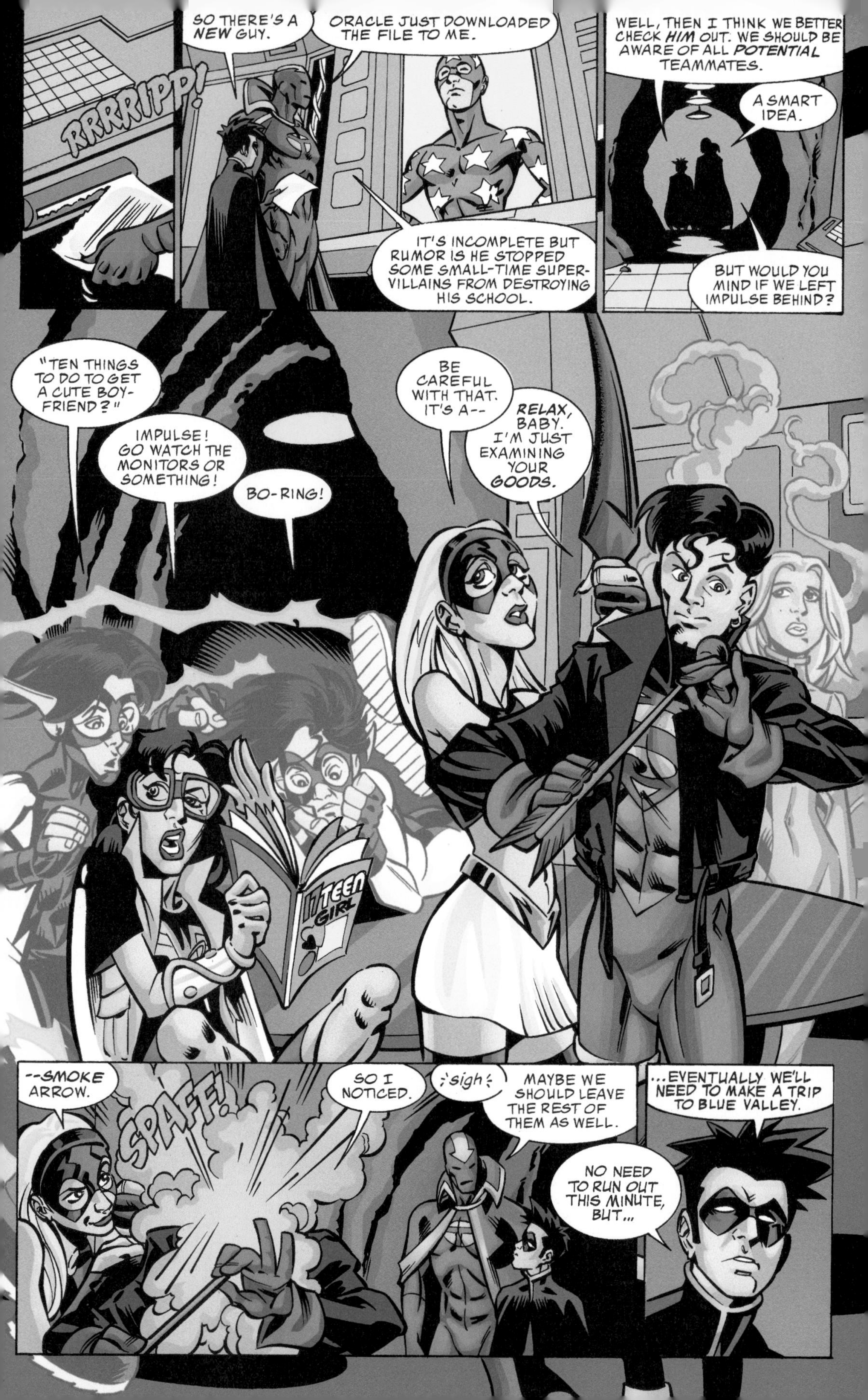
RRRRIPP!
SO THERE'S A NEW GUY.
ORACLE JUST DOWNLOADED THE FILE TO ME.
IT'S INCOMPLETE BUT RUMOR IS HE STOPPED SOME SMALL-TIME SUPER-VILLAINS FROM DESTROYING HIS SCHOOL.
WELL, THEN I THINK WE BETTER CHECK HIM OUT. WE SHOULD BE AWARE OF ALL POTENTIAL TEAMMATES.
A SMART IDEA.
BUT WOULD YOU MIND IF WE LEFT IMPULSE BEHIND?
"TEN THINGS TO DO TO GET A CUTE BOY-FRIEND?"
IMPULSE! GO WATCH THE MONITORS OR SOMETHING!
BO-RING!
BE CAREFUL WITH THAT. IT'S A--
RELAX, BABY. I'M JUST EXAMINING YOUR GOODS.
TEEN GIRL
--SMOKE ARROW.
SPAFF!
SO I NOTICED.
sigh
MAYBE WE SHOULD LEAVE THE REST OF THEM AS WELL.
NO NEED TO RUN OUT THIS MINUTE, BUT...
...EVENTUALLY WE'LL NEED TO MAKE A TRIP TO BLUE VALLEY.

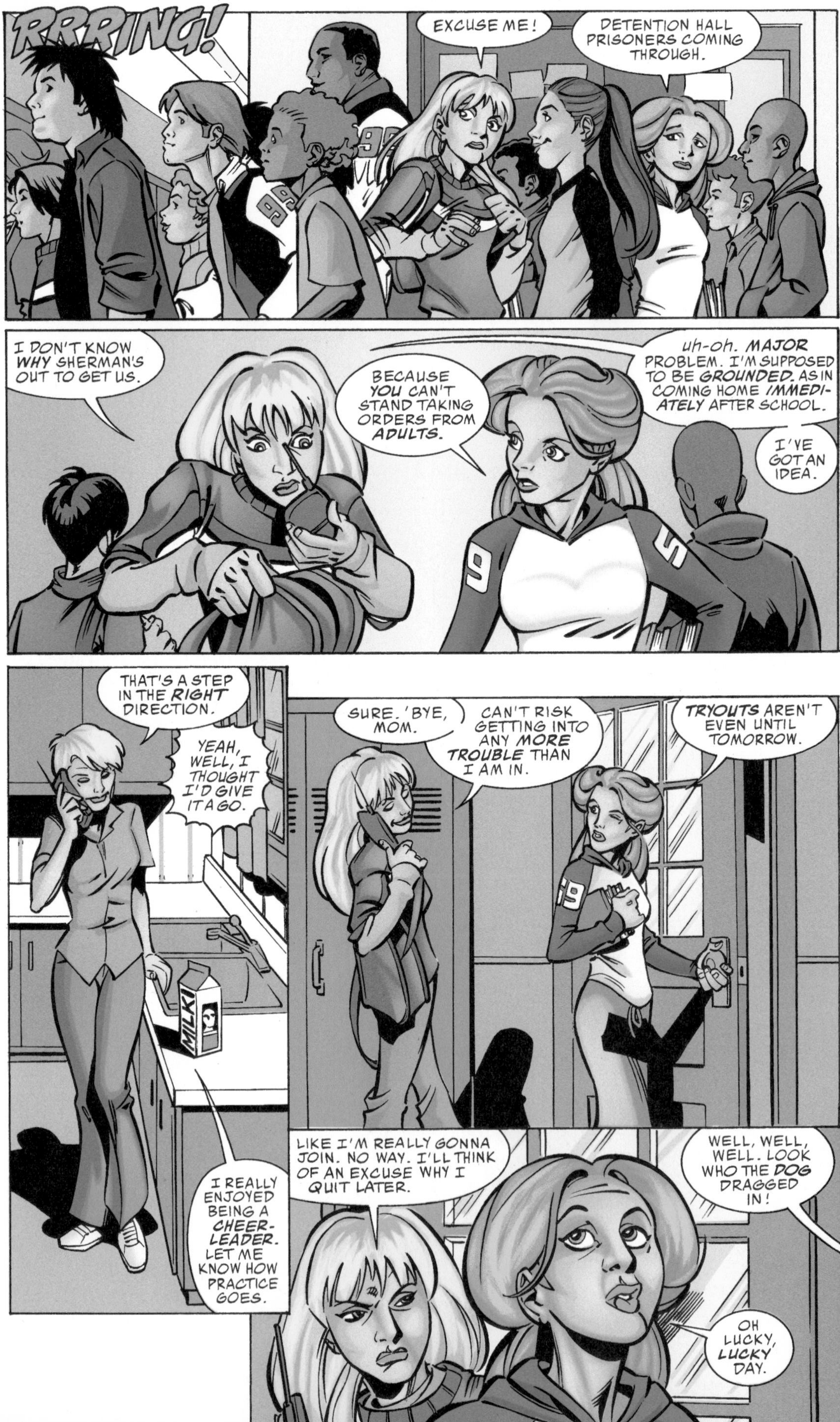
RRRING!
EXCUSE ME!
DETENTION HALL PRISONERS COMING THROUGH.
I DON'T KNOW WHY SHERMAN'S OUT TO GET US.
BECAUSE YOU CAN'T STAND TAKING ORDERS FROM ADULTS.
uh-oh. MAJOR PROBLEM. I'M SUPPOSED TO BE GROUNDED. AS IN COMING HOME IMMEDI-ATELY AFTER SCHOOL.
I'VE GOT AN IDEA.
THAT'S A STEP IN THE RIGHT DIRECTION.
YEAH, WELL, I THOUGHT I'D GIVE IT A GO.
I REALLY ENJOYED BEING A CHEER-LEADER. LET ME KNOW HOW PRACTICE GOES.
SURE. 'BYE, MOM.
CAN'T RISK GETTING INTO ANY MORE TROUBLE THAN I AM IN.
TRYOUTS AREN'T EVEN UNTIL TOMORROW.
MILK!
LIKE I'M REALLY GONNA JOIN. NO WAY. I'LL THINK OF AN EXCUSE WHY I QUIT LATER.
WELL, WELL, WELL. LOOK WHO THE DOG DRAGGED IN!
OH LUCKY, LUCKY DAY.

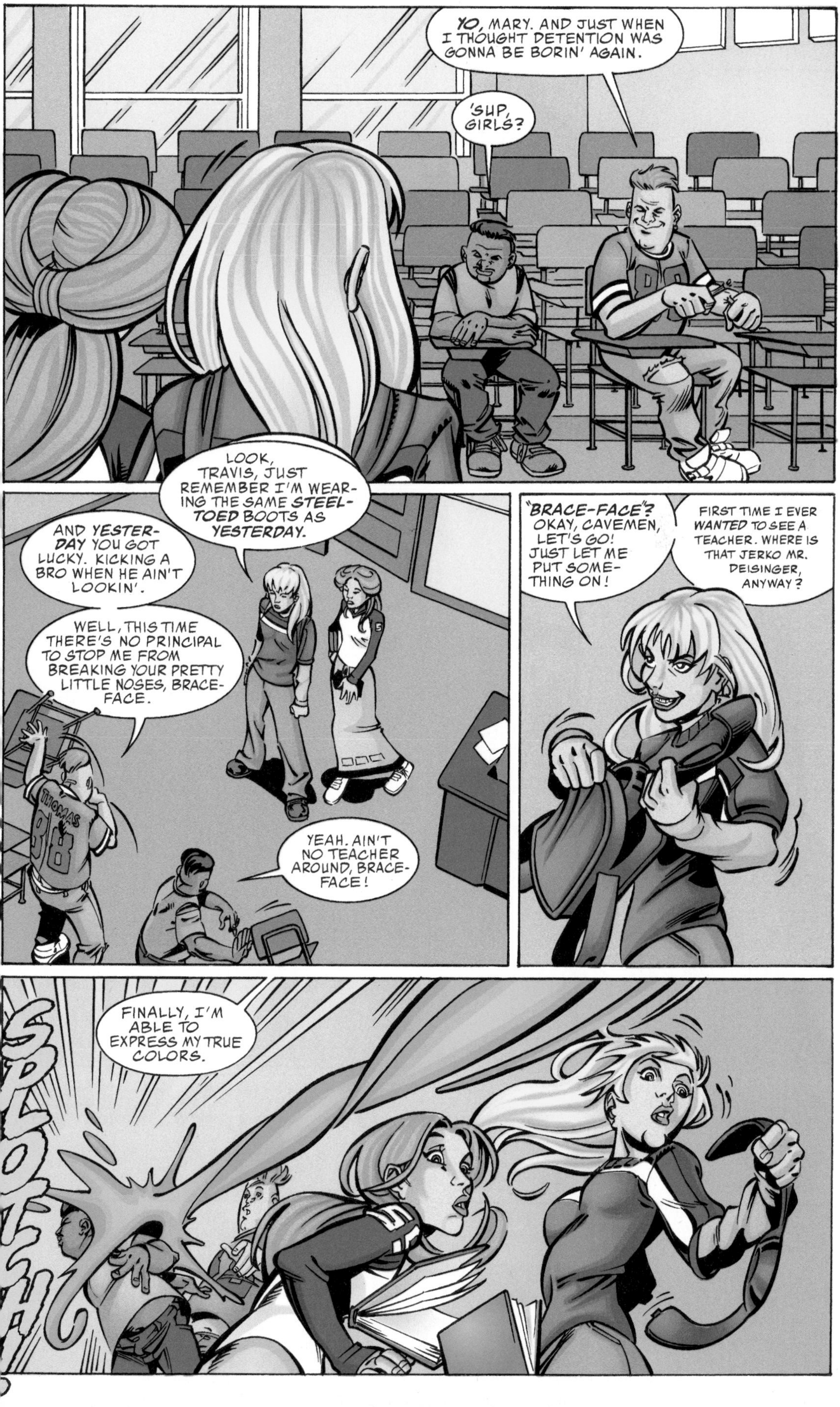
'SUP, GIRLS?
YO, MARY. AND JUST WHEN I THOUGHT DETENTION WAS GONNA BE BORIN' AGAIN.
LOOK, TRAVIS, JUST REMEMBER I'M WEARING THE SAME STEEL-TOED BOOTS AS YESTERDAY.
AND YESTERDAY YOU GOT LUCKY. KICKING A BRO WHEN HE AIN'T LOOKIN'.
WELL, THIS TIME THERE'S NO PRINCIPAL TO STOP ME FROM BREAKING YOUR PRETTY LITTLE NOSES, BRACE-FACE.
YEAH. AIN'T NO TEACHER AROUND, BRACE-FACE!
"BRACE-FACE"? OKAY, CAVEMEN, LET'S GO! JUST LET ME PUT SOMETHING ON!
FIRST TIME I EVER WANTED TO SEE A TEACHER. WHERE IS THAT JERKO MR. DEISINGER, ANYWAY?
FINALLY, I'M ABLE TO EXPRESS MY TRUE COLORS.
SPLOTCH

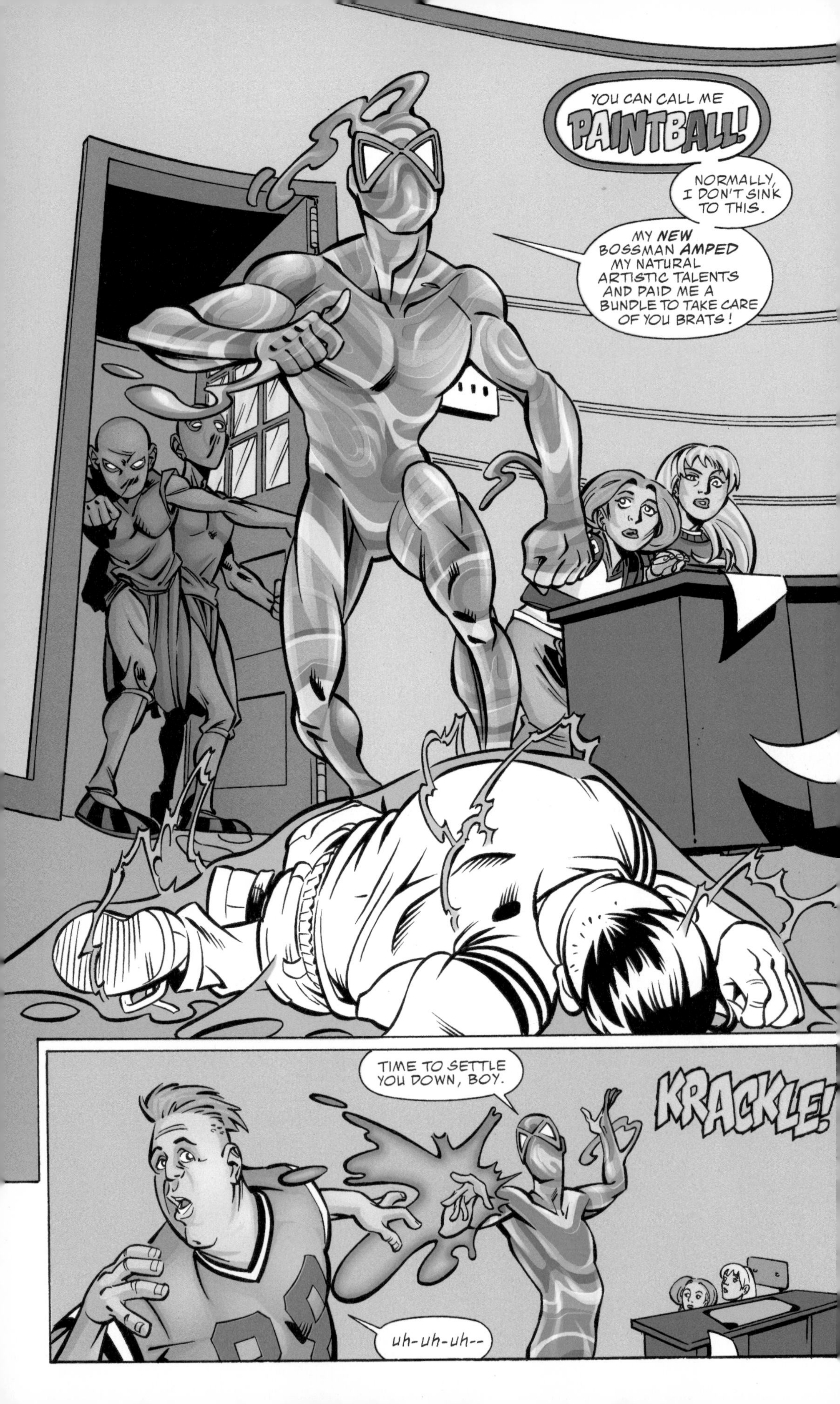

YOU CAN CALL ME PAINTBALL!
NORMALLY, I DON'T SINK TO THIS.
MY NEW BOSSMAN AMPED MY NATURAL ARTISTIC TALENTS AND PAID ME A BUNDLE TO TAKE CARE OF YOU BRATS!
TIME TO SETTLE YOU DOWN, BOY.
KRACKLE!
uh-uh-uh--

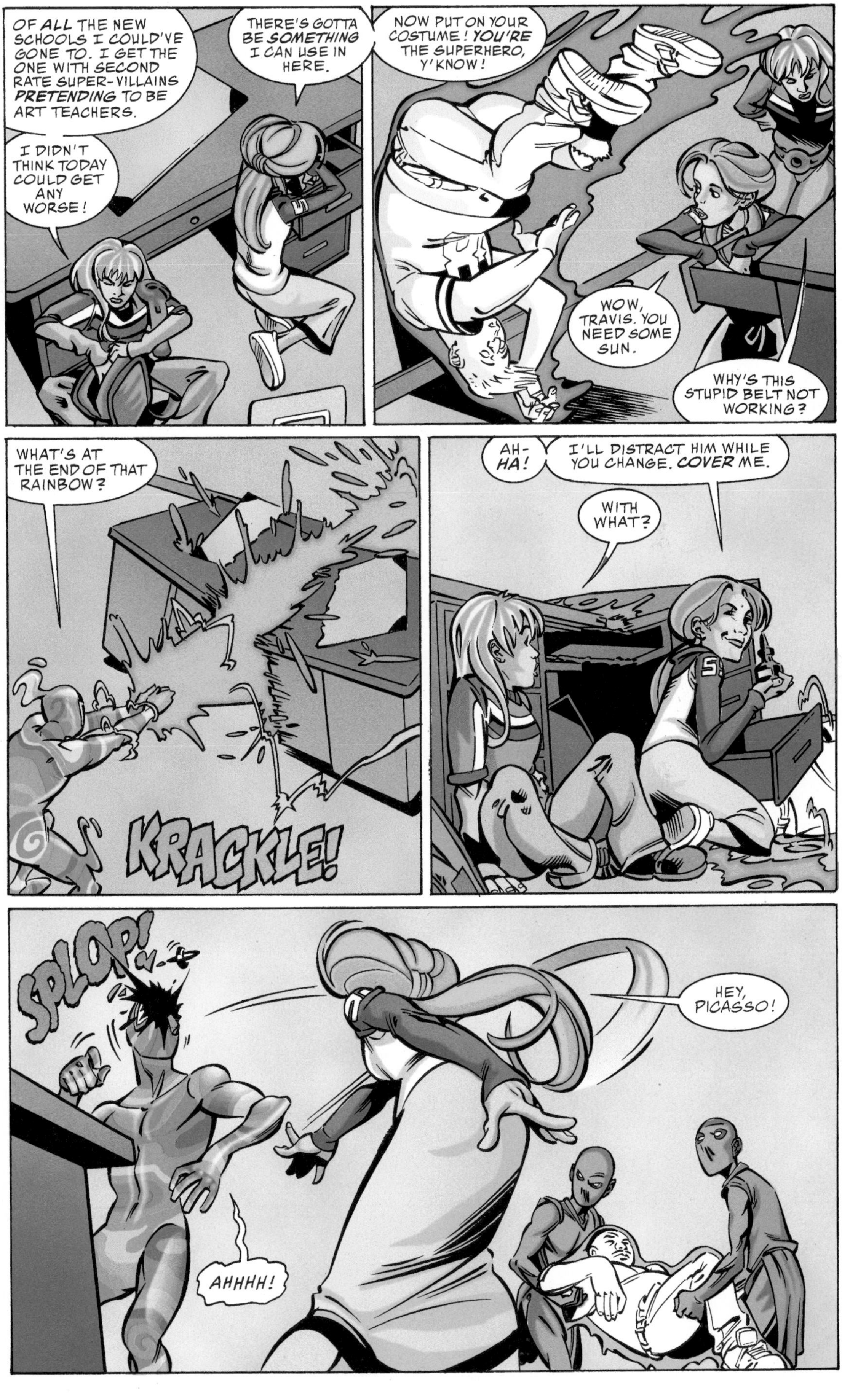

OF ALL THE NEW SCHOOLS I COULD'VE GONE TO. I GET THE ONE WITH SECOND RATE SUPER-VILLAINS PRETENDING TO BE ART TEACHERS.
I DIDN'T THINK TODAY COULD GET ANY WORSE!
THERE'S GOTTA BE SOMETHING I CAN USE IN HERE.
NOW PUT ON YOUR COSTUME! YOU'RE THE SUPERHERO, Y'KNOW!
WOW, TRAVIS. YOU NEED SOME SUN.
WHY'S THIS STUPID BELT NOT WORKING?
WHAT'S AT THE END OF THAT RAINBOW?
KRACKLE!
AH-HA!
I'LL DISTRACT HIM WHILE YOU CHANGE. COVER ME.
WITH WHAT?
SPLOP!
HEY, PICASSO!
AHHHH!

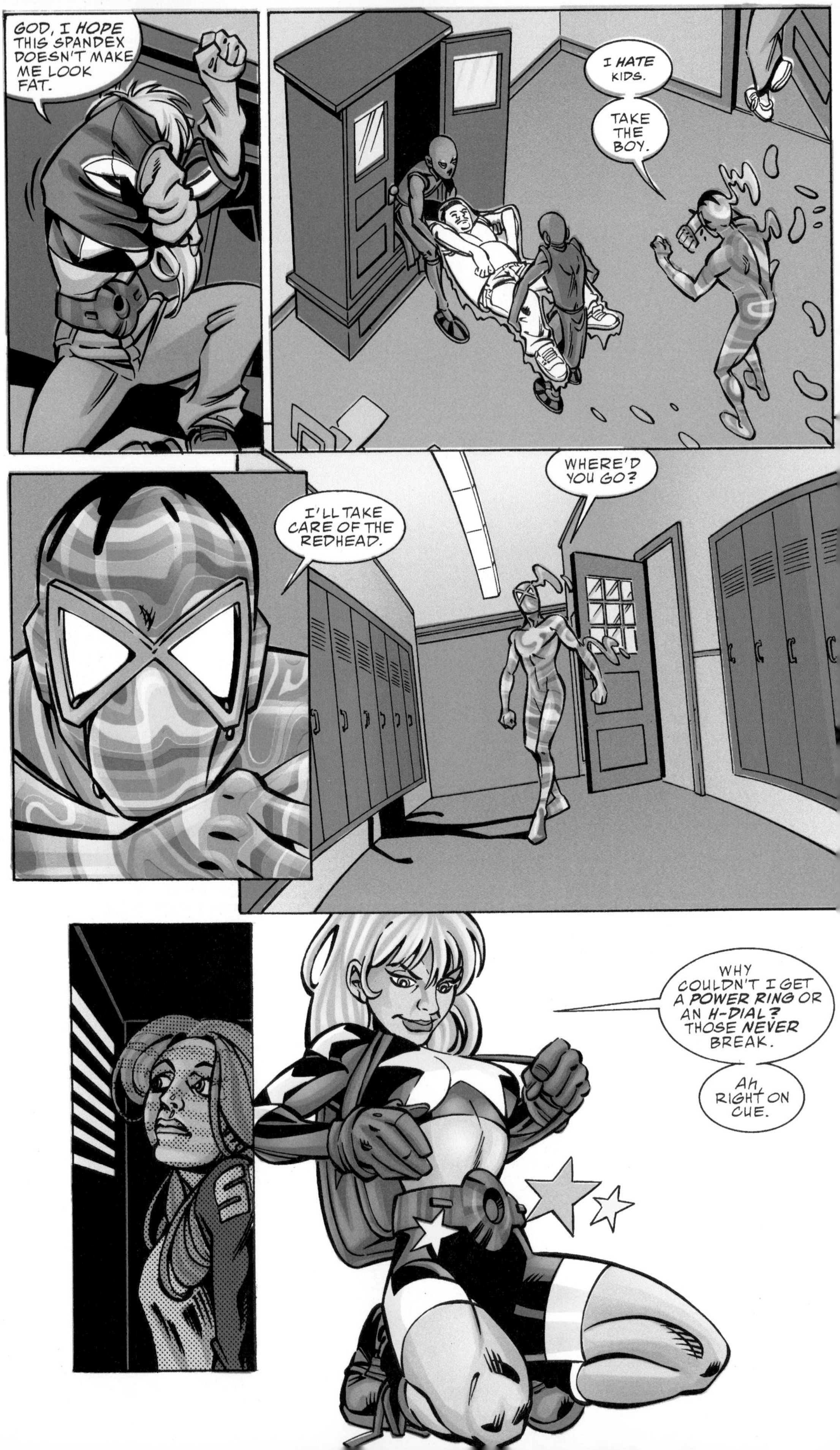
GOD, I HOPE THIS SPANDEX DOESN'T MAKE ME LOOK FAT.
I HATE KIDS.
TAKE THE BOY.
I'LL TAKE CARE OF THE REDHEAD.
WHERE'D YOU GO?
WHY COULDN'T I GET A POWER RING OR AN H-DIAL? THOSE NEVER BREAK.
AH, RIGHT ON CUE.

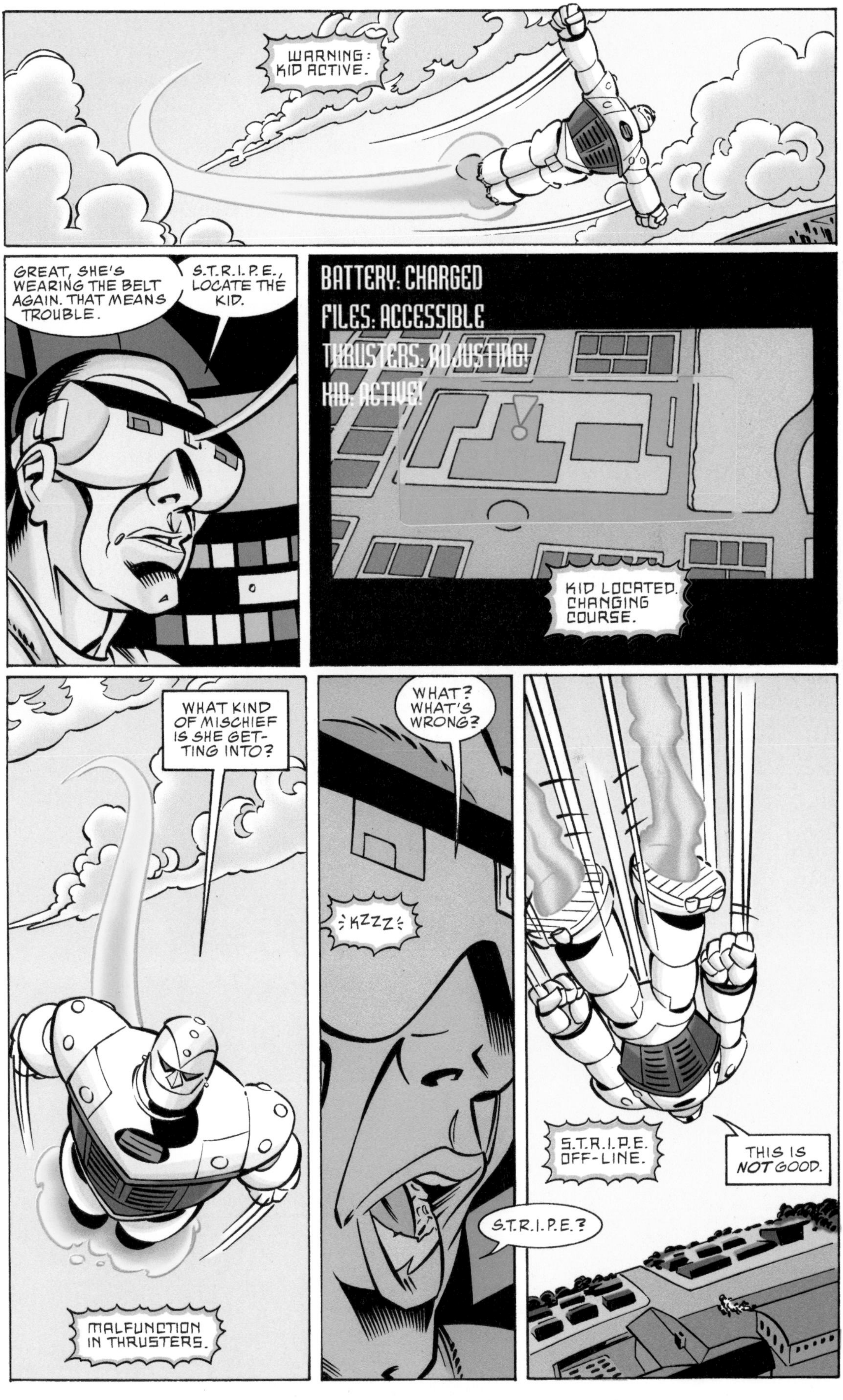
WARNING: KID ACTIVE.
GREAT, SHE'S WEARING THE BELT AGAIN. THAT MEANS TROUBLE.
S.T.R.I.P.E., LOCATE THE KID.
BATTERY: CHARGED
FILES: ACCESSIBLE
THRUSTERS: ADJUSTING!
KID: ACTIVE!
KID LOCATED. CHANGING COURSE.
WHAT KIND OF MISCHIEF IS SHE GETTING INTO?
MALFUNCTION IN THRUSTERS.
WHAT? WHAT'S WRONG?
KZZZ
S.T.R.I.P.E.?
S.T.R.I.P.E. OFF-LINE.
THIS IS *NOT* GOOD.

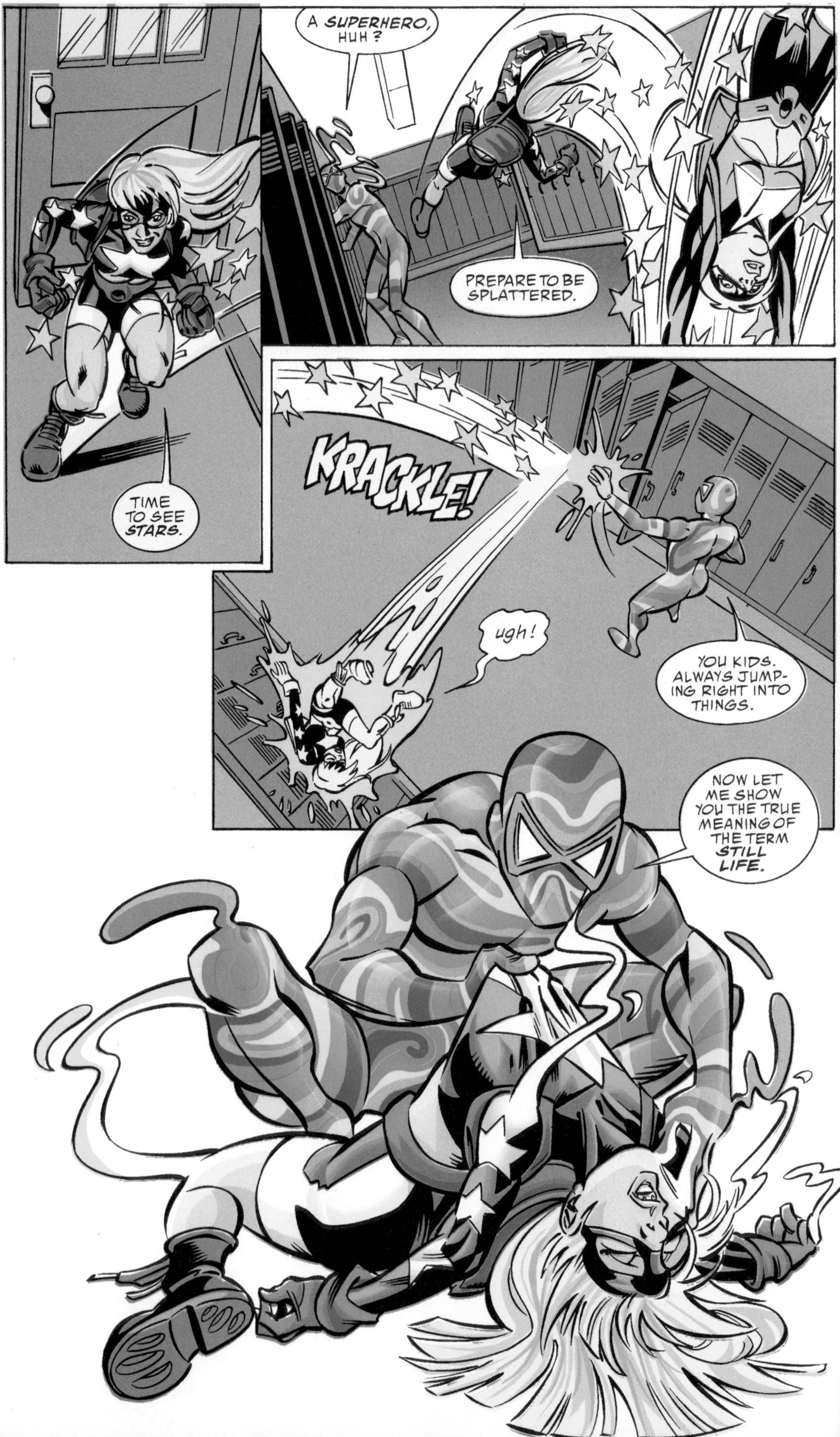
TIME TO SEE STARS.
A SUPERHERO, HUH?
PREPARE TO BE SPLATTERED.
KRACKLE!
ugh!
YOU KIDS. ALWAYS JUMPING RIGHT INTO THINGS.
NOW LET ME SHOW YOU THE TRUE MEANING OF THE TERM STILL LIFE.

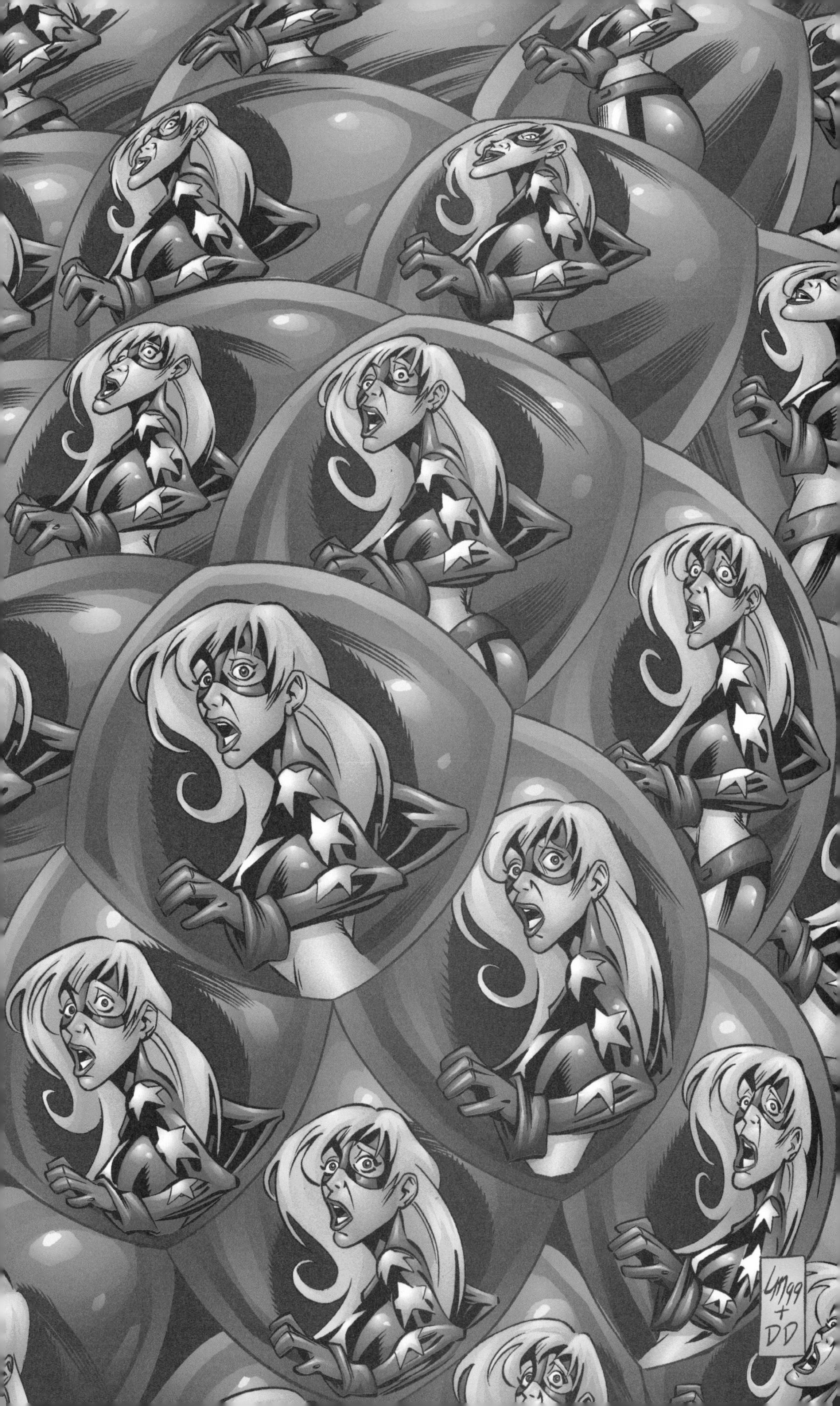
LM99
+
DD

STARS AND S.T.R.I.P.E. #3

Written by GEOFF JOHNS
Pencils by LEE MODER
Inks by DAN DAVIS
Colors by TOM McCRAW
Letters by BILL OAKLEY
Cover art by LEE MODER and DAN DAVIS
Cover color by RICHARD & TANYA HORIE

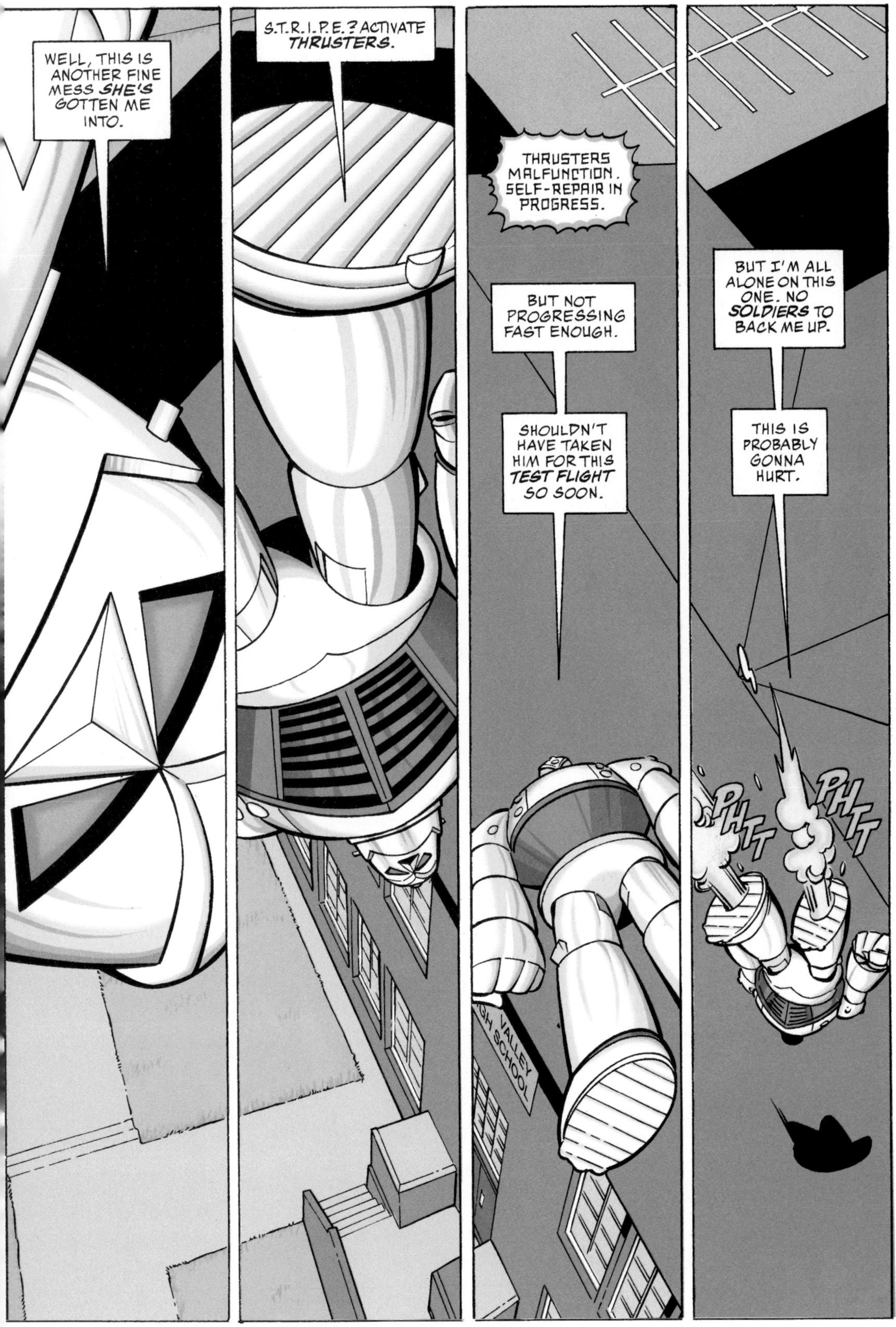
WELL, THIS IS ANOTHER FINE MESS SHE'S GOTTEN ME INTO.
S.T.R.I.P.E.? ACTIVATE THRUSTERS.
THRUSTERS MALFUNCTION. SELF-REPAIR IN PROGRESS.
BUT NOT PROGRESSING FAST ENOUGH.
SHOULDN'T HAVE TAKEN HIM FOR THIS TEST FLIGHT SO SOON.
VALLEY
GH SCHOOL
BUT I'M ALL ALONE ON THIS ONE. NO SOLDIERS TO BACK ME UP.
THIS IS PROBABLY GONNA HURT.
PHTT
PHTT

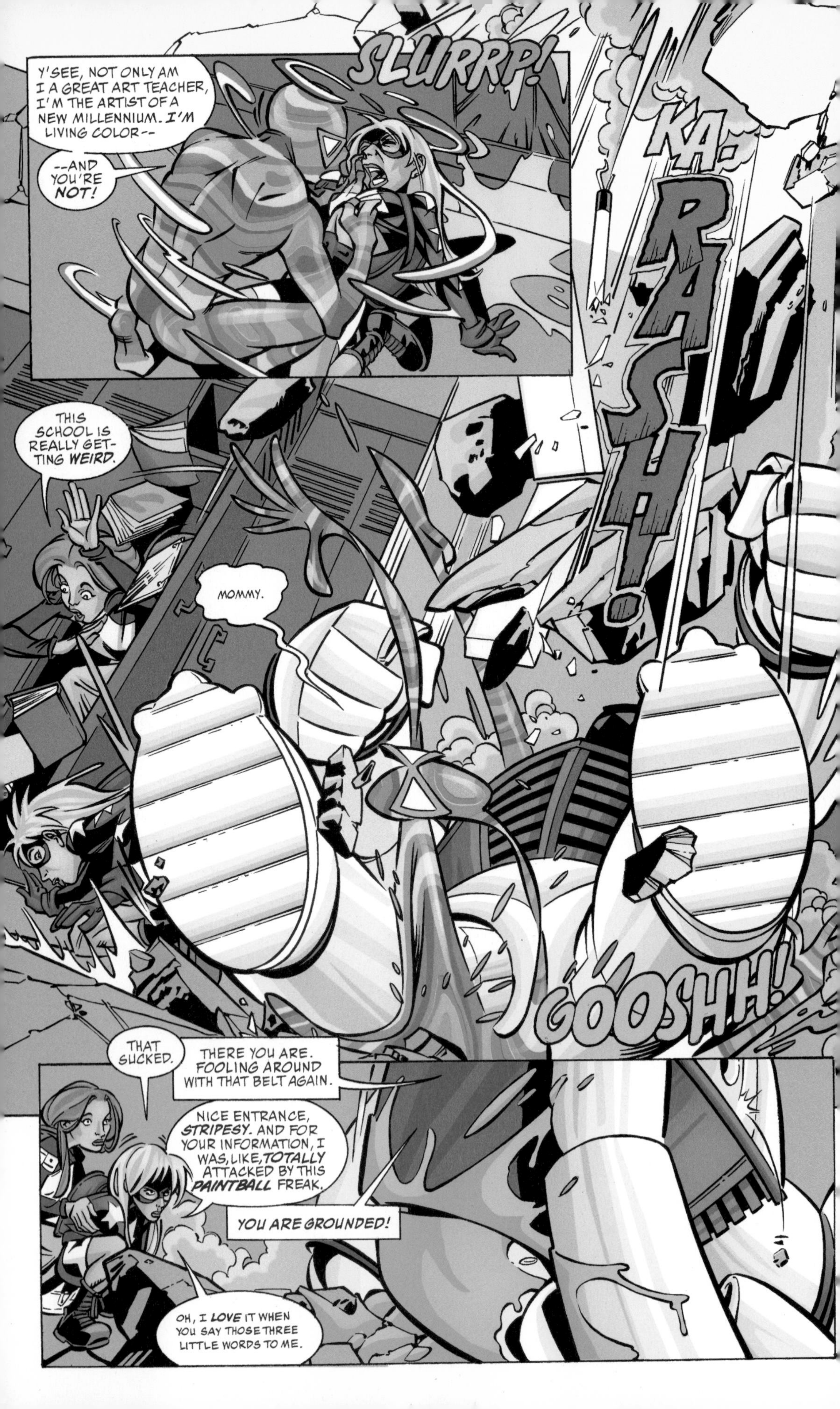
Y'SEE, NOT ONLY AM I A GREAT ART TEACHER, I'M THE ARTIST OF A NEW MILLENNIUM. I'M LIVING COLOR--
--AND YOU'RE NOT!
SLURRP!
KA-RASH!
THIS SCHOOL IS REALLY GETTING WEIRD.
MOMMY.
GOOSHH!
THAT SUCKED.
THERE YOU ARE. FOOLING AROUND WITH THAT BELT AGAIN.
NICE ENTRANCE, STRIPESY. AND FOR YOUR INFORMATION, I WAS, LIKE, TOTALLY ATTACKED BY THIS PAINTBALL FREAK.
YOU ARE GROUNDED!
OH, I LOVE IT WHEN YOU SAY THOSE THREE LITTLE WORDS TO ME.

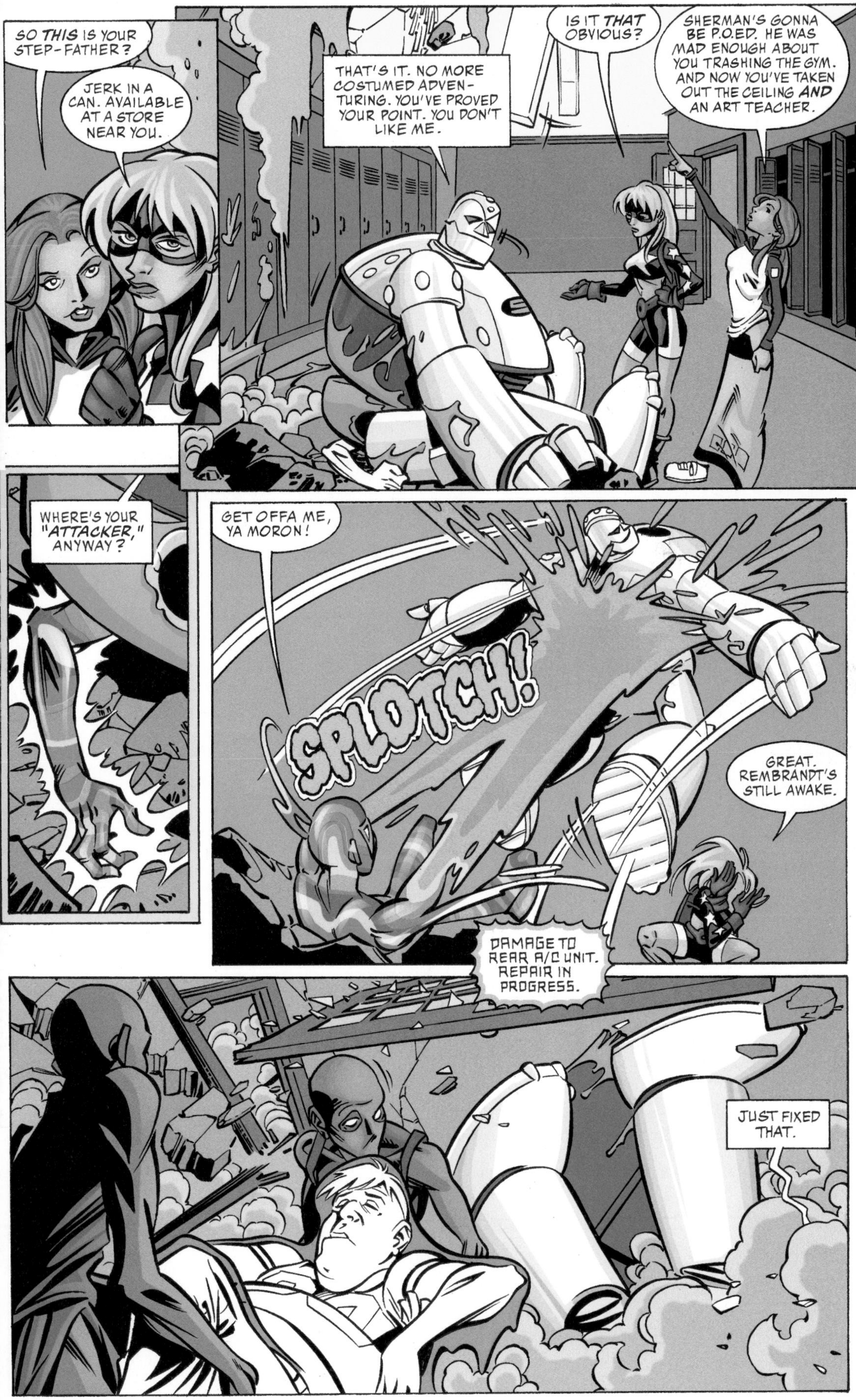

SO THIS IS YOUR STEP-FATHER?
JERK IN A CAN. AVAILABLE AT A STORE NEAR YOU.
THAT'S IT. NO MORE COSTUMED ADVENTURING. YOU'VE PROVED YOUR POINT. YOU DON'T LIKE ME.
IS IT THAT OBVIOUS?
SHERMAN'S GONNA BE P.O.ED. HE WAS MAD ENOUGH ABOUT YOU TRASHING THE GYM. AND NOW YOU'VE TAKEN OUT THE CEILING AND AN ART TEACHER.
WHERE'S YOUR "ATTACKER," ANYWAY?
GET OFFA ME, YA MORON!
SPLOTCH!
GREAT. REMBRANDT'S STILL AWAKE.
DAMAGE TO REAR A/C UNIT. REPAIR IN PROGRESS.
JUST FIXED THAT.

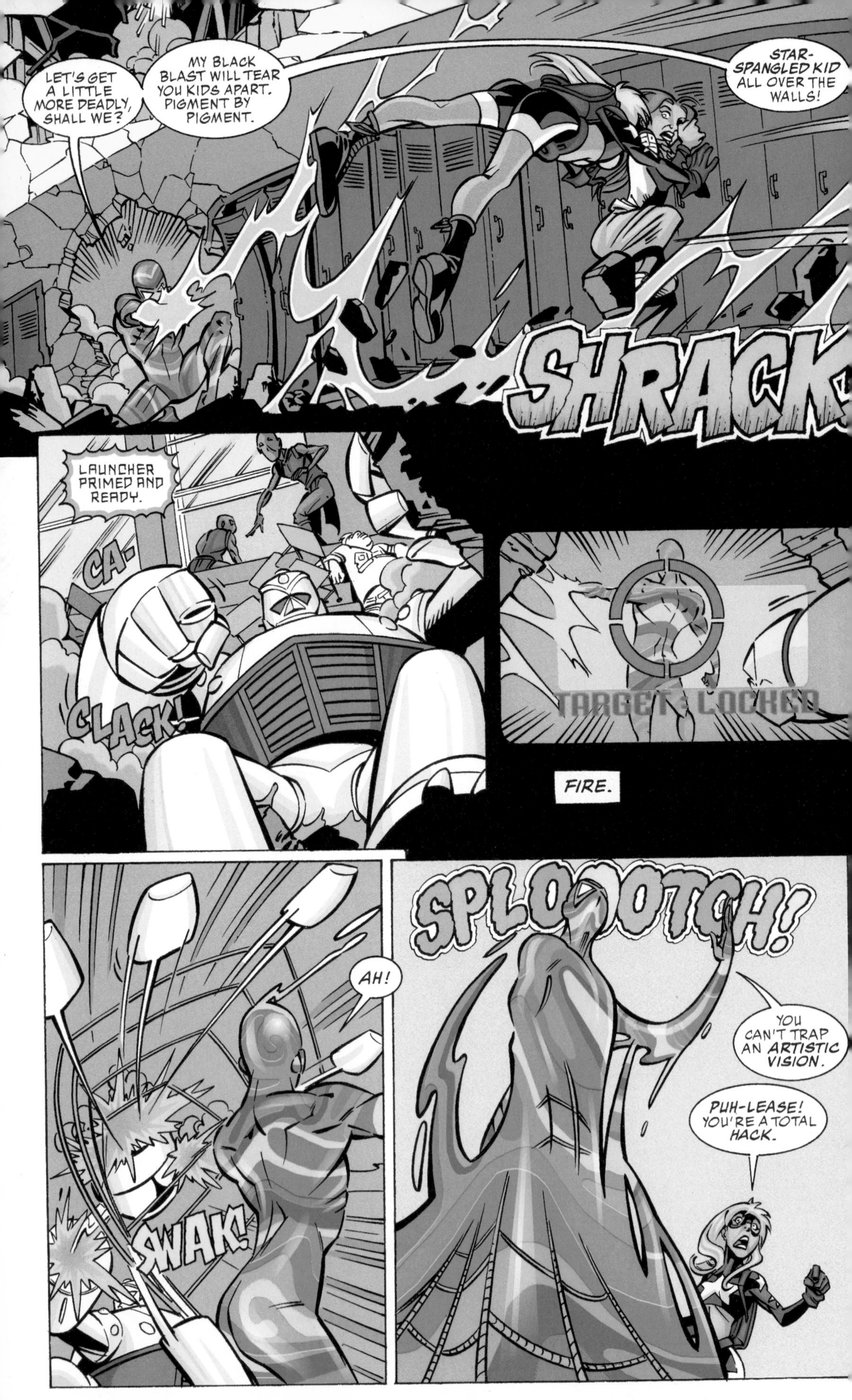

LET'S GET A LITTLE MORE DEADLY, SHALL WE?
MY BLACK BLAST WILL TEAR YOU KIDS APART. PIGMENT BY PIGMENT.
STAR-SPANGLED KID ALL OVER THE WALLS!
SHRACK
LAUNCHER PRIMED AND READY.
CA-
CLACK!
TARGET: LOCKED
FIRE.
AH!
SWAK!
SPLOOOTCH!
YOU CAN'T TRAP AN ARTISTIC VISION.
PUH-LEASE! YOU'RE A TOTAL HACK.

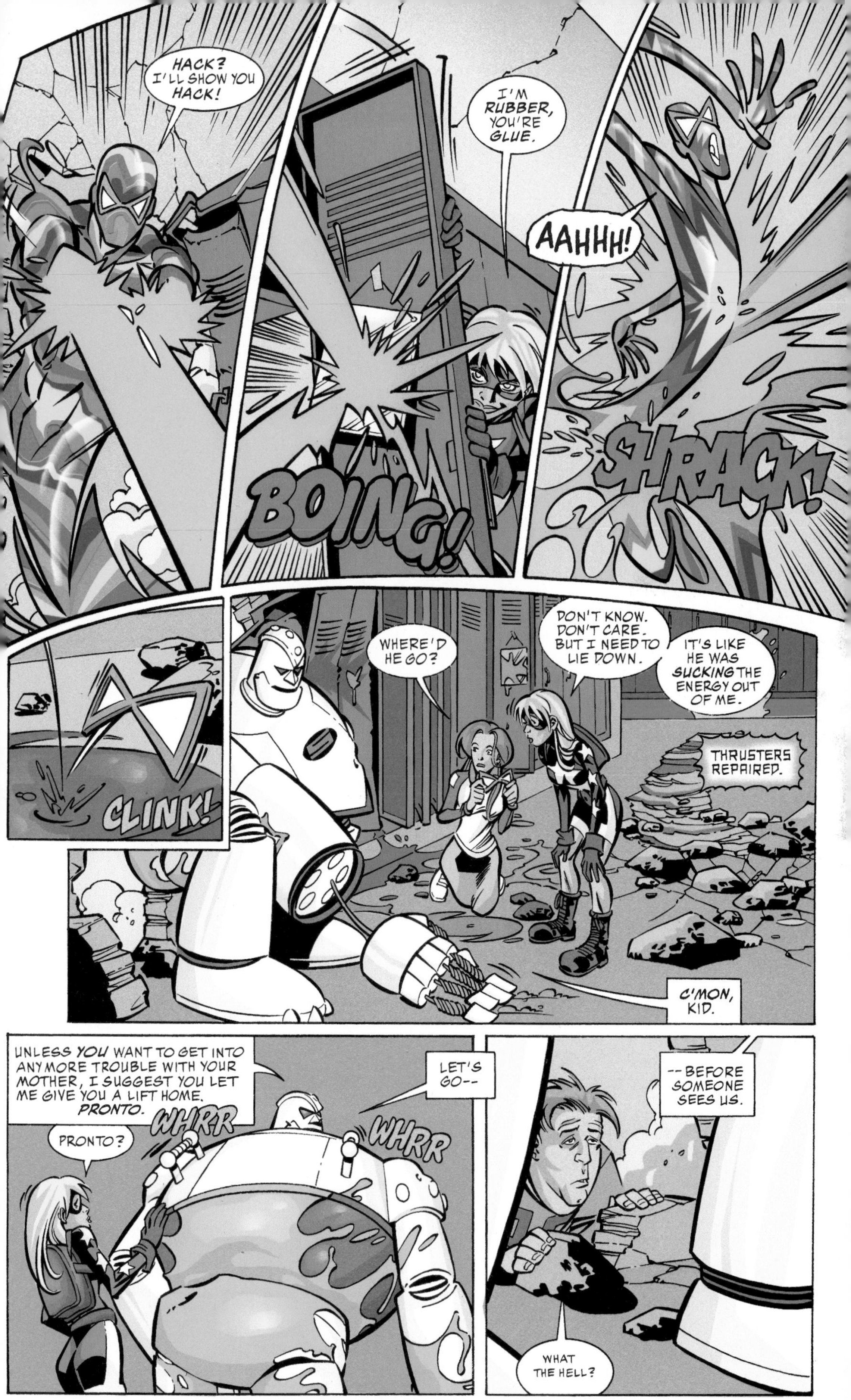
HACK? I'LL SHOW YOU HACK!
I'M RUBBER, YOU'RE GLUE.
BOING!
AAHHH!
SHRACK!
CLINK!
WHERE'D HE GO?
DON'T KNOW. DON'T CARE. BUT I NEED TO LIE DOWN.
IT'S LIKE HE WAS SUCKING THE ENERGY OUT OF ME.
THRUSTERS REPAIRED.
C'MON, KID.
UNLESS YOU WANT TO GET INTO ANYMORE TROUBLE WITH YOUR MOTHER, I SUGGEST YOU LET ME GIVE YOU A LIFT HOME. PRONTO.
PRONTO?
WHRR
WHRR
LET'S GO--
--BEFORE SOMEONE SEES US.
WHAT THE HELL?

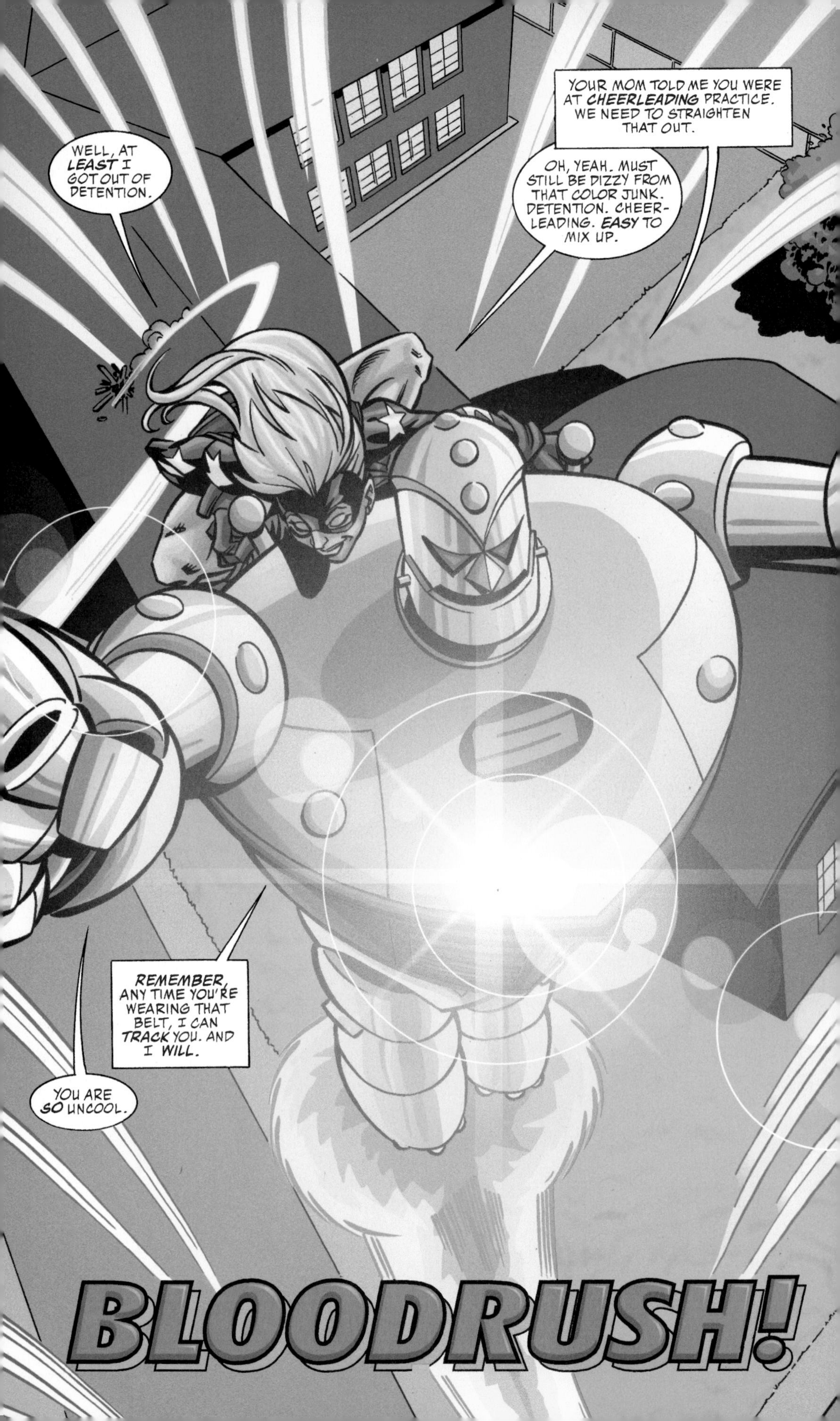
WELL, AT LEAST I GOT OUT OF DETENTION.
YOUR MOM TOLD ME YOU WERE AT CHEERLEADING PRACTICE. WE NEED TO STRAIGHTEN THAT OUT.
OH, YEAH. MUST STILL BE DIZZY FROM THAT COLOR JUNK. DETENTION. CHEER-LEADING. EASY TO MIX UP.
REMEMBER, ANY TIME YOU'RE WEARING THAT BELT, I CAN TRACK YOU. AND I WILL.
YOU ARE SO UNCOOL.
BLOODRUSH!

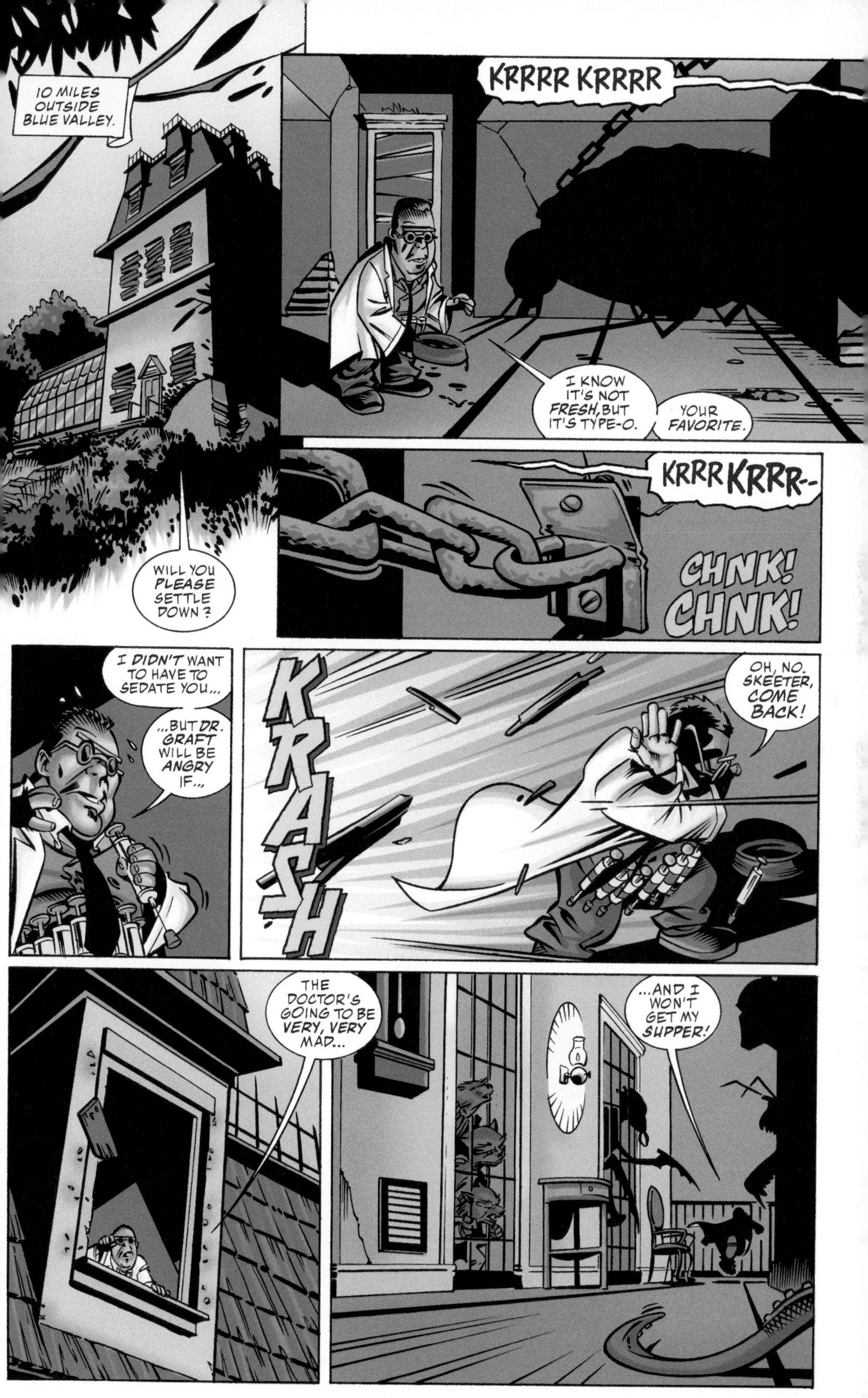
10 MILES OUTSIDE BLUE VALLEY.
KRRRR KRRRR
I KNOW IT'S NOT FRESH, BUT IT'S TYPE-O.
YOUR FAVORITE.
WILL YOU PLEASE SETTLE DOWN?
KRRR KRRR--
CHNK! CHNK!
I DIDN'T WANT TO HAVE TO SEDATE YOU...
...BUT DR. GRAFT WILL BE ANGRY IF...
KRASH
OH, NO. SKEETER, COME BACK!
THE DOCTOR'S GOING TO BE VERY, VERY MAD...
...AND I WON'T GET MY SUPPER!

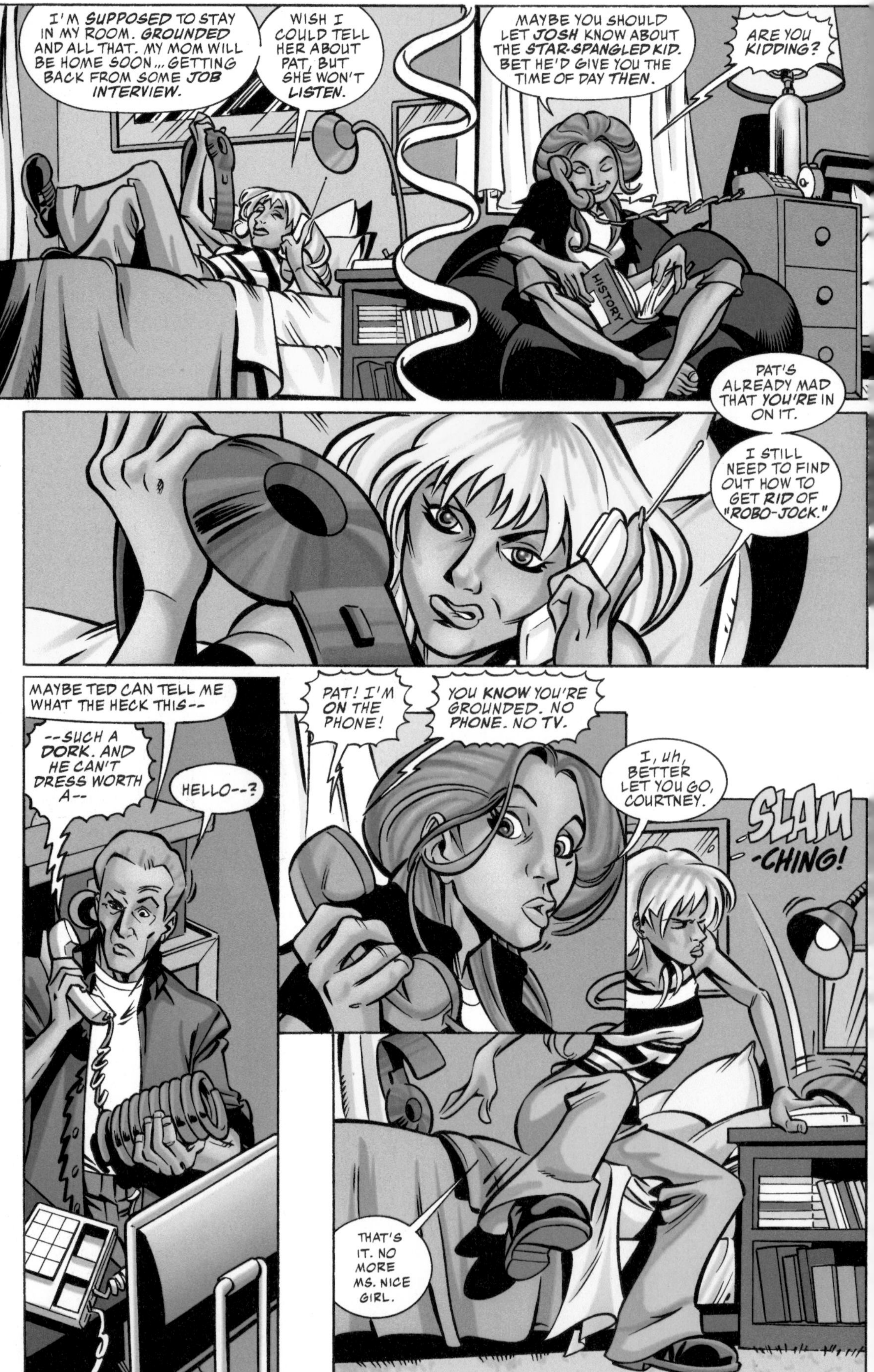

I'M SUPPOSED TO STAY IN MY ROOM. GROUNDED AND ALL THAT. MY MOM WILL BE HOME SOON... GETTING BACK FROM SOME JOB INTERVIEW.
WISH I COULD TELL HER ABOUT PAT, BUT SHE WON'T LISTEN.
MAYBE YOU SHOULD LET JOSH KNOW ABOUT THE STAR-SPANGLED KID. BET HE'D GIVE YOU THE TIME OF DAY THEN.
ARE YOU KIDDING?
HISTORY
PAT'S ALREADY MAD THAT YOU'RE IN ON IT.
I STILL NEED TO FIND OUT HOW TO GET RID OF "ROBO-JOCK."
MAYBE TED CAN TELL ME WHAT THE HECK THIS--
--SUCH A DORK. AND HE CAN'T DRESS WORTH A--
HELLO--?
PAT! I'M ON THE PHONE!
YOU KNOW YOU'RE GROUNDED. NO PHONE. NO TV.
I, uh, BETTER LET YOU GO, COURTNEY.
SLAM
-CHING!
THAT'S IT. NO MORE MS. NICE GIRL.

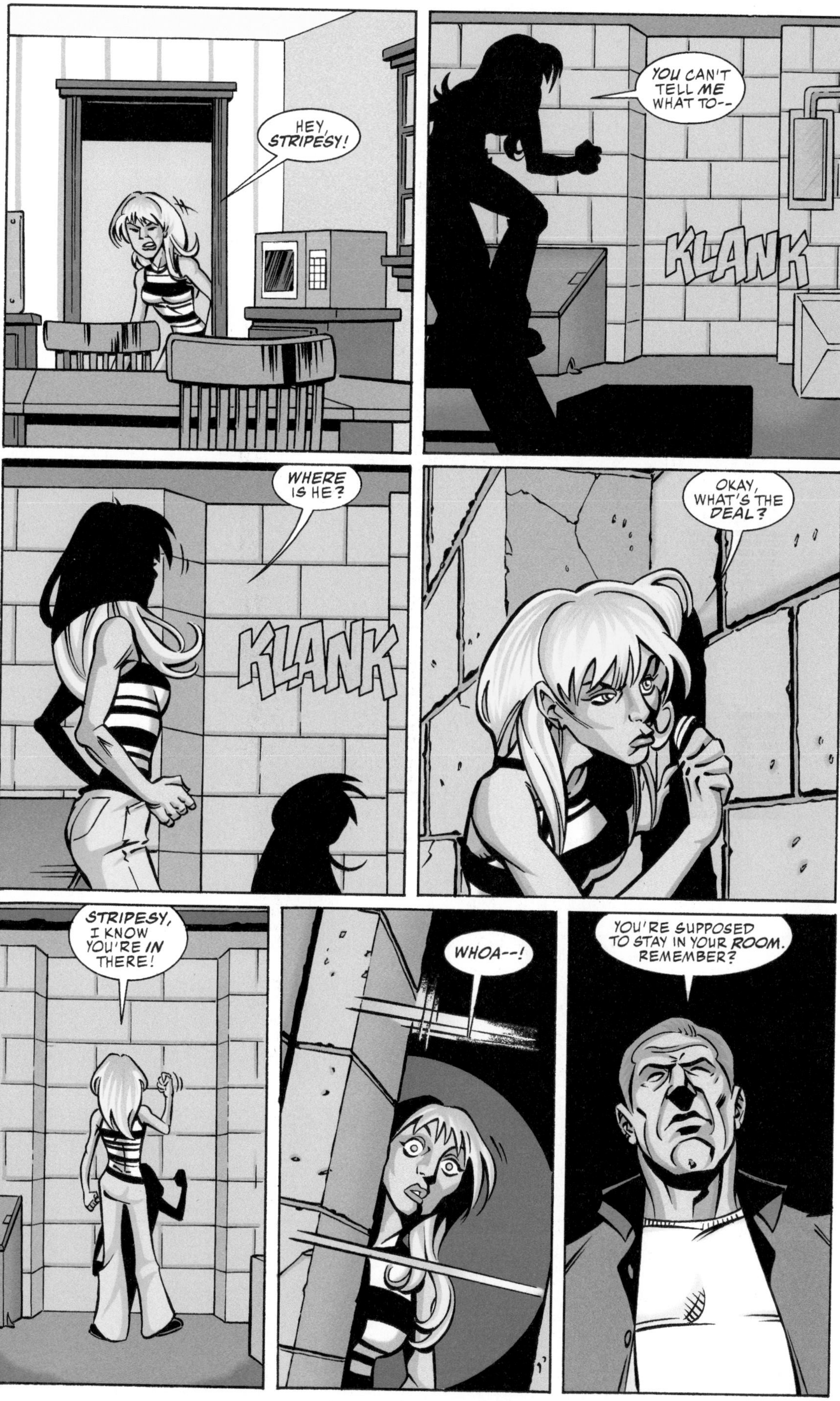
HEY, STRIPESY!
YOU CAN'T TELL ME WHAT TO--
KLANK
WHERE IS HE?
KLANK
OKAY, WHAT'S THE DEAL?
STRIPESY, I KNOW YOU'RE IN THERE!
WHOA--!
YOU'RE SUPPOSED TO STAY IN YOUR ROOM. REMEMBER?

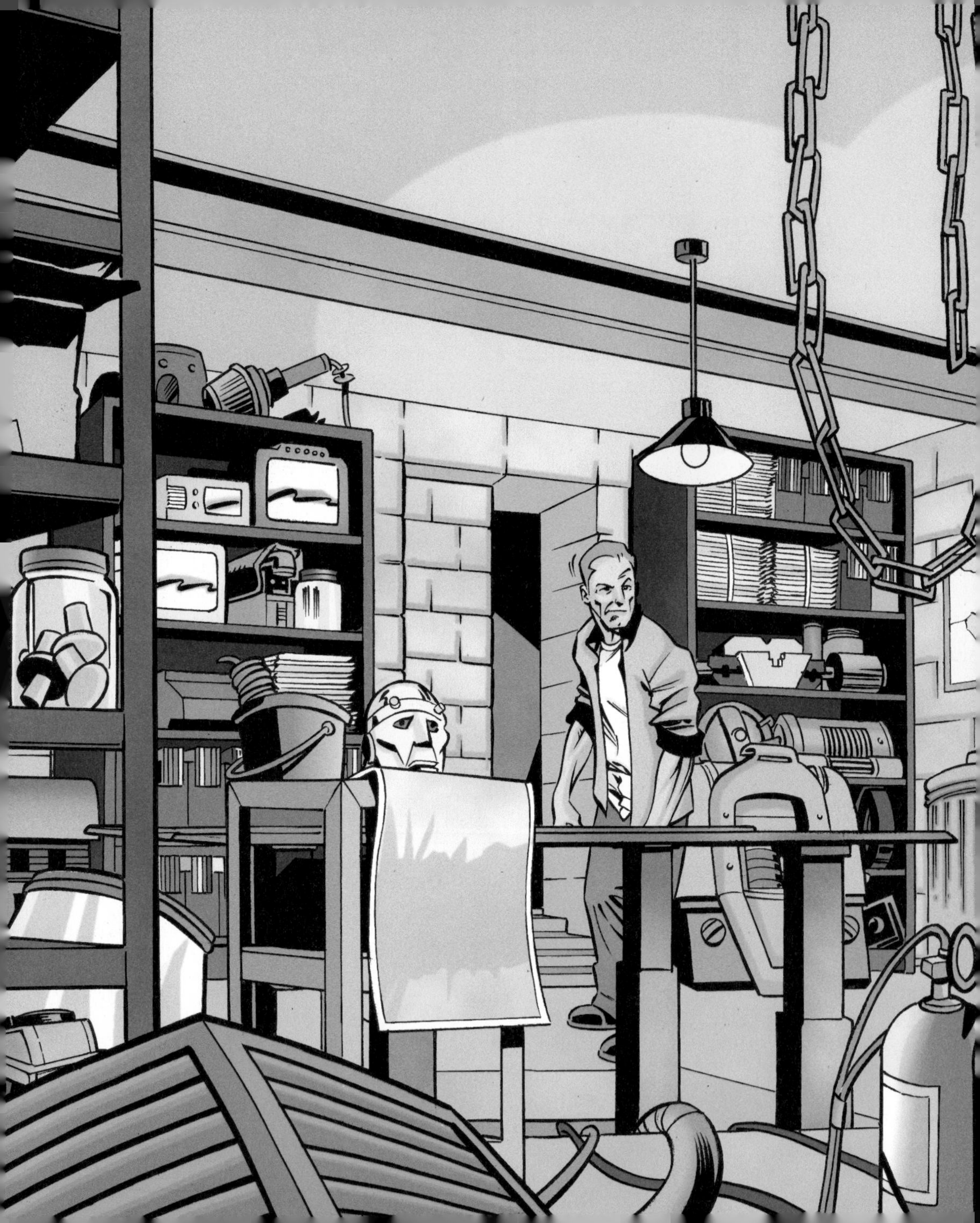

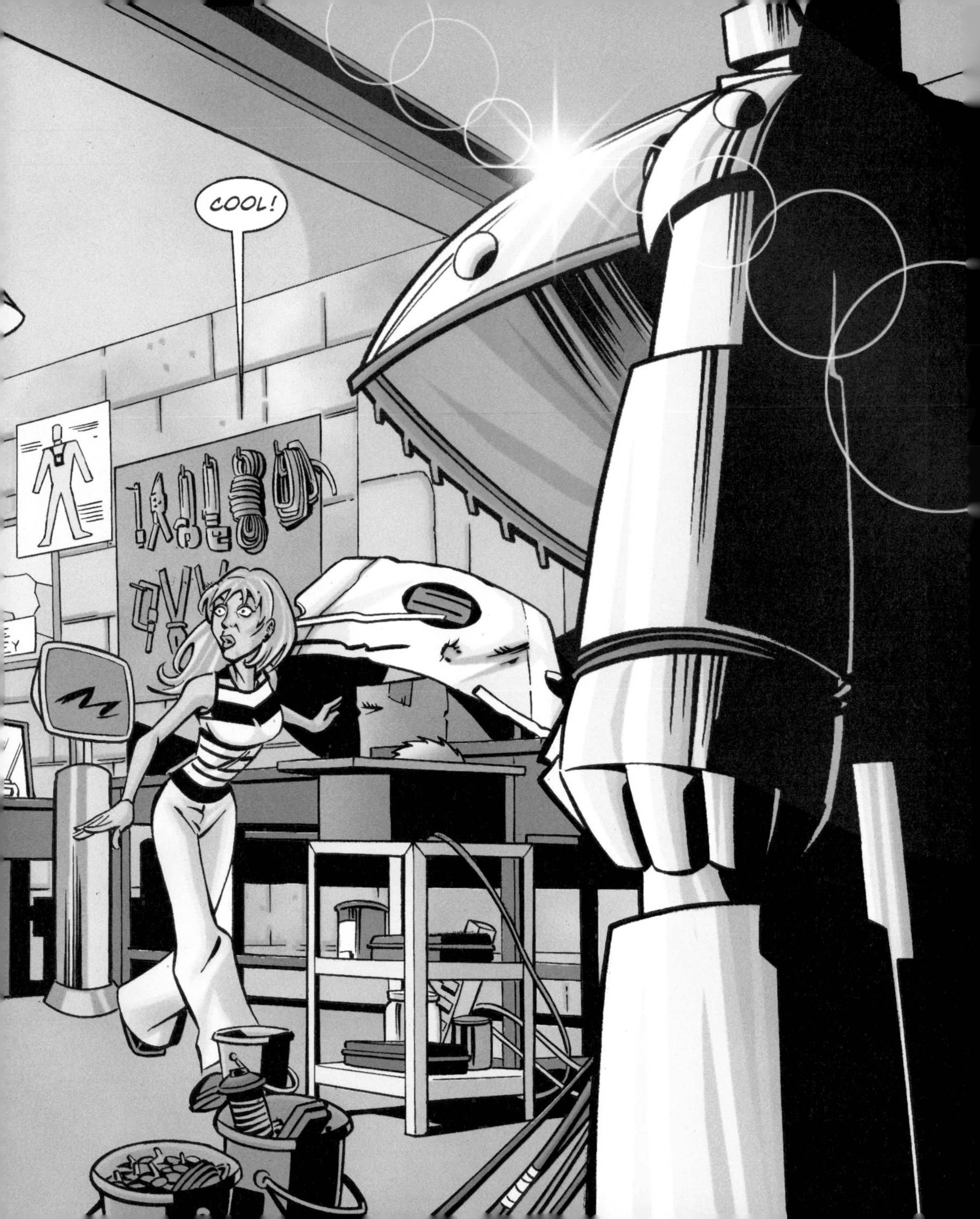
COOL!

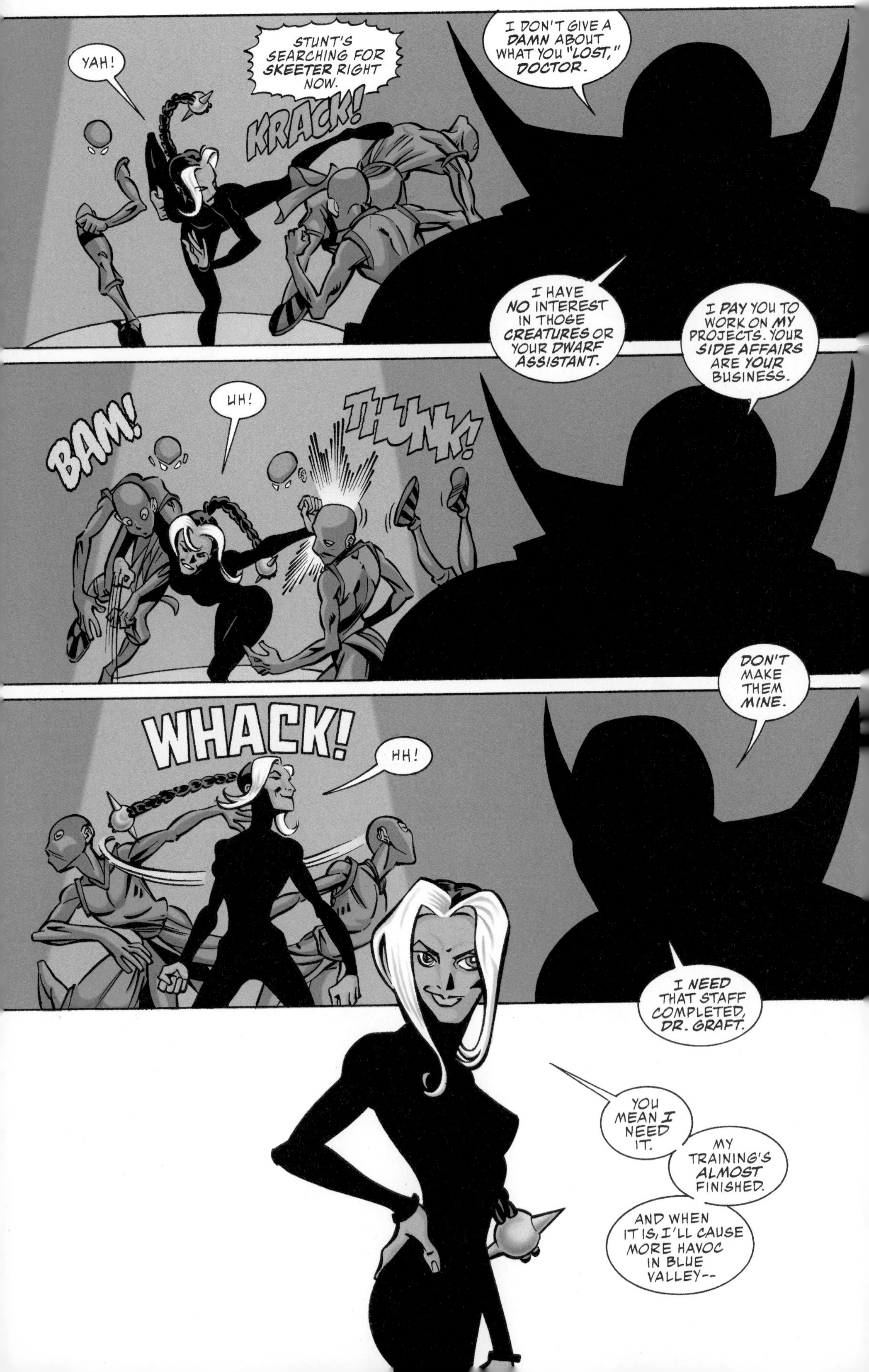
YAH!
STUNT'S SEARCHING FOR SKEETER RIGHT NOW.
KRACK!
I DON'T GIVE A DAMN ABOUT WHAT YOU "LOST," DOCTOR.
I HAVE NO INTEREST IN THOSE CREATURES OR YOUR DWARF ASSISTANT.
I PAY YOU TO WORK ON MY PROJECTS. YOUR SIDE AFFAIRS ARE YOUR BUSINESS.
BAM!
UH!
THUNK!
DON'T MAKE THEM MINE.
WHACK!
HH!
I NEED THAT STAFF COMPLETED, DR. GRAFT.
YOU MEAN I NEED IT.
MY TRAINING'S ALMOST FINISHED.
AND WHEN IT IS, I'LL CAUSE MORE HAVOC IN BLUE VALLEY--

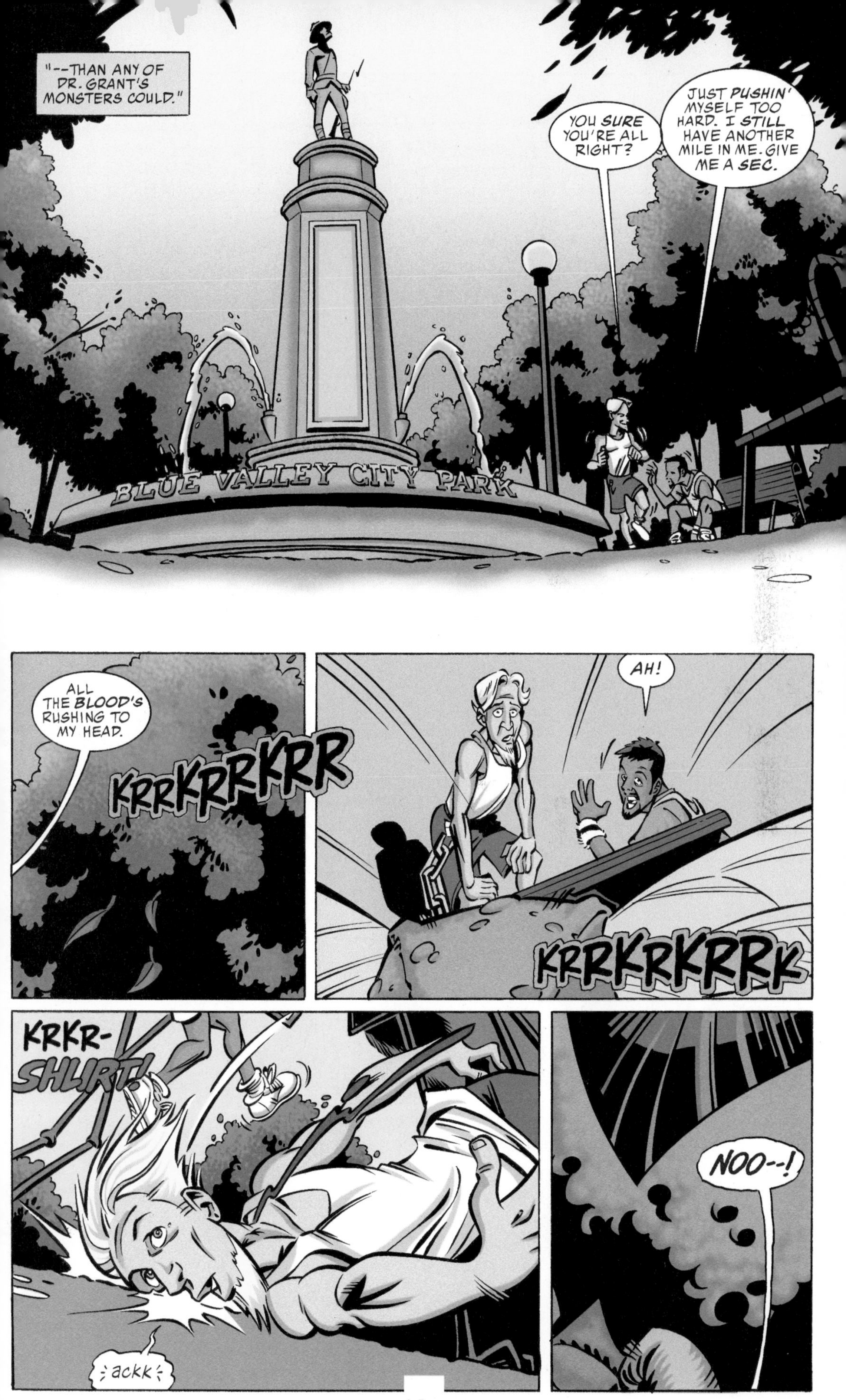
"--THAN ANY OF DR. GRANT'S MONSTERS COULD."
BLUE VALLEY CITY PARK
YOU SURE YOU'RE ALL RIGHT?
JUST PUSHIN' MYSELF TOO HARD. I STILL HAVE ANOTHER MILE IN ME. GIVE ME A SEC.
ALL THE BLOOD'S RUSHING TO MY HEAD.
KRRKRRKRR
AH!
KRRKRKRRK
KRKR-SHLIRT!
ackk
NOO--!

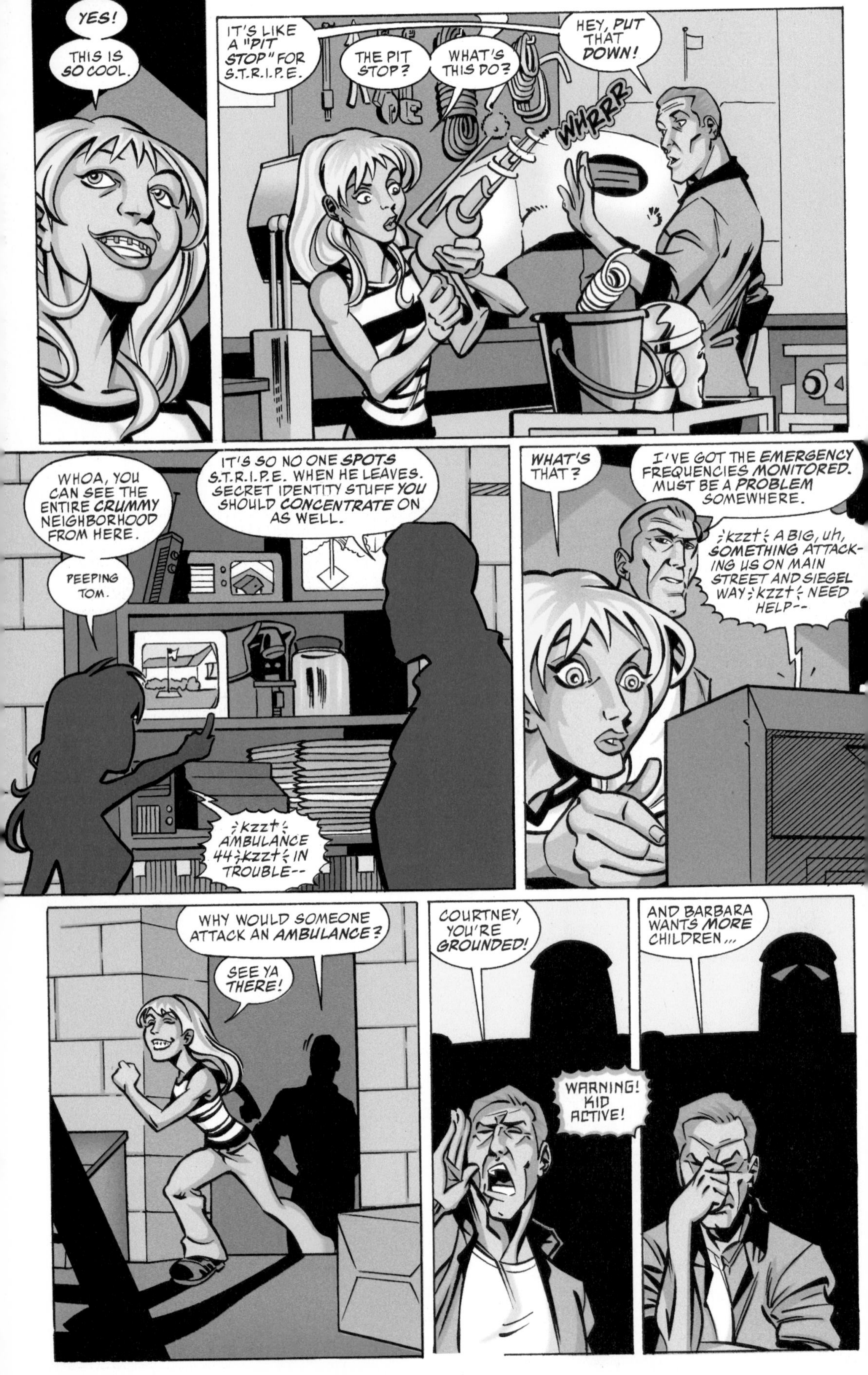
YES!
THIS IS SO COOL.
IT'S LIKE A "PIT STOP" FOR S.T.R.I.P.E.
THE PIT STOP?
WHAT'S THIS DO?
HEY, PUT THAT DOWN!
WHRRR
WHOA, YOU CAN SEE THE ENTIRE CRUMMY NEIGHBORHOOD FROM HERE.
PEEPING TOM.
IT'S SO NO ONE SPOTS S.T.R.I.P.E. WHEN HE LEAVES. SECRET IDENTITY STUFF YOU SHOULD CONCENTRATE ON AS WELL.
kzzt AMBULANCE 44 kzzt IN TROUBLE--
WHAT'S THAT?
I'VE GOT THE EMERGENCY FREQUENCIES MONITORED. MUST BE A PROBLEM SOMEWHERE.
kzzt A BIG, uh, SOMETHING ATTACKING US ON MAIN STREET AND SIEGEL WAY kzzt NEED HELP--
WHY WOULD SOMEONE ATTACK AN AMBULANCE?
SEE YA THERE!
COURTNEY, YOU'RE GROUNDED!
WARNING! KID ACTIVE!
AND BARBARA WANTS MORE CHILDREN...

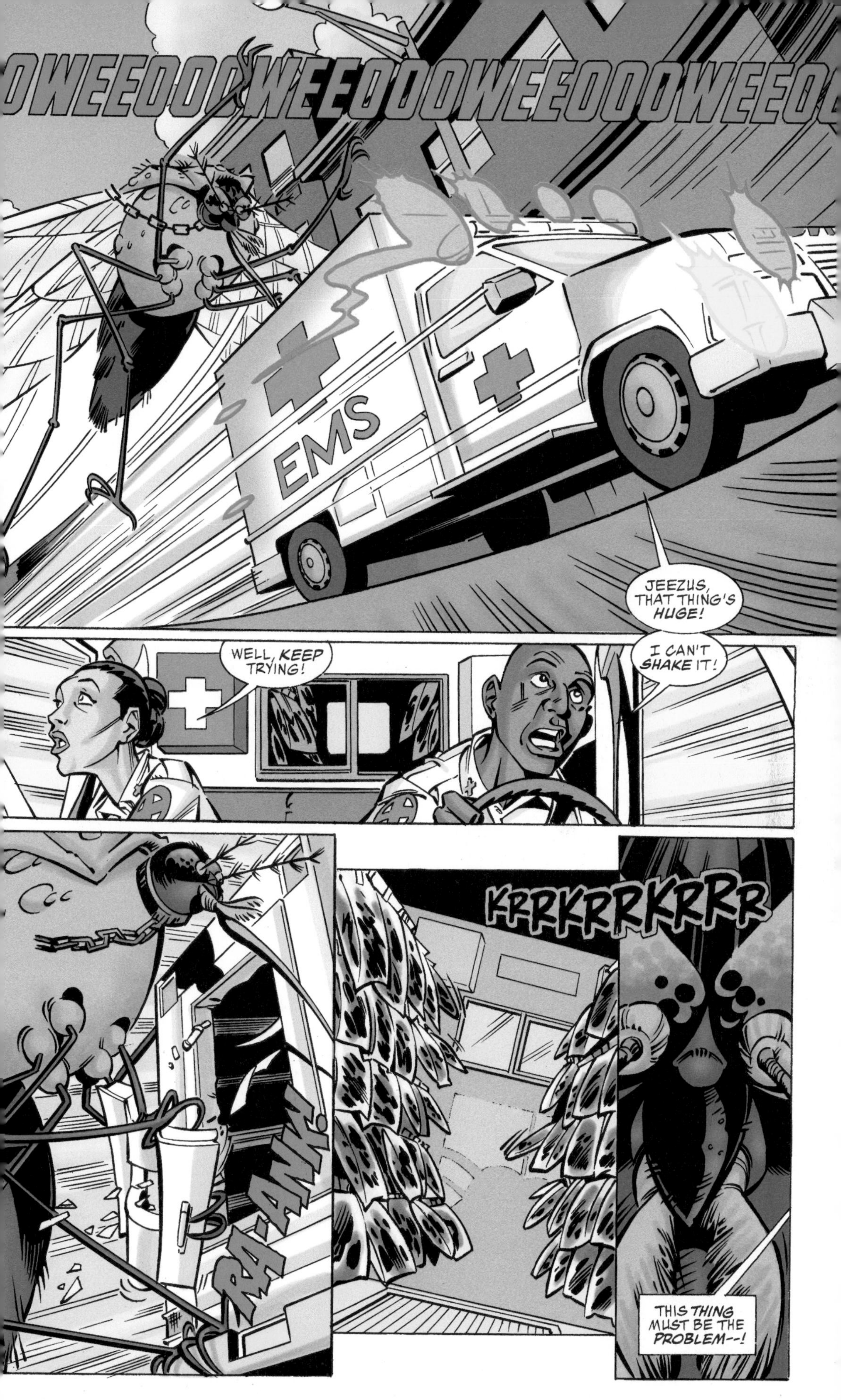
OWEEOOOWEEOOOWEEOOOWEEOO
JEEZUS, THAT THING'S HUGE!
WELL, KEEP TRYING!
I CAN'T SHAKE IT!
KRRKRRKRRR
RA-AMM
THIS THING MUST BE THE PROBLEM--!

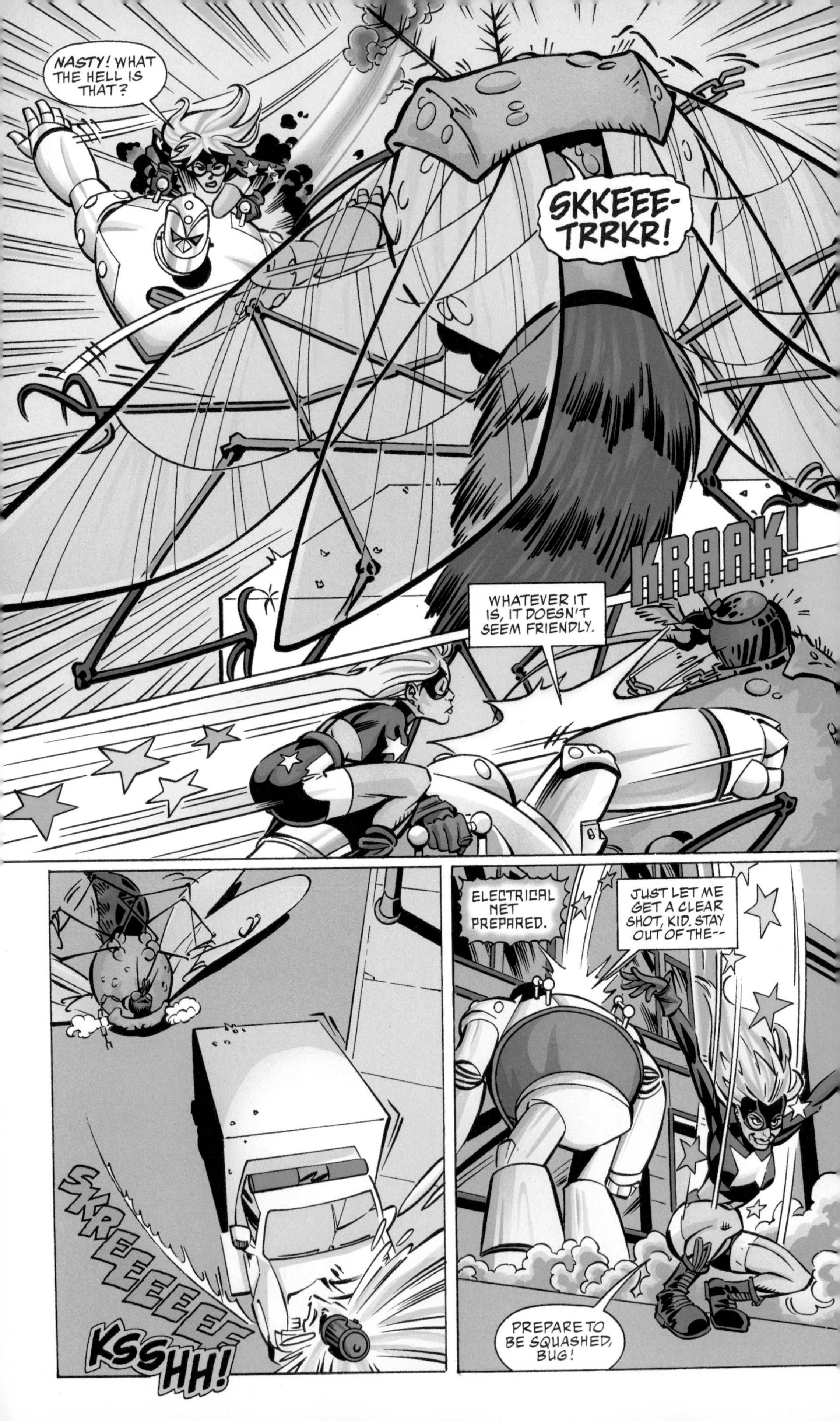
NASTY! WHAT THE HELL IS THAT?
SKKEEE-TRRKR!
KRAAK!
WHATEVER IT IS, IT DOESN'T SEEM FRIENDLY.
SKREEEEEEE
KSSHH!
ELECTRICAL NET PREPARED.
JUST LET ME GET A CLEAR SHOT, KID. STAY OUT OF THE--
PREPARE TO BE SQUASHED, BUG!

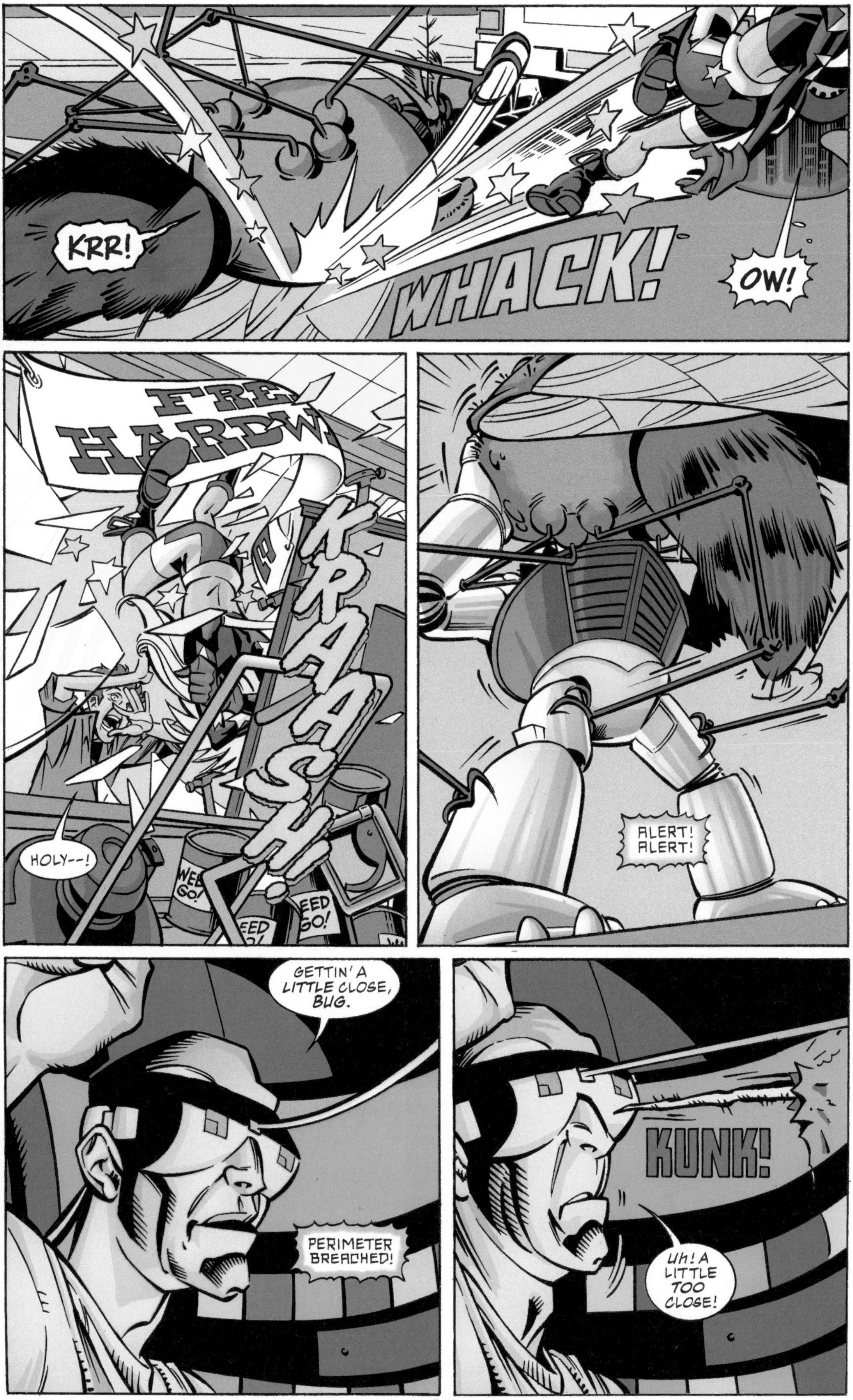
KRR!
WHACK!
OW!
FREE HARDW
KRAASH
HOLY--!
ALERT! ALERT!
GETTIN' A LITTLE CLOSE, BUG.
PERIMETER BREACHED!
KUNK!
UH! A LITTLE TOO CLOSE!

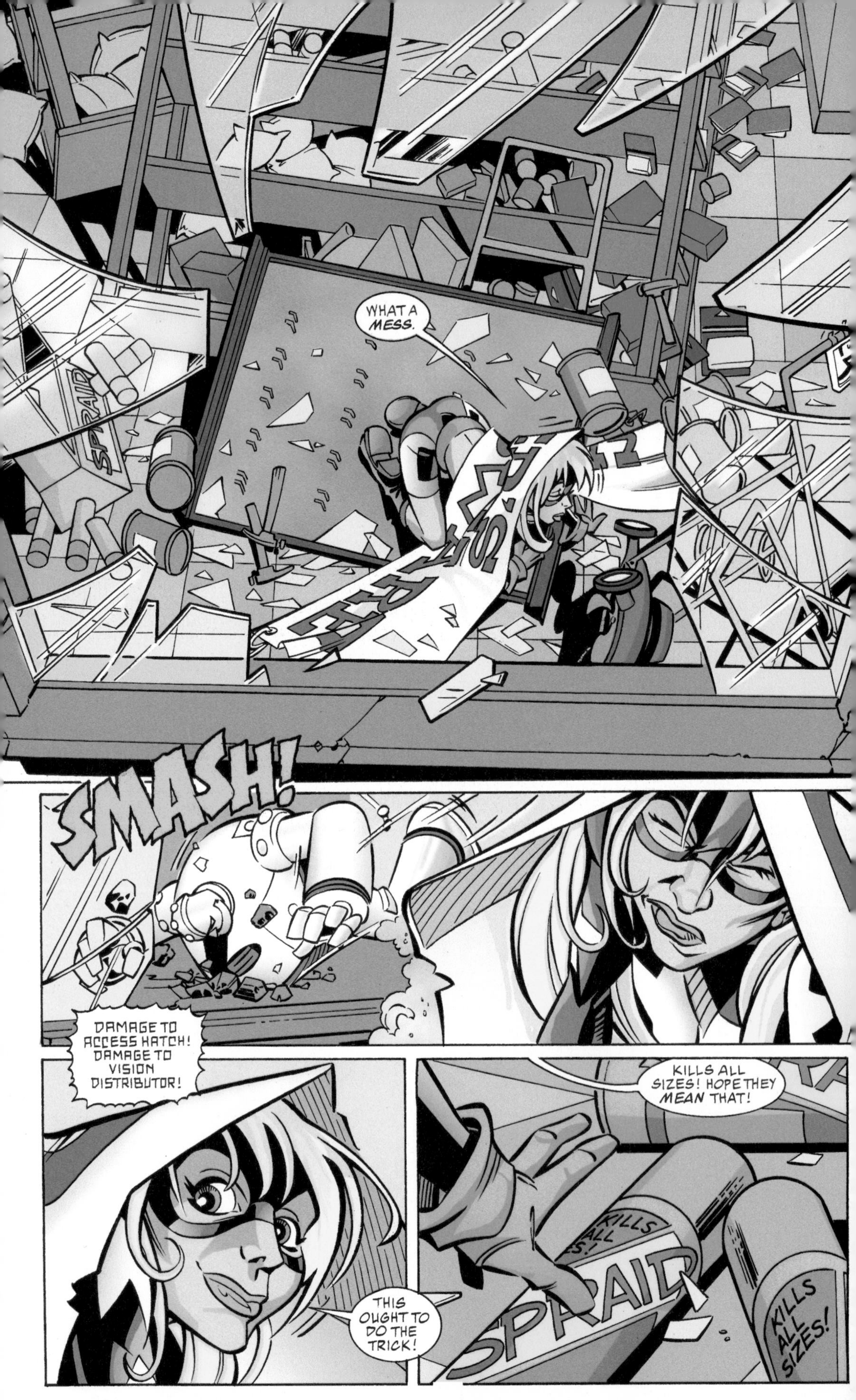
WHAT A MESS.
SPRAID
SMASH!
DAMAGE TO ACCESS HATCH! DAMAGE TO VISION DISTRIBUTOR!
THIS OUGHT TO DO THE TRICK!
KILLS ALL SIZES! HOPE THEY MEAN THAT!
SPRAID
KILLS ALL SIZES!

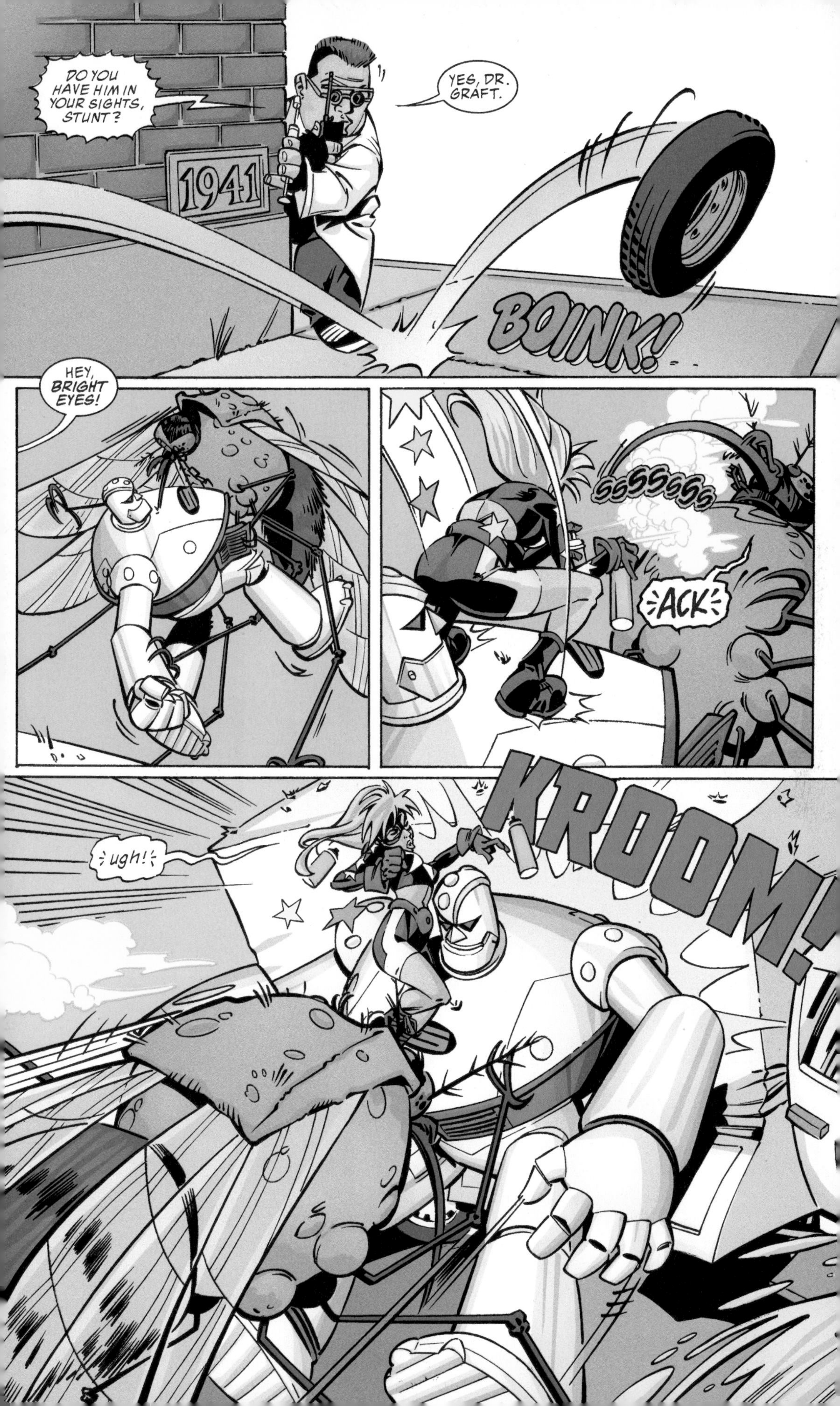

DO YOU HAVE HIM IN YOUR SIGHTS, STUNT?
YES, DR. GRAFT.
1941
BOINK!
HEY, BRIGHT EYES!
SSSSSSSS
ACK
ugh!
KROOM!

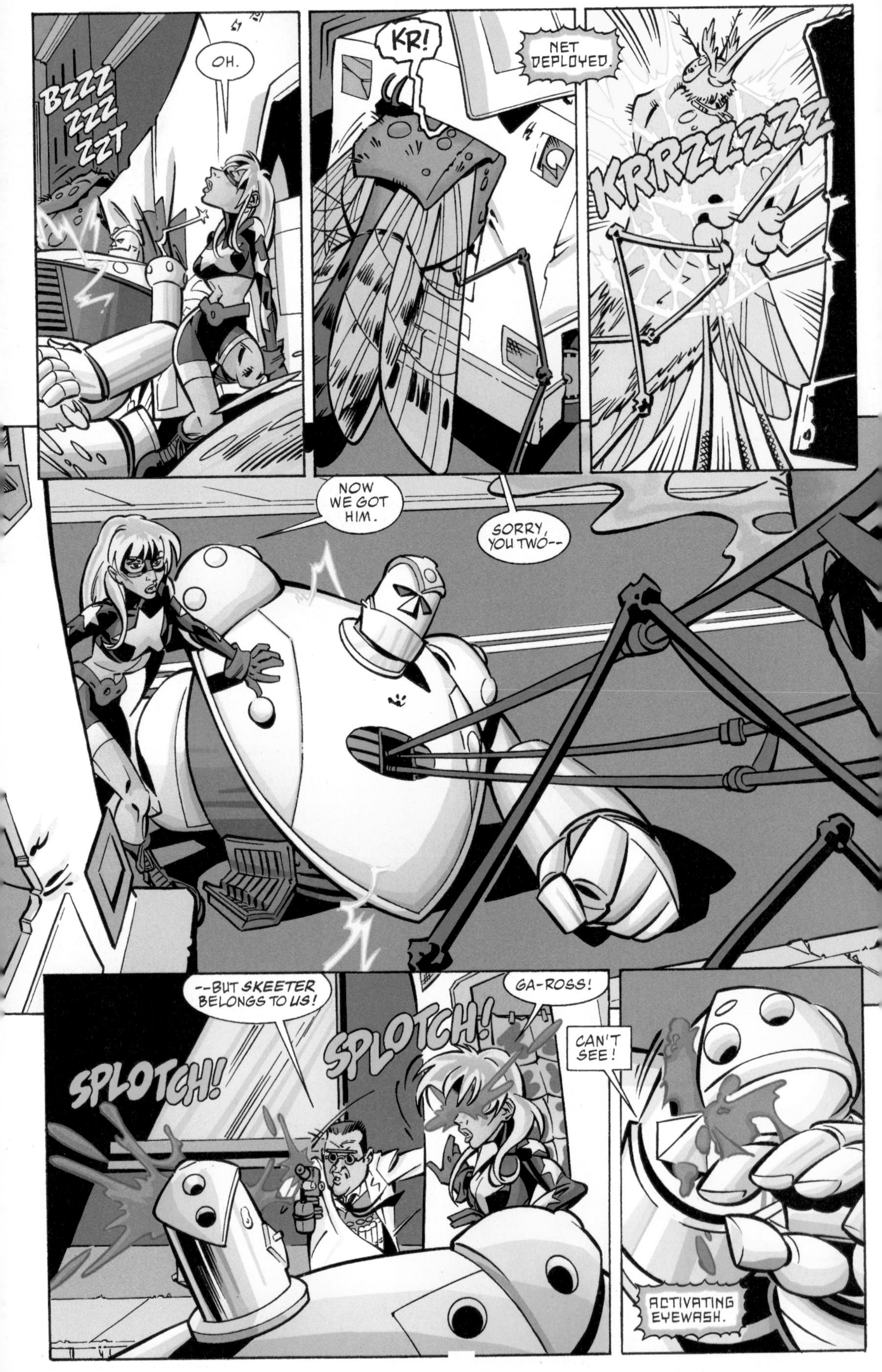
BZZZ ZZZ ZZT
OH.
KR!
NET DEPLOYED.
KRRZZZZZ
NOW WE GOT HIM.
SORRY, YOU TWO--
--BUT SKEETER BELONGS TO US!
SPLOTCH!
SPLOTCH!
GA-ROSS!
CAN'T SEE!
ACTIVATING EYEWASH.

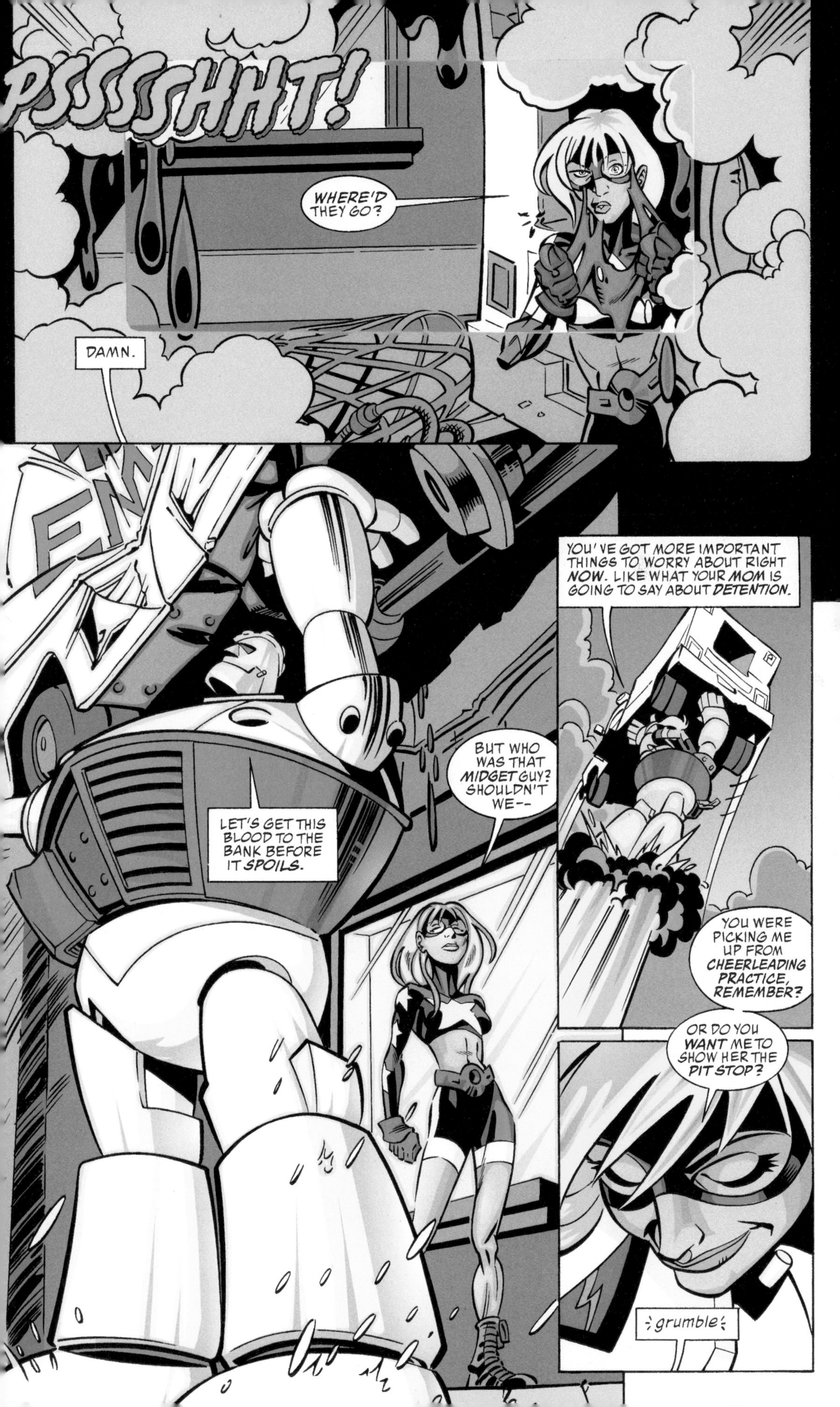
PSSSSHHT!
WHERE'D THEY GO?
DAMN.
YOU'VE GOT MORE IMPORTANT THINGS TO WORRY ABOUT RIGHT NOW. LIKE WHAT YOUR MOM IS GOING TO SAY ABOUT DETENTION.
BUT WHO WAS THAT MIDGET GUY? SHOULDN'T WE--
LET'S GET THIS BLOOD TO THE BANK BEFORE IT SPOILS.
YOU WERE PICKING ME UP FROM CHEERLEADING PRACTICE, REMEMBER?
OR DO YOU WANT ME TO SHOW HER THE PIT STOP?
grumble

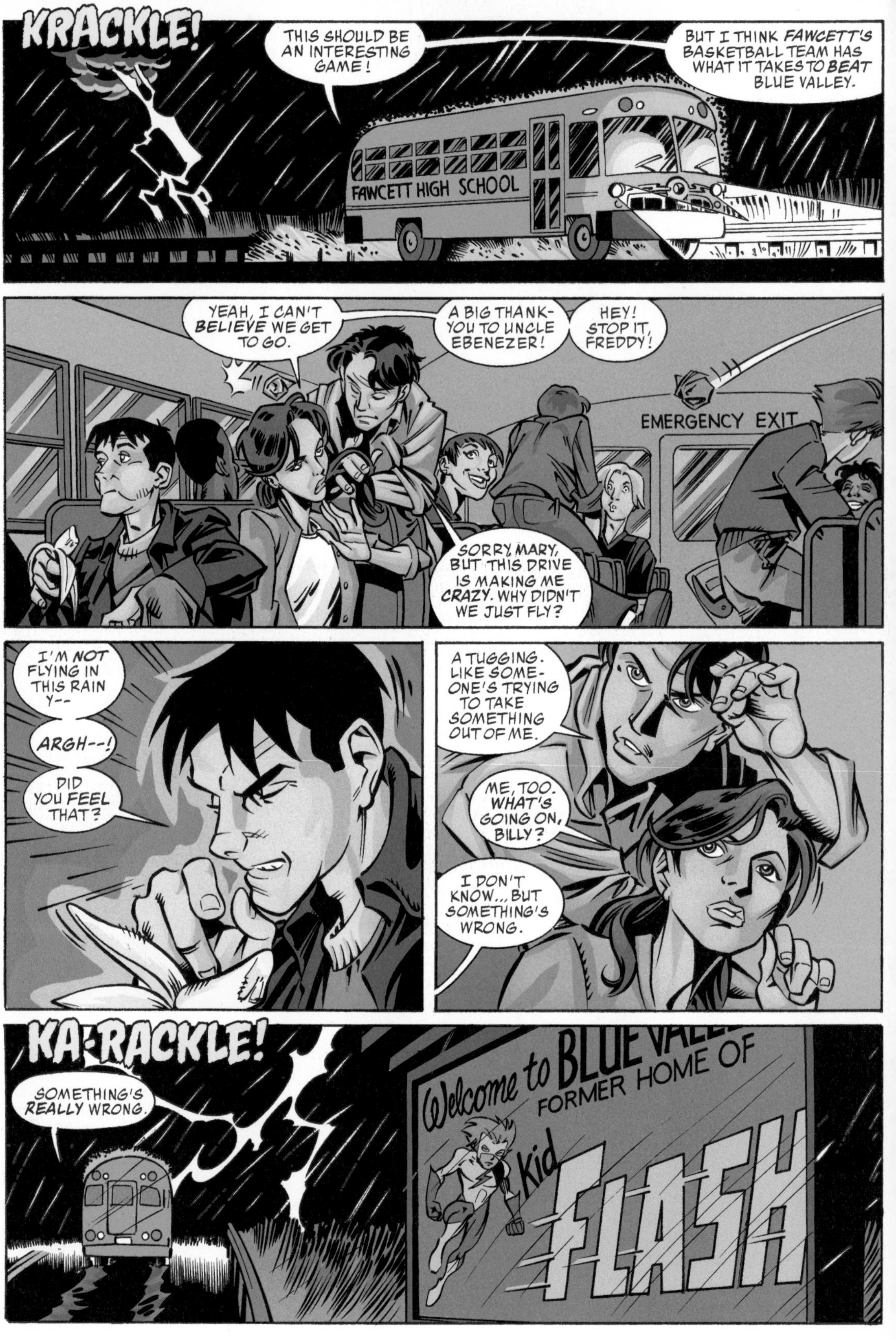
KRACKLE!
THIS SHOULD BE AN INTERESTING GAME!
BUT I THINK FAWCETT'S BASKETBALL TEAM HAS WHAT IT TAKES TO BEAT BLUE VALLEY.
FAWCETT HIGH SCHOOL
YEAH, I CAN'T BELIEVE WE GET TO GO.
A BIG THANK-YOU TO UNCLE EBENEZER!
HEY! STOP IT, FREDDY!
EMERGENCY EXIT
SORRY, MARY, BUT THIS DRIVE IS MAKING ME CRAZY. WHY DIDN'T WE JUST FLY?
I'M NOT FLYING IN THIS RAIN Y--
ARGH--!
DID YOU FEEL THAT?
A TUGGING. LIKE SOME-ONE'S TRYING TO TAKE SOMETHING OUT OF ME.
ME, TOO. WHAT'S GOING ON, BILLY?
I DON'T KNOW... BUT SOMETHING'S WRONG.
KA-RACKLE!
SOMETHING'S REALLY WRONG.
Welcome to BLUE VALL
FORMER HOME OF
Kid FLASH

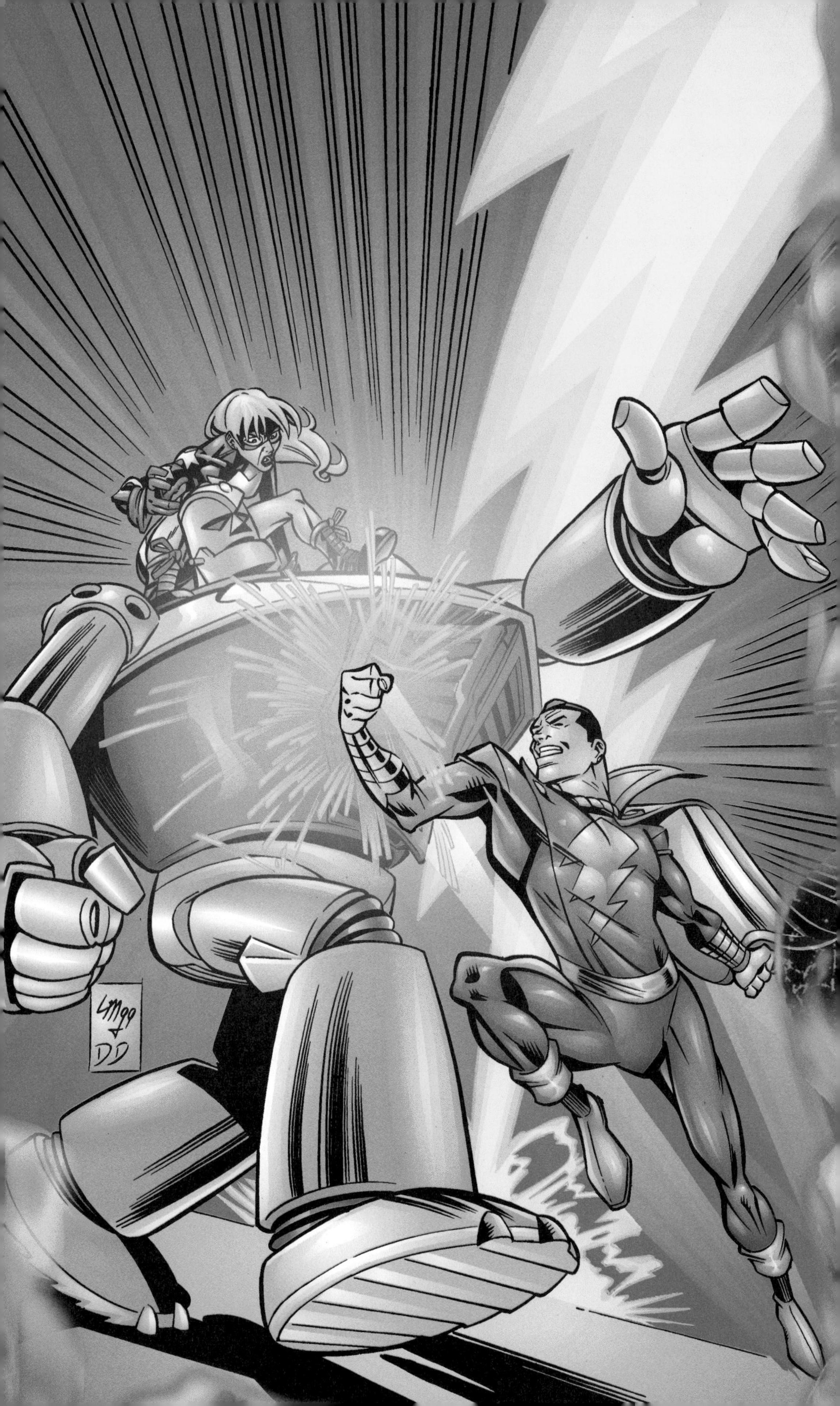

STARS AND S.T.R.I.P.E. #4

Written by GEOFF JOHNS
Pencils by LEE MODER
Inks by DAN DAVIS
Colors by TOM McCRAW
Letters by BILL OAKLEY
Cover art by LEE MODER and DAN DAVIS
Cover color by RICHARD & TANYA HORIE

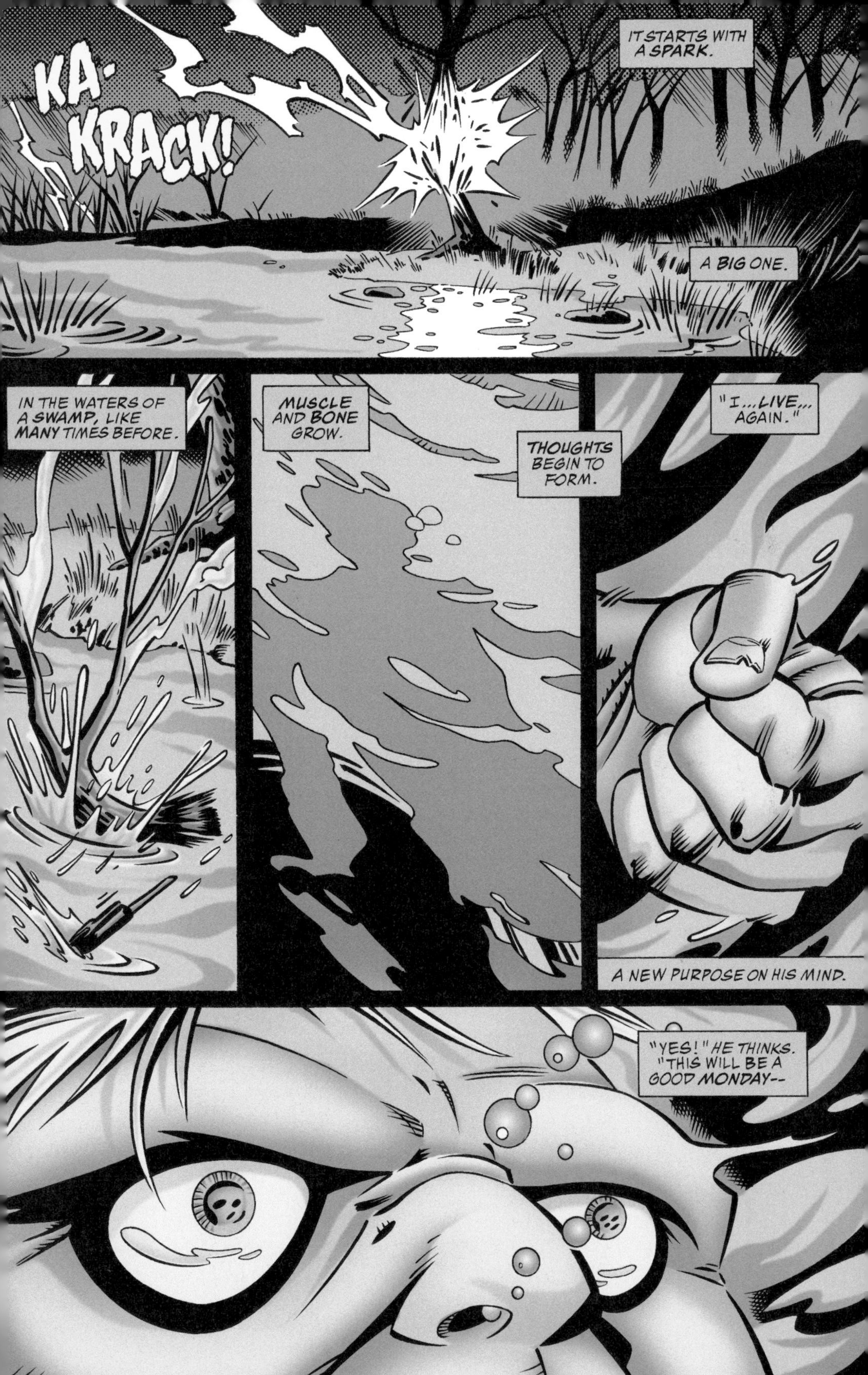
KA-KRACK!
IT STARTS WITH A SPARK.
A BIG ONE.
IN THE WATERS OF A SWAMP, LIKE MANY TIMES BEFORE.
MUSCLE AND BONE GROW.
THOUGHTS BEGIN TO FORM.
"I...LIVE... AGAIN."
A NEW PURPOSE ON HIS MIND.
"YES!" HE THINKS. "THIS WILL BE A GOOD MONDAY--

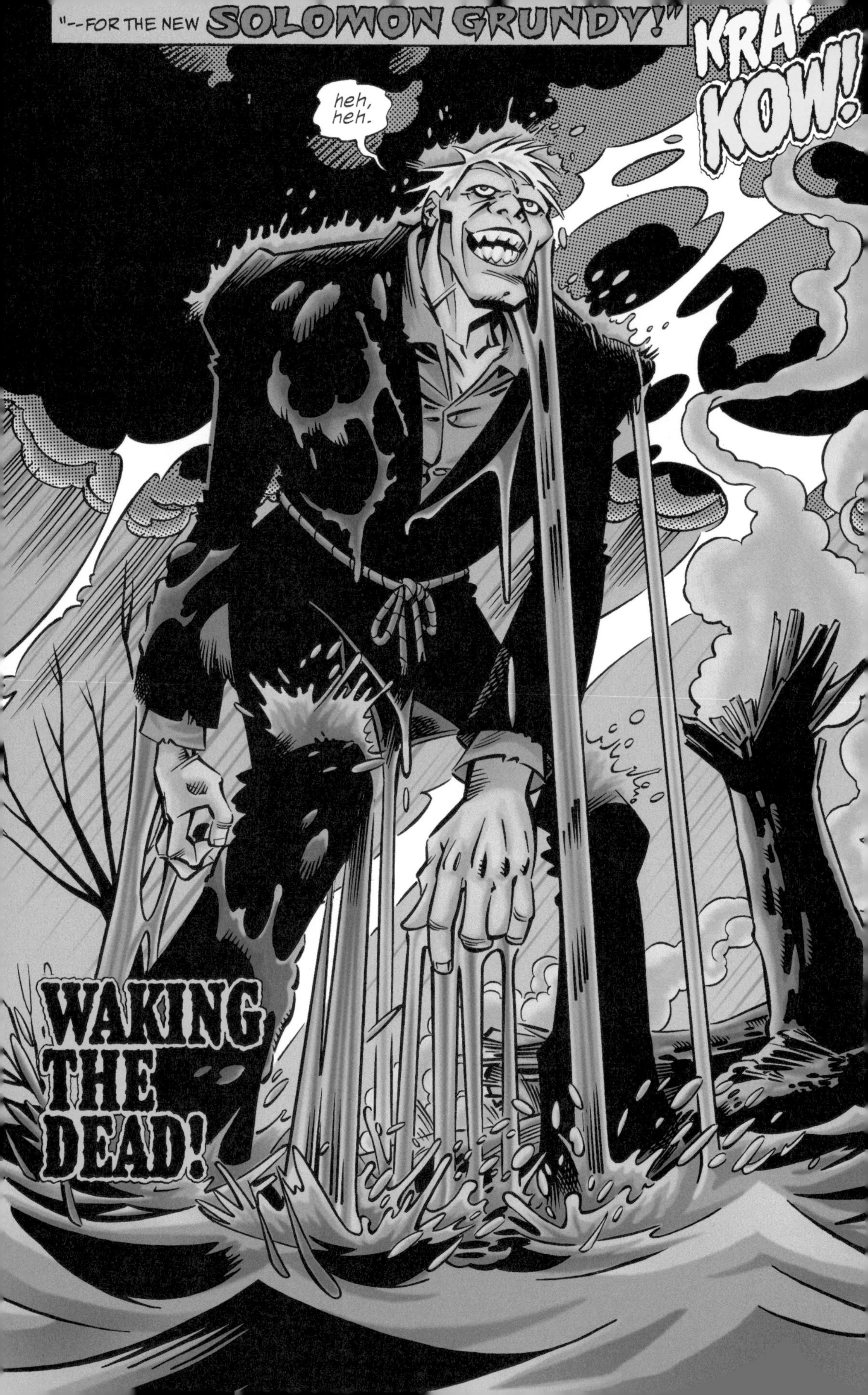

"--FOR THE NEW SOLOMON GRUNDY!"
KRA-KOW!
heh, heh.
WAKING THE DEAD!

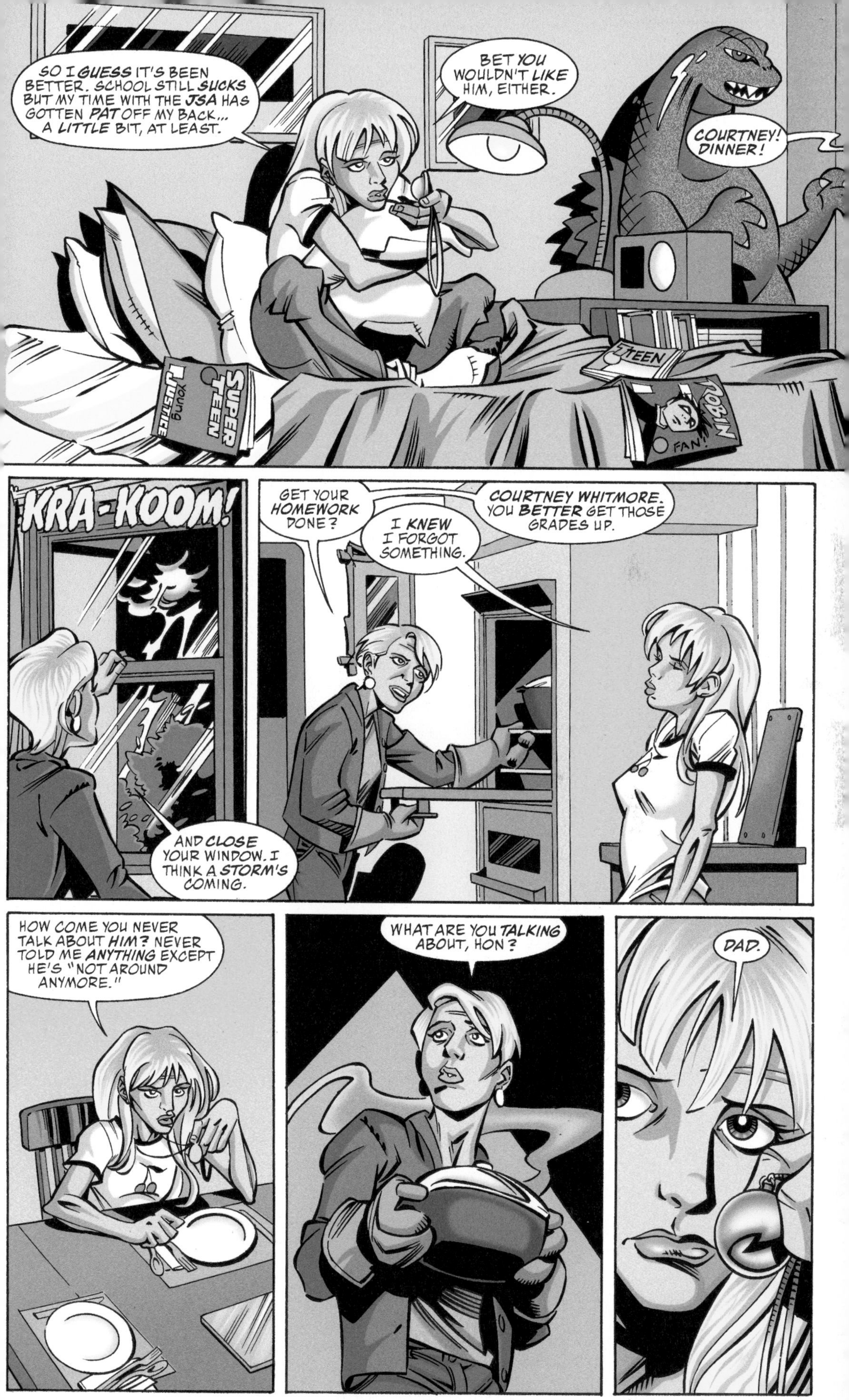
SO I GUESS IT'S BEEN BETTER. SCHOOL STILL SUCKS BUT MY TIME WITH THE JSA HAS GOTTEN PAT OFF MY BACK... A LITTLE BIT, AT LEAST.
BET YOU WOULDN'T LIKE HIM, EITHER.
COURTNEY! DINNER!
SUPER TEEN
YOUNG JUSTICE
TEEN
ROBIN FAN!
KRA-KOOM!
AND CLOSE YOUR WINDOW. I THINK A STORM'S COMING.
GET YOUR HOMEWORK DONE?
I KNEW I FORGOT SOMETHING.
COURTNEY WHITMORE. YOU BETTER GET THOSE GRADES UP.
HOW COME YOU NEVER TALK ABOUT HIM? NEVER TOLD ME ANYTHING EXCEPT HE'S "NOT AROUND ANYMORE."
WHAT ARE YOU TALKING ABOUT, HON?
DAD.

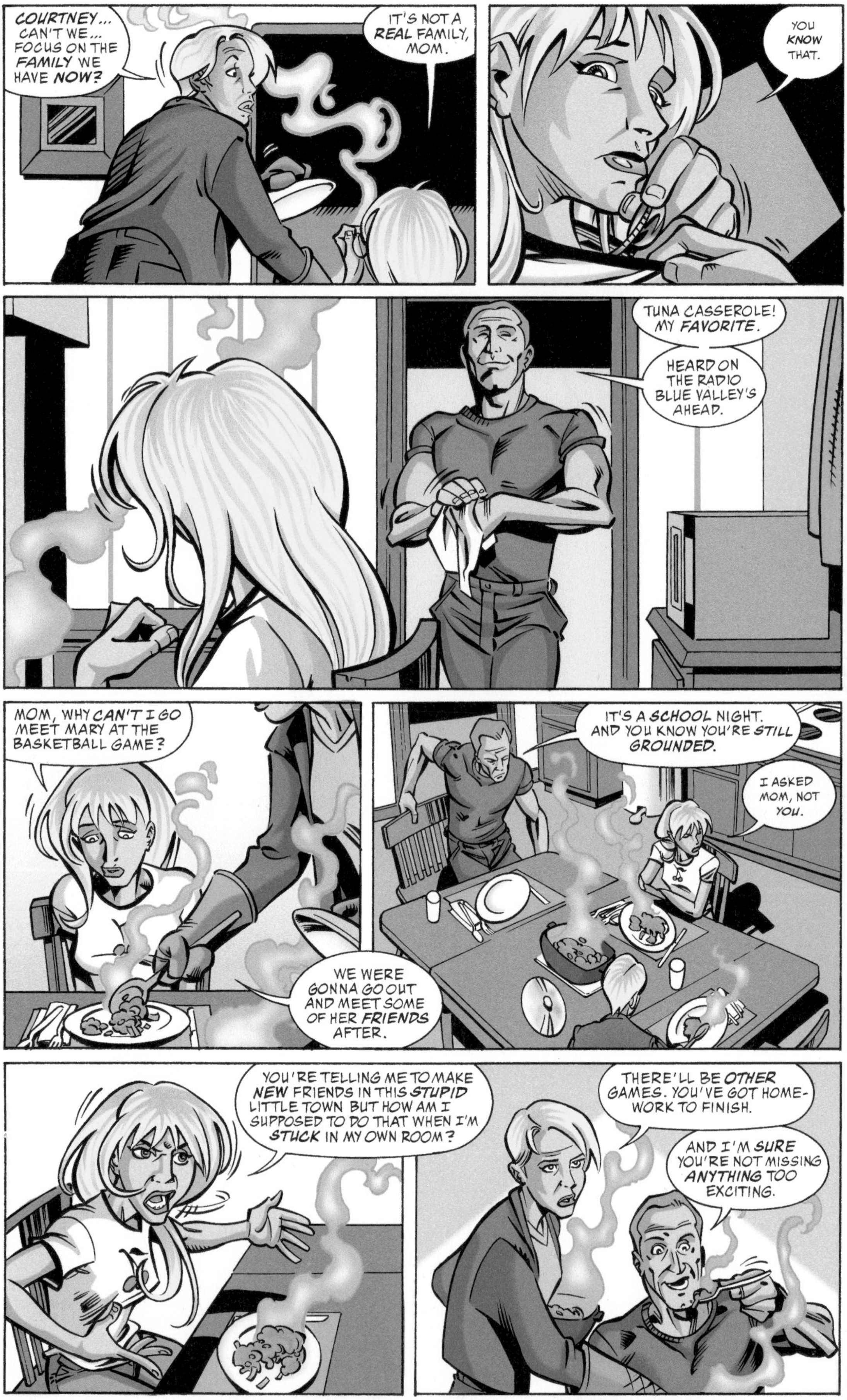
COURTNEY... CAN'T WE... FOCUS ON THE FAMILY WE HAVE NOW?
IT'S NOT A REAL FAMILY, MOM.
YOU KNOW THAT.
TUNA CASSEROLE! MY FAVORITE.
HEARD ON THE RADIO BLUE VALLEY'S AHEAD.
MOM, WHY CAN'T I GO MEET MARY AT THE BASKETBALL GAME?
WE WERE GONNA GO OUT AND MEET SOME OF HER FRIENDS AFTER.
IT'S A SCHOOL NIGHT. AND YOU KNOW YOU'RE STILL GROUNDED.
I ASKED MOM, NOT YOU.
YOU'RE TELLING ME TO MAKE NEW FRIENDS IN THIS STUPID LITTLE TOWN BUT HOW AM I SUPPOSED TO DO THAT WHEN I'M STUCK IN MY OWN ROOM?
THERE'LL BE OTHER GAMES. YOU'VE GOT HOME-WORK TO FINISH.
AND I'M SURE YOU'RE NOT MISSING ANYTHING TOO EXCITING.

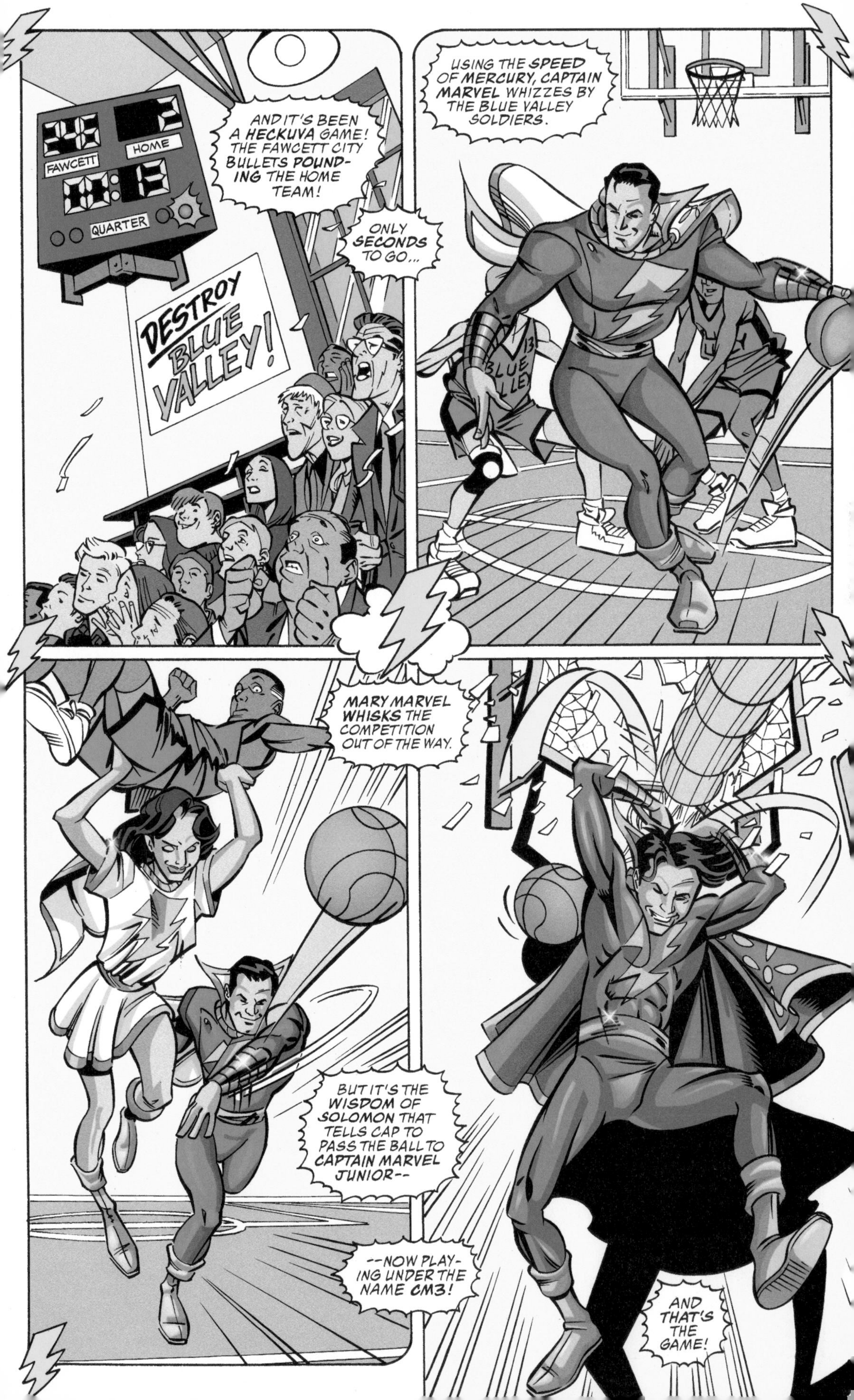
24 2
FAWCETT
HOME
00:13
QUARTER
AND IT'S BEEN A HECKUVA GAME! THE FAWCETT CITY BULLETS POUNDING THE HOME TEAM!
ONLY SECONDS TO GO...
DESTROY BLUE VALLEY!
USING THE SPEED OF MERCURY, CAPTAIN MARVEL WHIZZES BY THE BLUE VALLEY SOLDIERS.
MARY MARVEL WHISKS THE COMPETITION OUT OF THE WAY.
BUT IT'S THE WISDOM OF SOLOMON THAT TELLS CAP TO PASS THE BALL TO CAPTAIN MARVEL JUNIOR--
--NOW PLAYING UNDER THE NAME CM3!
AND THAT'S THE GAME!

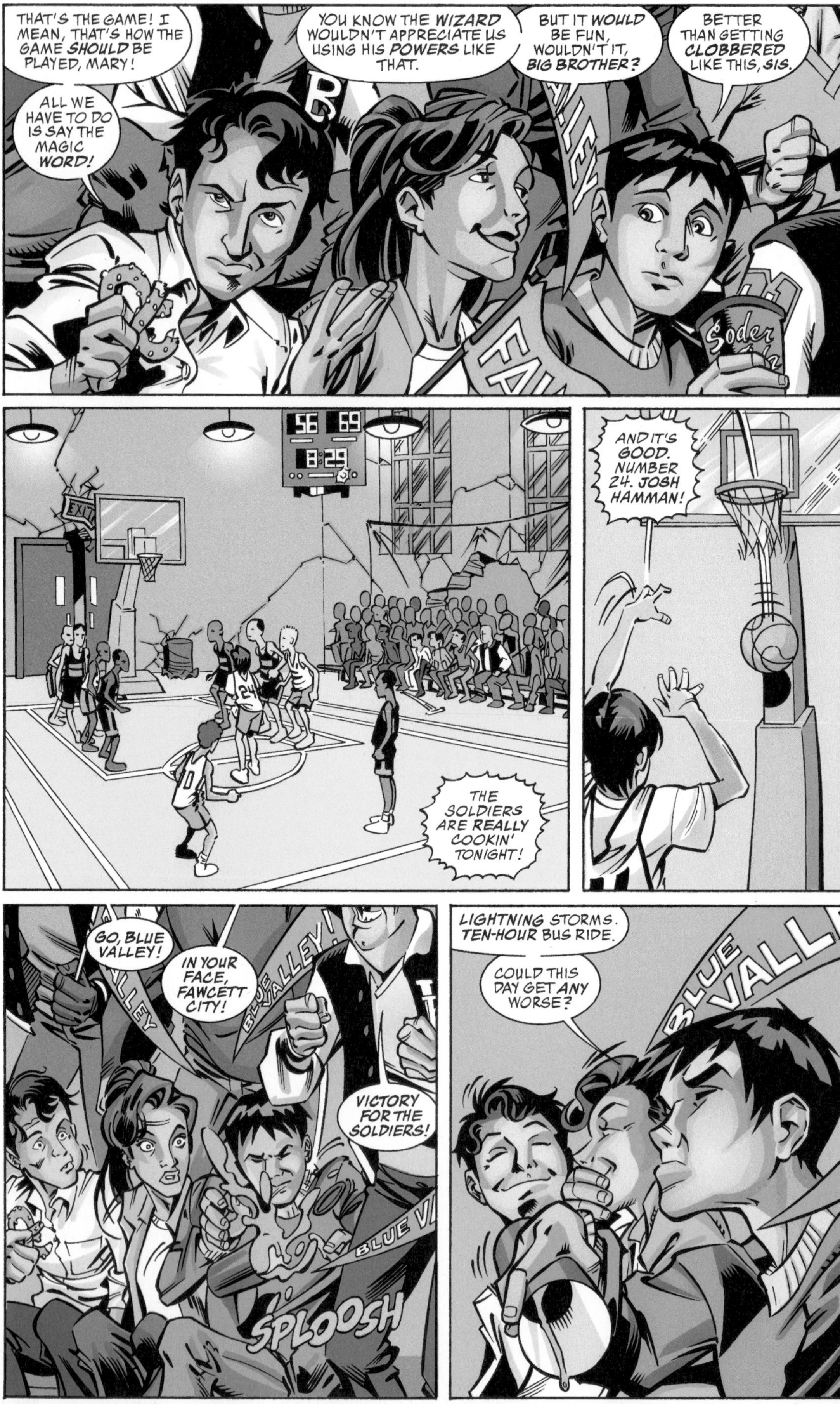
THAT'S THE GAME! I MEAN, THAT'S HOW THE GAME SHOULD BE PLAYED, MARY!
ALL WE HAVE TO DO IS SAY THE MAGIC WORD!
YOU KNOW THE WIZARD WOULDN'T APPRECIATE US USING HIS POWERS LIKE THAT.
BUT IT WOULD BE FUN, WOULDN'T IT, BIG BROTHER?
BETTER THAN GETTING CLOBBERED LIKE THIS, SIS.
56 69
8:29
EXIT
THE SOLDIERS ARE REALLY COOKIN' TONIGHT!
AND IT'S GOOD. NUMBER 24. JOSH HAMMAN!
GO, BLUE VALLEY!
IN YOUR FACE, FAWCETT CITY!
BLUE VALLEY!
VICTORY FOR THE SOLDIERS!
SPLOOSH
LIGHTNING STORMS. TEN-HOUR BUS RIDE.
COULD THIS DAY GET ANY WORSE?
BLUE VALLEY

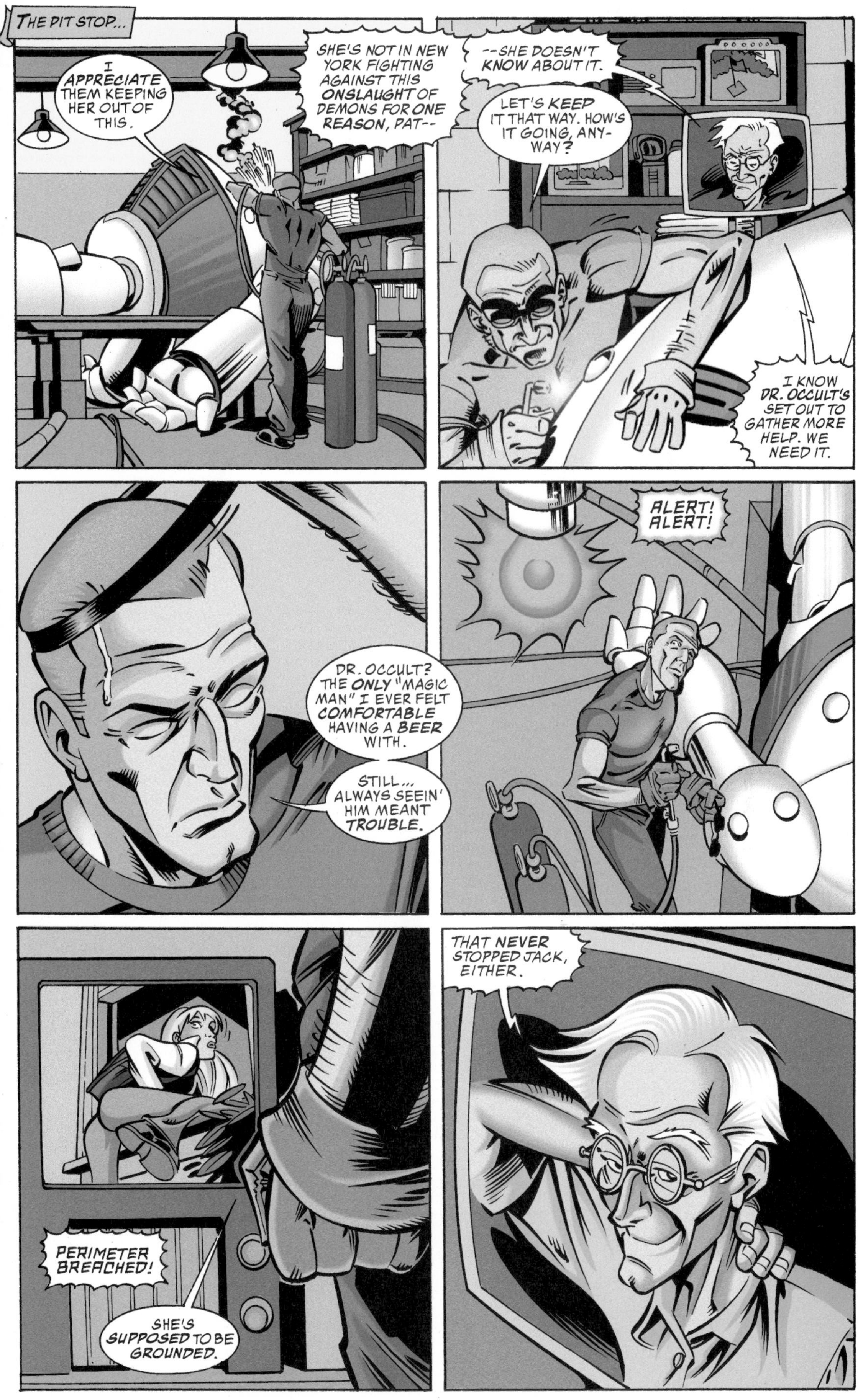
THE PIT STOP...
I APPRECIATE THEM KEEPING HER OUT OF THIS.
SHE'S NOT IN NEW YORK FIGHTING AGAINST THIS ONSLAUGHT OF DEMONS FOR ONE REASON, PAT--
--SHE DOESN'T KNOW ABOUT IT.
LET'S KEEP IT THAT WAY. HOW'S IT GOING, ANYWAY?
I KNOW DR. OCCULT'S SET OUT TO GATHER MORE HELP. WE NEED IT.
DR. OCCULT? THE ONLY "MAGIC MAN" I EVER FELT COMFORTABLE HAVING A BEER WITH.
STILL... ALWAYS SEEIN' HIM MEANT TROUBLE.
ALERT! ALERT!
PERIMETER BREACHED!
SHE'S SUPPOSED TO BE GROUNDED.
THAT NEVER STOPPED JACK, EITHER.

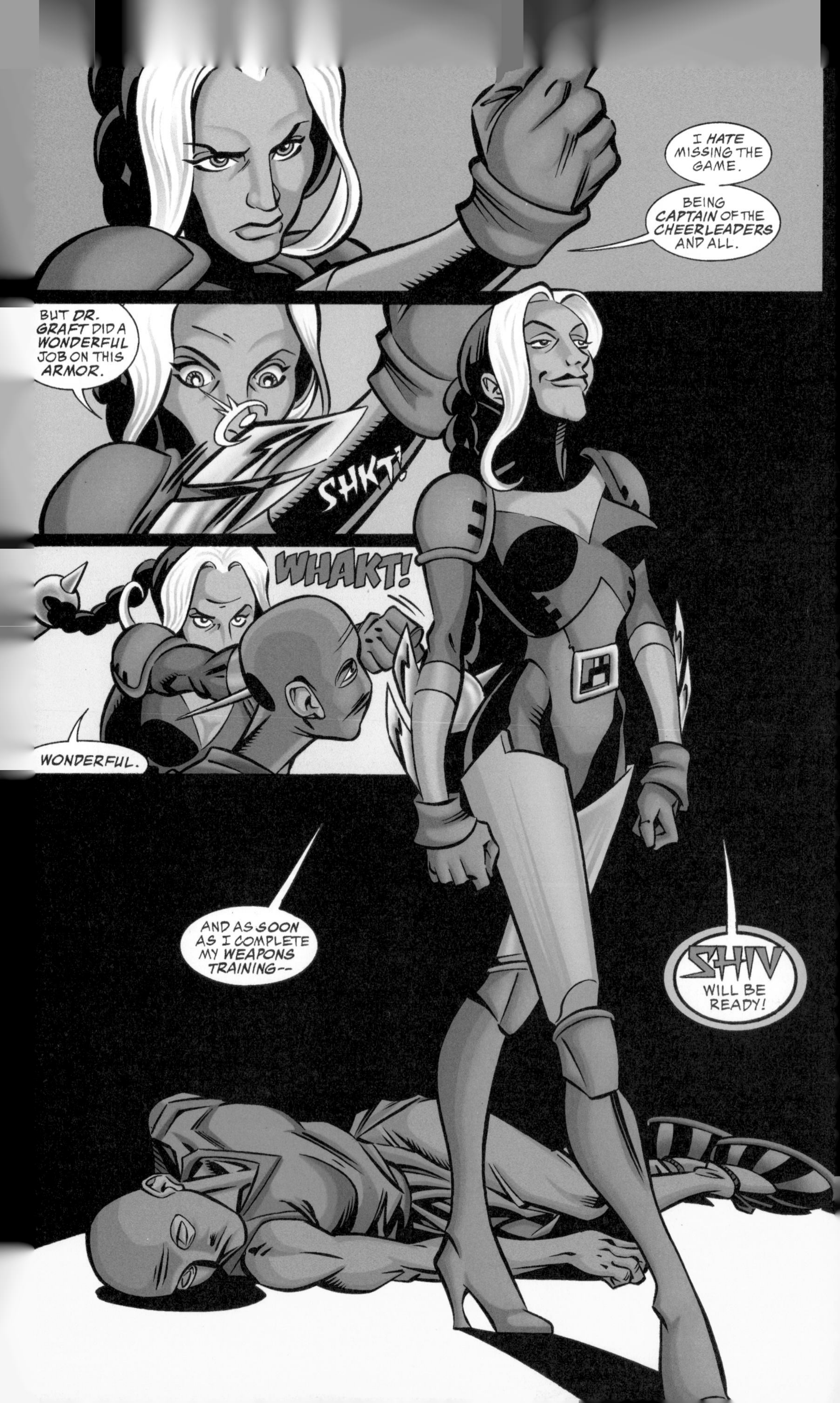

I HATE MISSING THE GAME.
BEING CAPTAIN OF THE CHEERLEADERS AND ALL.
BUT DR. GRAFT DID A WONDERFUL JOB ON THIS ARMOR.
SHKT!
WHAKT!
WONDERFUL.
AND AS SOON AS I COMPLETE MY WEAPONS TRAINING--
SHIV WILL BE READY!

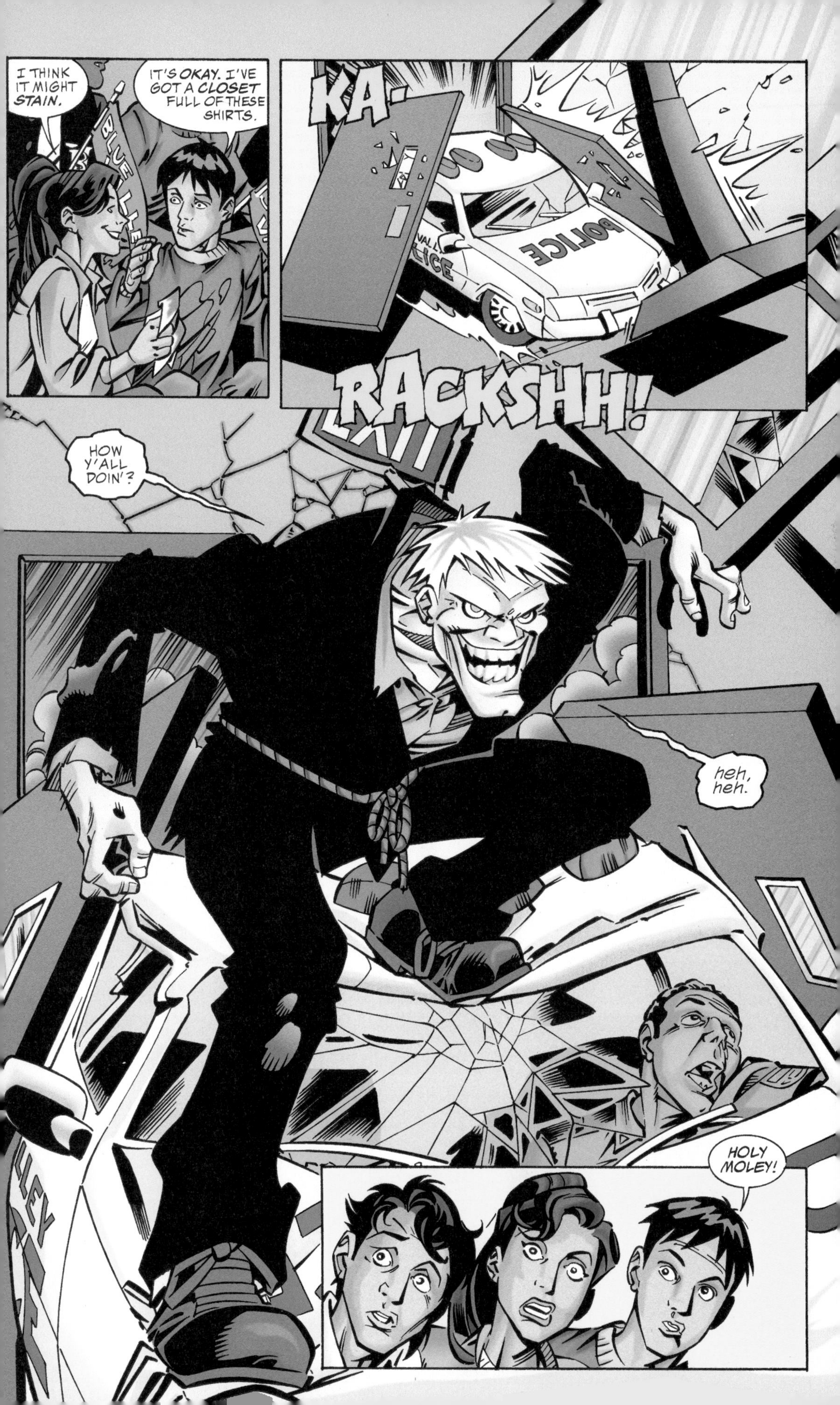

I THINK IT MIGHT STAIN.
IT'S OKAY. I'VE GOT A CLOSET FULL OF THESE SHIRTS.
KA-
RACKSHH!
POLICE
HOW Y'ALL DOIN'?
heh, heh.
HOLY MOLEY!

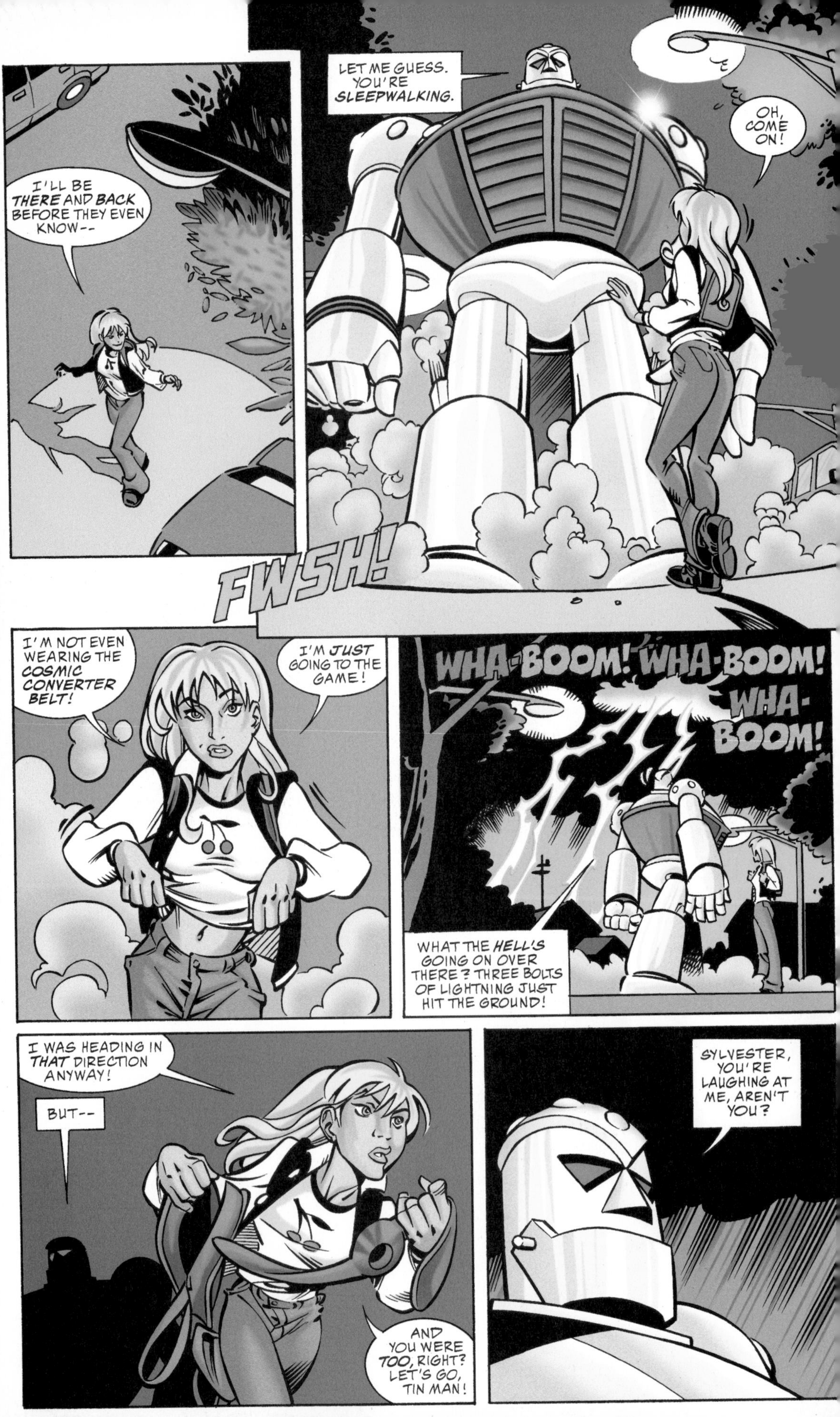
I'LL BE THERE AND BACK BEFORE THEY EVEN KNOW--
LET ME GUESS. YOU'RE SLEEPWALKING.
OH, COME ON!
FWSH!
I'M NOT EVEN WEARING THE COSMIC CONVERTER BELT!
I'M JUST GOING TO THE GAME!
WHA-BOOM! WHA-BOOM! WHA-BOOM!
WHAT THE HELL'S GOING ON OVER THERE? THREE BOLTS OF LIGHTNING JUST HIT THE GROUND!
I WAS HEADING IN THAT DIRECTION ANYWAY!
BUT--
AND YOU WERE TOO, RIGHT? LET'S GO, TIN MAN!
SYLVESTER, YOU'RE LAUGHING AT ME, AREN'T YOU?

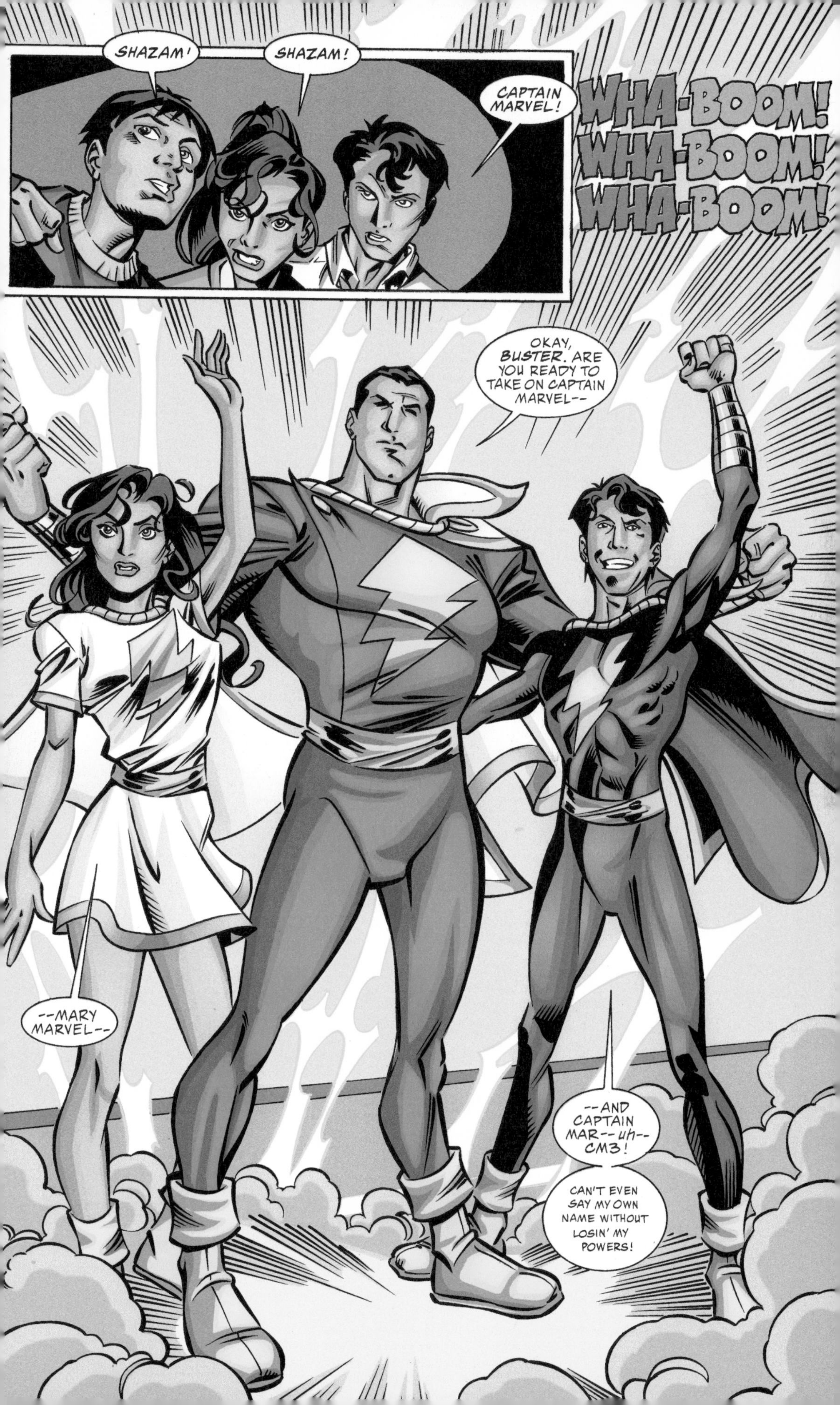
SHAZAM!
SHAZAM!
CAPTAIN MARVEL!
WHA-BOOM! WHA-BOOM! WHA-BOOM!
OKAY, BUSTER. ARE YOU READY TO TAKE ON CAPTAIN MARVEL--
--MARY MARVEL--
--AND CAPTAIN MAR--UH--CM3!
CAN'T EVEN SAY MY OWN NAME WITHOUT LOSIN' MY POWERS!

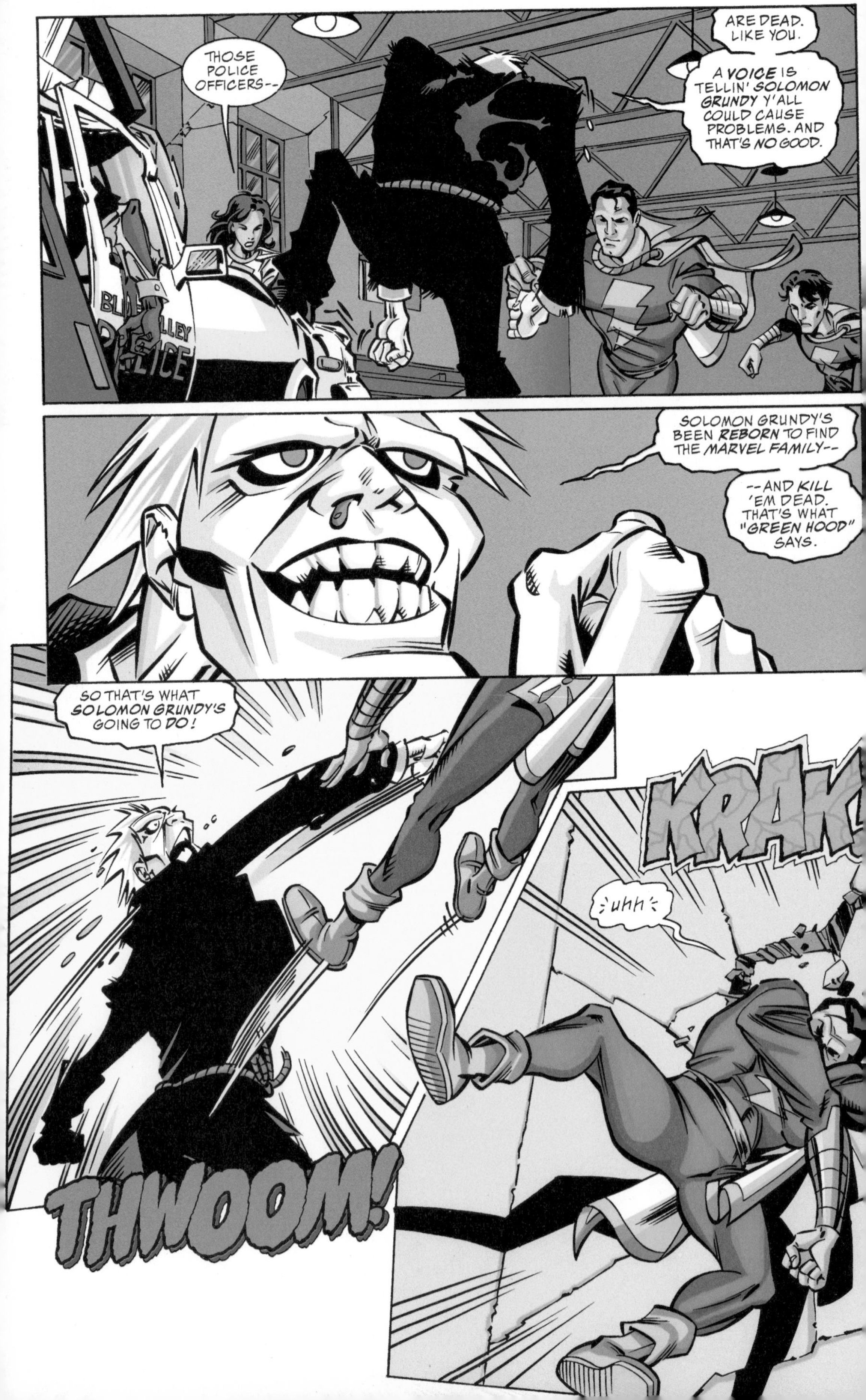
THOSE POLICE OFFICERS--
ARE DEAD. LIKE YOU.
A VOICE IS TELLIN' SOLOMON GRUNDY Y'ALL COULD CAUSE PROBLEMS. AND THAT'S NO GOOD.
BLUDVALLEY POLICE
SOLOMON GRUNDY'S BEEN REBORN TO FIND THE MARVEL FAMILY--
--AND KILL 'EM DEAD. THAT'S WHAT "GREEN HOOD" SAYS.
SO THAT'S WHAT SOLOMON GRUNDY'S GOING TO DO!
THWOOM!
KRAK
uhh

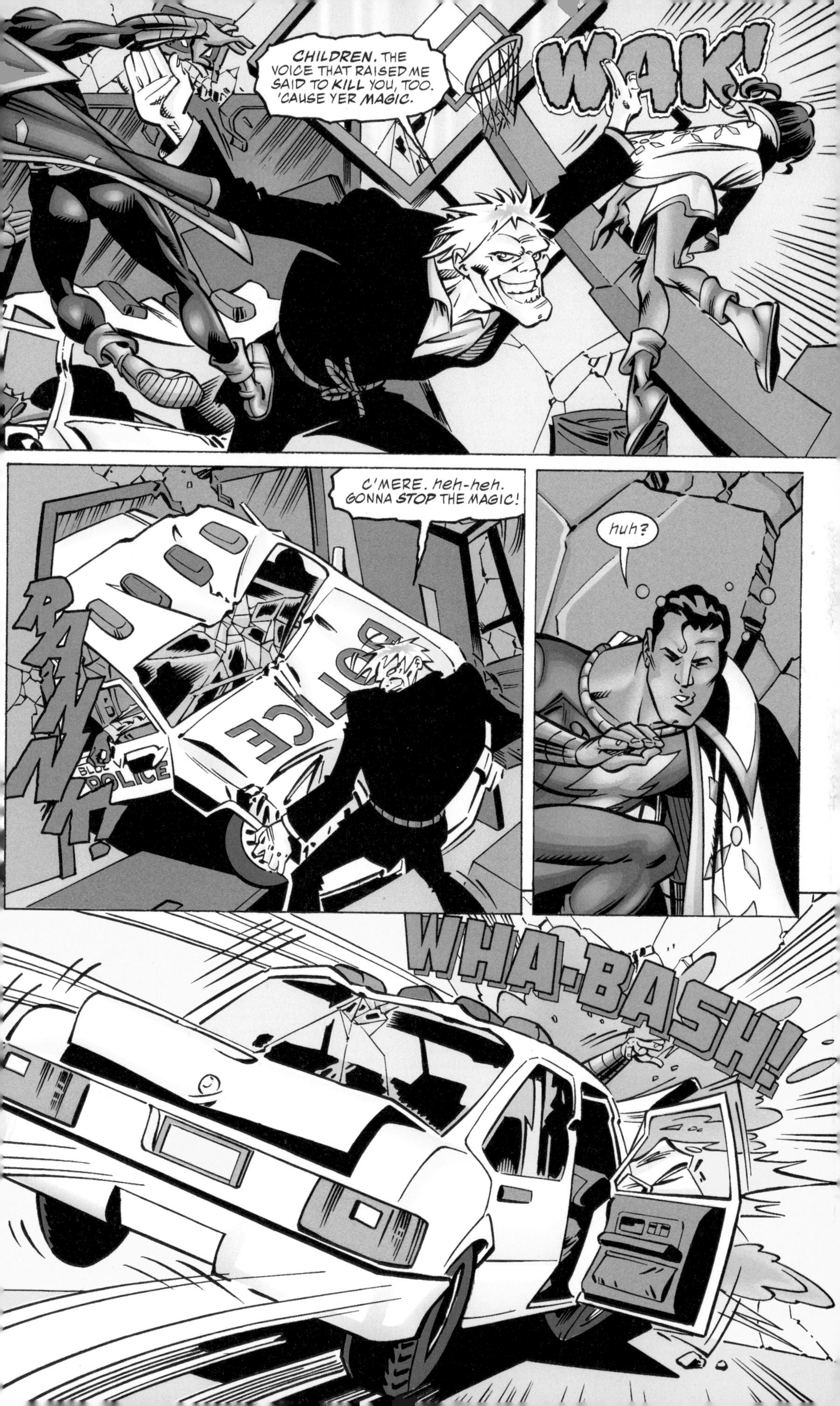

CHILDREN. THE VOICE THAT RAISED ME SAID TO KILL YOU, TOO. 'CAUSE YER MAGIC.
WAK!
C'MERE. heh-heh. GONNA STOP THE MAGIC!
RANNK!
POLICE
huh?
WHA-BASH!!

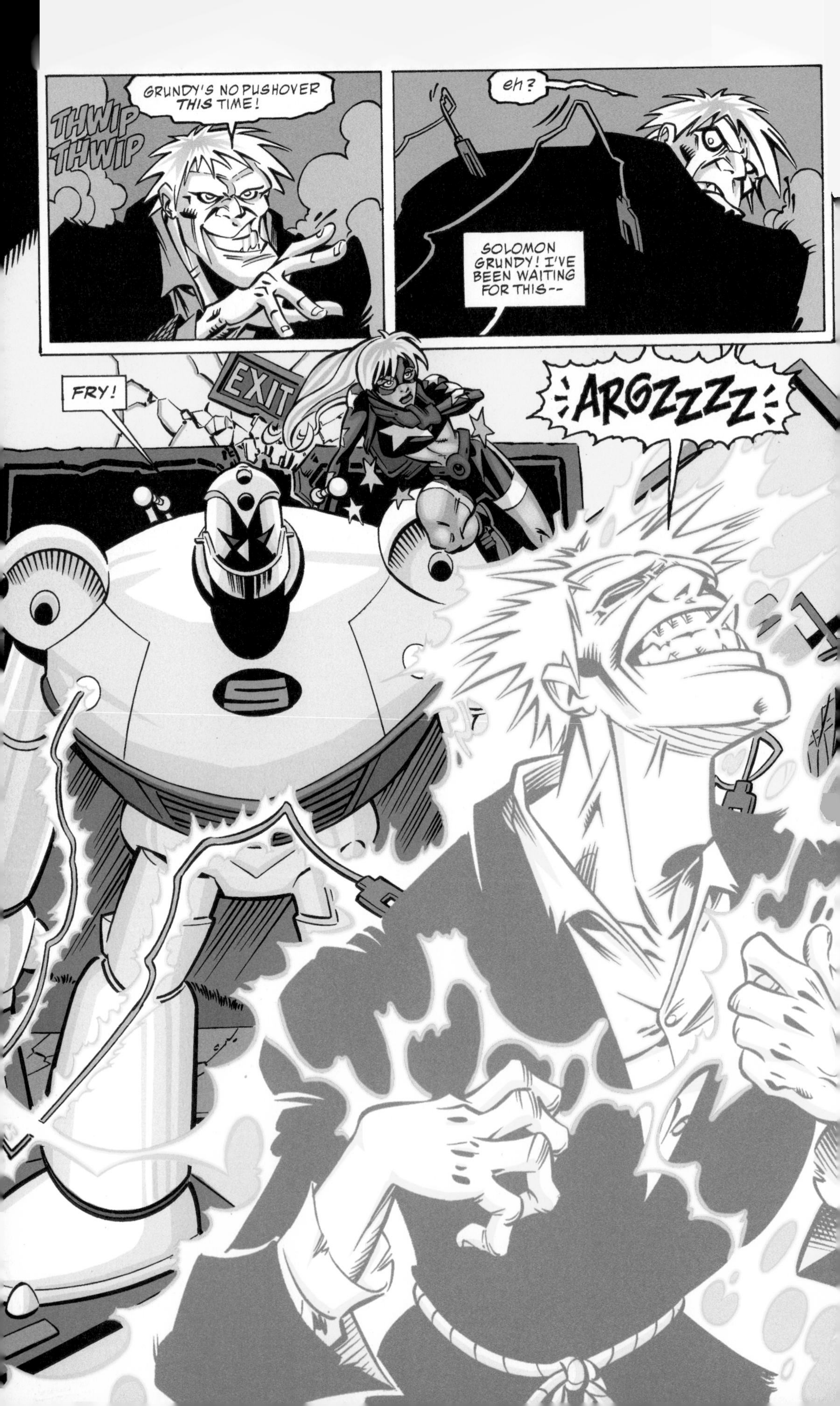

THWIP THWIP
GRUNDY'S NO PUSHOVER THIS TIME!
eh?
SOLOMON GRUNDY! I'VE BEEN WAITING FOR THIS--
EXIT
FRY!
ARGZZZZZ

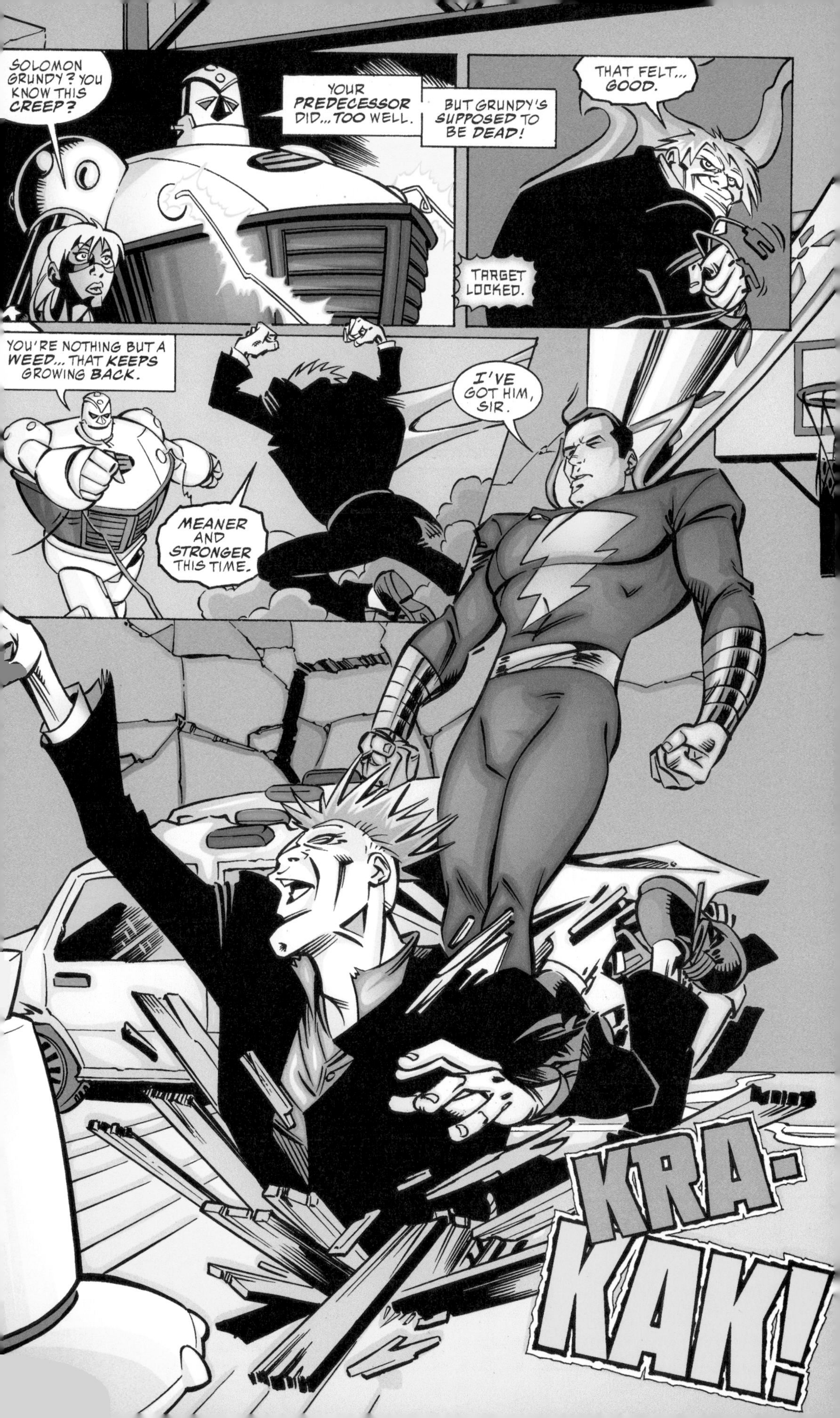
SOLOMON GRUNDY? YOU KNOW THIS CREEP?
YOUR PREDECESSOR DID... TOO WELL.
BUT GRUNDY'S SUPPOSED TO BE DEAD!
THAT FELT... GOOD.
TARGET LOCKED.
YOU'RE NOTHING BUT A WEED... THAT KEEPS GROWING BACK.
MEANER AND STRONGER THIS TIME.
I'VE GOT HIM, SIR.
KRA-KAK!

WHOA! THE MARVEL FAMILY!

I MEAN... YO, FELLOW HEROES. I'M THE STAR-SPANGLED KID. THIS IS MY SIDE-KICK, S.T.R.I.P.E.

THIS CREATURE'S ON A RAMPAGE. HE'S ALREADY KILLED SOME COPS.

NICE... BRACES.

UH... LET'S GO KICK HIS BIG WHITE BUTT!

I'M WITH YOU, KID!

DUMB BRACES.

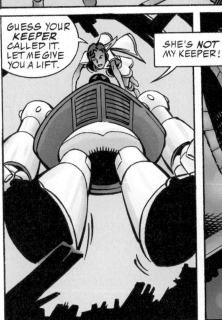

GUESS YOUR KEEPER CALLED IT. LET ME GIVE YOU A LIFT.

SHE'S NOT MY KEEPER!

HEY, CAP!

WHERE'D THEY GO? CAN'T YOU USE YOUR X-RAY VISION?

THAT'S SUPERMAN, NOT CAPTAIN MARV--

DANGIT! ALMOST DID IT AGAIN!

KID, C'MERE!

WHAT? CAN'T IT WAIT? WE'RE IN THE MIDDLE OF A TEAM-UP HERE!

COURTNEY... THIS MONSTER... HE KILLED SYLVESTER PEMBERTON--

--THE ORIGINAL STAR-SPANGLED KID.

HE WHAT...?

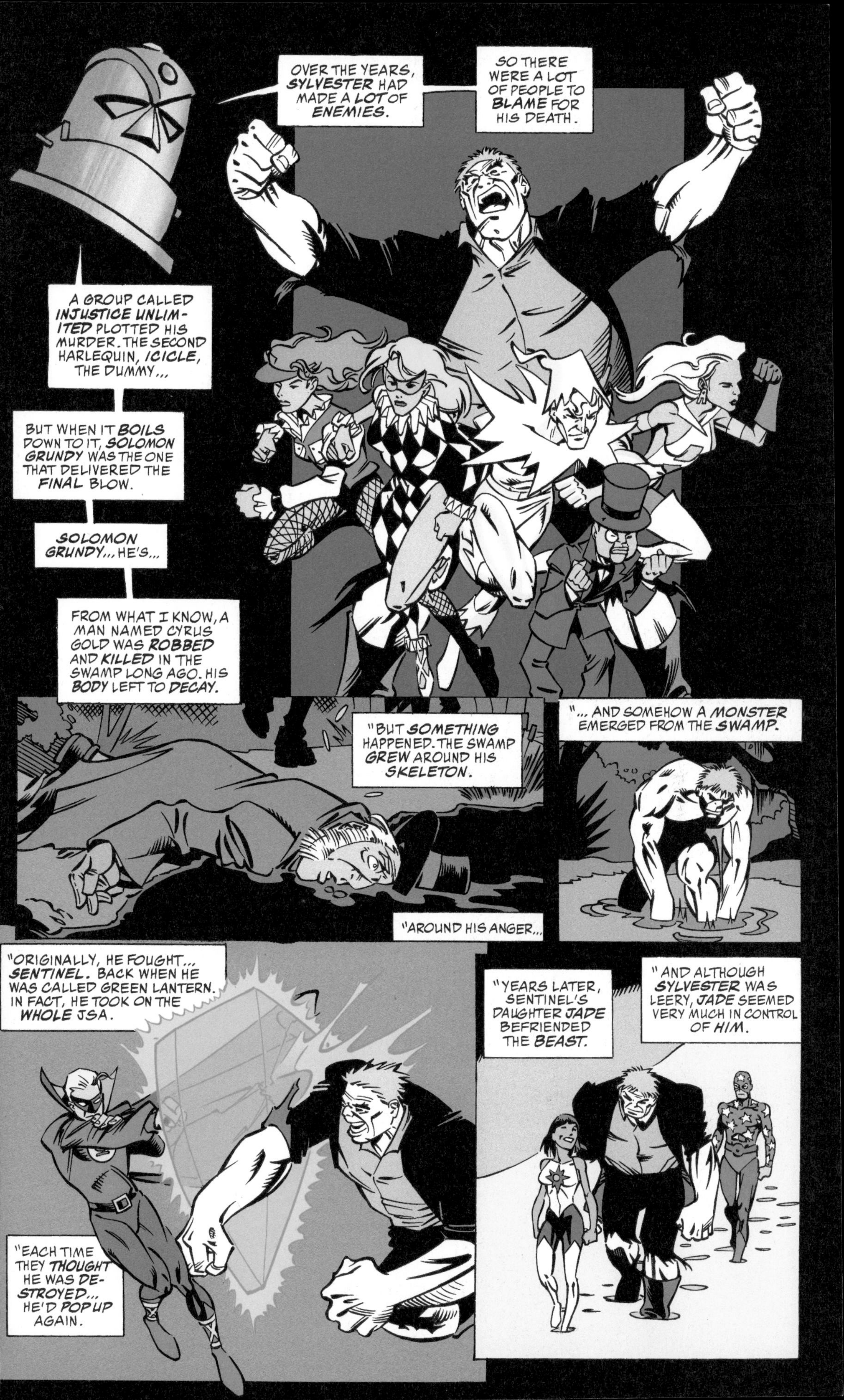
OVER THE YEARS, SYLVESTER HAD MADE A LOT OF ENEMIES.
SO THERE WERE A LOT OF PEOPLE TO BLAME FOR HIS DEATH.
A GROUP CALLED INJUSTICE UNLIMITED PLOTTED HIS MURDER. THE SECOND HARLEQUIN, ICICLE, THE DUMMY...
BUT WHEN IT BOILS DOWN TO IT, SOLOMON GRUNDY WAS THE ONE THAT DELIVERED THE FINAL BLOW.
SOLOMON GRUNDY... HE'S...
FROM WHAT I KNOW, A MAN NAMED CYRUS GOLD WAS ROBBED AND KILLED IN THE SWAMP LONG AGO. HIS BODY LEFT TO DECAY.
"BUT SOMETHING HAPPENED. THE SWAMP GREW AROUND HIS SKELETON.
"AROUND HIS ANGER...
"... AND SOMEHOW A MONSTER EMERGED FROM THE SWAMP.
"ORIGINALLY, HE FOUGHT... SENTINEL. BACK WHEN HE WAS CALLED GREEN LANTERN. IN FACT, HE TOOK ON THE WHOLE JSA.
"EACH TIME THEY THOUGHT HE WAS DESTROYED... HE'D POP UP AGAIN.
"YEARS LATER, SENTINEL'S DAUGHTER JADE BEFRIENDED THE BEAST.
"AND ALTHOUGH SYLVESTER WAS LEERY, JADE SEEMED VERY MUCH IN CONTROL OF HIM.

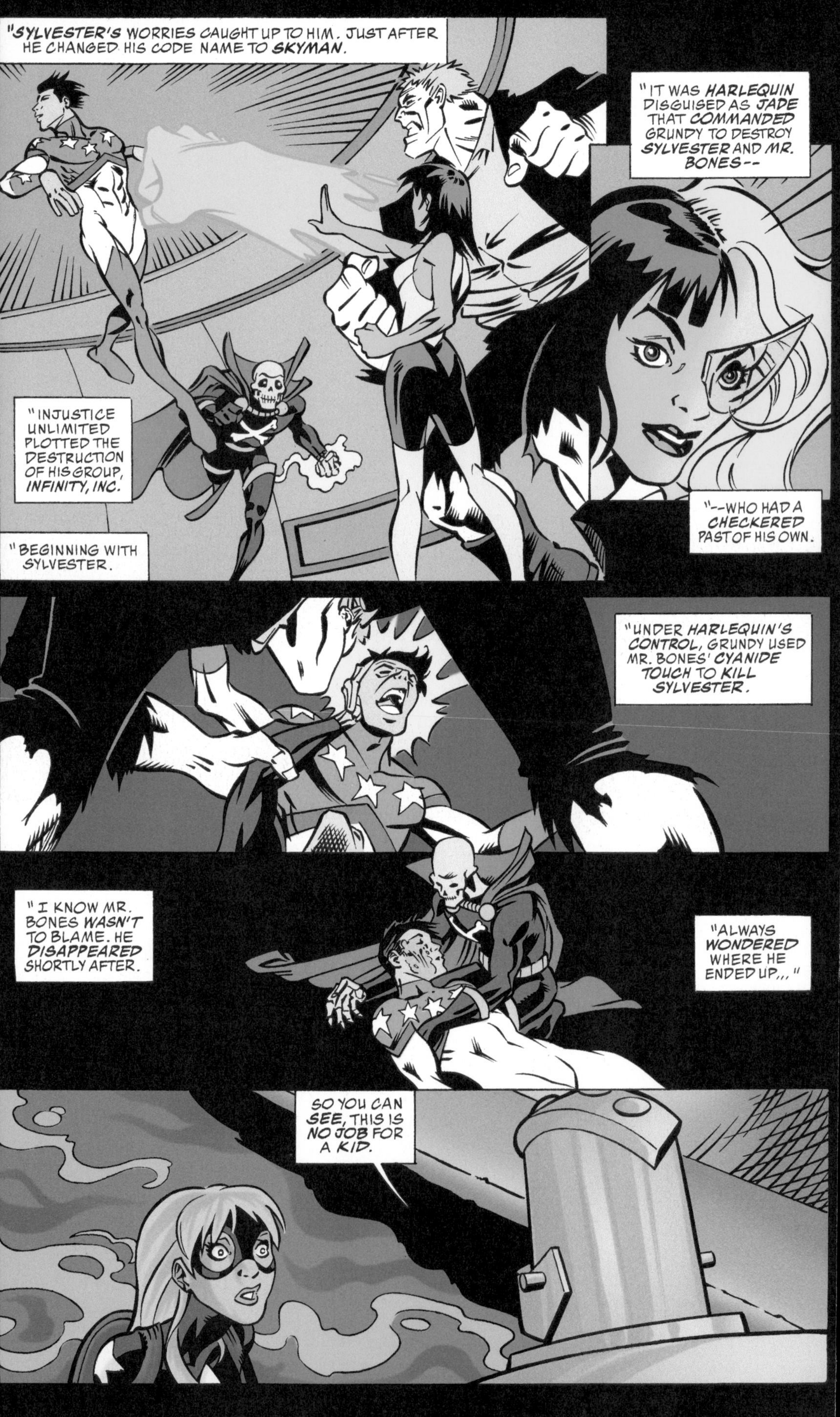
"SYLVESTER'S WORRIES CAUGHT UP TO HIM. JUST AFTER HE CHANGED HIS CODE NAME TO SKYMAN.
"INJUSTICE UNLIMITED PLOTTED THE DESTRUCTION OF HIS GROUP, INFINITY, INC.
"BEGINNING WITH SYLVESTER.
"IT WAS HARLEQUIN DISGUISED AS JADE THAT COMMANDED GRUNDY TO DESTROY SYLVESTER AND MR. BONES--
"--WHO HAD A CHECKERED PAST OF HIS OWN.
"UNDER HARLEQUIN'S CONTROL, GRUNDY USED MR. BONES' CYANIDE TOUCH TO KILL SYLVESTER.
"I KNOW MR. BONES WASN'T TO BLAME. HE DISAPPEARED SHORTLY AFTER.
"ALWAYS WONDERED WHERE HE ENDED UP..."
SO YOU CAN SEE, THIS IS NO JOB FOR A KID.

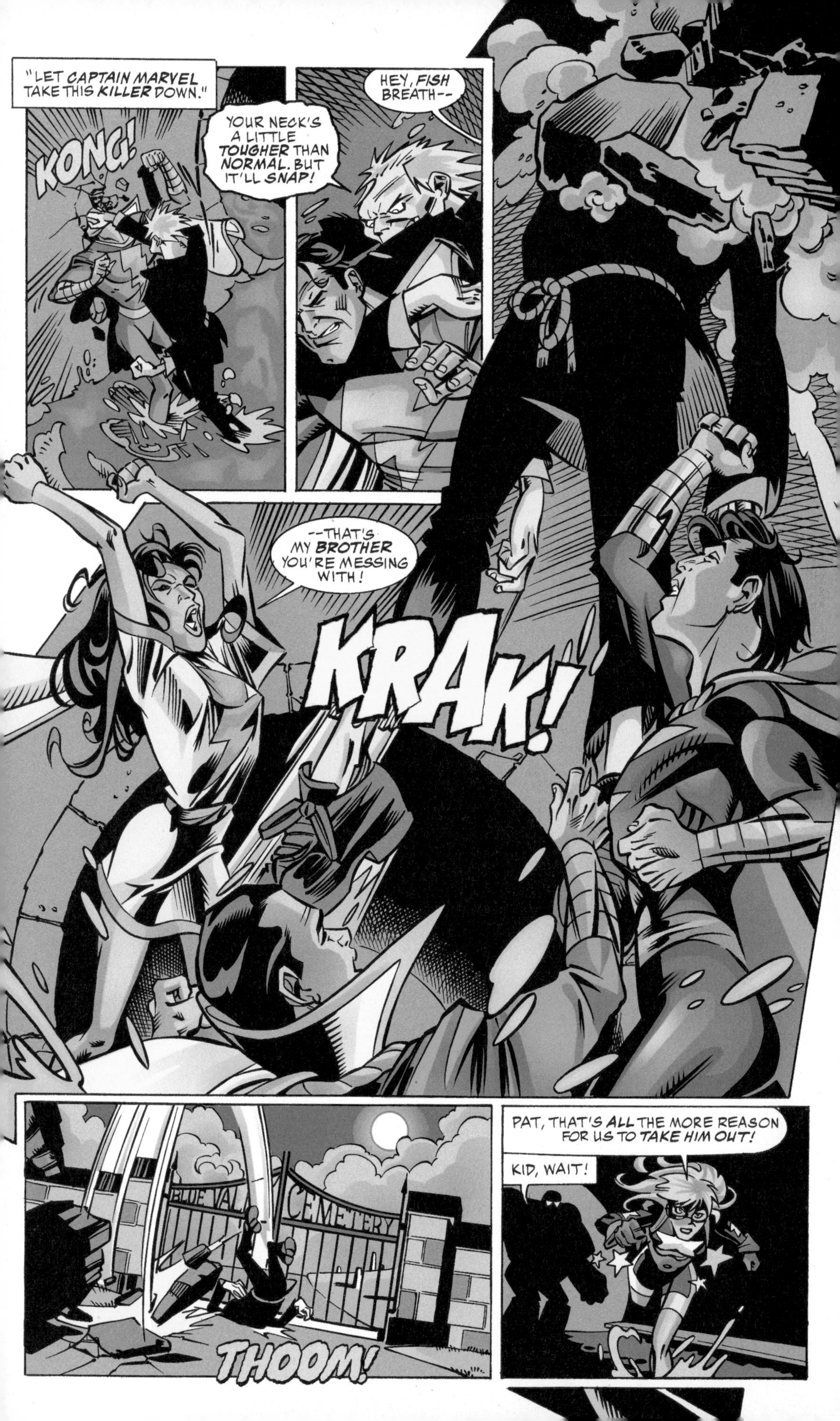
"LET CAPTAIN MARVEL TAKE THIS KILLER DOWN."
KONG!
YOUR NECK'S A LITTLE TOUGHER THAN NORMAL. BUT IT'LL SNAP!
HEY, FISH BREATH--
--THAT'S MY BROTHER YOU'RE MESSING WITH!
KRAK!
BLUE VAL CEMETERY
THOOM!
PAT, THAT'S ALL THE MORE REASON FOR US TO TAKE HIM OUT!
KID, WAIT!

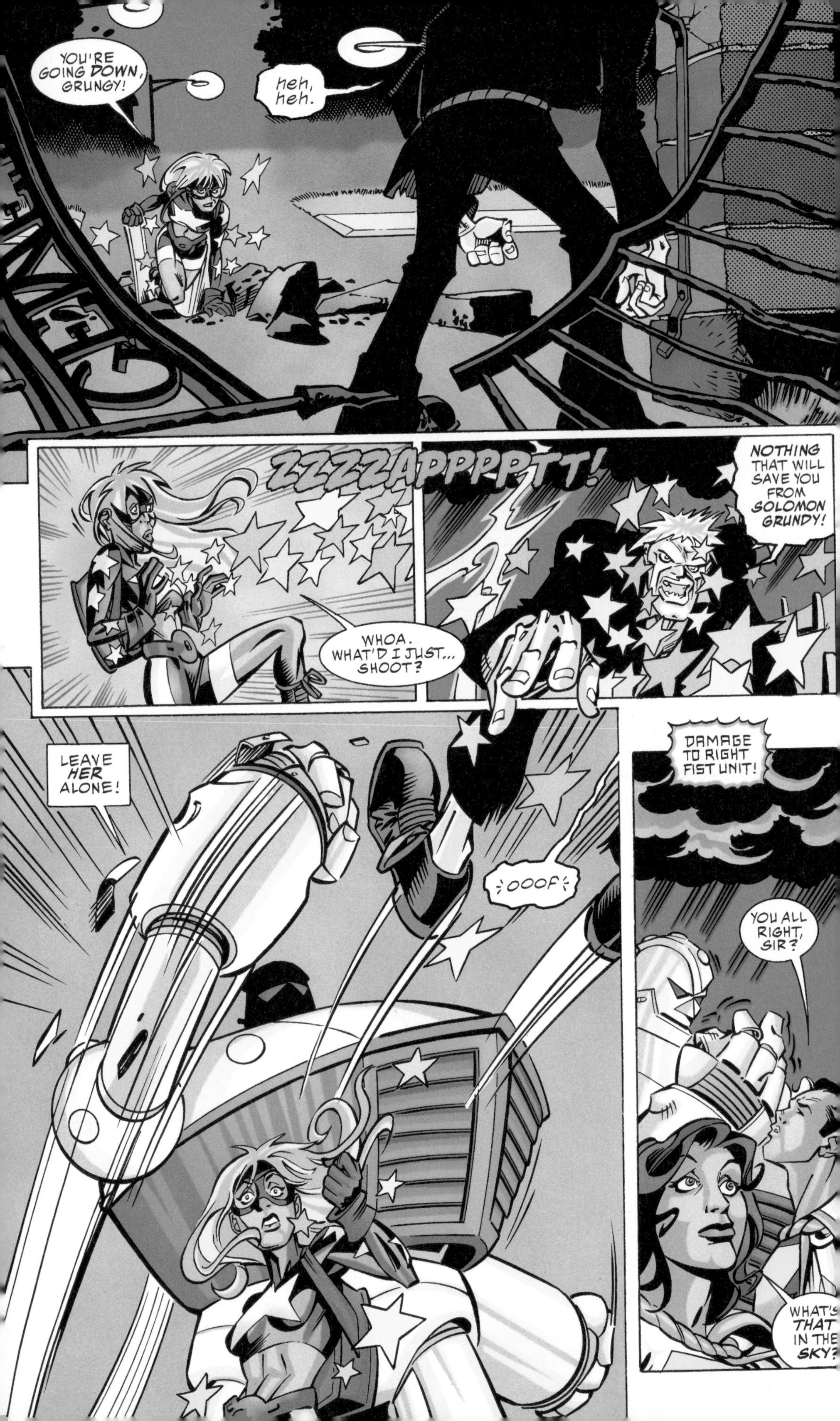
YOU'RE GOING DOWN, GRUNGY!
heh, heh.
ZZZZZAPPPPPTTT!
WHOA. WHAT'D I JUST... SHOOT?
NOTHING THAT WILL SAVE YOU FROM SOLOMON GRUNDY!
LEAVE HER ALONE!
OOOF
DAMAGE TO RIGHT FIST UNIT!
YOU ALL RIGHT, SIR?
WHAT'S THAT IN THE SKY?

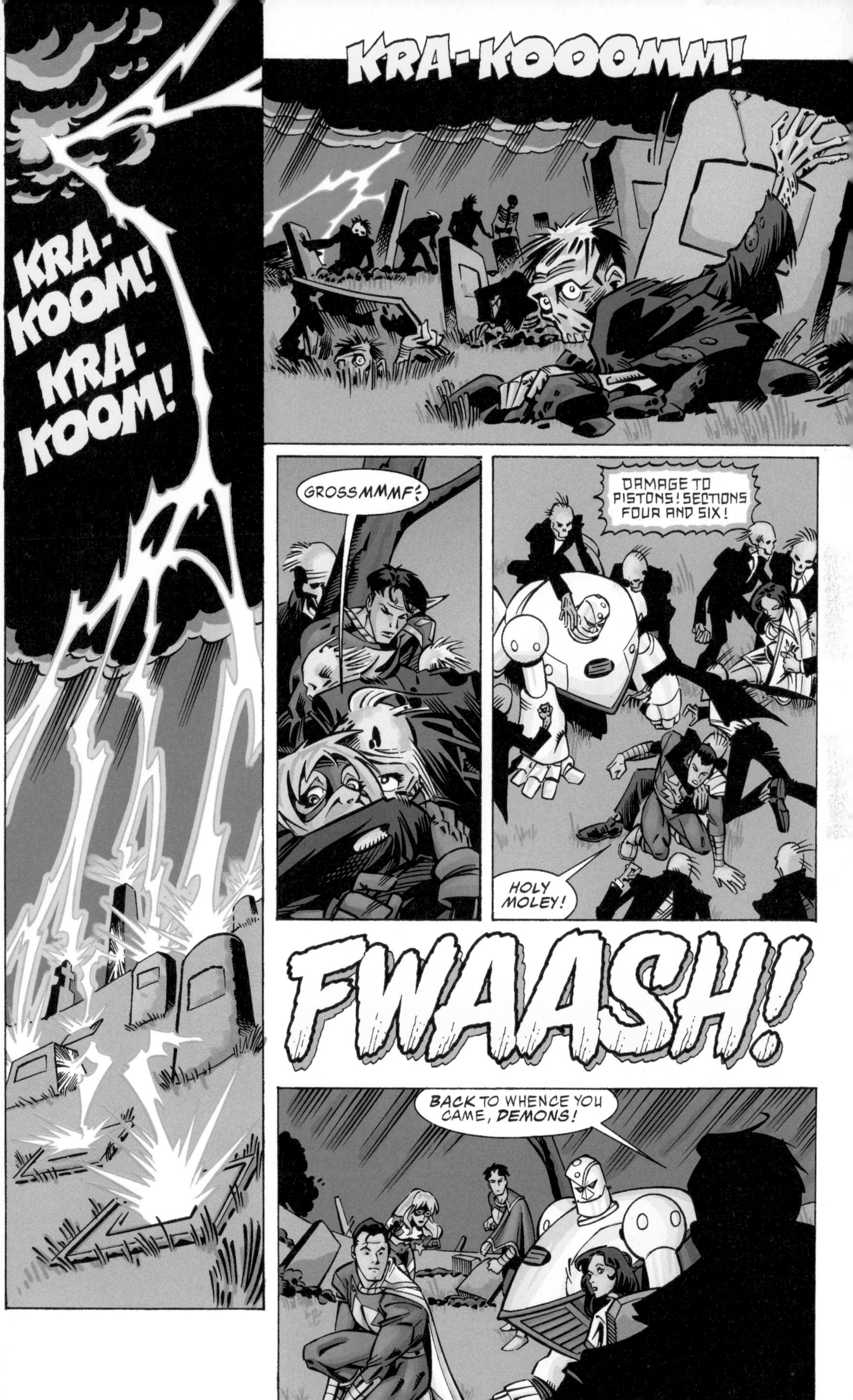
KRA-KOOM! KRA-KOOM!
KRA-KOOOMM!
GROSSMMMF!
DAMAGE TO PISTONS! SECTIONS FOUR AND SIX!
HOLY MOLEY!
FWAASH!
BACK TO WHENCE YOU CAME, DEMONS!

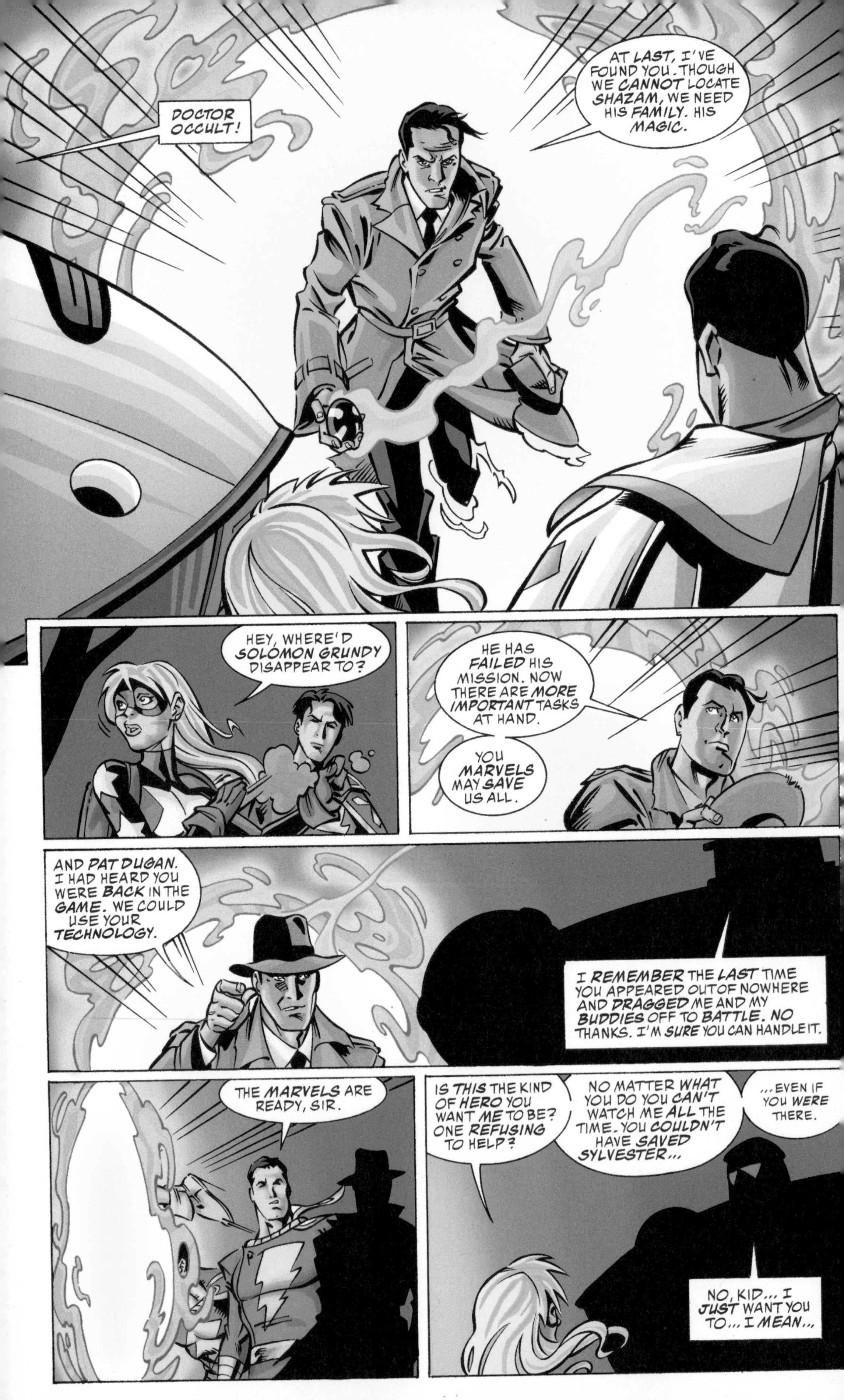
DOCTOR OCCULT!
AT LAST, I'VE FOUND YOU. THOUGH WE CANNOT LOCATE SHAZAM, WE NEED HIS FAMILY. HIS MAGIC.
HEY, WHERE'D SOLOMON GRUNDY DISAPPEAR TO?
HE HAS FAILED HIS MISSION. NOW THERE ARE MORE IMPORTANT TASKS AT HAND.
YOU MARVELS MAY SAVE US ALL.
AND PAT DUGAN. I HAD HEARD YOU WERE BACK IN THE GAME. WE COULD USE YOUR TECHNOLOGY.
I REMEMBER THE LAST TIME YOU APPEARED OUT OF NOWHERE AND DRAGGED ME AND MY BUDDIES OFF TO BATTLE. NO THANKS. I'M SURE YOU CAN HANDLE IT.
THE MARVELS ARE READY, SIR.
IS THIS THE KIND OF HERO YOU WANT ME TO BE? ONE REFUSING TO HELP?
NO MATTER WHAT YOU DO YOU CAN'T WATCH ME ALL THE TIME. YOU COULDN'T HAVE SAVED SYLVESTER...
...EVEN IF YOU WERE THERE.
NO, KID... I JUST WANT YOU TO... I MEAN...

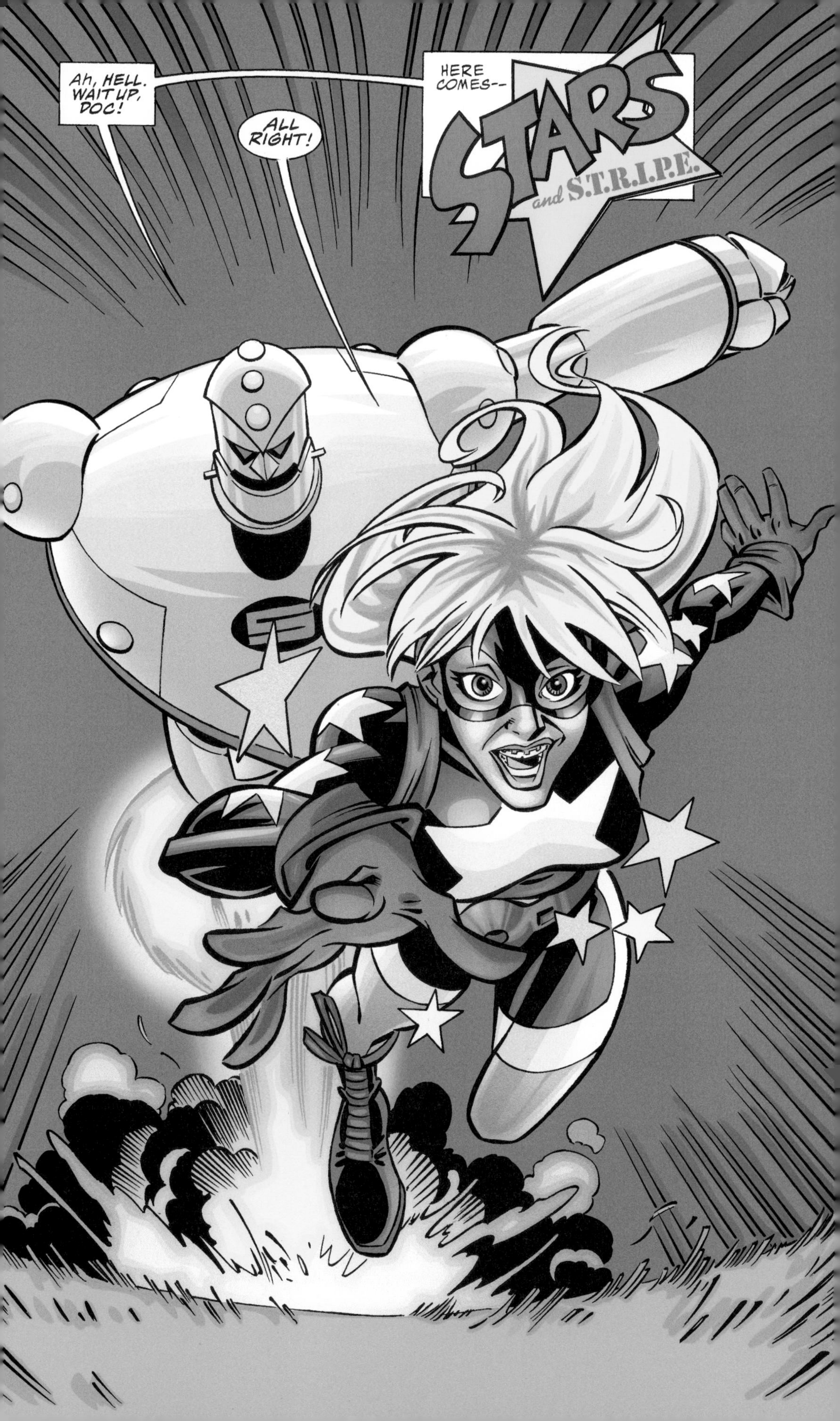
Ah, HELL. WAIT UP, DOC!
ALL RIGHT!
HERE COMES--
STARS and S.T.R.I.P.E.

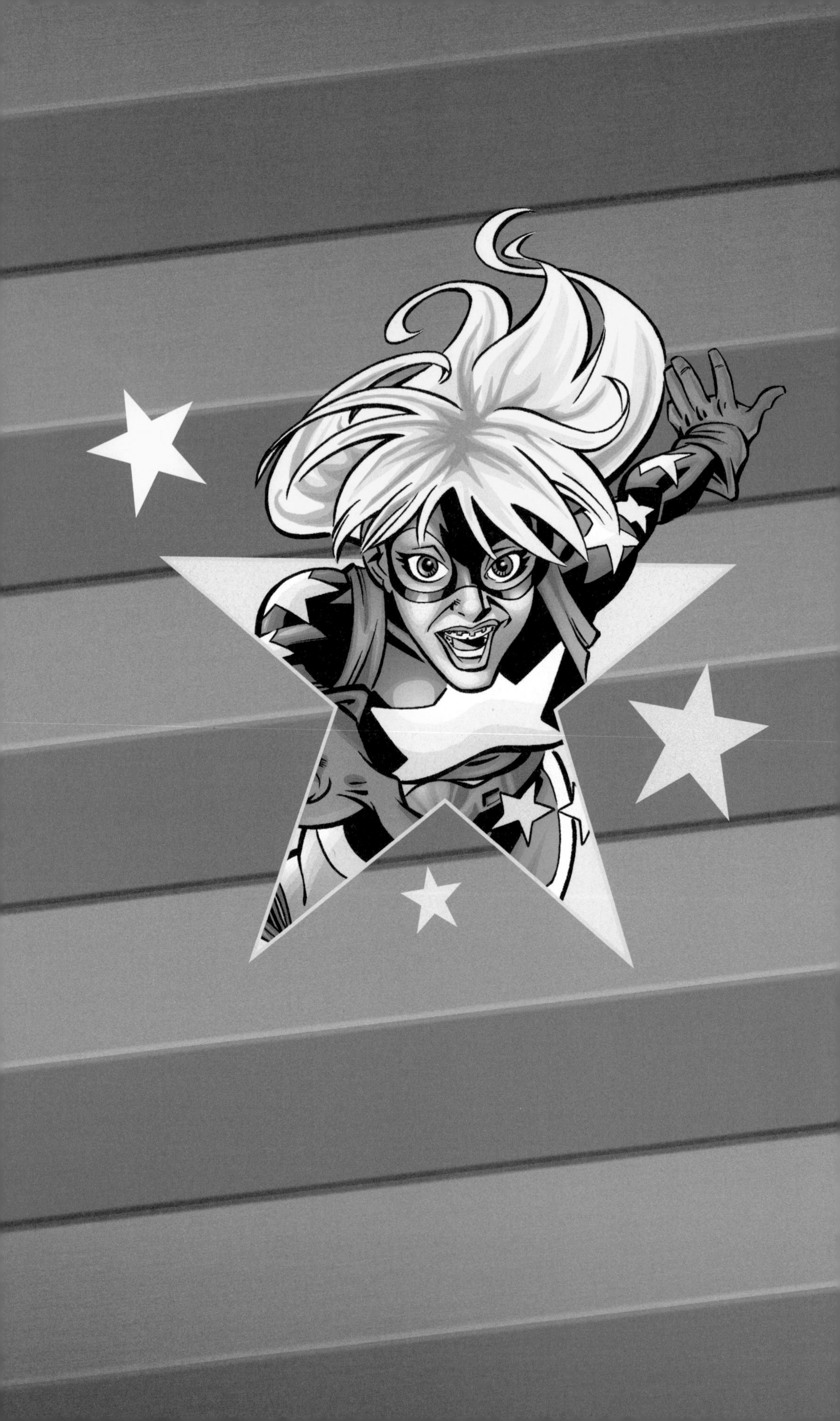

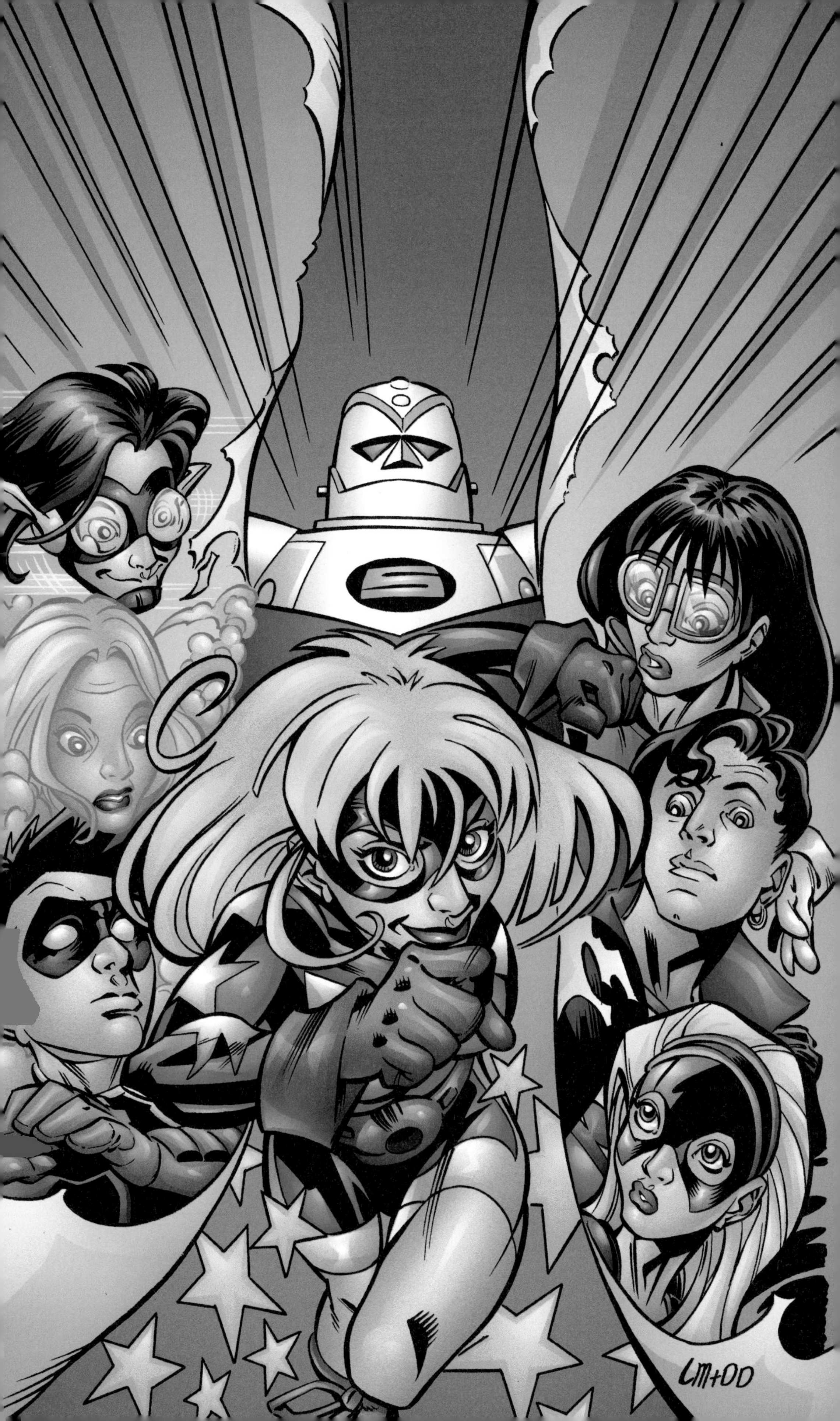
LM+OD

STARS AND S.T.R.I.P.E. #5

Written by GEOFF JOHNS
Pencils by LEE MODER
Inks by DAN DAVIS
Colors by TOM McCRAW
Letters by BILL OAKLEY
Cover art by LEE MODER and DAN DAVIS
Cover color by RICHARD & TANYA HORIE

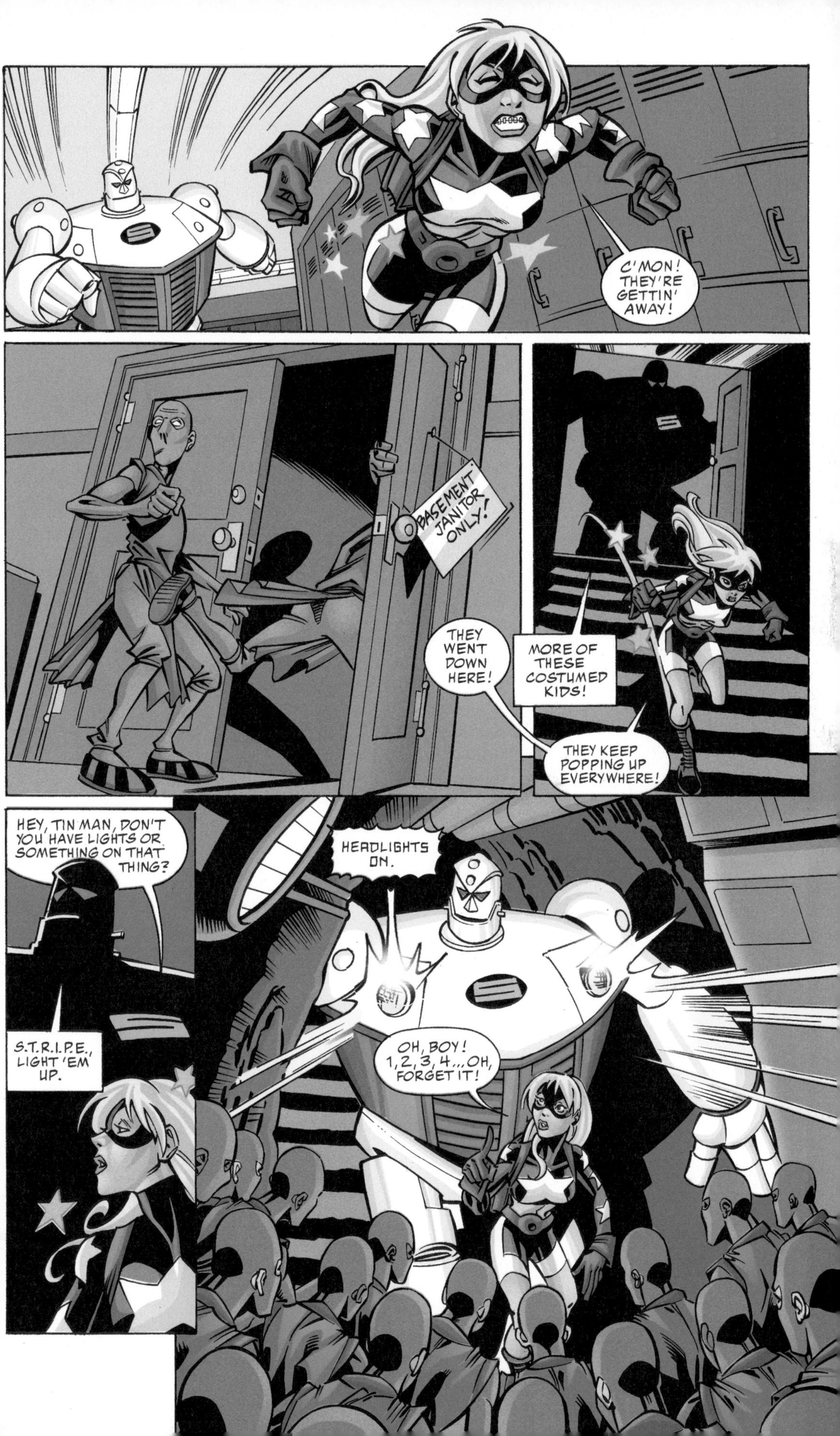
C'MON! THEY'RE GETTIN' AWAY!
BASEMENT JANITOR ONLY!
THEY WENT DOWN HERE!
MORE OF THESE COSTUMED KIDS!
THEY KEEP POPPING UP EVERYWHERE!
HEY, TIN MAN, DON'T YOU HAVE LIGHTS OR SOMETHING ON THAT THING?
HEADLIGHTS ON.
S.T.R.I.P.E., LIGHT 'EM UP.
OH, BOY! 1,2,3,4...OH, FORGET IT!

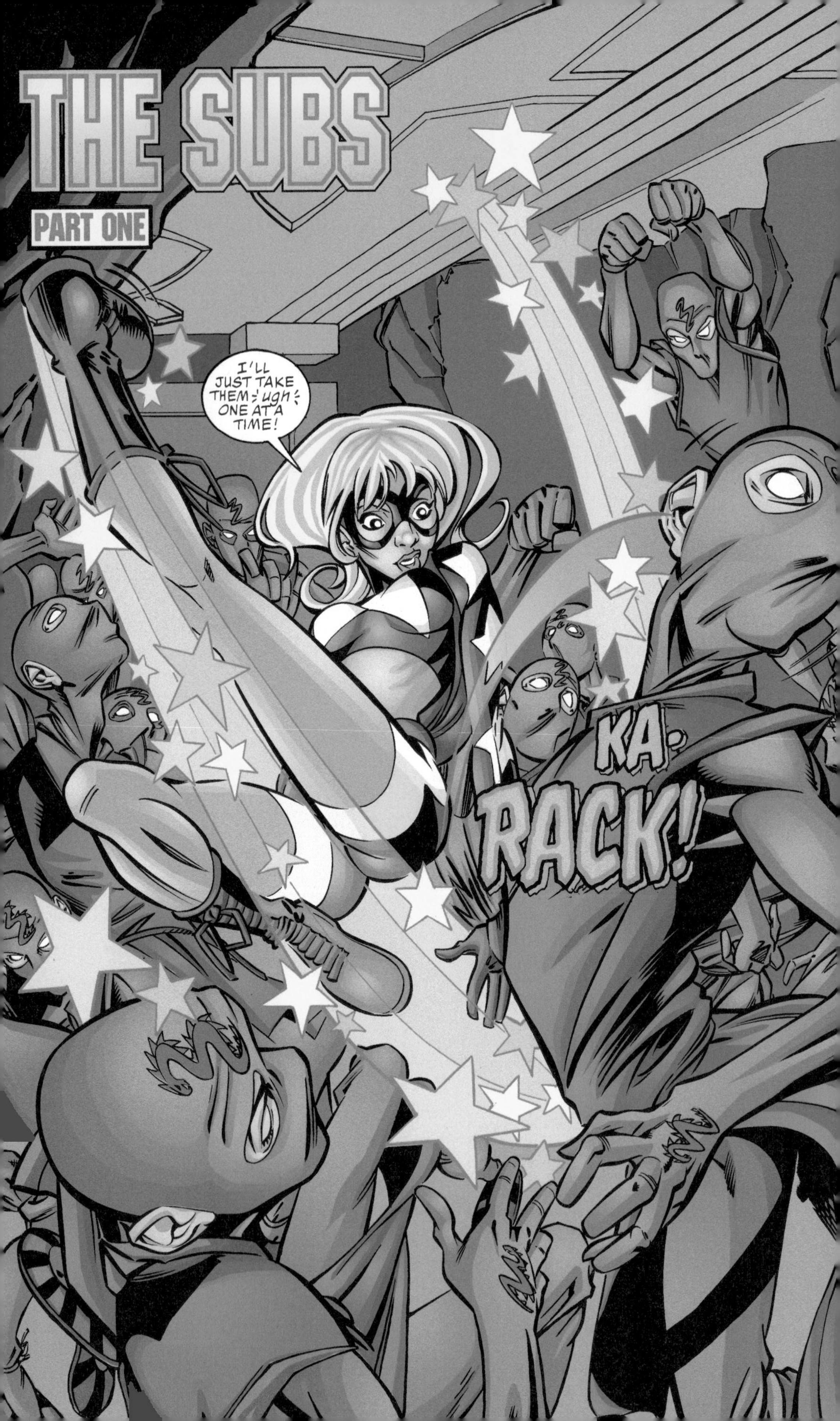
THE SUBS
PART ONE
I'LL JUST TAKE THEM -ugh- ONE AT A TIME!
KA-RACK!

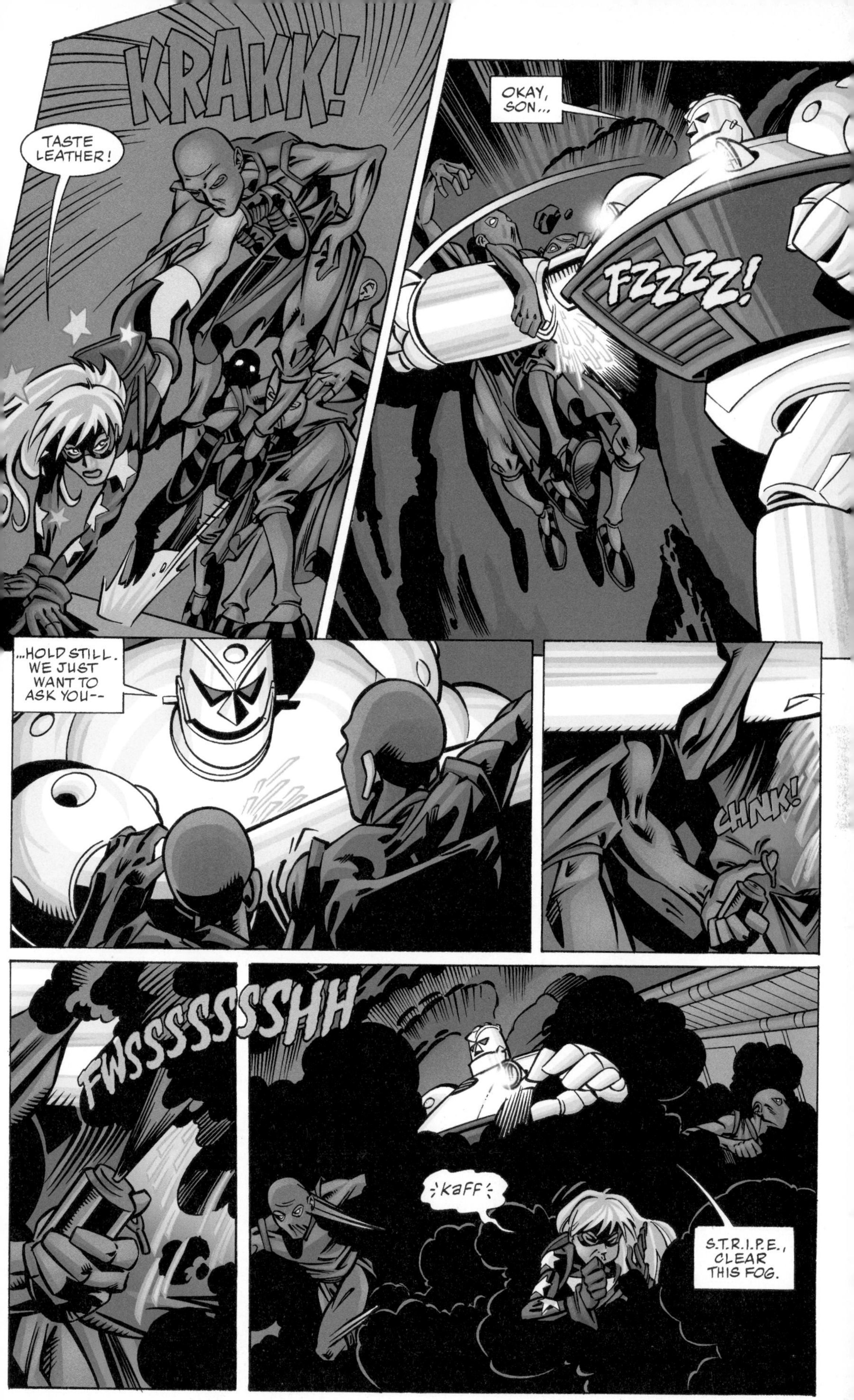
KRAKK!
TASTE LEATHER!
OKAY, SON...
FZZZZ!
...HOLD STILL. WE JUST WANT TO ASK YOU--
CHNK!
FWSSSSSSSHH
KAFF
S.T.R.I.P.E., CLEAR THIS FOG.

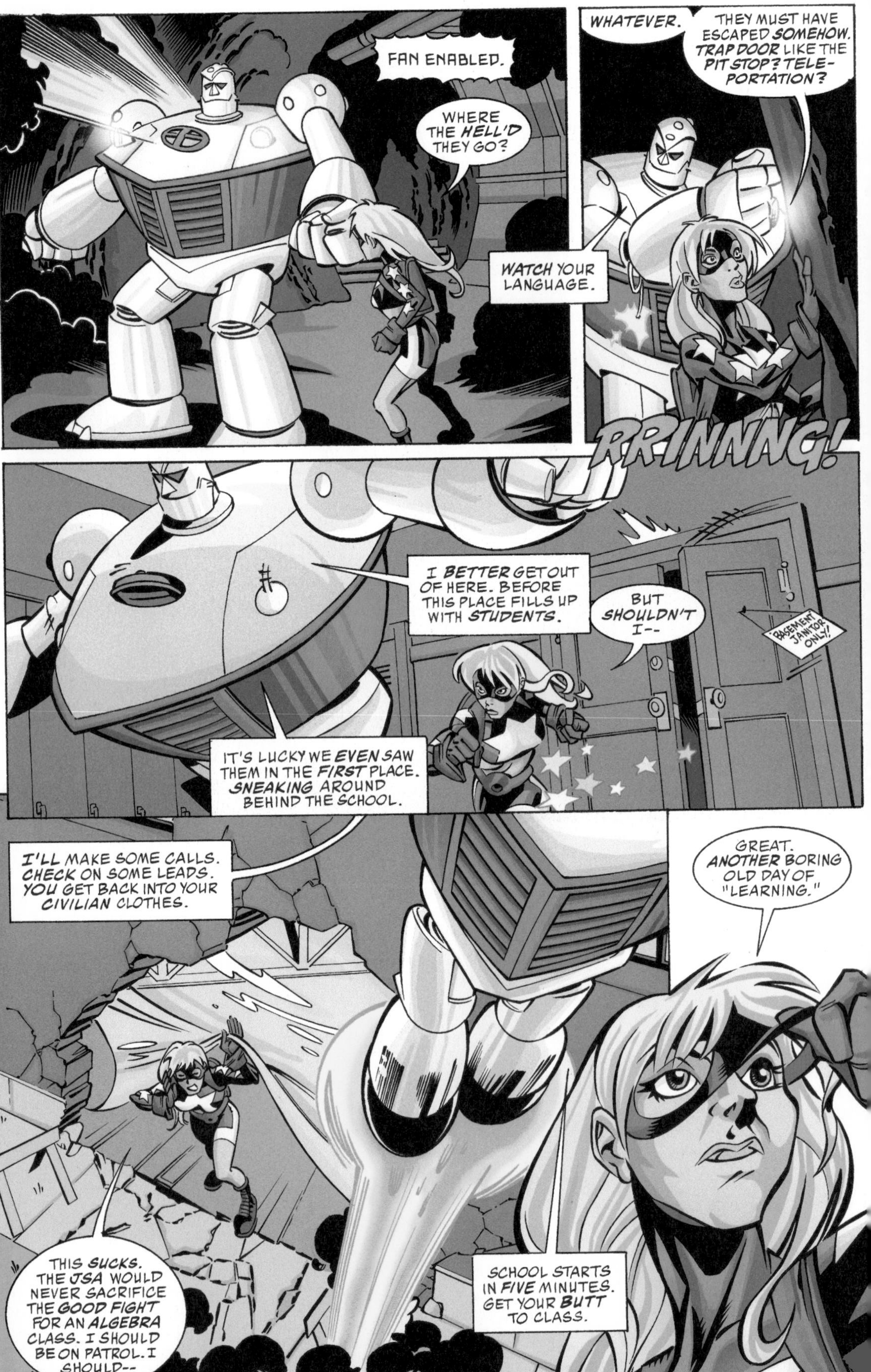
FAN ENABLED.
WHERE THE HELL'D THEY GO?
WHATEVER.
THEY MUST HAVE ESCAPED SOMEHOW. TRAP DOOR LIKE THE PIT STOP? TELE-PORTATION?
WATCH YOUR LANGUAGE.
RRINNNG!
I BETTER GET OUT OF HERE. BEFORE THIS PLACE FILLS UP WITH STUDENTS.
BUT SHOULDN'T I--
BASEMENT JANITOR ONLY!
IT'S LUCKY WE EVEN SAW THEM IN THE FIRST PLACE. SNEAKING AROUND BEHIND THE SCHOOL.
I'LL MAKE SOME CALLS. CHECK ON SOME LEADS. YOU GET BACK INTO YOUR CIVILIAN CLOTHES.
THIS SUCKS. THE JSA WOULD NEVER SACRIFICE THE GOOD FIGHT FOR AN ALGEBRA CLASS. I SHOULD BE ON PATROL. I SHOULD--
SCHOOL STARTS IN FIVE MINUTES. GET YOUR BUTT TO CLASS.
GREAT. ANOTHER BORING OLD DAY OF "LEARNING."

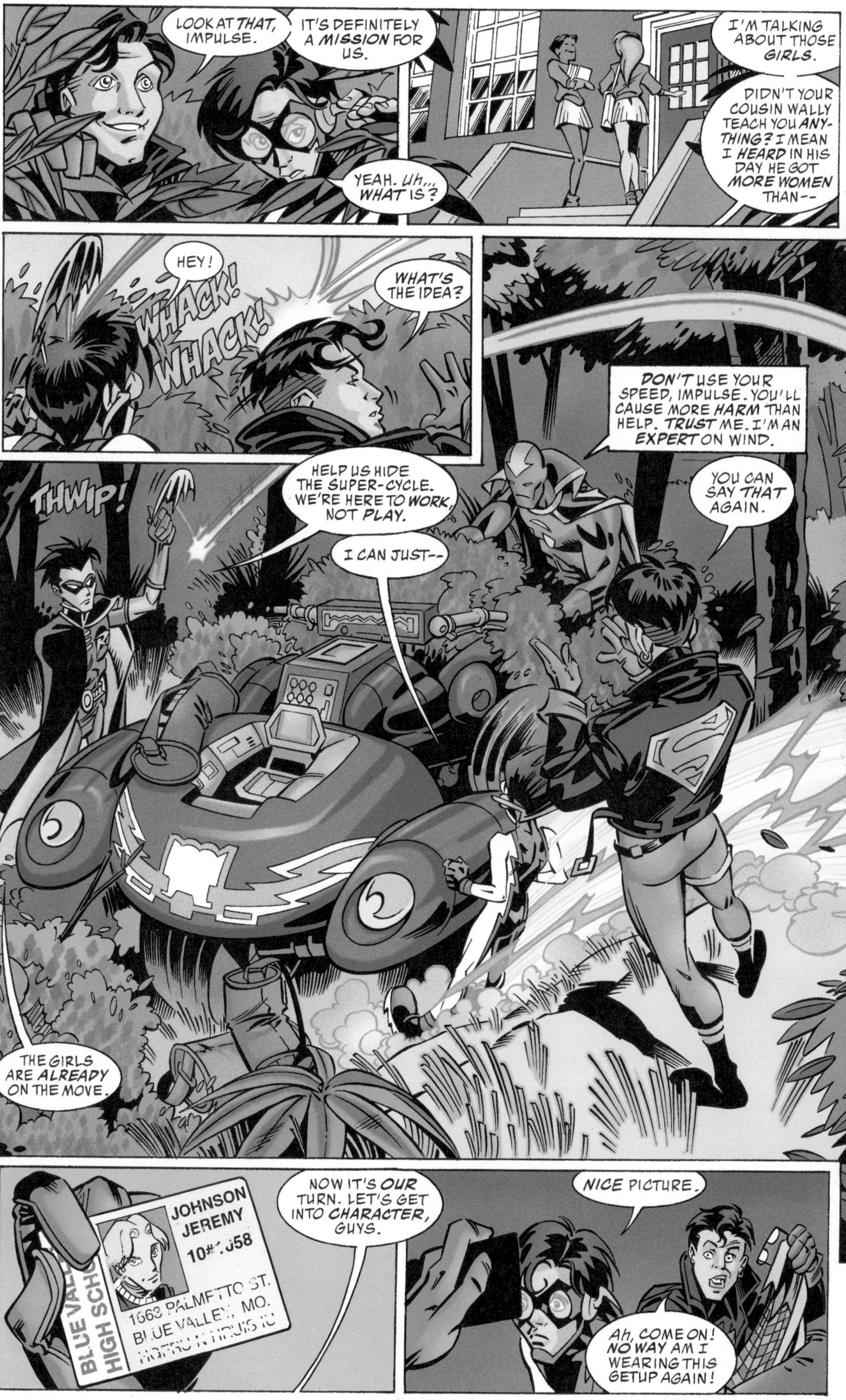

LOOK AT THAT, IMPULSE.
IT'S DEFINITELY A MISSION FOR US.
YEAH. Uh... WHAT IS?
I'M TALKING ABOUT THOSE GIRLS.
DIDN'T YOUR COUSIN WALLY TEACH YOU ANYTHING? I MEAN I HEARD IN HIS DAY HE GOT MORE WOMEN THAN--
HEY!
WHACK!
WHACK!
WHAT'S THE IDEA?
DON'T USE YOUR SPEED, IMPULSE. YOU'LL CAUSE MORE HARM THAN HELP. TRUST ME. I'M AN EXPERT ON WIND.
THWIP!
HELP US HIDE THE SUPER-CYCLE. WE'RE HERE TO WORK, NOT PLAY.
YOU CAN SAY THAT AGAIN.
I CAN JUST--
THE GIRLS ARE ALREADY ON THE MOVE.
JOHNSON JEREMY
1663 PALMETTO ST. BLUE VALLEY, MO.
BLUE VALLEY HIGH SCHOOL
NOW IT'S OUR TURN. LET'S GET INTO CHARACTER, GUYS.
NICE PICTURE.
Ah, COME ON! NO WAY AM I WEARING THIS GETUP AGAIN!

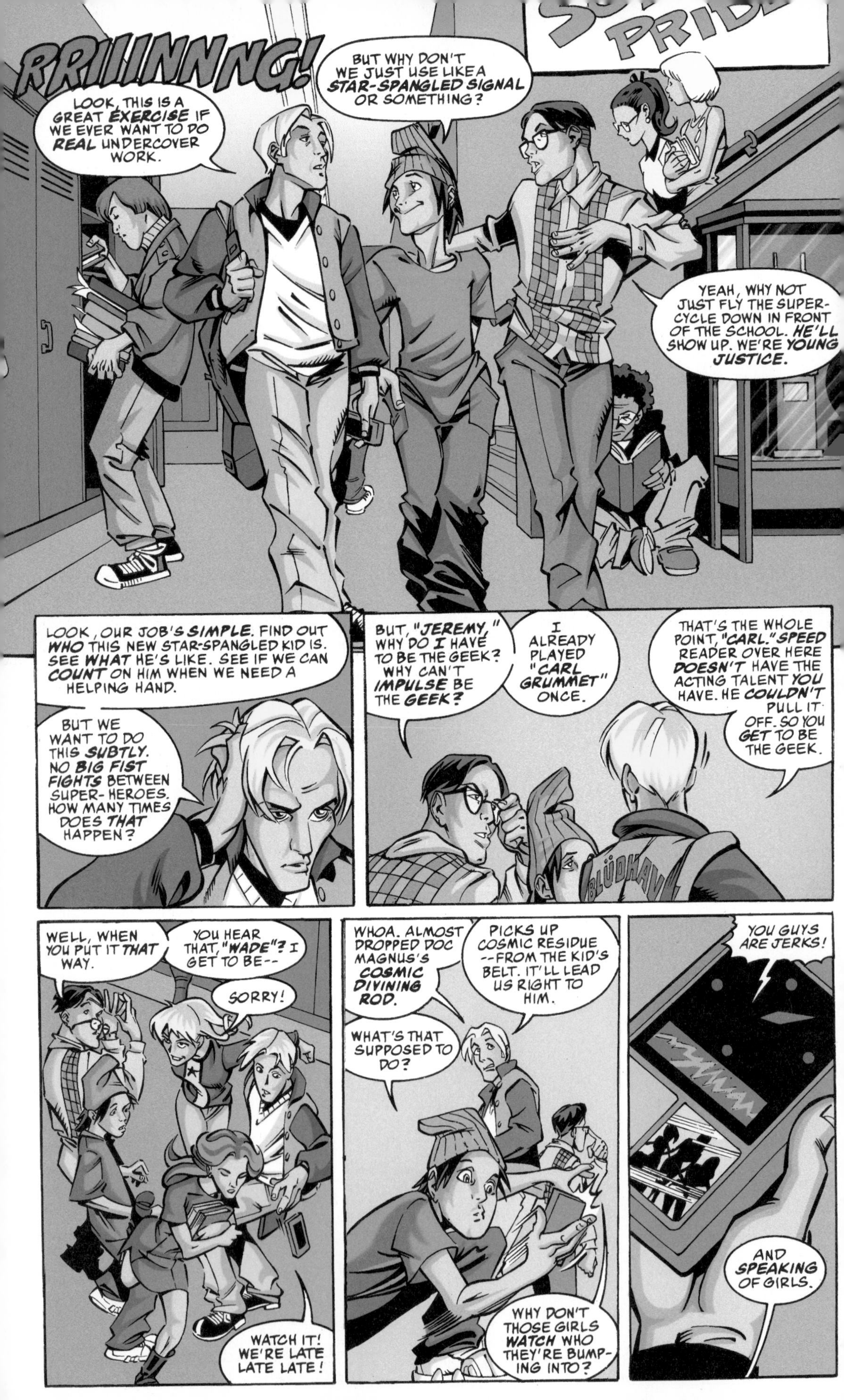
RRIIINNNNG!
LOOK, THIS IS A GREAT EXERCISE IF WE EVER WANT TO DO REAL UNDERCOVER WORK.
BUT WHY DON'T WE JUST USE LIKE A STAR-SPANGLED SIGNAL OR SOMETHING?
YEAH, WHY NOT JUST FLY THE SUPER-CYCLE DOWN IN FRONT OF THE SCHOOL. HE'LL SHOW UP. WE'RE YOUNG JUSTICE.
LOOK, OUR JOB'S SIMPLE. FIND OUT WHO THIS NEW STAR-SPANGLED KID IS. SEE WHAT HE'S LIKE. SEE IF WE CAN COUNT ON HIM WHEN WE NEED A HELPING HAND.
BUT WE WANT TO DO THIS SUBTLY. NO BIG FIST FIGHTS BETWEEN SUPER-HEROES. HOW MANY TIMES DOES THAT HAPPEN?
BUT, "JEREMY," WHY DO I HAVE TO BE THE GEEK? WHY CAN'T IMPULSE BE THE GEEK?
I ALREADY PLAYED "CARL GRUMMET" ONCE.
THAT'S THE WHOLE POINT, "CARL." SPEED READER OVER HERE DOESN'T HAVE THE ACTING TALENT YOU HAVE. HE COULDN'T PULL IT OFF. SO YOU GET TO BE THE GEEK.
BLÜDHAV
WELL, WHEN YOU PUT IT THAT WAY.
YOU HEAR THAT, "WADE"? I GET TO BE--
SORRY!
WATCH IT! WE'RE LATE LATE LATE!
WHOA. ALMOST DROPPED DOC MAGNUS'S COSMIC DIVINING ROD.
PICKS UP COSMIC RESIDUE --FROM THE KID'S BELT. IT'LL LEAD US RIGHT TO HIM.
WHAT'S THAT SUPPOSED TO DO?
WHY DON'T THOSE GIRLS WATCH WHO THEY'RE BUMPING INTO?
YOU GUYS ARE JERKS!
AND SPEAKING OF GIRLS.

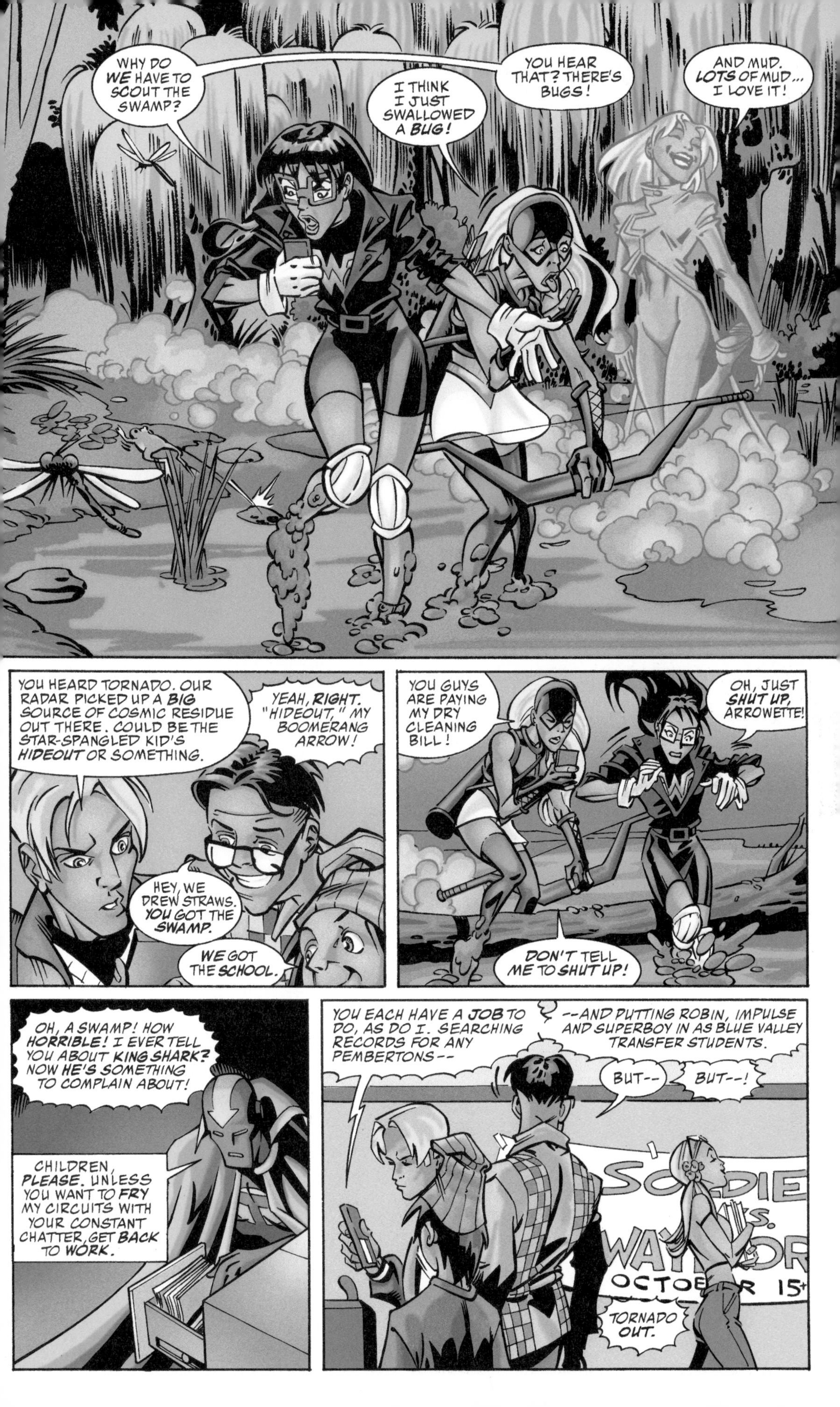

WHY DO WE HAVE TO SCOUT THE SWAMP?
I THINK I JUST SWALLOWED A BUG!
YOU HEAR THAT? THERE'S BUGS!
AND MUD. LOTS OF MUD... I LOVE IT!
YOU HEARD TORNADO. OUR RADAR PICKED UP A BIG SOURCE OF COSMIC RESIDUE OUT THERE. COULD BE THE STAR-SPANGLED KID'S HIDEOUT OR SOMETHING.
YEAH, RIGHT. "HIDEOUT," MY BOOMERANG ARROW!
HEY, WE DREW STRAWS. YOU GOT THE SWAMP.
WE GOT THE SCHOOL.
YOU GUYS ARE PAYING MY DRY CLEANING BILL!
OH, JUST SHUT UP, ARROWETTE!
DON'T TELL ME TO SHUT UP!
OH, A SWAMP! HOW HORRIBLE! I EVER TELL YOU ABOUT KING SHARK? NOW HE'S SOMETHING TO COMPLAIN ABOUT!
CHILDREN, PLEASE. UNLESS YOU WANT TO FRY MY CIRCUITS WITH YOUR CONSTANT CHATTER, GET BACK TO WORK.
YOU EACH HAVE A JOB TO DO, AS DO I. SEARCHING RECORDS FOR ANY PEMBERTONS--
--AND PUTTING ROBIN, IMPULSE AND SUPERBOY IN AS BLUE VALLEY TRANSFER STUDENTS.
BUT--
BUT--!
OCTOBER 15
TORNADO OUT.

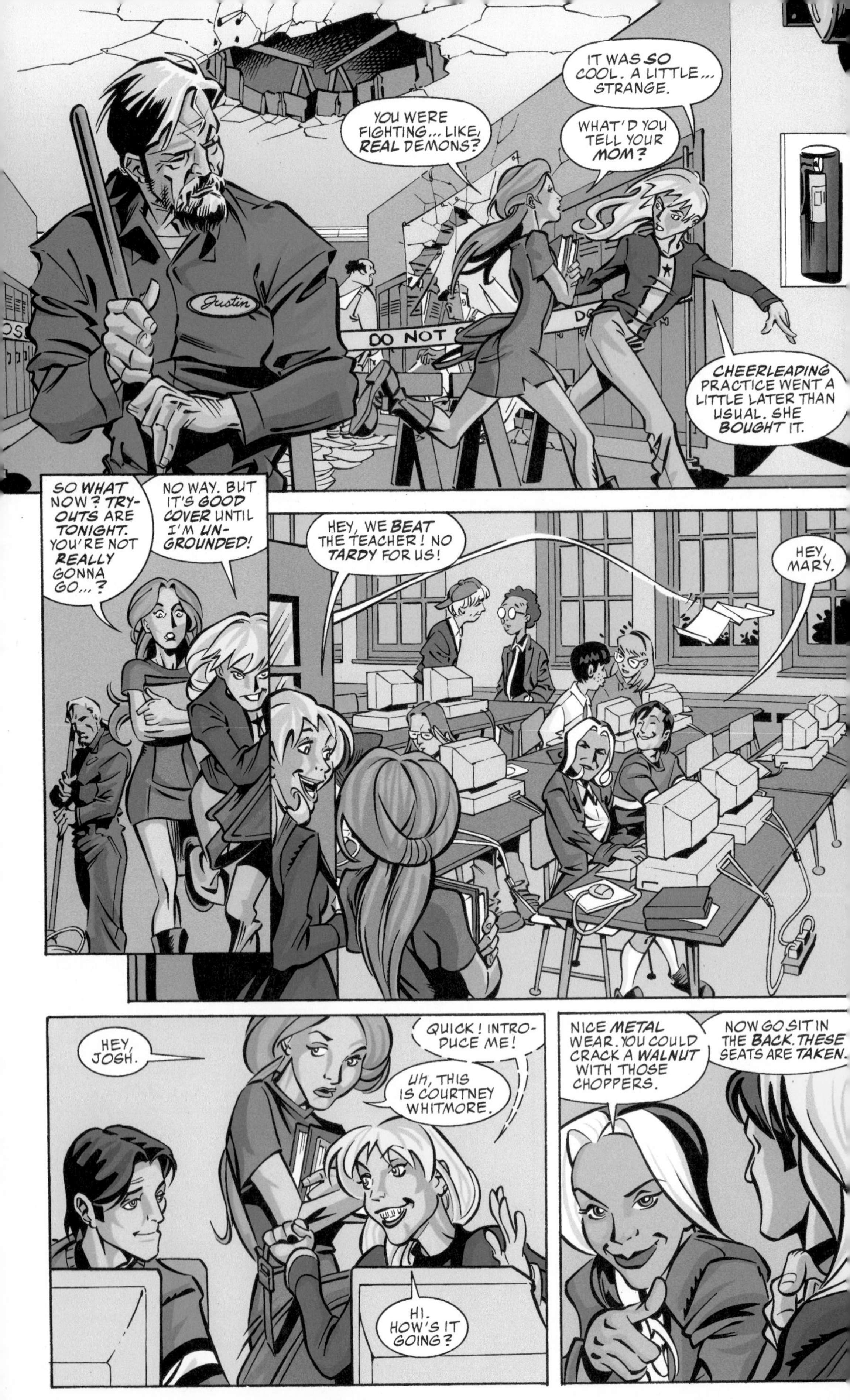

YOU WERE FIGHTING... LIKE, REAL DEMONS?
IT WAS SO COOL. A LITTLE... STRANGE.
WHAT'D YOU TELL YOUR MOM?
CHEERLEADING PRACTICE WENT A LITTLE LATER THAN USUAL. SHE BOUGHT IT.
JUSTIN
DO NOT
SO WHAT NOW? TRY-OUTS ARE TONIGHT. YOU'RE NOT REALLY GONNA GO...?
NO WAY. BUT IT'S GOOD COVER UNTIL I'M UN-GROUNDED!
HEY, WE BEAT THE TEACHER! NO TARDY FOR US!
HEY, MARY.
HEY, JOSH.
QUICK! INTRO-DUCE ME!
UH, THIS IS COURTNEY WHITMORE.
HI. HOW'S IT GOING?
NICE METAL WEAR. YOU COULD CRACK A WALNUT WITH THOSE CHOPPERS.
NOW GO SIT IN THE BACK. THESE SEATS ARE TAKEN.

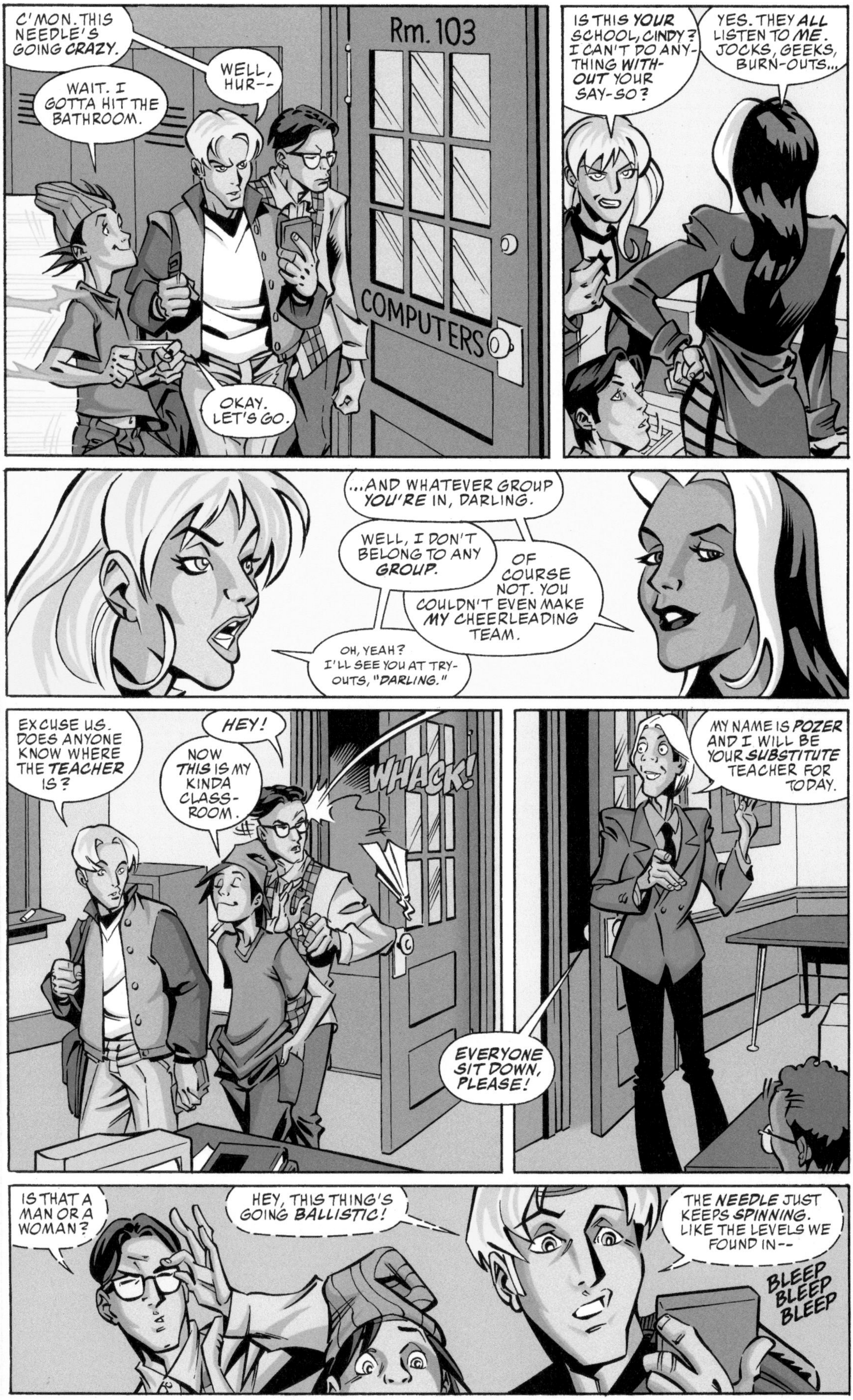

C'MON. THIS NEEDLE'S GOING CRAZY.
WAIT. I GOTTA HIT THE BATHROOM.
WELL, HUR--
OKAY. LET'S GO.
Rm. 103
COMPUTERS
IS THIS YOUR SCHOOL, CINDY? I CAN'T DO ANYTHING WITHOUT YOUR SAY-SO?
YES. THEY ALL LISTEN TO ME. JOCKS, GEEKS, BURN-OUTS...
...AND WHATEVER GROUP YOU'RE IN, DARLING.
WELL, I DON'T BELONG TO ANY GROUP.
OF COURSE NOT. YOU COULDN'T EVEN MAKE MY CHEERLEADING TEAM.
OH, YEAH? I'LL SEE YOU AT TRY-OUTS, "DARLING."
EXCUSE US. DOES ANYONE KNOW WHERE THE TEACHER IS?
HEY!
NOW THIS IS MY KINDA CLASSROOM.
WHACK!
MY NAME IS POZER AND I WILL BE YOUR SUBSTITUTE TEACHER FOR TODAY.
EVERYONE SIT DOWN, PLEASE!
IS THAT A MAN OR A WOMAN?
HEY, THIS THING'S GOING BALLISTIC!
THE NEEDLE JUST KEEPS SPINNING. LIKE THE LEVELS WE FOUND IN--
BLEEP BLEEP BLEEP

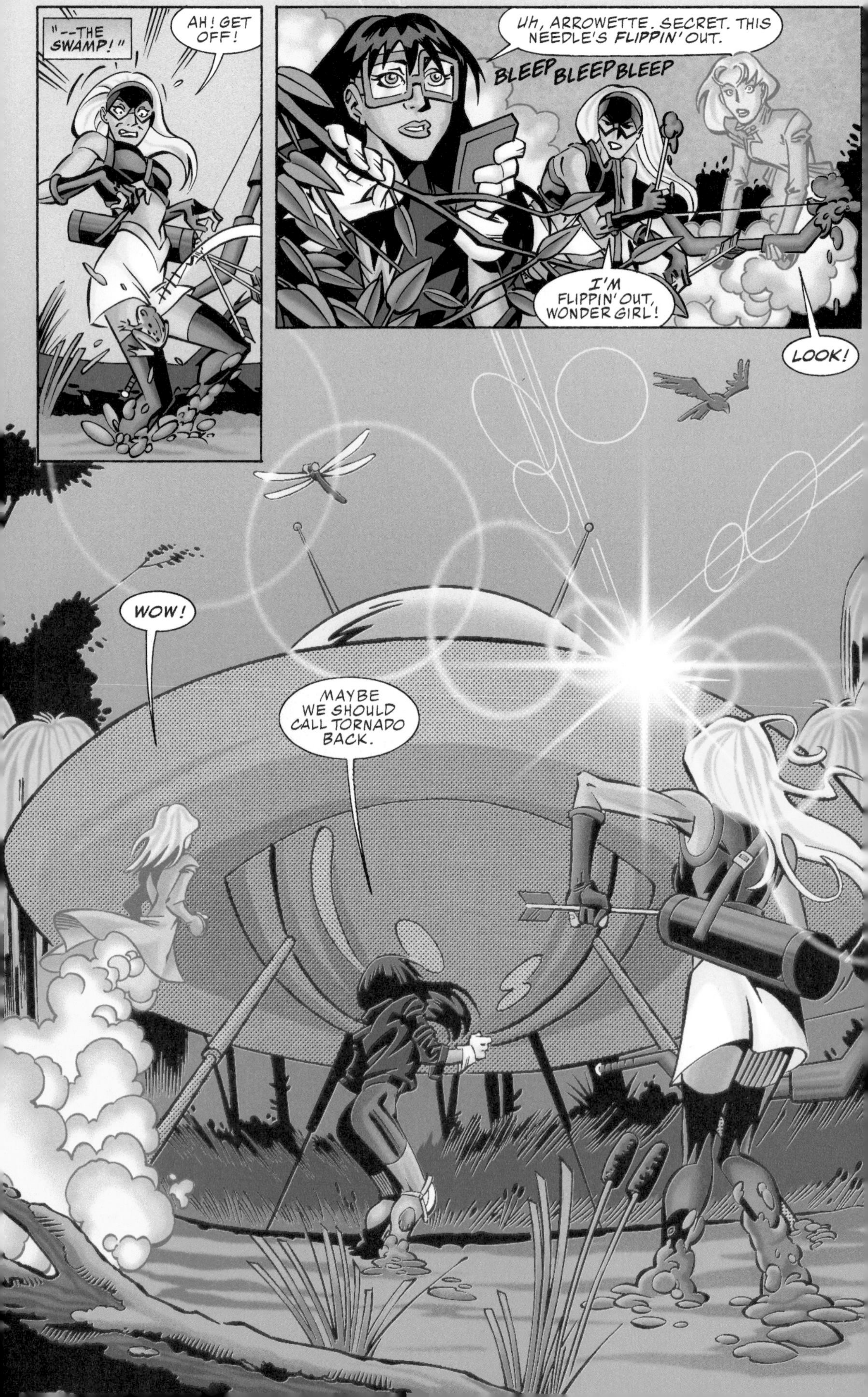
"--THE SWAMP!"
AH! GET OFF!
UH, ARROWETTE. SECRET. THIS NEEDLE'S FLIPPIN' OUT.
BLEEP BLEEP BLEEP
I'M FLIPPIN' OUT, WONDER GIRL!
LOOK!
WOW!
MAYBE WE SHOULD CALL TORNADO BACK.

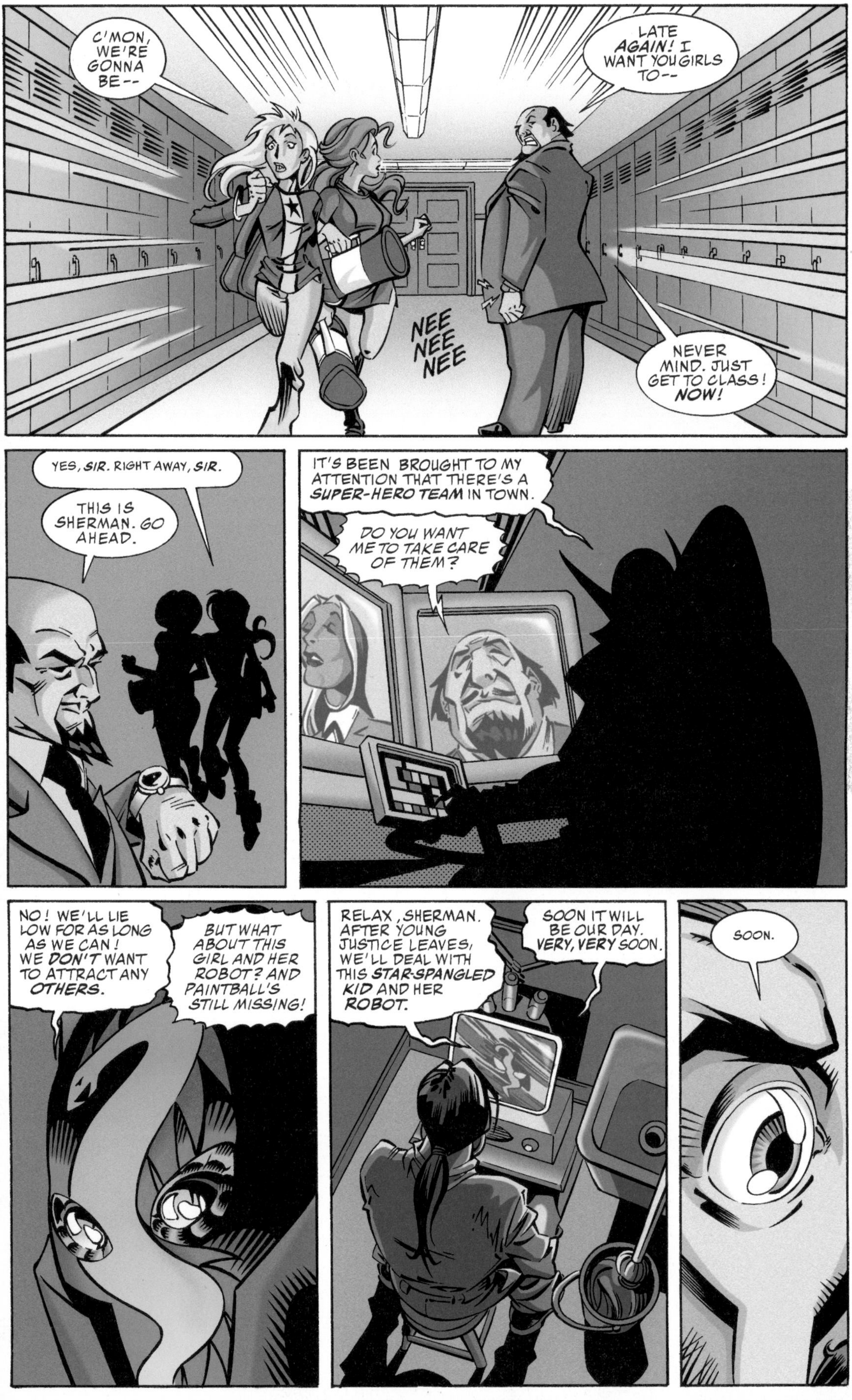
C'MON, WE'RE GONNA BE--
LATE AGAIN! I WANT YOU GIRLS TO--
NEE NEE NEE
NEVER MIND. JUST GET TO CLASS! NOW!
YES, SIR. RIGHT AWAY, SIR.
THIS IS SHERMAN. GO AHEAD.
IT'S BEEN BROUGHT TO MY ATTENTION THAT THERE'S A SUPER-HERO TEAM IN TOWN.
DO YOU WANT ME TO TAKE CARE OF THEM?
NO! WE'LL LIE LOW FOR AS LONG AS WE CAN! WE DON'T WANT TO ATTRACT ANY OTHERS.
BUT WHAT ABOUT THIS GIRL AND HER ROBOT? AND PAINTBALL'S STILL MISSING!
RELAX, SHERMAN. AFTER YOUNG JUSTICE LEAVES, WE'LL DEAL WITH THIS STAR-SPANGLED KID AND HER ROBOT.
SOON IT WILL BE OUR DAY. VERY, VERY SOON.
SOON.

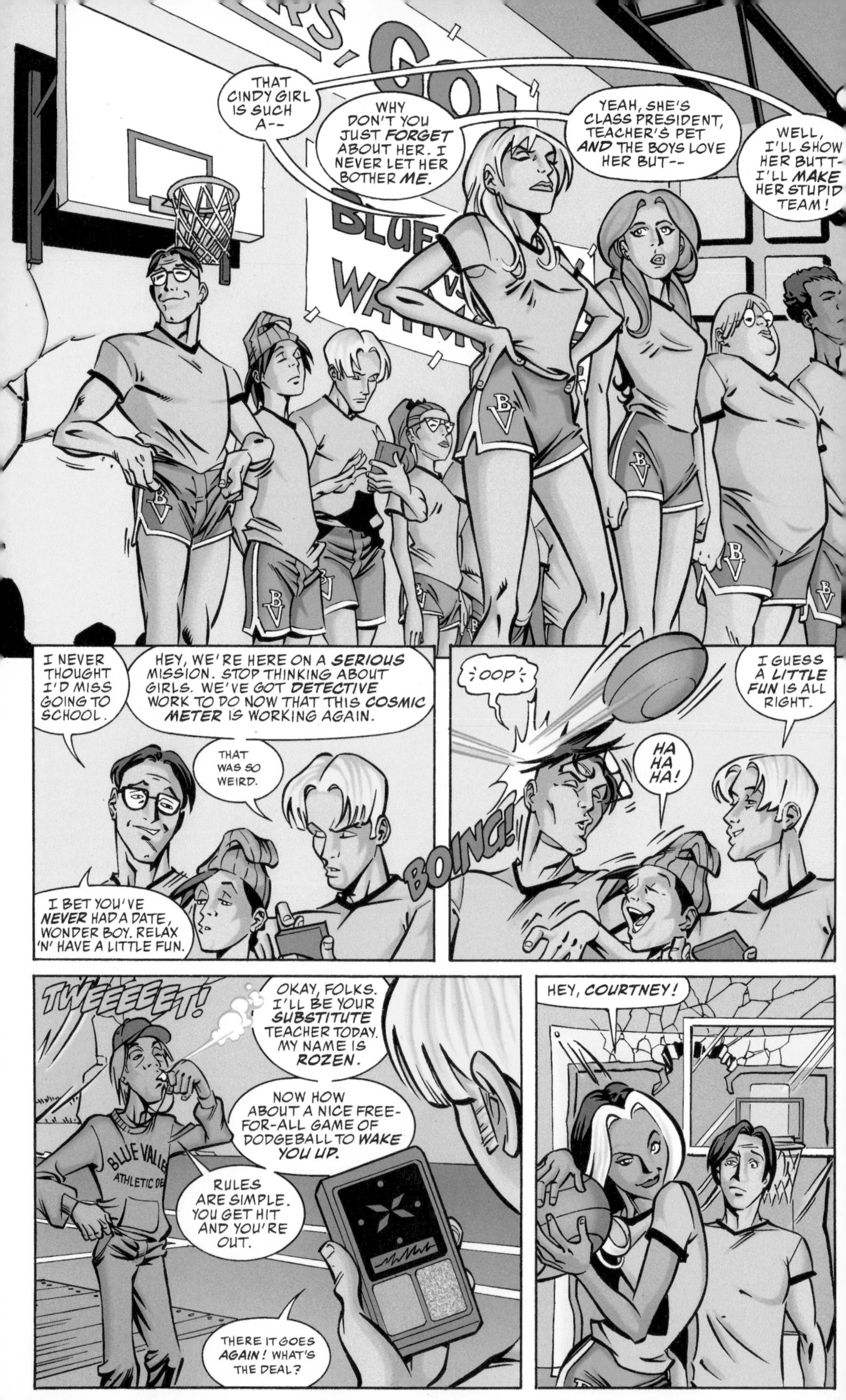

THAT CINDY GIRL IS SUCH A--
WHY DON'T YOU JUST FORGET ABOUT HER. I NEVER LET HER BOTHER ME.
YEAH, SHE'S CLASS PRESIDENT, TEACHER'S PET AND THE BOYS LOVE HER BUT--
WELL, I'LL SHOW HER BUTT-I'LL MAKE HER STUPID TEAM!
BLUE V
WA
I NEVER THOUGHT I'D MISS GOING TO SCHOOL.
HEY, WE'RE HERE ON A SERIOUS MISSION. STOP THINKING ABOUT GIRLS. WE'VE GOT DETECTIVE WORK TO DO NOW THAT THIS COSMIC METER IS WORKING AGAIN.
THAT WAS SO WEIRD.
I BET YOU'VE NEVER HAD A DATE, WONDER BOY. RELAX 'N' HAVE A LITTLE FUN.
OOP
BOING!
HA HA HA!
I GUESS A LITTLE FUN IS ALL RIGHT.
TWEEEEET!
OKAY, FOLKS. I'LL BE YOUR SUBSTITUTE TEACHER TODAY. MY NAME IS ROZEN.
NOW HOW ABOUT A NICE FREE-FOR-ALL GAME OF DODGEBALL TO WAKE YOU UP.
RULES ARE SIMPLE. YOU GET HIT AND YOU'RE OUT.
BLUE VALLE
ATHLETIC DE
THERE IT GOES AGAIN! WHAT'S THE DEAL?
HEY, COURTNEY!

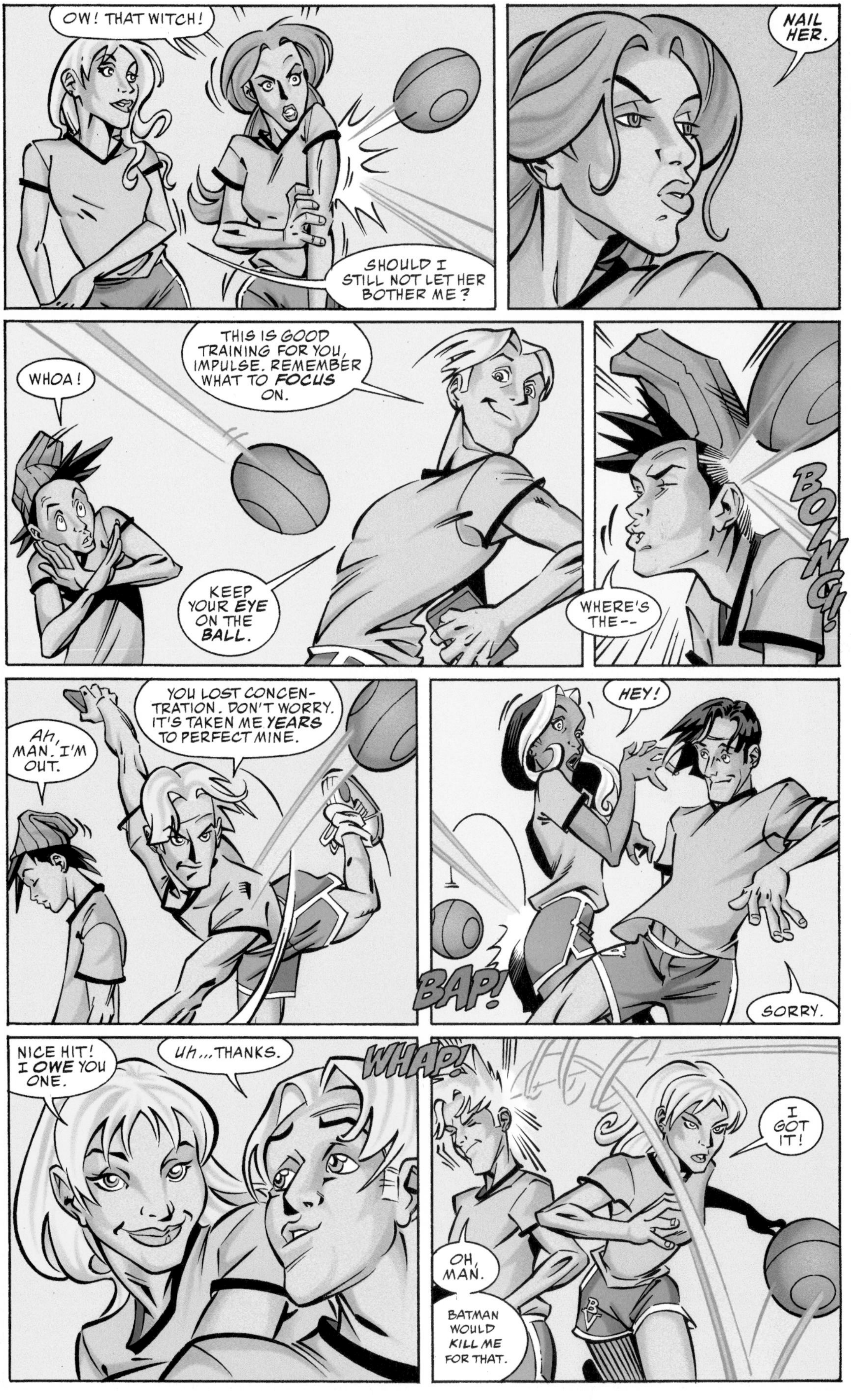

OW! THAT WITCH!
SHOULD I STILL NOT LET HER BOTHER ME?
NAIL HER.
WHOA!
THIS IS GOOD TRAINING FOR YOU, IMPULSE. REMEMBER WHAT TO FOCUS ON.
KEEP YOUR EYE ON THE BALL.
BOING!
WHERE'S THE--
Ah, MAN. I'M OUT.
YOU LOST CONCEN-TRATION. DON'T WORRY. IT'S TAKEN ME YEARS TO PERFECT MINE.
HEY!
BAP!
SORRY.
NICE HIT! I OWE YOU ONE.
Uh... THANKS.
WHAP!
I GOT IT!
OH, MAN.
BATMAN WOULD KILL ME FOR THAT.

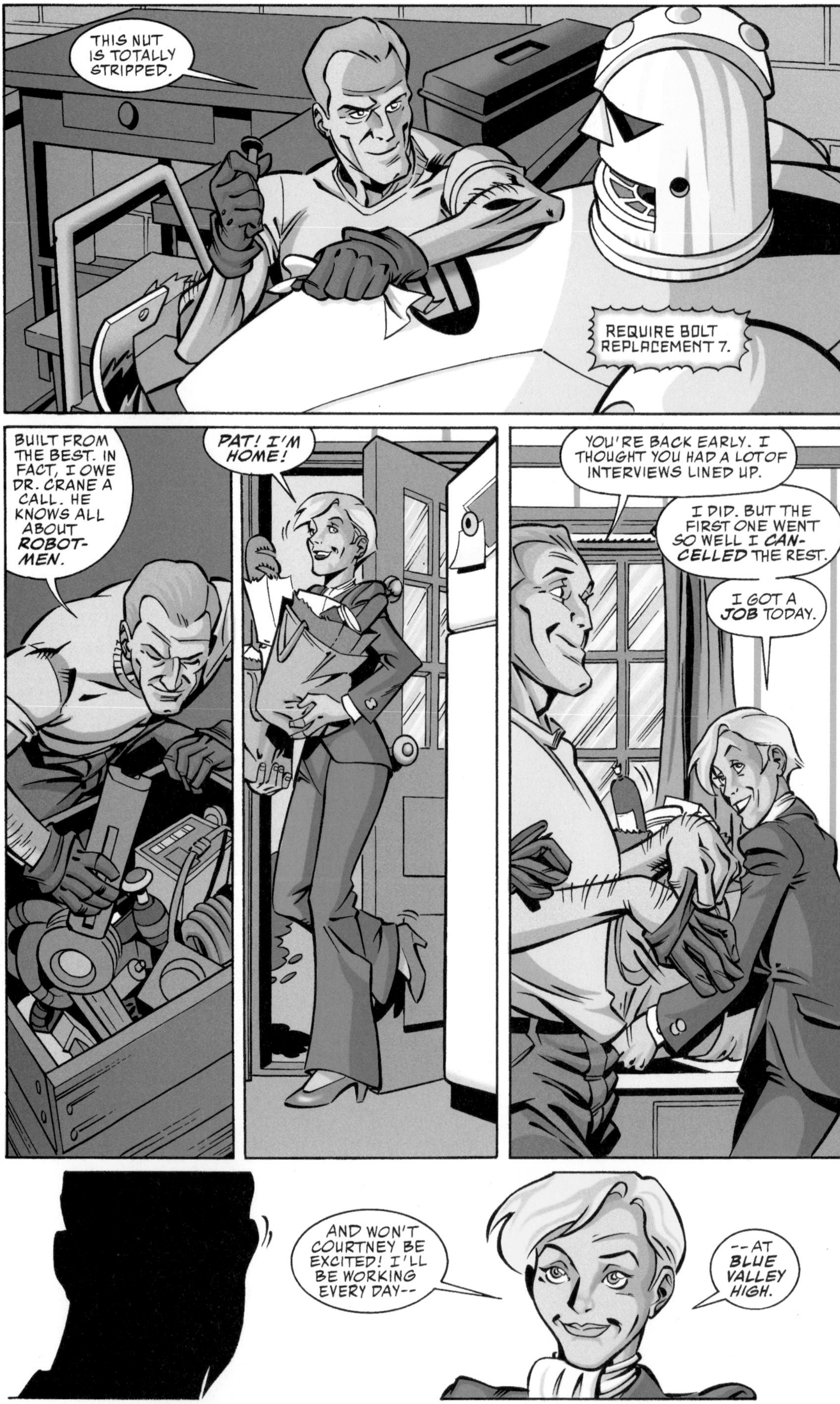
THIS NUT IS TOTALLY STRIPPED.
REQUIRE BOLT REPLACEMENT 7.
BUILT FROM THE BEST. IN FACT, I OWE DR. CRANE A CALL. HE KNOWS ALL ABOUT ROBOT-MEN.
PAT! I'M HOME!
YOU'RE BACK EARLY. I THOUGHT YOU HAD A LOT OF INTERVIEWS LINED UP.
I DID. BUT THE FIRST ONE WENT SO WELL I CANCELLED THE REST.
I GOT A JOB TODAY.
AND WON'T COURTNEY BE EXCITED! I'LL BE WORKING EVERY DAY--
--AT BLUE VALLEY HIGH.

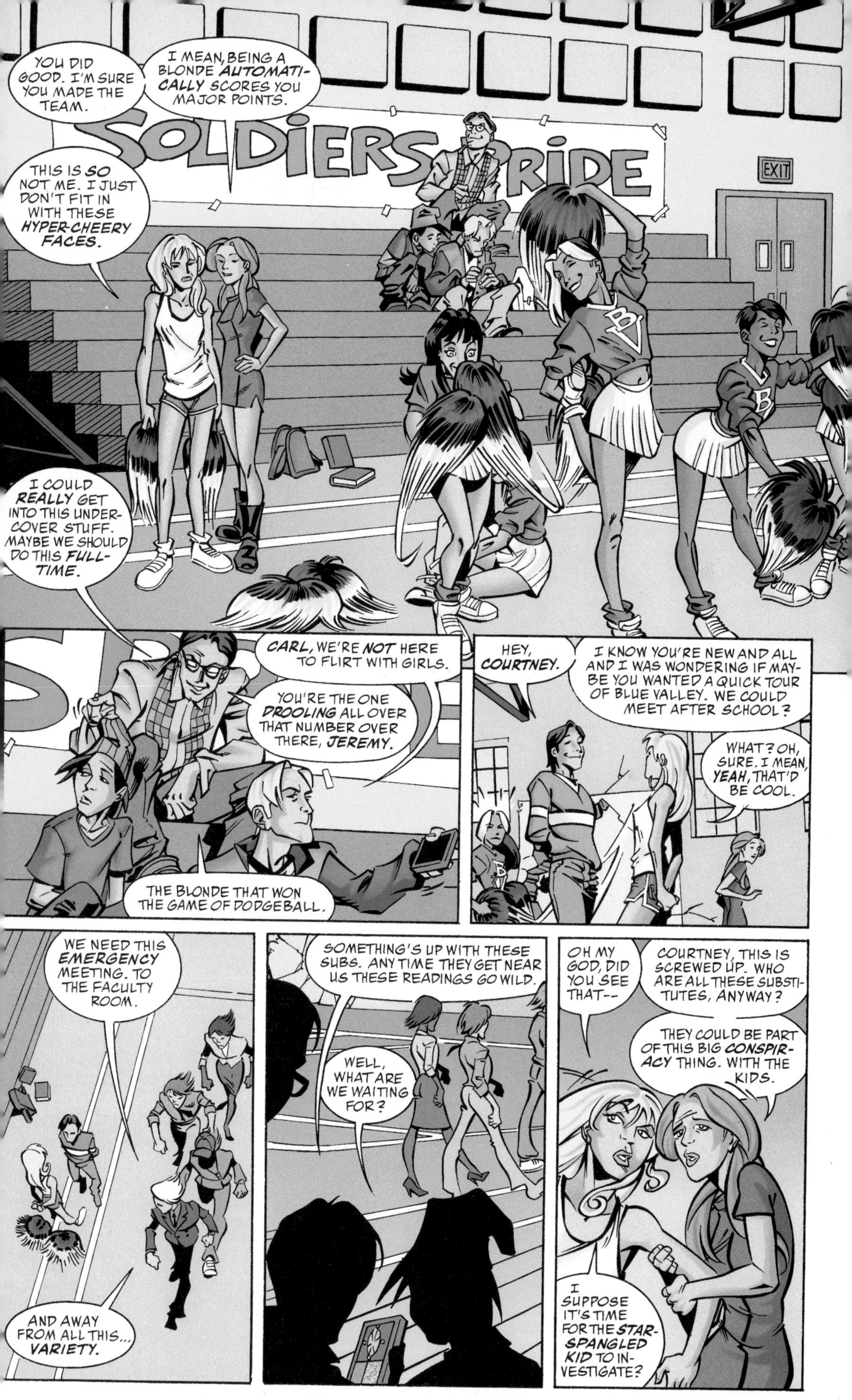
YOU DID GOOD. I'M SURE YOU MADE THE TEAM.
I MEAN, BEING A BLONDE AUTOMATICALLY SCORES YOU MAJOR POINTS.
SOLDIERS PRIDE
EXIT
THIS IS SO NOT ME. I JUST DON'T FIT IN WITH THESE HYPER-CHEERY FACES.
I COULD REALLY GET INTO THIS UNDERCOVER STUFF. MAYBE WE SHOULD DO THIS FULL-TIME.
CARL, WE'RE NOT HERE TO FLIRT WITH GIRLS.
YOU'RE THE ONE DROOLING ALL OVER THAT NUMBER OVER THERE, JEREMY.
THE BLONDE THAT WON THE GAME OF DODGEBALL.
HEY, COURTNEY.
I KNOW YOU'RE NEW AND ALL AND I WAS WONDERING IF MAYBE YOU WANTED A QUICK TOUR OF BLUE VALLEY. WE COULD MEET AFTER SCHOOL?
WHAT? OH, SURE. I MEAN, YEAH, THAT'D BE COOL.
WE NEED THIS EMERGENCY MEETING. TO THE FACULTY ROOM.
AND AWAY FROM ALL THIS... VARIETY.
SOMETHING'S UP WITH THESE SUBS. ANY TIME THEY GET NEAR US THESE READINGS GO WILD.
WELL, WHAT ARE WE WAITING FOR?
OH MY GOD, DID YOU SEE THAT--
COURTNEY, THIS IS SCREWED UP. WHO ARE ALL THESE SUBSTITUTES, ANYWAY?
THEY COULD BE PART OF THIS BIG CONSPIRACY THING. WITH THE KIDS.
I SUPPOSE IT'S TIME FOR THE STAR-SPANGLED KID TO INVESTIGATE?

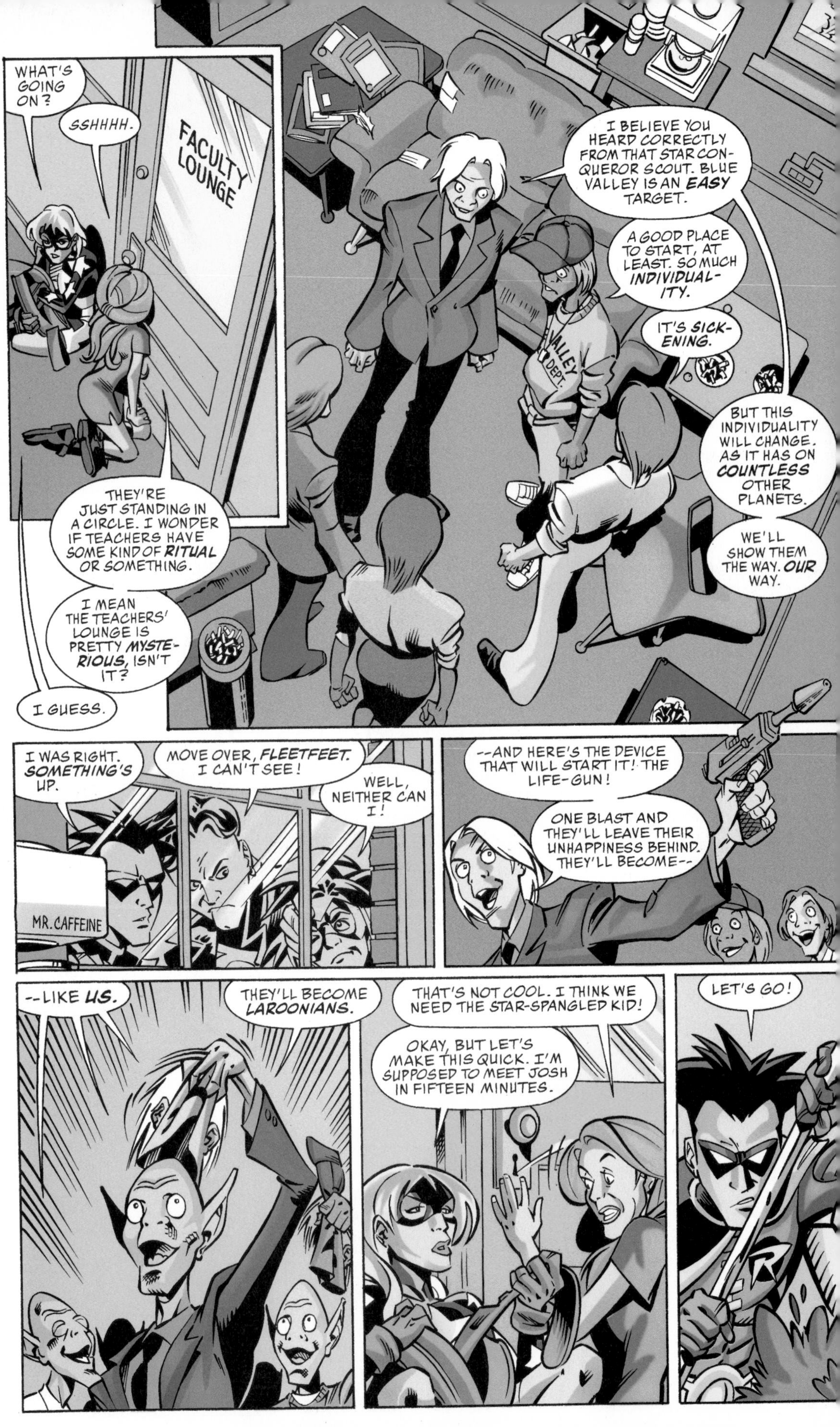
WHAT'S GOING ON?
SSHHHH.
FACULTY LOUNGE
I BELIEVE YOU HEARD CORRECTLY FROM THAT STAR CONQUEROR SCOUT. BLUE VALLEY IS AN EASY TARGET.
A GOOD PLACE TO START, AT LEAST. SO MUCH INDIVIDUALITY.
IT'S SICKENING.
BUT THIS INDIVIDUALITY WILL CHANGE. AS IT HAS ON COUNTLESS OTHER PLANETS.
WE'LL SHOW THEM THE WAY. OUR WAY.
THEY'RE JUST STANDING IN A CIRCLE. I WONDER IF TEACHERS HAVE SOME KIND OF RITUAL OR SOMETHING.
I MEAN THE TEACHERS' LOUNGE IS PRETTY MYSTERIOUS, ISN'T IT?
I GUESS.
I WAS RIGHT. SOMETHING'S UP.
MOVE OVER, FLEETFEET. I CAN'T SEE!
WELL, NEITHER CAN I!
MR. CAFFEINE
--AND HERE'S THE DEVICE THAT WILL START IT! THE LIFE-GUN!
ONE BLAST AND THEY'LL LEAVE THEIR UNHAPPINESS BEHIND. THEY'LL BECOME--
--LIKE US.
THEY'LL BECOME LAROONIANS.
THAT'S NOT COOL. I THINK WE NEED THE STAR-SPANGLED KID!
OKAY, BUT LET'S MAKE THIS QUICK. I'M SUPPOSED TO MEET JOSH IN FIFTEEN MINUTES.
LET'S GO!

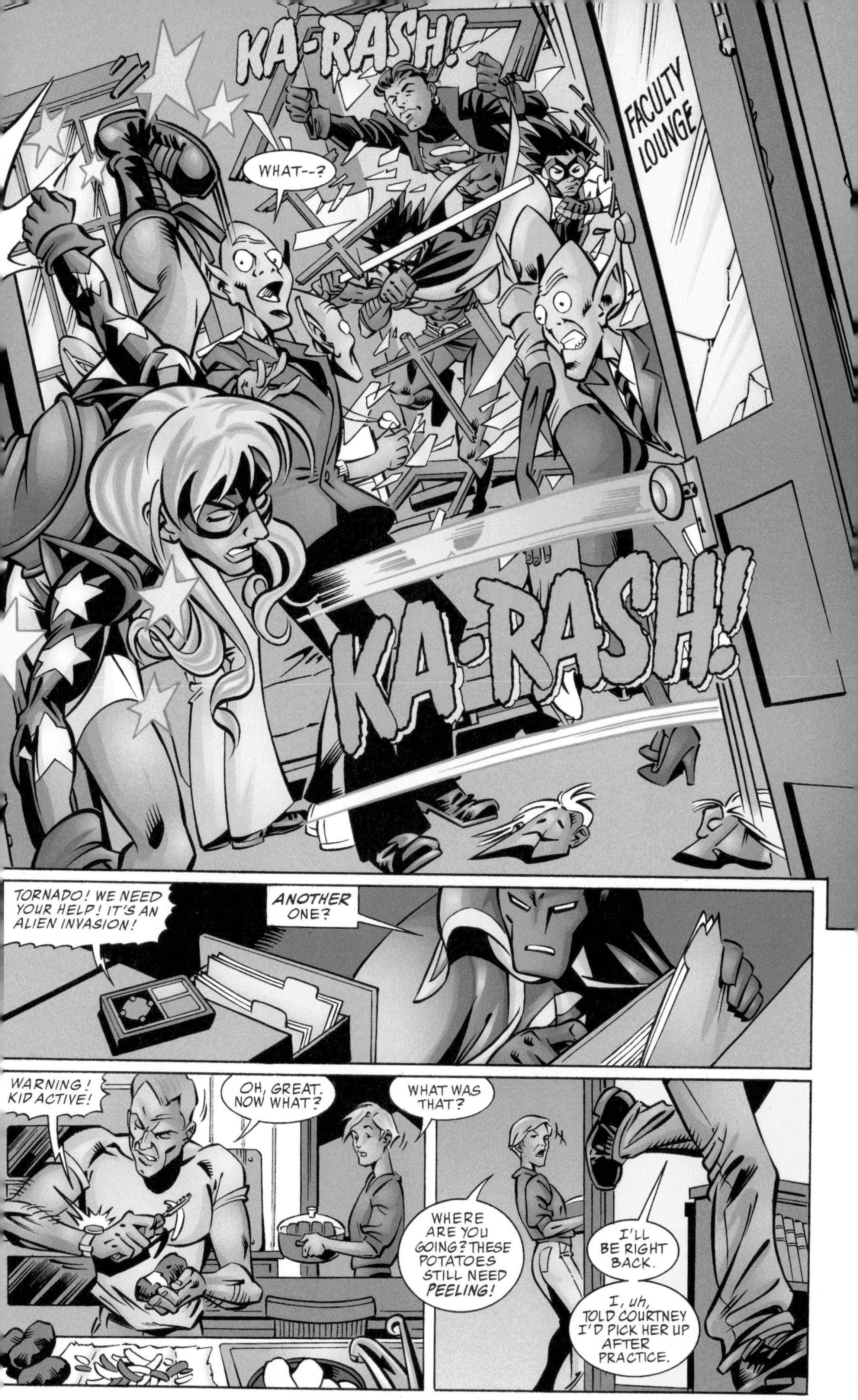
KA-RASH!
FACULTY LOUNGE
WHAT--?
KA-RASH!
TORNADO! WE NEED YOUR HELP! IT'S AN ALIEN INVASION!
ANOTHER ONE?
WARNING! KID ACTIVE!
OH, GREAT. NOW WHAT?
WHAT WAS THAT?
WHERE ARE YOU GOING? THESE POTATOES STILL NEED PEELING!
I'LL BE RIGHT BACK.
I, uh, TOLD COURTNEY I'D PICK HER UP AFTER PRACTICE.

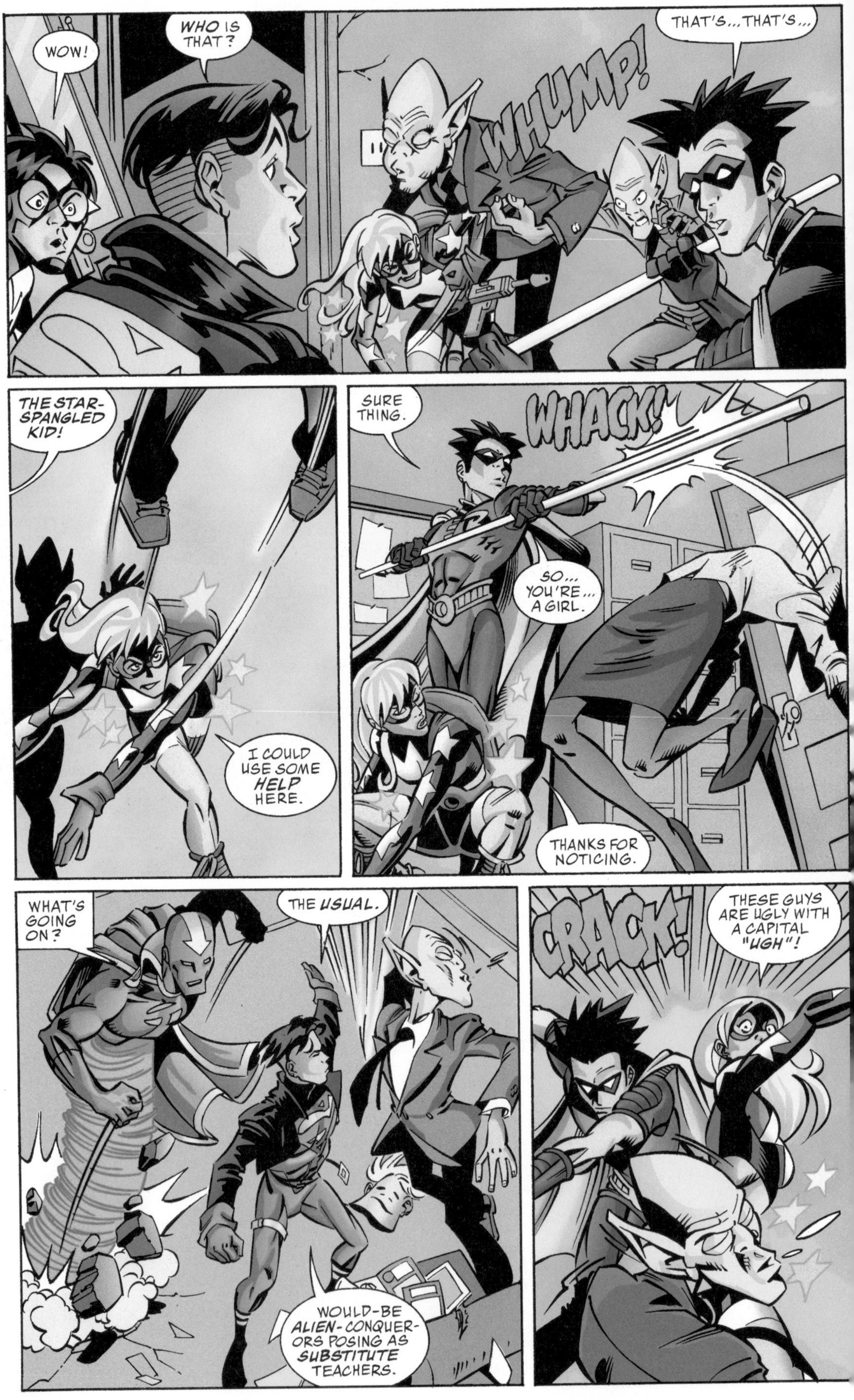
WOW!
WHO IS THAT?
WHUMP!
THAT'S... THAT'S...
THE STAR-SPANGLED KID!
I COULD USE SOME HELP HERE.
SURE THING.
WHACK!
SO... YOU'RE... A GIRL.
THANKS FOR NOTICING.
WHAT'S GOING ON?
THE USUAL.
WOULD-BE ALIEN-CONQUERORS POSING AS SUBSTITUTE TEACHERS.
CRACK!
THESE GUYS ARE UGLY WITH A CAPITAL "UGH"!

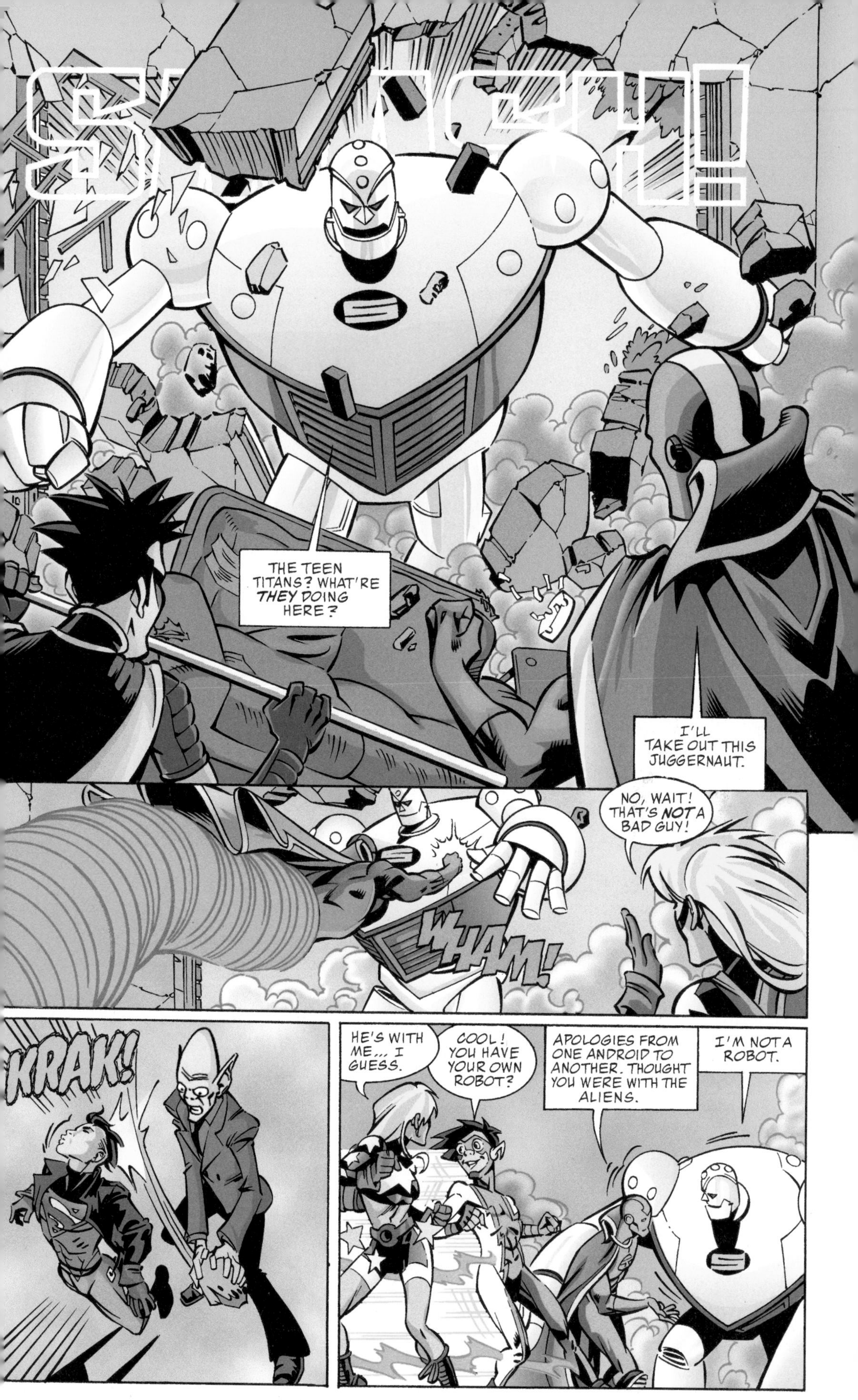
THE TEEN TITANS? WHAT'RE *THEY* DOING HERE?
I'LL TAKE OUT THIS JUGGERNAUT.
NO, WAIT! THAT'S *NOT* A BAD GUY!
WHAM!
KRAK!
HE'S WITH ME... I GUESS.
COOL! YOU HAVE YOUR OWN ROBOT?
APOLOGIES FROM ONE ANDROID TO ANOTHER. THOUGHT YOU WERE WITH THE ALIENS.
I'M NOT A ROBOT.

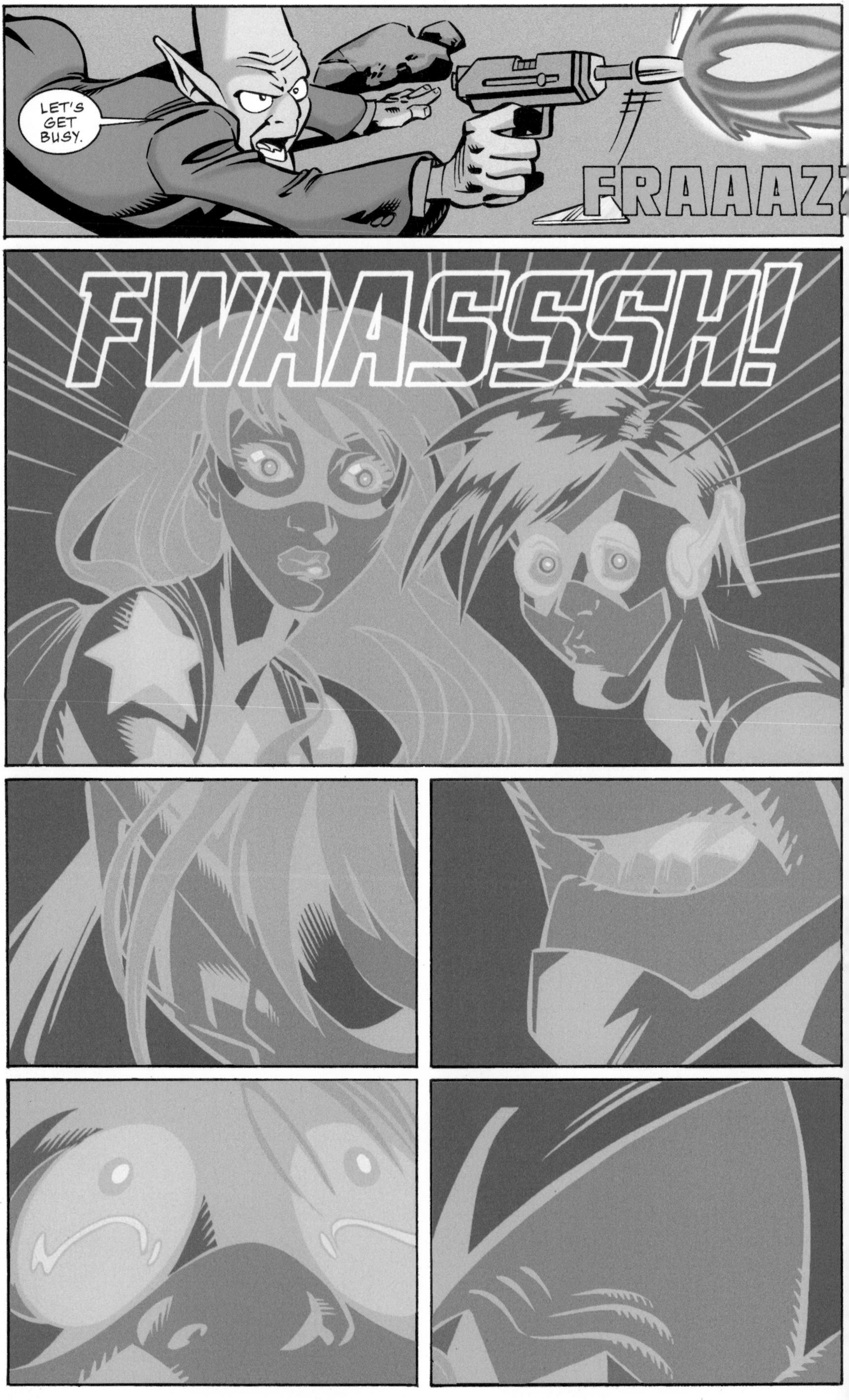

LET'S GET BUSY.
FRAAAZ
FWAASSSH!

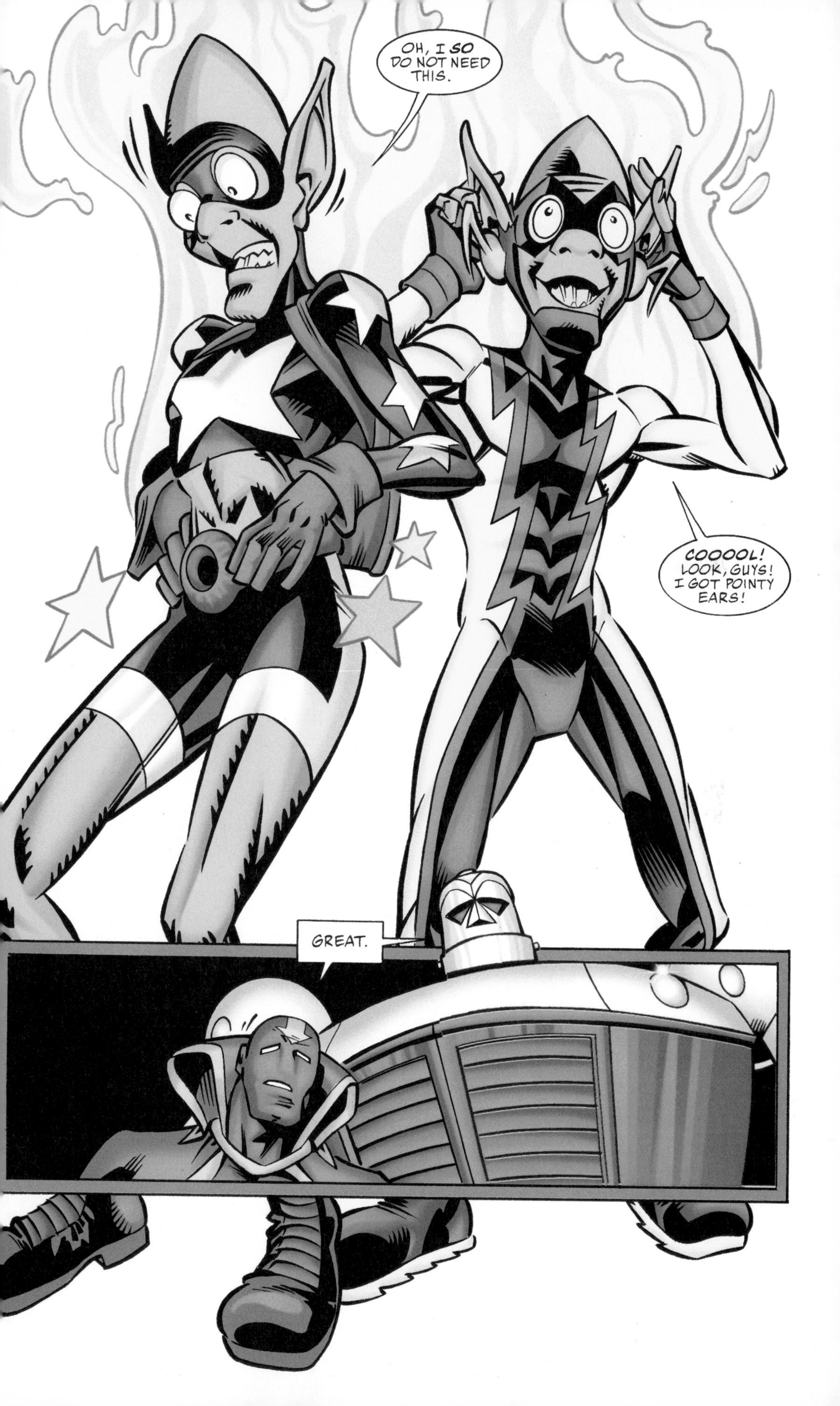

OH, I SO DO NOT NEED THIS.
COOOOL! LOOK, GUYS! I GOT POINTY EARS!
GREAT.

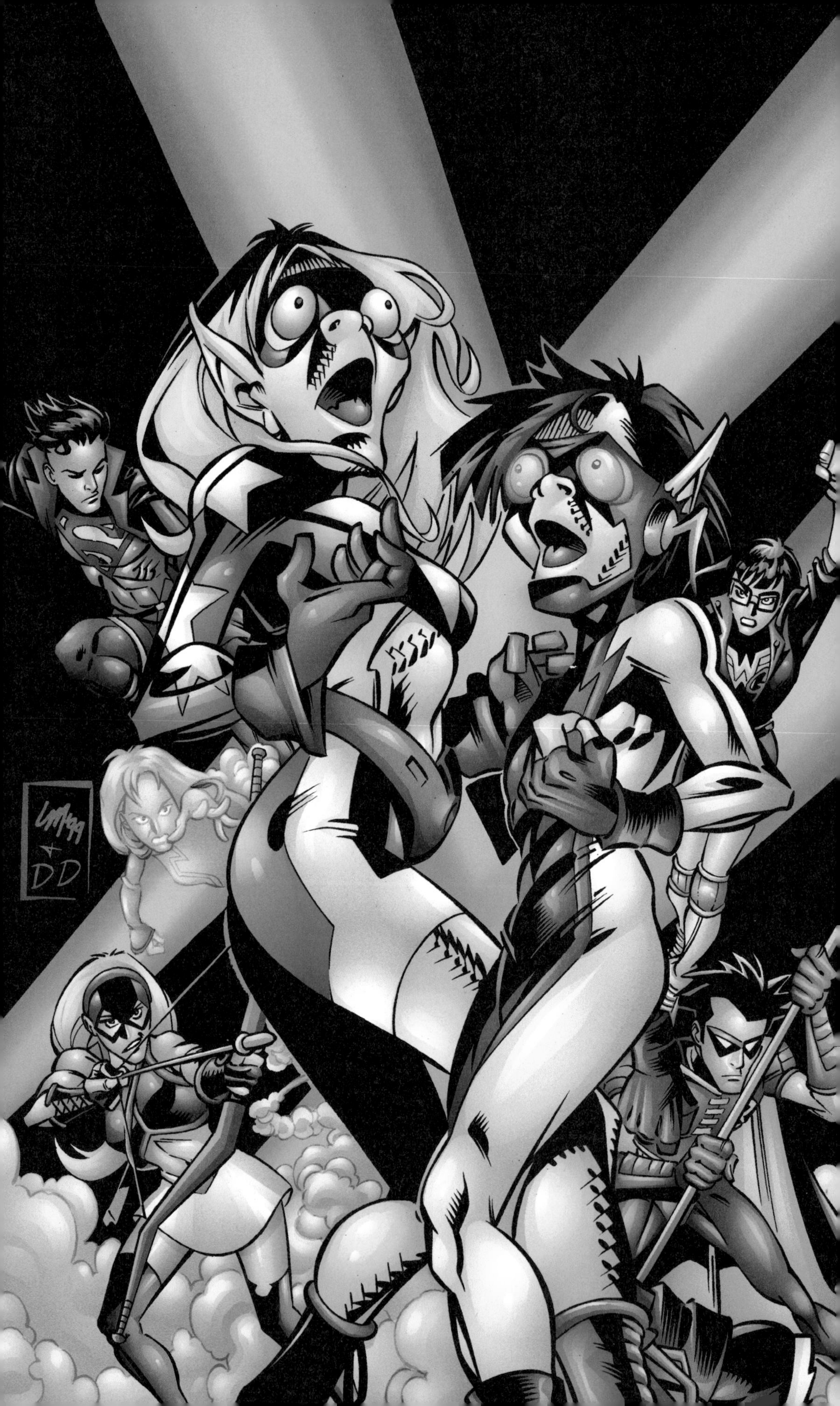

STARS AND S.T.R.I.P.E. #6

Written by GEOFF JOHNS
Pencils by LEE MODER
Inks by DAN DAVIS
Colors by TOM McCRAW
Letters by BILL OAKLEY
Cover art by LEE MODER and DAN DAVIS
Cover color by RICHARD & TANYA HORIE

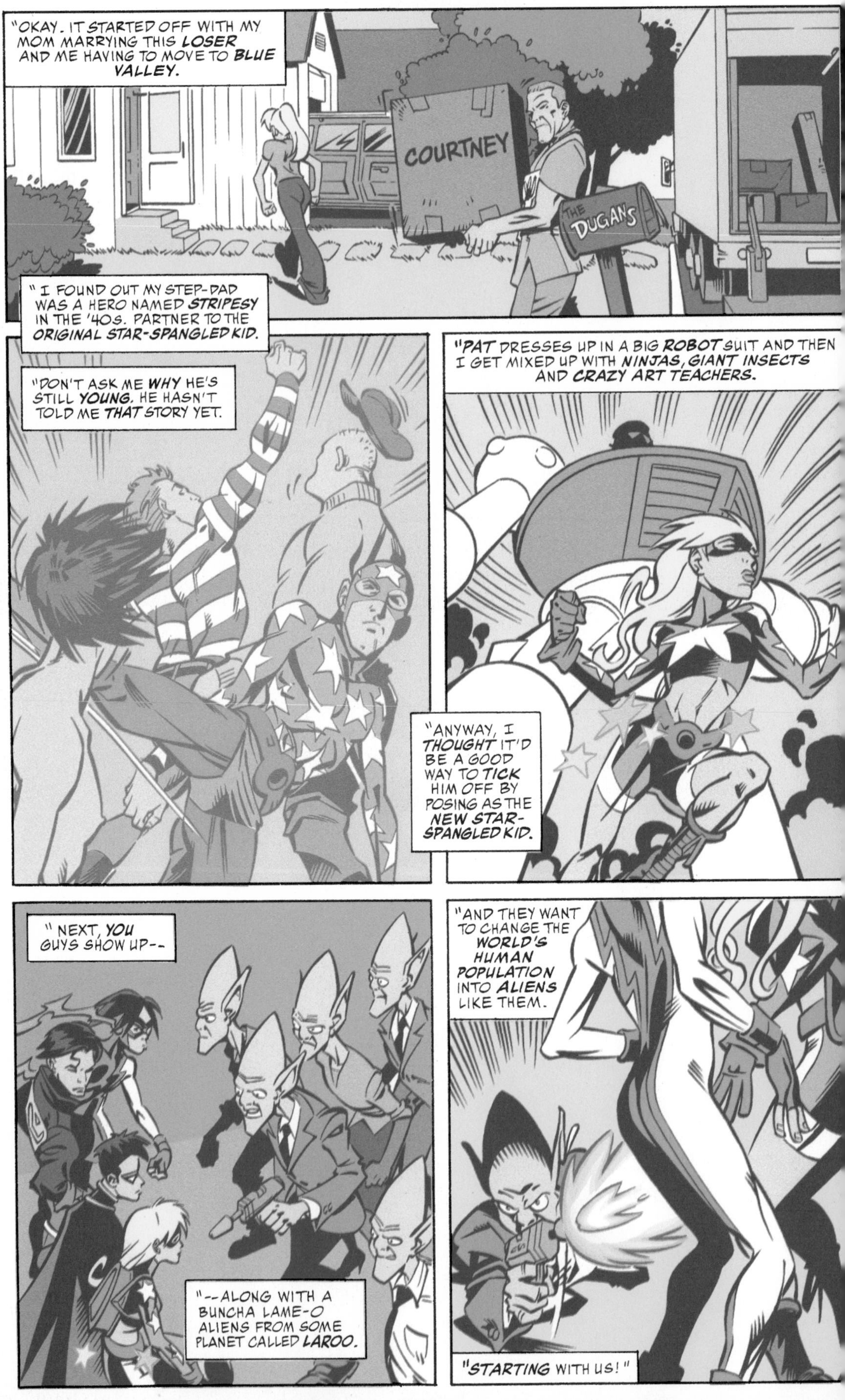
"OKAY. IT STARTED OFF WITH MY MOM MARRYING THIS LOSER AND ME HAVING TO MOVE TO BLUE VALLEY.
COURTNEY
THE DUGANS
"I FOUND OUT MY STEP-DAD WAS A HERO NAMED STRIPESY IN THE '40s. PARTNER TO THE ORIGINAL STAR-SPANGLED KID.
"DON'T ASK ME WHY HE'S STILL YOUNG. HE HASN'T TOLD ME THAT STORY YET.
"PAT DRESSES UP IN A BIG ROBOT SUIT AND THEN I GET MIXED UP WITH NINJAS, GIANT INSECTS AND CRAZY ART TEACHERS.
"ANYWAY, I THOUGHT IT'D BE A GOOD WAY TO TICK HIM OFF BY POSING AS THE NEW STAR-SPANGLED KID.
"NEXT, YOU GUYS SHOW UP--
"--ALONG WITH A BUNCHA LAME-O ALIENS FROM SOME PLANET CALLED LAROO.
"AND THEY WANT TO CHANGE THE WORLD'S HUMAN POPULATION INTO ALIENS LIKE THEM.
"STARTING WITH US!"

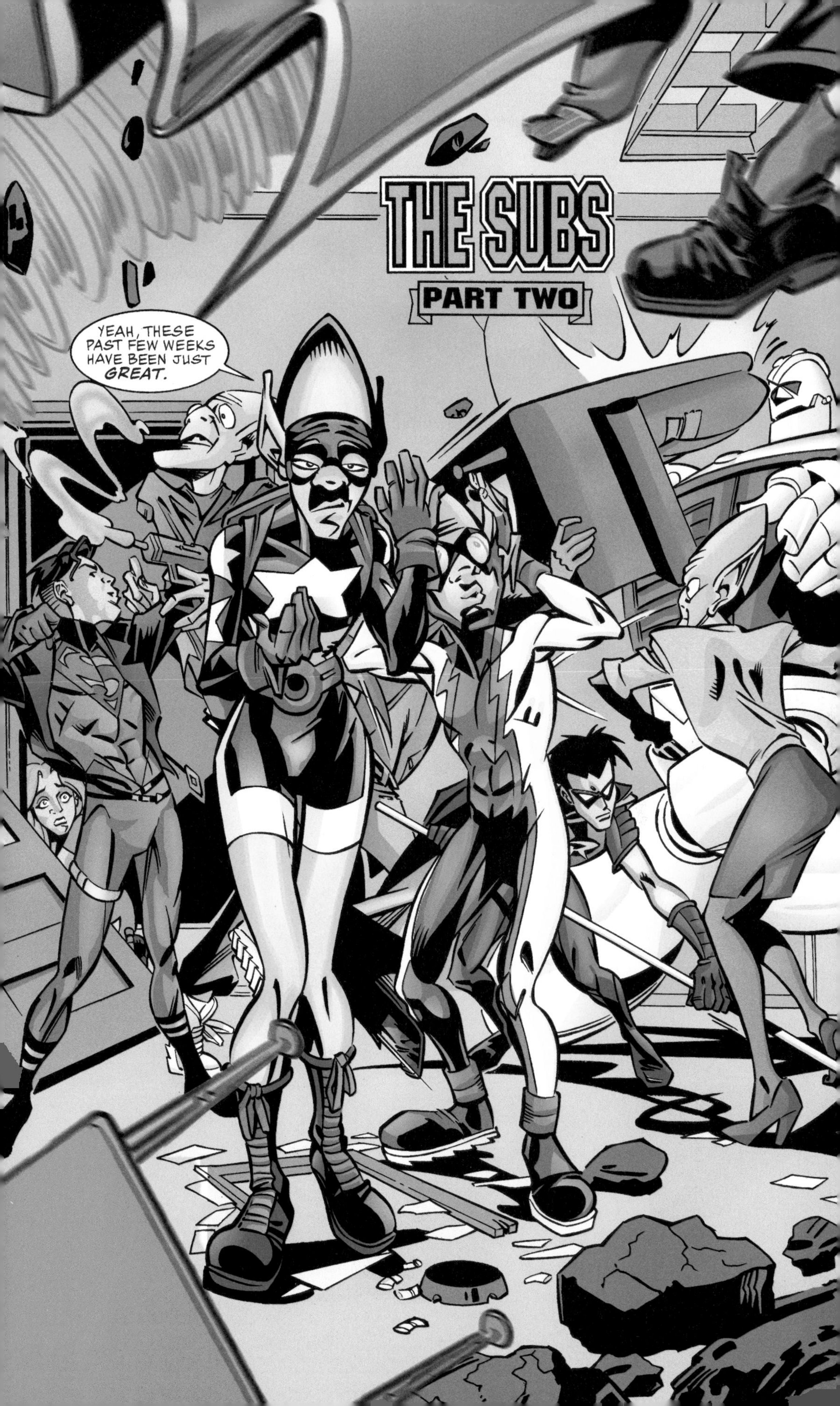
THE SUBS
PART TWO
YEAH, THESE PAST FEW WEEKS HAVE BEEN JUST *GREAT.*

YOU LOOK LIKE YOU COULD LOSE SOME INDIVIDUALITY.

HEY, PAL, LET ME INTRODUCE YOU TO A LITTLE POWER OF MINE--

--IT'S CALLED TACTILE TELEKINESIS!

FRAZZT!

SUPERBOY! WE NEED THAT DEVICE INTACT TO CHANGE IMPULSE AND THE STAR-SPANGLED KID BACK!

HEY, HE WAS ABOUT TO TRANSFORM THIS CUTE REDHEAD INTO A BLUE-SKINNED BASKET CASE!

CRACK!

HOW AM I GONNA EXPLAIN THIS TO YOUR MOM?

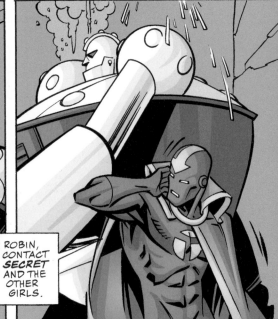

ROBIN, CONTACT SECRET AND THE OTHER GIRLS.

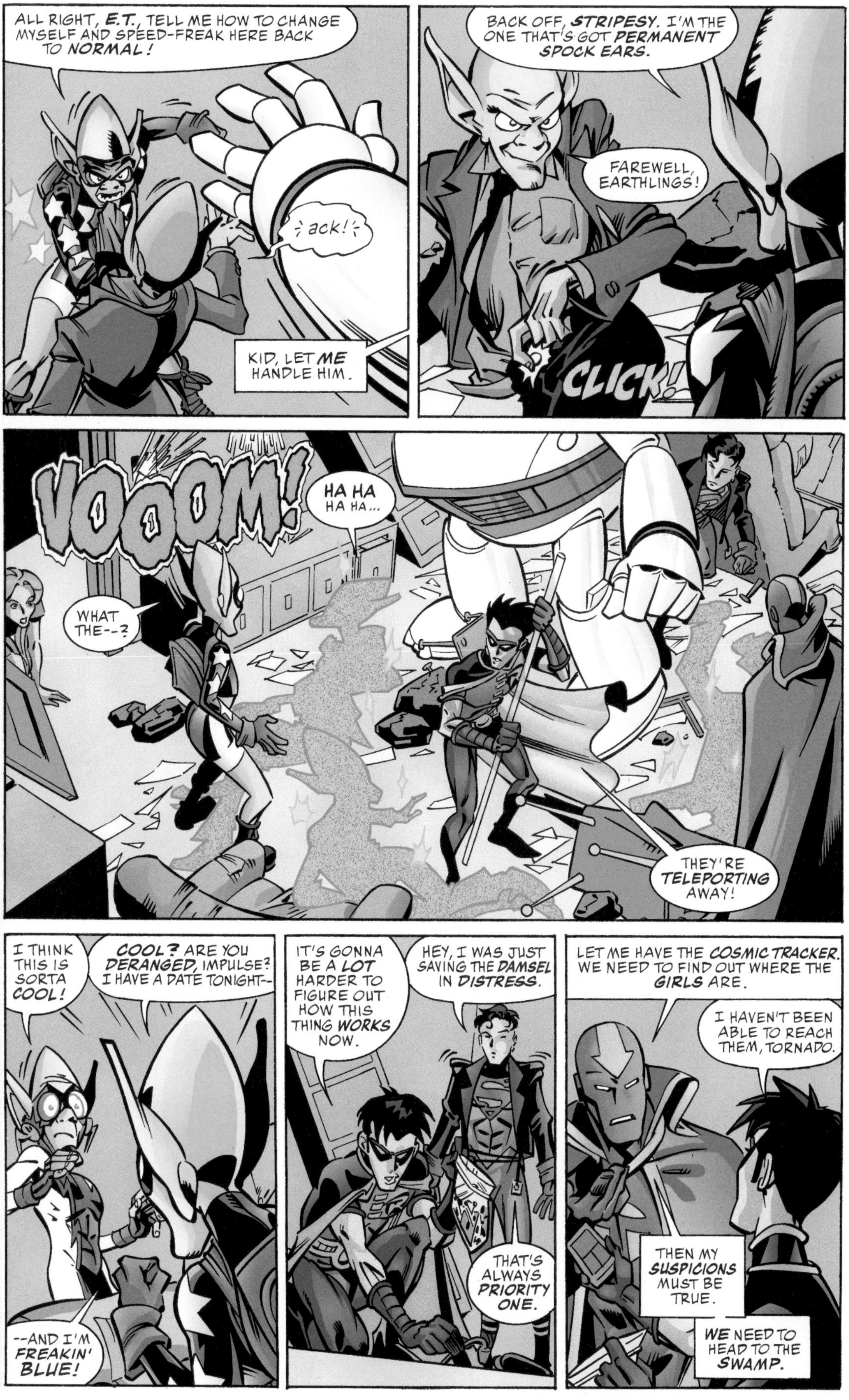

ALL RIGHT, E.T., TELL ME HOW TO CHANGE MYSELF AND SPEED-FREAK HERE BACK TO NORMAL!
ack!
KID, LET ME HANDLE HIM.
BACK OFF, STRIPESY. I'M THE ONE THAT'S GOT PERMANENT SPOCK EARS.
FAREWELL, EARTHLINGS!
CLICK!
VOOOM!
HA HA HA HA...
WHAT THE--?
THEY'RE TELEPORTING AWAY!
I THINK THIS IS SORTA COOL!
COOL? ARE YOU DERANGED, IMPULSE? I HAVE A DATE TONIGHT--
--AND I'M FREAKIN' BLUE!
IT'S GONNA BE A LOT HARDER TO FIGURE OUT HOW THIS THING WORKS NOW.
HEY, I WAS JUST SAVING THE DAMSEL IN DISTRESS.
THAT'S ALWAYS PRIORITY ONE.
LET ME HAVE THE COSMIC TRACKER. WE NEED TO FIND OUT WHERE THE GIRLS ARE.
I HAVEN'T BEEN ABLE TO REACH THEM, TORNADO.
THEN MY SUSPICIONS MUST BE TRUE.
WE NEED TO HEAD TO THE SWAMP.

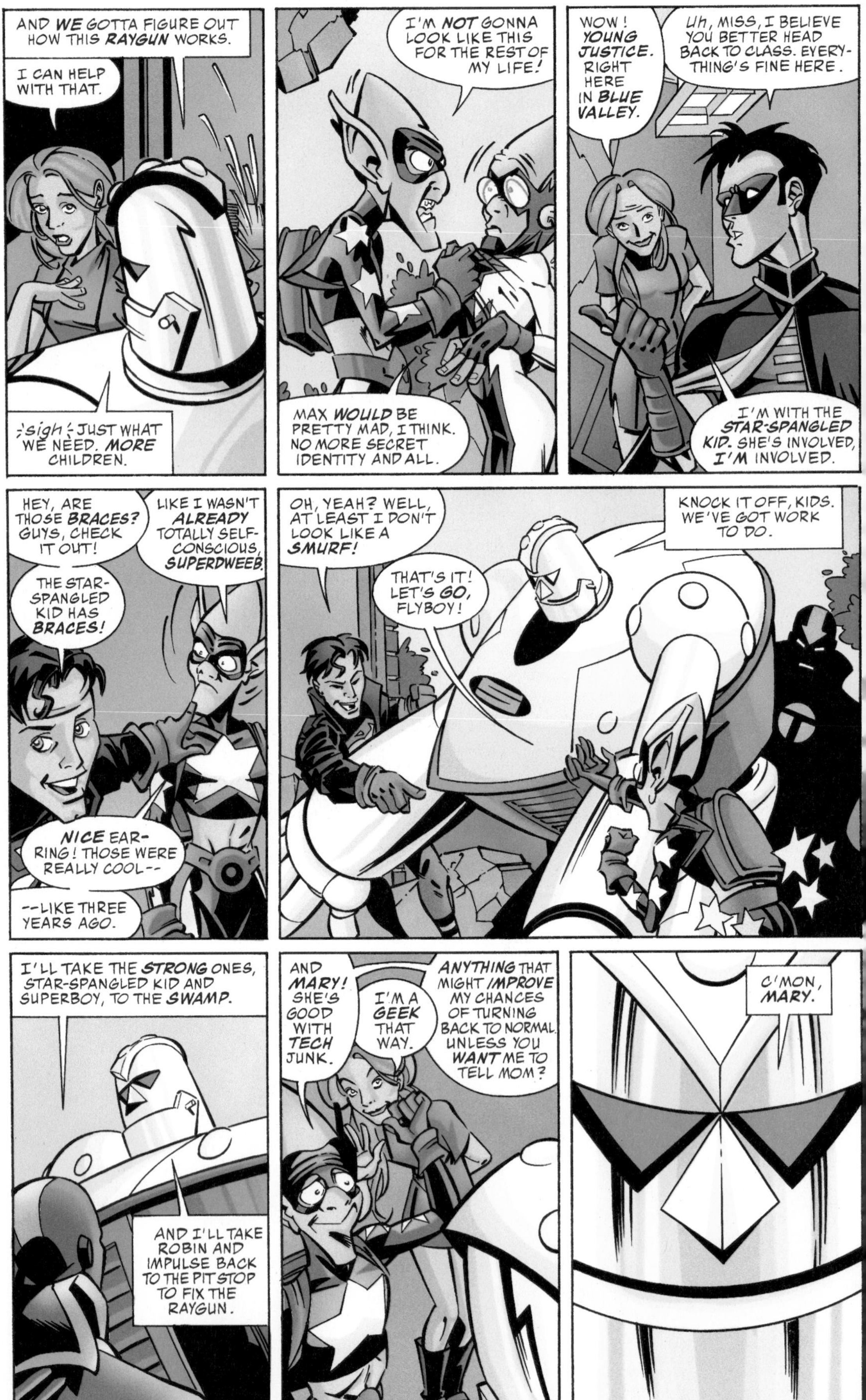
AND WE GOTTA FIGURE OUT HOW THIS RAYGUN WORKS.
I CAN HELP WITH THAT.
-sigh- JUST WHAT WE NEED. MORE CHILDREN.
I'M NOT GONNA LOOK LIKE THIS FOR THE REST OF MY LIFE!
MAX WOULD BE PRETTY MAD, I THINK. NO MORE SECRET IDENTITY AND ALL.
WOW! YOUNG JUSTICE. RIGHT HERE IN BLUE VALLEY.
Uh, MISS, I BELIEVE YOU BETTER HEAD BACK TO CLASS. EVERYTHING'S FINE HERE.
I'M WITH THE STAR-SPANGLED KID. SHE'S INVOLVED, I'M INVOLVED.
HEY, ARE THOSE BRACES? GUYS, CHECK IT OUT!
LIKE I WASN'T ALREADY TOTALLY SELF-CONSCIOUS, SUPERDWEEB.
THE STAR-SPANGLED KID HAS BRACES!
NICE EAR-RING! THOSE WERE REALLY COOL--
--LIKE THREE YEARS AGO.
OH, YEAH? WELL, AT LEAST I DON'T LOOK LIKE A SMURF!
THAT'S IT! LET'S GO, FLYBOY!
KNOCK IT OFF, KIDS. WE'VE GOT WORK TO DO.
I'LL TAKE THE STRONG ONES, STAR-SPANGLED KID AND SUPERBOY, TO THE SWAMP.
AND I'LL TAKE ROBIN AND IMPULSE BACK TO THE PIT STOP TO FIX THE RAYGUN.
AND MARY! SHE'S GOOD WITH TECH JUNK.
I'M A GEEK THAT WAY.
ANYTHING THAT MIGHT IMPROVE MY CHANCES OF TURNING BACK TO NORMAL. UNLESS YOU WANT ME TO TELL MOM?
C'MON, MARY.

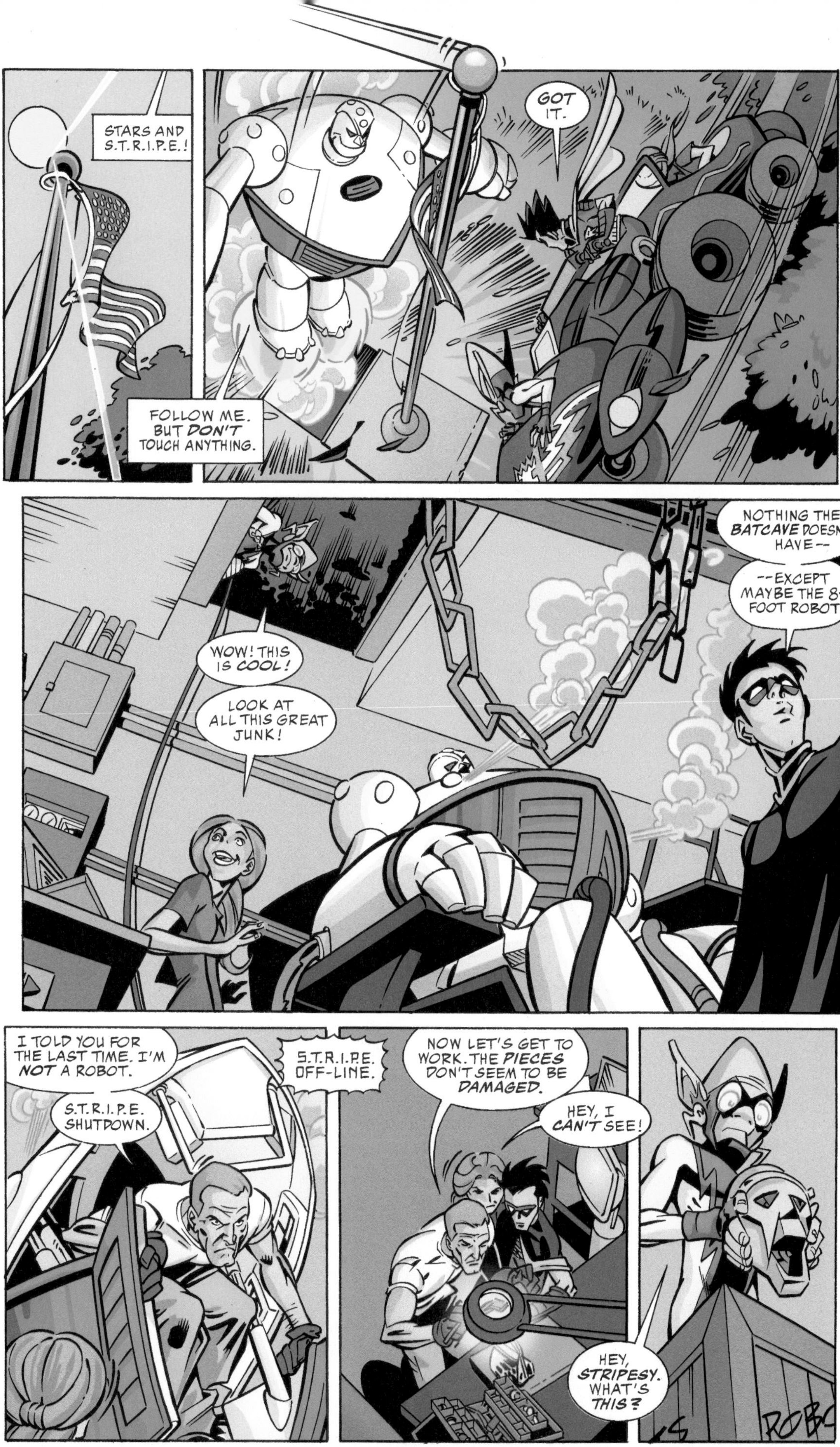
STARS AND S.T.R.I.P.E.!
FOLLOW ME. BUT DON'T TOUCH ANYTHING.
GOT IT.
NOTHING THE BATCAVE DOESN'T HAVE--
--EXCEPT MAYBE THE 8-FOOT ROBOT.
WOW! THIS IS COOL!
LOOK AT ALL THIS GREAT JUNK!
I TOLD YOU FOR THE LAST TIME. I'M NOT A ROBOT.
S.T.R.I.P.E. SHUTDOWN.
S.T.R.I.P.E. OFF-LINE.
NOW LET'S GET TO WORK. THE PIECES DON'T SEEM TO BE DAMAGED.
HEY, I CAN'T SEE!
HEY, STRIPESY. WHAT'S THIS?

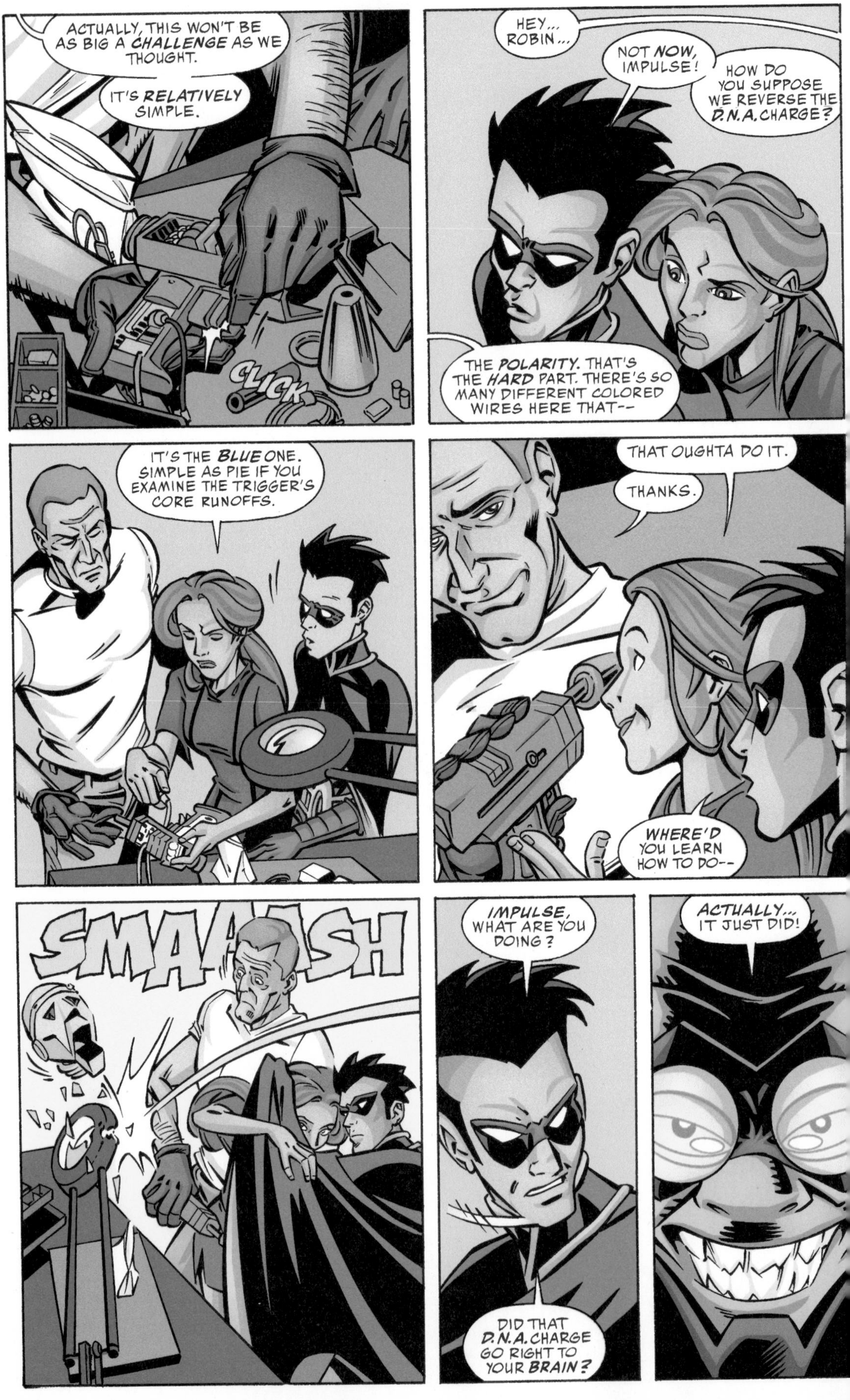
ACTUALLY, THIS WON'T BE AS BIG A CHALLENGE AS WE THOUGHT.
IT'S RELATIVELY SIMPLE.
CLICK
HEY... ROBIN...
NOT NOW, IMPULSE!
HOW DO YOU SUPPOSE WE REVERSE THE D.N.A. CHARGE?
THE POLARITY. THAT'S THE HARD PART. THERE'S SO MANY DIFFERENT COLORED WIRES HERE THAT--
IT'S THE BLUE ONE. SIMPLE AS PIE IF YOU EXAMINE THE TRIGGER'S CORE RUNOFFS.
THAT OUGHTA DO IT.
THANKS.
WHERE'D YOU LEARN HOW TO DO--
SMAAASH
IMPULSE, WHAT ARE YOU DOING?
DID THAT D.N.A. CHARGE GO RIGHT TO YOUR BRAIN?
ACTUALLY... IT JUST DID!

WHAK! WHAK!

WHOOSH

SO, THE *RAY* CHANGES MORE THAN JUST YOUR HAIRSTYLE.

JOIN US. IT'S ONLY A MATTER OF *TIME*, ANYWAY.

LOOK, HOW CAN YOU *HOPE* TO BEAT US? RIGHT NOW YOU'RE FACED WITH A BEING THAT HAS *UNLIMITED* ACCESS TO THE *SPEED FORCE*.

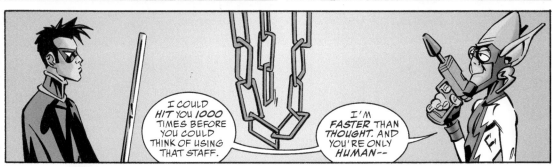

I COULD *HIT* YOU *1000* TIMES BEFORE YOU COULD THINK OF USING THAT STAFF.

I'M *FASTER* THAN *THOUGHT*. AND YOU'RE ONLY *HUMAN*--

--FOR NOW.

LET'S GO, PAL.

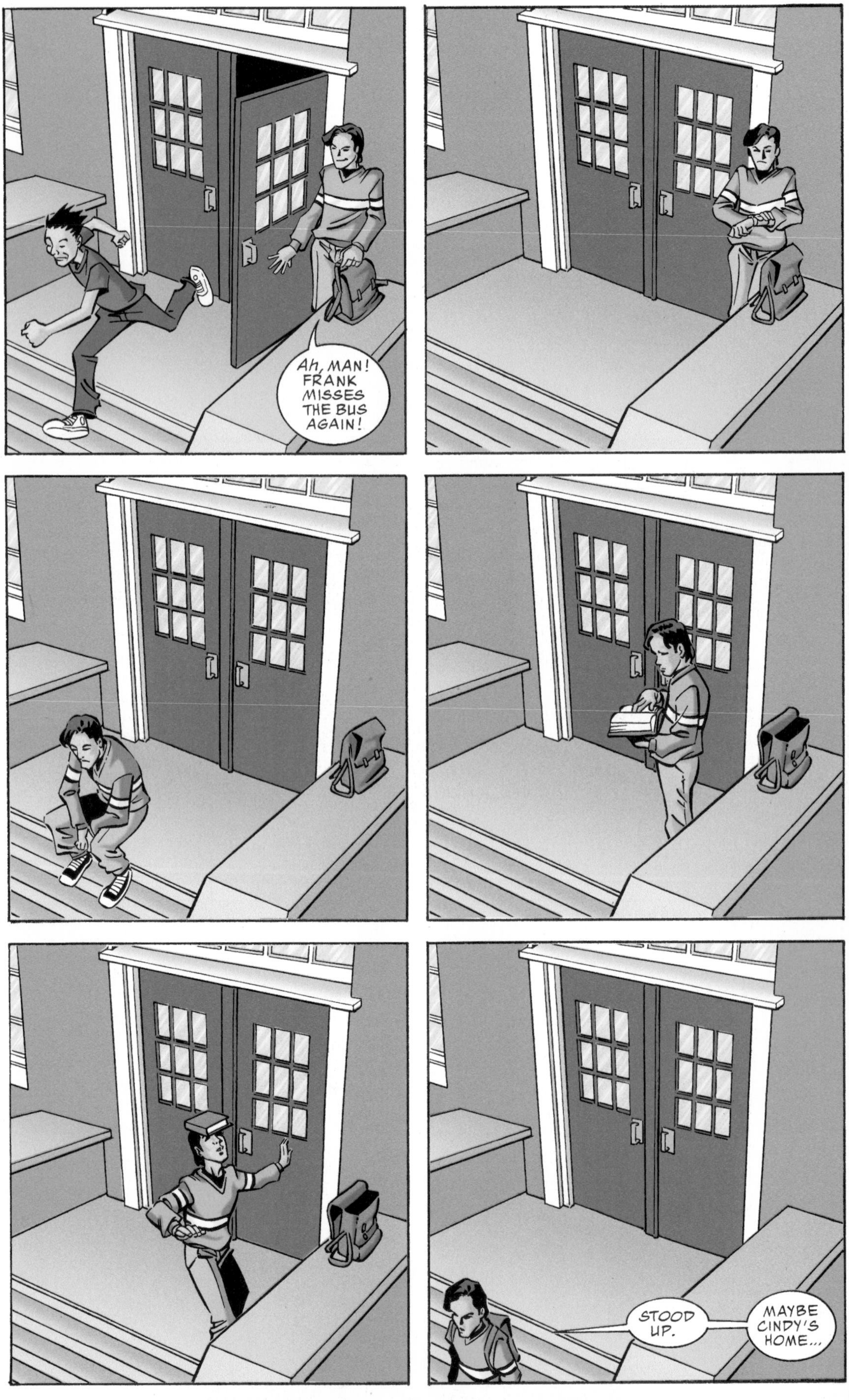
Ah, MAN! FRANK MISSES THE BUS AGAIN!
STOOD UP.
MAYBE CINDY'S HOME...

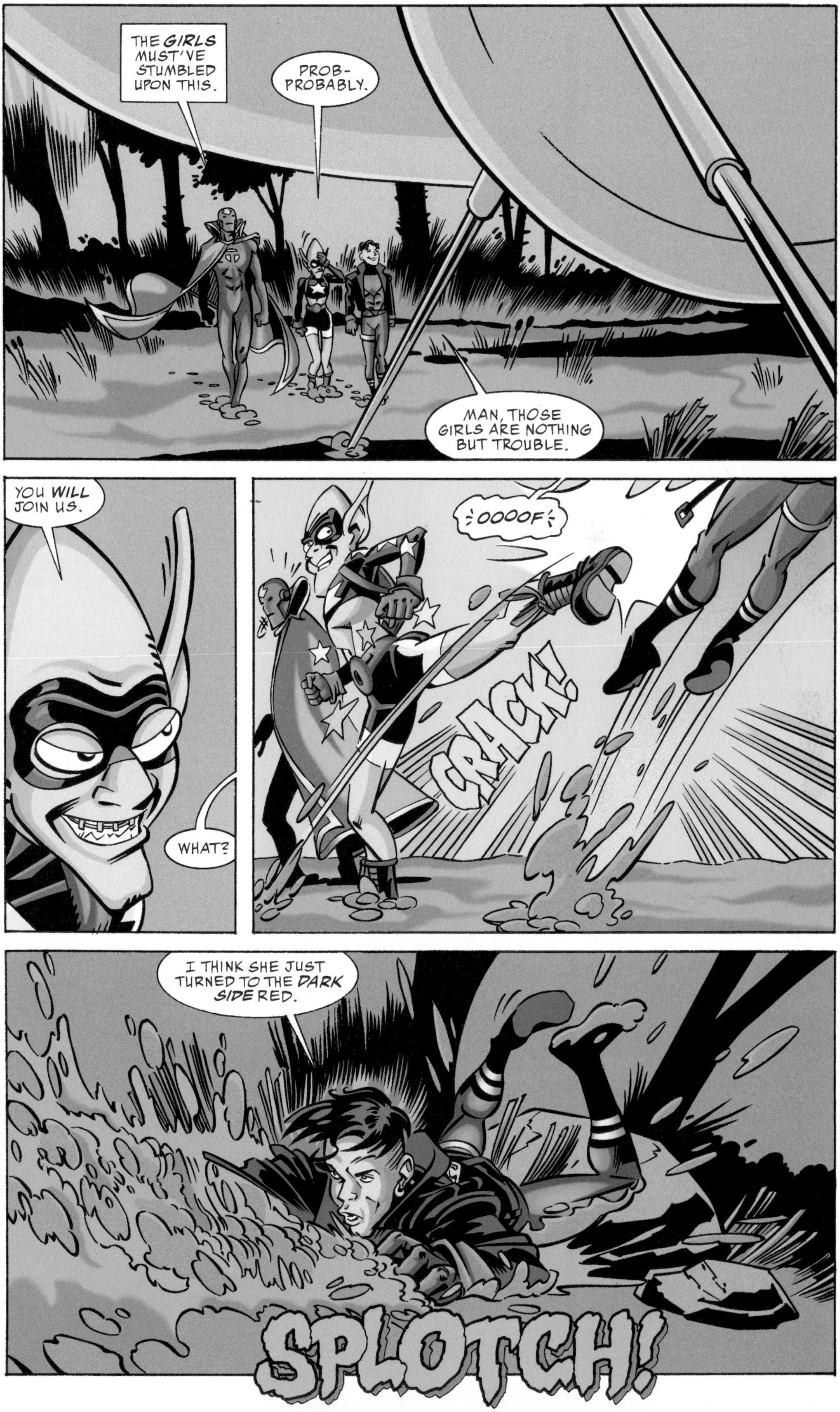
THE GIRLS MUST'VE STUMBLED UPON THIS.
PROB-PROBABLY.
MAN, THOSE GIRLS ARE NOTHING BUT TROUBLE.
YOU WILL JOIN US.
WHAT?
OOOOF
CRACK!
I THINK SHE JUST TURNED TO THE DARK SIDE RED.
SPLOTCH!

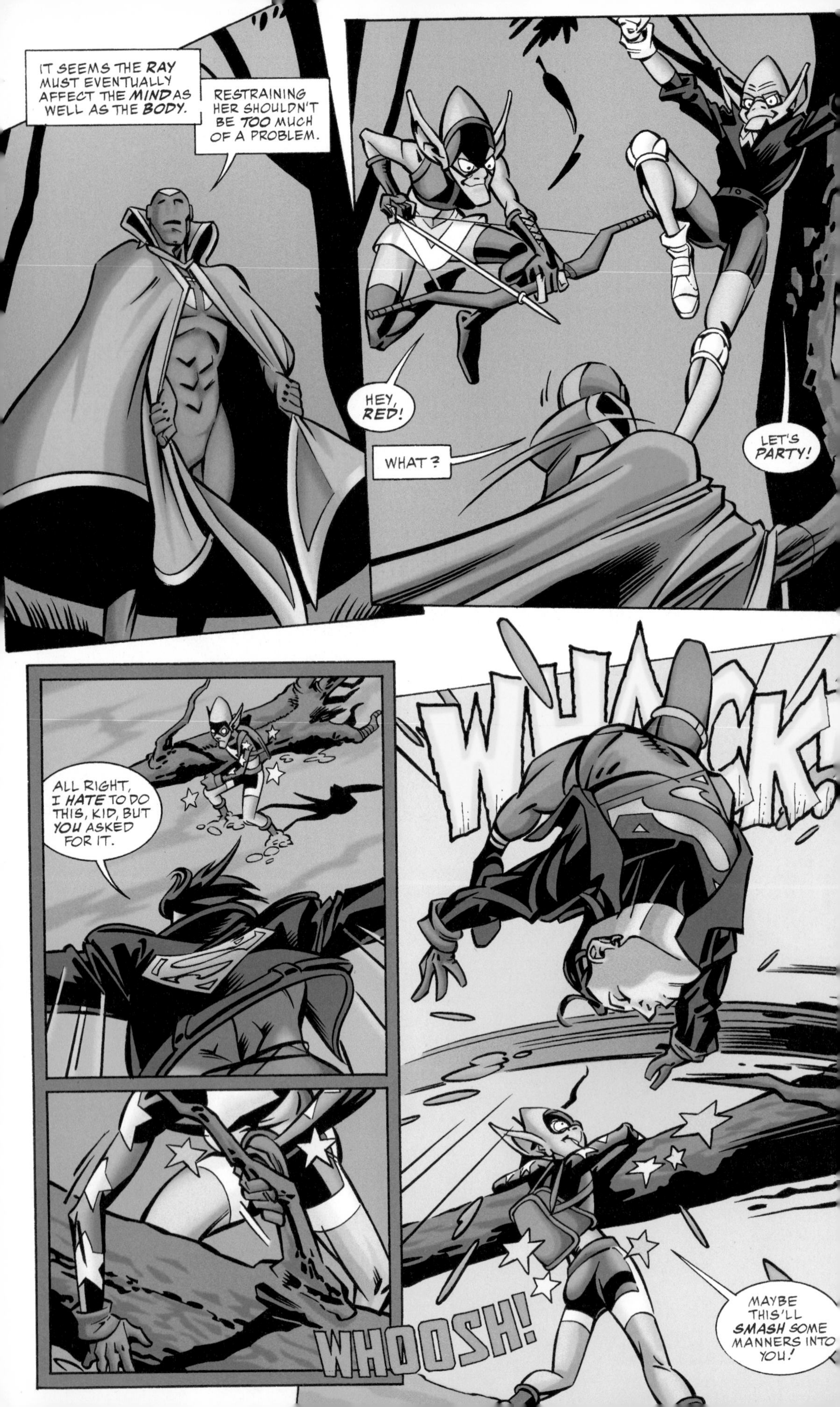
IT SEEMS THE RAY MUST EVENTUALLY AFFECT THE MIND AS WELL AS THE BODY.
RESTRAINING HER SHOULDN'T BE TOO MUCH OF A PROBLEM.
HEY, RED!
WHAT?
LET'S PARTY!
ALL RIGHT, I HATE TO DO THIS, KID, BUT YOU ASKED FOR IT.
WHOOSH!
WHACK!
MAYBE THIS'LL SMASH SOME MANNERS INTO YOU!

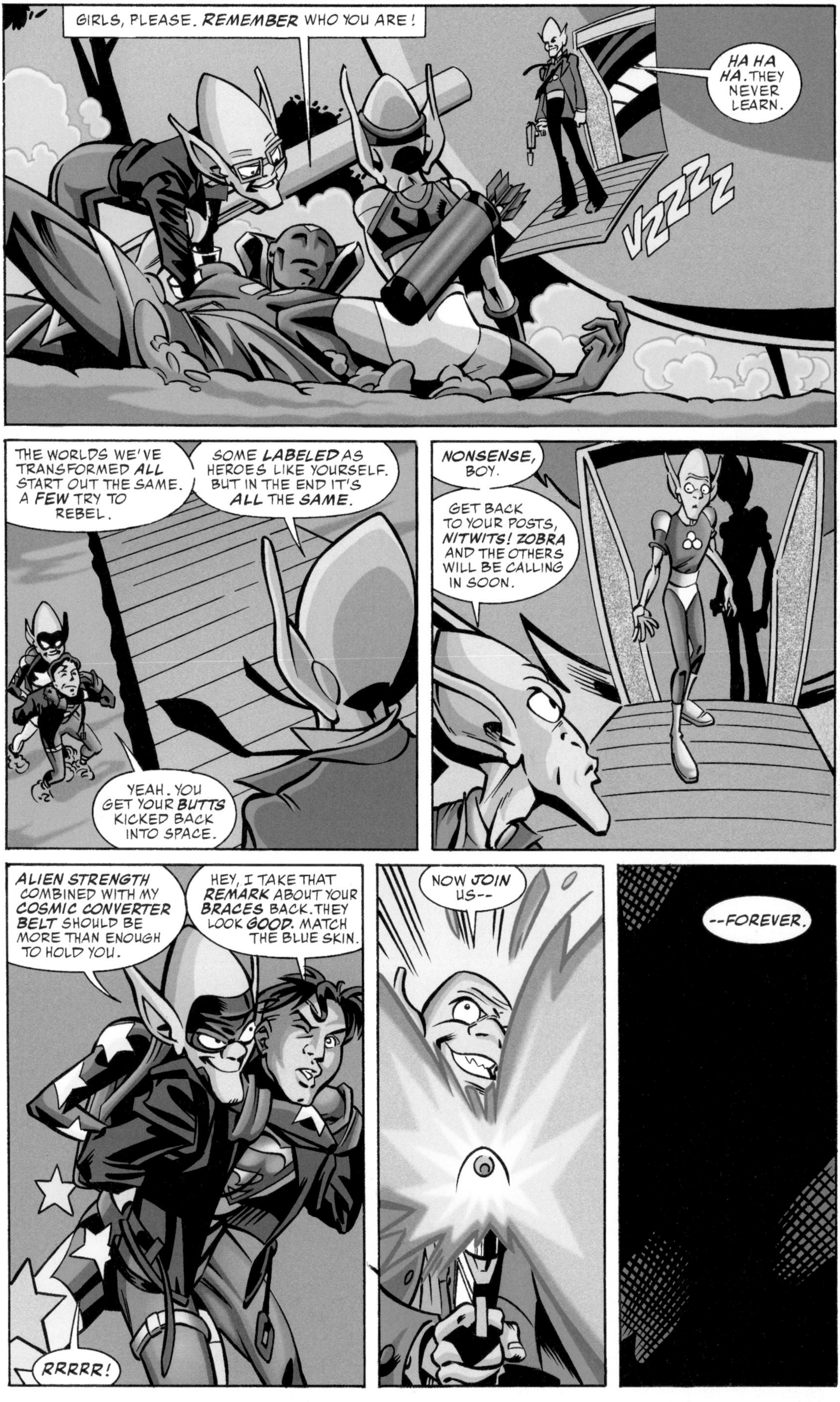
GIRLS, PLEASE. REMEMBER WHO YOU ARE!
HA HA HA. THEY NEVER LEARN.
VZZZZ
THE WORLDS WE'VE TRANSFORMED ALL START OUT THE SAME. A FEW TRY TO REBEL.
SOME LABELED AS HEROES LIKE YOURSELF. BUT IN THE END IT'S ALL THE SAME.
YEAH. YOU GET YOUR BUTTS KICKED BACK INTO SPACE.
NONSENSE, BOY.
GET BACK TO YOUR POSTS, NITWITS! ZOBRA AND THE OTHERS WILL BE CALLING IN SOON.
ALIEN STRENGTH COMBINED WITH MY COSMIC CONVERTER BELT SHOULD BE MORE THAN ENOUGH TO HOLD YOU.
HEY, I TAKE THAT REMARK ABOUT YOUR BRACES BACK. THEY LOOK GOOD. MATCH THE BLUE SKIN.
RRRRR!
NOW JOIN US--
--FOREVER.

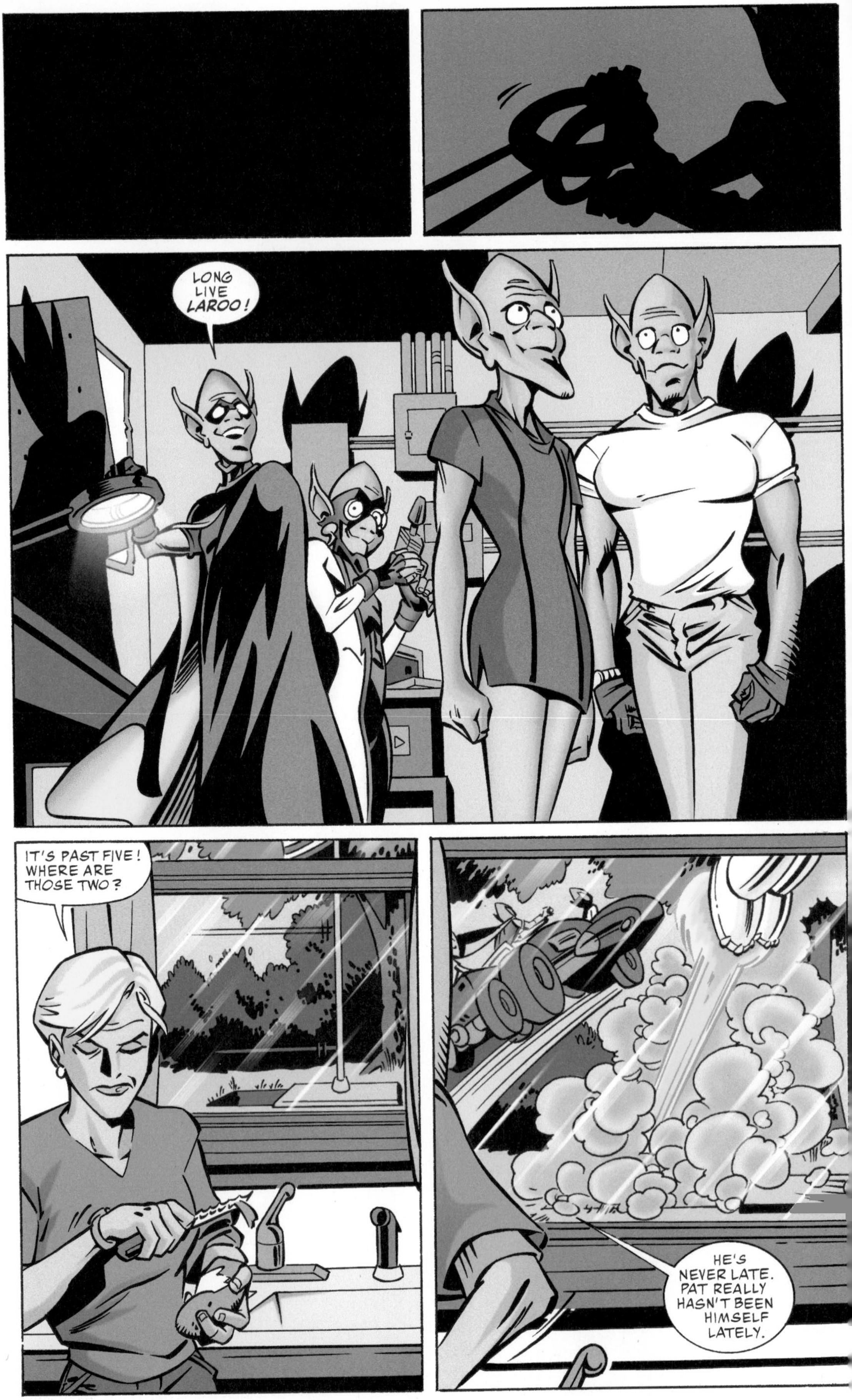
LONG LIVE LAROO!
IT'S PAST FIVE! WHERE ARE THOSE TWO?
HE'S NEVER LATE. PAT REALLY HASN'T BEEN HIMSELF LATELY.

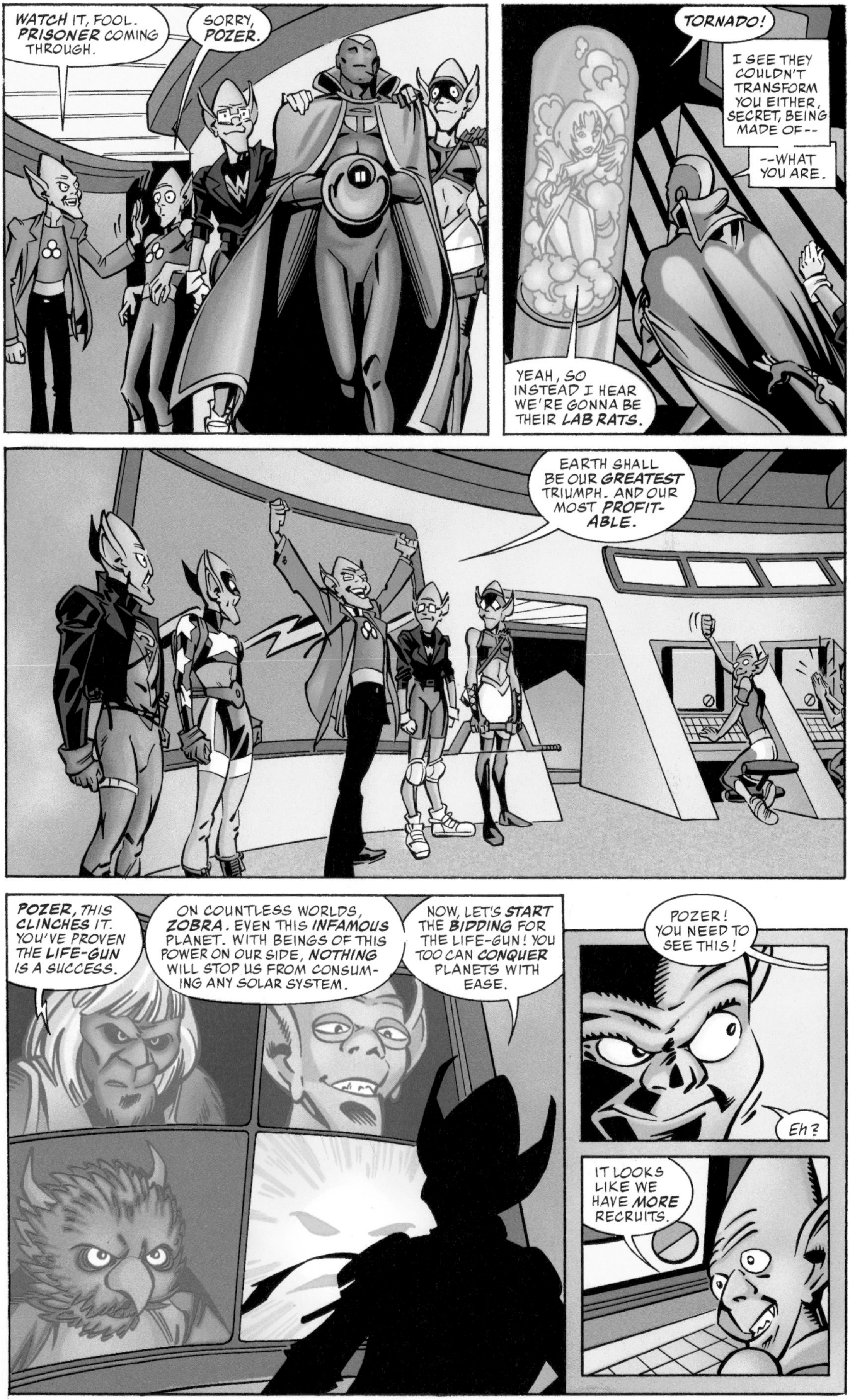

WATCH IT, FOOL. PRISONER COMING THROUGH.
SORRY, POZER.
TORNADO!
I SEE THEY COULDN'T TRANSFORM YOU EITHER, SECRET, BEING MADE OF --
--WHAT YOU ARE.
YEAH, SO INSTEAD I HEAR WE'RE GONNA BE THEIR LAB RATS.
EARTH SHALL BE OUR GREATEST TRIUMPH. AND OUR MOST PROFIT-ABLE.
POZER, THIS CLINCHES IT. YOU'VE PROVEN THE LIFE-GUN IS A SUCCESS.
ON COUNTLESS WORLDS, ZOBRA. EVEN THIS INFAMOUS PLANET. WITH BEINGS OF THIS POWER ON OUR SIDE, NOTHING WILL STOP US FROM CONSUM-ING ANY SOLAR SYSTEM.
NOW, LET'S START THE BIDDING FOR THE LIFE-GUN! YOU TOO CAN CONQUER PLANETS WITH EASE.
POZER! YOU NEED TO SEE THIS!
Eh?
IT LOOKS LIKE WE HAVE MORE RECRUITS.

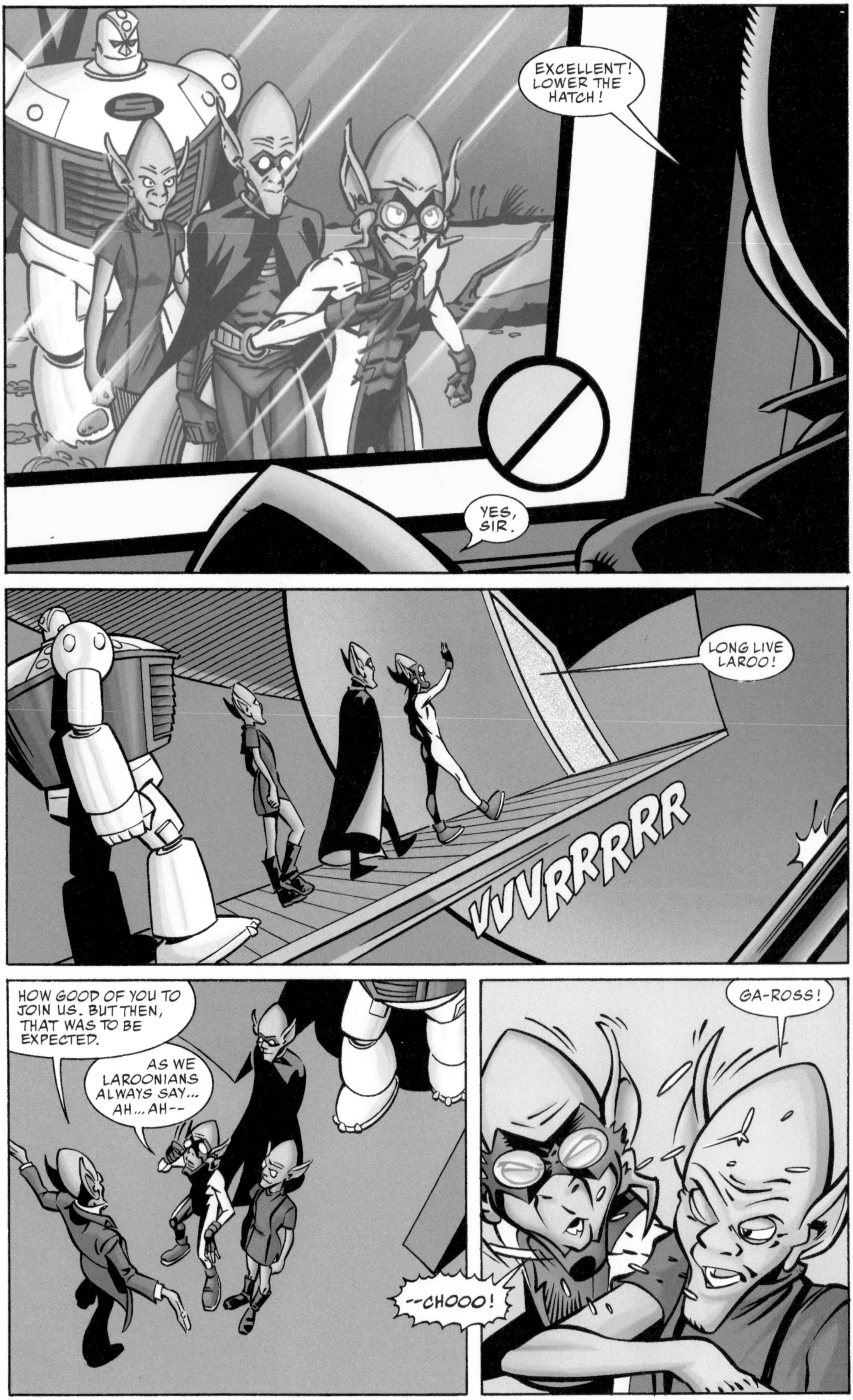

EXCELLENT! LOWER THE HATCH!
YES, SIR.
LONG LIVE LAROO!
VVVRRRRRR
HOW GOOD OF YOU TO JOIN US. BUT THEN, THAT WAS TO BE EXPECTED.
AS WE LAROONIANS ALWAYS SAY... AH... AH--
GA-ROSS!
--CHOOO!

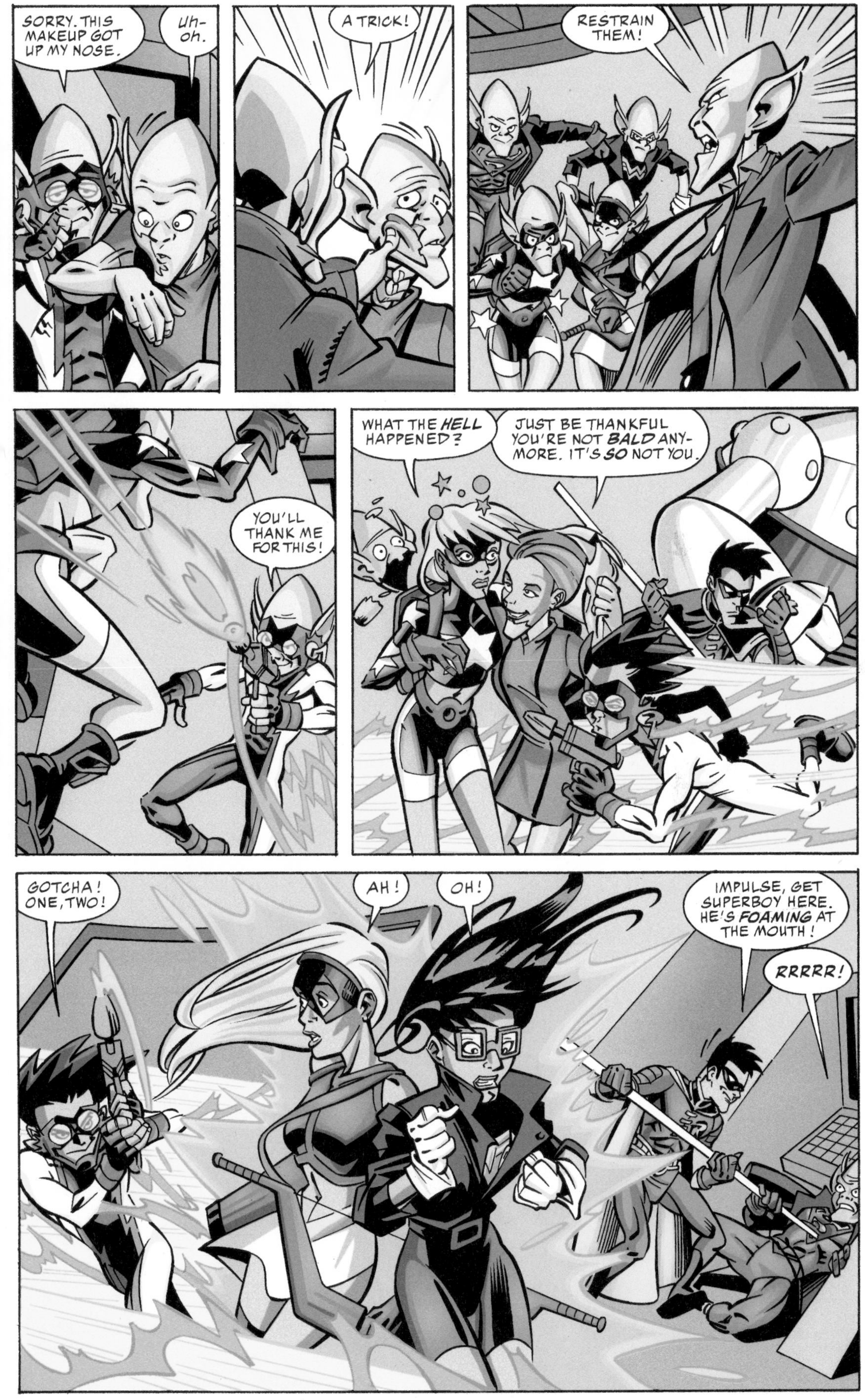

SORRY. THIS MAKEUP GOT UP MY NOSE.
Uh-oh.
A TRICK!
RESTRAIN THEM!
YOU'LL THANK ME FOR THIS!
WHAT THE HELL HAPPENED?
JUST BE THANKFUL YOU'RE NOT BALD ANYMORE. IT'S SO NOT YOU.
GOTCHA! ONE, TWO!
AH!
OH!
IMPULSE, GET SUPERBOY HERE. HE'S FOAMING AT THE MOUTH!
RRRRR!

CHANGE *MY* GENETIC STRUCTURE, *WILLYA*?

AAAHH!

GOING *UP!*

WATCH IT, *GIRLS!*

EXCUSE ME!

--AND THEN SHE *SOCKED* ME. *LUCKY* KICK!

WISH I COULDA *SEEN* THAT!

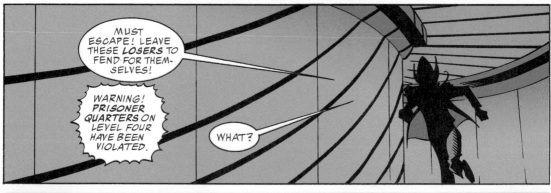

MUST ESCAPE! LEAVE THESE *LOSERS* TO *FEND* FOR THEMSELVES!

WARNING! PRISONER *QUARTERS* ON *LEVEL FOUR* HAVE BEEN *VIOLATED.*

WHAT?

AH... WE WERE JUST TALKING ABOUT YOU.

YOU AREN'T VERY *NICE,* Y'KNOW.

WEAPONS PRIMED AND READY!

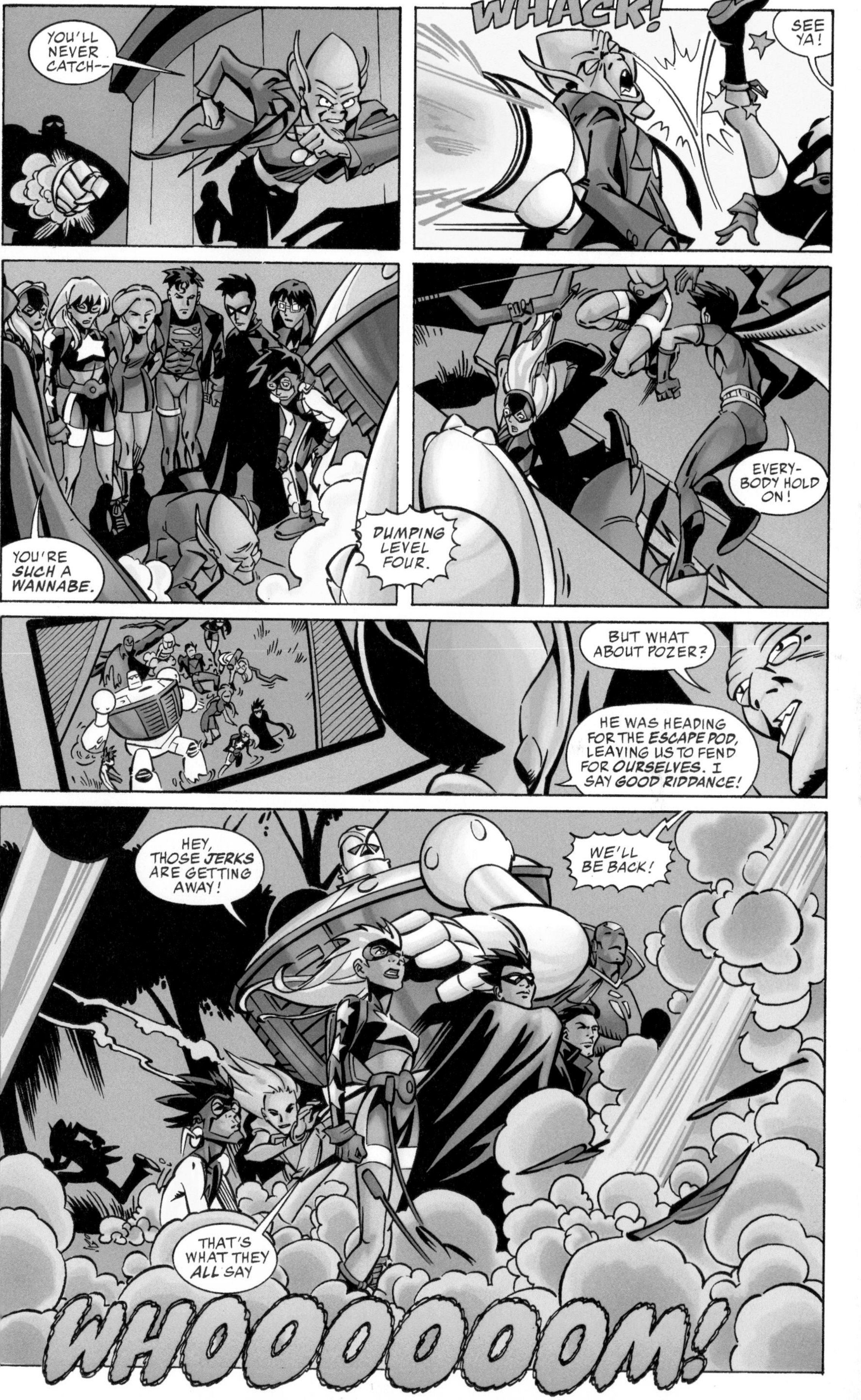
YOU'LL NEVER CATCH--
WHACK!
SEE YA!
YOU'RE SUCH A WANNABE.
DUMPING LEVEL FOUR.
EVERY-BODY HOLD ON!
BUT WHAT ABOUT POZER?
HE WAS HEADING FOR THE ESCAPE POD, LEAVING US TO FEND FOR OURSELVES. I SAY GOOD RIDDANCE!
HEY, THOSE JERKS ARE GETTING AWAY!
WE'LL BE BACK!
THAT'S WHAT THEY ALL SAY
WHOOOOOOOM!

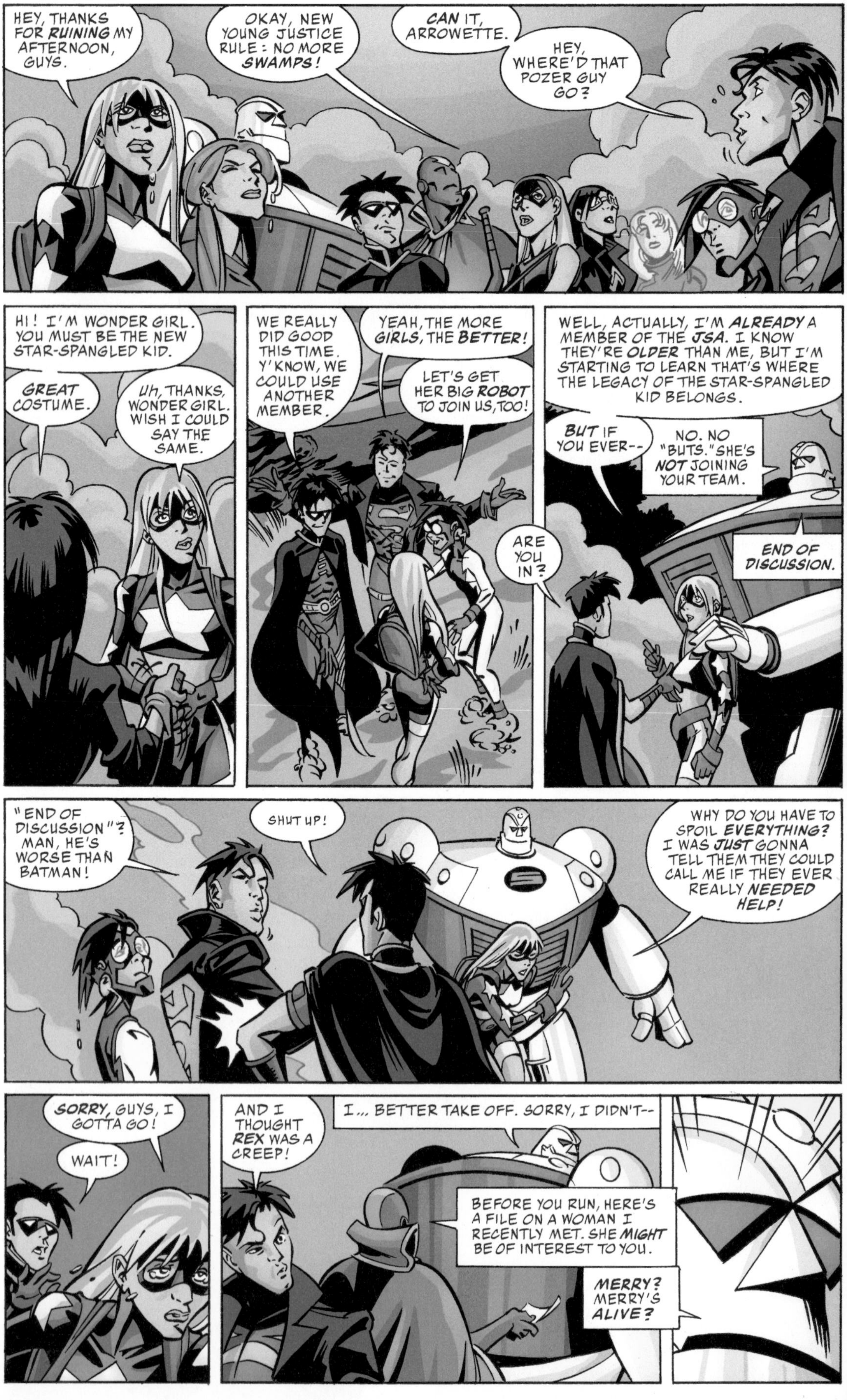

HEY, THANKS FOR RUINING MY AFTERNOON, GUYS.
OKAY, NEW YOUNG JUSTICE RULE: NO MORE SWAMPS!
CAN IT, ARROWETTE.
HEY, WHERE'D THAT POZER GUY GO?
HI! I'M WONDER GIRL. YOU MUST BE THE NEW STAR-SPANGLED KID.
GREAT COSTUME.
UH, THANKS, WONDER GIRL. WISH I COULD SAY THE SAME.
WE REALLY DID GOOD THIS TIME. Y'KNOW, WE COULD USE ANOTHER MEMBER.
YEAH, THE MORE GIRLS, THE BETTER!
LET'S GET HER BIG ROBOT TO JOIN US, TOO!
WELL, ACTUALLY, I'M ALREADY A MEMBER OF THE JSA. I KNOW THEY'RE OLDER THAN ME, BUT I'M STARTING TO LEARN THAT'S WHERE THE LEGACY OF THE STAR-SPANGLED KID BELONGS.
BUT IF YOU EVER--
NO. NO "BUTS." SHE'S NOT JOINING YOUR TEAM.
ARE YOU IN?
END OF DISCUSSION.
"END OF DISCUSSION"? MAN, HE'S WORSE THAN BATMAN!
SHUT UP!
WHY DO YOU HAVE TO SPOIL EVERYTHING? I WAS JUST GONNA TELL THEM THEY COULD CALL ME IF THEY EVER REALLY NEEDED HELP!
SORRY, GUYS, I GOTTA GO!
WAIT!
AND I THOUGHT REX WAS A CREEP!
I... BETTER TAKE OFF. SORRY, I DIDN'T--
BEFORE YOU RUN, HERE'S A FILE ON A WOMAN I RECENTLY MET. SHE MIGHT BE OF INTEREST TO YOU.
MERRY? MERRY'S ALIVE?

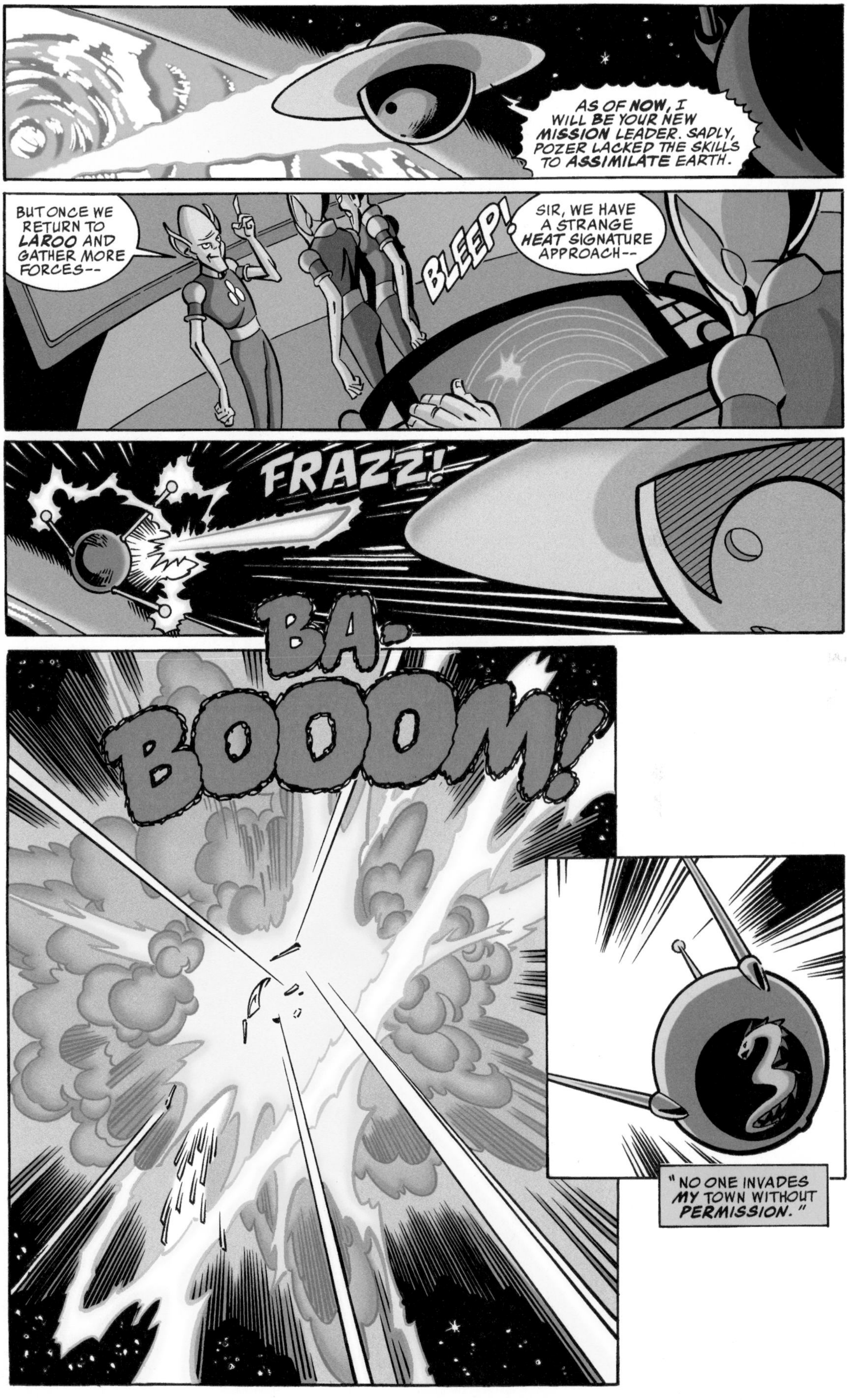
AS OF NOW, I WILL BE YOUR NEW MISSION LEADER. SADLY, POZER LACKED THE SKILLS TO ASSIMILATE EARTH.
BUT ONCE WE RETURN TO LAROO AND GATHER MORE FORCES--
BLEEP!
SIR, WE HAVE A STRANGE HEAT SIGNATURE APPROACH--
FRAZZ!
BA-BOOOM!
"NO ONE INVADES MY TOWN WITHOUT PERMISSION."

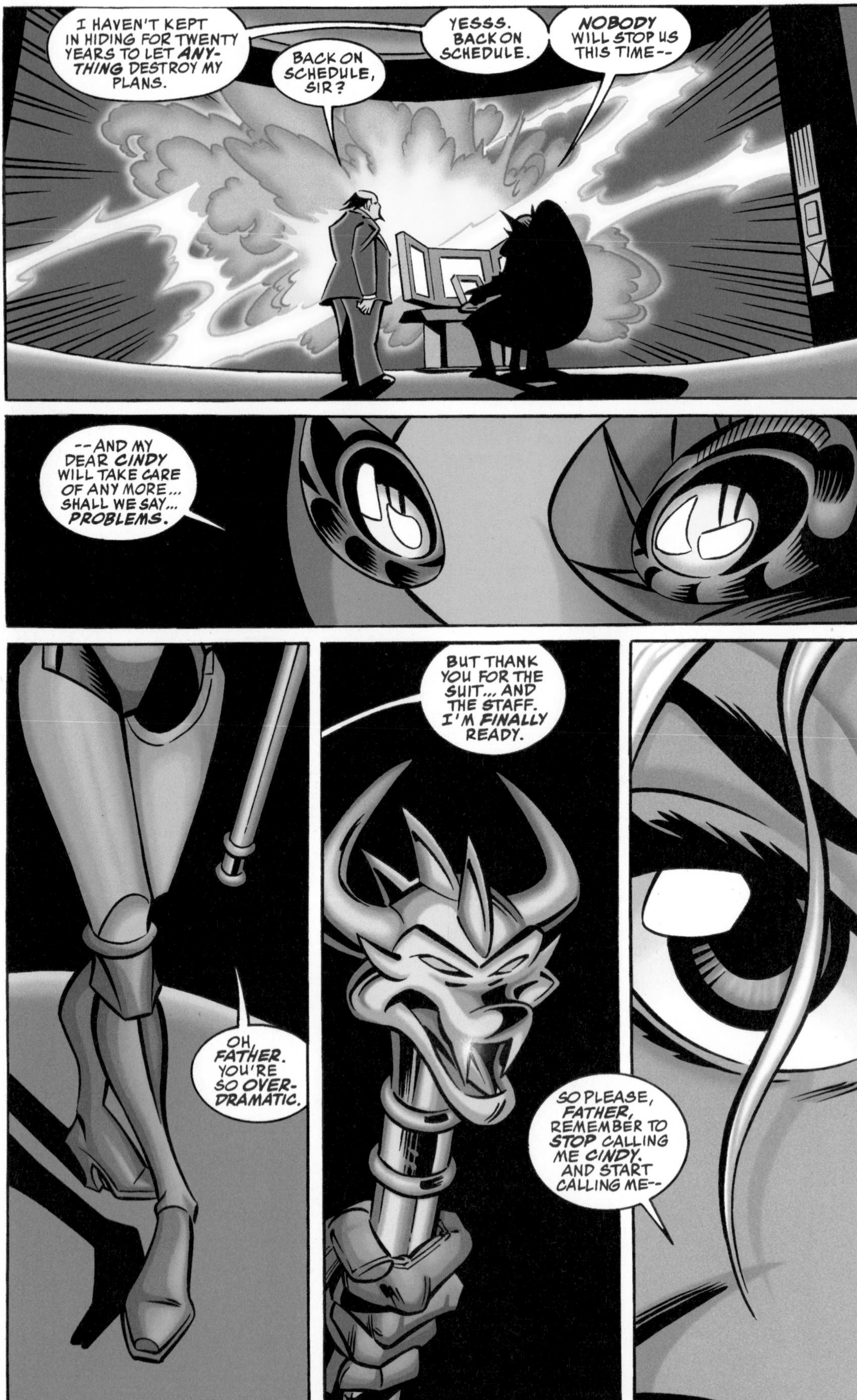
I HAVEN'T KEPT IN HIDING FOR TWENTY YEARS TO LET ANYTHING DESTROY MY PLANS.
BACK ON SCHEDULE, SIR?
YESSS. BACK ON SCHEDULE.
NOBODY WILL STOP US THIS TIME--
--AND MY DEAR CINDY WILL TAKE CARE OF ANY MORE... SHALL WE SAY... PROBLEMS.
OH, FATHER. YOU'RE SO OVER-DRAMATIC.
BUT THANK YOU FOR THE SUIT... AND THE STAFF. I'M FINALLY READY.
SO PLEASE, FATHER, REMEMBER TO STOP CALLING ME CINDY. AND START CALLING ME--

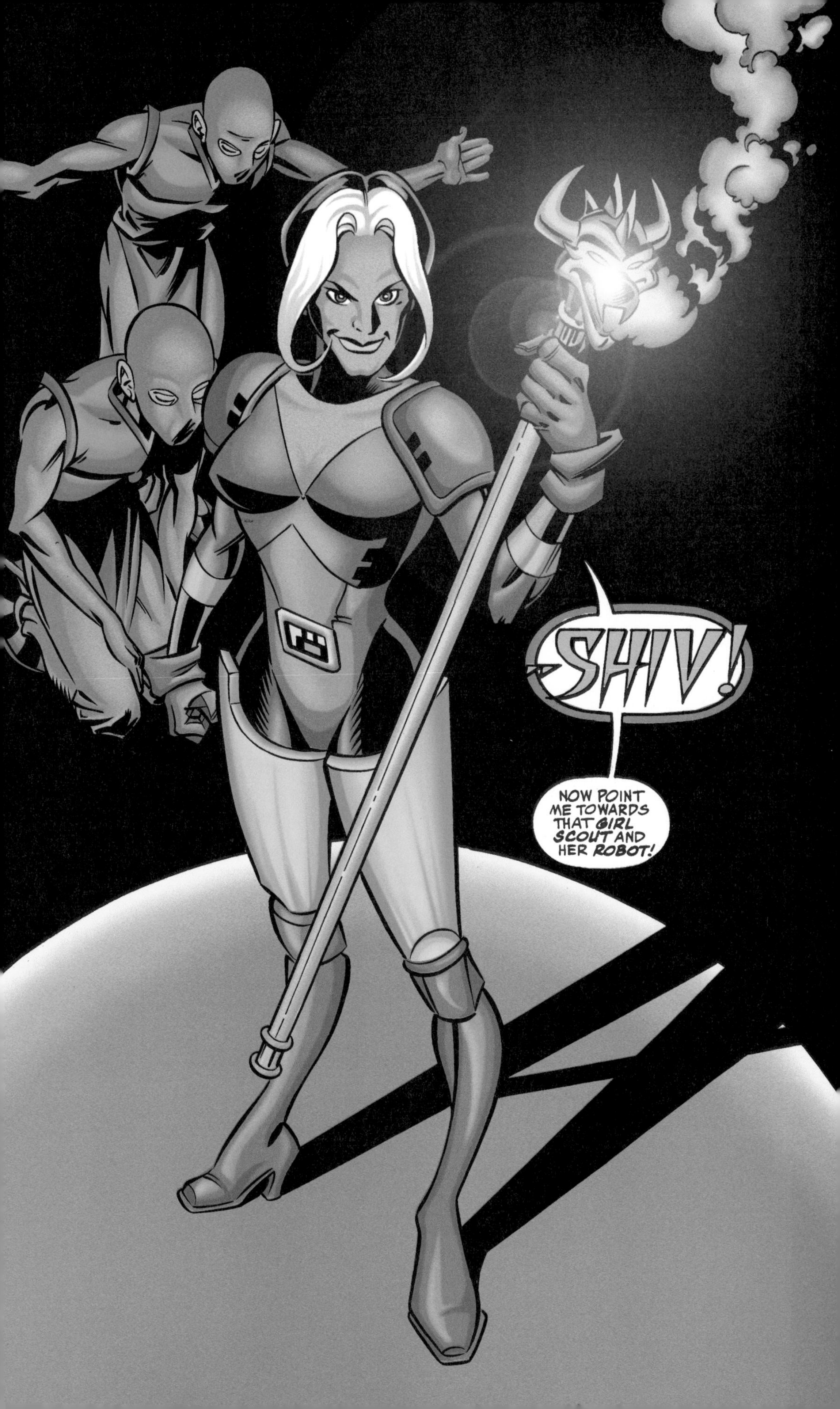
SHIV!
NOW POINT ME TOWARDS THAT GIRL SCOUT AND HER ROBOT!

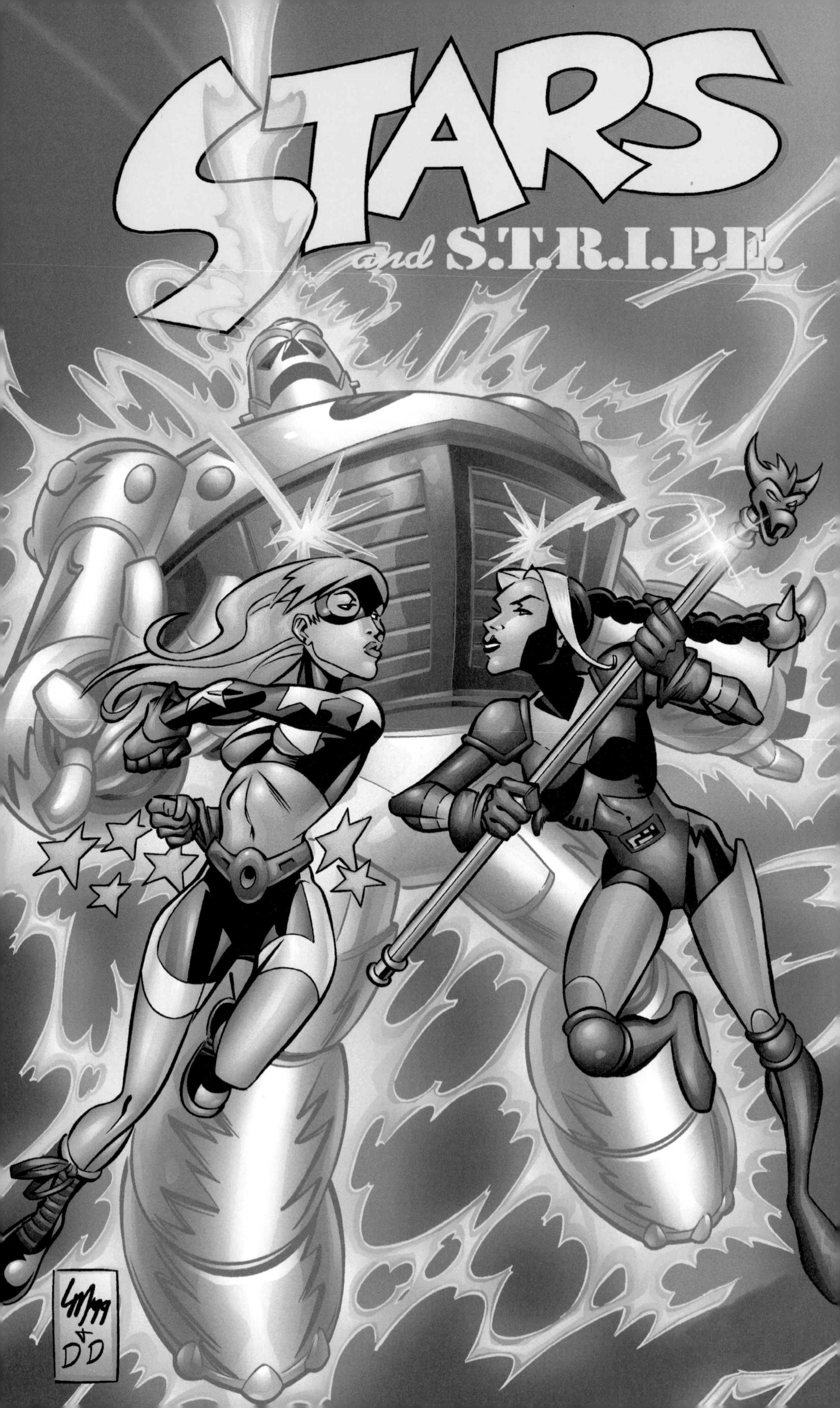
STARS
and S.T.R.I.P.E.

STARS AND S.T.R.I.P.E. #7

Written by GEOFF JOHNS
Pencils by LEE MODER
Inks by DAN DAVIS
Colors by TOM McCRAW
Letters by BILL OAKLEY
Cover art by LEE MODER and DAN DAVIS
Cover color by RICHARD & TANYA HORIE

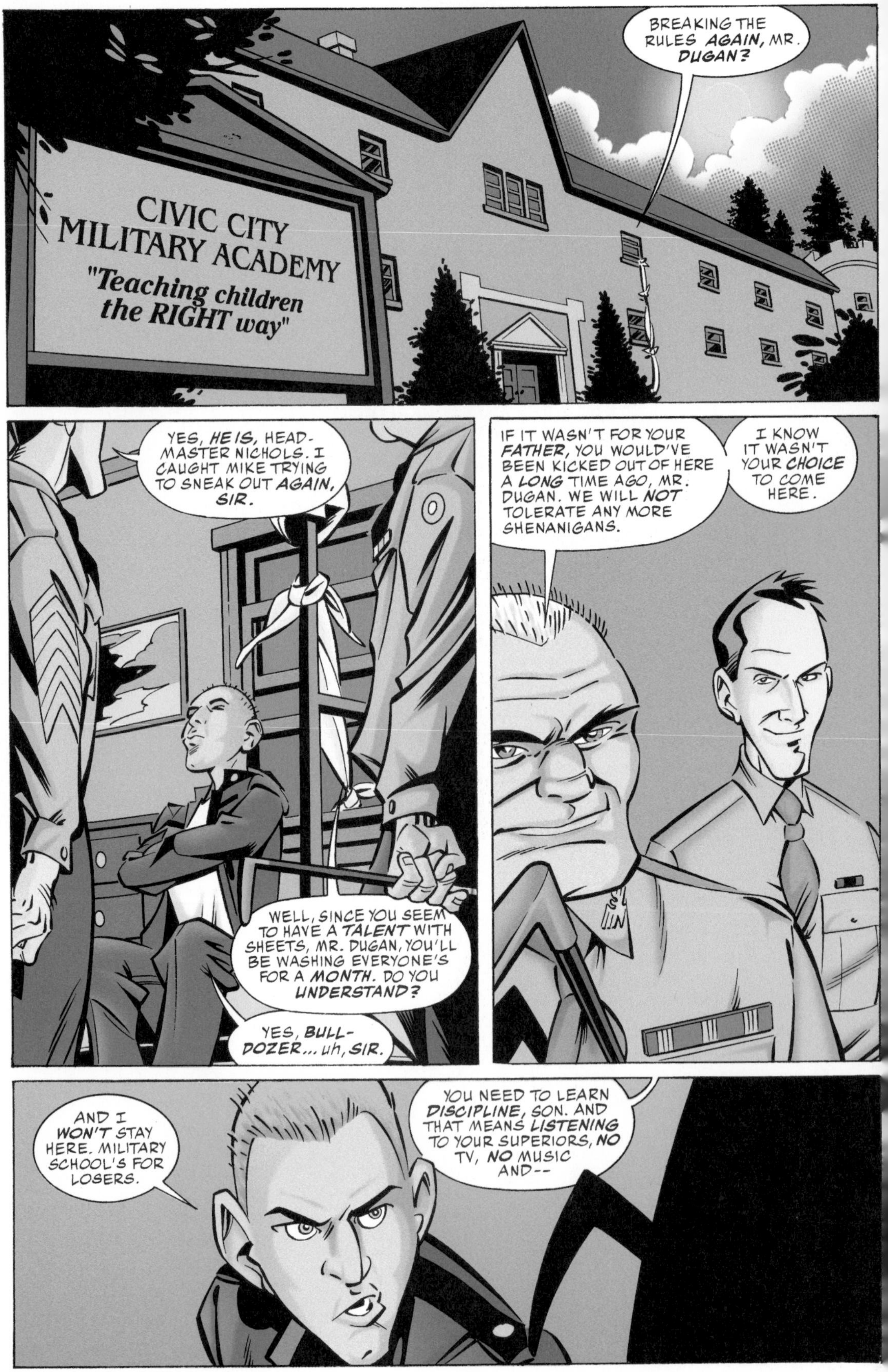
CIVIC CITY MILITARY ACADEMY
"Teaching children the RIGHT way"
BREAKING THE RULES AGAIN, MR. DUGAN?
YES, HE IS, HEADMASTER NICHOLS. I CAUGHT MIKE TRYING TO SNEAK OUT AGAIN, SIR.
WELL, SINCE YOU SEEM TO HAVE A TALENT WITH SHEETS, MR. DUGAN, YOU'LL BE WASHING EVERYONE'S FOR A MONTH. DO YOU UNDERSTAND?
YES, BULL-DOZER... uh, SIR.
IF IT WASN'T FOR YOUR FATHER, YOU WOULD'VE BEEN KICKED OUT OF HERE A LONG TIME AGO, MR. DUGAN. WE WILL NOT TOLERATE ANY MORE SHENANIGANS.
I KNOW IT WASN'T YOUR CHOICE TO COME HERE.
YOU NEED TO LEARN DISCIPLINE, SON. AND THAT MEANS LISTENING TO YOUR SUPERIORS, NO TV, NO MUSIC AND--
AND I WON'T STAY HERE. MILITARY SCHOOL'S FOR LOSERS.

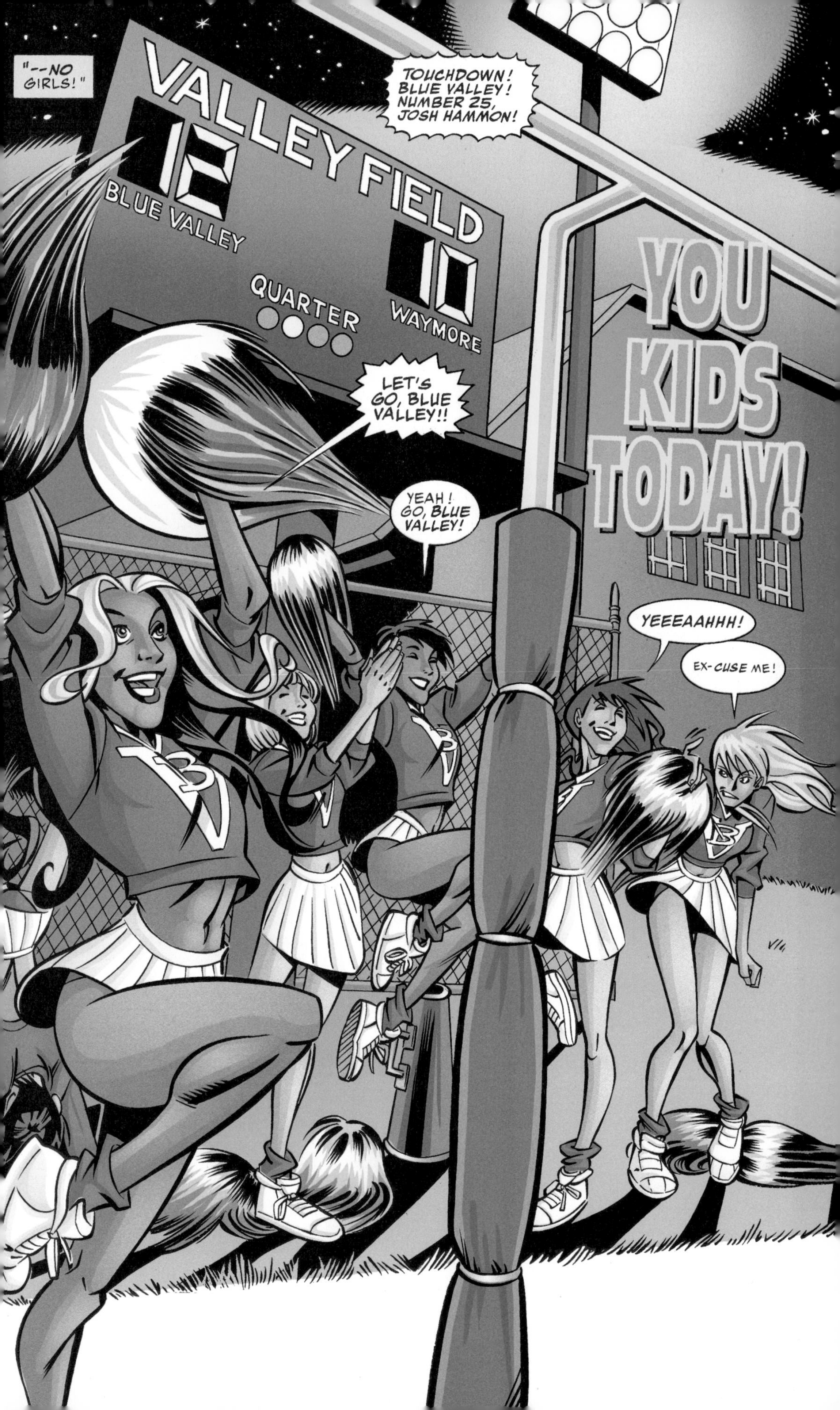
"--NO GIRLS!"
VALLEY FIELD
12
BLUE VALLEY
10
WAYMORE
QUARTER
TOUCHDOWN! BLUE VALLEY! NUMBER 25, JOSH HAMMON!
YOU KIDS TODAY!
LET'S GO, BLUE VALLEY!!
YEAH! GO, BLUE VALLEY!
YEEEAAHHH!
EX-CUSE ME!

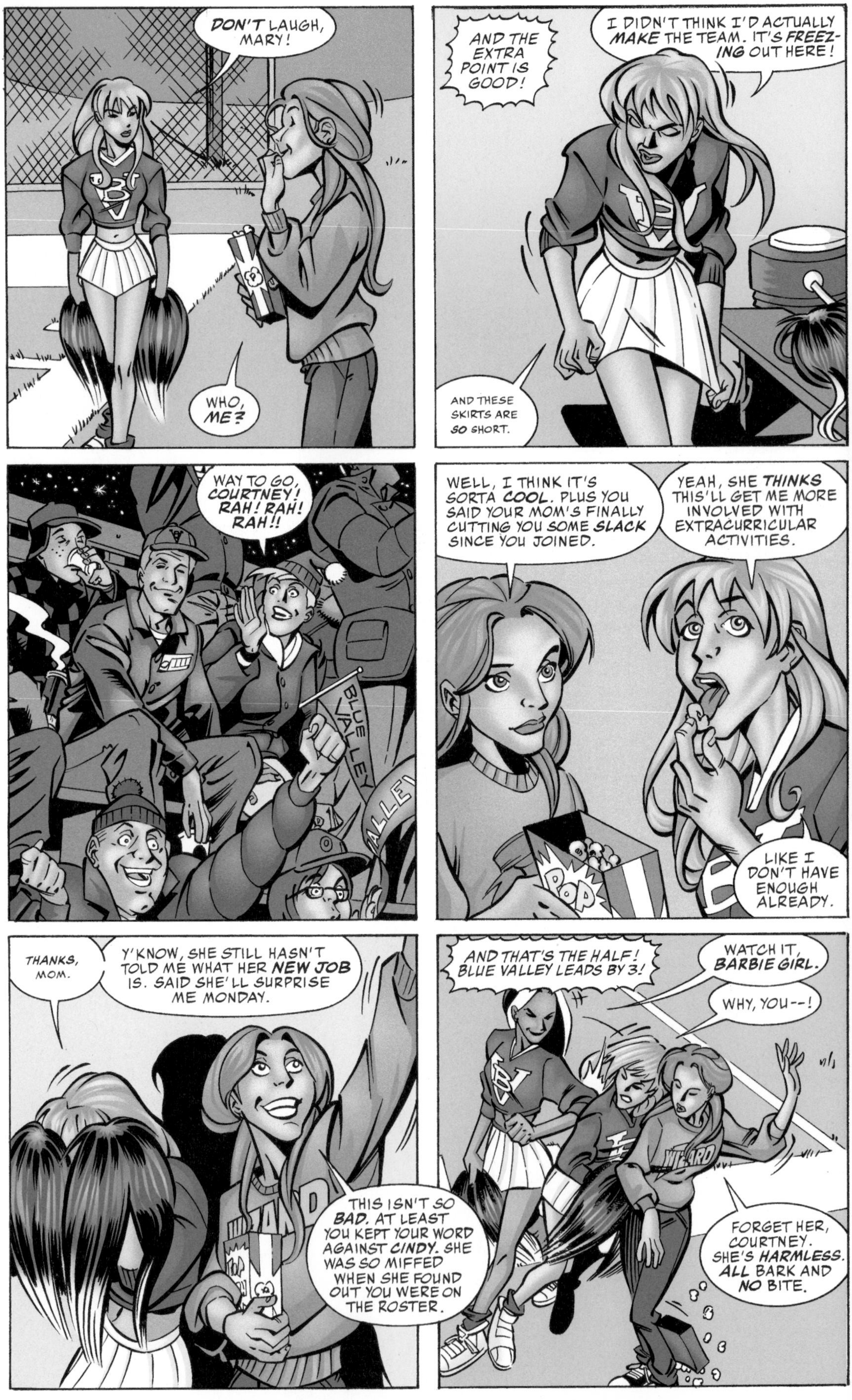
DON'T LAUGH, MARY!
WHO, ME?
AND THE EXTRA POINT IS GOOD!
I DIDN'T THINK I'D ACTUALLY MAKE THE TEAM. IT'S FREEZ-ING OUT HERE!
AND THESE SKIRTS ARE SO SHORT.
WAY TO GO, COURTNEY! RAH! RAH! RAH!!
BLUE VALLEY
VALLEY
WELL, I THINK IT'S SORTA COOL. PLUS YOU SAID YOUR MOM'S FINALLY CUTTING YOU SOME SLACK SINCE YOU JOINED.
YEAH, SHE THINKS THIS'LL GET ME MORE INVOLVED WITH EXTRACURRICULAR ACTIVITIES.
LIKE I DON'T HAVE ENOUGH ALREADY.
POP
THANKS, MOM.
Y'KNOW, SHE STILL HASN'T TOLD ME WHAT HER NEW JOB IS. SAID SHE'LL SURPRISE ME MONDAY.
THIS ISN'T SO BAD. AT LEAST YOU KEPT YOUR WORD AGAINST CINDY. SHE WAS SO MIFFED WHEN SHE FOUND OUT YOU WERE ON THE ROSTER.
AND THAT'S THE HALF! BLUE VALLEY LEADS BY 3!
WATCH IT, BARBIE GIRL.
WHY, YOU--!
FORGET HER, COURTNEY. SHE'S HARMLESS. ALL BARK AND NO BITE.

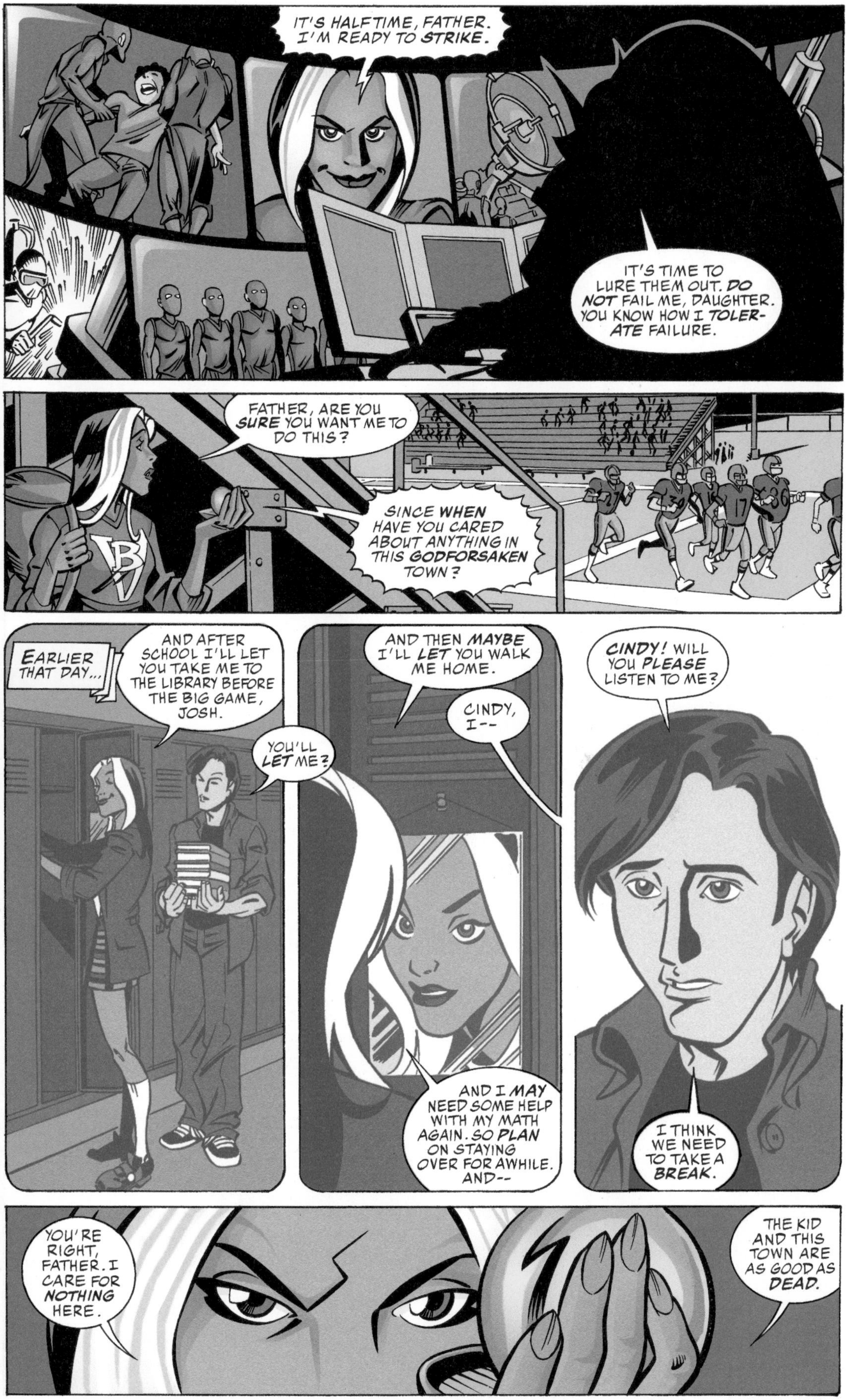
IT'S HALFTIME, FATHER. I'M READY TO STRIKE.
IT'S TIME TO LURE THEM OUT. DO NOT FAIL ME, DAUGHTER. YOU KNOW HOW I TOLERATE FAILURE.
FATHER, ARE YOU SURE YOU WANT ME TO DO THIS?
SINCE WHEN HAVE YOU CARED ABOUT ANYTHING IN THIS GODFORSAKEN TOWN?
EARLIER THAT DAY...
AND AFTER SCHOOL I'LL LET YOU TAKE ME TO THE LIBRARY BEFORE THE BIG GAME, JOSH.
YOU'LL LET ME?
AND THEN MAYBE I'LL LET YOU WALK ME HOME.
CINDY, I--
AND I MAY NEED SOME HELP WITH MY MATH AGAIN. SO PLAN ON STAYING OVER FOR AWHILE. AND--
CINDY! WILL YOU PLEASE LISTEN TO ME?
I THINK WE NEED TO TAKE A BREAK.
YOU'RE RIGHT, FATHER. I CARE FOR NOTHING HERE.
THE KID AND THIS TOWN ARE AS GOOD AS DEAD.

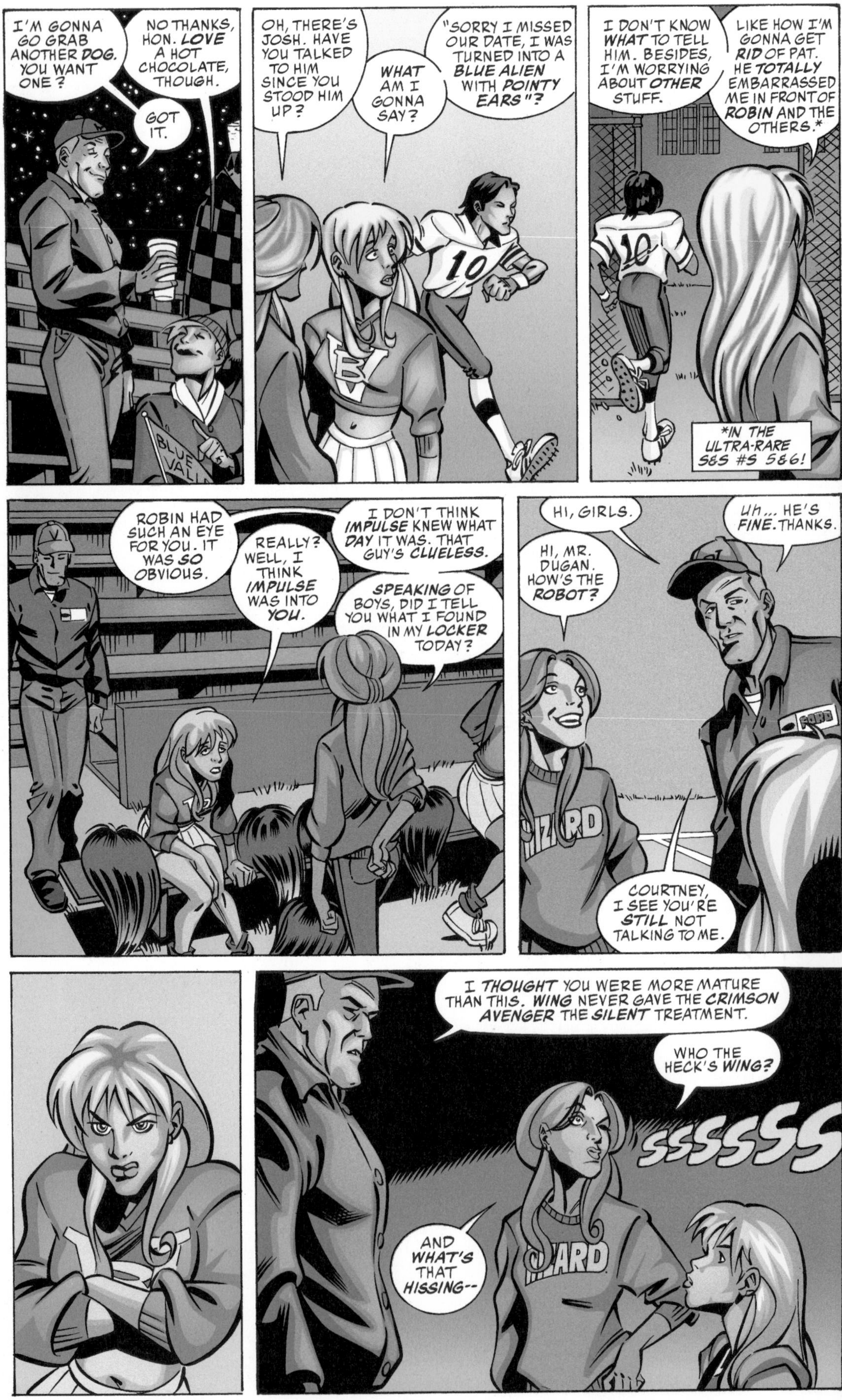

I'M GONNA GO GRAB ANOTHER DOG. YOU WANT ONE?
NO THANKS, HON. LOVE A HOT CHOCOLATE, THOUGH.
GOT IT.
BLUE VALL
OH, THERE'S JOSH. HAVE YOU TALKED TO HIM SINCE YOU STOOD HIM UP?
WHAT AM I GONNA SAY?
"SORRY I MISSED OUR DATE, I WAS TURNED INTO A BLUE ALIEN WITH POINTY EARS"?
I DON'T KNOW WHAT TO TELL HIM. BESIDES, I'M WORRYING ABOUT OTHER STUFF.
LIKE HOW I'M GONNA GET RID OF PAT. HE TOTALLY EMBARRASSED ME IN FRONT OF ROBIN AND THE OTHERS.*
*IN THE ULTRA-RARE S&S #S 5&6!
ROBIN HAD SUCH AN EYE FOR YOU. IT WAS SO OBVIOUS.
REALLY? WELL, I THINK IMPULSE WAS INTO YOU.
I DON'T THINK IMPULSE KNEW WHAT DAY IT WAS. THAT GUY'S CLUELESS.
SPEAKING OF BOYS, DID I TELL YOU WHAT I FOUND IN MY LOCKER TODAY?
HI, GIRLS.
HI, MR. DUGAN. HOW'S THE ROBOT?
UH... HE'S FINE. THANKS.
COURTNEY, I SEE YOU'RE STILL NOT TALKING TO ME.
I THOUGHT YOU WERE MORE MATURE THAN THIS. WING NEVER GAVE THE CRIMSON AVENGER THE SILENT TREATMENT.
WHO THE HECK'S WING?
SSSSSS
AND WHAT'S THAT HISSING--

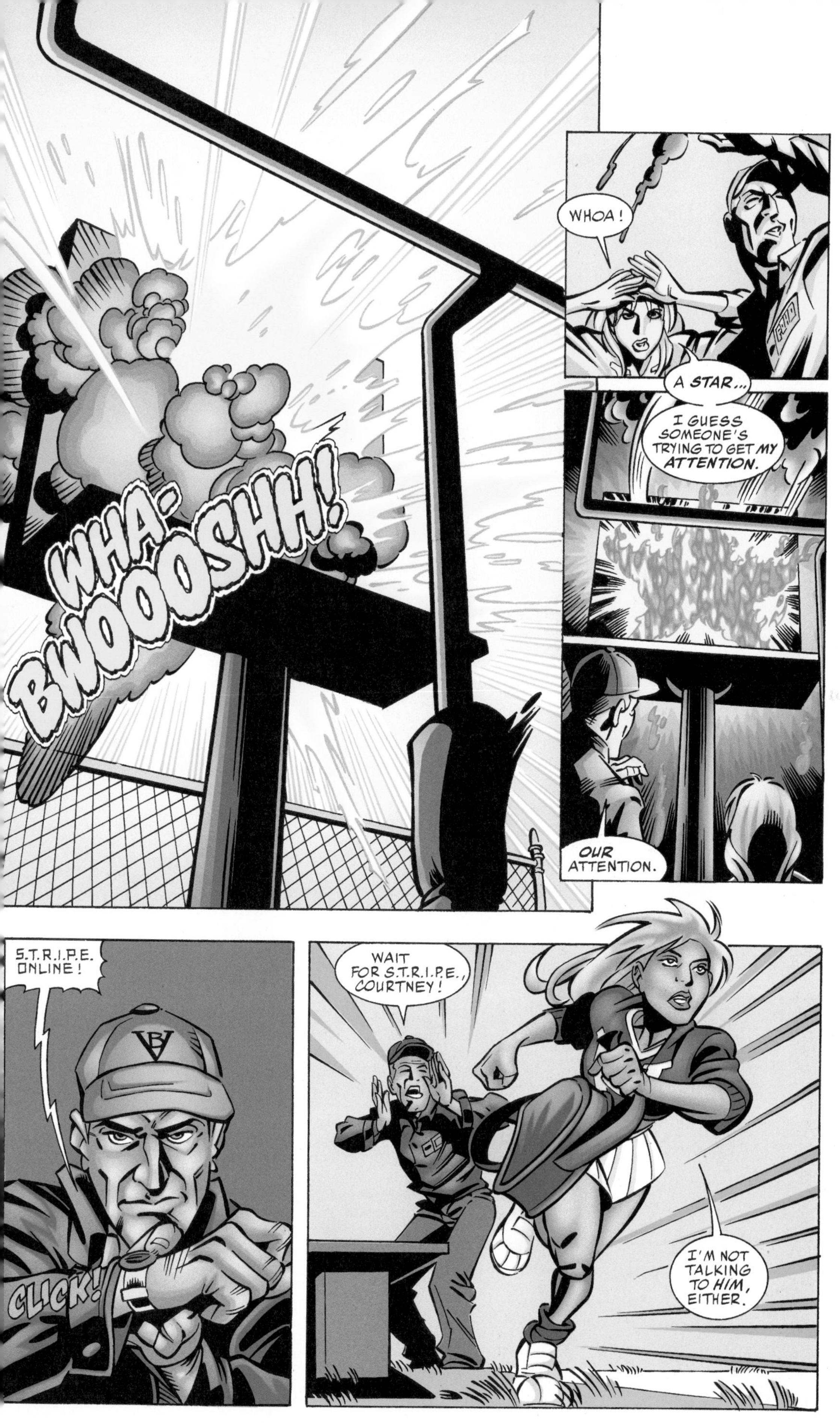
WHA-BWOOOSHH!
WHOA!
A STAR...
I GUESS SOMEONE'S TRYING TO GET MY ATTENTION.
OUR ATTENTION.
S.T.R.I.P.E. ONLINE!
CLICK!
WAIT FOR S.T.R.I.P.E., COURTNEY!
I'M NOT TALKING TO HIM, EITHER.

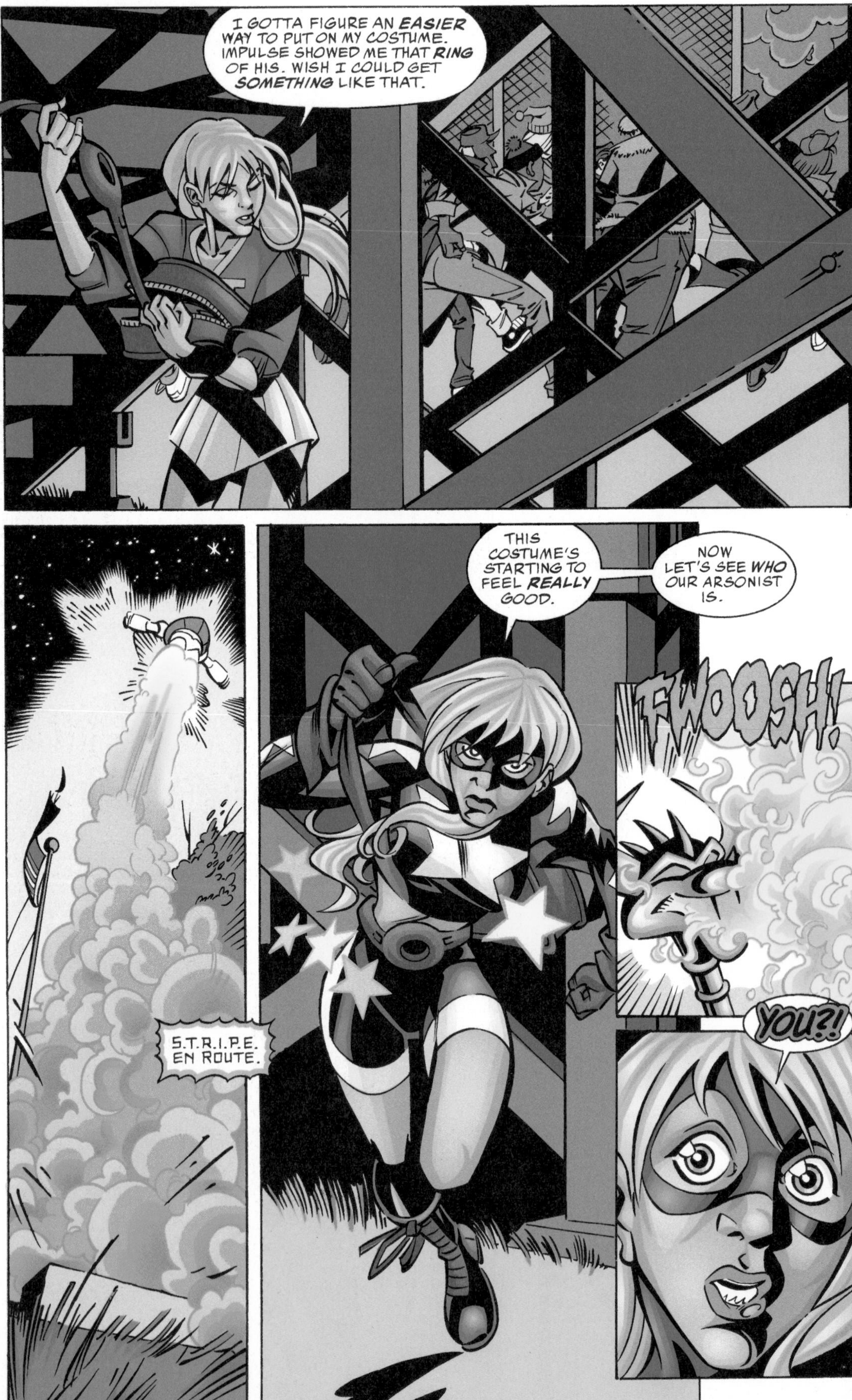

I GOTTA FIGURE AN *EASIER* WAY TO PUT ON MY COSTUME. IMPULSE SHOWED ME THAT *RING* OF HIS. WISH I COULD GET *SOMETHING* LIKE THAT.
S.T.R.I.P.E. EN ROUTE.
THIS COSTUME'S STARTING TO FEEL *REALLY* GOOD.
NOW LET'S SEE *WHO* OUR ARSONIST IS.
FWOOSH!
YOU?!

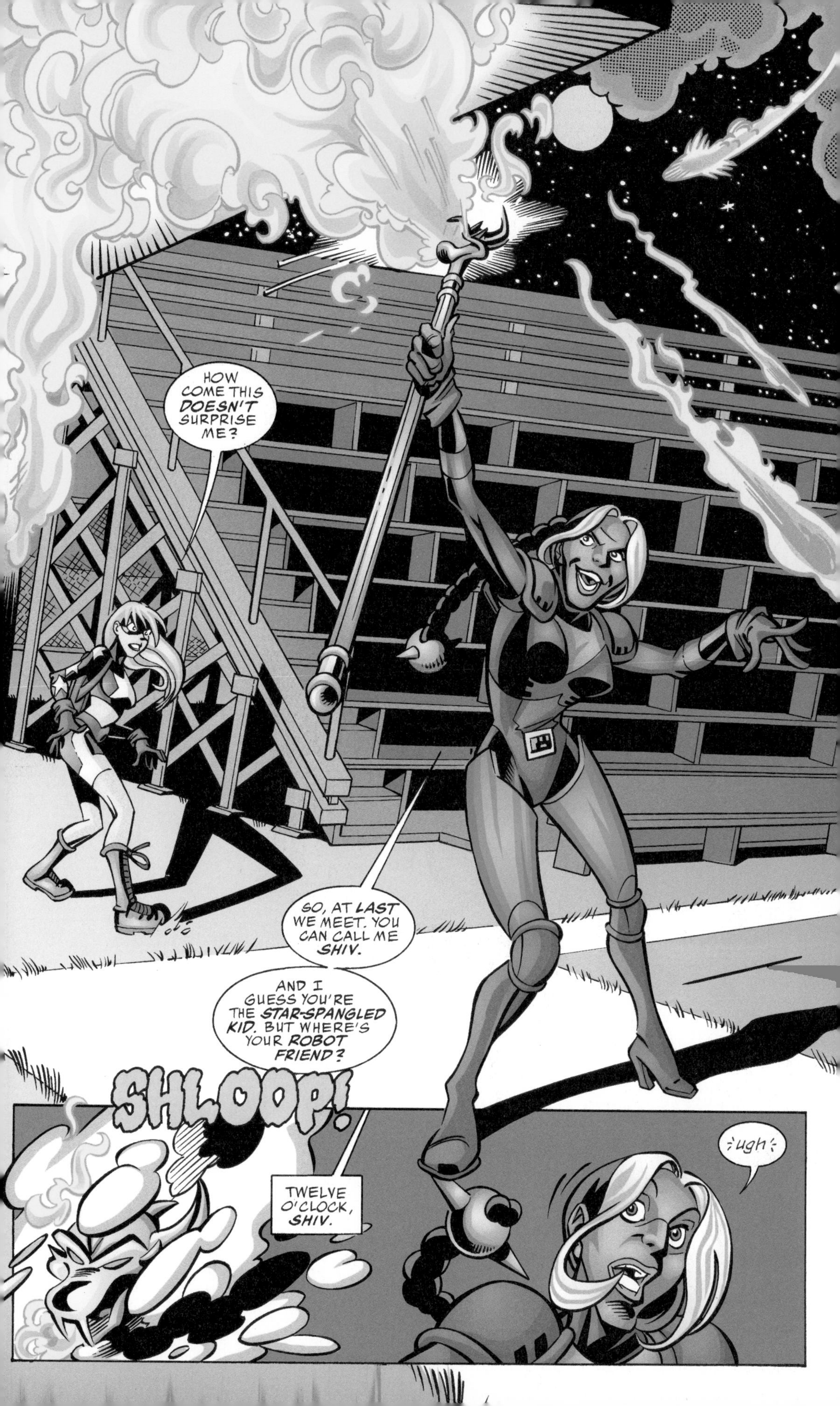

HOW COME THIS DOESN'T SURPRISE ME?
SO, AT LAST WE MEET. YOU CAN CALL ME SHIV.
AND I GUESS YOU'RE THE STAR-SPANGLED KID. BUT WHERE'S YOUR ROBOT FRIEND?
SHLOOP!
TWELVE O'CLOCK, SHIV.
ugh

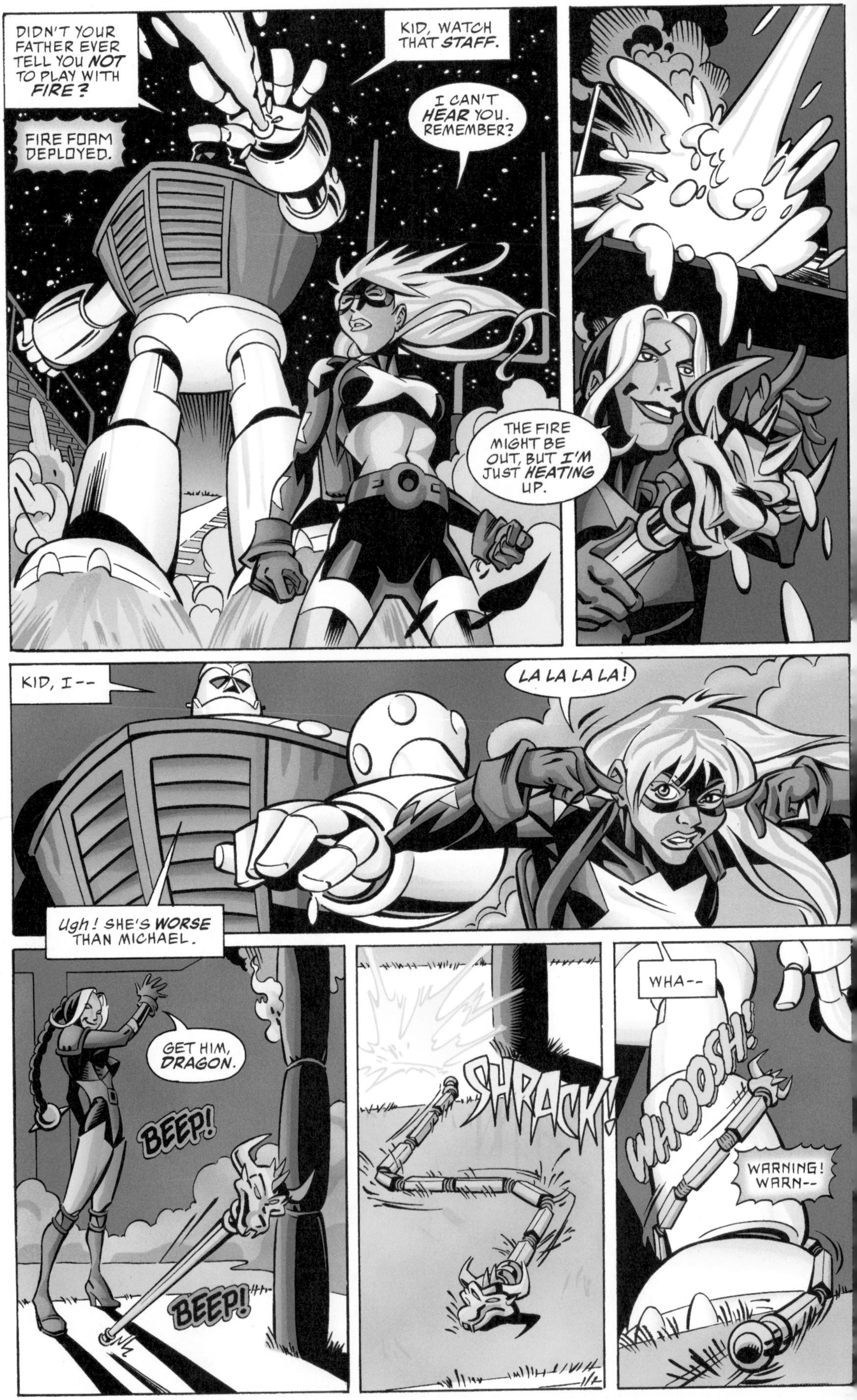

DIDN'T YOUR FATHER EVER TELL YOU NOT TO PLAY WITH FIRE?
KID, WATCH THAT STAFF.
FIRE FOAM DEPLOYED.
I CAN'T HEAR YOU. REMEMBER?
THE FIRE MIGHT BE OUT, BUT I'M JUST HEATING UP.
KID, I--
LA LA LA LA!
Ugh! SHE'S WORSE THAN MICHAEL.
GET HIM, DRAGON.
BEEP!
BEEP!
SHRACK!
WHA--
WHOOSH!
WARNING! WARN--

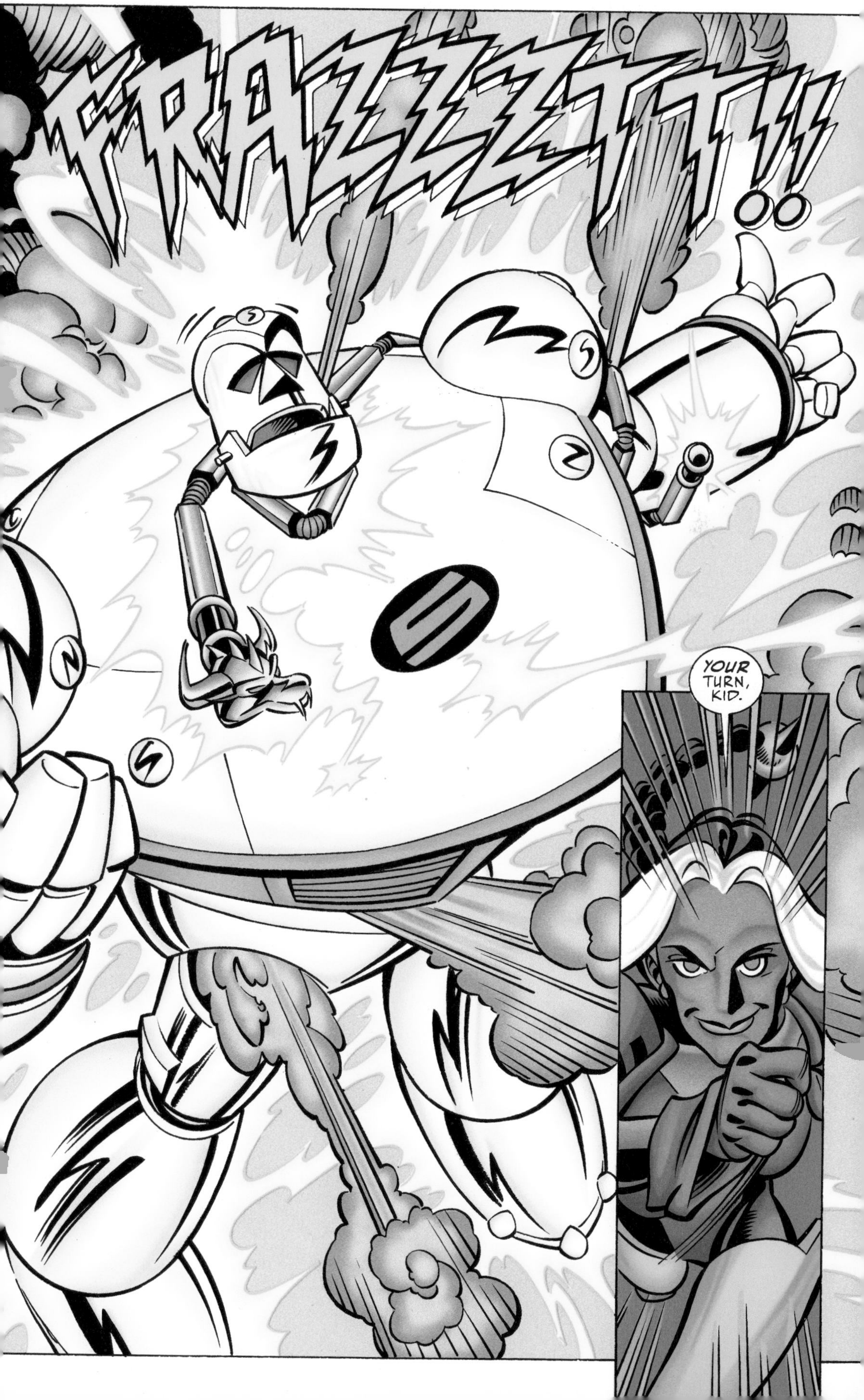
FRAZZZTT!!
YOUR TURN, KID.

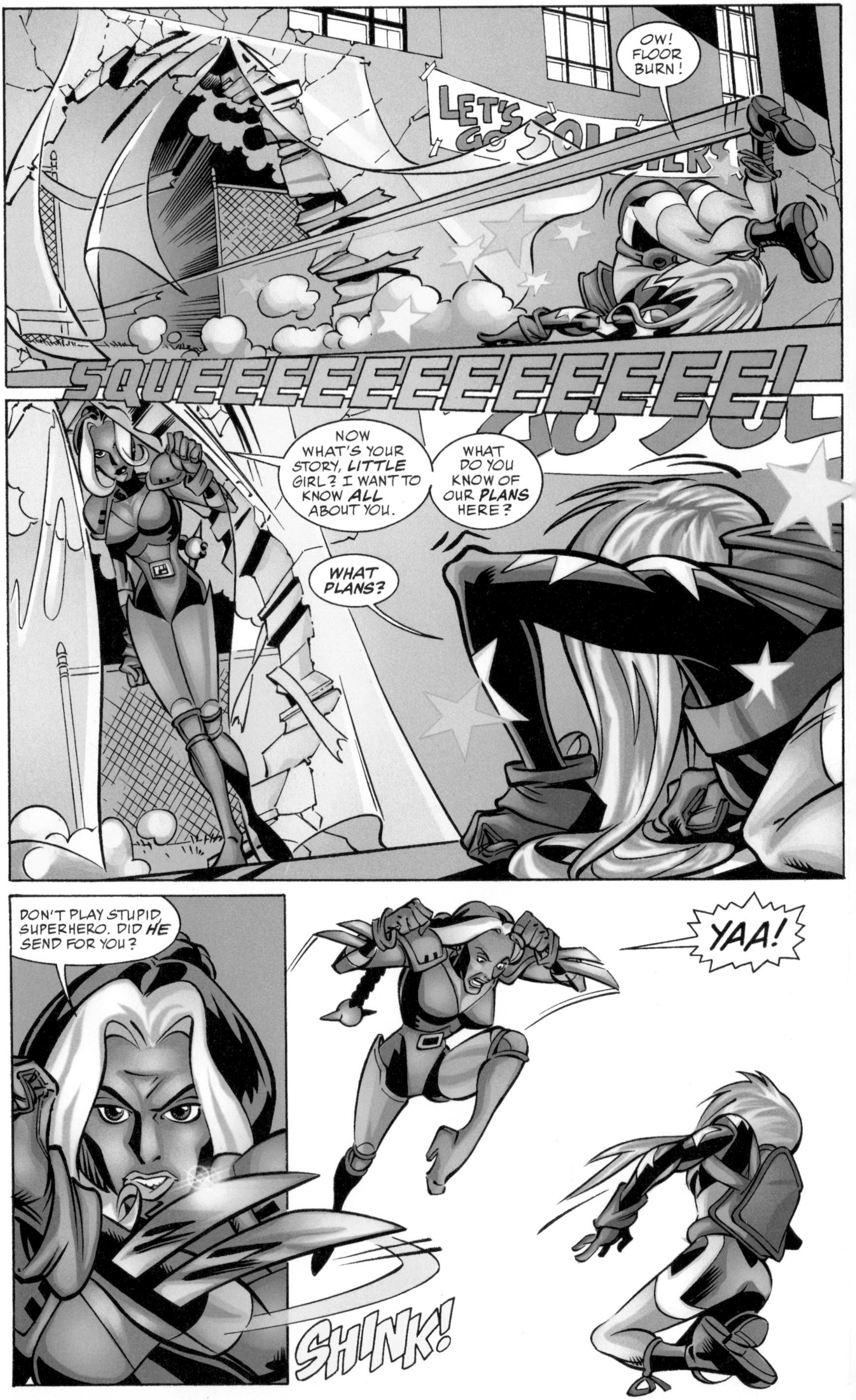
OW! FLOOR BURN!
LET'S GO SOLDIERS
SQUEEEEEEEEEEEEEE!
NOW WHAT'S YOUR STORY, LITTLE GIRL? I WANT TO KNOW ALL ABOUT YOU.
WHAT DO YOU KNOW OF OUR PLANS HERE?
WHAT PLANS?
DON'T PLAY STUPID, SUPERHERO. DID HE SEND FOR YOU?
SHINK!
YAA!

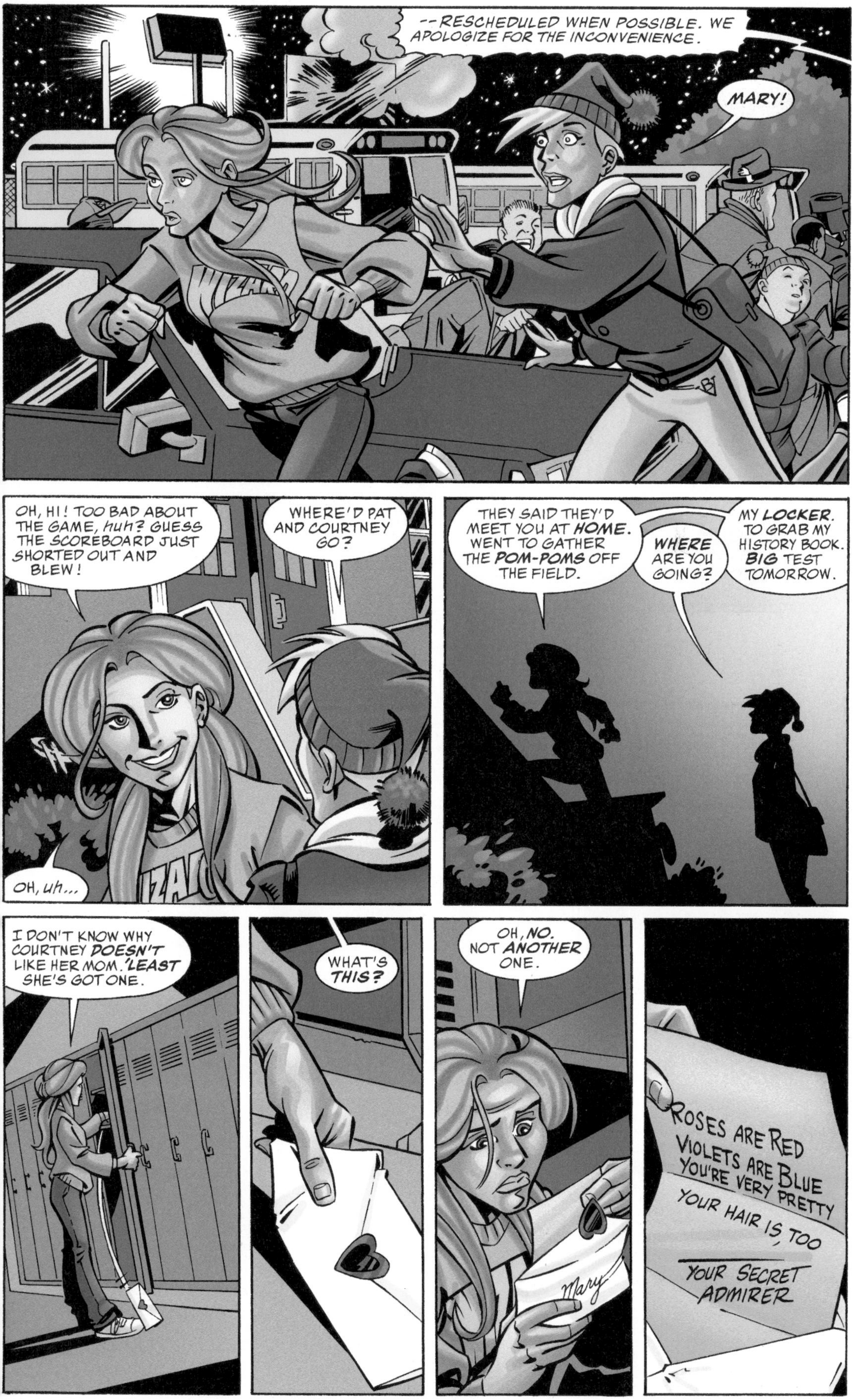

--RESCHEDULED WHEN POSSIBLE. WE APOLOGIZE FOR THE INCONVENIENCE.
MARY!
OH, HI! TOO BAD ABOUT THE GAME, huh? GUESS THE SCOREBOARD JUST SHORTED OUT AND BLEW!
WHERE'D PAT AND COURTNEY GO?
OH, uh...
THEY SAID THEY'D MEET YOU AT HOME. WENT TO GATHER THE POM-POMS OFF THE FIELD.
WHERE ARE YOU GOING?
MY LOCKER. TO GRAB MY HISTORY BOOK. BIG TEST TOMORROW.
I DON'T KNOW WHY COURTNEY DOESN'T LIKE HER MOM. 'LEAST SHE'S GOT ONE.
WHAT'S THIS?
OH, NO. NOT ANOTHER ONE.
Mary
ROSES ARE RED
VIOLETS ARE BLUE
YOU'RE VERY PRETTY
YOUR HAIR IS, TOO
YOUR SECRET ADMIRER

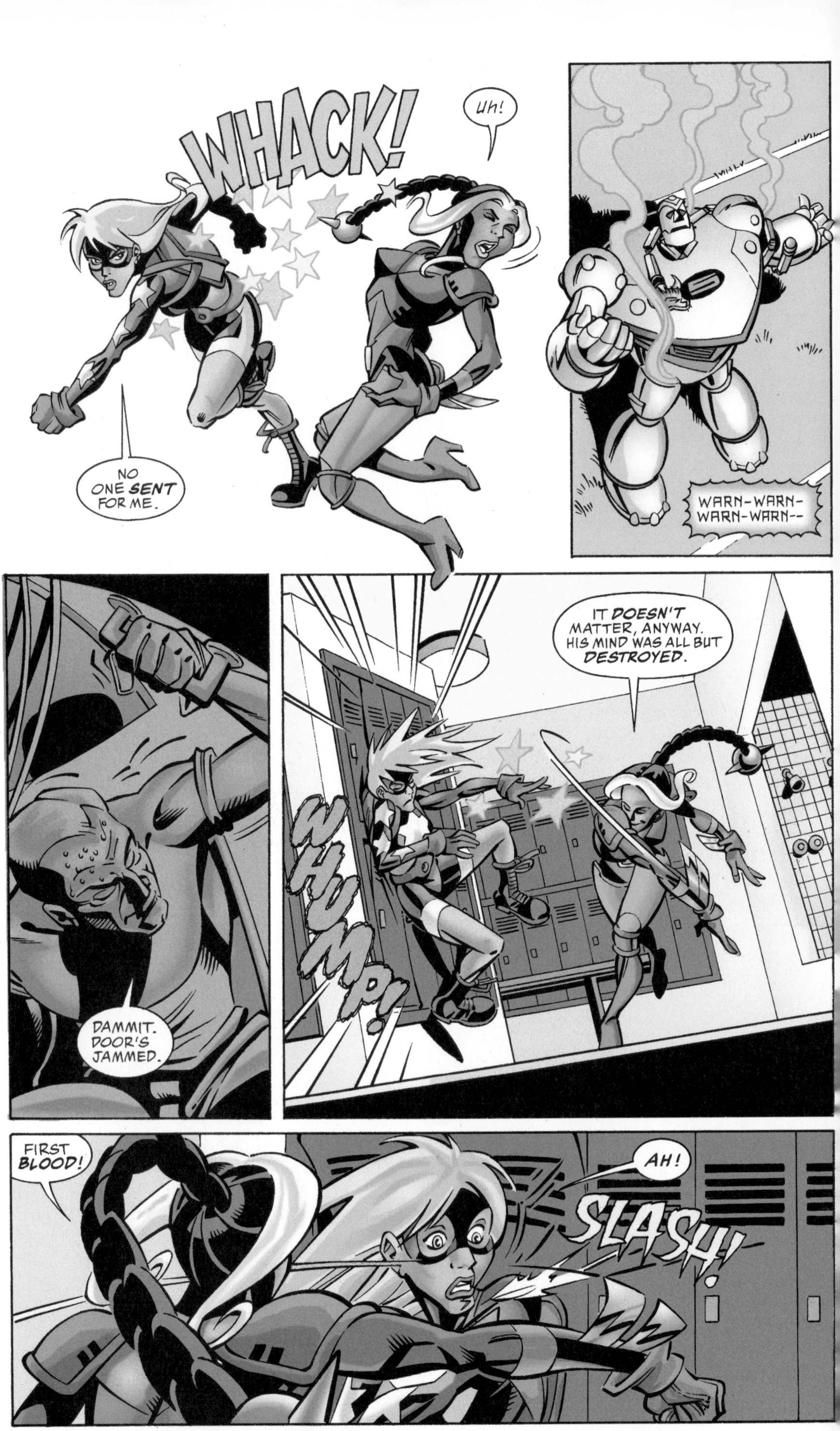
WHACK!
UH!
NO ONE SENT FOR ME.
WARN-WARN-WARN-WARN--
DAMMIT. DOOR'S JAMMED.
IT DOESN'T MATTER, ANYWAY. HIS MIND WAS ALL BUT DESTROYED.
WHUMP!
FIRST BLOOD!
AH!
SLASH!

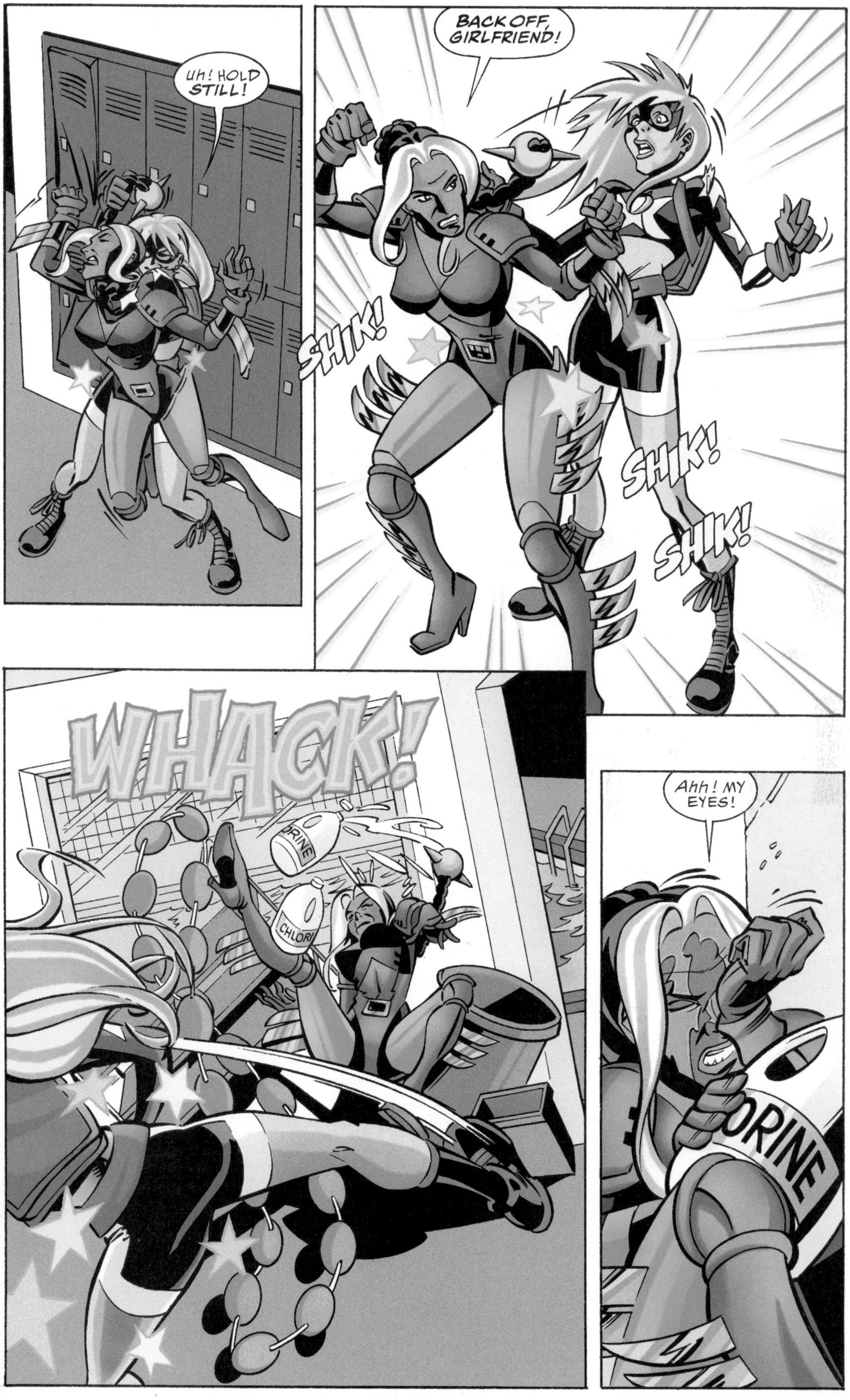
UH! HOLD STILL!
BACK OFF, GIRLFRIEND!
SHIK!
SHIK!
SHIK!
WHACK!
CHLORINE
CHLORI
Ahh! MY EYES!
ORINE

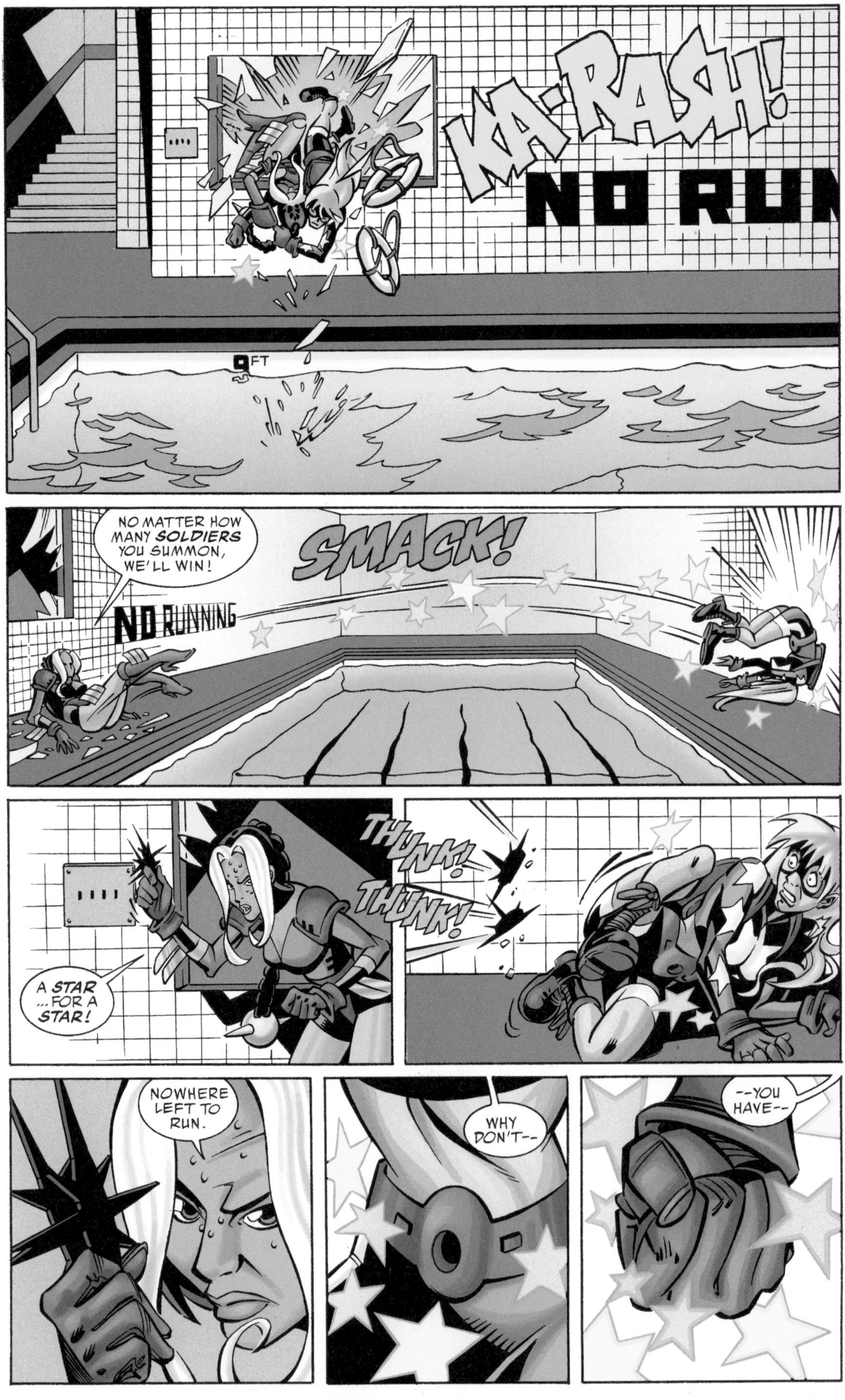
KA-RASH!
NO RUN
9 FT
NO MATTER HOW MANY SOLDIERS YOU SUMMON, WE'LL WIN!
SMACK!
NO RUNNING
A STAR ...FOR A STAR!
THUNK!
THUNK!
NOWHERE LEFT TO RUN.
WHY DON'T--
--YOU HAVE--

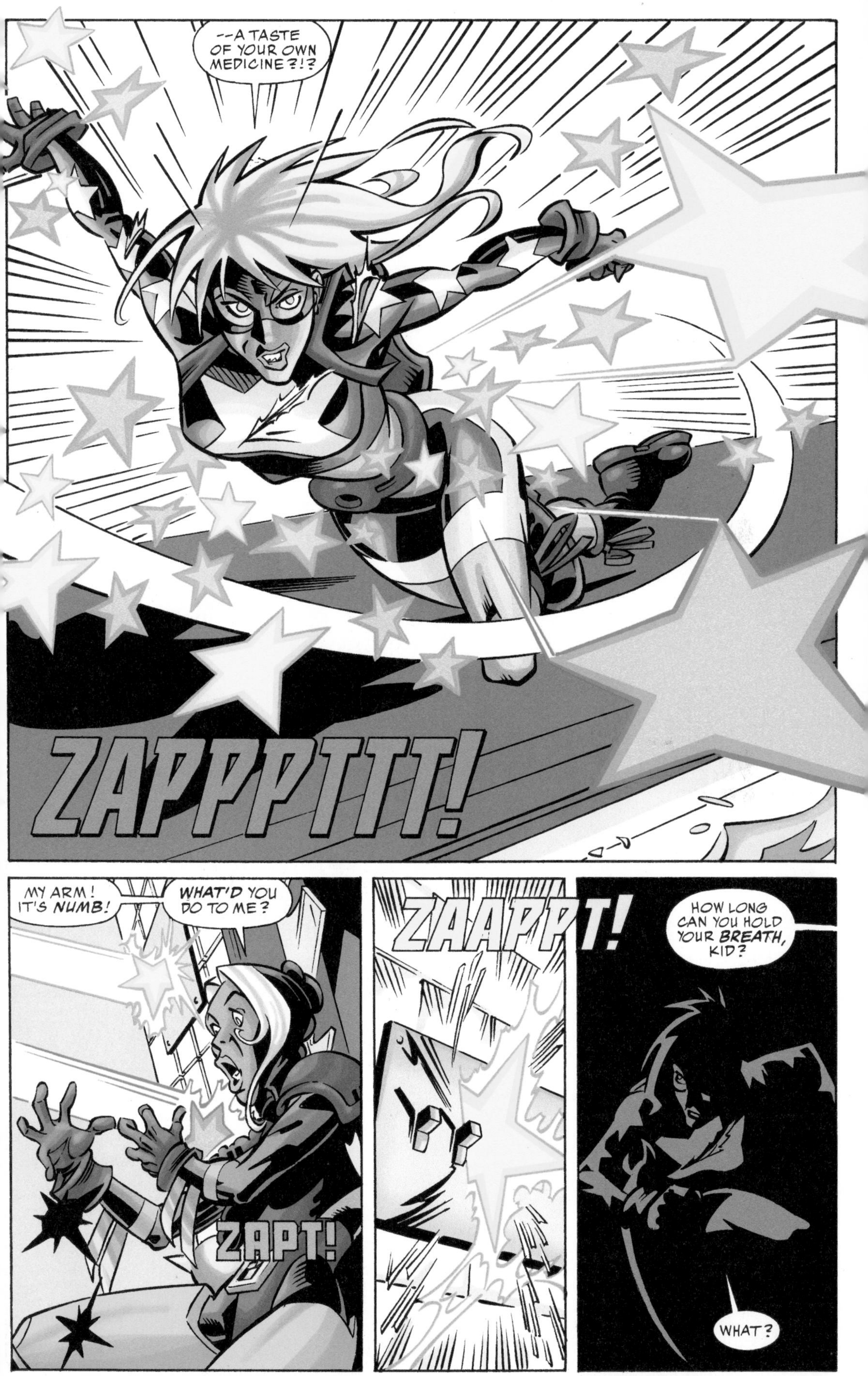
--A TASTE OF YOUR OWN MEDICINE?!?
ZAPPPTTT!
MY ARM! IT'S NUMB!
WHAT'D YOU DO TO ME?
ZAPT!
ZAAPPT!
HOW LONG CAN YOU HOLD YOUR BREATH, KID?
WHAT?

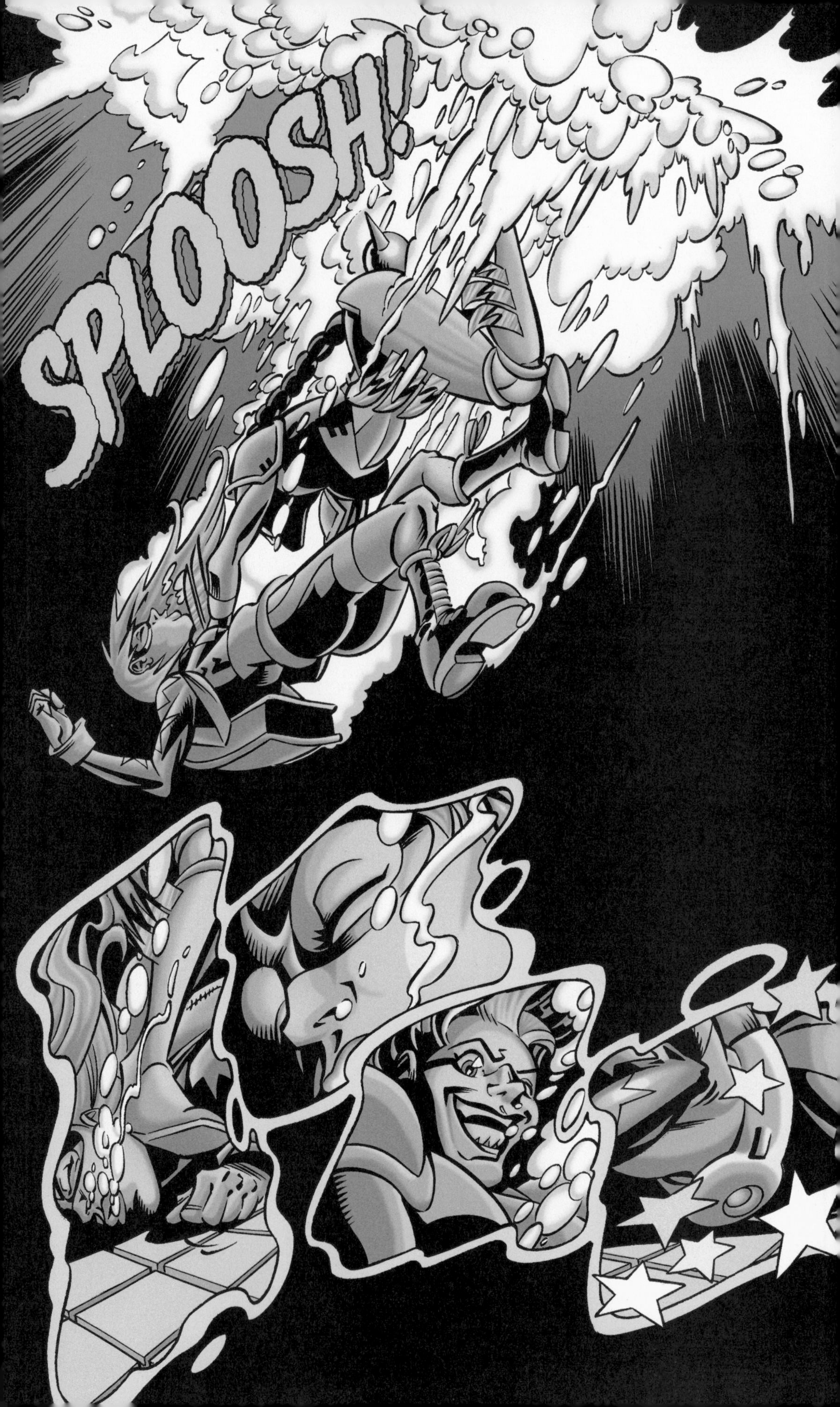
SPLOOSH!

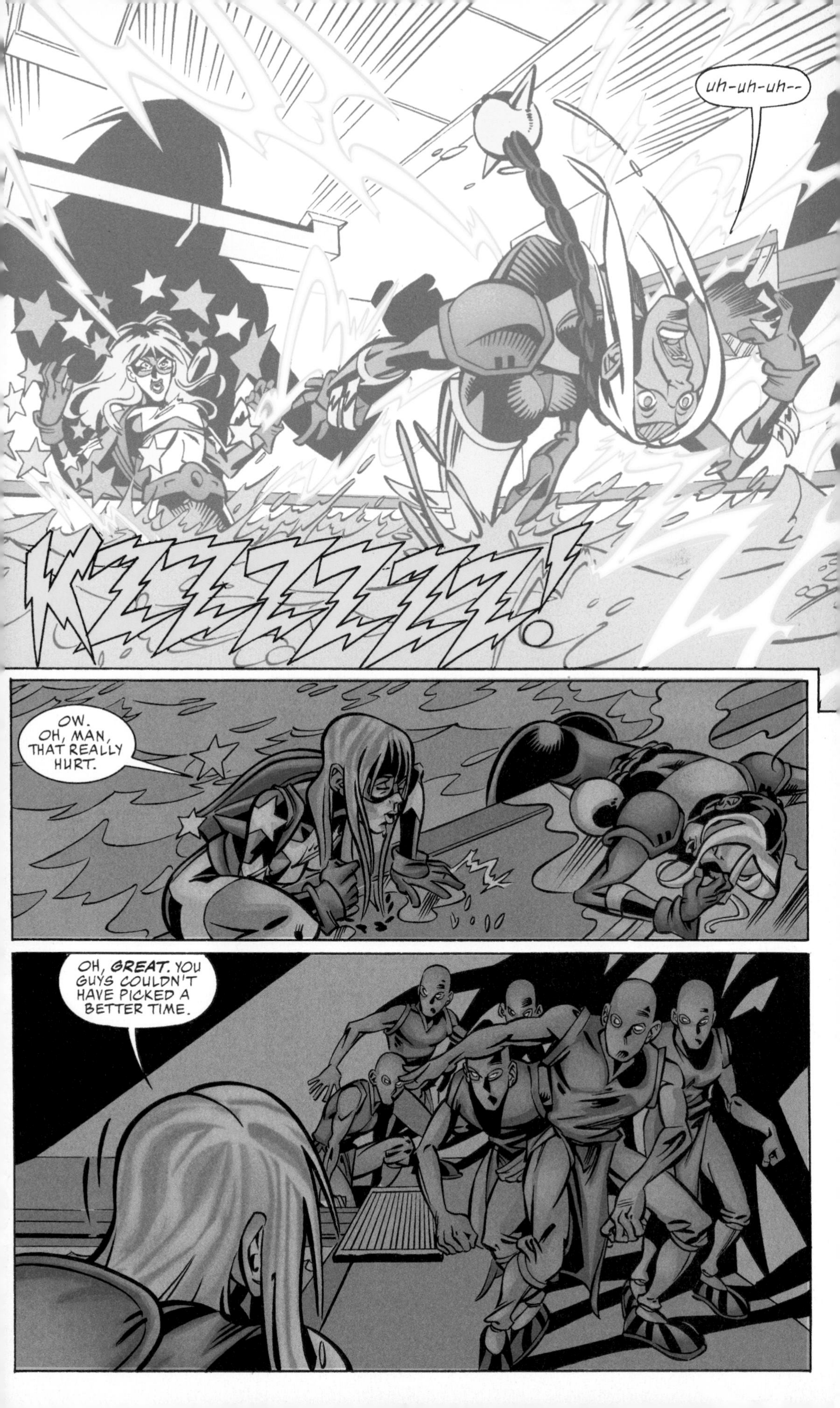
uh-uh-uh--
KZZZZZZT!
OW. OH, MAN, THAT REALLY HURT.
OH, GREAT. YOU GUYS COULDN'T HAVE PICKED A BETTER TIME.

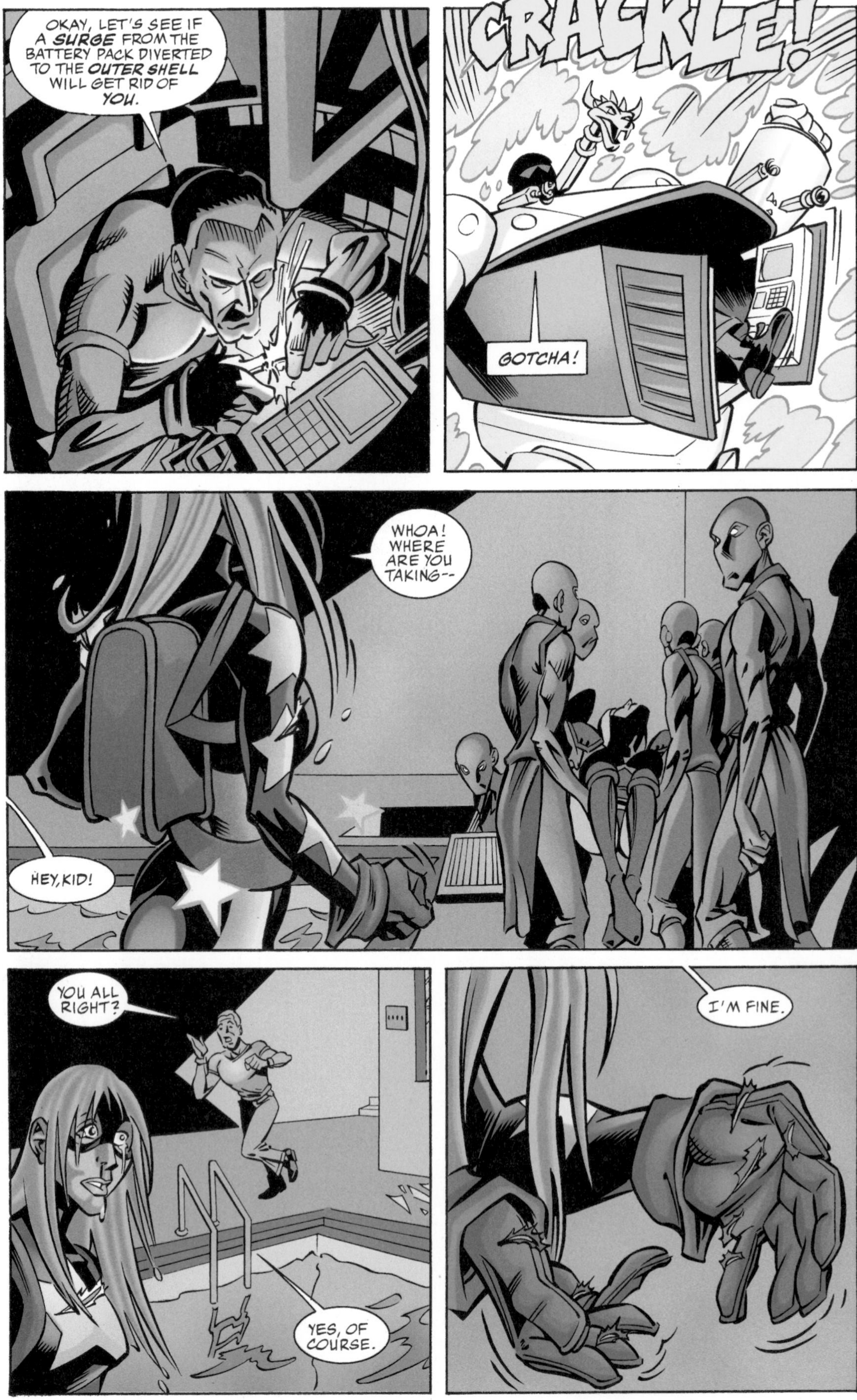
OKAY, LET'S SEE IF A SURGE FROM THE BATTERY PACK DIVERTED TO THE OUTER SHELL WILL GET RID OF YOU.
CRACKLE!
GOTCHA!
WHOA! WHERE ARE YOU TAKING--
HEY, KID!
YOU ALL RIGHT?
YES, OF COURSE.
I'M FINE.

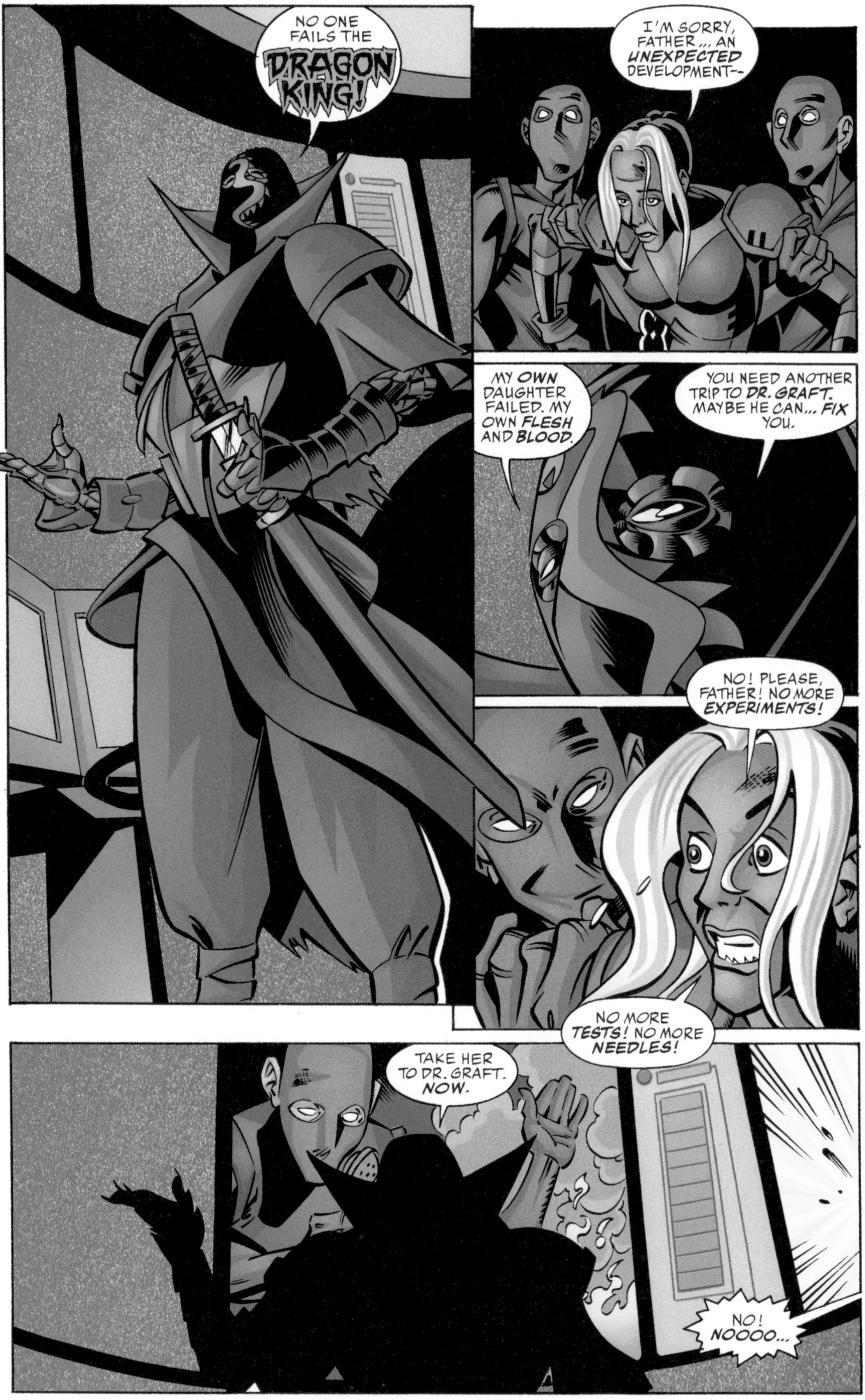
NO ONE FAILS THE DRAGON KING!
I'M SORRY, FATHER... AN UNEXPECTED DEVELOPMENT--
MY OWN DAUGHTER FAILED. MY OWN FLESH AND BLOOD.
YOU NEED ANOTHER TRIP TO DR. GRAFT. MAYBE HE CAN... FIX YOU.
NO! PLEASE, FATHER! NO MORE EXPERIMENTS!
NO MORE TESTS! NO MORE NEEDLES!
TAKE HER TO DR. GRAFT. NOW.
NO! NOOOO...

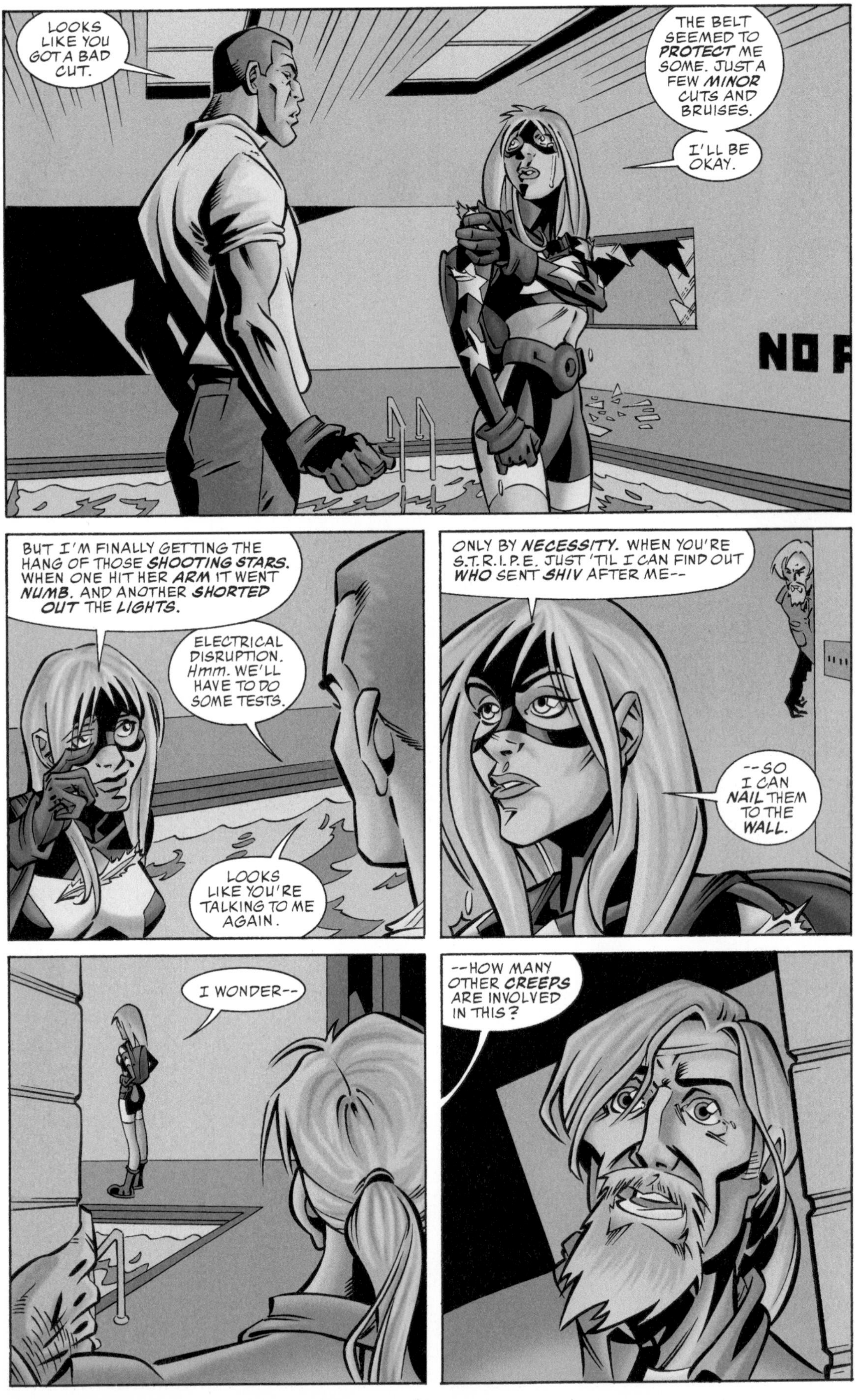
LOOKS LIKE YOU GOT A BAD CUT.
THE BELT SEEMED TO PROTECT ME SOME. JUST A FEW MINOR CUTS AND BRUISES.
I'LL BE OKAY.
NO P
BUT I'M FINALLY GETTING THE HANG OF THOSE SHOOTING STARS. WHEN ONE HIT HER ARM IT WENT NUMB. AND ANOTHER SHORTED OUT THE LIGHTS.
ELECTRICAL DISRUPTION. Hmm. WE'LL HAVE TO DO SOME TESTS.
LOOKS LIKE YOU'RE TALKING TO ME AGAIN.
ONLY BY NECESSITY. WHEN YOU'RE S.T.R.I.P.E. JUST 'TIL I CAN FIND OUT WHO SENT SHIV AFTER ME--
--SO I CAN NAIL THEM TO THE WALL.
I WONDER--
--HOW MANY OTHER CREEPS ARE INVOLVED IN THIS?

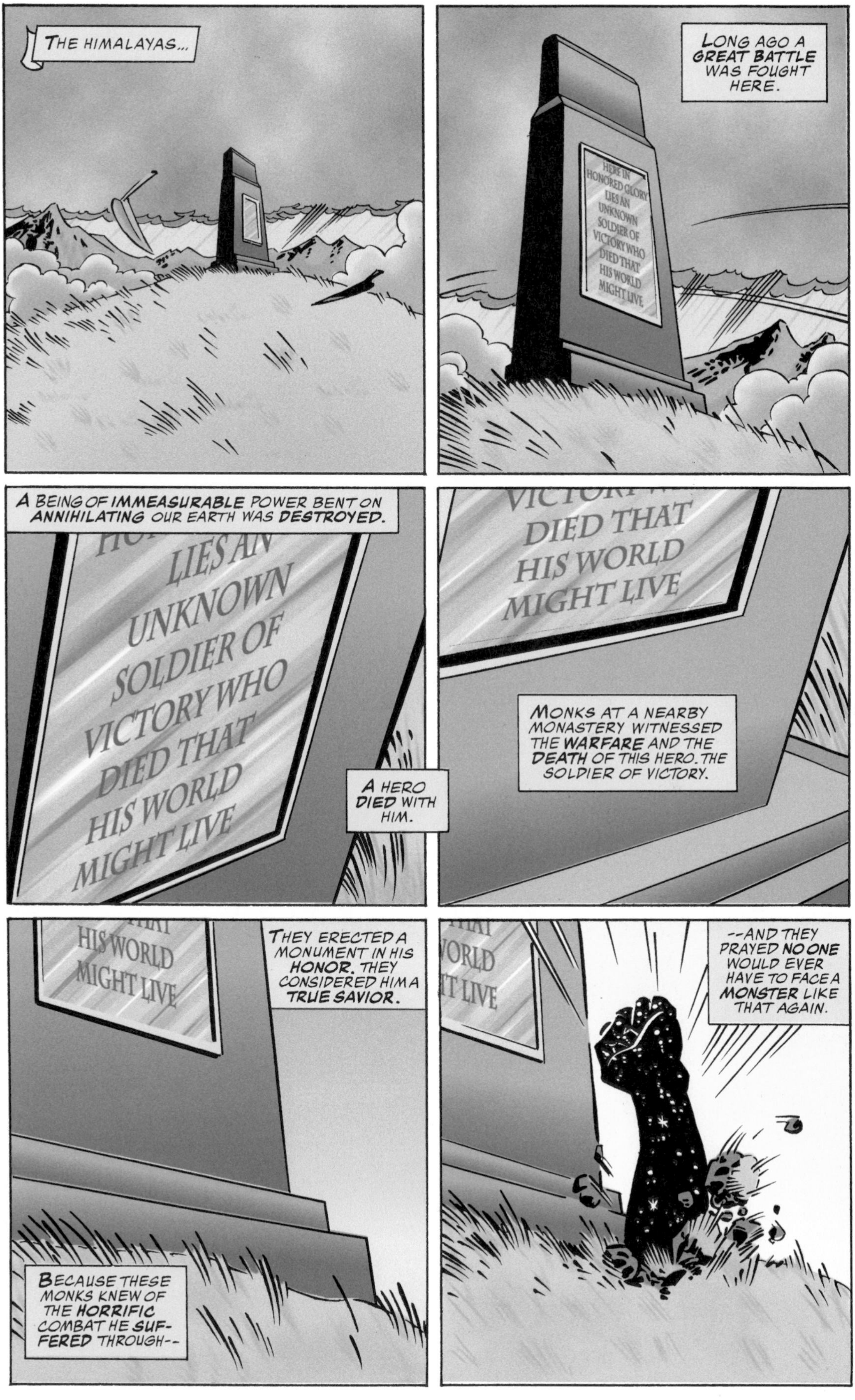
THE HIMALAYAS...
LONG AGO A GREAT BATTLE WAS FOUGHT HERE.
HERE IN HONORED GLORY LIES AN UNKNOWN SOLDIER OF VICTORY WHO DIED THAT HIS WORLD MIGHT LIVE
A BEING OF IMMEASURABLE POWER BENT ON ANNIHILATING OUR EARTH WAS DESTROYED.
LIES AN UNKNOWN SOLDIER OF VICTORY WHO DIED THAT HIS WORLD MIGHT LIVE
A HERO DIED WITH HIM.
DIED THAT HIS WORLD MIGHT LIVE
MONKS AT A NEARBY MONASTERY WITNESSED THE WARFARE AND THE DEATH OF THIS HERO. THE SOLDIER OF VICTORY.
HIS WORLD MIGHT LIVE
THEY ERECTED A MONUMENT IN HIS HONOR. THEY CONSIDERED HIM A TRUE SAVIOR.
BECAUSE THESE MONKS KNEW OF THE HORRIFIC COMBAT HE SUF-FERED THROUGH--
--AND THEY PRAYED NO ONE WOULD EVER HAVE TO FACE A MONSTER LIKE THAT AGAIN.

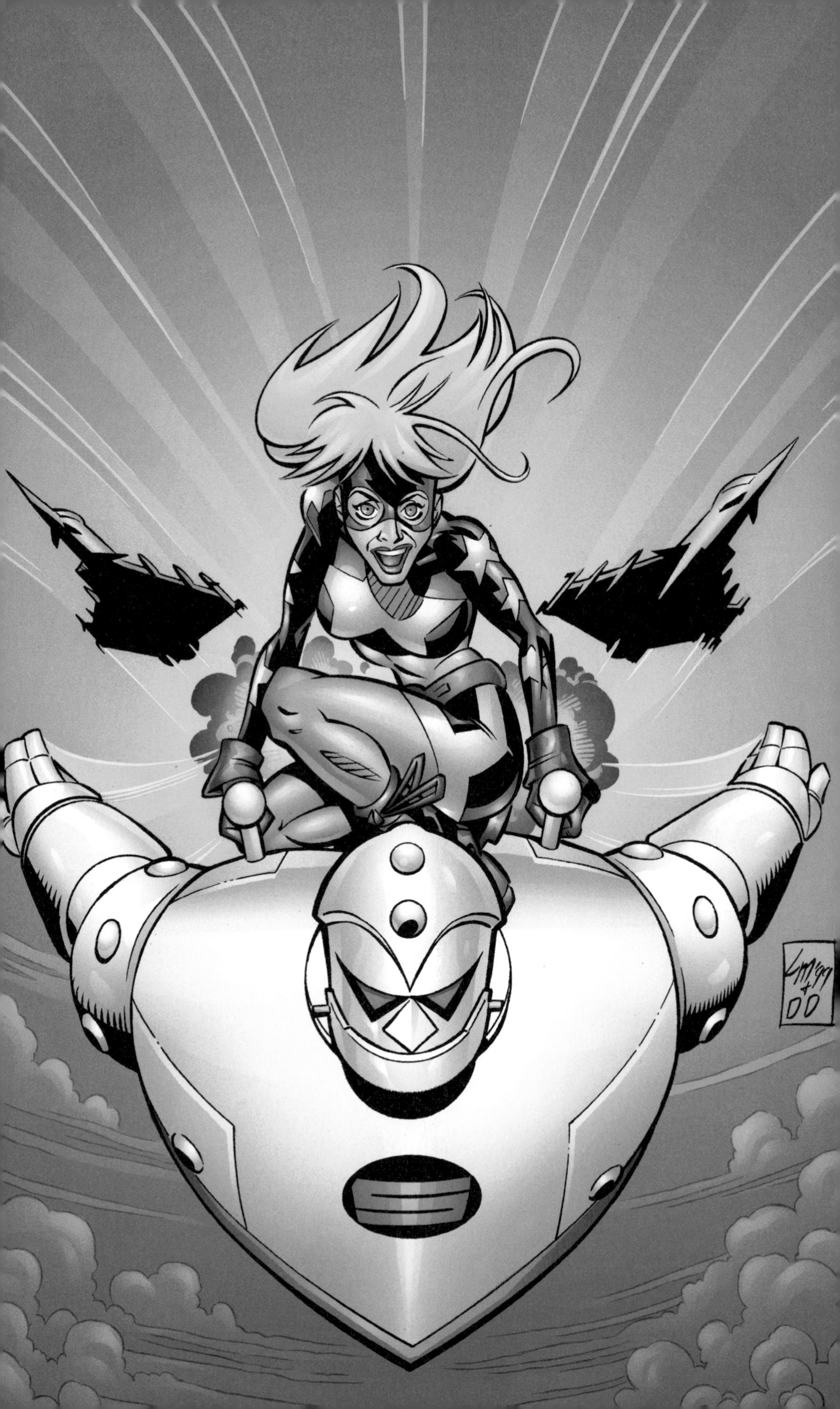

STARS AND S.T.R.I.P.E. #8

Written by GEOFF JOHNS
Pencils by LEE MODER
Inks by DAN DAVIS
Colors by TOM McCRAW
Letters by BILL OAKLEY
Cover art by LEE MODER and DAN DAVIS
Cover color by RICHARD & TANYA HORIE

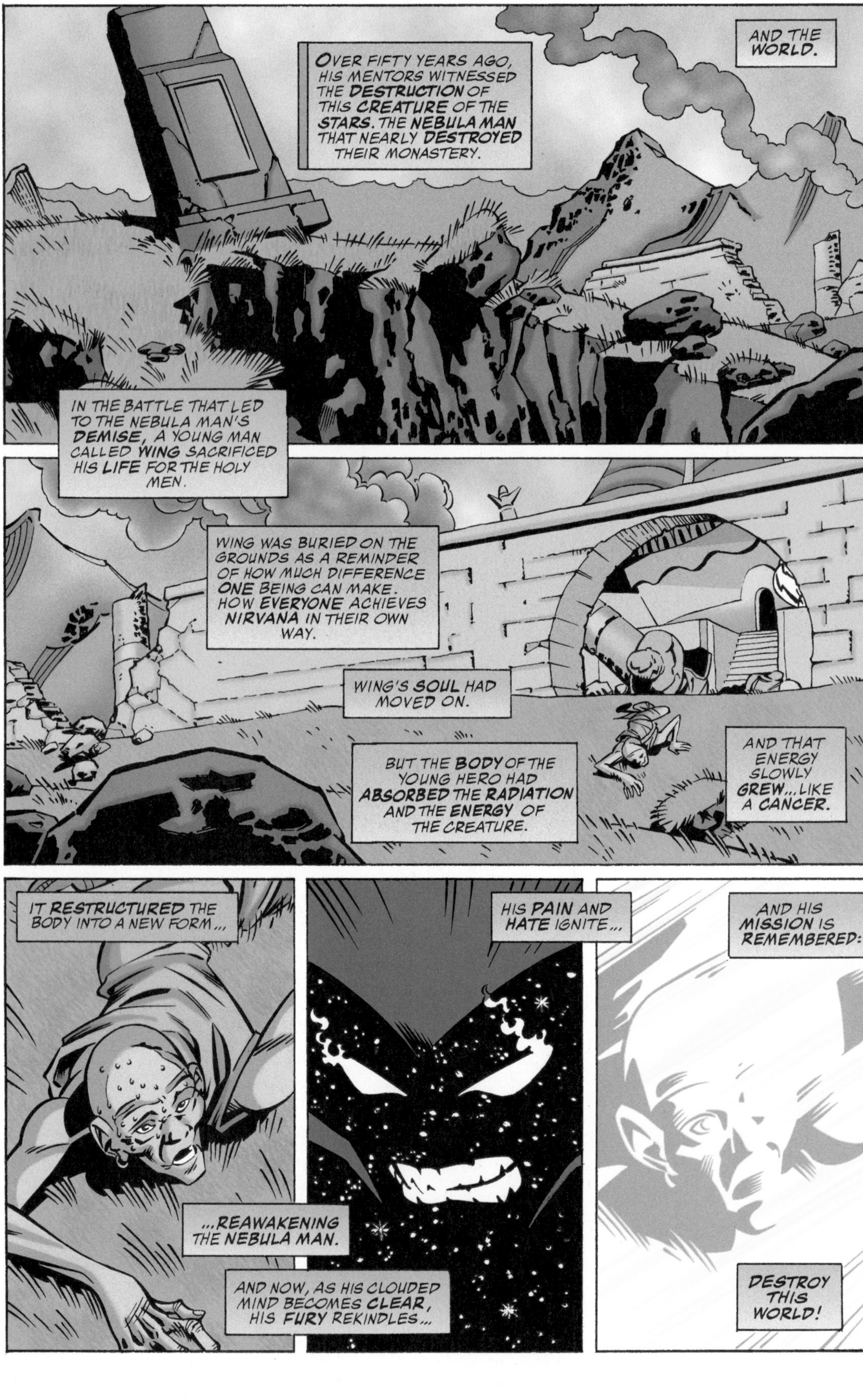

OVER FIFTY YEARS AGO, HIS MENTORS WITNESSED THE DESTRUCTION OF THIS CREATURE OF THE STARS. THE NEBULA MAN THAT NEARLY DESTROYED THEIR MONASTERY.
AND THE WORLD.
IN THE BATTLE THAT LED TO THE NEBULA MAN'S DEMISE, A YOUNG MAN CALLED WING SACRIFICED HIS LIFE FOR THE HOLY MEN.
WING WAS BURIED ON THE GROUNDS AS A REMINDER OF HOW MUCH DIFFERENCE ONE BEING CAN MAKE. HOW EVERYONE ACHIEVES NIRVANA IN THEIR OWN WAY.
WING'S SOUL HAD MOVED ON.
BUT THE BODY OF THE YOUNG HERO HAD ABSORBED THE RADIATION AND THE ENERGY OF THE CREATURE.
AND THAT ENERGY SLOWLY GREW... LIKE A CANCER.
IT RESTRUCTURED THE BODY INTO A NEW FORM...
...REAWAKENING THE NEBULA MAN.
AND NOW, AS HIS CLOUDED MIND BECOMES CLEAR, HIS FURY REKINDLES...
HIS PAIN AND HATE IGNITE...
AND HIS MISSION IS REMEMBERED:
DESTROY THIS WORLD!

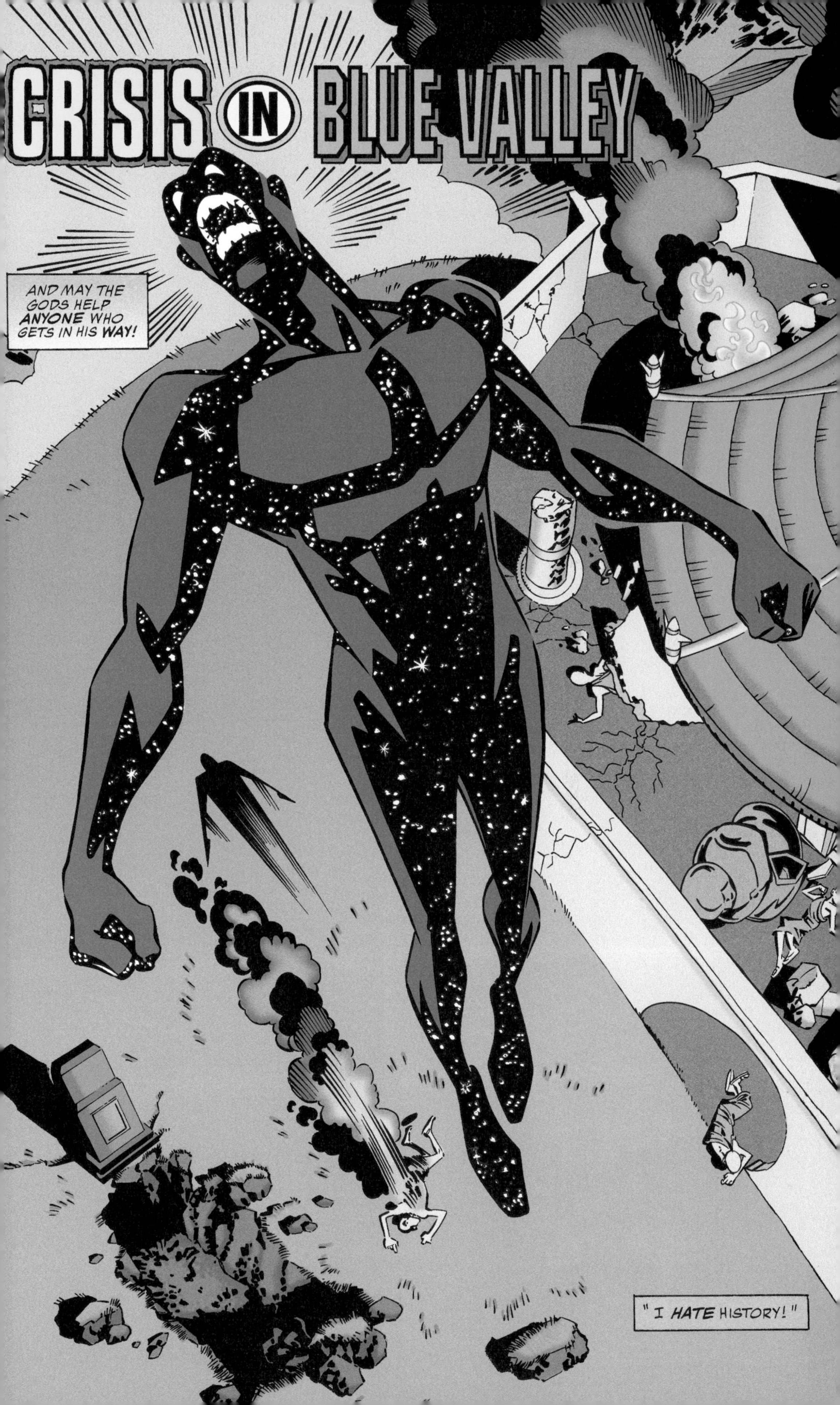
CRISIS IN BLUE VALLEY
AND MAY THE GODS HELP ANYONE WHO GETS IN HIS WAY!
"I HATE HISTORY!"

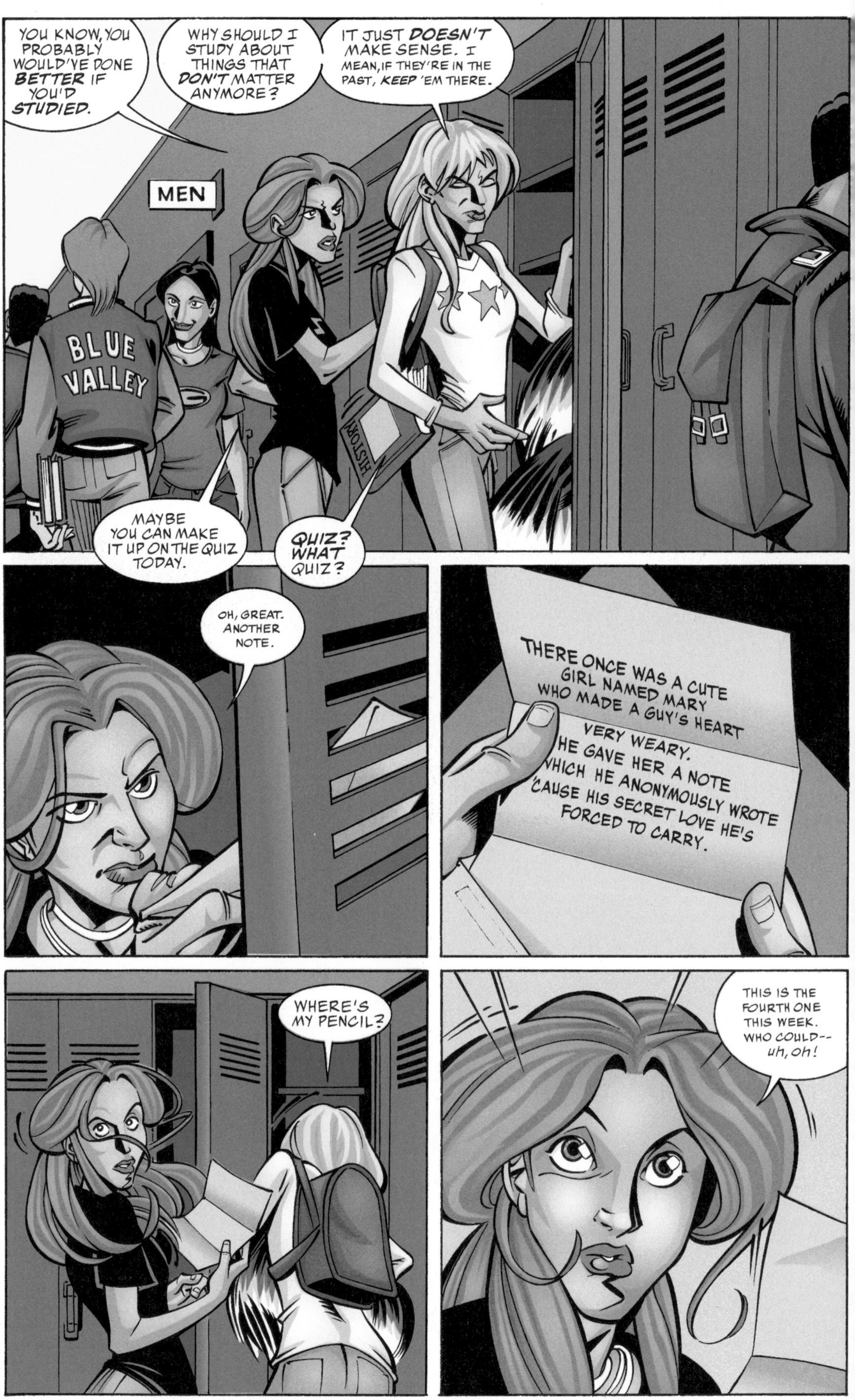

YOU KNOW, YOU PROBABLY WOULD'VE DONE BETTER IF YOU'D STUDIED.
WHY SHOULD I STUDY ABOUT THINGS THAT DON'T MATTER ANYMORE?
IT JUST DOESN'T MAKE SENSE. I MEAN, IF THEY'RE IN THE PAST, KEEP 'EM THERE.
MEN
BLUE VALLEY
HISTORY
MAYBE YOU CAN MAKE IT UP ON THE QUIZ TODAY.
QUIZ? WHAT QUIZ?
OH, GREAT. ANOTHER NOTE.
THERE ONCE WAS A CUTE GIRL NAMED MARY WHO MADE A GUY'S HEART VERY WEARY.
HE GAVE HER A NOTE WHICH HE ANONYMOUSLY WROTE 'CAUSE HIS SECRET LOVE HE'S FORCED TO CARRY.
WHERE'S MY PENCIL?
THIS IS THE FOURTH ONE THIS WEEK. WHO COULD-- uh, oh!

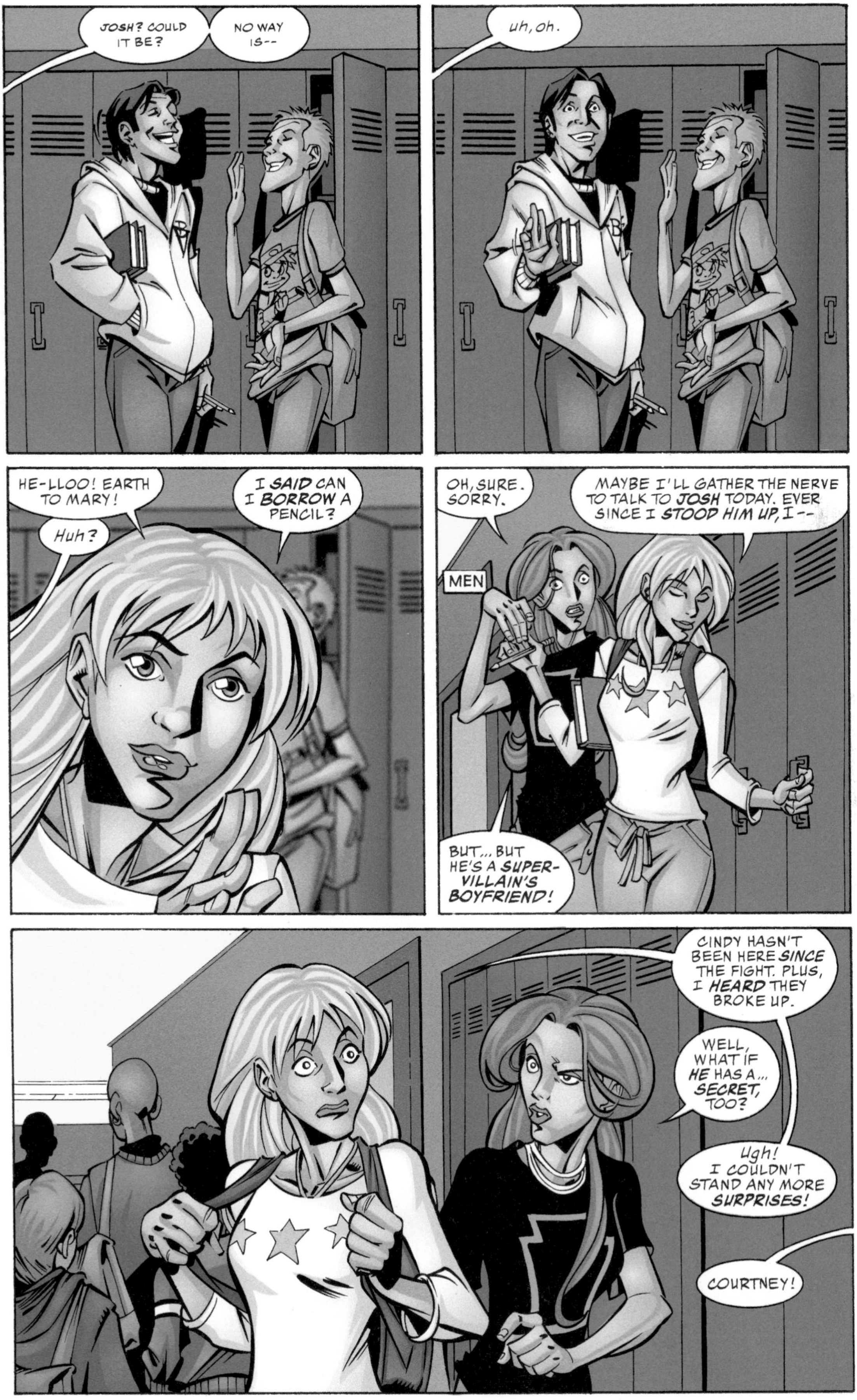
JOSH? COULD IT BE?
NO WAY IS--
uh, oh.
HE-LLOO! EARTH TO MARY!
Huh?
I SAID CAN I BORROW A PENCIL?
OH, SURE. SORRY.
MAYBE I'LL GATHER THE NERVE TO TALK TO JOSH TODAY. EVER SINCE I STOOD HIM UP, I--
MEN
BUT... BUT HE'S A SUPER-VILLAIN'S BOYFRIEND!
CINDY HASN'T BEEN HERE SINCE THE FIGHT. PLUS, I HEARD THEY BROKE UP.
WELL, WHAT IF HE HAS A... SECRET, TOO?
Ugh! I COULDN'T STAND ANY MORE SURPRISES!
COURTNEY!

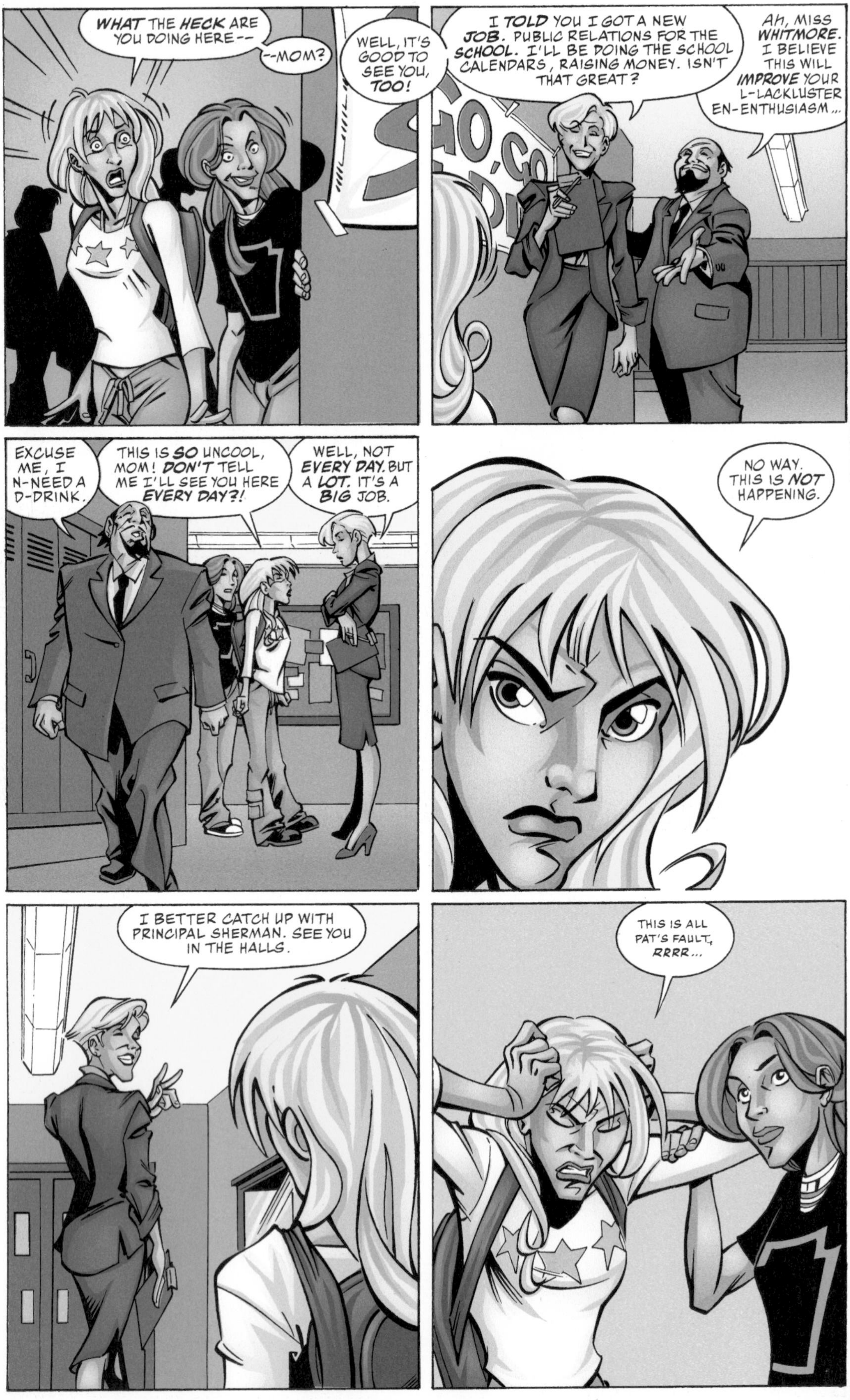
WHAT THE HECK ARE YOU DOING HERE--
--MOM?
WELL, IT'S GOOD TO SEE YOU, TOO!
I TOLD YOU I GOT A NEW JOB. PUBLIC RELATIONS FOR THE SCHOOL. I'LL BE DOING THE SCHOOL CALENDARS, RAISING MONEY. ISN'T THAT GREAT?
Ah, MISS WHITMORE. I BELIEVE THIS WILL IMPROVE YOUR L-LACKLUSTER EN-ENTHUSIASM...
GO, GO
EXCUSE ME, I N-NEED A D-DRINK.
THIS IS SO UNCOOL, MOM! DON'T TELL ME I'LL SEE YOU HERE EVERY DAY?!
WELL, NOT EVERY DAY. BUT A LOT. IT'S A BIG JOB.
NO WAY. THIS IS NOT HAPPENING.
I BETTER CATCH UP WITH PRINCIPAL SHERMAN. SEE YOU IN THE HALLS.
THIS IS ALL PAT'S FAULT, RRRR...

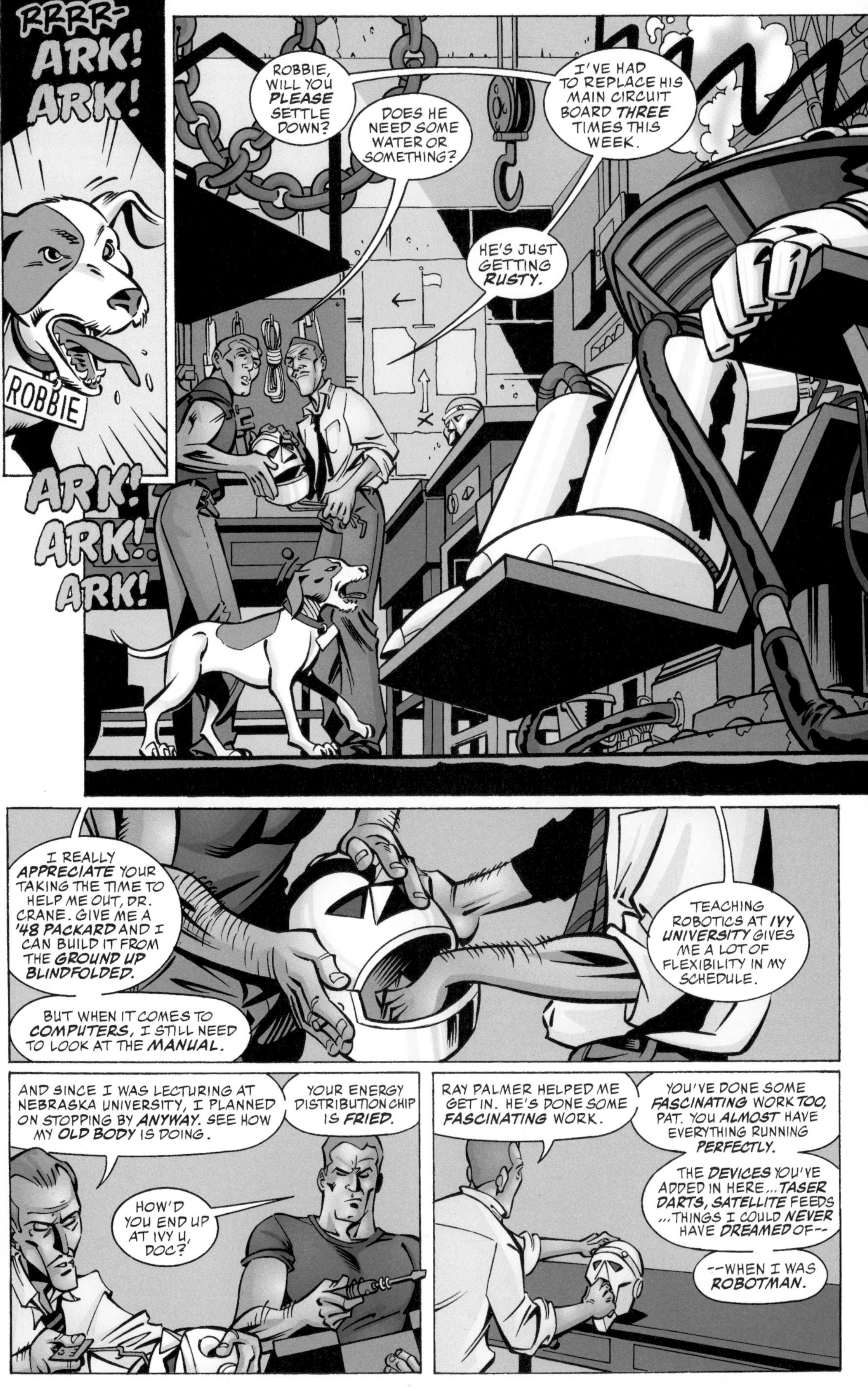

RRRR-ARK! ARK!
ROBBIE
ARK! ARK! ARK!
ROBBIE, WILL YOU PLEASE SETTLE DOWN?
DOES HE NEED SOME WATER OR SOMETHING?
I'VE HAD TO REPLACE HIS MAIN CIRCUIT BOARD THREE TIMES THIS WEEK.
HE'S JUST GETTING RUSTY.
I REALLY APPRECIATE YOUR TAKING THE TIME TO HELP ME OUT, DR. CRANE. GIVE ME A '48 PACKARD AND I CAN BUILD IT FROM THE GROUND UP BLINDFOLDED.
BUT WHEN IT COMES TO COMPUTERS, I STILL NEED TO LOOK AT THE MANUAL.
TEACHING ROBOTICS AT IVY UNIVERSITY GIVES ME A LOT OF FLEXIBILITY IN MY SCHEDULE.
AND SINCE I WAS LECTURING AT NEBRASKA UNIVERSITY, I PLANNED ON STOPPING BY ANYWAY. SEE HOW MY OLD BODY IS DOING.
YOUR ENERGY DISTRIBUTION CHIP IS FRIED.
HOW'D YOU END UP AT IVY U, DOC?
RAY PALMER HELPED ME GET IN. HE'S DONE SOME FASCINATING WORK.
YOU'VE DONE SOME FASCINATING WORK TOO, PAT. YOU ALMOST HAVE EVERYTHING RUNNING PERFECTLY.
THE DEVICES YOU'VE ADDED IN HERE... TASER DARTS, SATELLITE FEEDS ...THINGS I COULD NEVER HAVE DREAMED OF--
--WHEN I WAS ROBOTMAN.

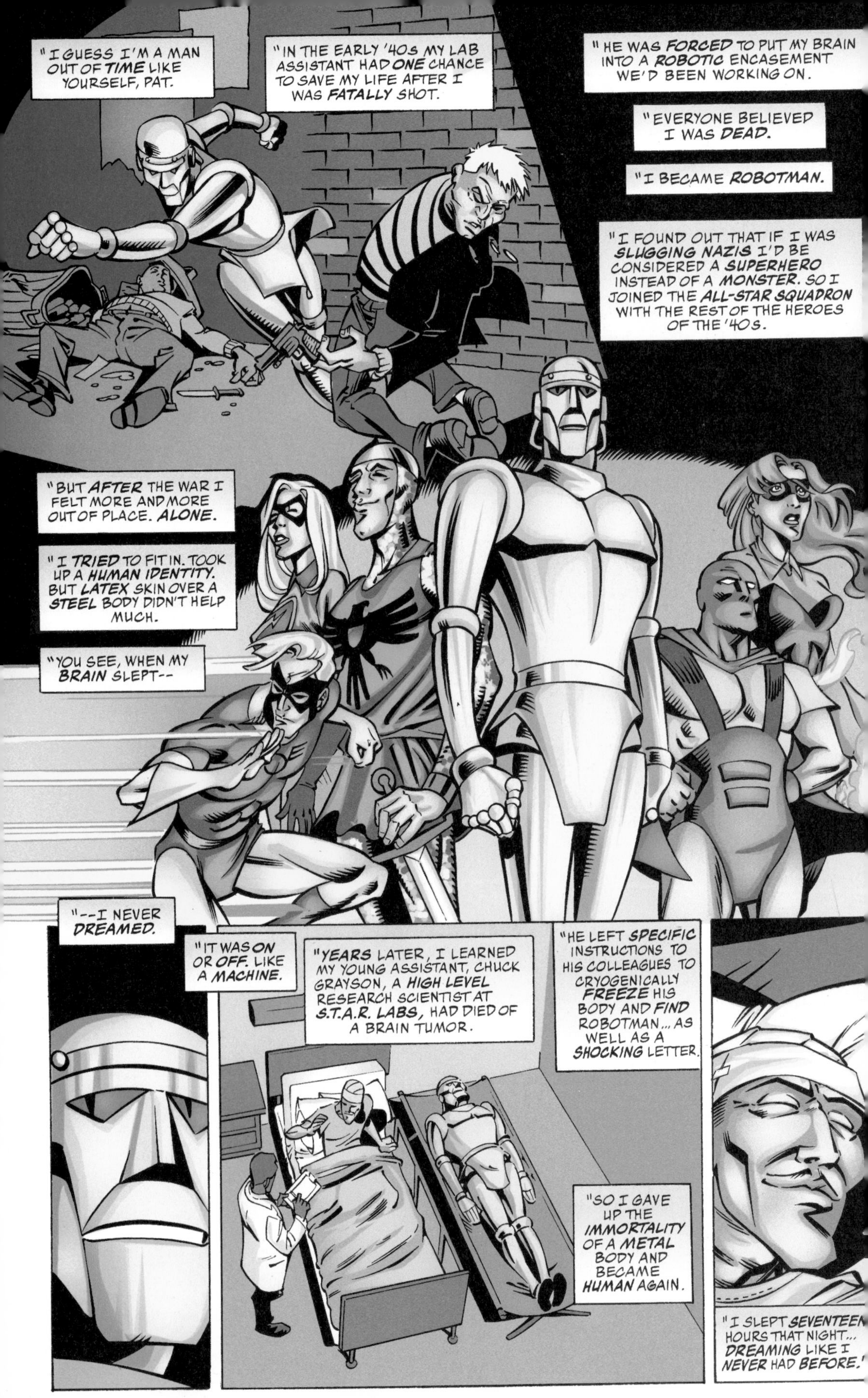
"I GUESS I'M A MAN OUT OF TIME LIKE YOURSELF, PAT.
"IN THE EARLY '40s MY LAB ASSISTANT HAD ONE CHANCE TO SAVE MY LIFE AFTER I WAS FATALLY SHOT.
"HE WAS FORCED TO PUT MY BRAIN INTO A ROBOTIC ENCASEMENT WE'D BEEN WORKING ON.
"EVERYONE BELIEVED I WAS DEAD.
"I BECAME ROBOTMAN.
"I FOUND OUT THAT IF I WAS SLUGGING NAZIS I'D BE CONSIDERED A SUPERHERO INSTEAD OF A MONSTER. SO I JOINED THE ALL-STAR SQUADRON WITH THE REST OF THE HEROES OF THE '40s.
"BUT AFTER THE WAR I FELT MORE AND MORE OUT OF PLACE. ALONE.
"I TRIED TO FIT IN. TOOK UP A HUMAN IDENTITY. BUT LATEX SKIN OVER A STEEL BODY DIDN'T HELP MUCH.
"YOU SEE, WHEN MY BRAIN SLEPT--
"--I NEVER DREAMED.
"IT WAS ON OR OFF. LIKE A MACHINE.
"YEARS LATER, I LEARNED MY YOUNG ASSISTANT, CHUCK GRAYSON, A HIGH LEVEL RESEARCH SCIENTIST AT S.T.A.R. LABS, HAD DIED OF A BRAIN TUMOR.
"HE LEFT SPECIFIC INSTRUCTIONS TO HIS COLLEAGUES TO CRYOGENICALLY FREEZE HIS BODY AND FIND ROBOTMAN... AS WELL AS A SHOCKING LETTER.
"SO I GAVE UP THE IMMORTALITY OF A METAL BODY AND BECAME HUMAN AGAIN.
"I SLEPT SEVENTEEN HOURS THAT NIGHT... DREAMING LIKE I NEVER HAD BEFORE."

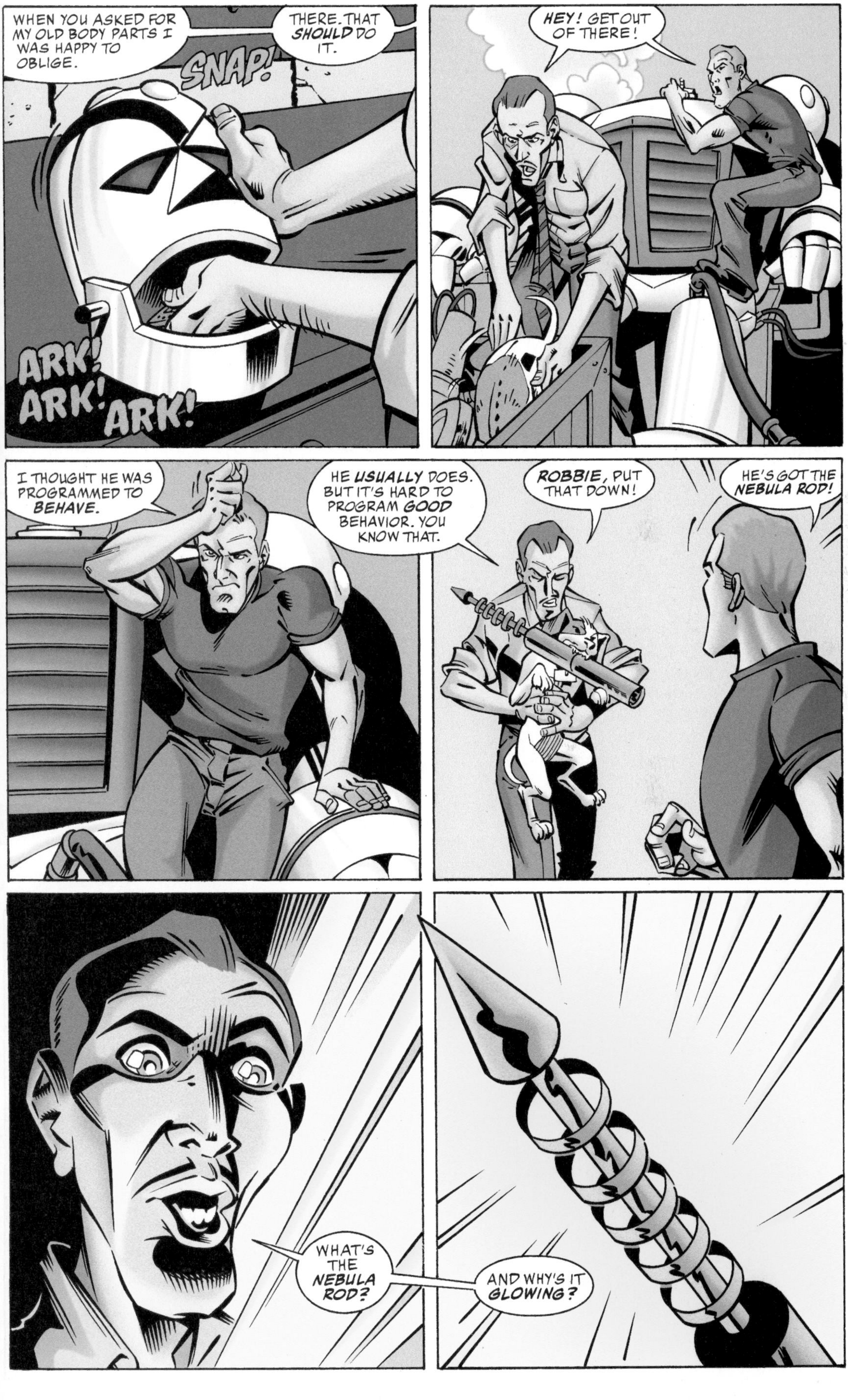
WHEN YOU ASKED FOR MY OLD BODY PARTS I WAS HAPPY TO OBLIGE.
THERE. THAT SHOULD DO IT.
SNAP!
ARK! ARK! ARK!
HEY! GET OUT OF THERE!
I THOUGHT HE WAS PROGRAMMED TO BEHAVE.
HE USUALLY DOES. BUT IT'S HARD TO PROGRAM GOOD BEHAVIOR. YOU KNOW THAT.
ROBBIE, PUT THAT DOWN!
HE'S GOT THE NEBULA ROD!
WHAT'S THE NEBULA ROD?
AND WHY'S IT GLOWING?

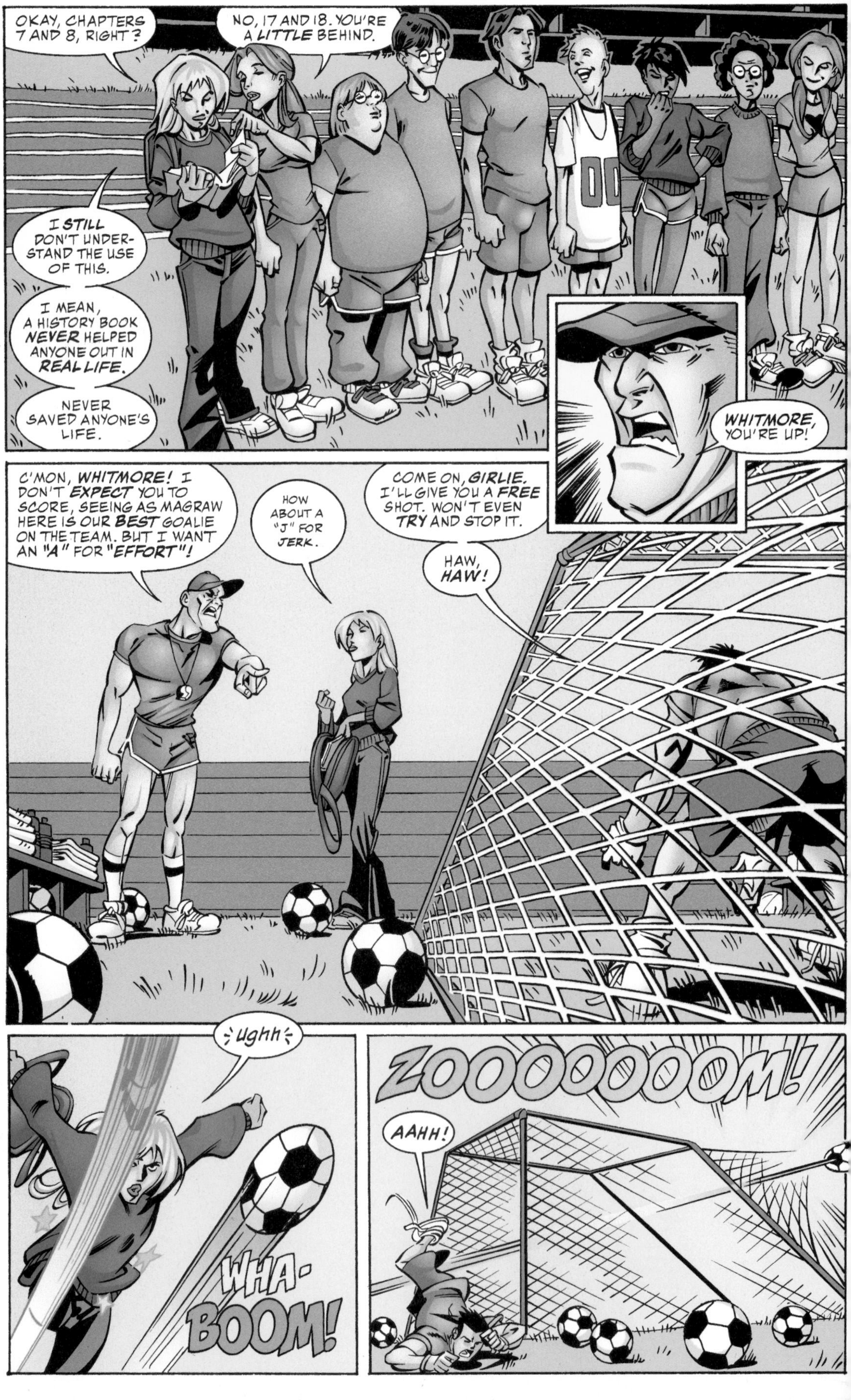

OKAY, CHAPTERS 7 AND 8, RIGHT?
NO, 17 AND 18. YOU'RE A LITTLE BEHIND.
I STILL DON'T UNDERSTAND THE USE OF THIS.
I MEAN, A HISTORY BOOK NEVER HELPED ANYONE OUT IN REAL LIFE.
NEVER SAVED ANYONE'S LIFE.
WHITMORE, YOU'RE UP!
C'MON, WHITMORE! I DON'T EXPECT YOU TO SCORE, SEEING AS MAGRAW HERE IS OUR BEST GOALIE ON THE TEAM. BUT I WANT AN "A" FOR "EFFORT"!
HOW ABOUT A "J" FOR JERK.
COME ON, GIRLIE. I'LL GIVE YOU A FREE SHOT. WON'T EVEN TRY AND STOP IT.
HAW, HAW!
ughh
WHA-BOOM!
ZOOOOOOOM!
AAHH!

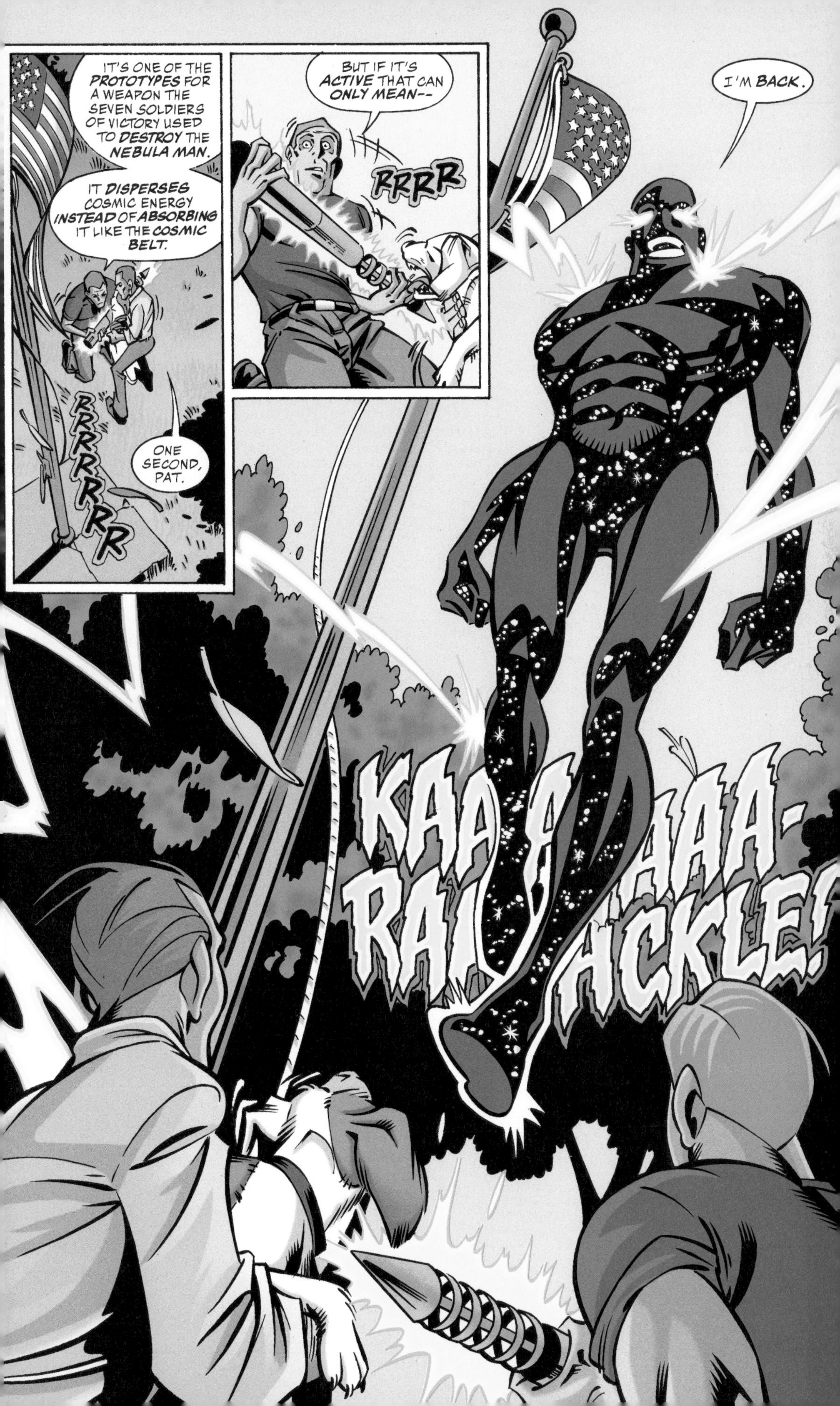
IT'S ONE OF THE PROTOTYPES FOR A WEAPON THE SEVEN SOLDIERS OF VICTORY USED TO DESTROY THE NEBULA MAN.
IT DISPERSES COSMIC ENERGY INSTEAD OF ABSORBING IT LIKE THE COSMIC BELT.
RRRRRRRR
ONE SECOND, PAT.
BUT IF IT'S ACTIVE THAT CAN ONLY MEAN--
RRRR
I'M BACK.

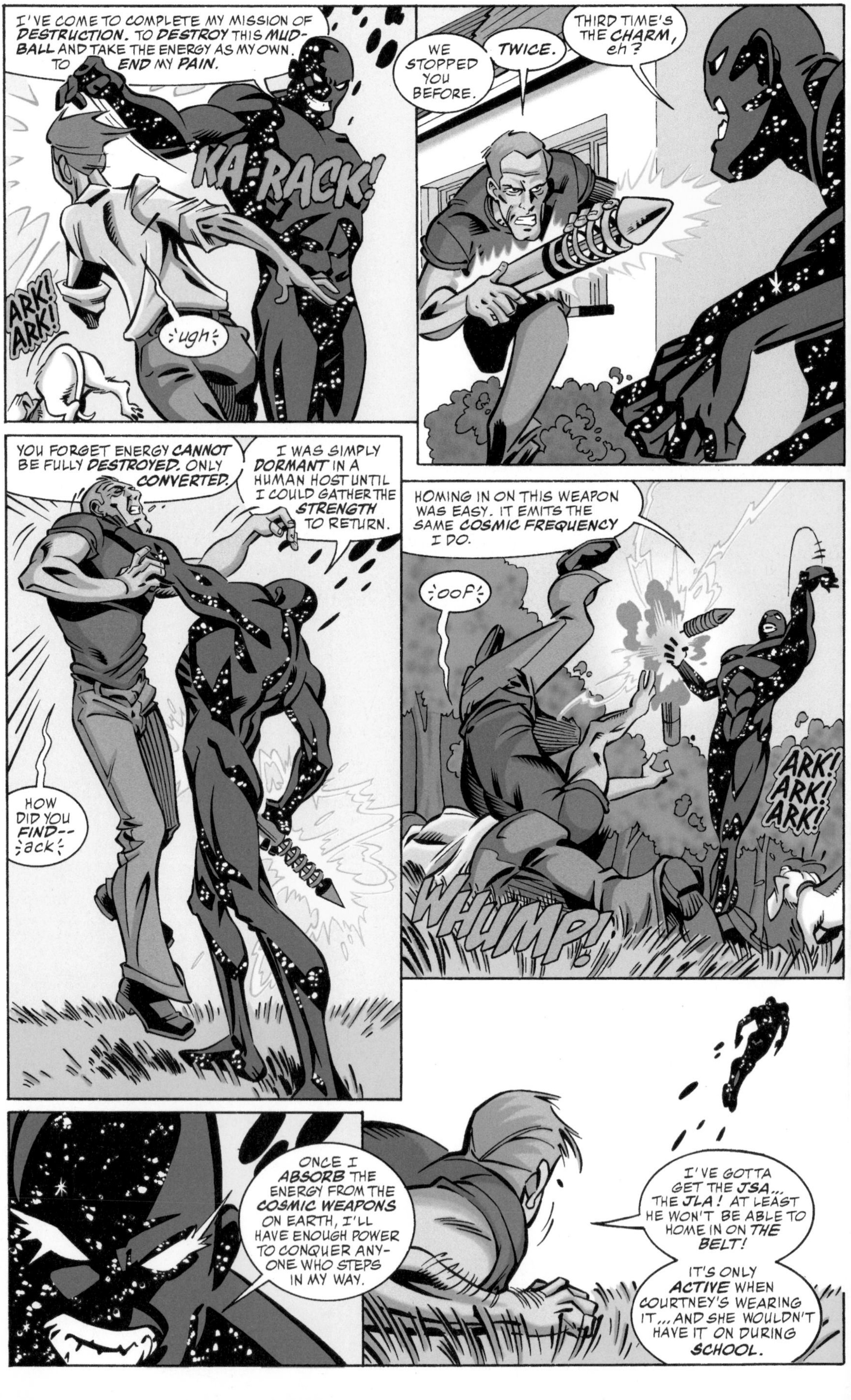

I'VE COME TO COMPLETE MY MISSION OF DESTRUCTION. TO DESTROY THIS MUD-BALL AND TAKE THE ENERGY AS MY OWN. TO END MY PAIN.
KA-RACK!
ARK! ARK!
ugh
WE STOPPED YOU BEFORE.
TWICE.
THIRD TIME'S THE CHARM, eh?
YOU FORGET ENERGY CANNOT BE FULLY DESTROYED. ONLY CONVERTED.
I WAS SIMPLY DORMANT IN A HUMAN HOST UNTIL I COULD GATHER THE STRENGTH TO RETURN.
HOW DID YOU FIND-- ack
HOMING IN ON THIS WEAPON WAS EASY. IT EMITS THE SAME COSMIC FREQUENCY I DO.
oof
ARK! ARK! ARK!
WHUMP!
ONCE I ABSORB THE ENERGY FROM THE COSMIC WEAPONS ON EARTH, I'LL HAVE ENOUGH POWER TO CONQUER ANY-ONE WHO STEPS IN MY WAY.
I'VE GOTTA GET THE JSA... THE JLA! AT LEAST HE WON'T BE ABLE TO HOME IN ON THE BELT!
IT'S ONLY ACTIVE WHEN COURTNEY'S WEARING IT... AND SHE WOULDN'T HAVE IT ON DURING SCHOOL.

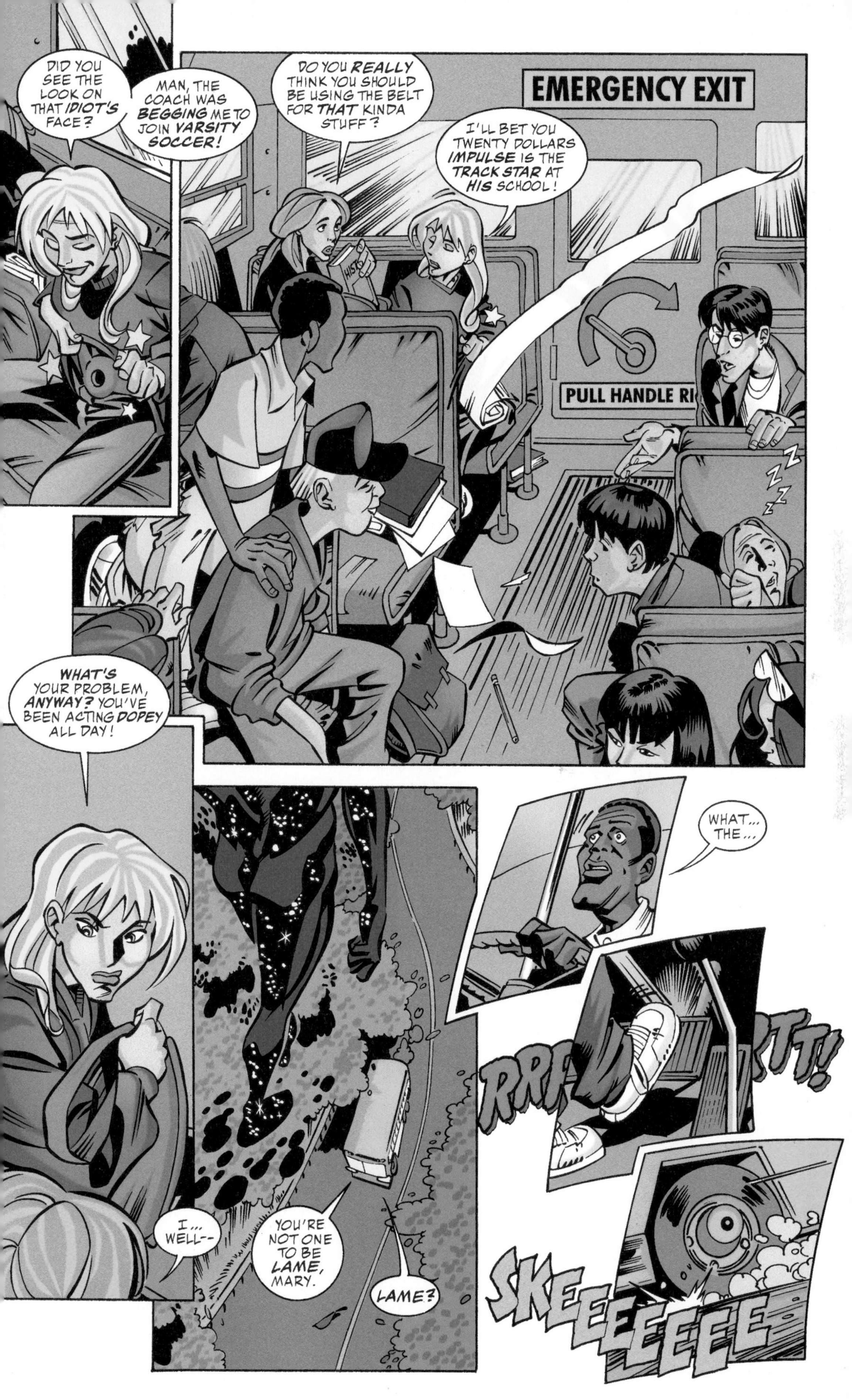

DID YOU SEE THE LOOK ON THAT IDIOT'S FACE?
MAN, THE COACH WAS BEGGING ME TO JOIN VARSITY SOCCER!
DO YOU REALLY THINK YOU SHOULD BE USING THE BELT FOR THAT KINDA STUFF?
EMERGENCY EXIT
I'LL BET YOU TWENTY DOLLARS IMPULSE IS THE TRACK STAR AT HIS SCHOOL!
PULL HANDLE RI
WHAT'S YOUR PROBLEM, ANYWAY? YOU'VE BEEN ACTING DOPEY ALL DAY!
WHAT... THE...
I... WELL--
YOU'RE NOT ONE TO BE LAME, MARY.
LAME?
SKEEEEEEEE

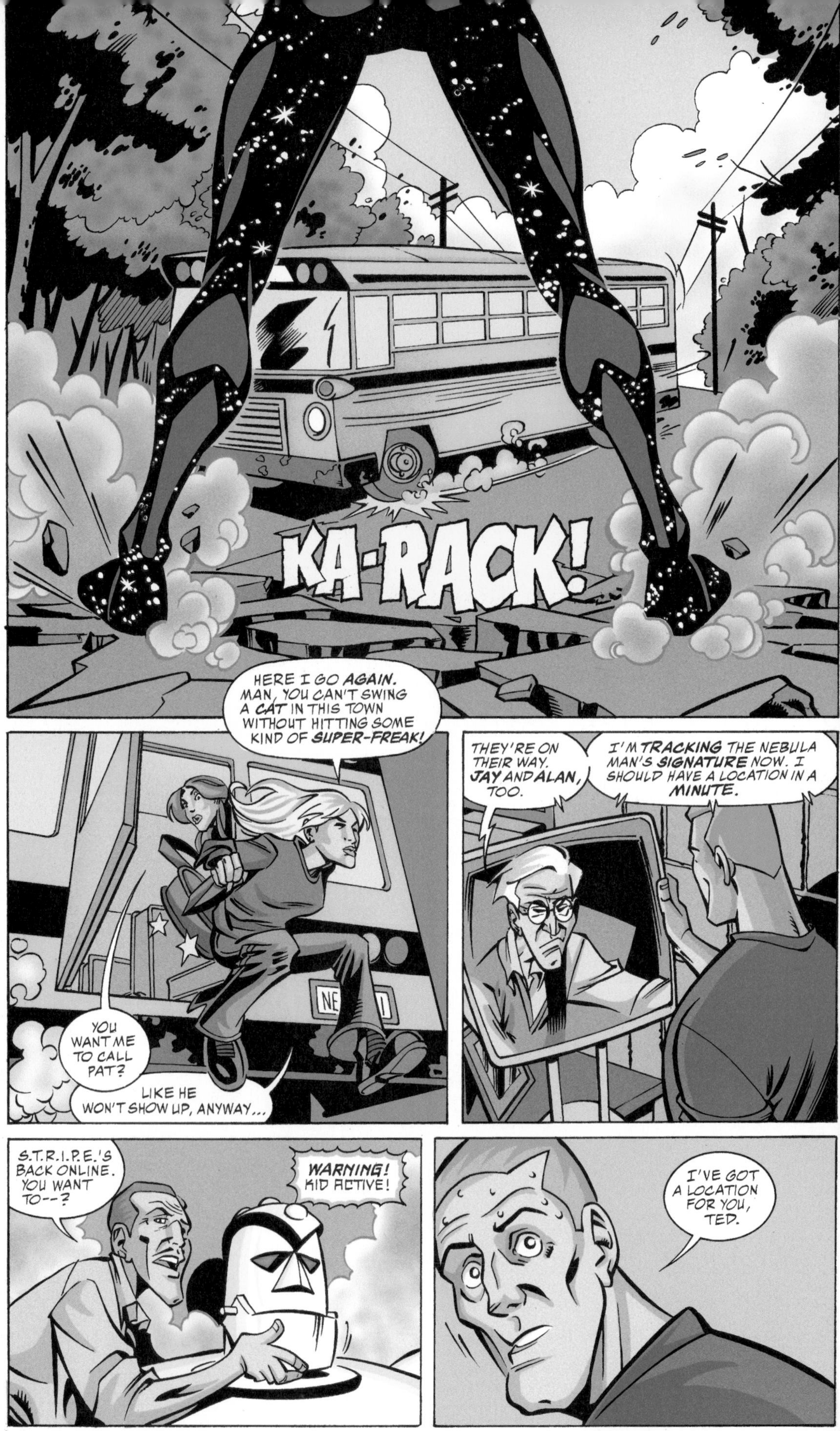
KA-RACK!
HERE I GO AGAIN. MAN, YOU CAN'T SWING A CAT IN THIS TOWN WITHOUT HITTING SOME KIND OF SUPER-FREAK!
YOU WANT ME TO CALL PAT?
LIKE HE WON'T SHOW UP, ANYWAY...
THEY'RE ON THEIR WAY. JAY AND ALAN, TOO.
I'M TRACKING THE NEBULA MAN'S SIGNATURE NOW. I SHOULD HAVE A LOCATION IN A MINUTE.
S.T.R.I.P.E.'S BACK ONLINE. YOU WANT TO--?
WARNING! KID ACTIVE!
I'VE GOT A LOCATION FOR YOU, TED.

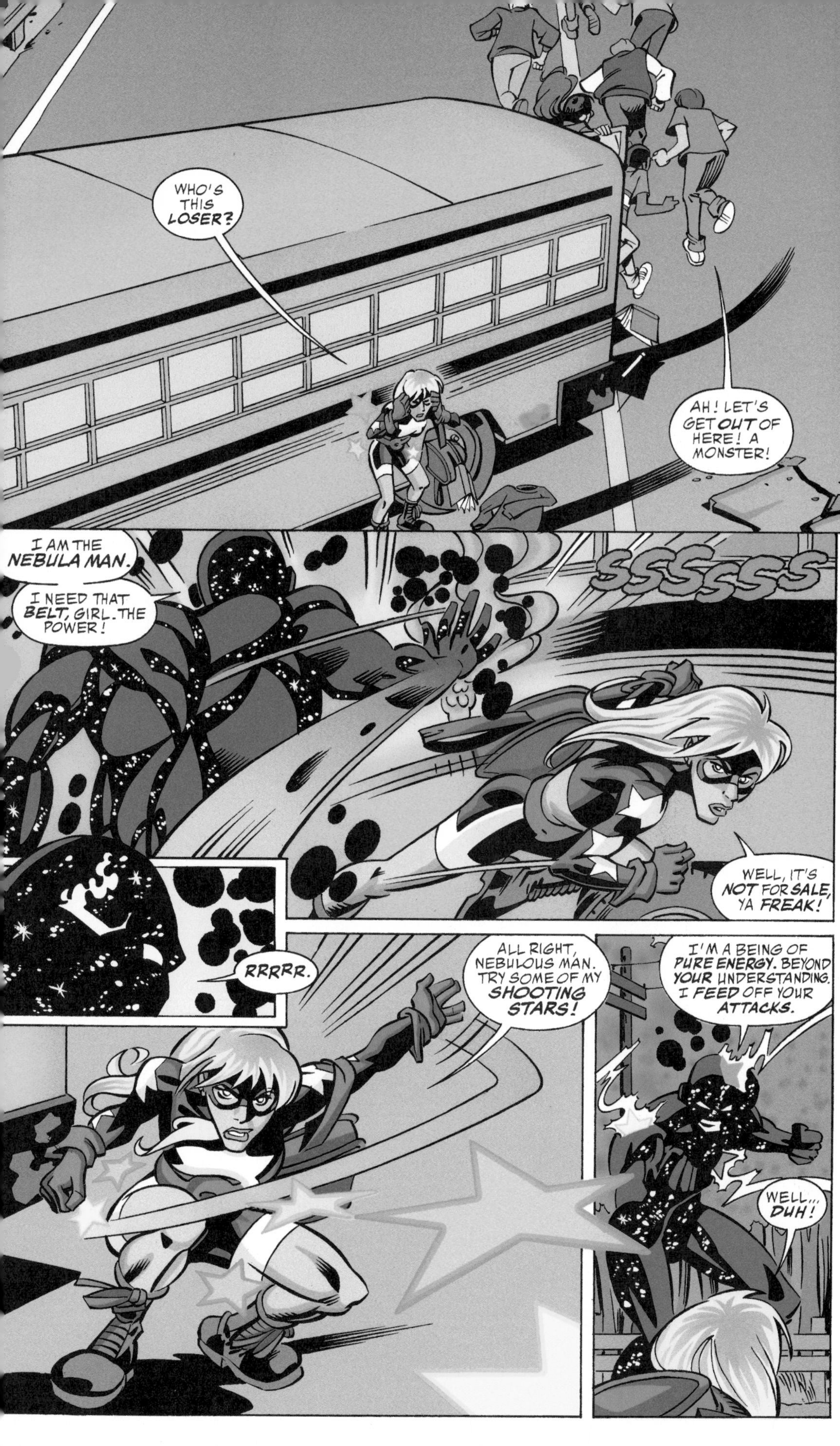
WHO'S THIS LOSER?
AH! LET'S GET OUT OF HERE! A MONSTER!
I AM THE NEBULA MAN.
I NEED THAT BELT, GIRL. THE POWER!
SSSSSSS
WELL, IT'S NOT FOR SALE, YA FREAK!
RRRRR.
ALL RIGHT, NEBULOUS MAN. TRY SOME OF MY SHOOTING STARS!
I'M A BEING OF PURE ENERGY. BEYOND YOUR UNDERSTANDING. I FEED OFF YOUR ATTACKS.
WELL... DUH!

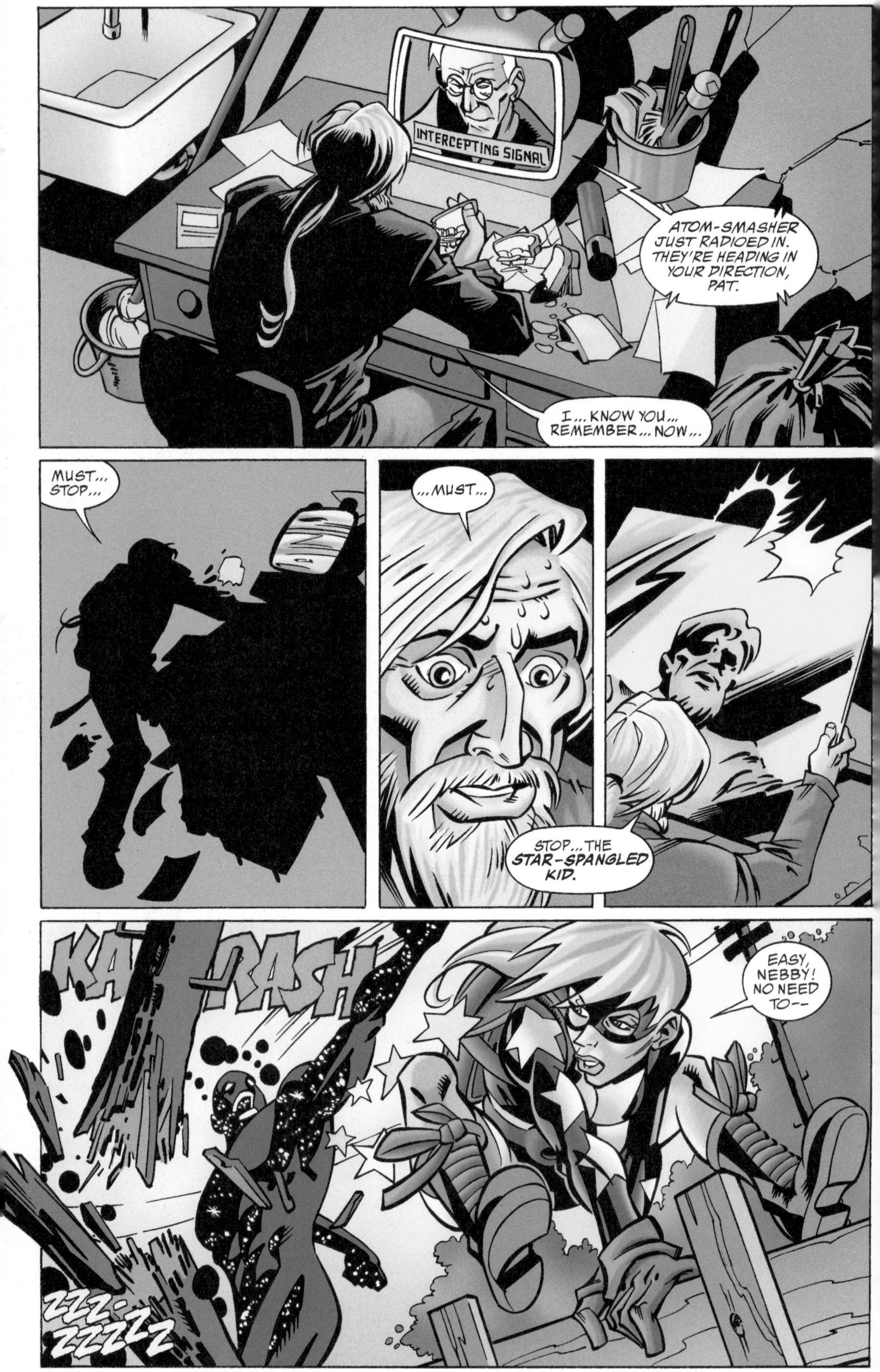
INTERCEPTING SIGNAL
ATOM-SMASHER JUST RADIOED IN. THEY'RE HEADING IN YOUR DIRECTION, PAT.
I... KNOW YOU... REMEMBER... NOW...
MUST... STOP...
...MUST...
STOP... THE STAR-SPANGLED KID.
KA-RASH
EASY, NEBBY! NO NEED TO--
ZZZ-ZZZZZ

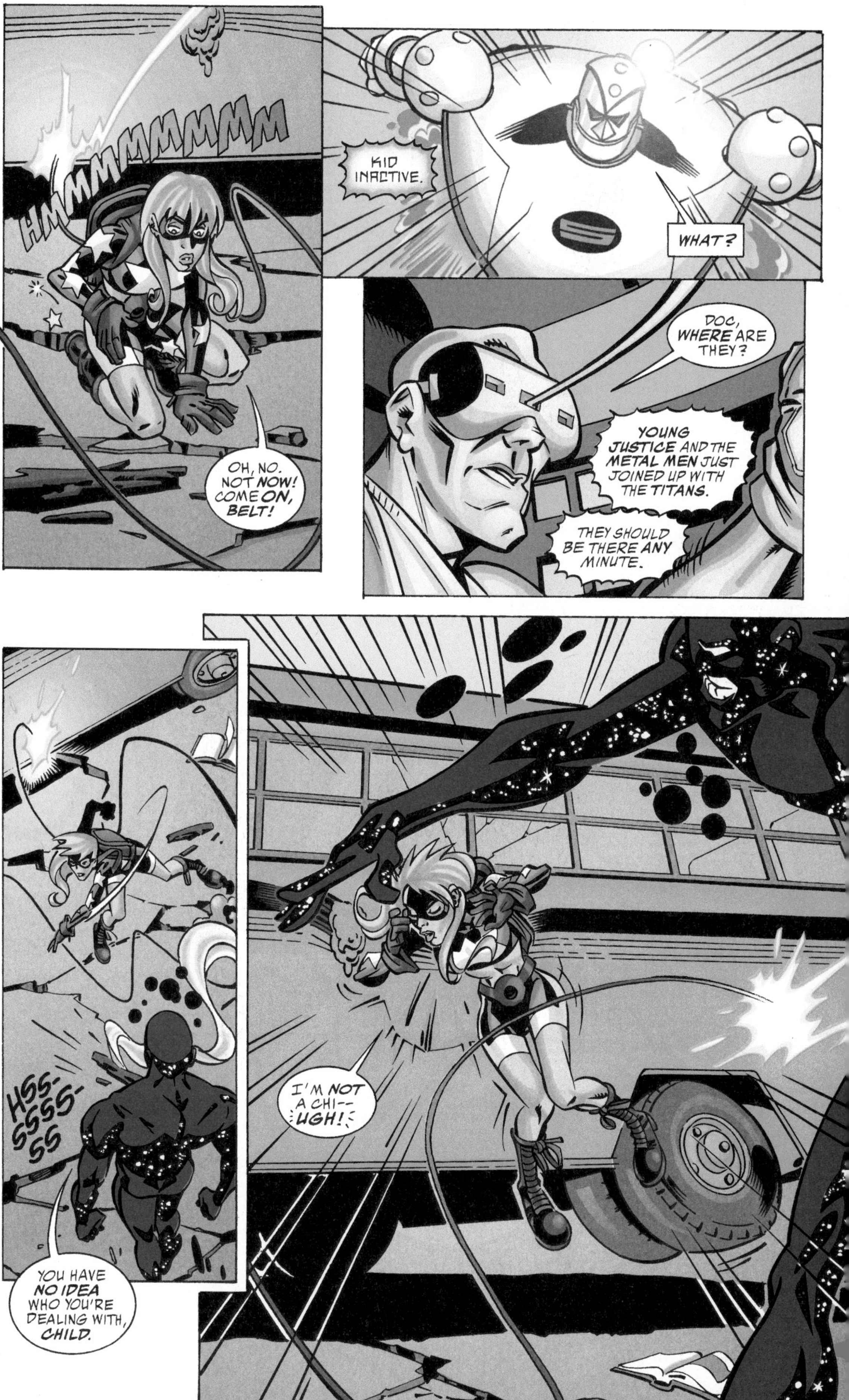

HMMMMMMMMMM
OH, NO. NOT NOW! COME ON, BELT!
KID INACTIVE.
WHAT?
DOC, WHERE ARE THEY?
YOUNG JUSTICE AND THE METAL MEN JUST JOINED UP WITH THE TITANS.
THEY SHOULD BE THERE ANY MINUTE.
HSS-SSSS-SSSS-SS
YOU HAVE NO IDEA WHO YOU'RE DEALING WITH, CHILD.
I'M NOT A CHI-- UGH!

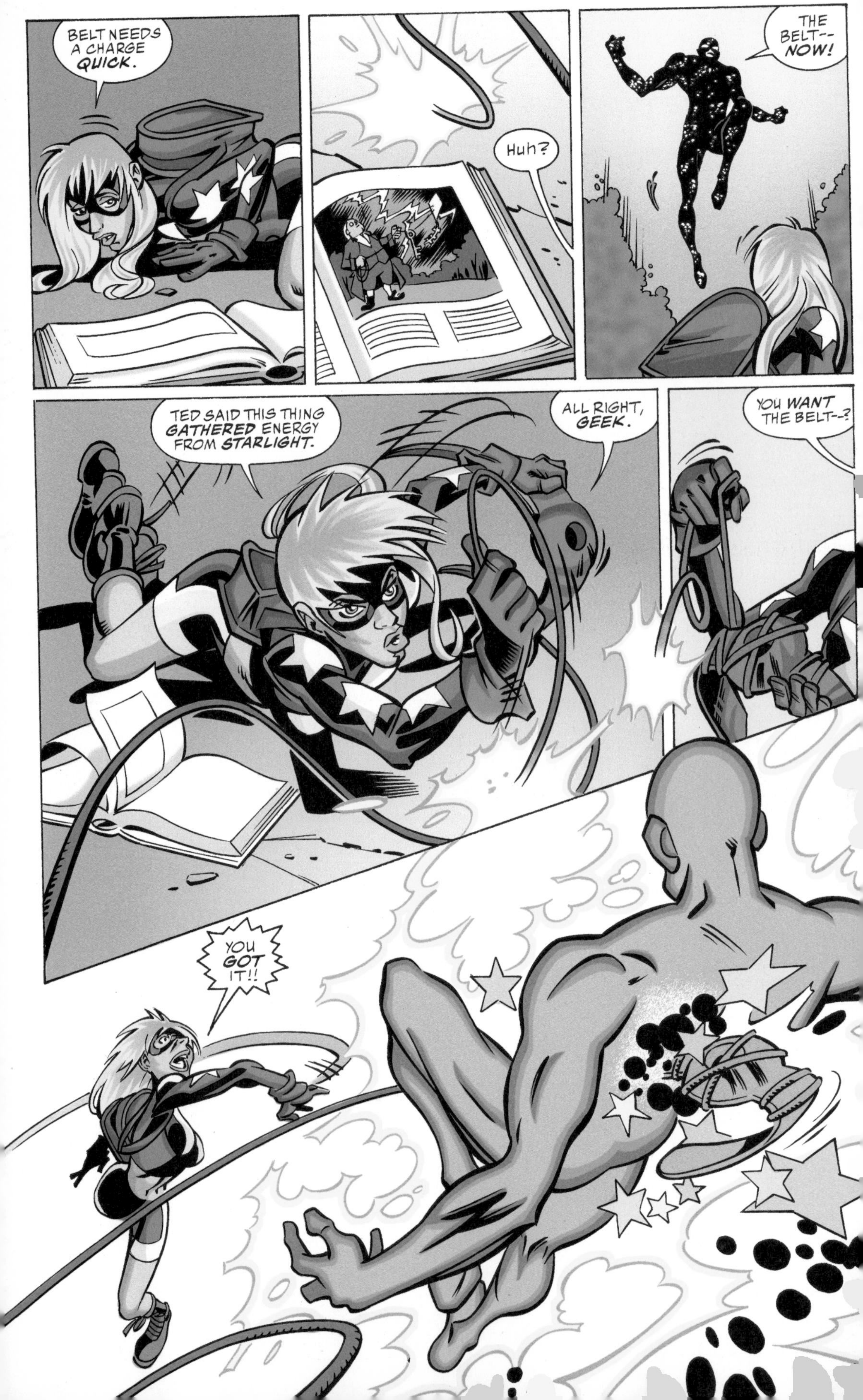

BELT NEEDS A CHARGE QUICK.
Huh?
THE BELT-- NOW!
TED SAID THIS THING GATHERED ENERGY FROM STARLIGHT.
ALL RIGHT, GEEK.
YOU WANT THE BELT--?
YOU GOT IT!!

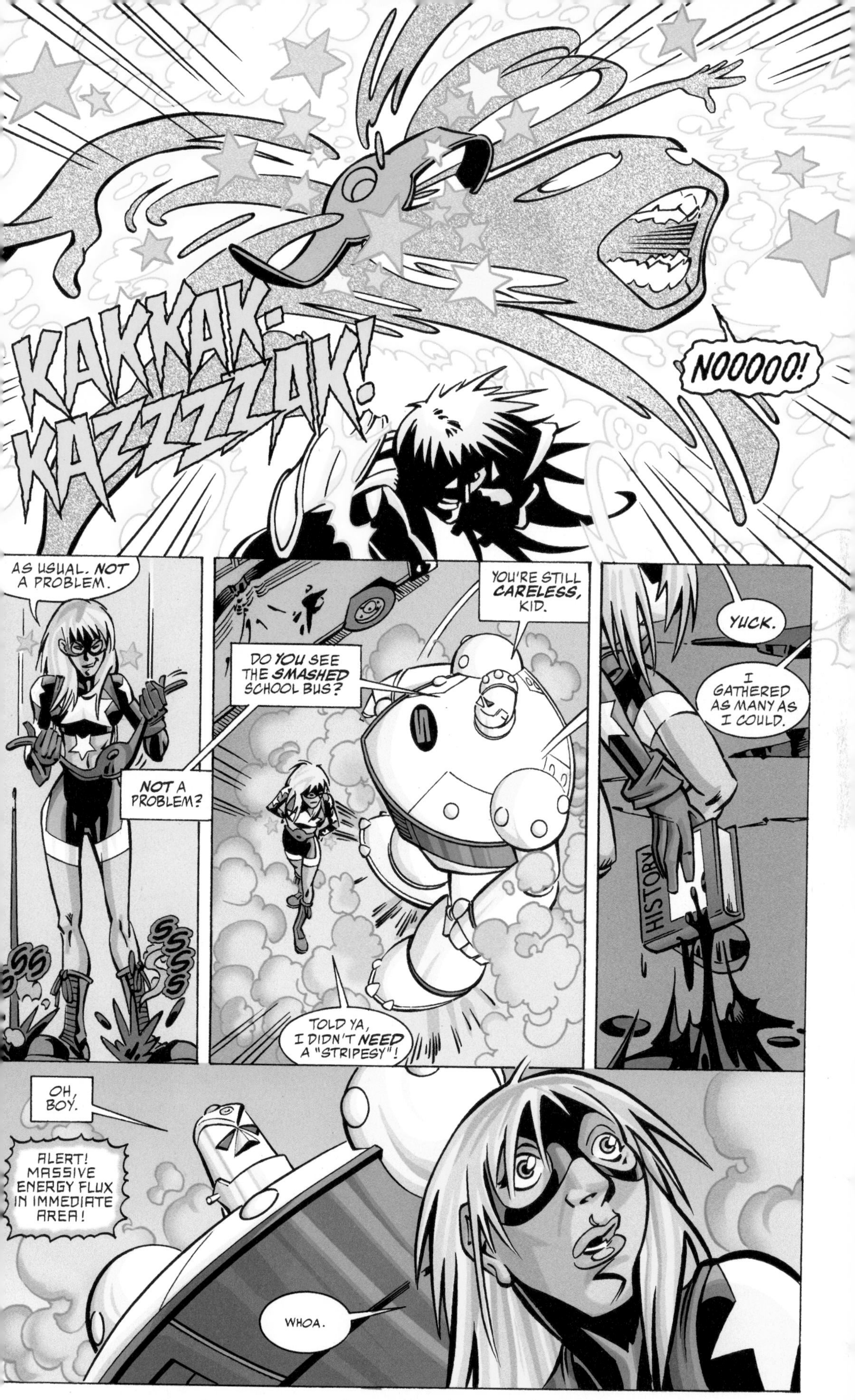
KAKKAK-KAZZZZAK!
NOOOOO!
AS USUAL. NOT A PROBLEM.
NOT A PROBLEM?
DO YOU SEE THE SMASHED SCHOOL BUS?
YOU'RE STILL CARELESS, KID.
TOLD YA, I DIDN'T NEED A "STRIPESY"!
YUCK.
I GATHERED AS MANY AS I COULD.
HISTORY
OH, BOY.
ALERT! MASSIVE ENERGY FLUX IN IMMEDIATE AREA!
WHOA.

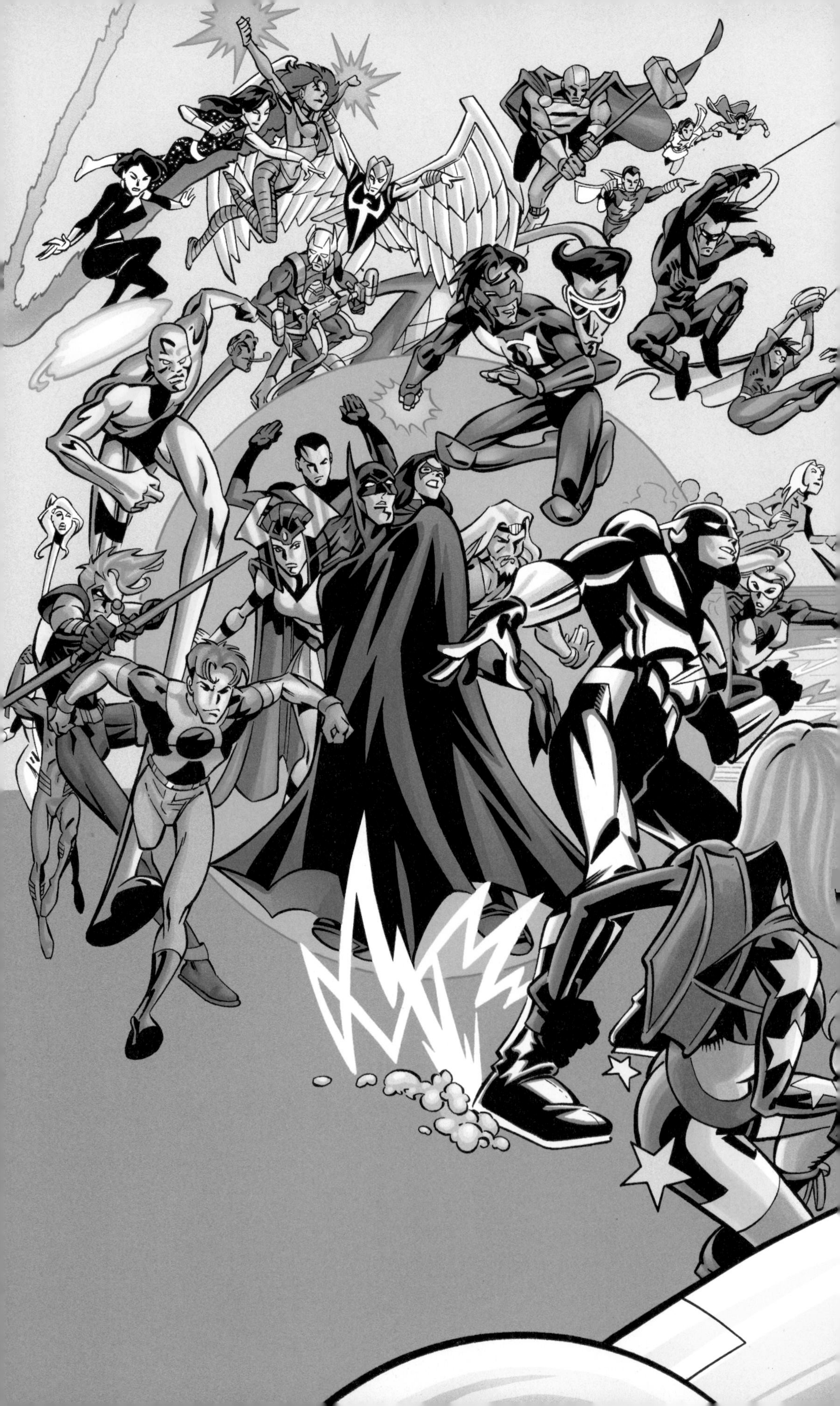

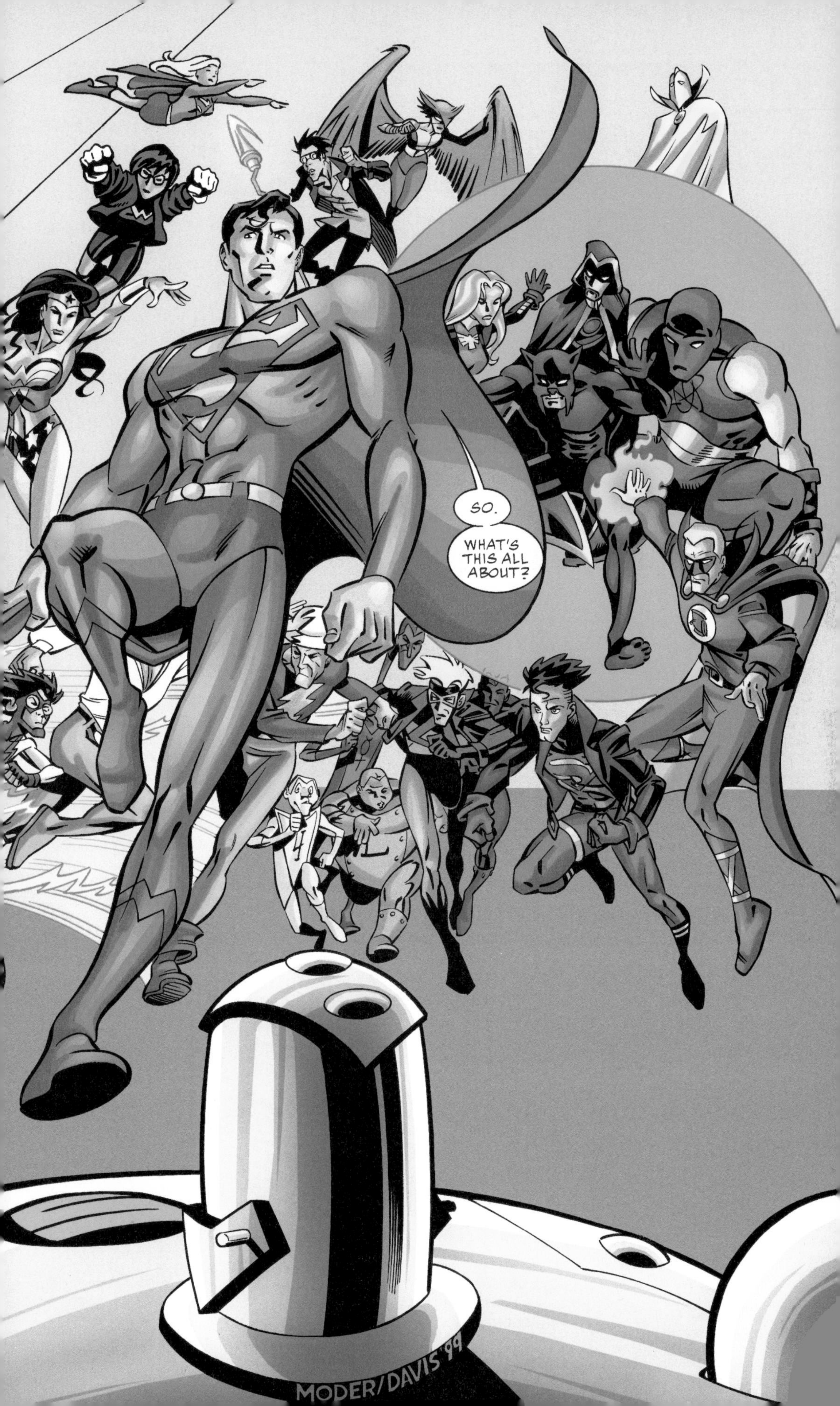
SO.
WHAT'S THIS ALL ABOUT?
MODER/DAVIS '99

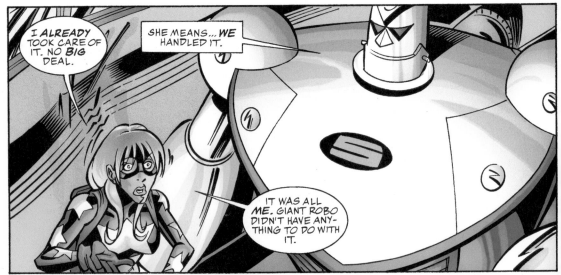

I ALREADY TOOK CARE OF IT. NO *BIG* DEAL.

SHE MEANS... *WE* HANDLED IT.

IT WAS ALL *ME*. GIANT ROBO DIDN'T HAVE ANYTHING TO DO WITH IT.

WE WERE *TOLD* THIS WAS A *SERIOUS* SITUATION. THE BEGINNING OF ANOTHER *CRISIS* OR--

RELAX, SUPERMAN.

I GUESS BLUE VALLEY'S NEW *SUPERHERO* HAS IT UNDER CONTROL.

YEAH, I *GUESS*.

SO YOU'RE LOOKING AFTER WALLY'S *HOMETOWN*, huh?

I GUESS... I *AM*.

SORRY FOR THE *DISTRESS* CALL, BUT YOU KNOW WHAT THE NEBULA MAN IS *CAPABLE* OF.

YES, I *RECALL*. BUT IT SEEMS YOU AND THE KID WORK QUITE WELL TOGETHER.

PARTNERS MAKE THIS KIND OF LIFE MUCH MORE ENJOYABLE.

RIGHT! SHE *HAS* BEEN HOLDING HER OWN IN THE JSA, PAT.

LET'S GO. SHE'S GOT IT UNDER CONTROL.

I'LL STOP IN SOMETIME, KID! SEE YA!

I BETTER GET HOME, PAT.

I'VE GOT SOME STUDYING TO DO!

HISTORY

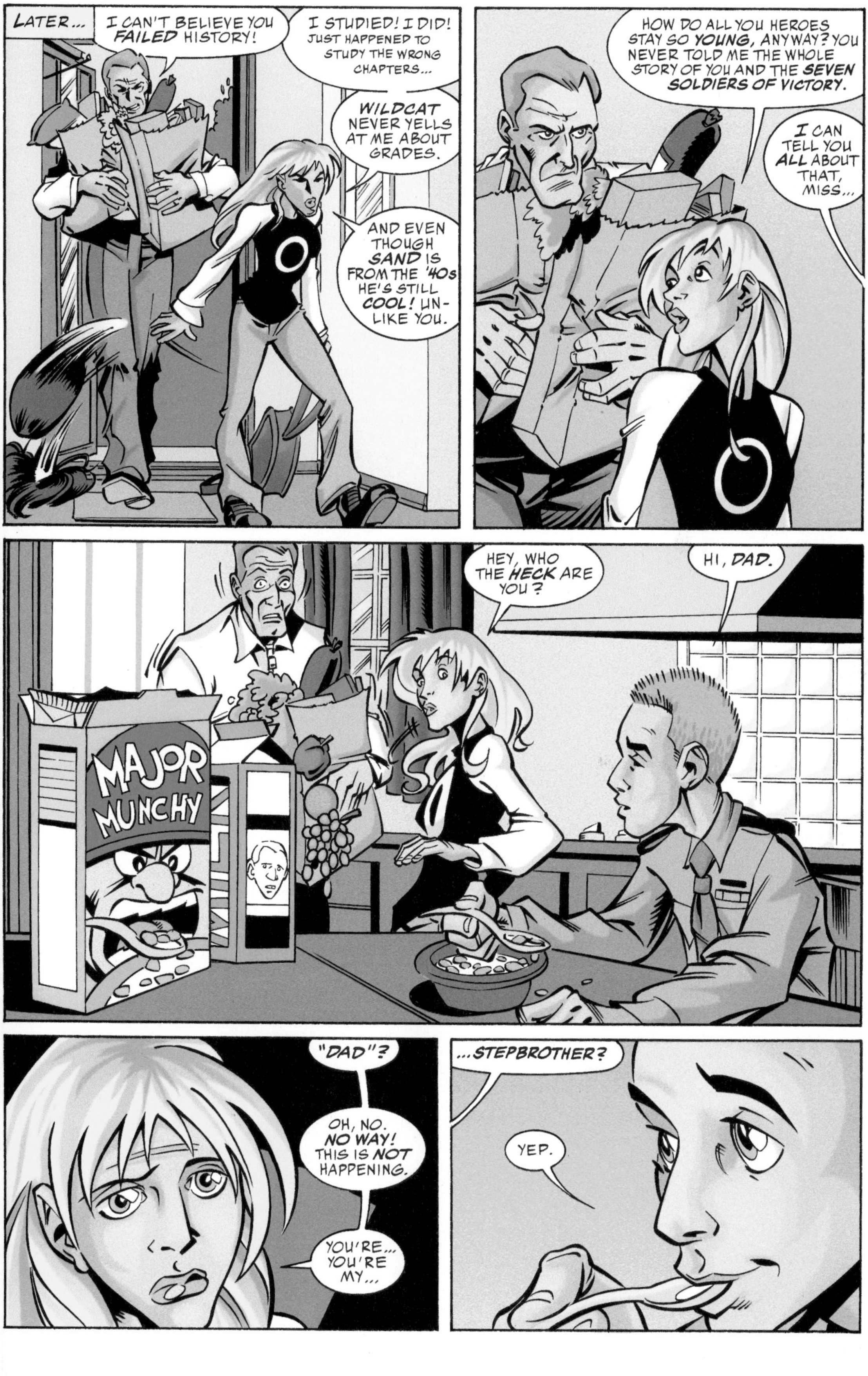
LATER...
I CAN'T BELIEVE YOU FAILED HISTORY!
I STUDIED! I DID! JUST HAPPENED TO STUDY THE WRONG CHAPTERS...
WILDCAT NEVER YELLS AT ME ABOUT GRADES.
AND EVEN THOUGH SAND IS FROM THE '40s HE'S STILL COOL! UN-LIKE YOU.
HOW DO ALL YOU HEROES STAY SO YOUNG, ANYWAY? YOU NEVER TOLD ME THE WHOLE STORY OF YOU AND THE SEVEN SOLDIERS OF VICTORY.
I CAN TELL YOU ALL ABOUT THAT, MISS...
MAJOR MUNCHY
HEY, WHO THE HECK ARE YOU?
HI, DAD.
"DAD"?
OH, NO. NO WAY! THIS IS NOT HAPPENING.
YOU'RE... YOU'RE MY...
...STEPBROTHER?
YEP.

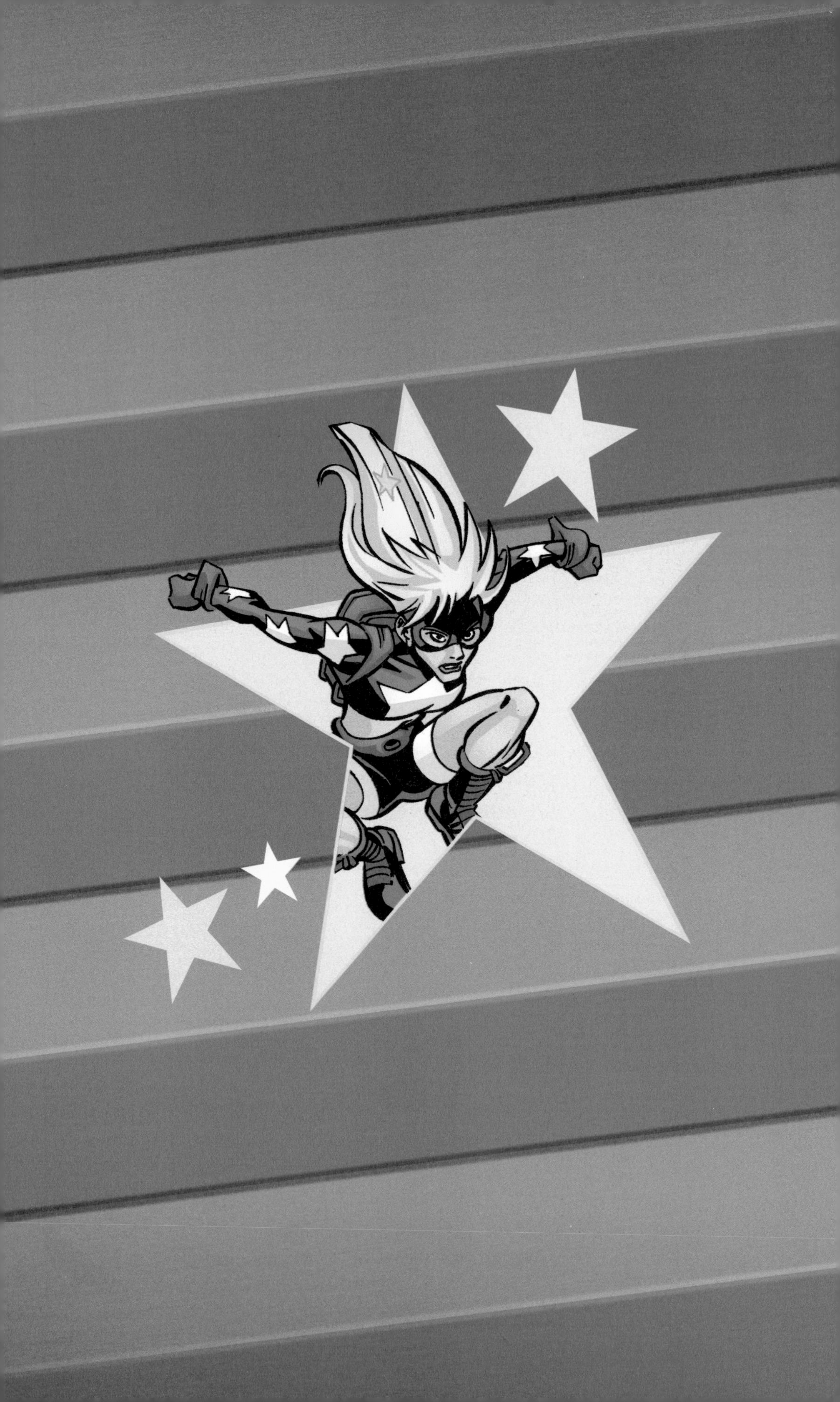

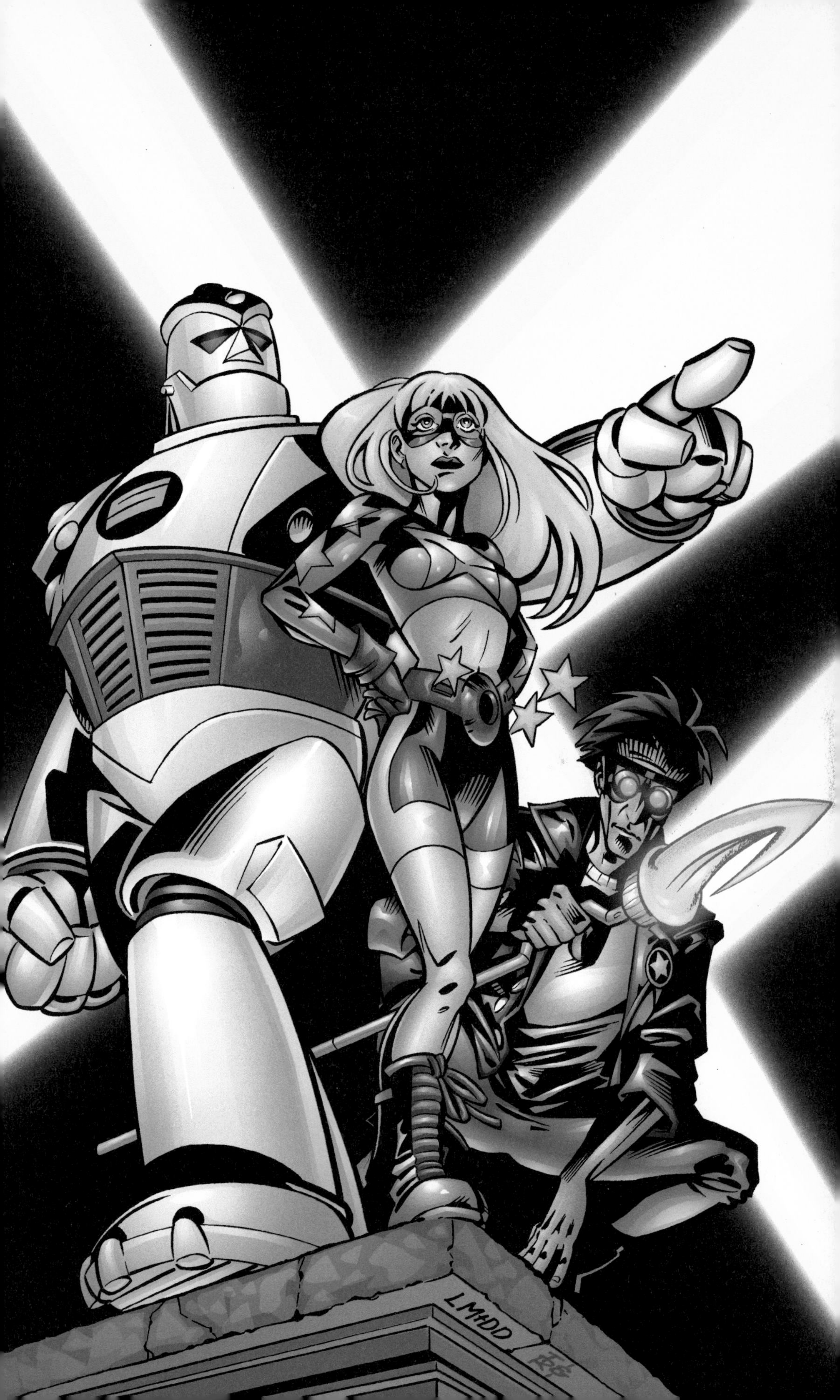

STARS AND S.T.R.I.P.E. #0

Written by GEOFF JOHNS and JAMES ROBINSON
Pencils by LEE MODER (present) and CHRIS WESTON (past)
Inks by DAN DAVIS (present) and JOHN STOKES (past)
Colors by TOM McCRAW (present) and CARLA FEENY (past)
Letters by BILL OAKLEY
Cover art by LEE MODER and DAN DAVIS
Cover color by RICHARD & TANYA HORIE

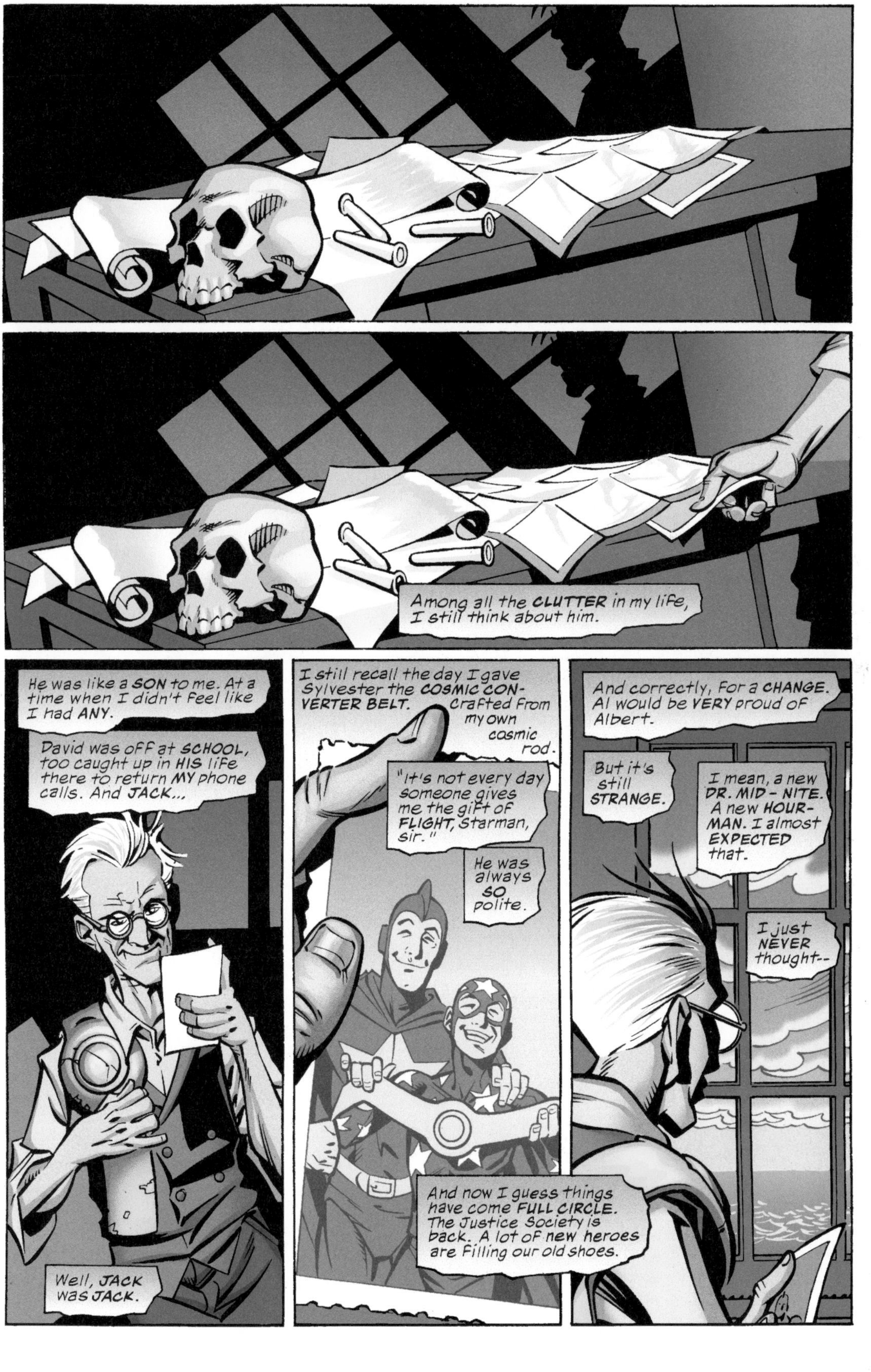

Among all the CLUTTER in my life, I still think about him.
He was like a SON to me. At a time when I didn't feel like I had ANY.
David was off at SCHOOL, too caught up in HIS life there to return MY phone calls. And JACK...
Well, JACK was JACK.
I still recall the day I gave Sylvester the COSMIC CONVERTER BELT.
Crafted from my own cosmic rod.
"It's not every day someone gives me the gift of FLIGHT, Starman, sir."
He was always SO polite.
And now I guess things have come FULL CIRCLE. The Justice Society is back. A lot of new heroes are filling our old shoes.
And correctly, for a CHANGE. Al would be VERY proud of Albert.
But it's still STRANGE.
I mean, a new DR. MID-NITE. A new HOURMAN. I almost EXPECTED that.
I just NEVER thought--

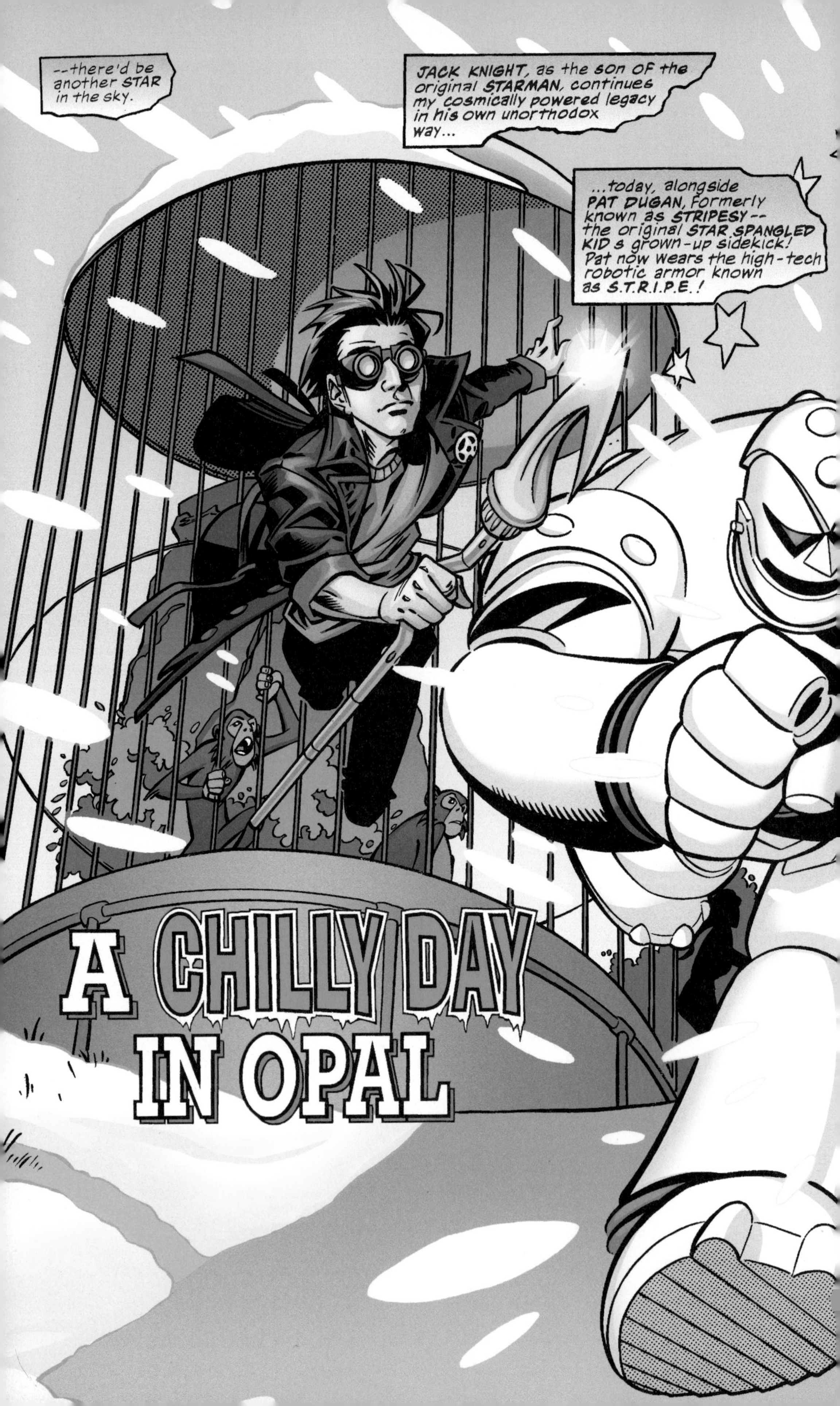
--there'd be another STAR in the sky.
JACK KNIGHT, as the son of the original STARMAN, continues my cosmically powered legacy in his own unorthodox way...
...today, alongside PAT DUGAN, formerly known as STRIPESY-- the original STAR SPANGLED KID's grown-up sidekick! Pat now wears the high-tech robotic armor known as S.T.R.I.P.E.!
A CHILLY DAY IN OPAL

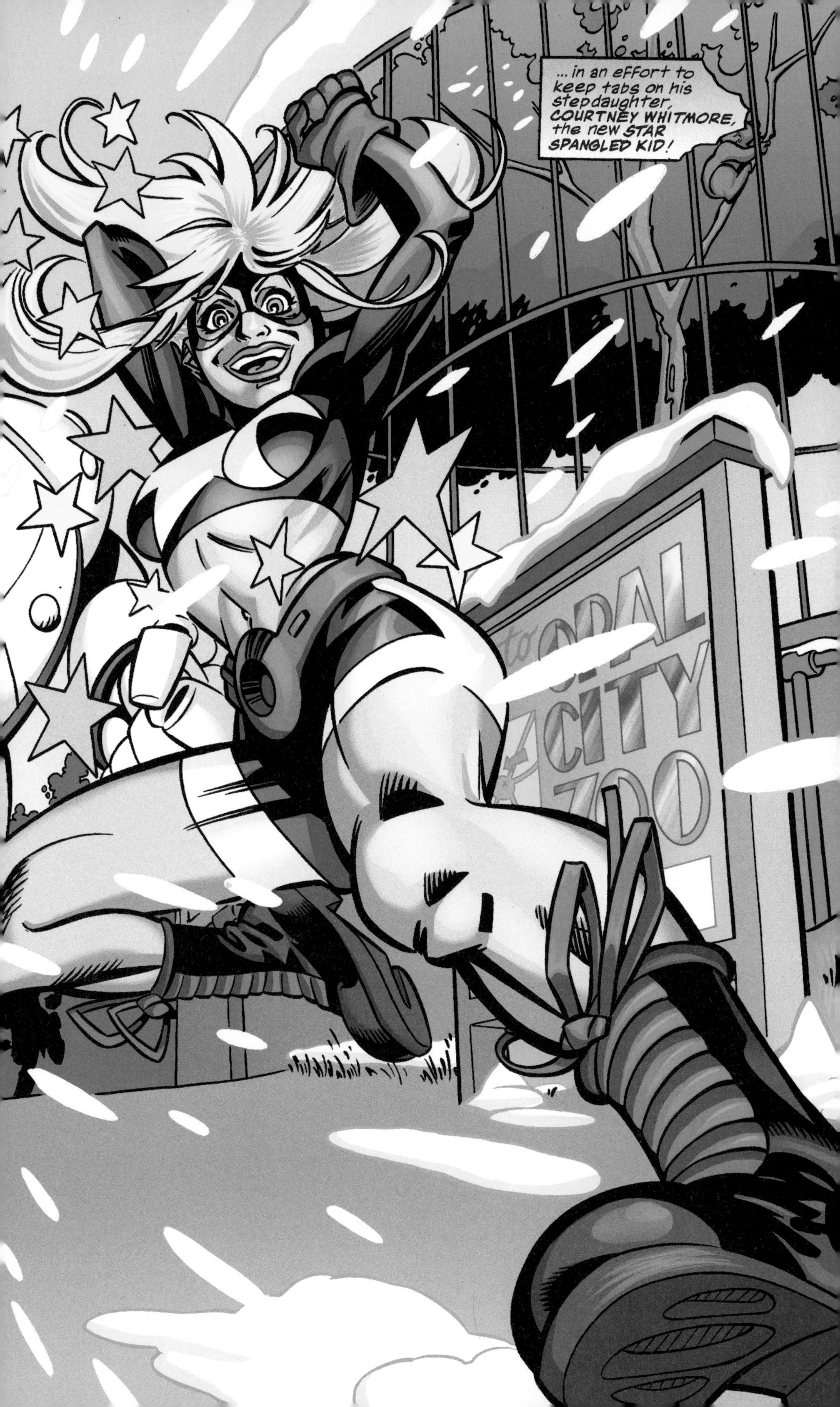
...in an effort to keep tabs on his stepdaughter, COURTNEY WHITMORE, the new STAR SPANGLED KID!
OPAL CITY ZOO

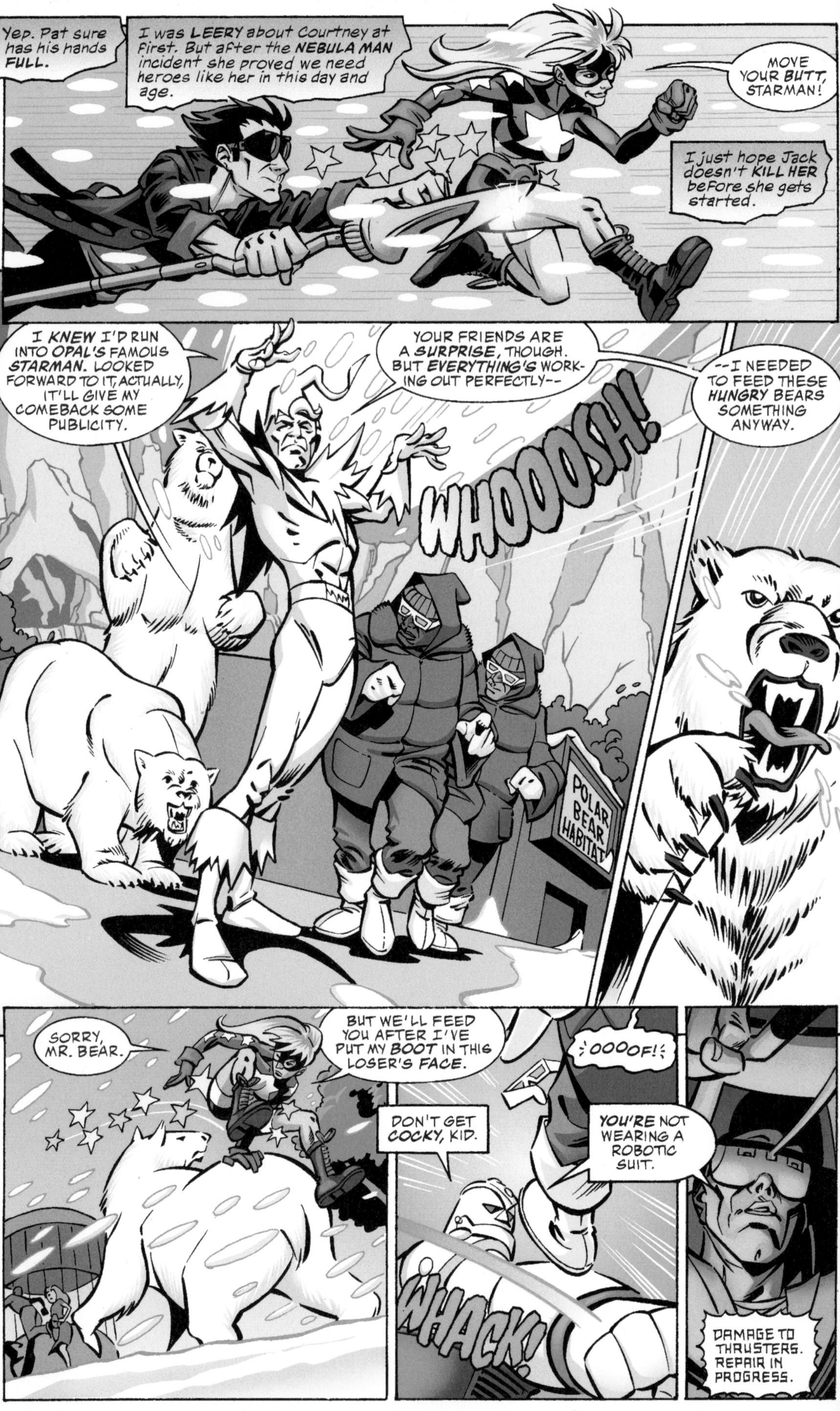
Yep. Pat sure has his hands FULL.
I was LEERY about Courtney at first. But after the NEBULA MAN incident she proved we need heroes like her in this day and age.
MOVE YOUR BUTT, STARMAN!
I just hope Jack doesn't KILL HER before she gets started.
I KNEW I'D RUN INTO OPAL'S FAMOUS STARMAN. LOOKED FORWARD TO IT, ACTUALLY. IT'LL GIVE MY COMEBACK SOME PUBLICITY.
YOUR FRIENDS ARE A SURPRISE, THOUGH. BUT EVERYTHING'S WORKING OUT PERFECTLY--
--I NEEDED TO FEED THESE HUNGRY BEARS SOMETHING ANYWAY.
WHOOOSH!
POLAR BEAR HABITAT
SORRY, MR. BEAR.
BUT WE'LL FEED YOU AFTER I'VE PUT MY BOOT IN THIS LOSER'S FACE.
OOOOF!
DON'T GET COCKY, KID.
YOU'RE NOT WEARING A ROBOTIC SUIT.
WHACK!
DAMAGE TO THRUSTERS. REPAIR IN PROGRESS.

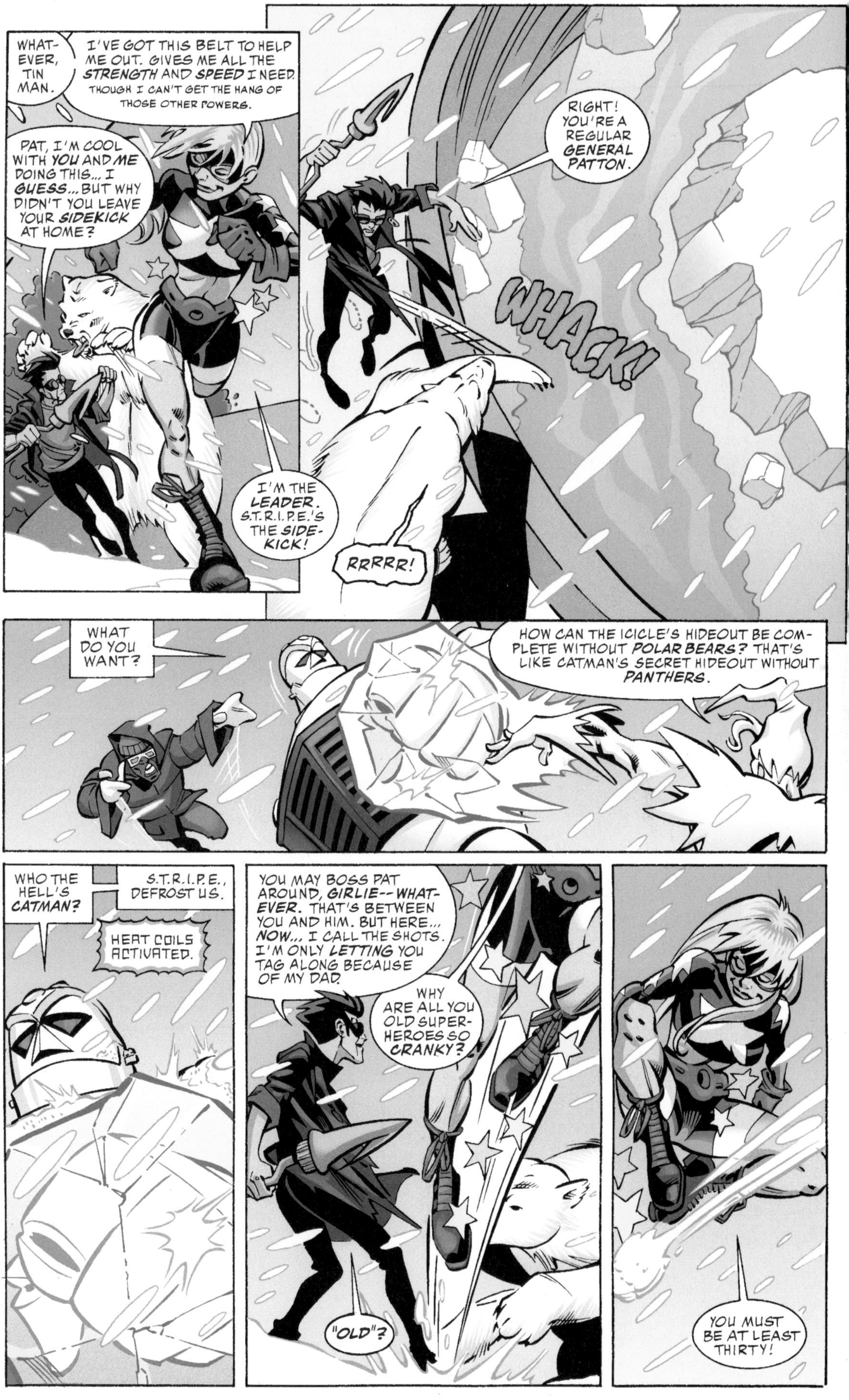
WHAT-EVER, TIN MAN.
I'VE GOT THIS BELT TO HELP ME OUT. GIVES ME ALL THE STRENGTH AND SPEED I NEED. THOUGH I CAN'T GET THE HANG OF THOSE OTHER POWERS.
PAT, I'M COOL WITH YOU AND ME DOING THIS... I GUESS... BUT WHY DIDN'T YOU LEAVE YOUR SIDEKICK AT HOME?
I'M THE LEADER. S.T.R.I.P.E.'S THE SIDE-KICK!
RIGHT! YOU'RE A REGULAR GENERAL PATTON.
WHACK!
RRRRR!
WHAT DO YOU WANT?
HOW CAN THE ICICLE'S HIDEOUT BE COM-PLETE WITHOUT POLAR BEARS? THAT'S LIKE CATMAN'S SECRET HIDEOUT WITHOUT PANTHERS.
WHO THE HELL'S CATMAN?
S.T.R.I.P.E., DEFROST US.
HEAT COILS ACTIVATED.
YOU MAY BOSS PAT AROUND, GIRLIE--WHAT-EVER. THAT'S BETWEEN YOU AND HIM. BUT HERE... NOW... I CALL THE SHOTS. I'M ONLY LETTING YOU TAG ALONG BECAUSE OF MY DAD.
WHY ARE ALL YOU OLD SUPER-HEROES SO CRANKY?
"OLD"?
YOU MUST BE AT LEAST THIRTY!

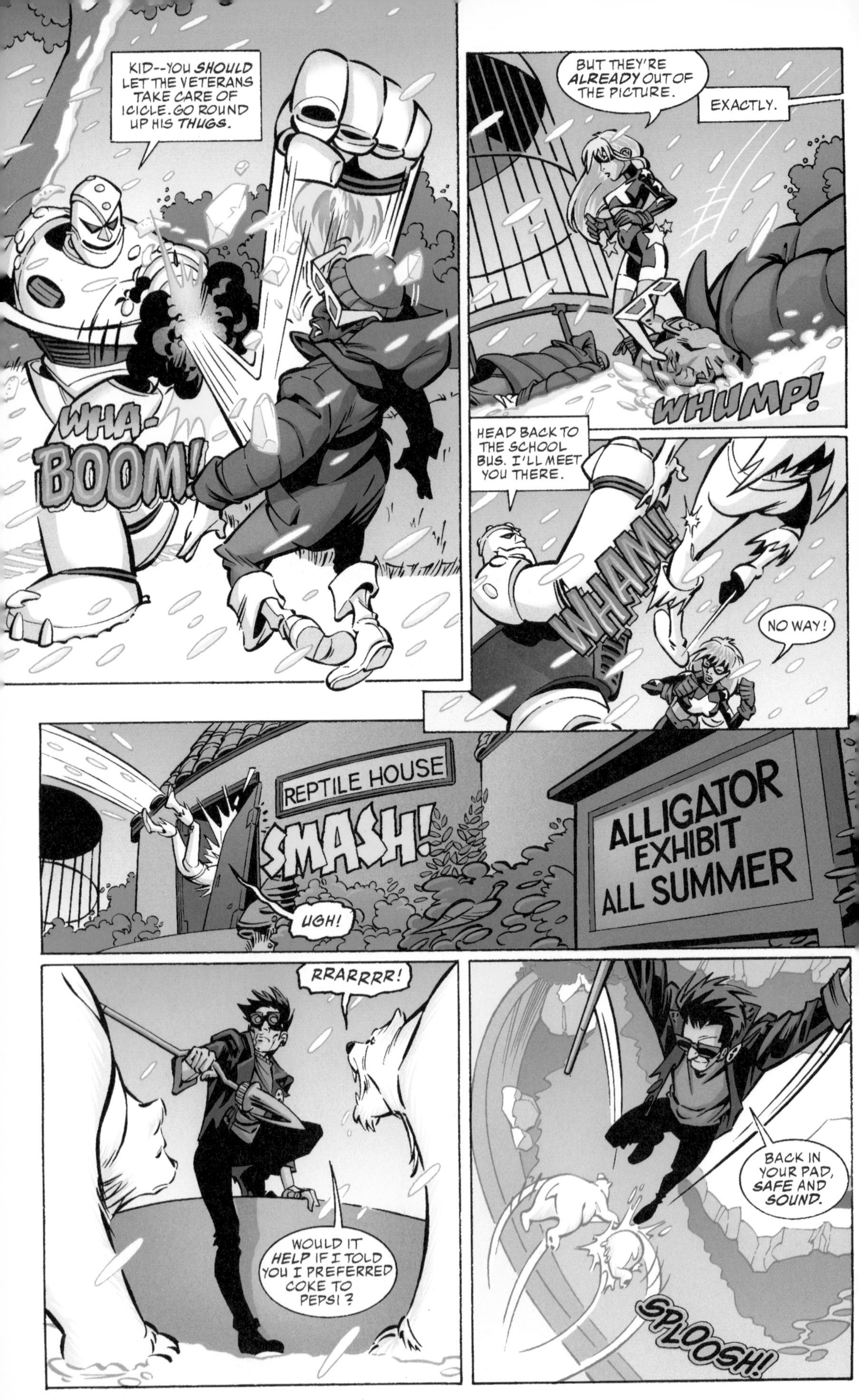
KID--YOU SHOULD LET THE VETERANS TAKE CARE OF ICICLE. GO ROUND UP HIS THUGS.
WHA-BOOM!
BUT THEY'RE ALREADY OUT OF THE PICTURE.
EXACTLY.
WHUMP!
HEAD BACK TO THE SCHOOL BUS. I'LL MEET YOU THERE.
WHAM!
NO WAY!
REPTILE HOUSE
SMASH!
UGH!
ALLIGATOR EXHIBIT ALL SUMMER
RRARRRR!
WOULD IT HELP IF I TOLD YOU I PREFERRED COKE TO PEPSI ?
BACK IN YOUR PAD, SAFE AND SOUND.
SPLOOSH!

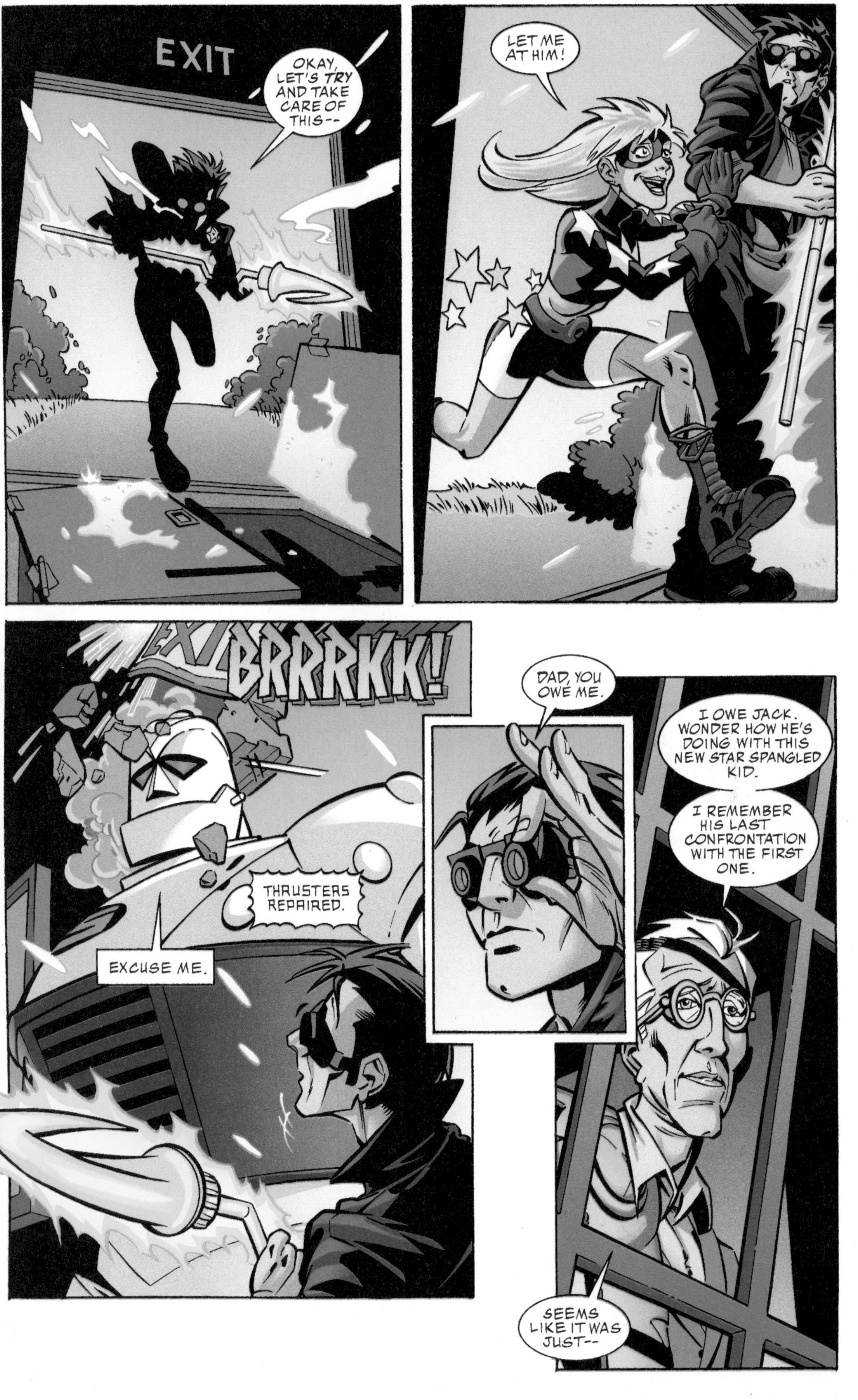
EXIT
OKAY, LET'S TRY AND TAKE CARE OF THIS--
LET ME AT HIM!
BRRRKK!
THRUSTERS REPAIRED.
EXCUSE ME.
DAD, YOU OWE ME.
I OWE JACK. WONDER HOW HE'S DOING WITH THIS NEW STAR SPANGLED KID.
I REMEMBER HIS LAST CONFRONTATION WITH THE FIRST ONE.
SEEMS LIKE IT WAS JUST--

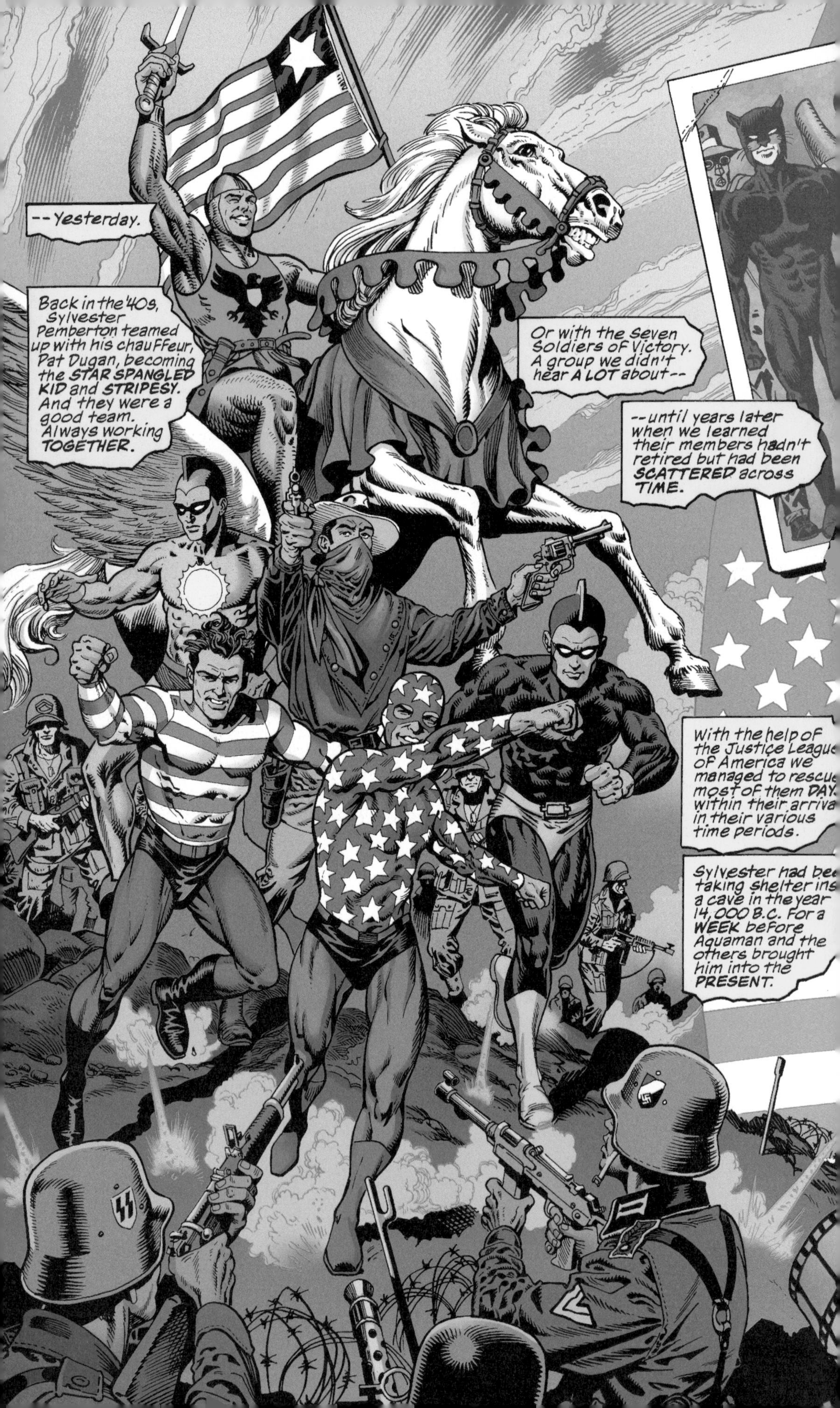

--Yesterday.
Back in the '40s, Sylvester Pemberton teamed up with his chauffeur, Pat Dugan, becoming the STAR SPANGLED KID and STRIPESY. And they were a good team. Always working TOGETHER.
Or with the Seven Soldiers of Victory. A group we didn't hear A LOT about--
--until years later when we learned their members hadn't retired but had been SCATTERED across TIME.
With the help of the Justice League of America we managed to rescu most of them DAY within their arriva in their various time periods.
Sylvester had be taking shelter ins a cave in the year 14,000 B.C. For a WEEK before Aquaman and the others brought him into the PRESENT.

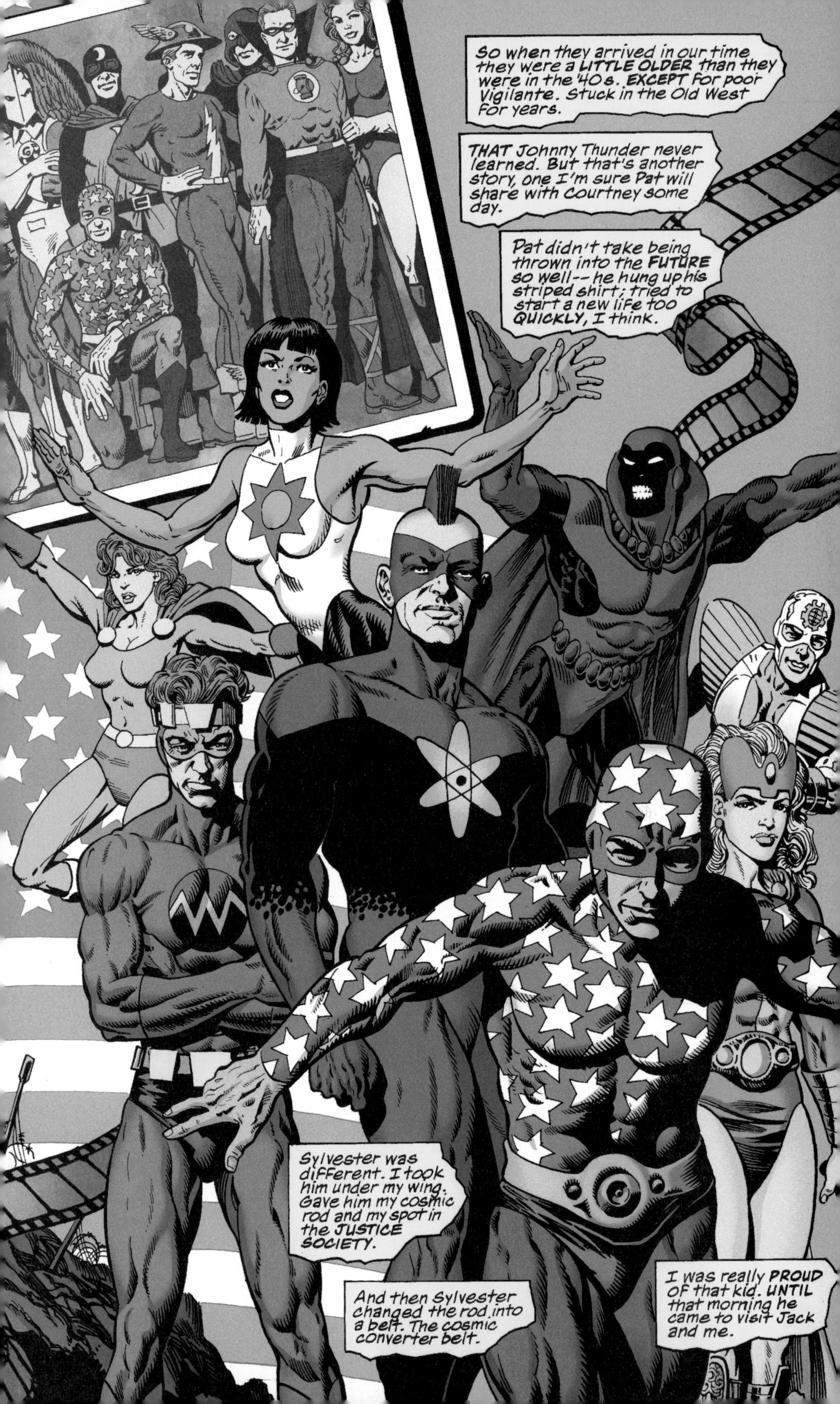
So when they arrived in our time they were a LITTLE OLDER than they were in the '40s. EXCEPT for poor Vigilante. Stuck in the Old West for years.
THAT Johnny Thunder never learned. But that's another story, one I'm sure Pat will share with Courtney some day.
Pat didn't take being thrown into the FUTURE so well-- he hung up his striped shirt; tried to start a new life too QUICKLY, I think.
Sylvester was different. I took him under my wing. Gave him my cosmic rod and my spot in the JUSTICE SOCIETY.
And then Sylvester changed the rod into a belt. The cosmic converter belt.
I was really PROUD of that kid. UNTIL that morning he came to visit Jack and me.

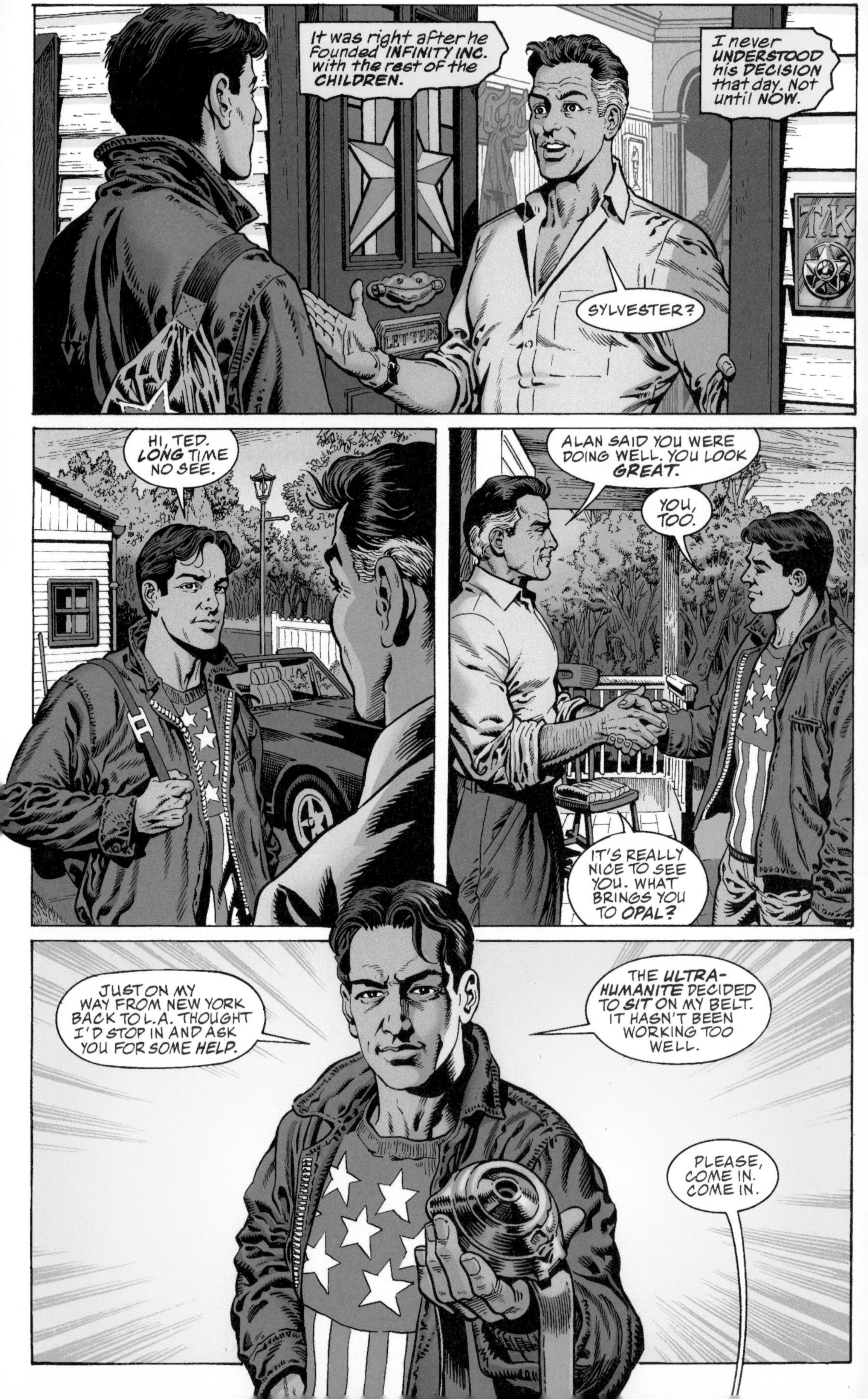

It was right after he founded INFINITY INC. with the rest of the CHILDREN.
I never UNDERSTOOD his DECISION that day. Not until NOW.
SYLVESTER?
LETTERS
HI, TED. LONG TIME NO SEE.
ALAN SAID YOU WERE DOING WELL. YOU LOOK GREAT.
YOU, TOO.
IT'S REALLY NICE TO SEE YOU. WHAT BRINGS YOU TO OPAL?
JUST ON MY WAY FROM NEW YORK BACK TO L.A. THOUGHT I'D STOP IN AND ASK YOU FOR SOME HELP.
THE ULTRA-HUMANITE DECIDED TO SIT ON MY BELT. IT HASN'T BEEN WORKING TOO WELL.
PLEASE, COME IN. COME IN.

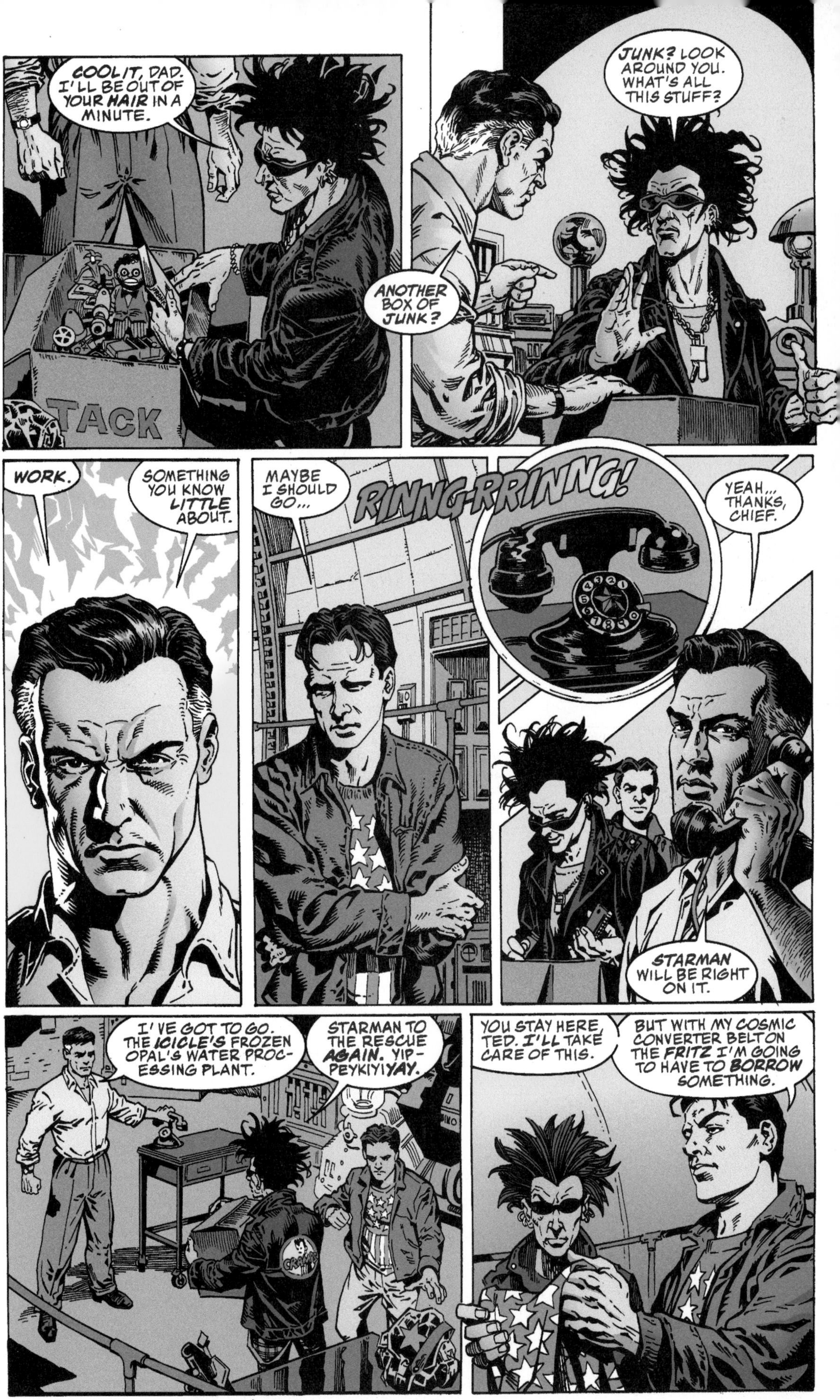

COOL IT, DAD. I'LL BE OUT OF YOUR HAIR IN A MINUTE.
TACK
ANOTHER BOX OF JUNK?
JUNK? LOOK AROUND YOU. WHAT'S ALL THIS STUFF?
WORK.
SOMETHING YOU KNOW LITTLE ABOUT.
MAYBE I SHOULD GO...
RINNG-RRINNG!
YEAH... THANKS, CHIEF.
STARMAN WILL BE RIGHT ON IT.
I'VE GOT TO GO. THE ICICLE'S FROZEN OPAL'S WATER PROCESSING PLANT.
STARMAN TO THE RESCUE AGAIN. YIP-PEYKIYIYAY.
YOU STAY HERE, TED. I'LL TAKE CARE OF THIS.
BUT WITH MY COSMIC CONVERTER BELT ON THE FRITZ I'M GOING TO HAVE TO BORROW SOMETHING.

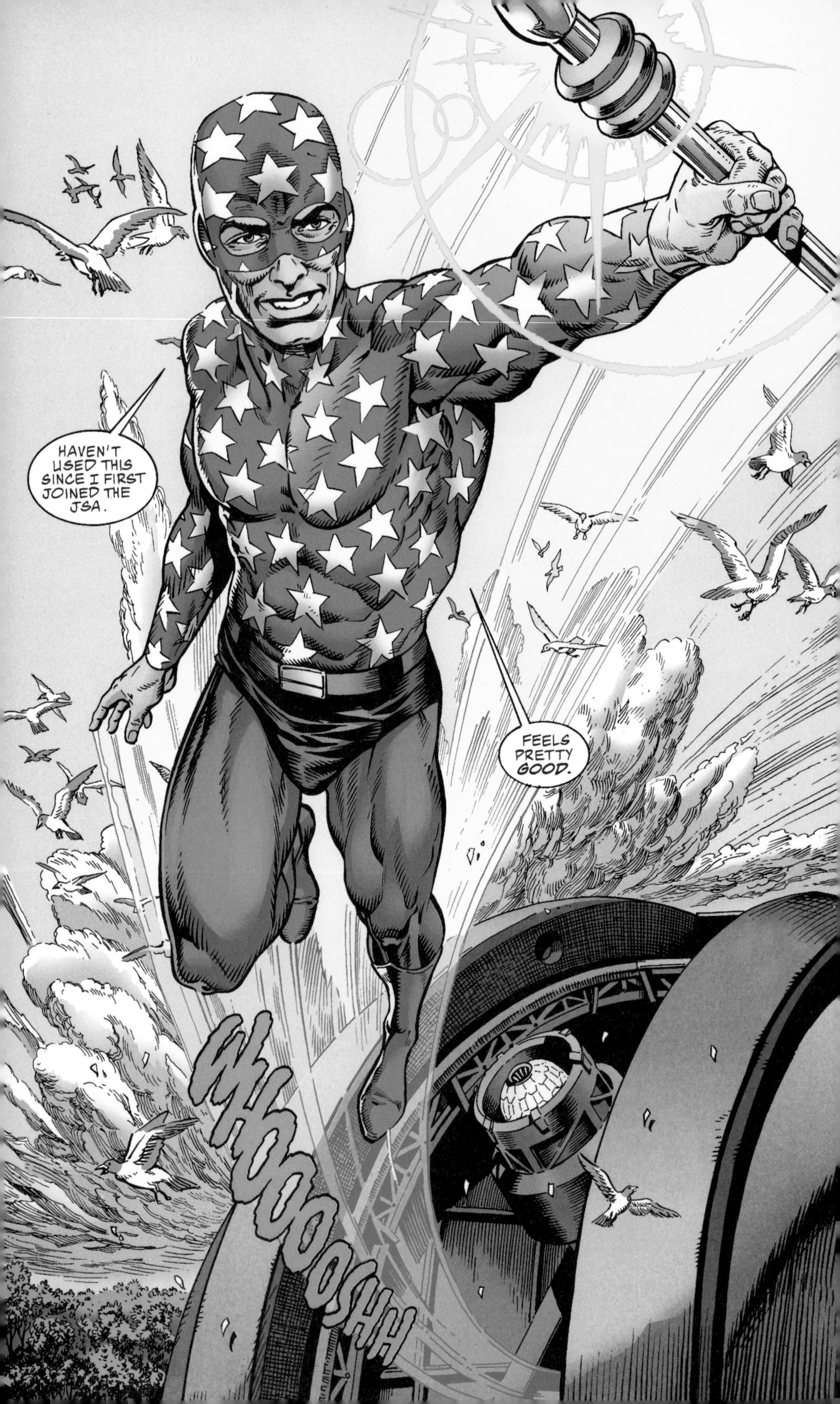

HAVEN'T USED THIS SINCE I FIRST JOINED THE JSA.
FEELS PRETTY GOOD.
WHOOOOSHH

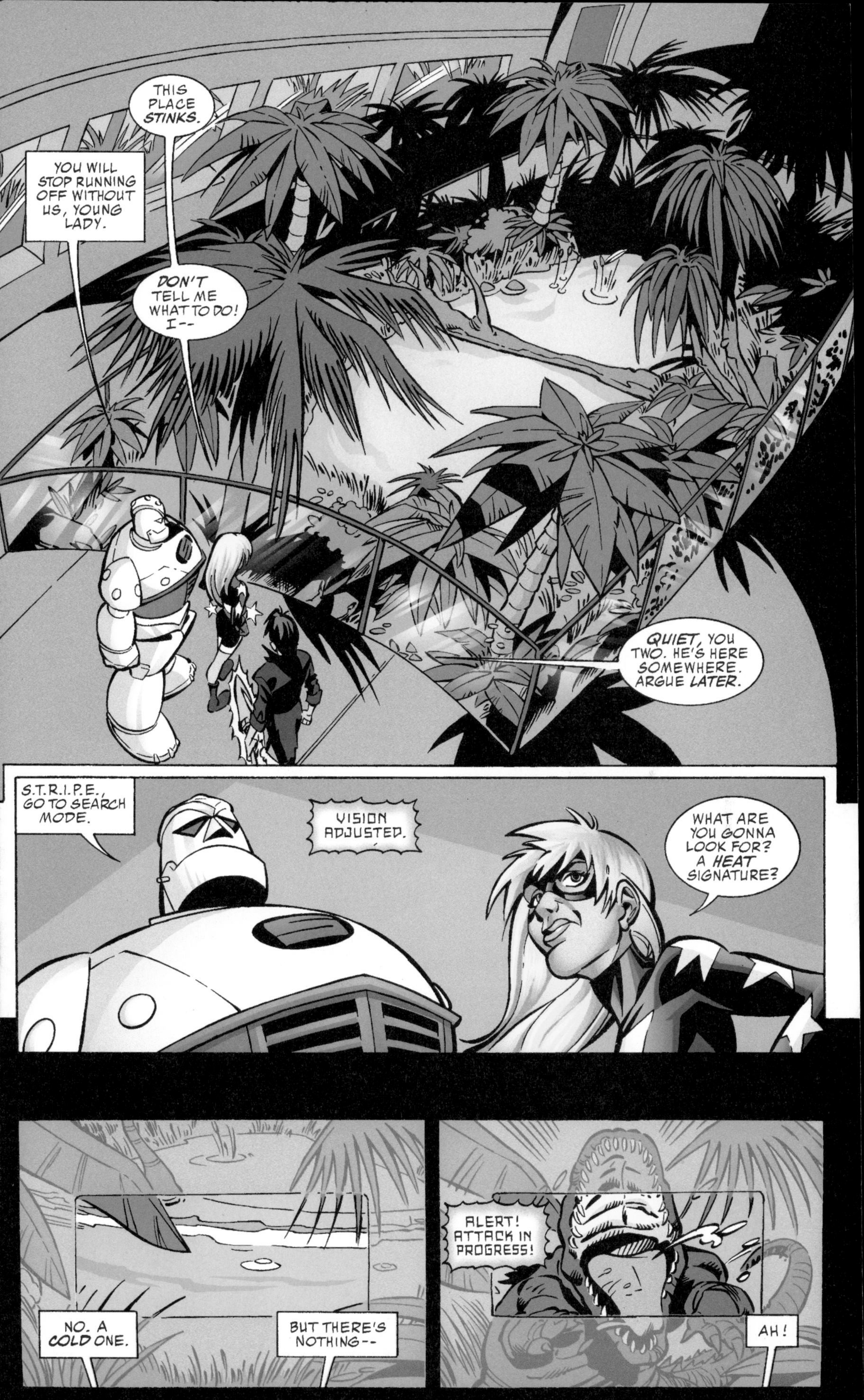
THIS PLACE STINKS.
YOU WILL STOP RUNNING OFF WITHOUT US, YOUNG LADY.
DON'T TELL ME WHAT TO DO! I--
QUIET, YOU TWO. HE'S HERE SOMEWHERE. ARGUE LATER.
S.T.R.I.P.E., GO TO SEARCH MODE.
VISION ADJUSTED.
WHAT ARE YOU GONNA LOOK FOR? A HEAT SIGNATURE?
NO. A COLD ONE.
BUT THERE'S NOTHING--
ALERT! ATTACK IN PROGRESS!
AH!

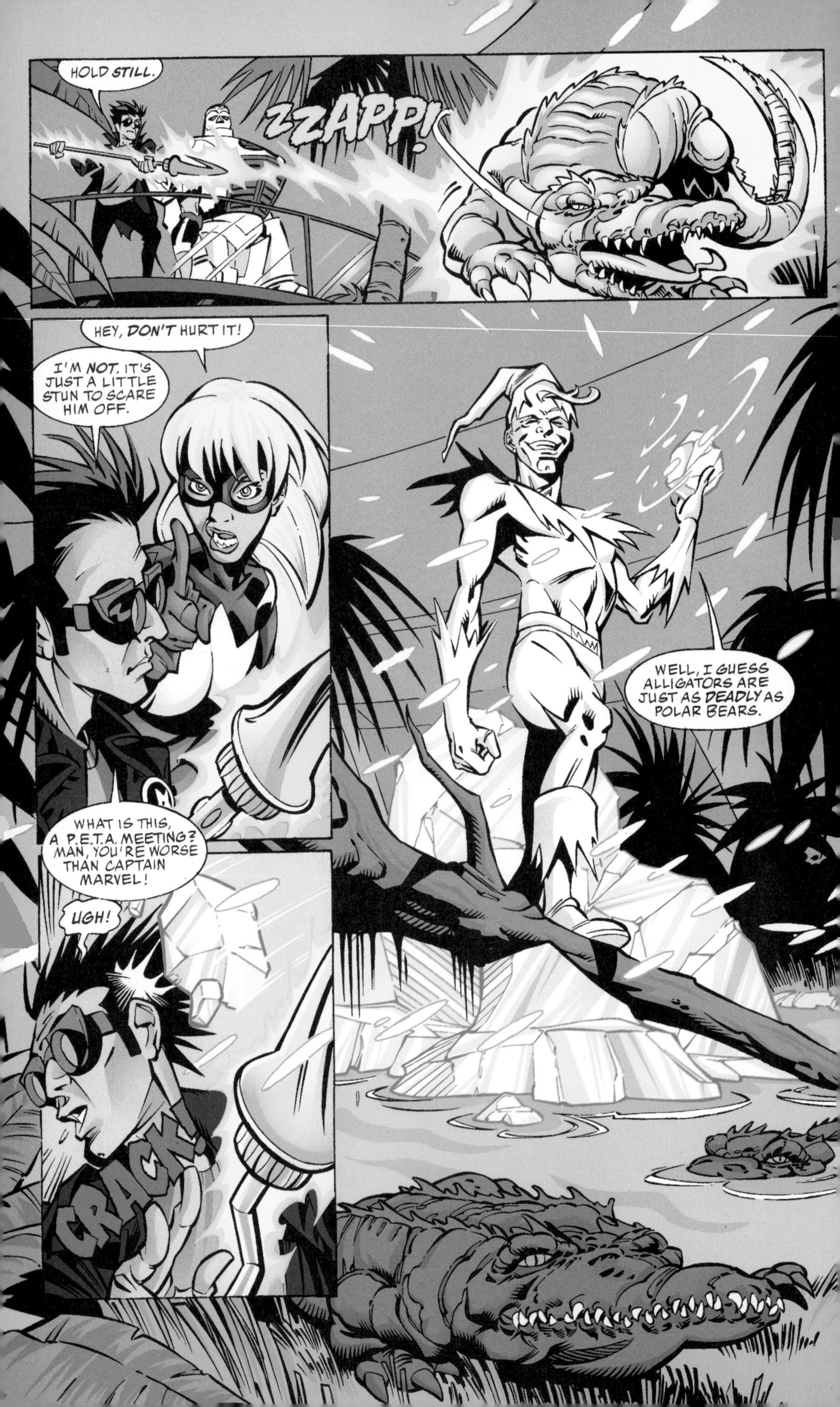
HOLD STILL.
ZZAPP!
HEY, DON'T HURT IT!
I'M NOT. IT'S JUST A LITTLE STUN TO SCARE HIM OFF.
WELL, I GUESS ALLIGATORS ARE JUST AS DEADLY AS POLAR BEARS.
WHAT IS THIS, A P.E.T.A. MEETING? MAN, YOU'RE WORSE THAN CAPTAIN MARVEL!
UGH!
CRACK

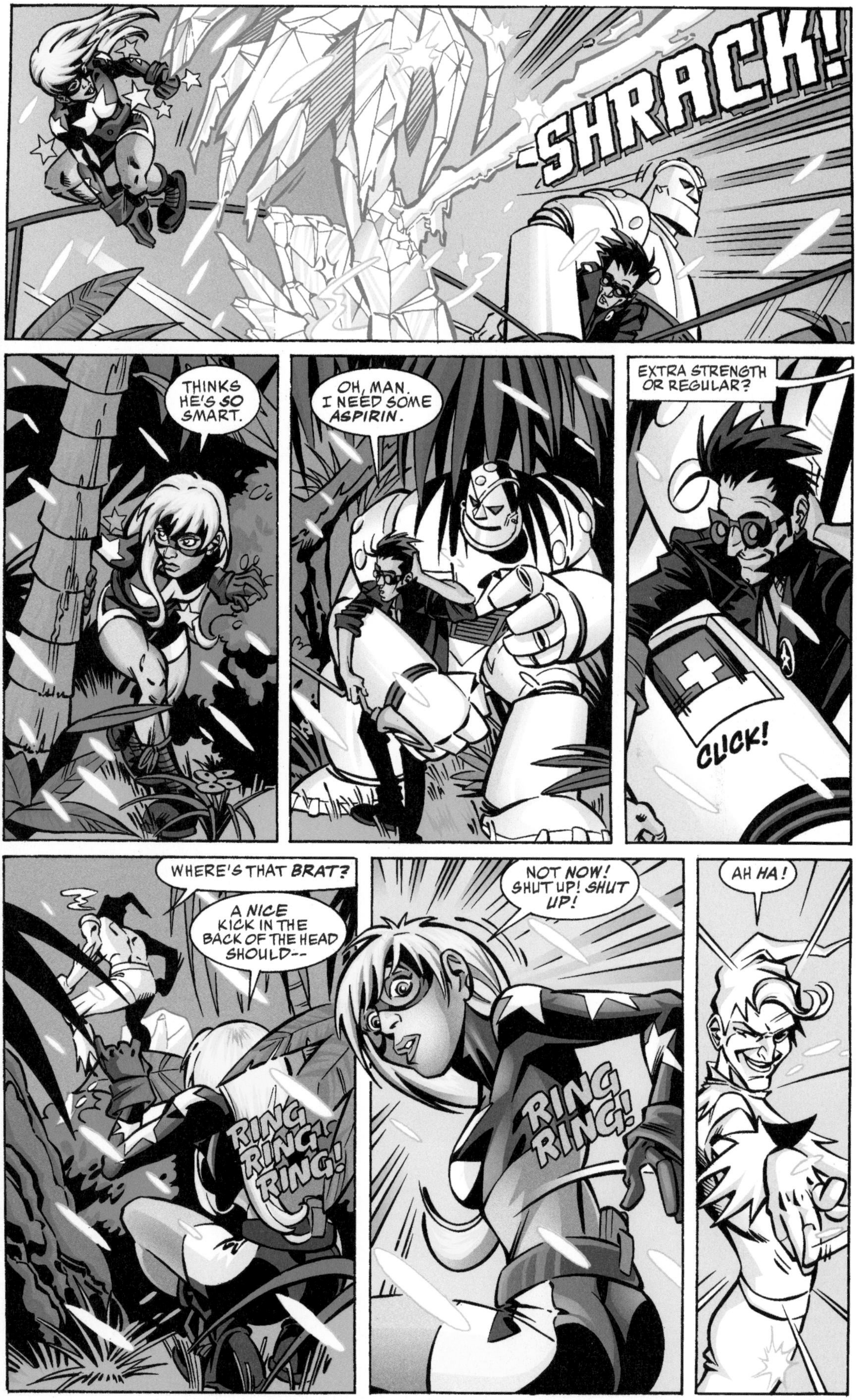
SHRACK!
THINKS HE'S SO SMART.
OH, MAN. I NEED SOME ASPIRIN.
EXTRA STRENGTH OR REGULAR?
CLICK!
WHERE'S THAT BRAT?
A NICE KICK IN THE BACK OF THE HEAD SHOULD--
RING RING RING!
NOT NOW! SHUT UP! SHUT UP!
RING RING!
AH HA!

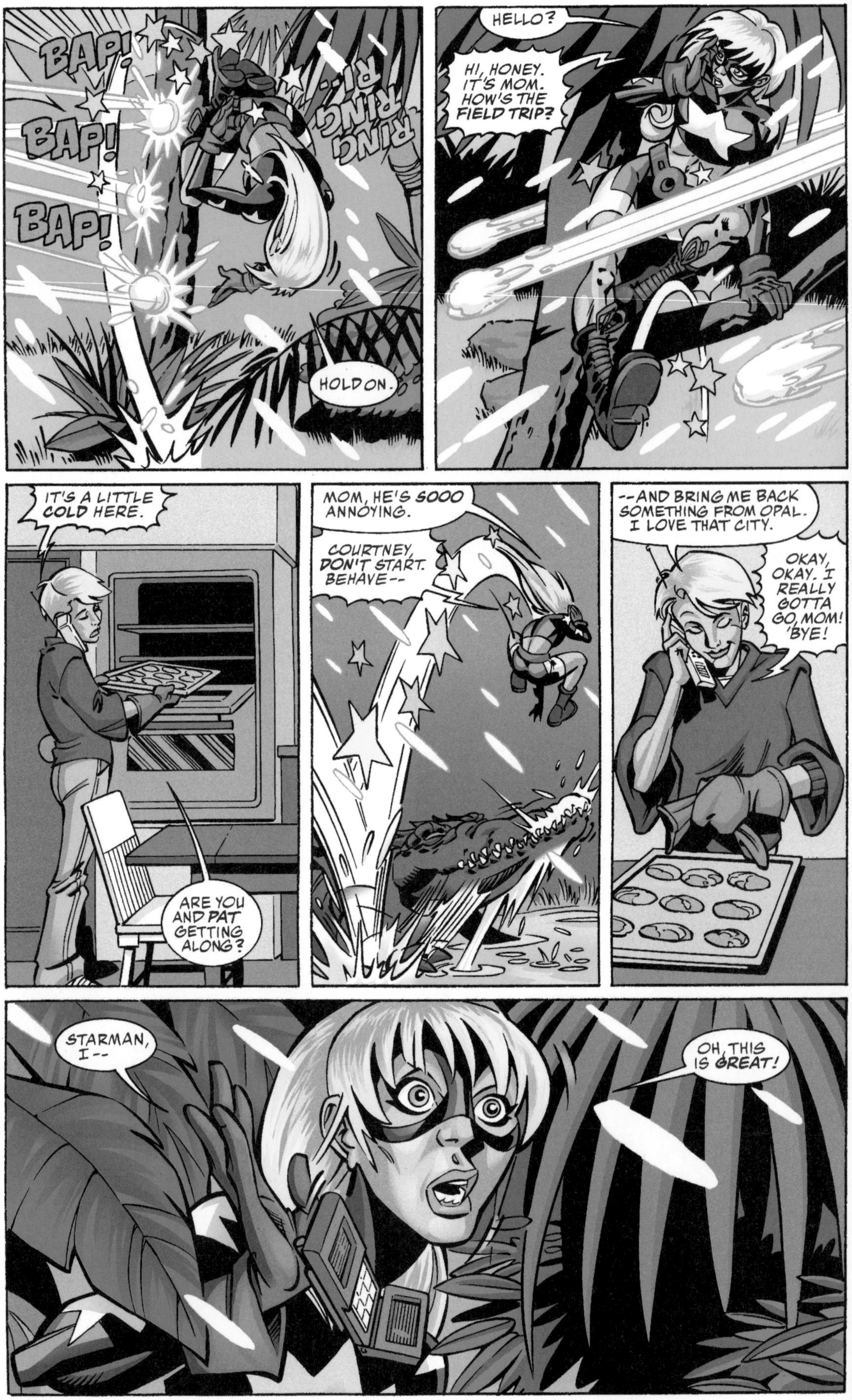
BAP!
BAP!
BAP!
RING RING RI--
HOLD ON.
HELLO?
HI, HONEY. IT'S MOM. HOW'S THE FIELD TRIP?
IT'S A LITTLE COLD HERE.
ARE YOU AND PAT GETTING ALONG?
MOM, HE'S SOOO ANNOYING.
COURTNEY, DON'T START. BEHAVE--
--AND BRING ME BACK SOMETHING FROM OPAL. I LOVE THAT CITY.
OKAY, OKAY. I REALLY GOTTA GO, MOM! 'BYE!
STARMAN, I--
OH, THIS IS GREAT!

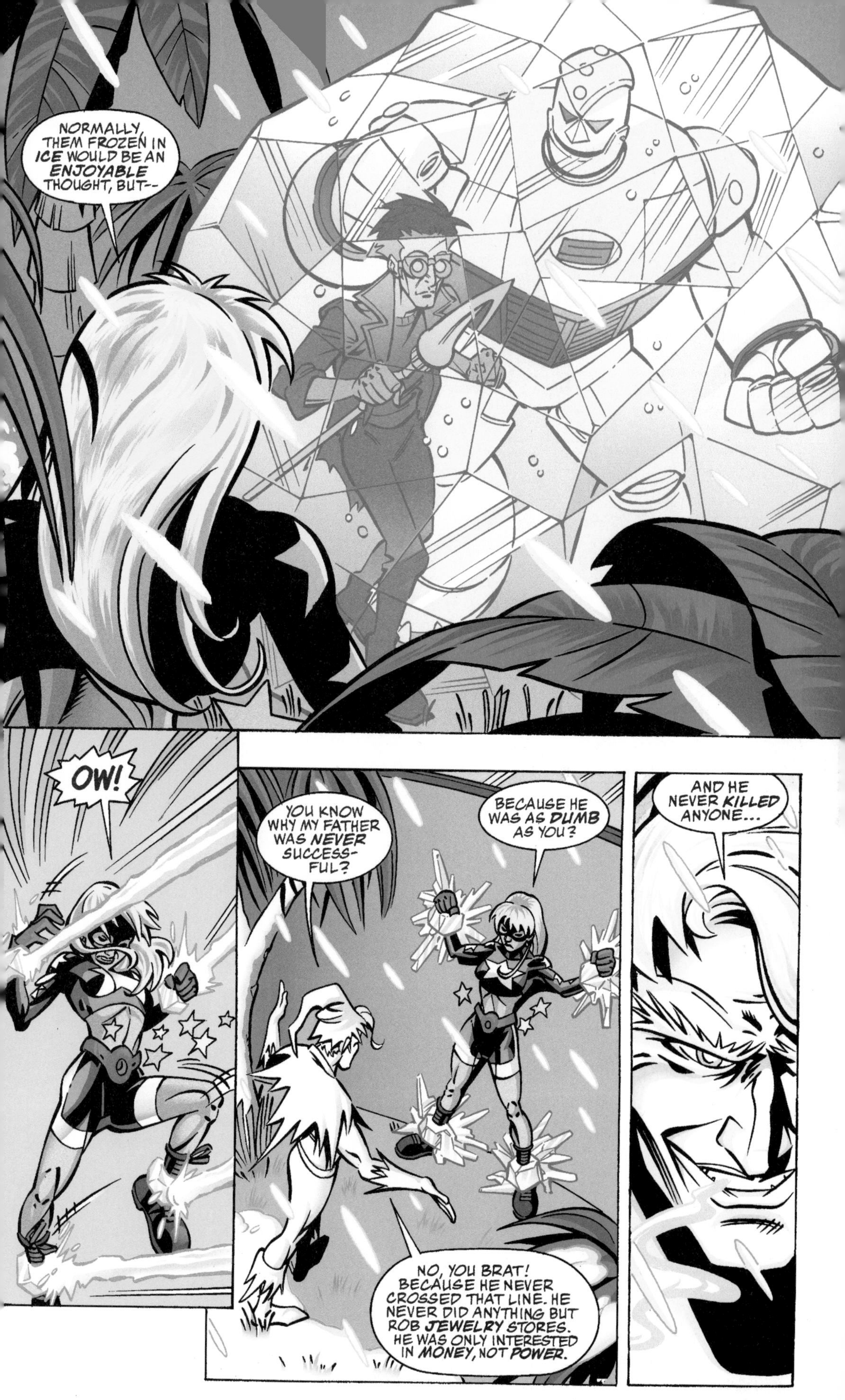
NORMALLY, THEM FROZEN IN ICE WOULD BE AN ENJOYABLE THOUGHT, BUT--
OW!
YOU KNOW WHY MY FATHER WAS NEVER SUCCESS-FUL?
BECAUSE HE WAS AS DUMB AS YOU?
NO, YOU BRAT! BECAUSE HE NEVER CROSSED THAT LINE. HE NEVER DID ANYTHING BUT ROB JEWELRY STORES. HE WAS ONLY INTERESTED IN MONEY, NOT POWER.
AND HE NEVER KILLED ANYONE...

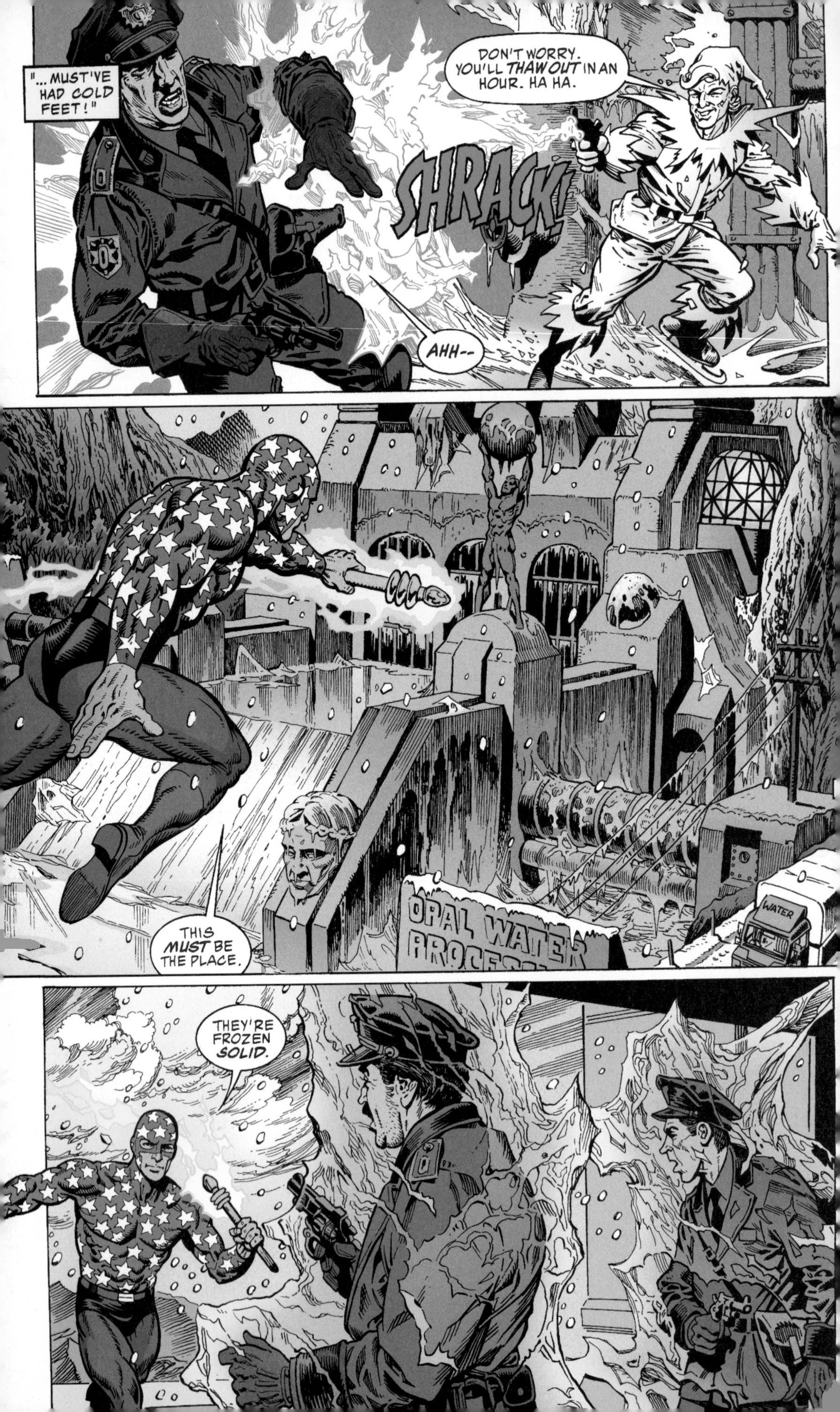
"...MUST'VE HAD COLD FEET!"
DON'T WORRY. YOU'LL THAW OUT IN AN HOUR. HA HA.
SHRACK!
AHH--
OPAL WATER
WATER
THIS MUST BE THE PLACE.
THEY'RE FROZEN SOLID.

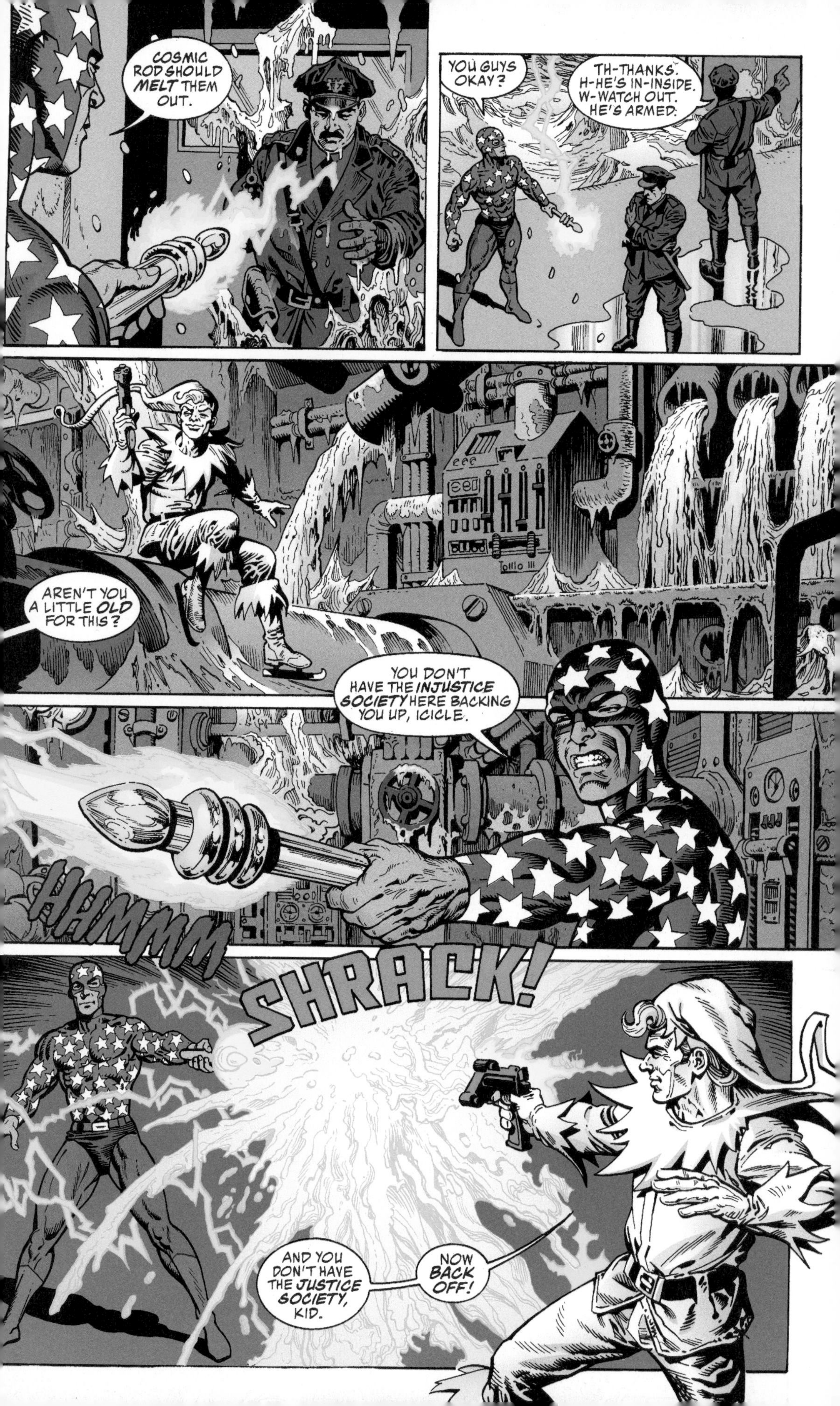
COSMIC ROD SHOULD MELT THEM OUT.
YOU GUYS OKAY?
TH-THANKS. H-HE'S IN-INSIDE. W-WATCH OUT. HE'S ARMED.
AREN'T YOU A LITTLE OLD FOR THIS?
YOU DON'T HAVE THE INJUSTICE SOCIETY HERE BACKING YOU UP, ICICLE.
HHMMMM
SHRACK!
AND YOU DON'T HAVE THE JUSTICE SOCIETY, KID.
NOW BACK OFF!

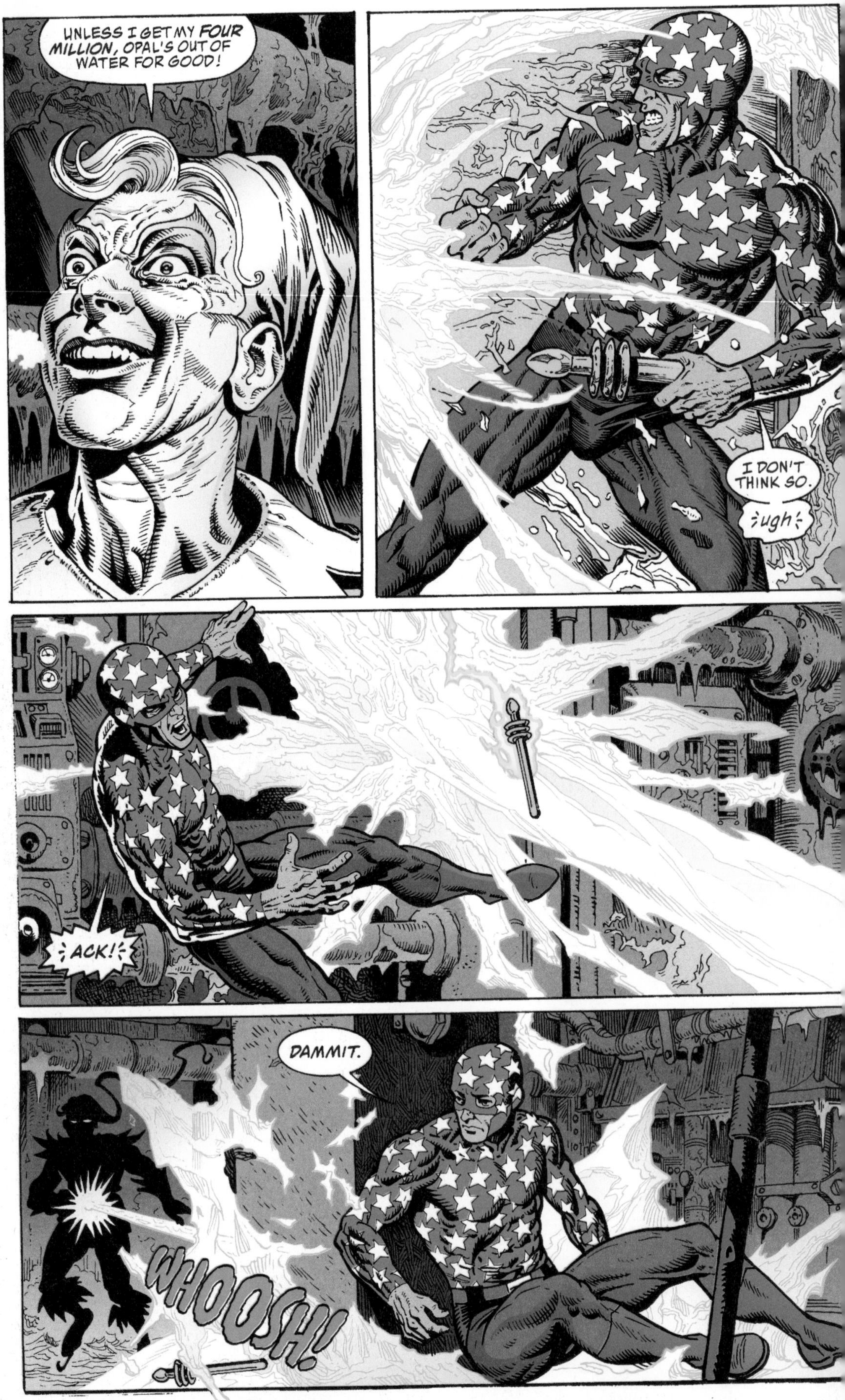
UNLESS I GET MY FOUR MILLION, OPAL'S OUT OF WATER FOR GOOD!
I DON'T THINK SO.
ugh
ACK!
DAMMIT.
WHOOSH!

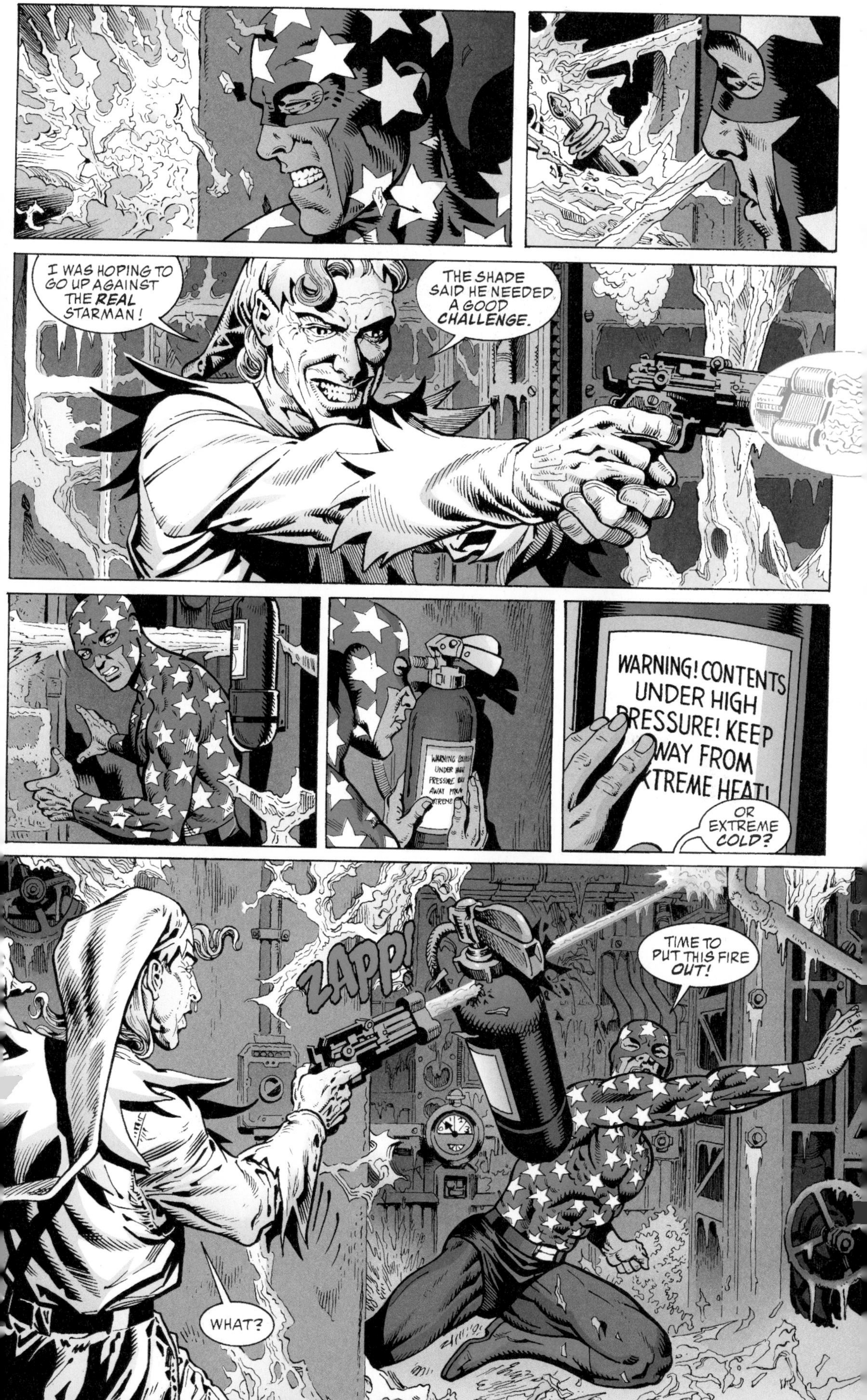

I WAS HOPING TO GO UP AGAINST THE REAL STARMAN!
THE SHADE SAID HE NEEDED A GOOD CHALLENGE.
WARNING! CONTENTS UNDER HIGH PRESSURE! KEEP AWAY FROM EXTREME HEAT!
OR EXTREME COLD?
ZAPP!
TIME TO PUT THIS FIRE OUT!
WHAT?

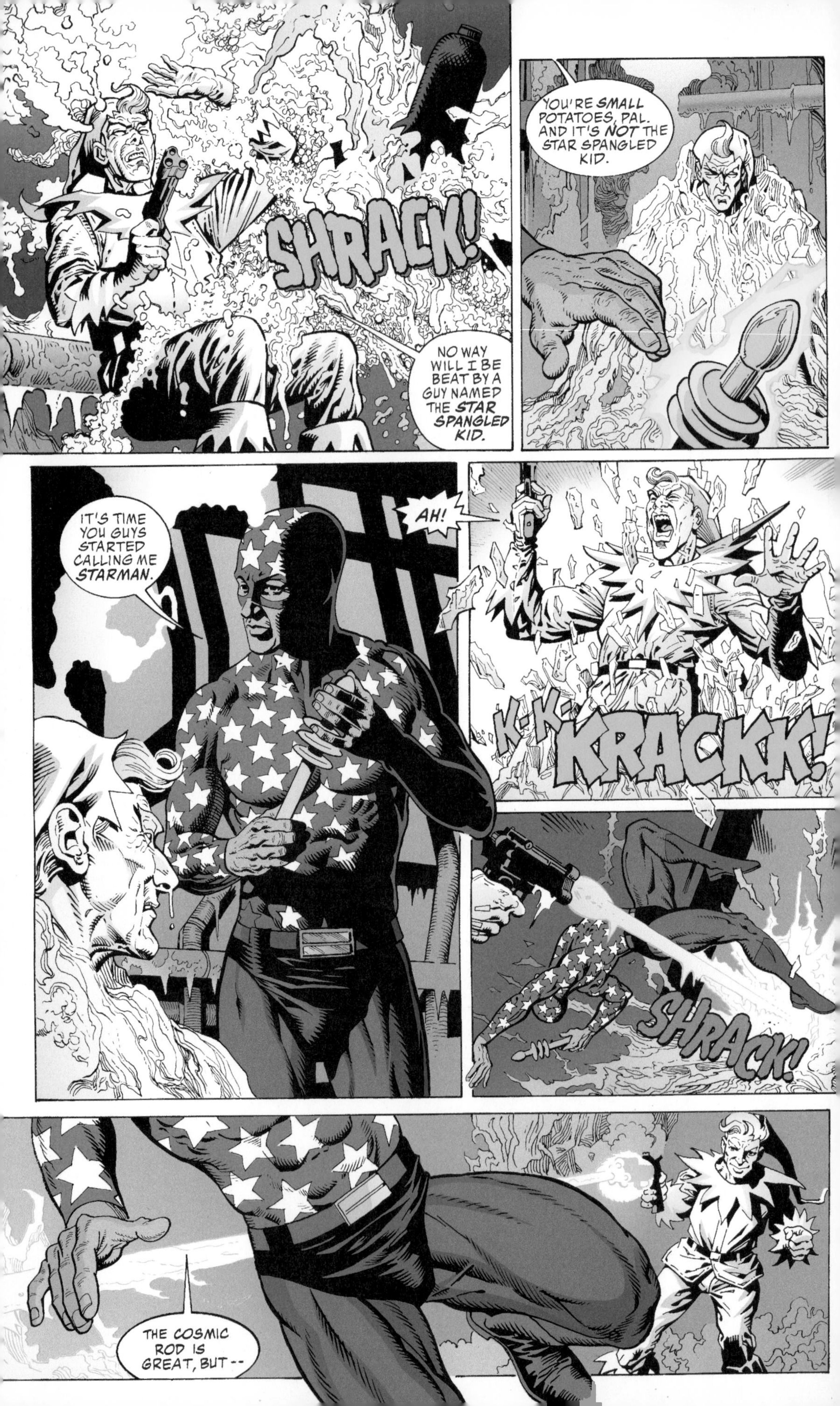
SHRACK!
NO WAY WILL I BE BEAT BY A GUY NAMED THE STAR SPANGLED KID.
YOU'RE SMALL POTATOES, PAL. AND IT'S NOT THE STAR SPANGLED KID.
IT'S TIME YOU GUYS STARTED CALLING ME STARMAN.
AH!
K-K-KRACKK!
SHRACK!
THE COSMIC ROD IS GREAT, BUT --

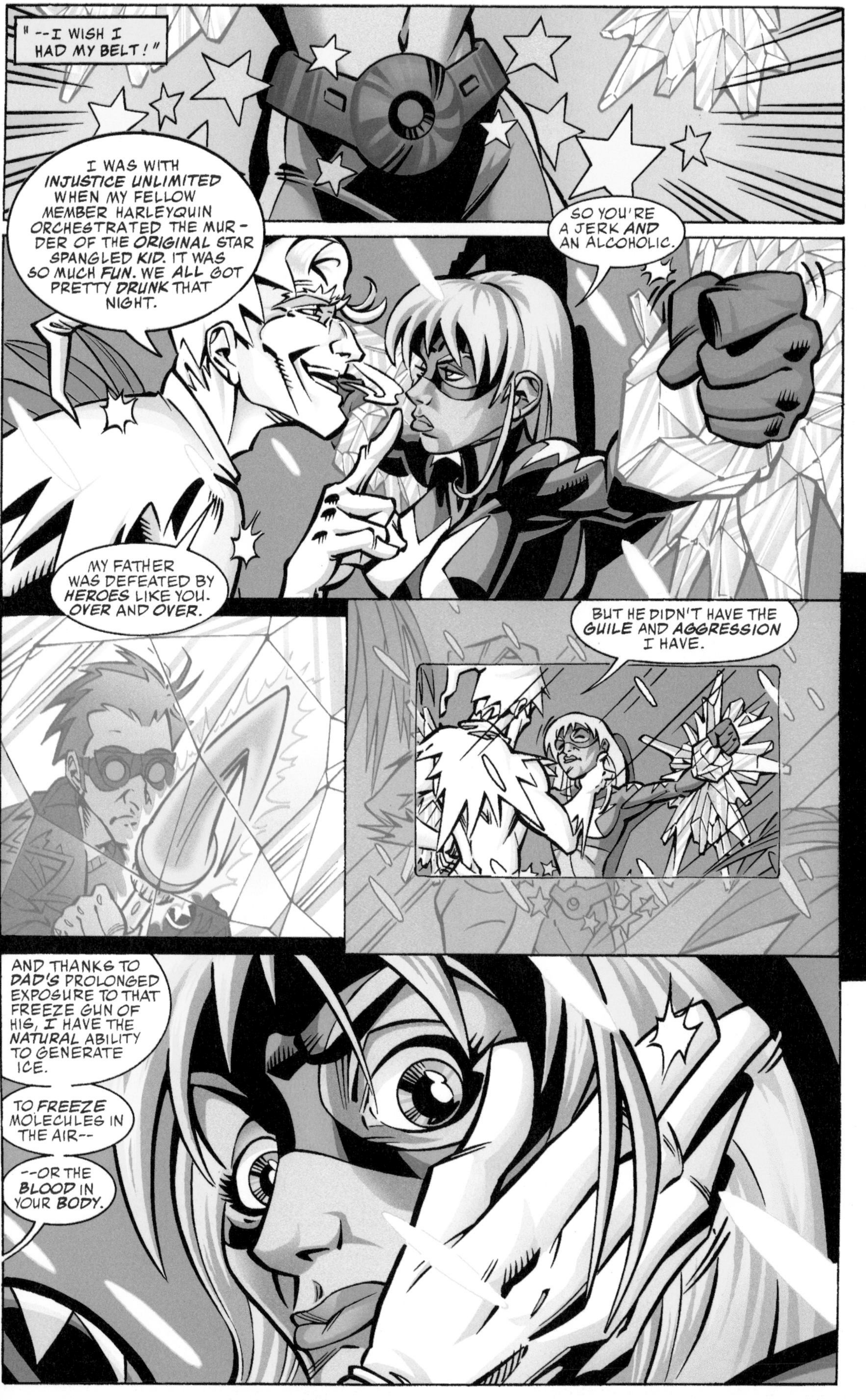
"--I WISH I HAD MY BELT!"
I WAS WITH INJUSTICE UNLIMITED WHEN MY FELLOW MEMBER HARLEYQUIN ORCHESTRATED THE MURDER OF THE ORIGINAL STAR SPANGLED KID. IT WAS SO MUCH FUN. WE ALL GOT PRETTY DRUNK THAT NIGHT.
SO YOU'RE A JERK AND AN ALCOHOLIC.
MY FATHER WAS DEFEATED BY HEROES LIKE YOU. OVER AND OVER.
BUT HE DIDN'T HAVE THE GUILE AND AGGRESSION I HAVE.
AND THANKS TO DAD'S PROLONGED EXPOSURE TO THAT FREEZE GUN OF HIS, I HAVE THE NATURAL ABILITY TO GENERATE ICE.
TO FREEZE MOLECULES IN THE AIR--
--OR THE BLOOD IN YOUR BODY.

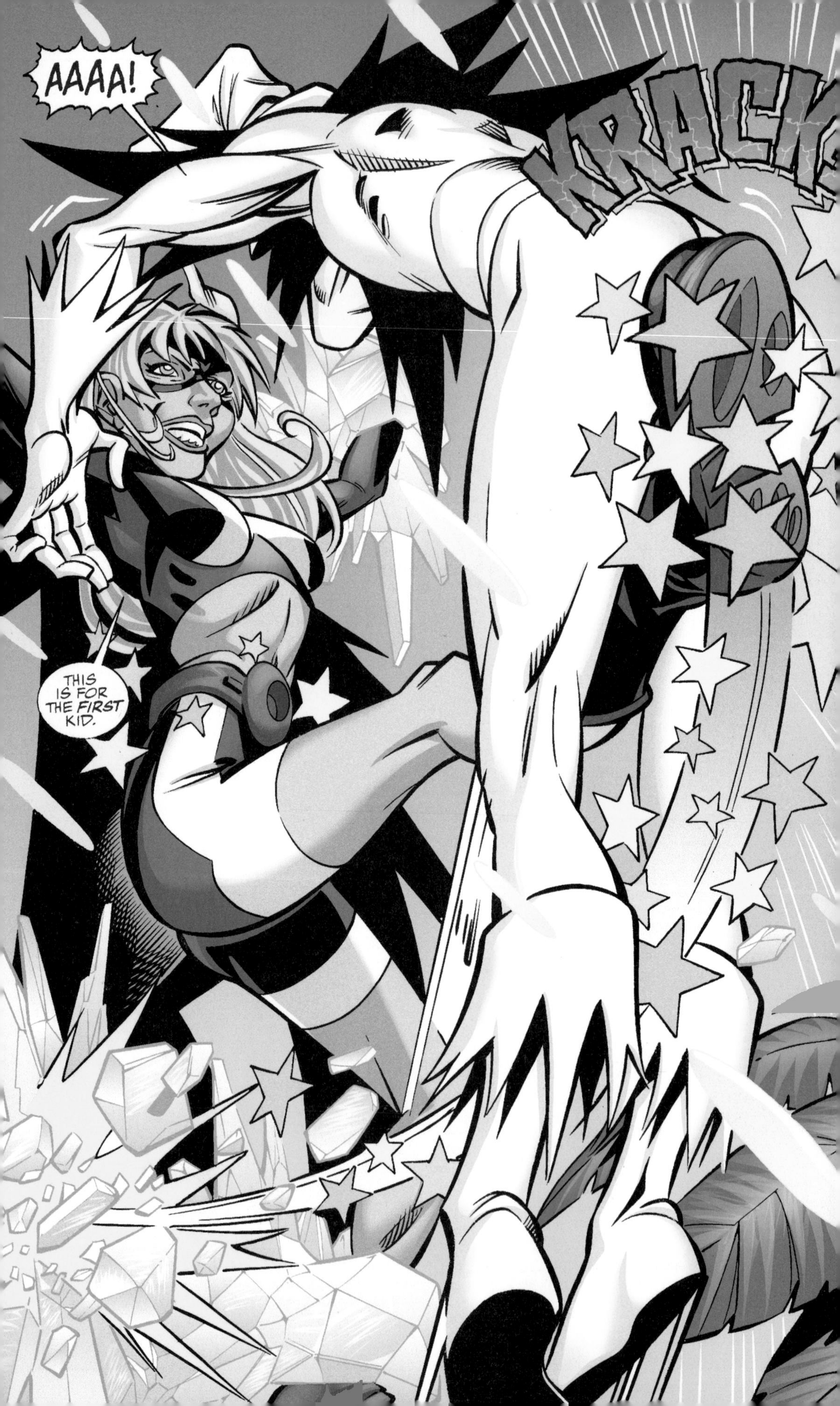
AAAA!
KRACK
THIS IS FOR THE *FIRST* KID.

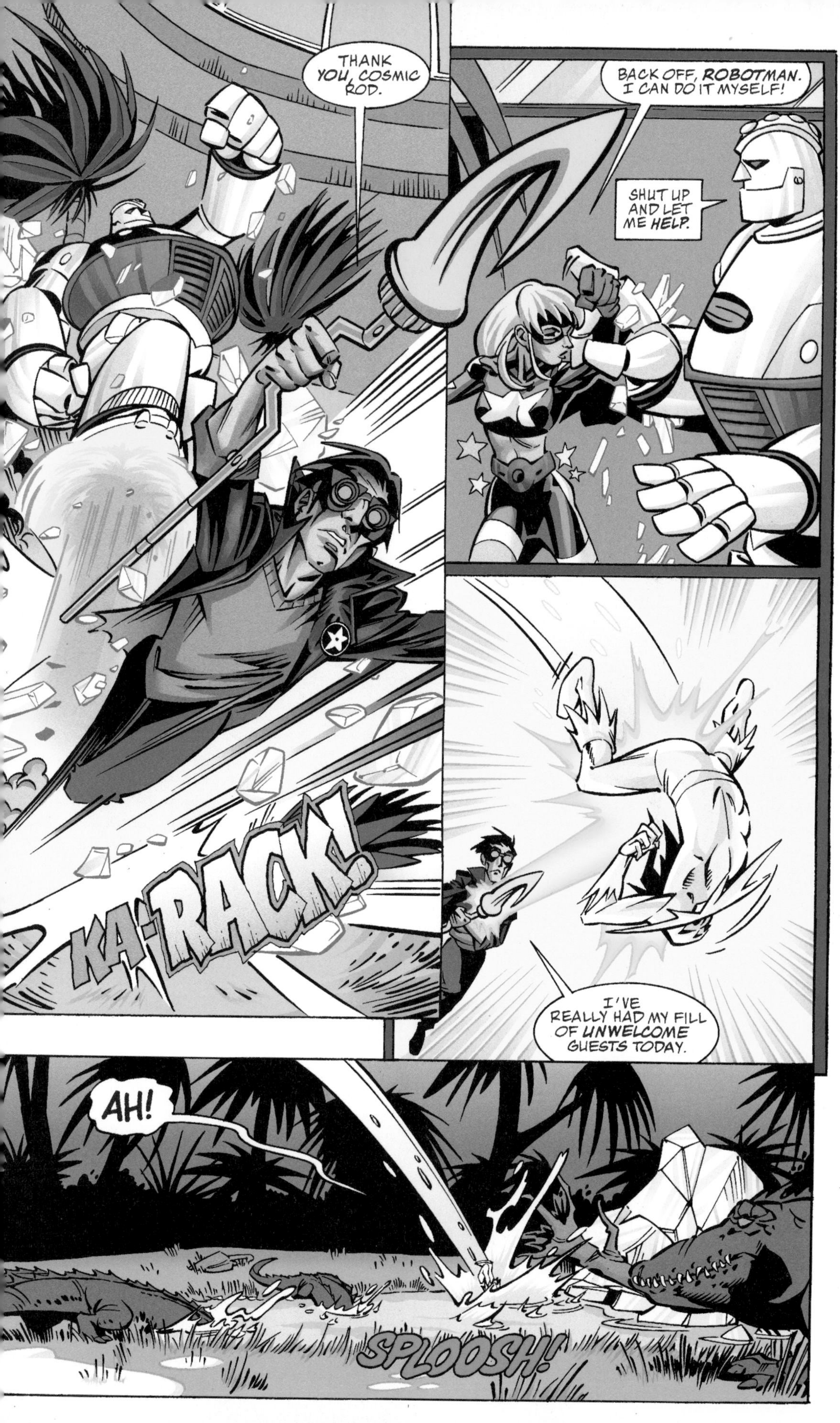
THANK YOU, COSMIC ROD.
KA-RACK!
BACK OFF, ROBOTMAN. I CAN DO IT MYSELF!
SHUT UP AND LET ME HELP.
I'VE REALLY HAD MY FILL OF UNWELCOME GUESTS TODAY.
AH!
SPLOOSH!

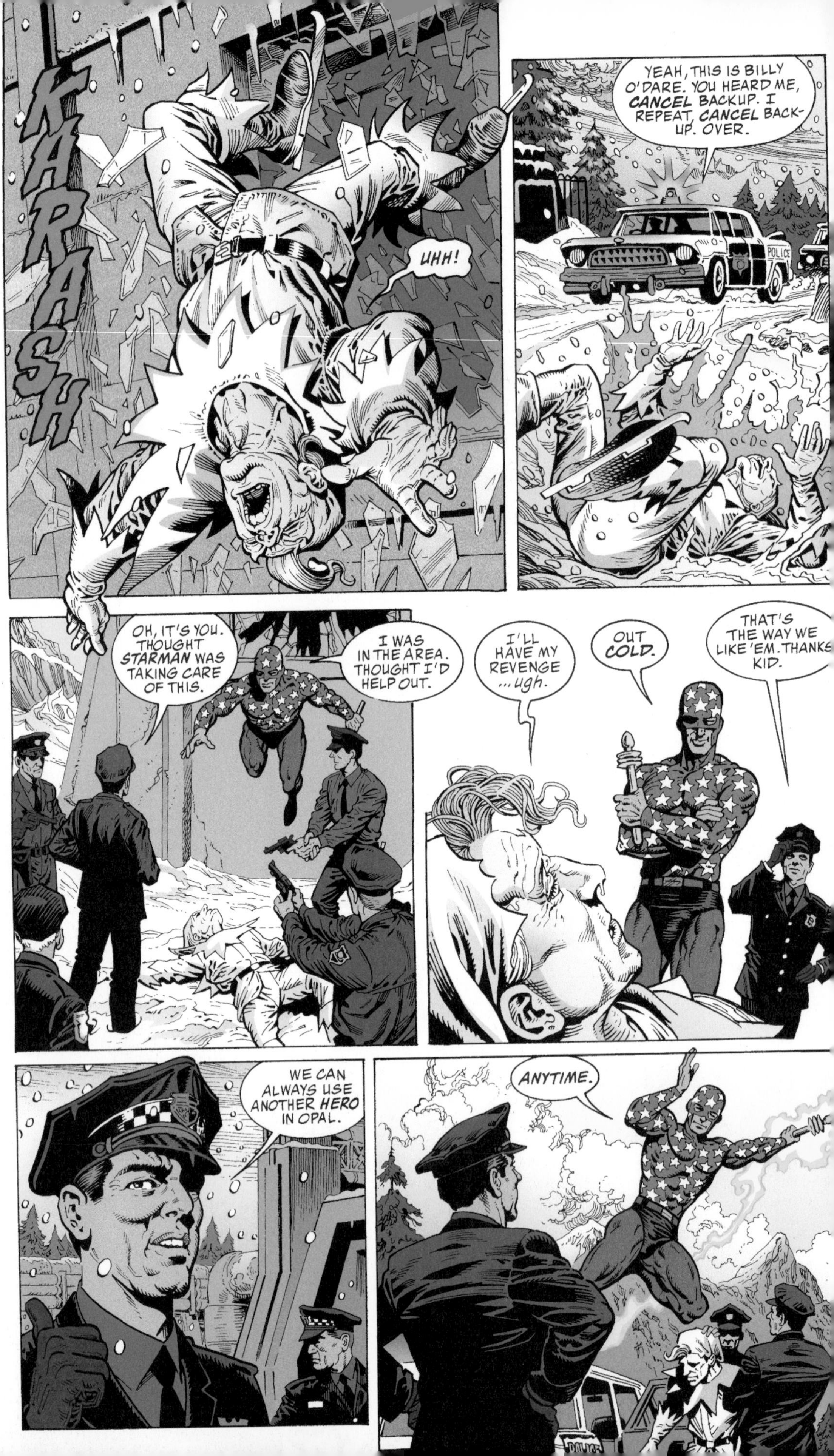

KARASH
UHH!
YEAH, THIS IS BILLY O'DARE. YOU HEARD ME, CANCEL BACKUP. I REPEAT, CANCEL BACK-UP. OVER.
POLICE
OH, IT'S YOU. THOUGHT STARMAN WAS TAKING CARE OF THIS.
I WAS IN THE AREA. THOUGHT I'D HELP OUT.
I'LL HAVE MY REVENGE ...ugh.
OUT COLD.
THAT'S THE WAY WE LIKE 'EM. THANKS KID.
WE CAN ALWAYS USE ANOTHER HERO IN OPAL.
ANYTIME.

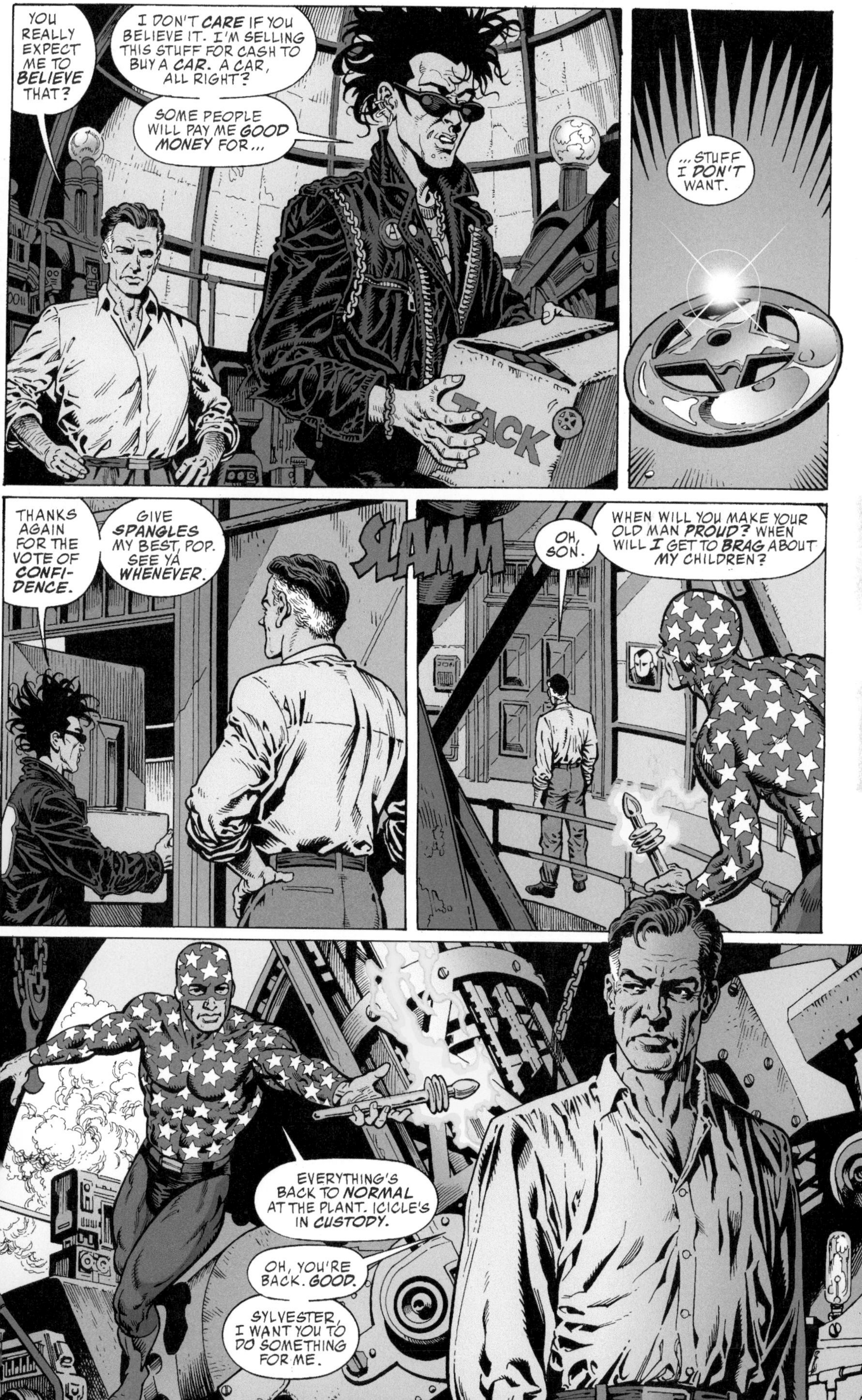
YOU REALLY EXPECT ME TO BELIEVE THAT?
I DON'T CARE IF YOU BELIEVE IT. I'M SELLING THIS STUFF FOR CASH TO BUY A CAR. A CAR, ALL RIGHT?
SOME PEOPLE WILL PAY ME GOOD MONEY FOR...
TACK
...STUFF I DON'T WANT.
THANKS AGAIN FOR THE VOTE OF CONFI-DENCE.
GIVE SPANGLES MY BEST, POP. SEE YA WHENEVER.
SLAMM
OH, SON.
WHEN WILL YOU MAKE YOUR OLD MAN PROUD? WHEN WILL I GET TO BRAG ABOUT MY CHILDREN?
EVERYTHING'S BACK TO NORMAL AT THE PLANT. ICICLE'S IN CUSTODY.
OH, YOU'RE BACK. GOOD.
SYLVESTER, I WANT YOU TO DO SOMETHING FOR ME.

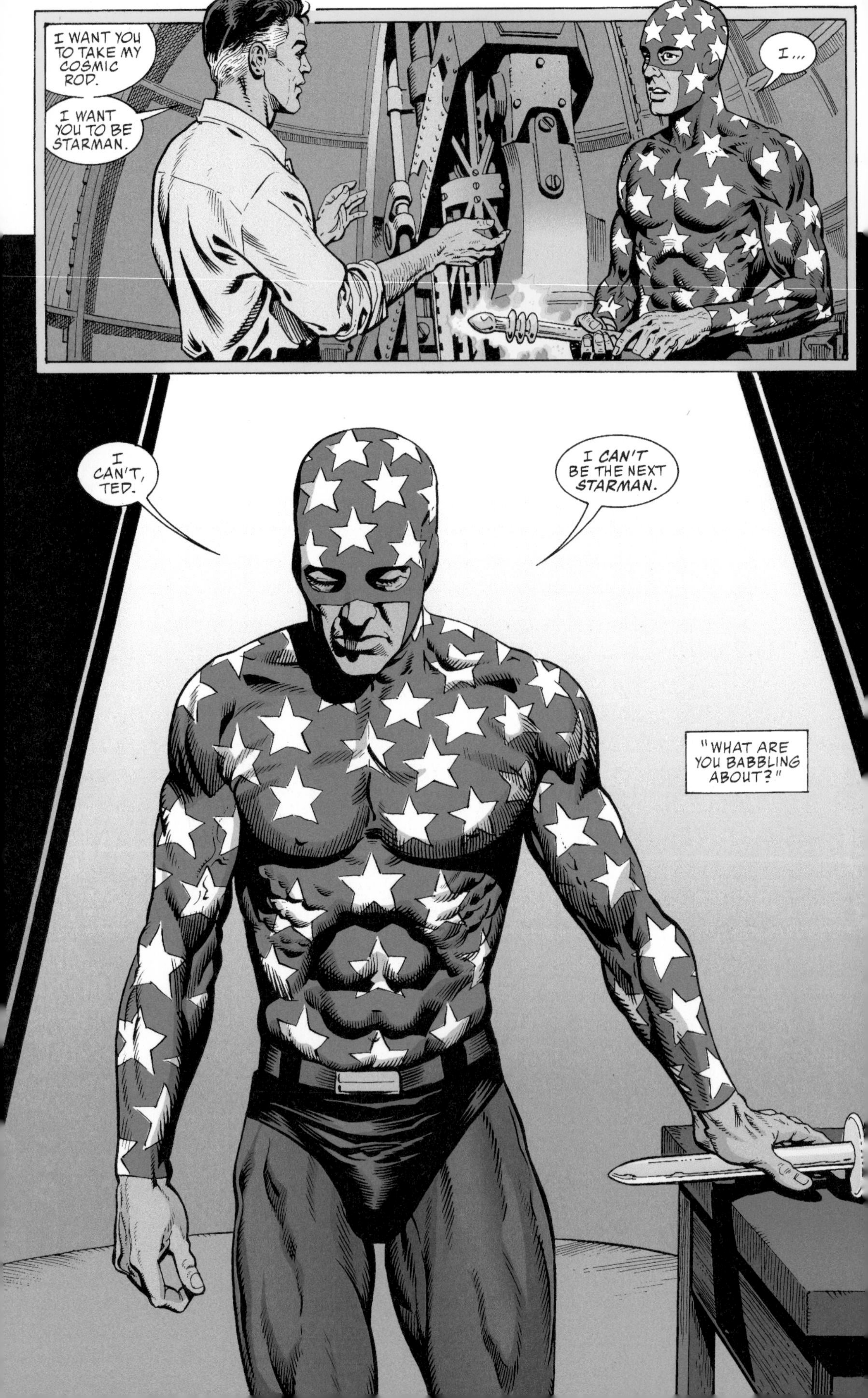

I WANT YOU TO TAKE MY COSMIC ROD.
I WANT YOU TO BE STARMAN.
I...
I CAN'T, TED.
I *CAN'T* BE THE NEXT *STARMAN.*
"WHAT ARE YOU BABBLING ABOUT?"

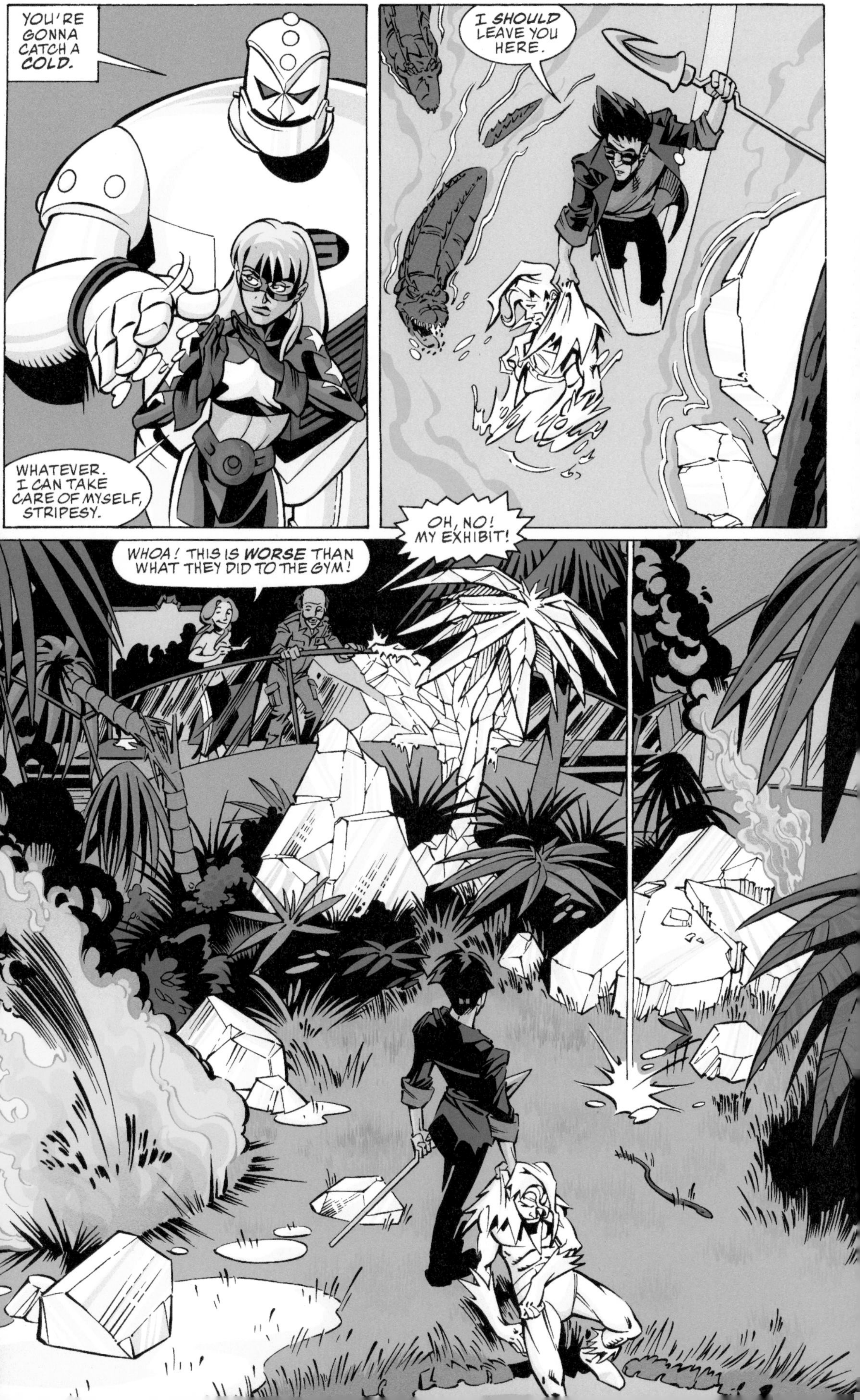
YOU'RE GONNA CATCH A COLD.
WHATEVER. I CAN TAKE CARE OF MYSELF, STRIPESY.
I SHOULD LEAVE YOU HERE.
OH, NO! MY EXHIBIT!
WHOA! THIS IS WORSE THAN WHAT THEY DID TO THE GYM!

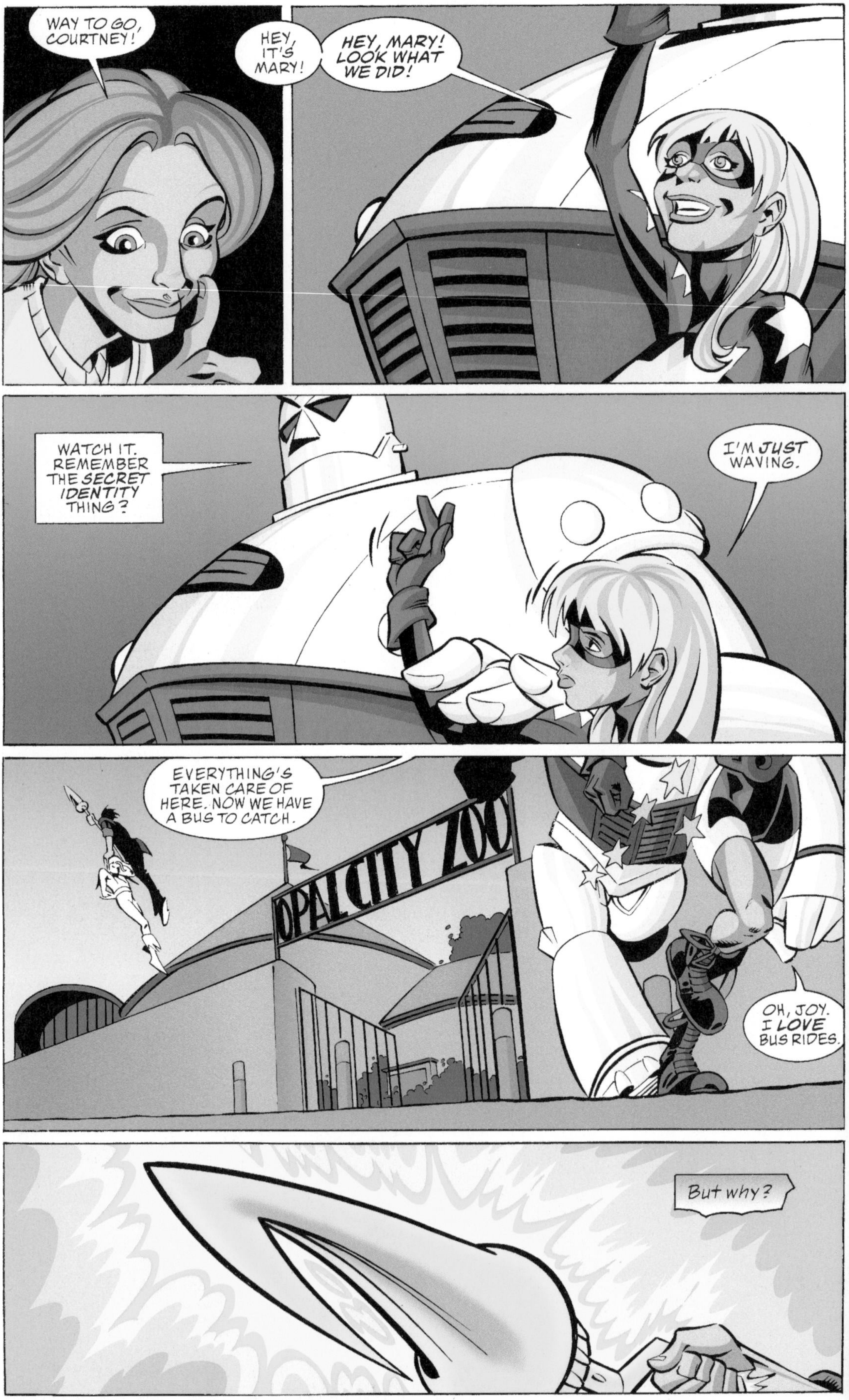

WAY TO GO, COURTNEY!
HEY, IT'S MARY!
HEY, MARY! LOOK WHAT WE DID!
WATCH IT. REMEMBER THE SECRET IDENTITY THING?
I'M JUST WAVING.
EVERYTHING'S TAKEN CARE OF HERE. NOW WE HAVE A BUS TO CATCH.
OPAL CITY ZOO
OH, JOY. I LOVE BUS RIDES.
But why?

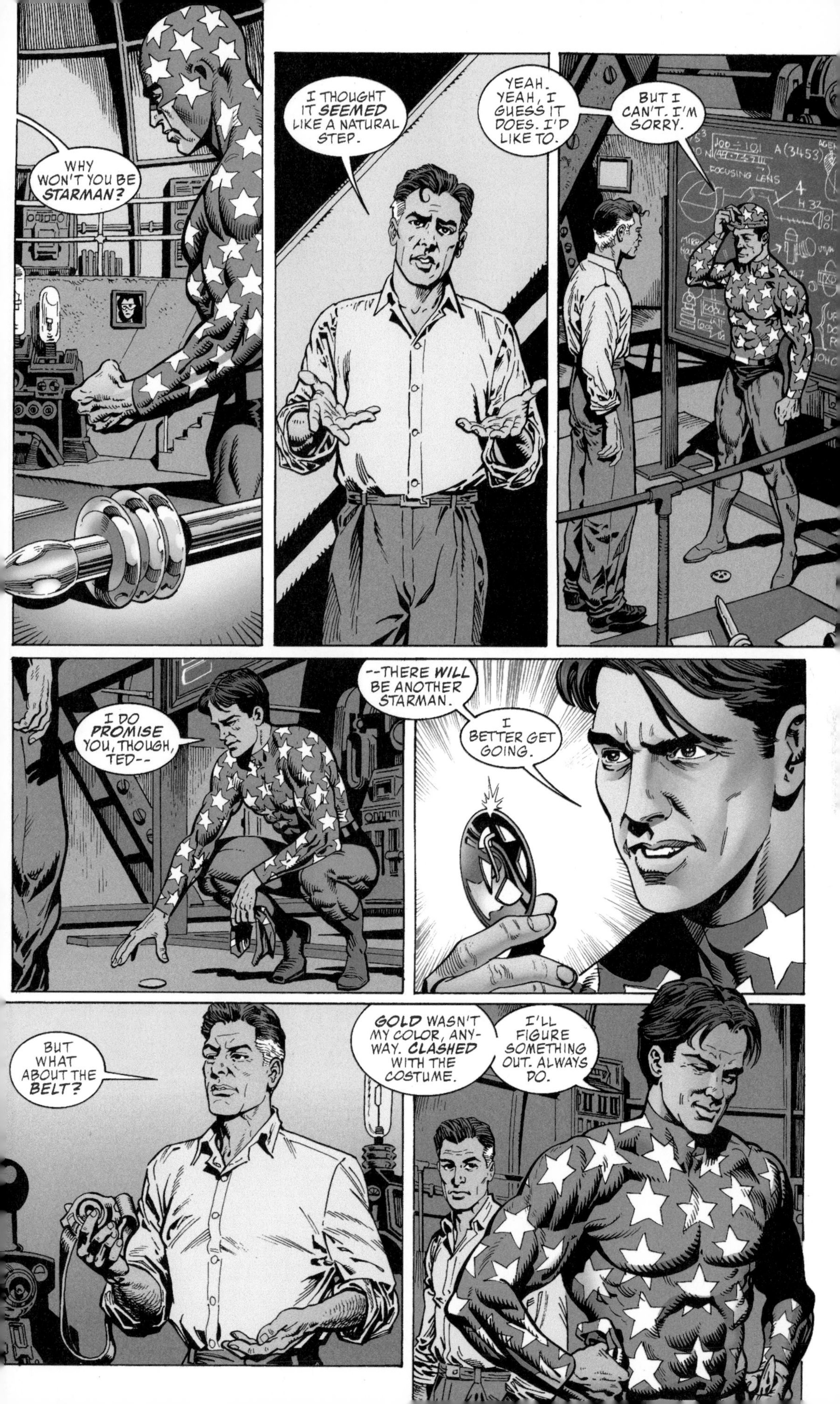

WHY WON'T YOU BE STARMAN?
I THOUGHT IT SEEMED LIKE A NATURAL STEP.
YEAH. YEAH, I GUESS IT DOES. I'D LIKE TO.
BUT I CAN'T. I'M SORRY.
FOCUSING LENS
I DO PROMISE YOU, THOUGH, TED--
--THERE WILL BE ANOTHER STARMAN.
I BETTER GET GOING.
BUT WHAT ABOUT THE BELT?
GOLD WASN'T MY COLOR, ANYWAY. CLASHED WITH THE COSTUME.
I'LL FIGURE SOMETHING OUT. ALWAYS DO.

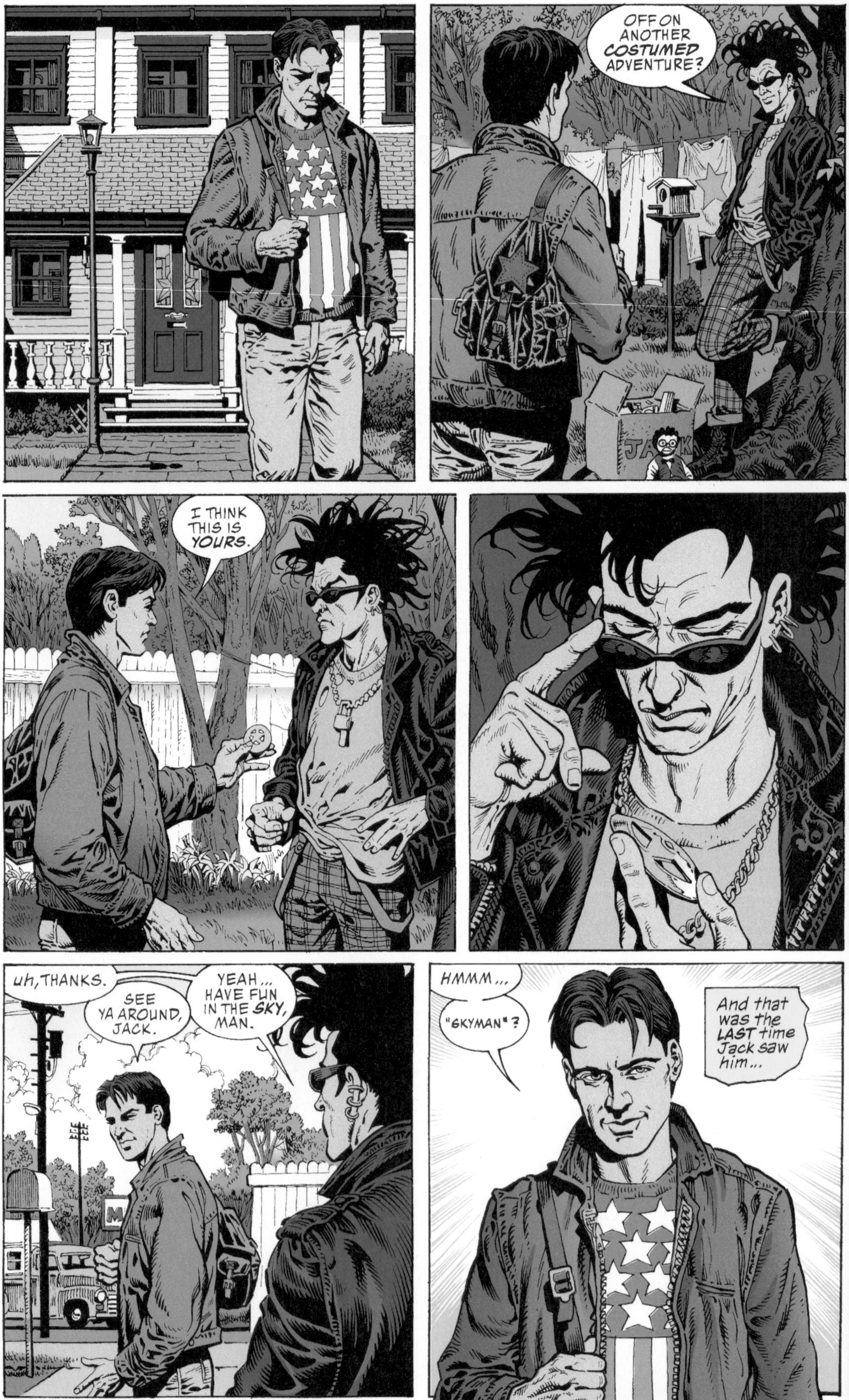

OFF ON ANOTHER COSTUMED ADVENTURE?
JACK
I THINK THIS IS YOURS.
uh, THANKS.
SEE YA AROUND, JACK.
YEAH... HAVE FUN IN THE SKY, MAN.
HMMM...
"SKYMAN"?
And that was the LAST time Jack saw him...

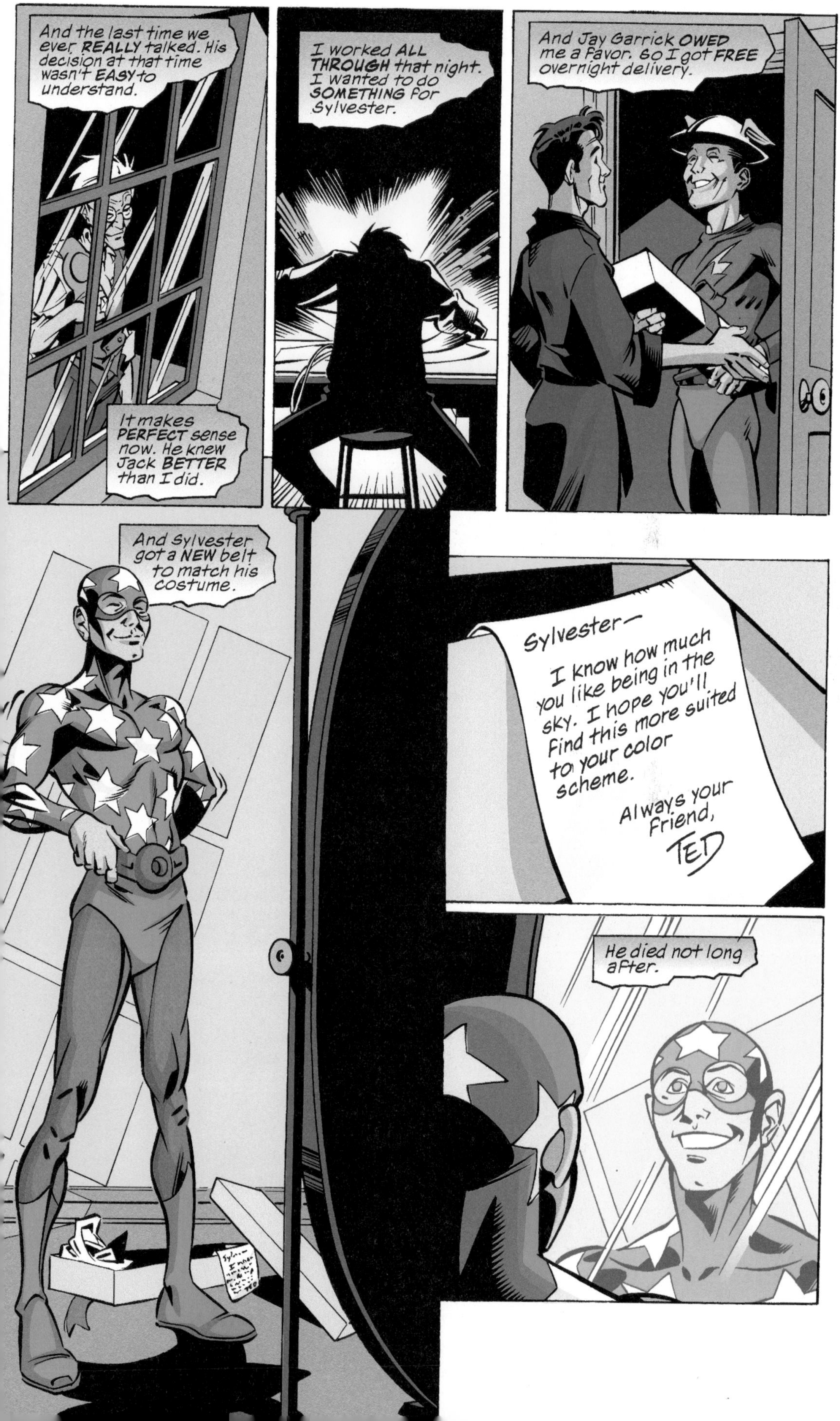
And the last time we ever REALLY talked. His decision at that time wasn't EASY to understand.
It makes PERFECT sense now. He knew Jack BETTER than I did.
I worked ALL THROUGH that night. I wanted to do SOMETHING for Sylvester.
And Jay Garrick OWED me a favor. So I got FREE overnight delivery.
And Sylvester got a NEW belt to match his costume.
Sylvester—
I know how much you like being in the sky. I hope you'll find this more suited to your color scheme.
Always your Friend,
TED
He died not long after.

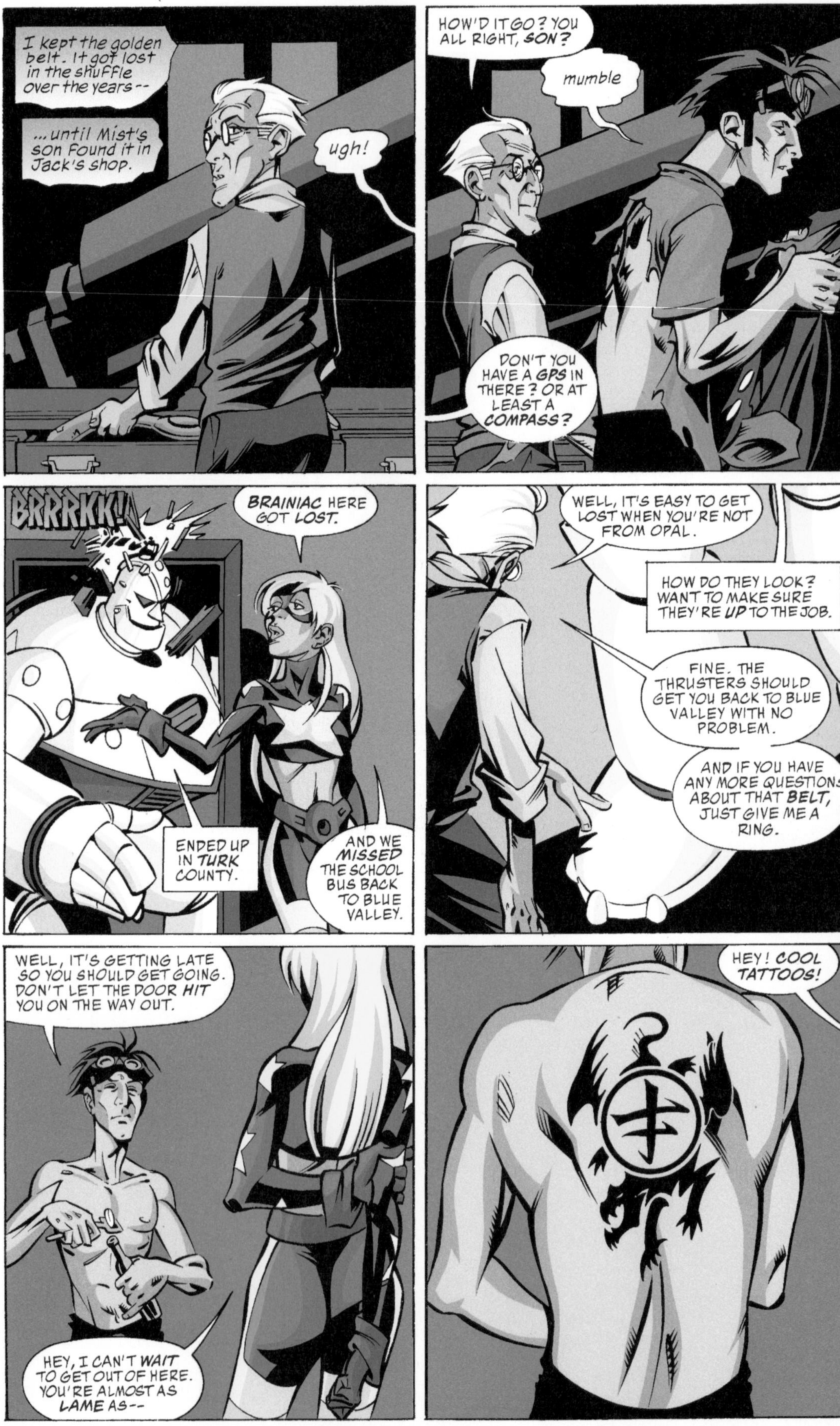
I kept the golden belt. It got lost in the shuffle over the years--
...until Mist's son found it in Jack's shop.
ugh!
HOW'D IT GO? YOU ALL RIGHT, SON?
mumble
DON'T YOU HAVE A GPS IN THERE? OR AT LEAST A COMPASS?
BRRRKK!
BRAINIAC HERE GOT LOST.
ENDED UP IN TURK COUNTY.
AND WE MISSED THE SCHOOL BUS BACK TO BLUE VALLEY.
WELL, IT'S EASY TO GET LOST WHEN YOU'RE NOT FROM OPAL.
HOW DO THEY LOOK? WANT TO MAKE SURE THEY'RE UP TO THE JOB.
FINE. THE THRUSTERS SHOULD GET YOU BACK TO BLUE VALLEY WITH NO PROBLEM.
AND IF YOU HAVE ANY MORE QUESTIONS ABOUT THAT BELT, JUST GIVE ME A RING.
WELL, IT'S GETTING LATE SO YOU SHOULD GET GOING. DON'T LET THE DOOR HIT YOU ON THE WAY OUT.
HEY, I CAN'T WAIT TO GET OUT OF HERE. YOU'RE ALMOST AS LAME AS--
HEY! COOL TATTOOS!

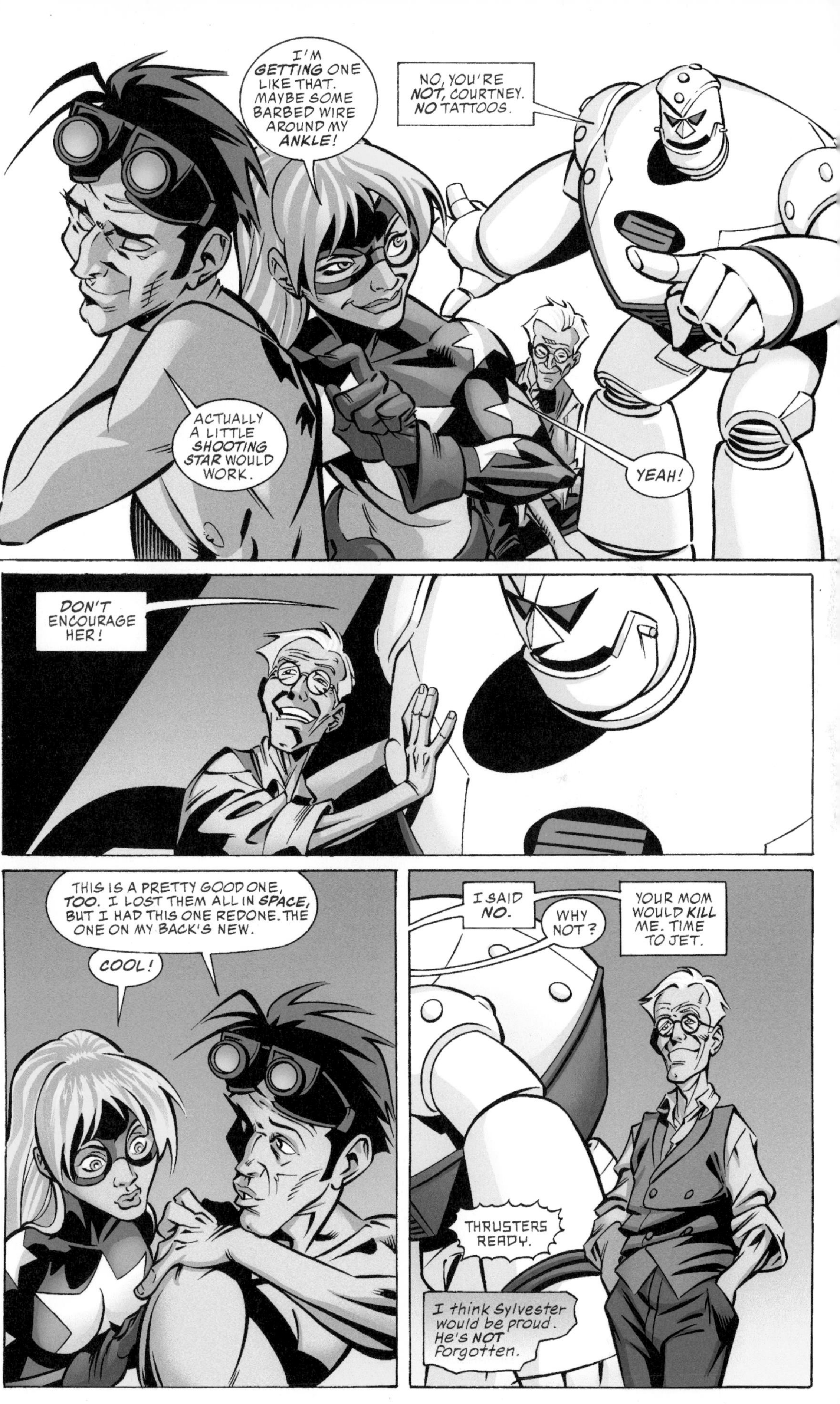
I'M GETTING ONE LIKE THAT. MAYBE SOME BARBED WIRE AROUND MY ANKLE!
NO, YOU'RE NOT, COURTNEY. NO TATTOOS.
ACTUALLY A LITTLE SHOOTING STAR WOULD WORK.
YEAH!
DON'T ENCOURAGE HER!
THIS IS A PRETTY GOOD ONE, TOO. I LOST THEM ALL IN SPACE, BUT I HAD THIS ONE REDONE. THE ONE ON MY BACK'S NEW.
COOL!
I SAID NO.
WHY NOT?
YOUR MOM WOULD KILL ME. TIME TO JET.
THRUSTERS READY.
I think Sylvester would be proud. He's NOT forgotten.

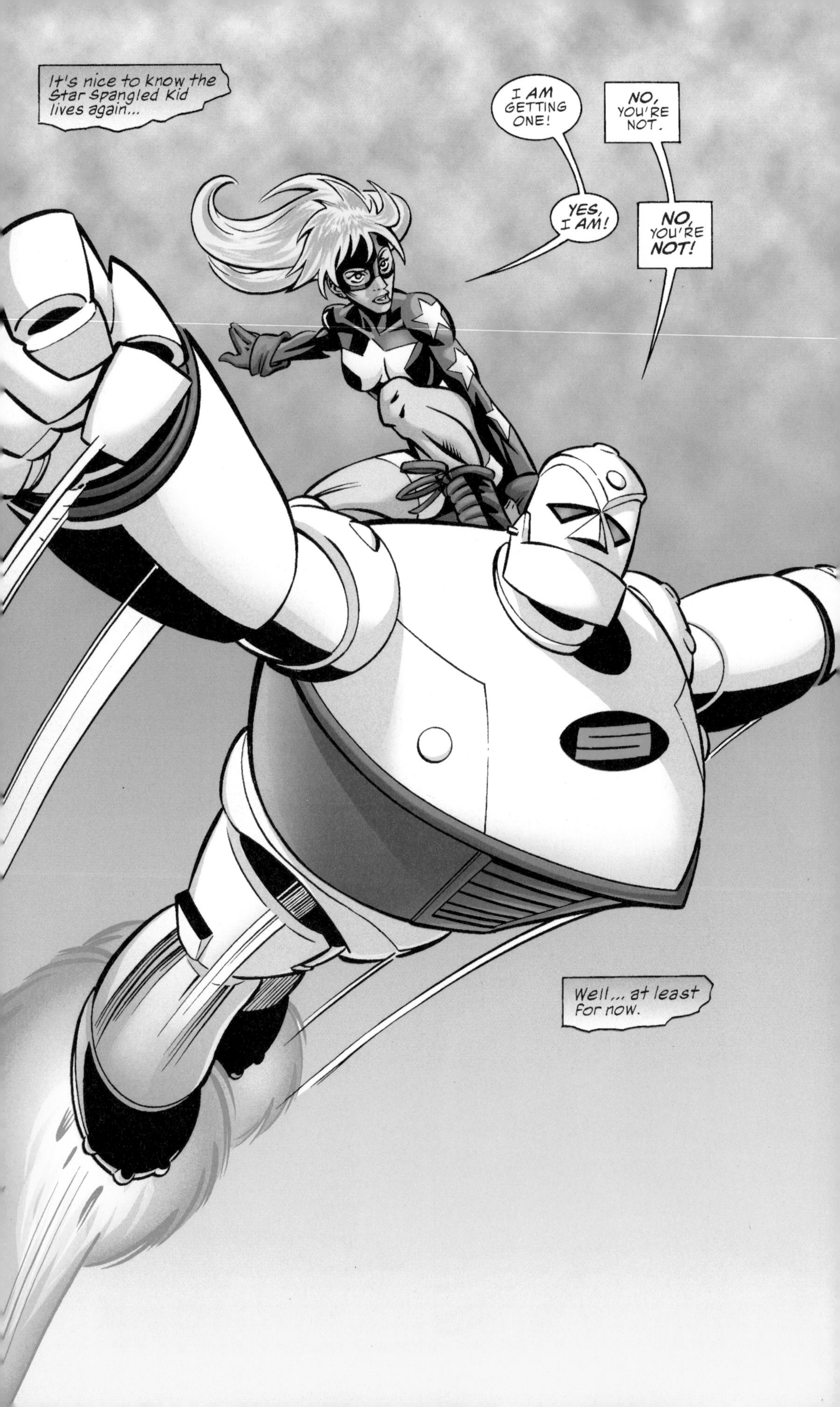
It's nice to know the Star Spangled Kid lives again...
I AM GETTING ONE!
NO, YOU'RE NOT.
YES, I AM!
NO, YOU'RE NOT!
Well... at least for now.

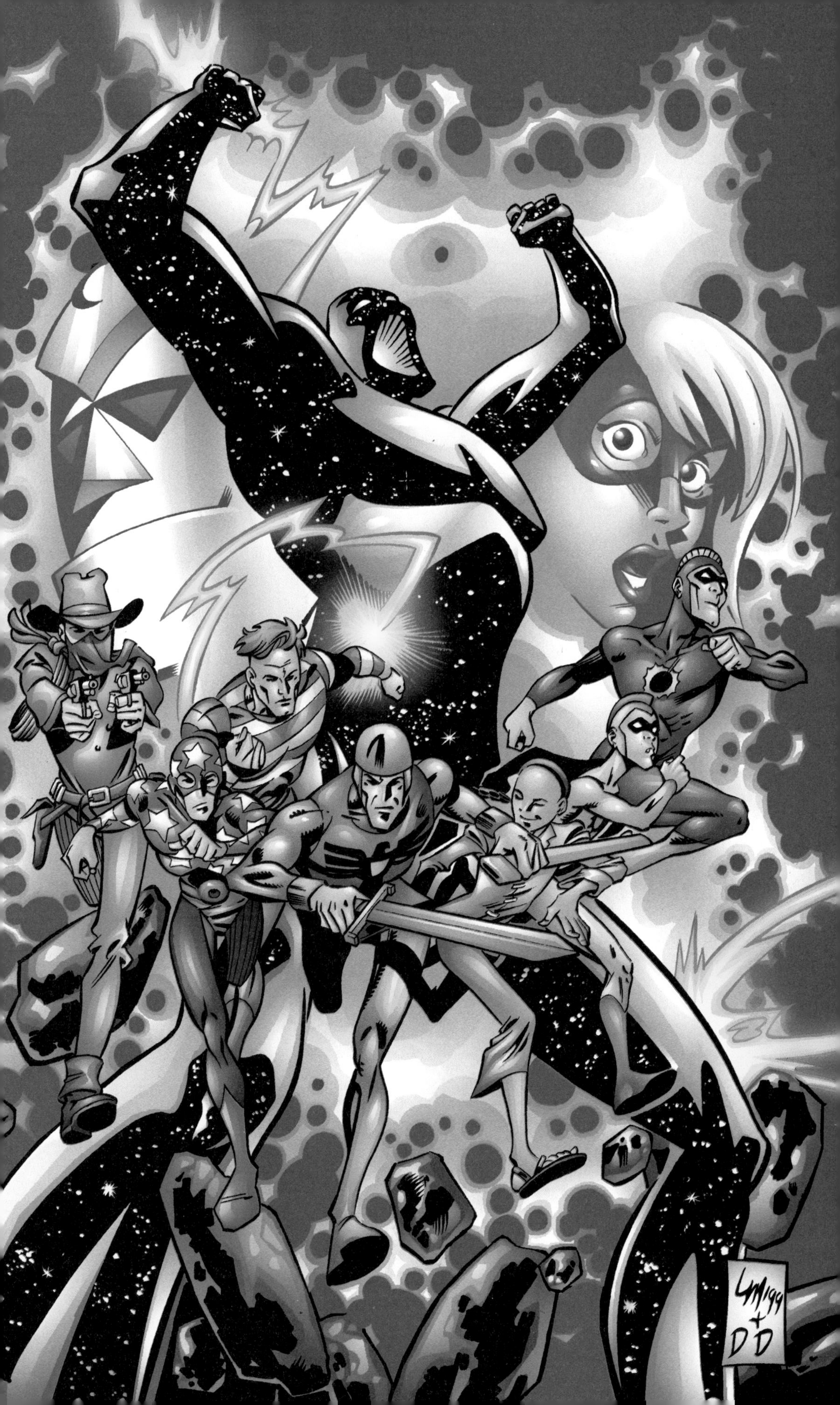

STARS AND S.T.R.I.P.E. #9

Written by GEOFF JOHNS
Pencils by SCOTT KOLINS
Inks by DAN DAVIS
Colors by TOM McCRAW
Letters by BILL OAKLEY
Cover art by LEE MODER and DAN DAVIS
Cover color by RICHARD & TANYA HORIE

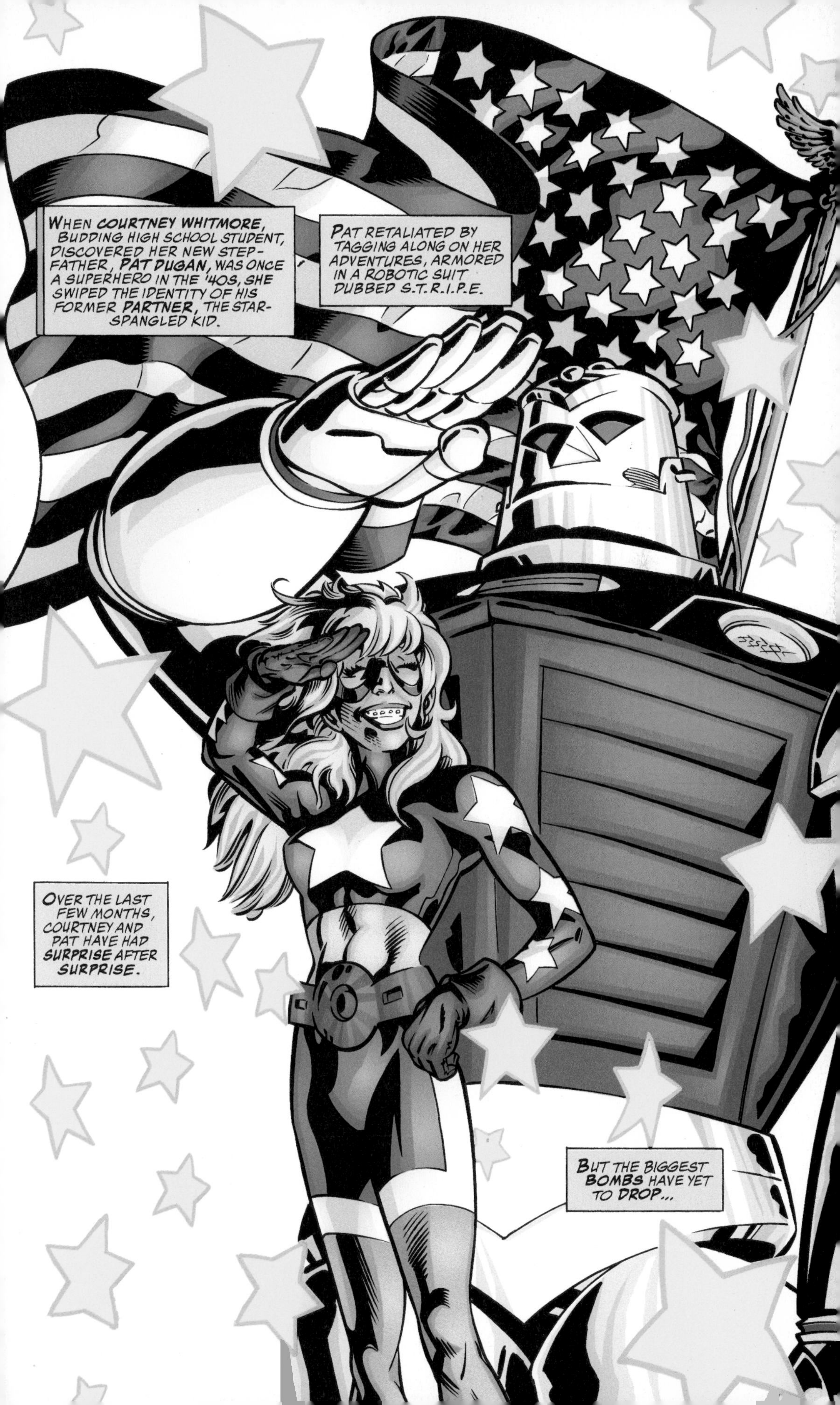

WHEN COURTNEY WHITMORE, BUDDING HIGH SCHOOL STUDENT, DISCOVERED HER NEW STEP-FATHER, PAT DUGAN, WAS ONCE A SUPERHERO IN THE '40S, SHE SWIPED THE IDENTITY OF HIS FORMER PARTNER, THE STAR-SPANGLED KID.
PAT RETALIATED BY TAGGING ALONG ON HER ADVENTURES, ARMORED IN A ROBOTIC SUIT DUBBED S.T.R.I.P.E.
OVER THE LAST FEW MONTHS, COURTNEY AND PAT HAVE HAD SURPRISE AFTER SURPRISE.
BUT THE BIGGEST BOMBS HAVE YET TO DROP...

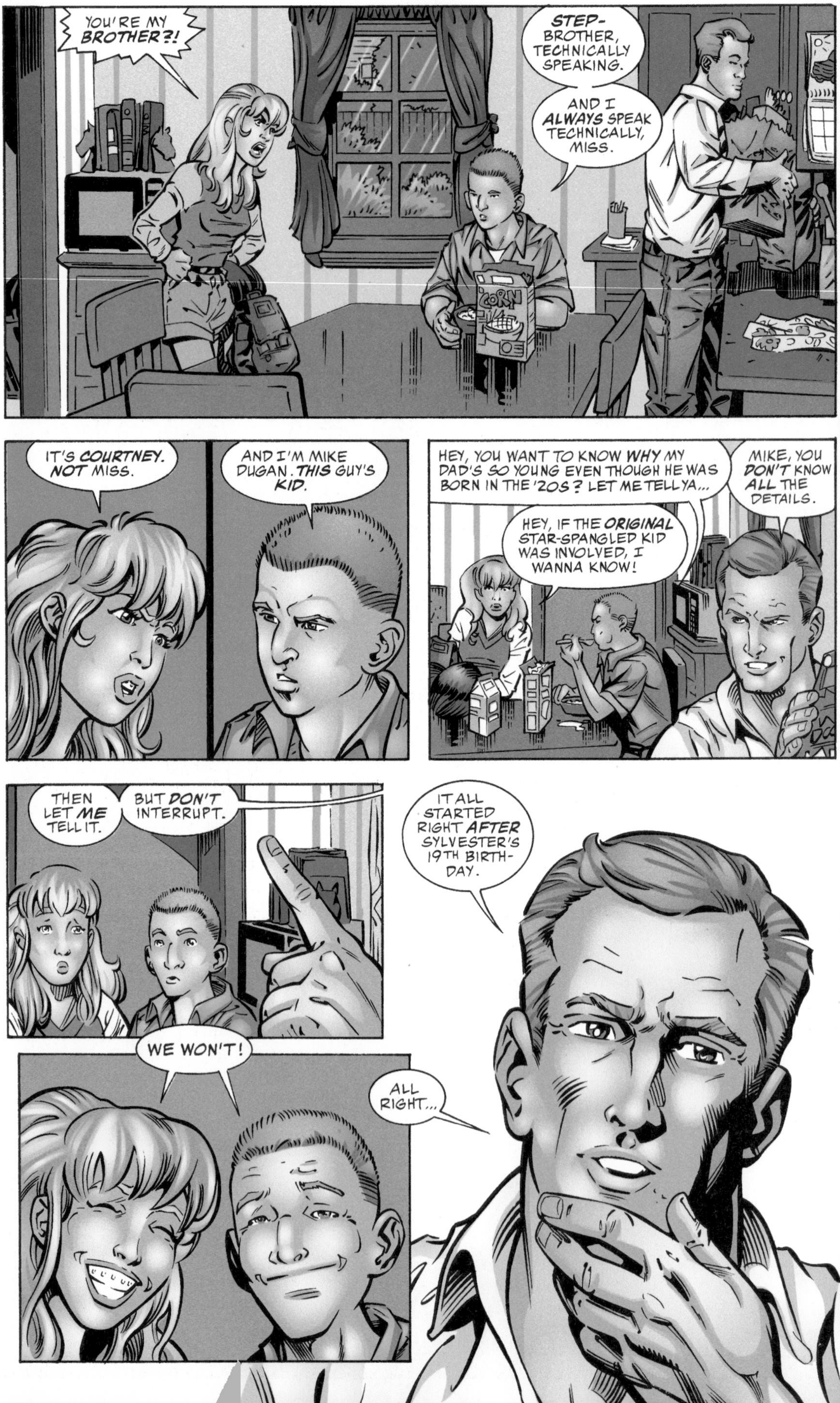
YOU'RE MY BROTHER?!
STEP-BROTHER, TECHNICALLY SPEAKING.
AND I ALWAYS SPEAK TECHNICALLY, MISS.
IT'S COURTNEY. NOT MISS.
AND I'M MIKE DUGAN. THIS GUY'S KID.
HEY, YOU WANT TO KNOW WHY MY DAD'S SO YOUNG EVEN THOUGH HE WAS BORN IN THE '20S? LET ME TELL YA...
MIKE, YOU DON'T KNOW ALL THE DETAILS.
HEY, IF THE ORIGINAL STAR-SPANGLED KID WAS INVOLVED, I WANNA KNOW!
THEN LET ME TELL IT.
BUT DON'T INTERRUPT.
IT ALL STARTED RIGHT AFTER SYLVESTER'S 19TH BIRTH-DAY.
WE WON'T!
ALL RIGHT...

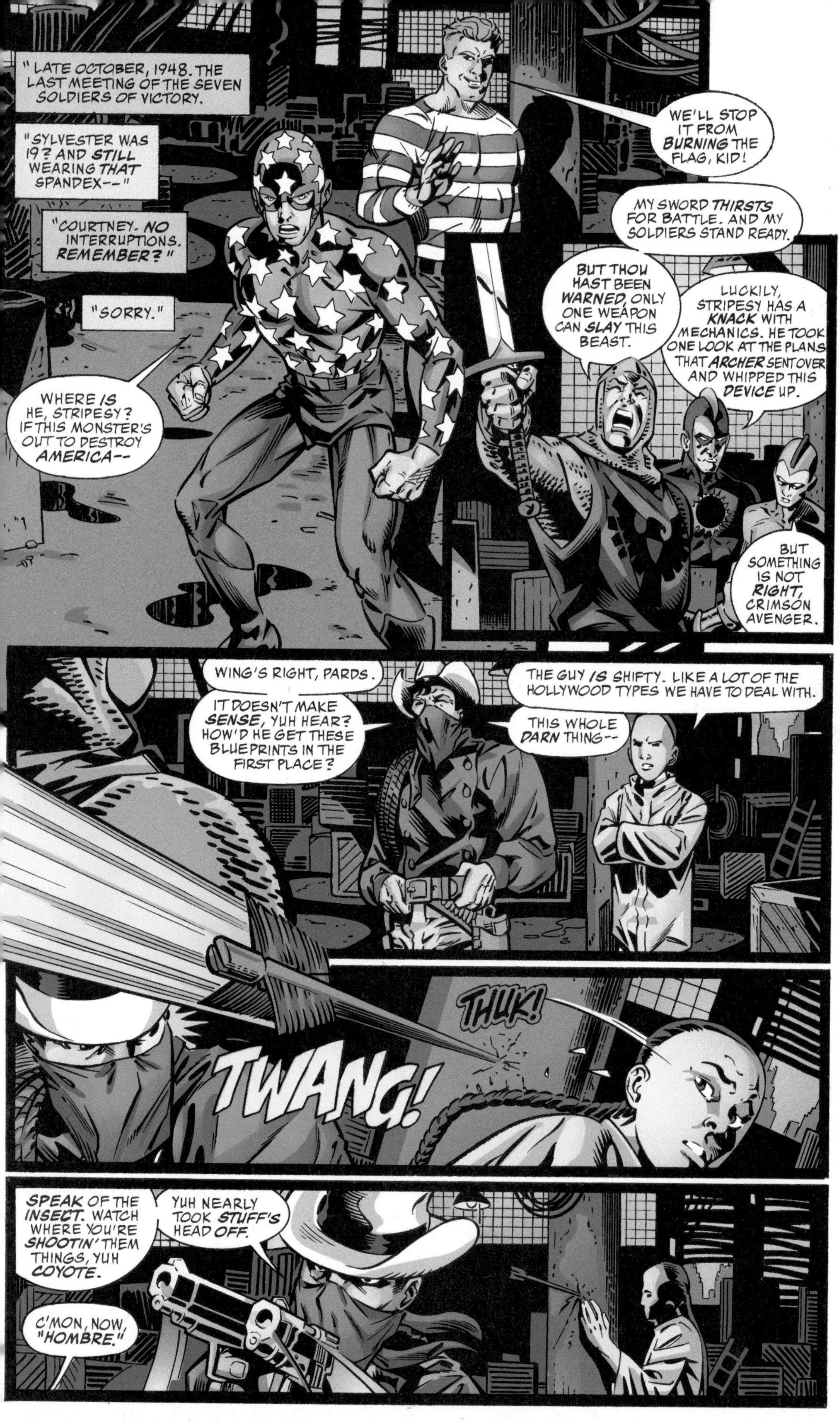
"LATE OCTOBER, 1948. THE LAST MEETING OF THE SEVEN SOLDIERS OF VICTORY.
"SYLVESTER WAS 19? AND STILL WEARING THAT SPANDEX--"
"COURTNEY. NO INTERRUPTIONS. REMEMBER?"
"SORRY."
WE'LL STOP IT FROM BURNING THE FLAG, KID!
WHERE IS HE, STRIPESY? IF THIS MONSTER'S OUT TO DESTROY AMERICA--
MY SWORD THIRSTS FOR BATTLE. AND MY SOLDIERS STAND READY.
BUT THOU HAST BEEN WARNED, ONLY ONE WEAPON CAN SLAY THIS BEAST.
LUCKILY, STRIPESY HAS A KNACK WITH MECHANICS. HE TOOK ONE LOOK AT THE PLANS THAT ARCHER SENT OVER AND WHIPPED THIS DEVICE UP.
BUT SOMETHING IS NOT RIGHT, CRIMSON AVENGER.
WING'S RIGHT, PARDS.
IT DOESN'T MAKE SENSE, YUH HEAR? HOW'D HE GET THESE BLUEPRINTS IN THE FIRST PLACE?
THE GUY IS SHIFTY. LIKE A LOT OF THE HOLLYWOOD TYPES WE HAVE TO DEAL WITH.
THIS WHOLE DARN THING--
THUK!
TWANG!
SPEAK OF THE INSECT. WATCH WHERE YOU'RE SHOOTIN' THEM THINGS, YUH COYOTE.
YUH NEARLY TOOK STUFF'S HEAD OFF.
C'MON, NOW, "HOMBRE."

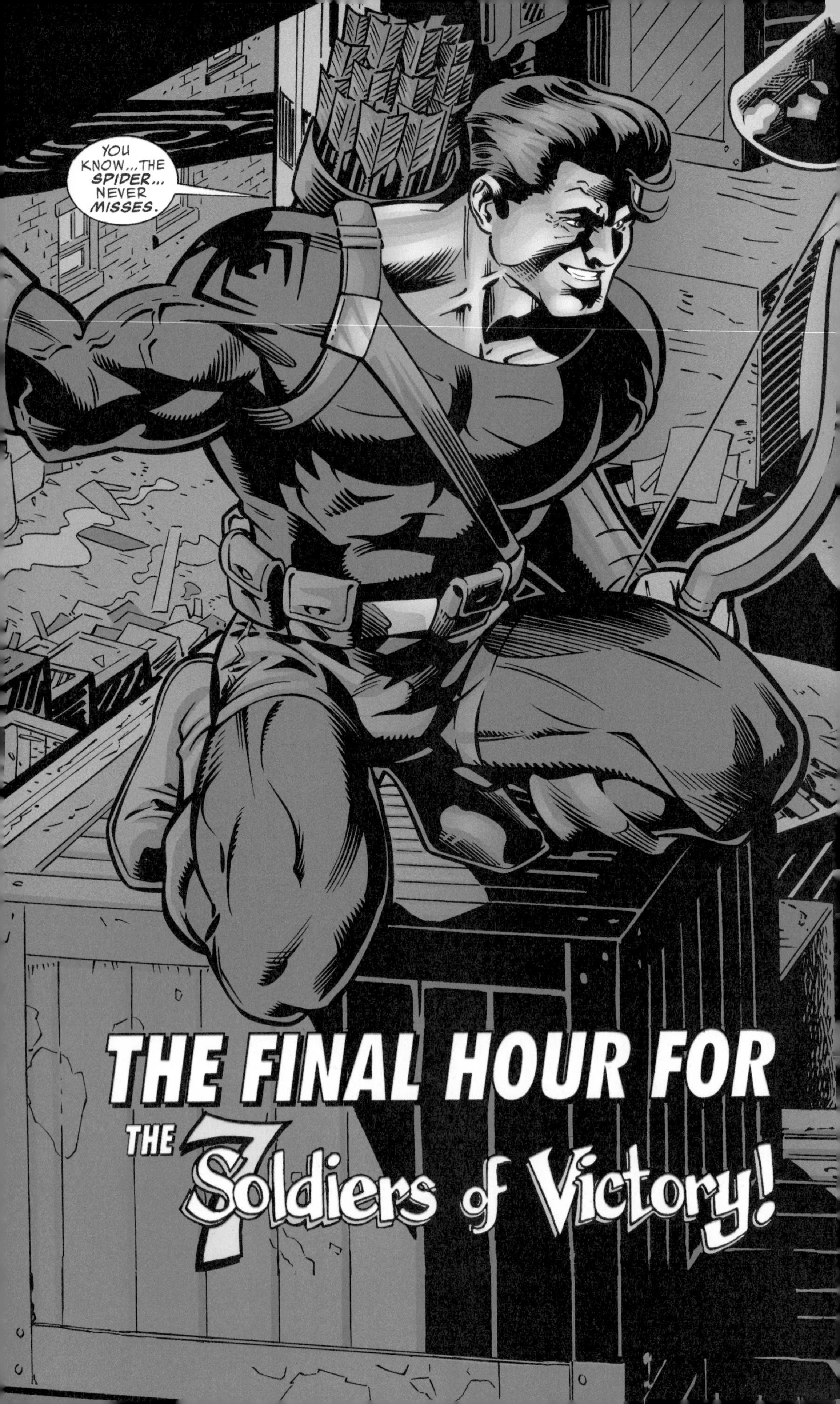
YOU KNOW... THE SPIDER... NEVER MISSES.
THE FINAL HOUR FOR
THE 7 Soldiers of Victory!

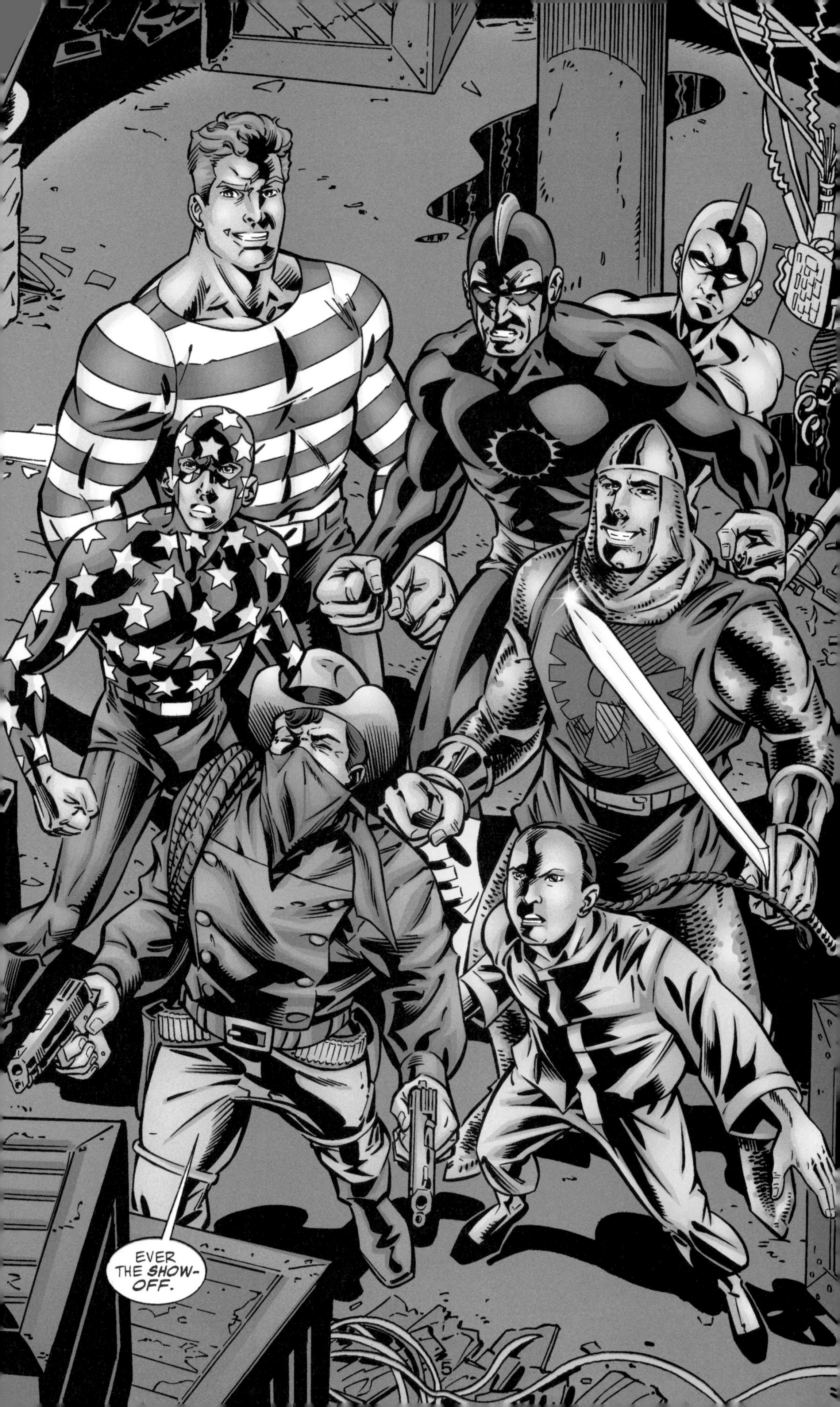
EVER THE SHOW-OFF.

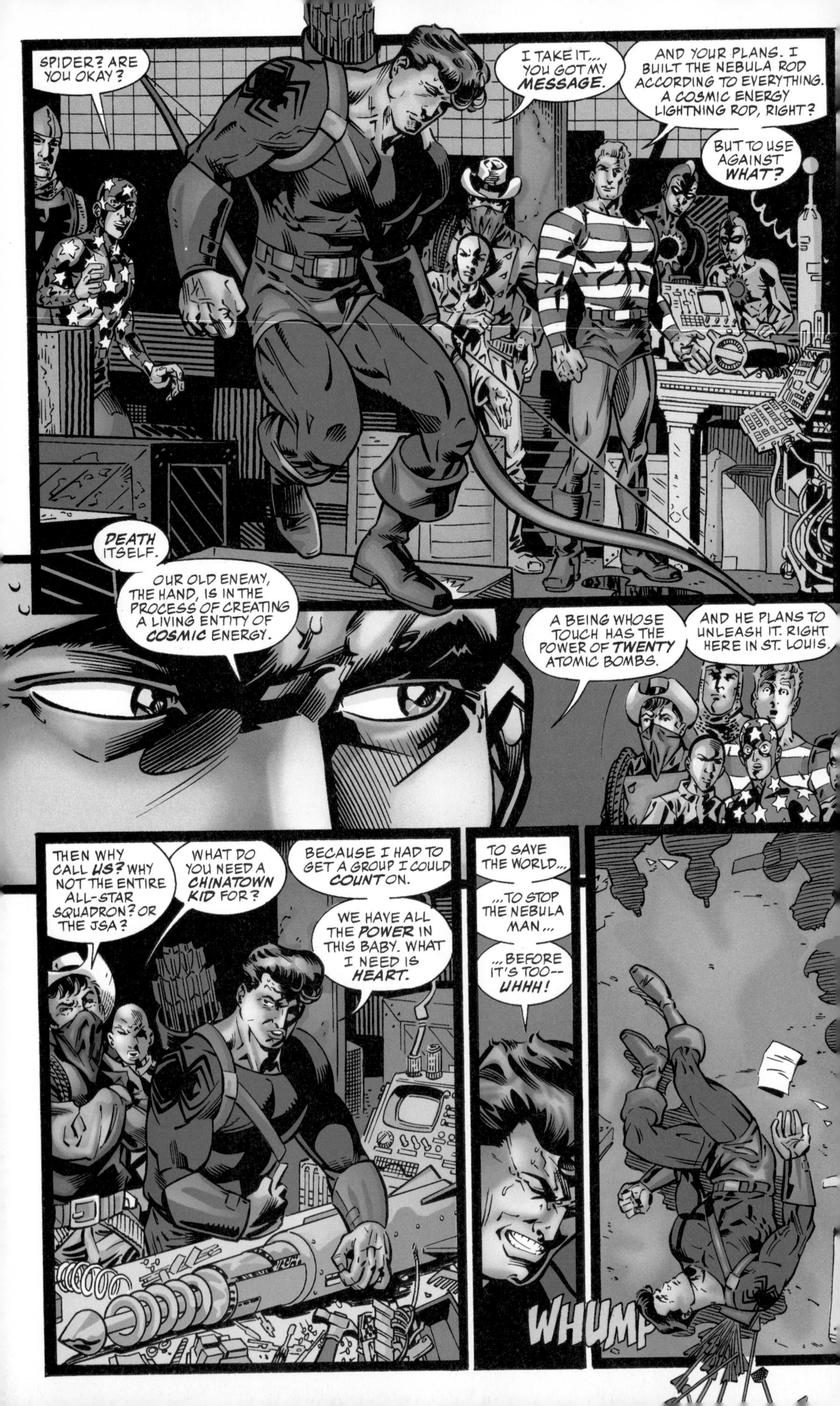
SPIDER? ARE YOU OKAY?
I TAKE IT... YOU GOT MY MESSAGE.
AND YOUR PLANS. I BUILT THE NEBULA ROD ACCORDING TO EVERYTHING. A COSMIC ENERGY LIGHTNING ROD, RIGHT?
BUT TO USE AGAINST WHAT?
DEATH ITSELF.
OUR OLD ENEMY, THE HAND, IS IN THE PROCESS OF CREATING A LIVING ENTITY OF COSMIC ENERGY.
A BEING WHOSE TOUCH HAS THE POWER OF TWENTY ATOMIC BOMBS.
AND HE PLANS TO UNLEASH IT. RIGHT HERE IN ST. LOUIS.
THEN WHY CALL US? WHY NOT THE ENTIRE ALL-STAR SQUADRON? OR THE JSA?
WHAT DO YOU NEED A CHINATOWN KID FOR?
BECAUSE I HAD TO GET A GROUP I COULD COUNT ON.
WE HAVE ALL THE POWER IN THIS BABY. WHAT I NEED IS HEART.
TO SAVE THE WORLD...
...TO STOP THE NEBULA MAN...
...BEFORE IT'S TOO-- UHHH!
WHUMP

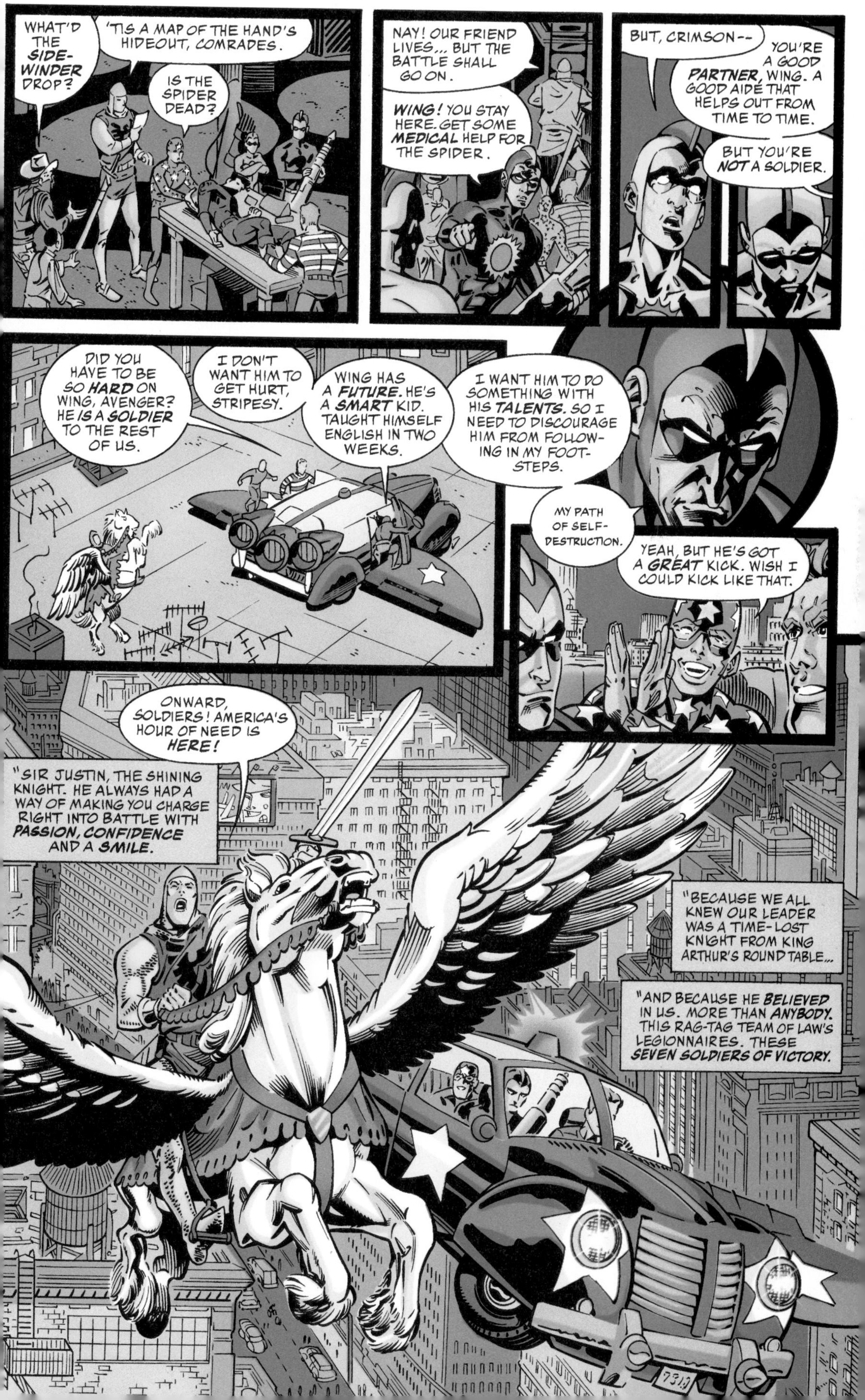
WHAT'D THE SIDE-WINDER DROP?
'TIS A MAP OF THE HAND'S HIDEOUT, COMRADES.
IS THE SPIDER DEAD?
NAY! OUR FRIEND LIVES... BUT THE BATTLE SHALL GO ON.
WING! YOU STAY HERE. GET SOME MEDICAL HELP FOR THE SPIDER.
BUT, CRIMSON--
YOU'RE A GOOD PARTNER, WING. A GOOD AIDE THAT HELPS OUT FROM TIME TO TIME.
BUT YOU'RE NOT A SOLDIER.
DID YOU HAVE TO BE SO HARD ON WING, AVENGER? HE IS A SOLDIER TO THE REST OF US.
I DON'T WANT HIM TO GET HURT, STRIPESY.
WING HAS A FUTURE. HE'S A SMART KID. TAUGHT HIMSELF ENGLISH IN TWO WEEKS.
I WANT HIM TO DO SOMETHING WITH HIS TALENTS. SO I NEED TO DISCOURAGE HIM FROM FOLLOWING IN MY FOOTSTEPS.
MY PATH OF SELF-DESTRUCTION.
YEAH, BUT HE'S GOT A GREAT KICK. WISH I COULD KICK LIKE THAT.
ONWARD, SOLDIERS! AMERICA'S HOUR OF NEED IS HERE!
"SIR JUSTIN, THE SHINING KNIGHT. HE ALWAYS HAD A WAY OF MAKING YOU CHARGE RIGHT INTO BATTLE WITH PASSION, CONFIDENCE AND A SMILE.
"BECAUSE WE ALL KNEW OUR LEADER WAS A TIME-LOST KNIGHT FROM KING ARTHUR'S ROUND TABLE...
"AND BECAUSE HE BELIEVED IN US. MORE THAN ANYBODY. THIS RAG-TAG TEAM OF LAW'S LEGIONNAIRES. THESE SEVEN SOLDIERS OF VICTORY.

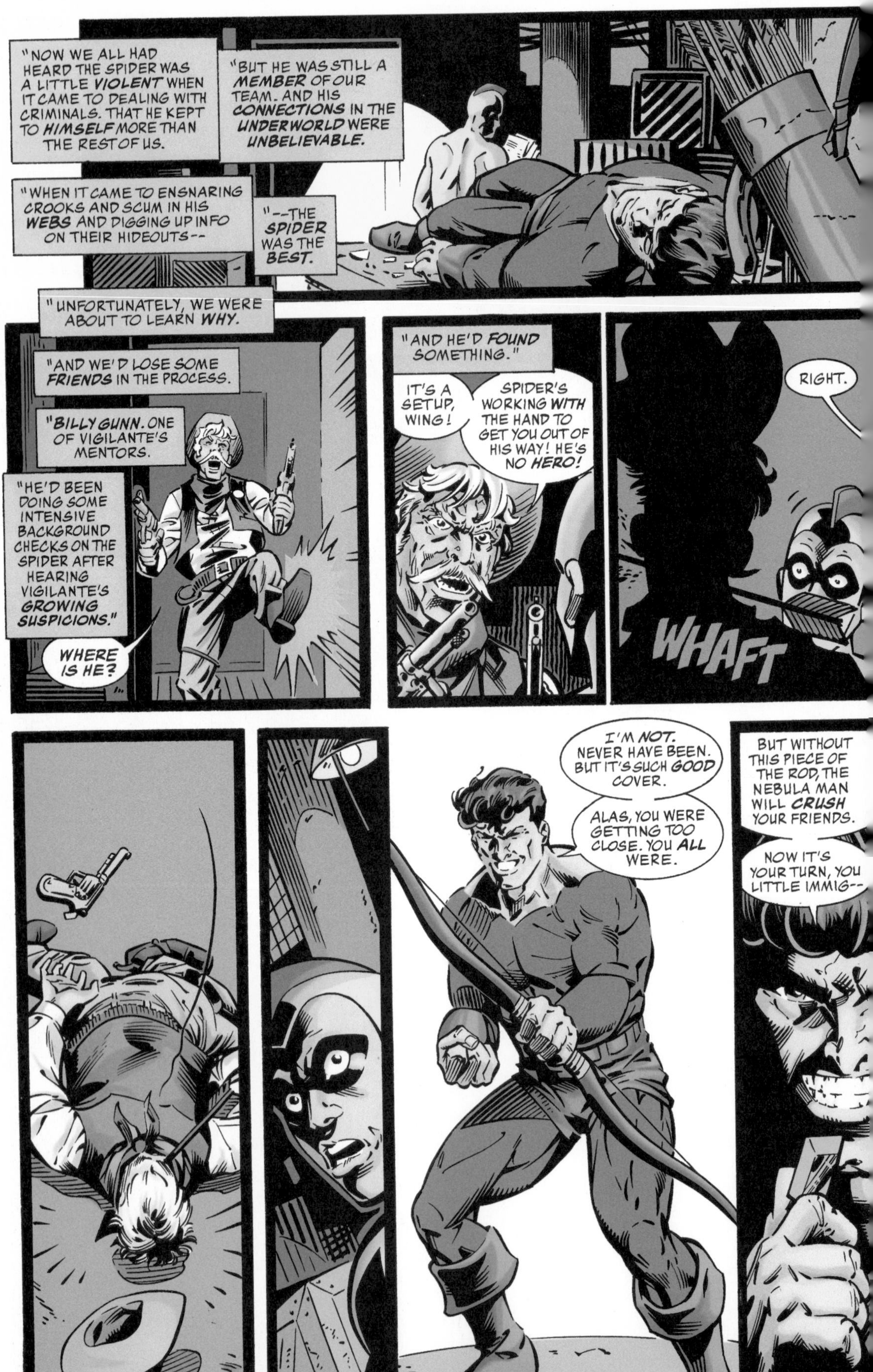

"NOW WE ALL HAD HEARD THE SPIDER WAS A LITTLE VIOLENT WHEN IT CAME TO DEALING WITH CRIMINALS. THAT HE KEPT TO HIMSELF MORE THAN THE REST OF US.
"BUT HE WAS STILL A MEMBER OF OUR TEAM. AND HIS CONNECTIONS IN THE UNDERWORLD WERE UNBELIEVABLE.
"WHEN IT CAME TO ENSNARING CROOKS AND SCUM IN HIS WEBS AND DIGGING UP INFO ON THEIR HIDEOUTS--
"--THE SPIDER WAS THE BEST.
"UNFORTUNATELY, WE WERE ABOUT TO LEARN WHY.
"AND WE'D LOSE SOME FRIENDS IN THE PROCESS.
"BILLY GUNN. ONE OF VIGILANTE'S MENTORS.
"HE'D BEEN DOING SOME INTENSIVE BACKGROUND CHECKS ON THE SPIDER AFTER HEARING VIGILANTE'S GROWING SUSPICIONS."
WHERE IS HE?
"AND HE'D FOUND SOMETHING."
IT'S A SETUP, WING!
SPIDER'S WORKING WITH THE HAND TO GET YOU OUT OF HIS WAY! HE'S NO HERO!
RIGHT.
WHAFT
I'M NOT. NEVER HAVE BEEN. BUT IT'S SUCH GOOD COVER.
ALAS, YOU WERE GETTING TOO CLOSE. YOU ALL WERE.
BUT WITHOUT THIS PIECE OF THE ROD, THE NEBULA MAN WILL CRUSH YOUR FRIENDS.
NOW IT'S YOUR TURN, YOU LITTLE IMMIG--

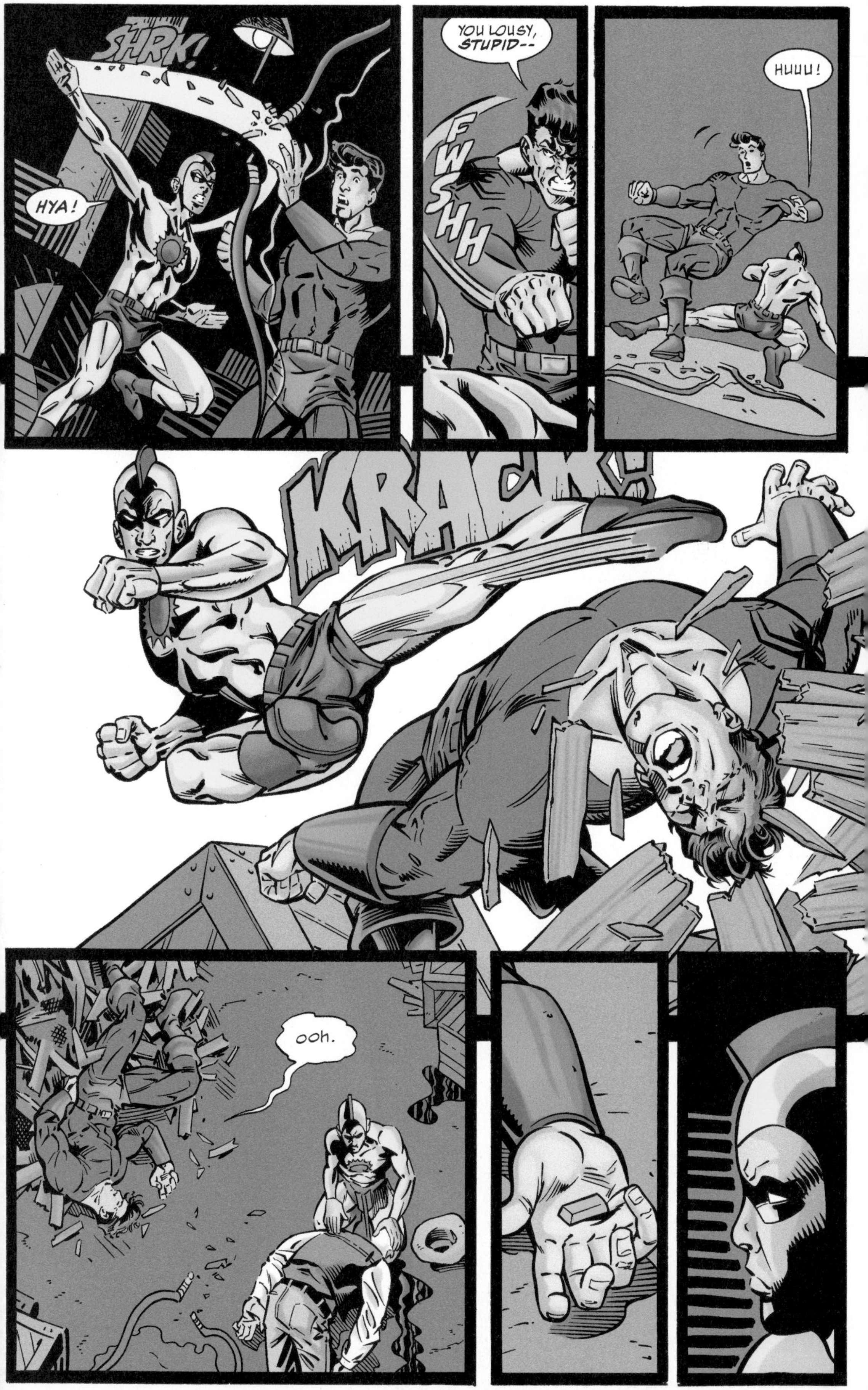
SHRK!
HYA!
YOU LOUSY, STUPID--
FWSHHH
HUUU!
KRACK!
ooh.

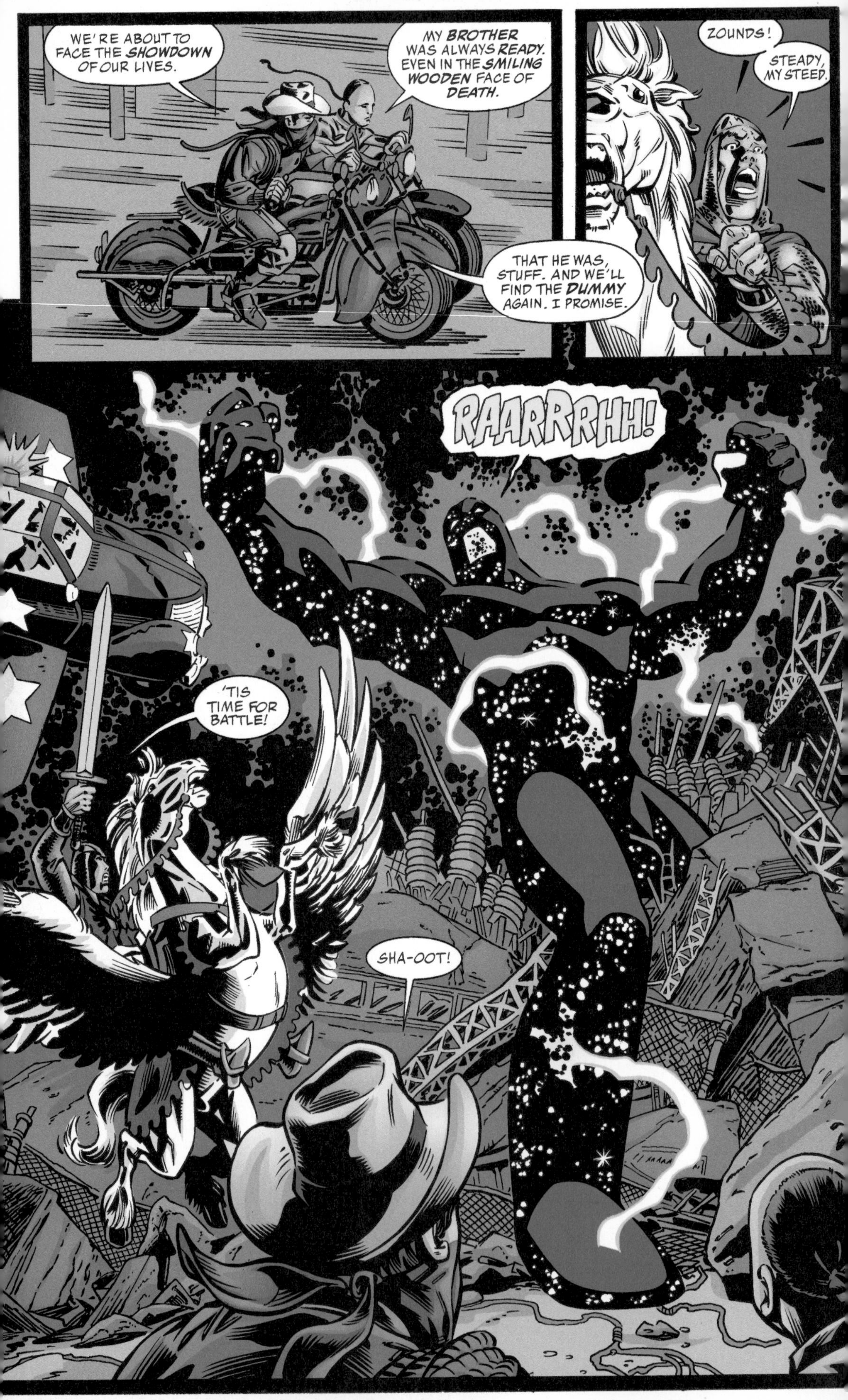
WE'RE ABOUT TO FACE THE SHOWDOWN OF OUR LIVES.
MY BROTHER WAS ALWAYS READY. EVEN IN THE SMILING WOODEN FACE OF DEATH.
ZOUNDS!
STEADY, MY STEED.
THAT HE WAS, STUFF. AND WE'LL FIND THE DUMMY AGAIN. I PROMISE.
RAARRRHH!
'TIS TIME FOR BATTLE!
SHA-OOT!

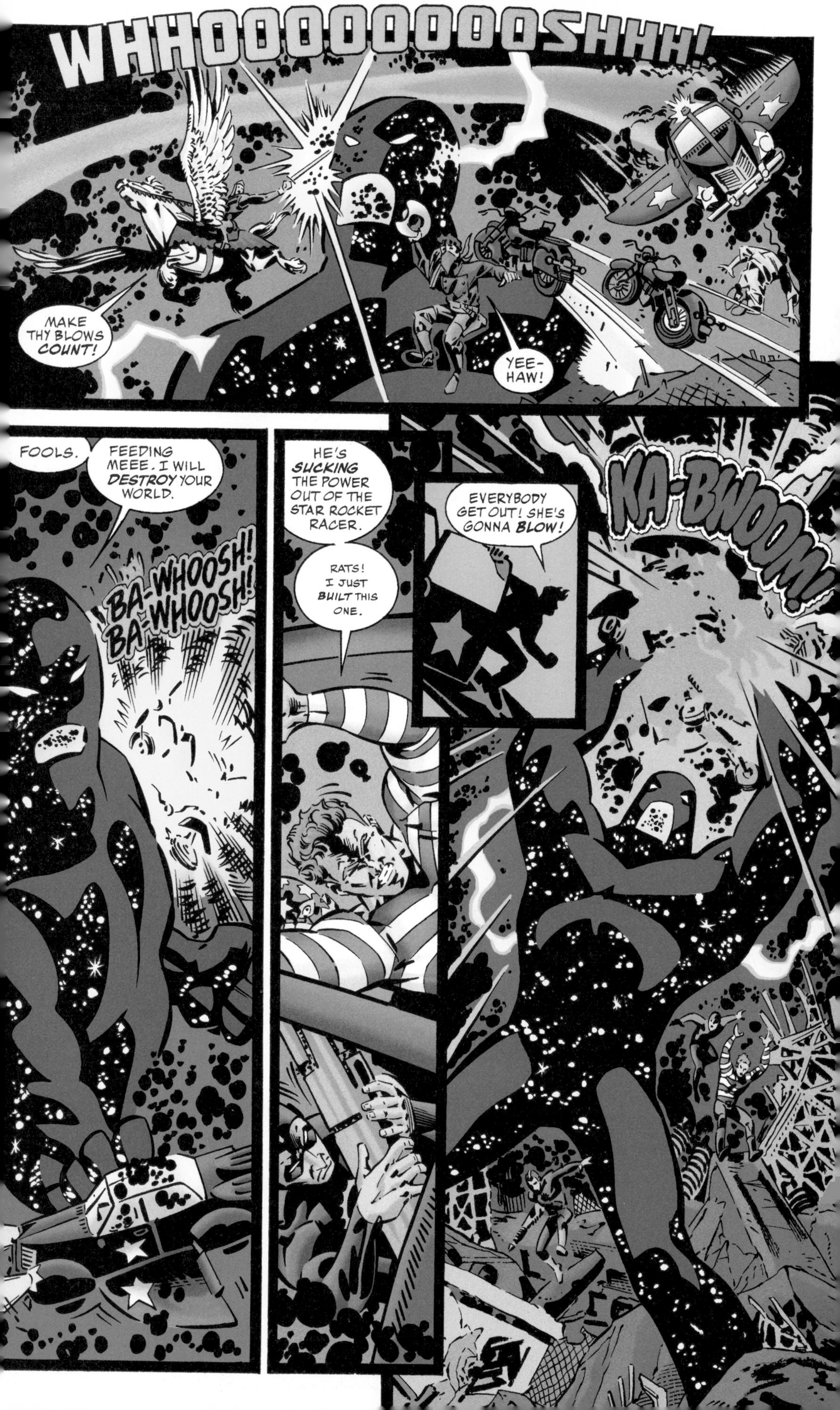
WHHOOOOOOOOOSHHH!
MAKE THY BLOWS COUNT!
YEE-HAW!
FOOLS.
FEEDING MEEE. I WILL DESTROY YOUR WORLD.
BA-WHOOSH! BA-WHOOSH!
HE'S SUCKING THE POWER OUT OF THE STAR ROCKET RACER.
RATS! I JUST BUILT THIS ONE.
EVERYBODY GET OUT! SHE'S GONNA BLOW!
KA-BWOOM!

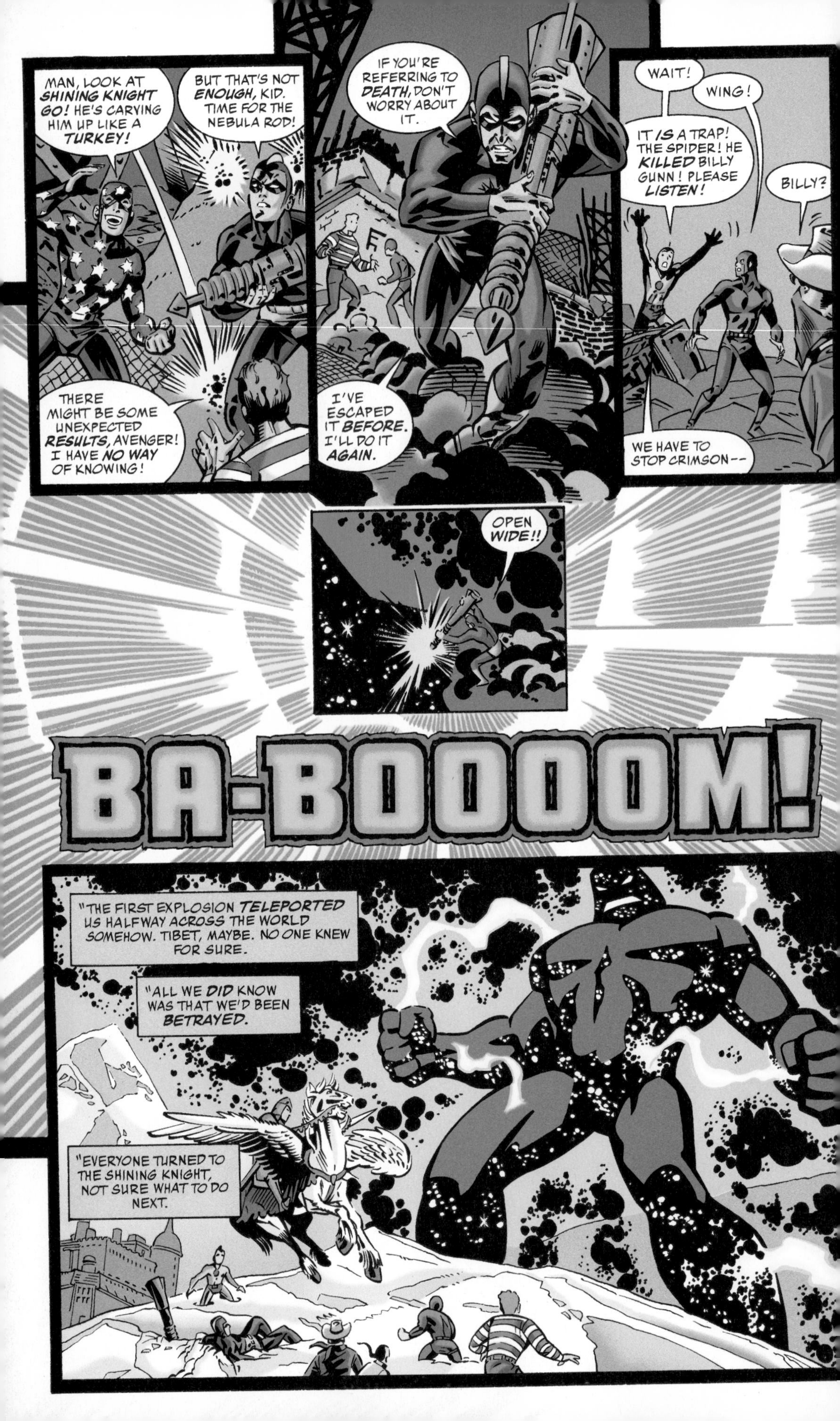
MAN, LOOK AT SHINING KNIGHT GO! HE'S CARVING HIM UP LIKE A TURKEY!
BUT THAT'S NOT ENOUGH, KID. TIME FOR THE NEBULA ROD!
THERE MIGHT BE SOME UNEXPECTED RESULTS, AVENGER! I HAVE NO WAY OF KNOWING!
IF YOU'RE REFERRING TO DEATH, DON'T WORRY ABOUT IT.
I'VE ESCAPED IT BEFORE. I'LL DO IT AGAIN.
WAIT!
WING!
IT IS A TRAP! THE SPIDER! HE KILLED BILLY GUNN! PLEASE LISTEN!
BILLY?
WE HAVE TO STOP CRIMSON--
OPEN WIDE!!
BA-BOOOOM!
"THE FIRST EXPLOSION TELEPORTED US HALFWAY ACROSS THE WORLD SOMEHOW. TIBET, MAYBE. NO ONE KNEW FOR SURE.
"ALL WE DID KNOW WAS THAT WE'D BEEN BETRAYED.
"EVERYONE TURNED TO THE SHINING KNIGHT, NOT SURE WHAT TO DO NEXT.

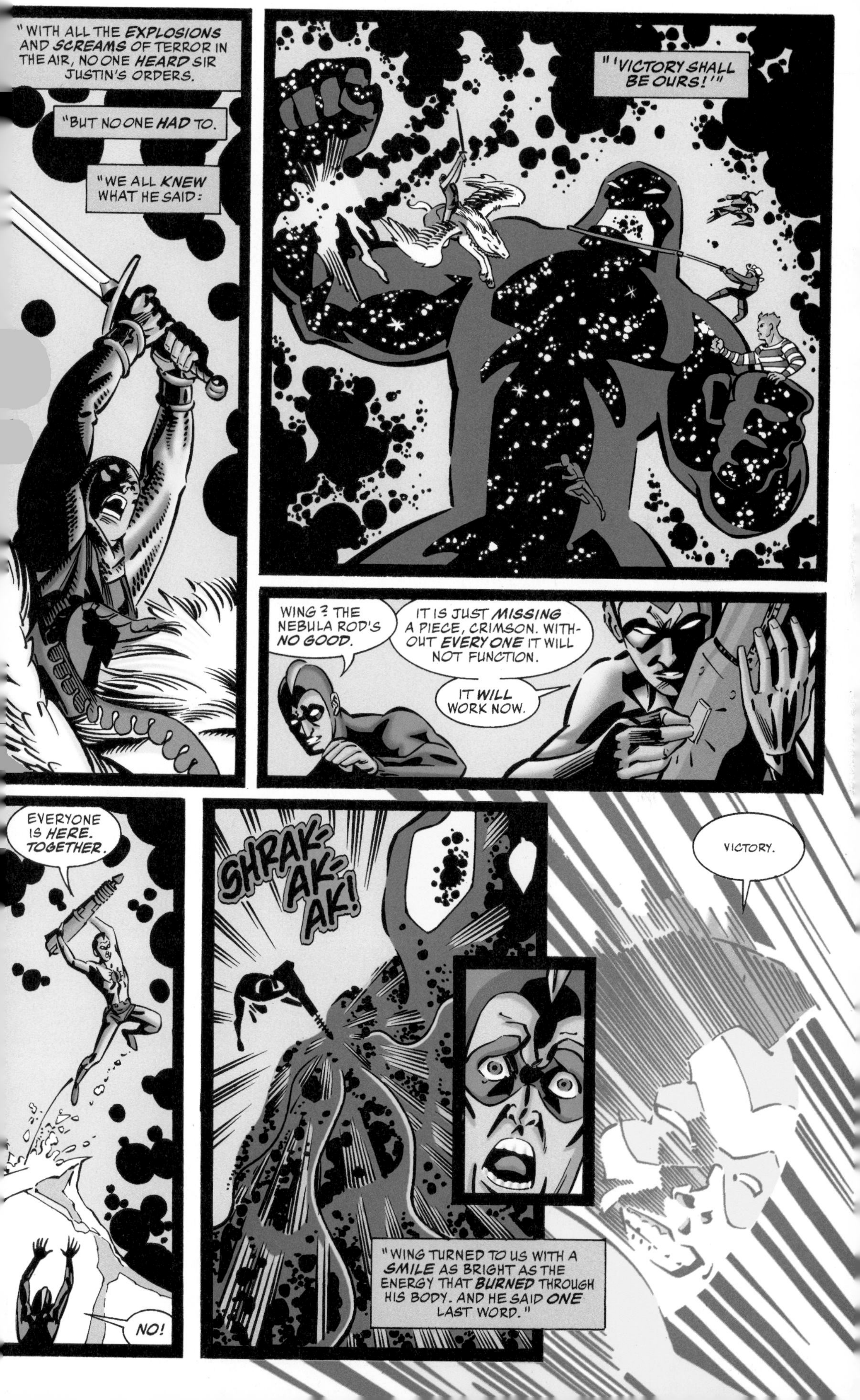
"WITH ALL THE EXPLOSIONS AND SCREAMS OF TERROR IN THE AIR, NO ONE HEARD SIR JUSTIN'S ORDERS.
"BUT NO ONE HAD TO.
"WE ALL KNEW WHAT HE SAID:
"'VICTORY SHALL BE OURS!'"
WING? THE NEBULA ROD'S NO GOOD.
IT IS JUST MISSING A PIECE, CRIMSON. WITHOUT EVERYONE IT WILL NOT FUNCTION.
IT WILL WORK NOW.
EVERYONE IS HERE. TOGETHER.
NO!
SHRAK-AK-AK!
"WING TURNED TO US WITH A SMILE AS BRIGHT AS THE ENERGY THAT BURNED THROUGH HIS BODY. AND HE SAID ONE LAST WORD."
VICTORY.

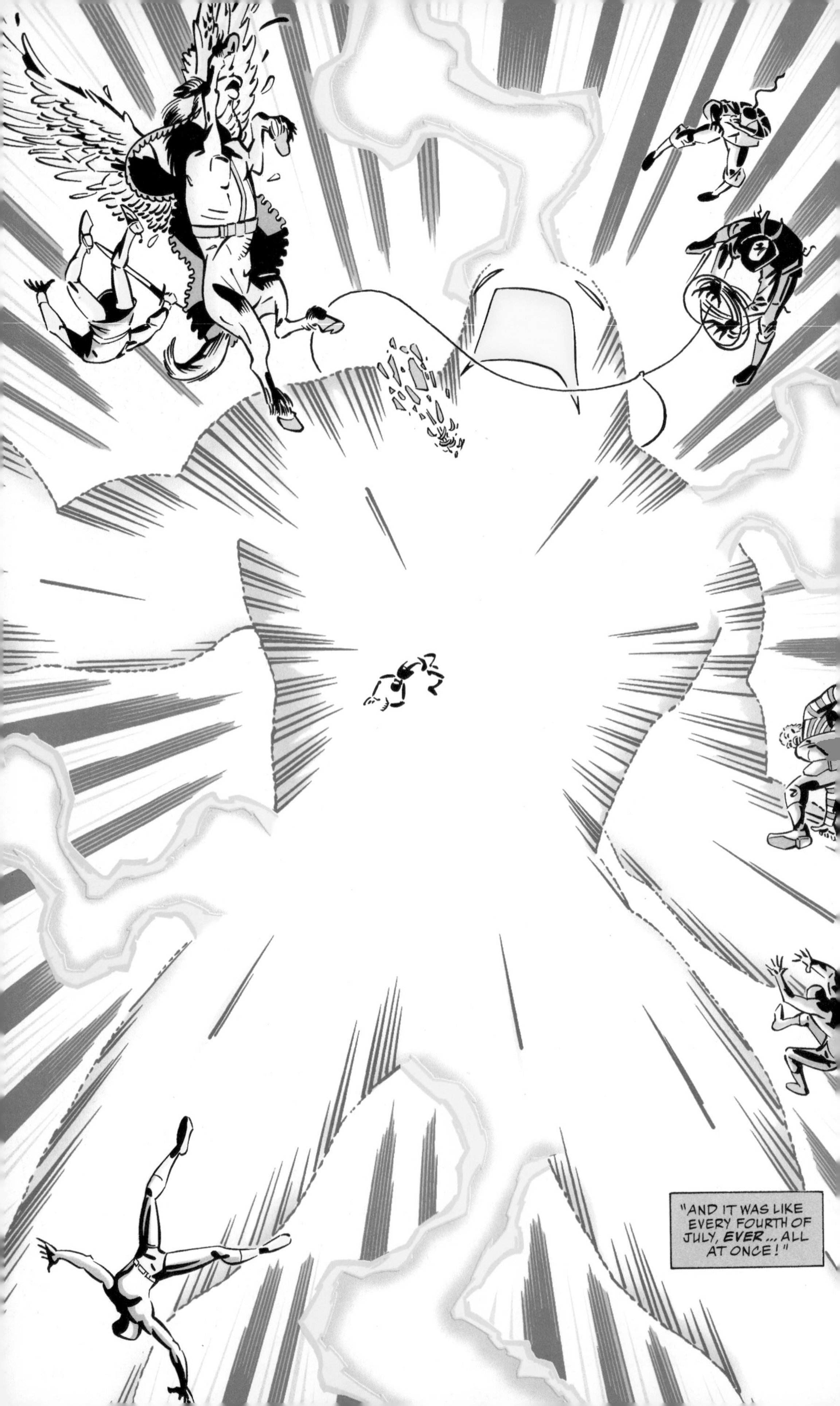
"AND IT WAS LIKE EVERY FOURTH OF JULY, EVER... ALL AT ONCE!"

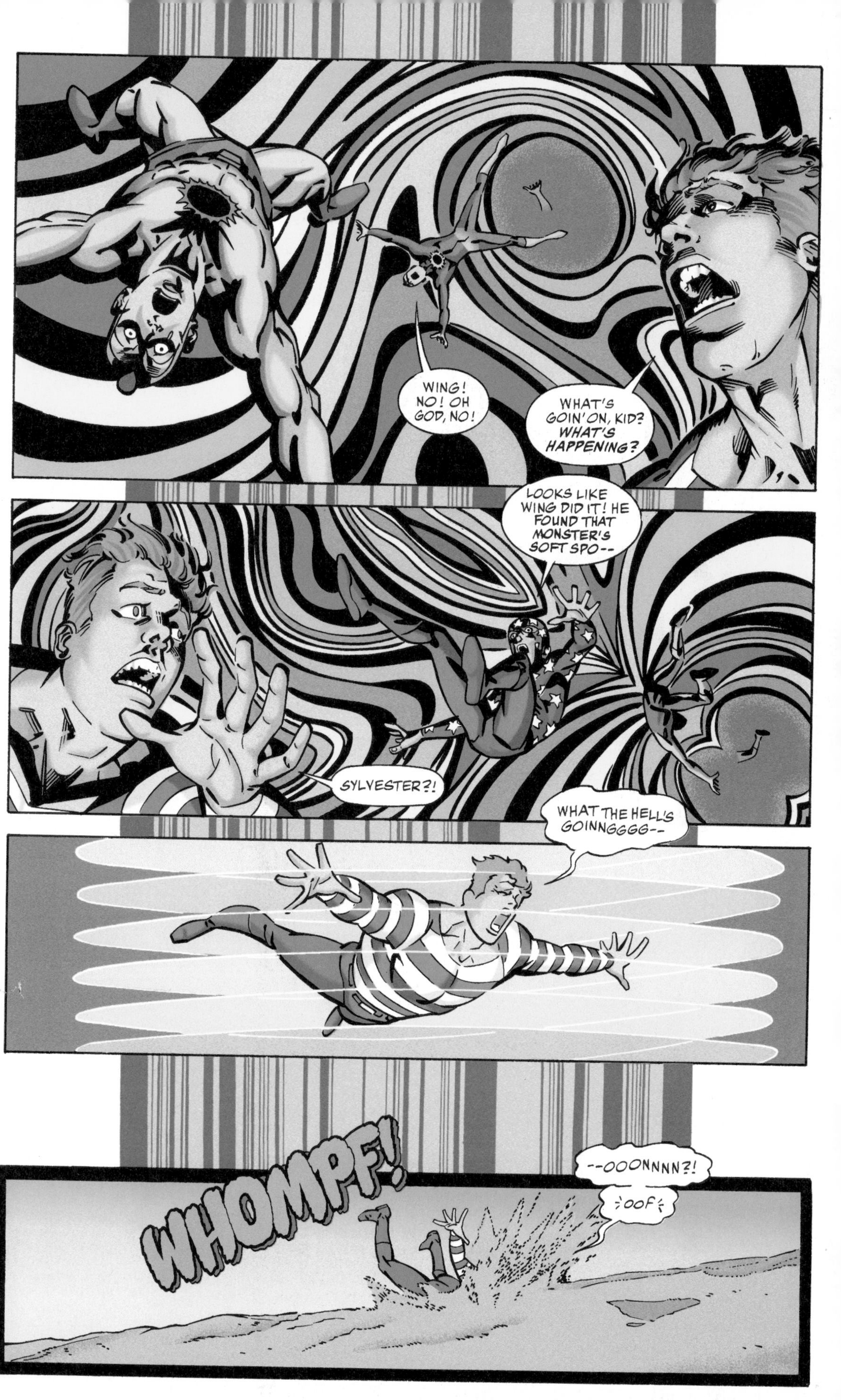

WING! NO! OH GOD, NO!
WHAT'S GOIN' ON, KID? WHAT'S HAPPENING?
LOOKS LIKE WING DID IT! HE FOUND THAT MONSTER'S SOFT SPO--
SYLVESTER?!
WHAT THE HELL'S GOINNGGGG--
WHOMPF!
--OOONNNN?!
OOF

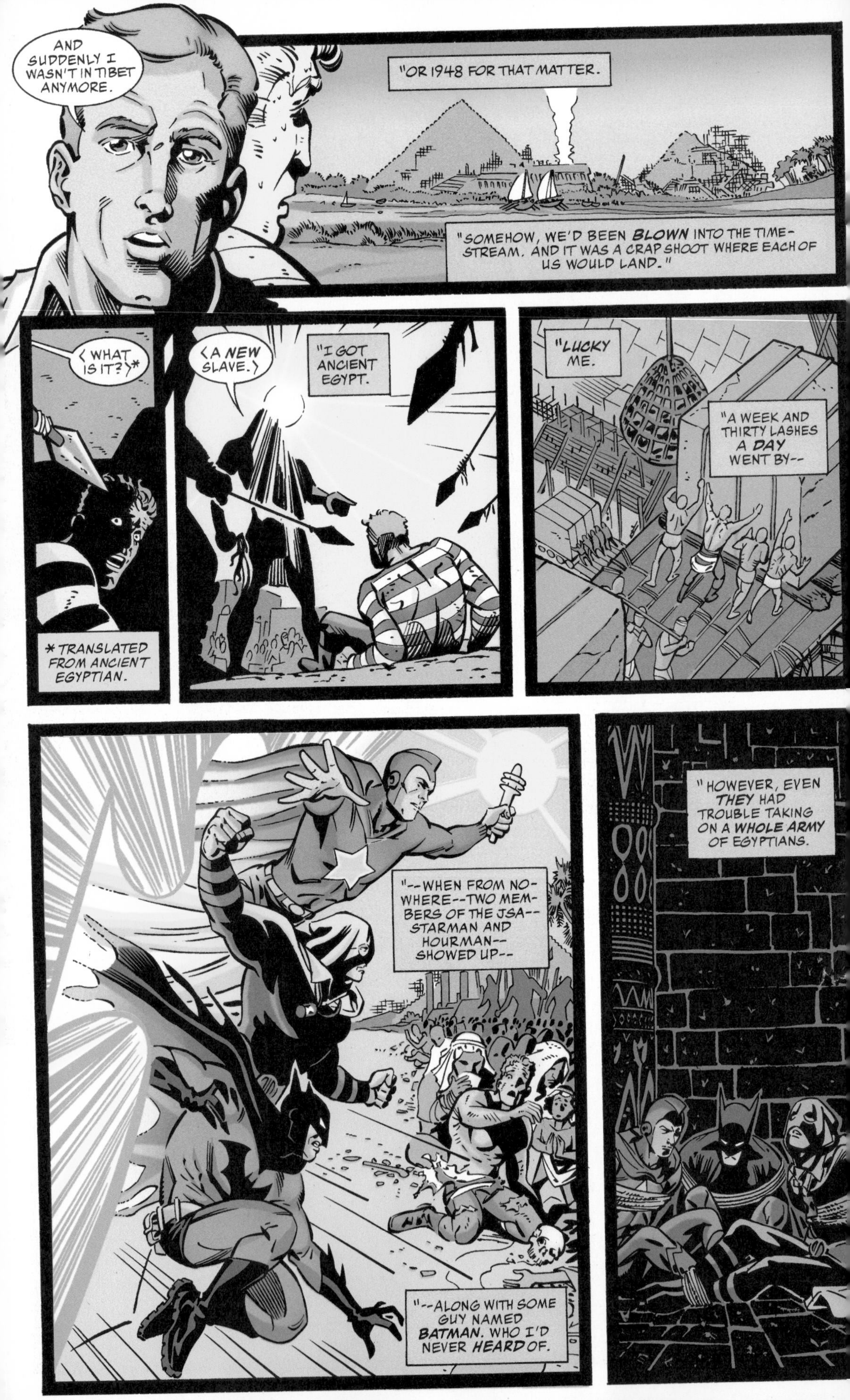
AND SUDDENLY I WASN'T IN TIBET ANYMORE.
"OR 1948 FOR THAT MATTER.
"SOMEHOW, WE'D BEEN BLOWN INTO THE TIME-STREAM. AND IT WAS A CRAP SHOOT WHERE EACH OF US WOULD LAND."
<WHAT IS IT?>*
*TRANSLATED FROM ANCIENT EGYPTIAN.
<A NEW SLAVE.>
"I GOT ANCIENT EGYPT.
"LUCKY ME.
"A WEEK AND THIRTY LASHES A DAY WENT BY--
"--WHEN FROM NO-WHERE--TWO MEMBERS OF THE JSA--STARMAN AND HOURMAN--SHOWED UP--
"--ALONG WITH SOME GUY NAMED BATMAN. WHO I'D NEVER HEARD OF.
"HOWEVER, EVEN THEY HAD TROUBLE TAKING ON A WHOLE ARMY OF EGYPTIANS.

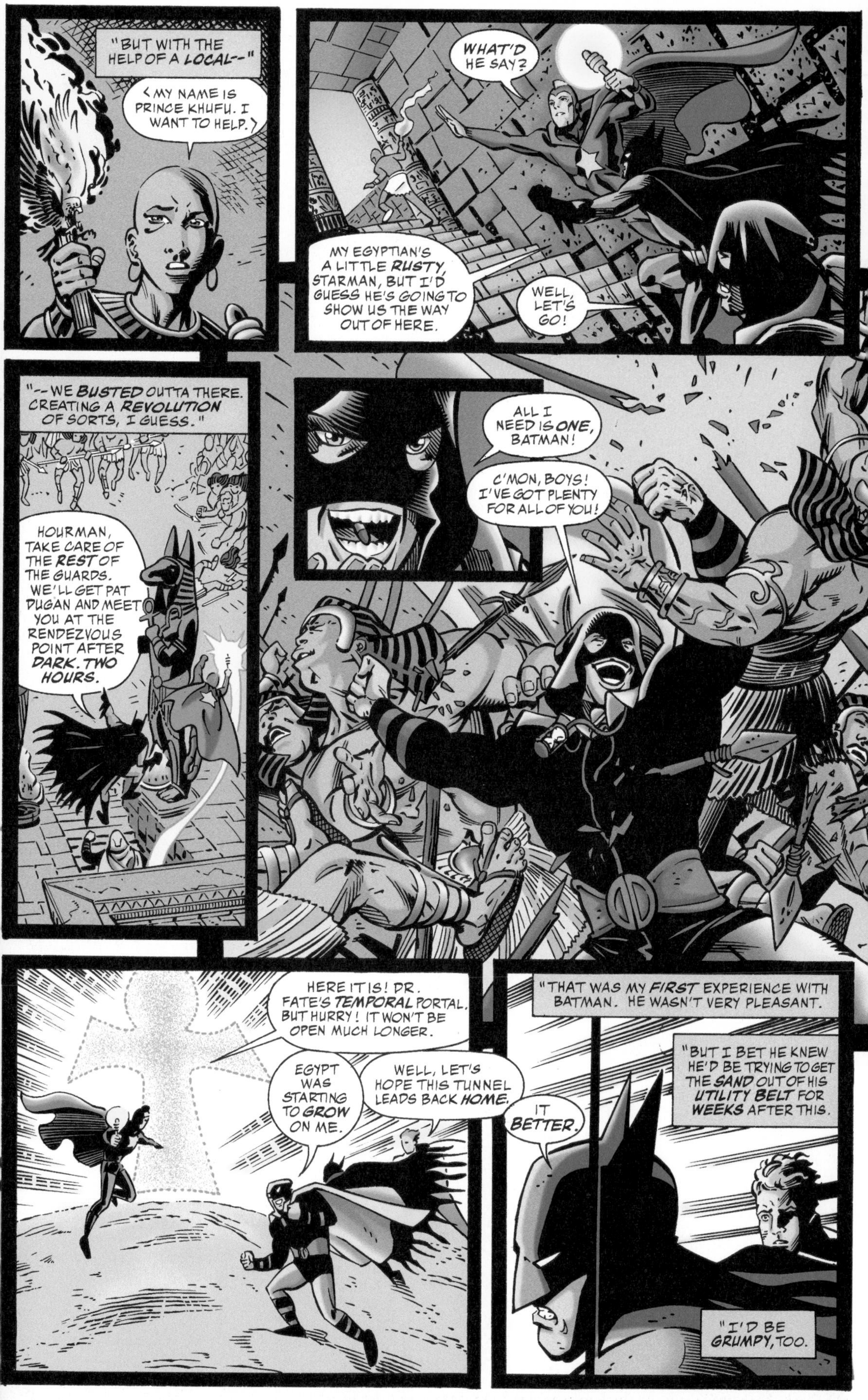

"BUT WITH THE HELP OF A LOCAL--"
<MY NAME IS PRINCE KHUFU. I WANT TO HELP.>
WHAT'D HE SAY?
MY EGYPTIAN'S A LITTLE RUSTY, STARMAN, BUT I'D GUESS HE'S GOING TO SHOW US THE WAY OUT OF HERE.
WELL, LET'S GO!
"--WE BUSTED OUTTA THERE. CREATING A REVOLUTION OF SORTS, I GUESS."
HOURMAN, TAKE CARE OF THE REST OF THE GUARDS. WE'LL GET PAT DUGAN AND MEET YOU AT THE RENDEZVOUS POINT AFTER DARK. TWO HOURS.
ALL I NEED IS ONE, BATMAN!
C'MON, BOYS! I'VE GOT PLENTY FOR ALL OF YOU!
HERE IT IS! DR. FATE'S TEMPORAL PORTAL. BUT HURRY! IT WON'T BE OPEN MUCH LONGER.
EGYPT WAS STARTING TO GROW ON ME.
WELL, LET'S HOPE THIS TUNNEL LEADS BACK HOME.
IT BETTER.
"THAT WAS MY FIRST EXPERIENCE WITH BATMAN. HE WASN'T VERY PLEASANT.
"BUT I BET HE KNEW HE'D BE TRYING TO GET THE SAND OUT OF HIS UTILITY BELT FOR WEEKS AFTER THIS.
"I'D BE GRUMPY, TOO.

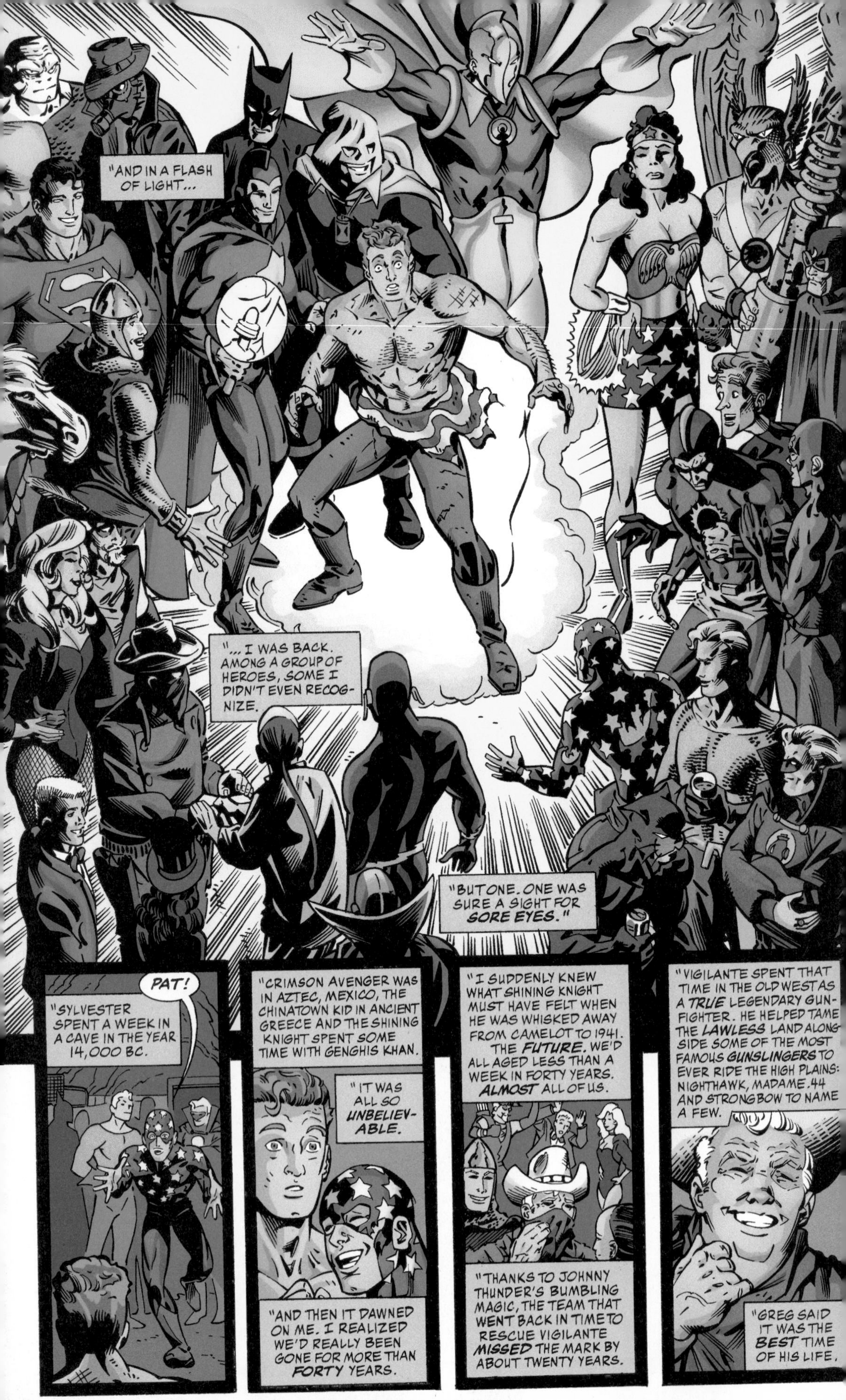
"AND IN A FLASH OF LIGHT...
"...I WAS BACK. AMONG A GROUP OF HEROES, SOME I DIDN'T EVEN RECOG-NIZE.
"BUT ONE. ONE WAS SURE A SIGHT FOR SORE EYES."
"SYLVESTER SPENT A WEEK IN A CAVE IN THE YEAR 14,000 BC.
PAT!
"CRIMSON AVENGER WAS IN AZTEC, MEXICO, THE CHINATOWN KID IN ANCIENT GREECE AND THE SHINING KNIGHT SPENT SOME TIME WITH GENGHIS KHAN.
"IT WAS ALL SO UNBELIEV-ABLE.
"AND THEN IT DAWNED ON ME. I REALIZED WE'D REALLY BEEN GONE FOR MORE THAN FORTY YEARS.
"I SUDDENLY KNEW WHAT SHINING KNIGHT MUST HAVE FELT WHEN HE WAS WHISKED AWAY FROM CAMELOT TO 1941. THE FUTURE. WE'D ALL AGED LESS THAN A WEEK IN FORTY YEARS. ALMOST ALL OF US.
"THANKS TO JOHNNY THUNDER'S BUMBLING MAGIC, THE TEAM THAT WENT BACK IN TIME TO RESCUE VIGILANTE MISSED THE MARK BY ABOUT TWENTY YEARS.
"VIGILANTE SPENT THAT TIME IN THE OLD WEST AS A TRUE LEGENDARY GUN-FIGHTER. HE HELPED TAME THE LAWLESS LAND ALONG SIDE SOME OF THE MOST FAMOUS GUNSLINGERS TO EVER RIDE THE HIGH PLAINS: NIGHTHAWK, MADAME .44 AND STRONGBOW TO NAME A FEW.
"GREG SAID IT WAS THE BEST TIME OF HIS LIFE.

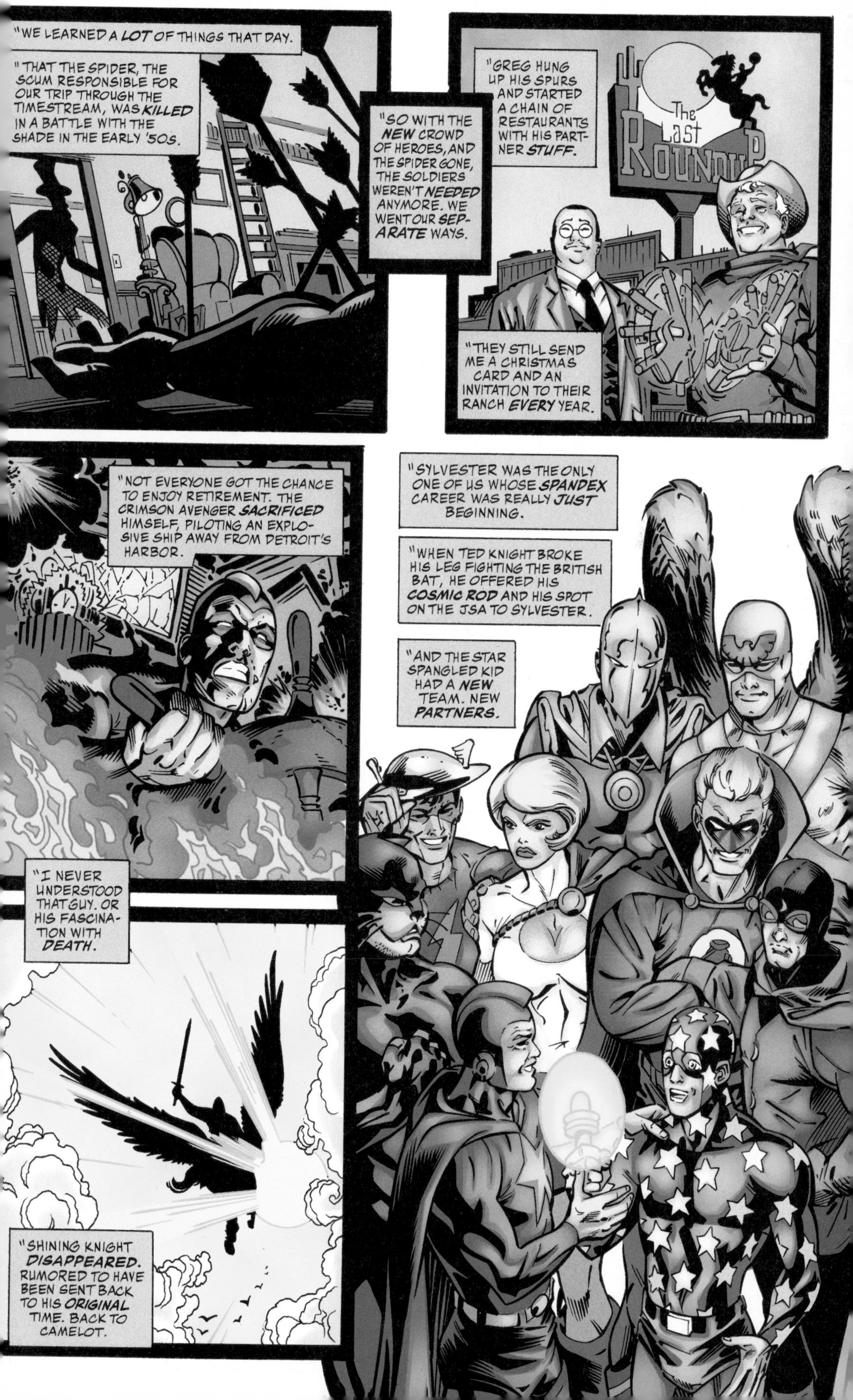

"WE LEARNED A LOT OF THINGS THAT DAY.
"THAT THE SPIDER, THE SCUM RESPONSIBLE FOR OUR TRIP THROUGH THE TIMESTREAM, WAS KILLED IN A BATTLE WITH THE SHADE IN THE EARLY '50s.
"SO WITH THE NEW CROWD OF HEROES, AND THE SPIDER GONE, THE SOLDIERS WEREN'T NEEDED ANYMORE. WE WENT OUR SEPARATE WAYS.
"GREG HUNG UP HIS SPURS AND STARTED A CHAIN OF RESTAURANTS WITH HIS PARTNER STUFF.
The Last Roundup
"THEY STILL SEND ME A CHRISTMAS CARD AND AN INVITATION TO THEIR RANCH EVERY YEAR.
"NOT EVERYONE GOT THE CHANCE TO ENJOY RETIREMENT. THE CRIMSON AVENGER SACRIFICED HIMSELF, PILOTING AN EXPLOSIVE SHIP AWAY FROM DETROIT'S HARBOR.
"I NEVER UNDERSTOOD THAT GUY. OR HIS FASCINATION WITH DEATH.
"SHINING KNIGHT DISAPPEARED. RUMORED TO HAVE BEEN SENT BACK TO HIS ORIGINAL TIME. BACK TO CAMELOT.
"SYLVESTER WAS THE ONLY ONE OF US WHOSE SPANDEX CAREER WAS REALLY JUST BEGINNING.
"WHEN TED KNIGHT BROKE HIS LEG FIGHTING THE BRITISH BAT, HE OFFERED HIS COSMIC ROD AND HIS SPOT ON THE JSA TO SYLVESTER.
"AND THE STAR SPANGLED KID HAD A NEW TEAM. NEW PARTNERS.

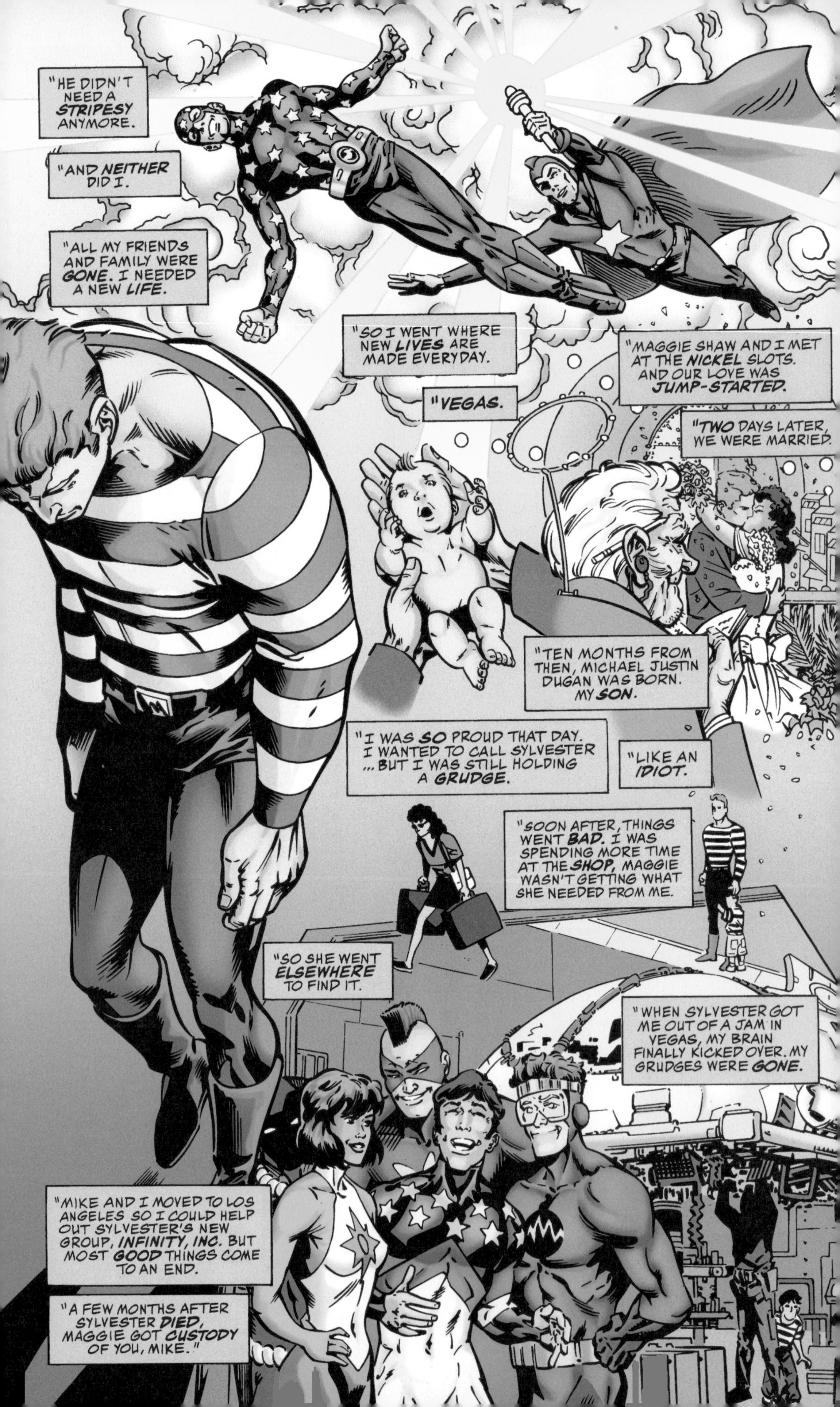
"HE DIDN'T NEED A STRIPESY ANYMORE.
"AND NEITHER DID I.
"ALL MY FRIENDS AND FAMILY WERE GONE. I NEEDED A NEW LIFE.
"SO I WENT WHERE NEW LIVES ARE MADE EVERYDAY.
"VEGAS.
"MAGGIE SHAW AND I MET AT THE NICKEL SLOTS. AND OUR LOVE WAS JUMP-STARTED.
"TWO DAYS LATER, WE WERE MARRIED.
"TEN MONTHS FROM THEN, MICHAEL JUSTIN DUGAN WAS BORN. MY SON.
"I WAS SO PROUD THAT DAY. I WANTED TO CALL SYLVESTER ...BUT I WAS STILL HOLDING A GRUDGE.
"LIKE AN IDIOT.
"SOON AFTER, THINGS WENT BAD. I WAS SPENDING MORE TIME AT THE SHOP, MAGGIE WASN'T GETTING WHAT SHE NEEDED FROM ME.
"SO SHE WENT ELSEWHERE TO FIND IT.
"WHEN SYLVESTER GOT ME OUT OF A JAM IN VEGAS, MY BRAIN FINALLY KICKED OVER. MY GRUDGES WERE GONE.
"MIKE AND I MOVED TO LOS ANGELES SO I COULD HELP OUT SYLVESTER'S NEW GROUP, INFINITY, INC. BUT MOST GOOD THINGS COME TO AN END.
"A FEW MONTHS AFTER SYLVESTER DIED, MAGGIE GOT CUSTODY OF YOU, MIKE."

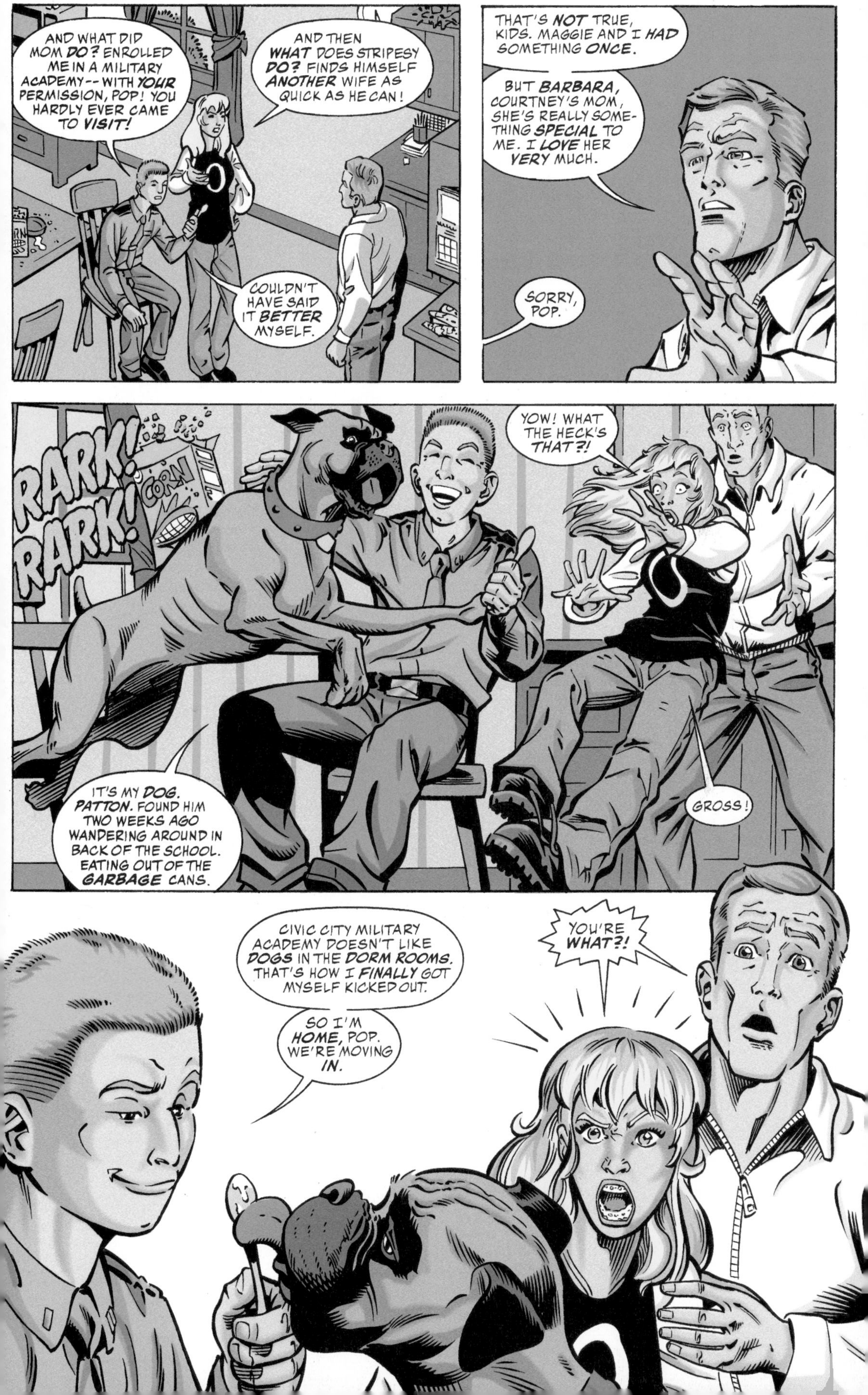
AND WHAT DID MOM DO? ENROLLED ME IN A MILITARY ACADEMY--WITH YOUR PERMISSION, POP! YOU HARDLY EVER CAME TO VISIT!
AND THEN WHAT DOES STRIPESY DO? FINDS HIMSELF ANOTHER WIFE AS QUICK AS HE CAN!
COULDN'T HAVE SAID IT BETTER MYSELF.
THAT'S NOT TRUE, KIDS. MAGGIE AND I HAD SOMETHING ONCE.
BUT BARBARA, COURTNEY'S MOM, SHE'S REALLY SOMETHING SPECIAL TO ME. I LOVE HER VERY MUCH.
SORRY, POP.
RARK! RARK!
YOW! WHAT THE HECK'S THAT?!
IT'S MY DOG. PATTON. FOUND HIM TWO WEEKS AGO WANDERING AROUND IN BACK OF THE SCHOOL. EATING OUT OF THE GARBAGE CANS.
GROSS!
CIVIC CITY MILITARY ACADEMY DOESN'T LIKE DOGS IN THE DORM ROOMS. THAT'S HOW I FINALLY GOT MYSELF KICKED OUT.
SO I'M HOME, POP. WE'RE MOVING IN.
YOU'RE WHAT?!

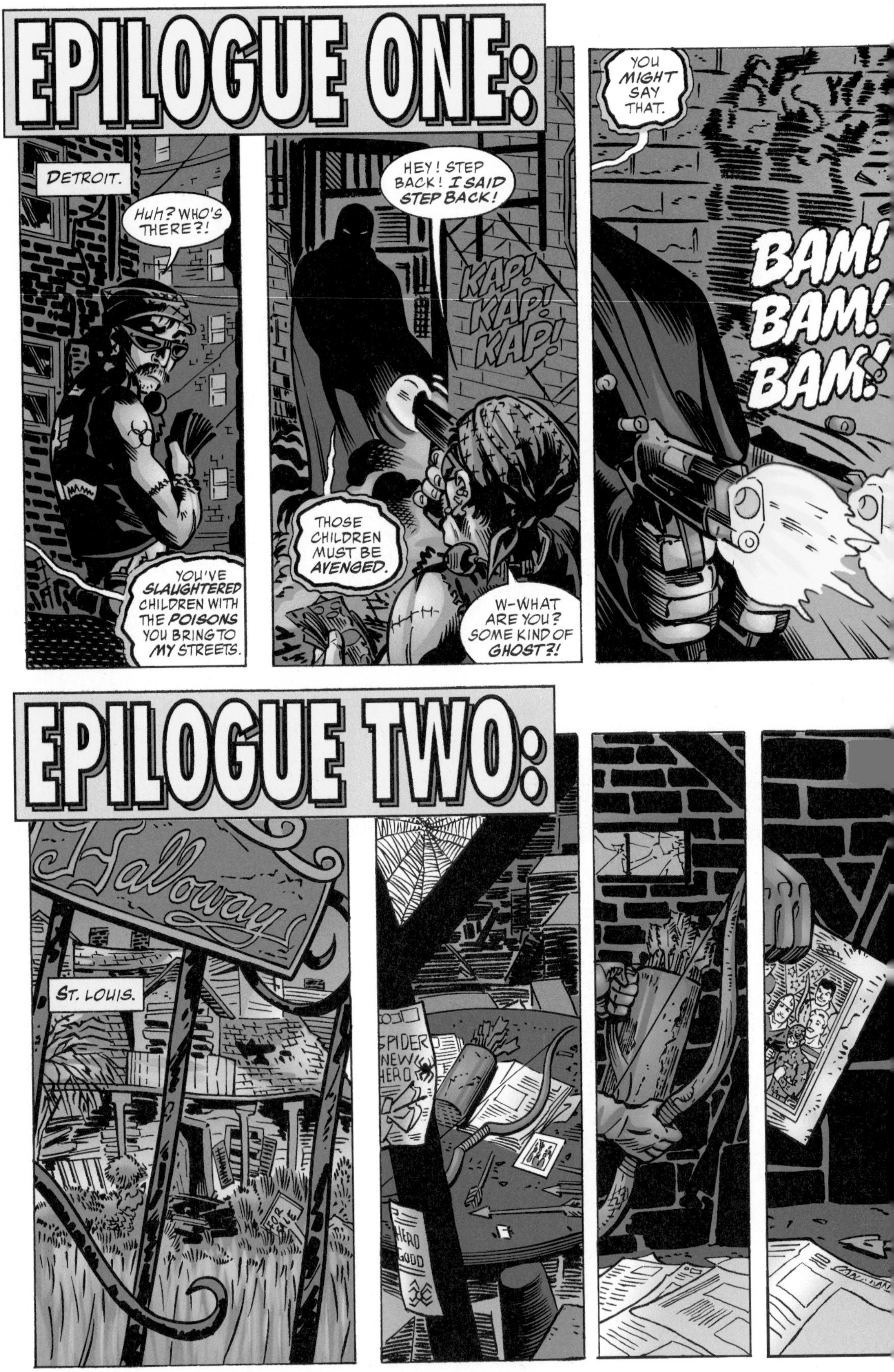
EPILOGUE ONE:
DETROIT.
Huh? WHO'S THERE?!
YOU'VE SLAUGHTERED CHILDREN WITH THE POISONS YOU BRING TO MY STREETS.
HEY! STEP BACK! I SAID STEP BACK!
KAP! KAP! KAP!
THOSE CHILDREN MUST BE AVENGED.
W-WHAT ARE YOU? SOME KIND OF GHOST?!
YOU MIGHT SAY THAT.
BAM! BAM! BAM!
EPILOGUE TWO:
ST. LOUIS.

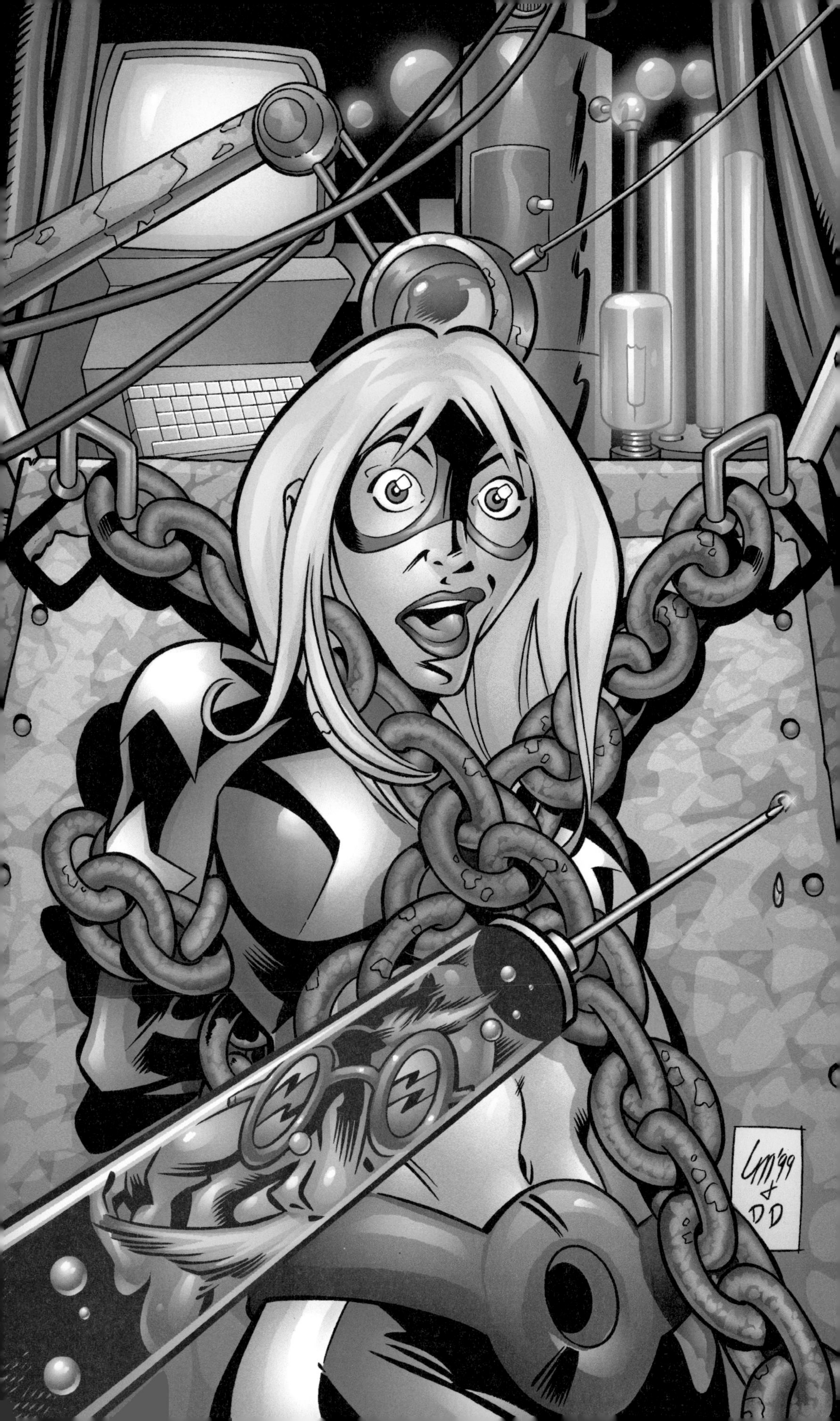

STARS AND S.T.R.I.P.E. #10

Written by GEOFF JOHNS
Pencils by SCOTT KOLINS
Inks by DAN DAVIS
Colors by TOM McCRAW
Letters by BILL OAKLEY
Cover art by LEE MODER and DAN DAVIS
Cover color by RICHARD & TANYA HORIE

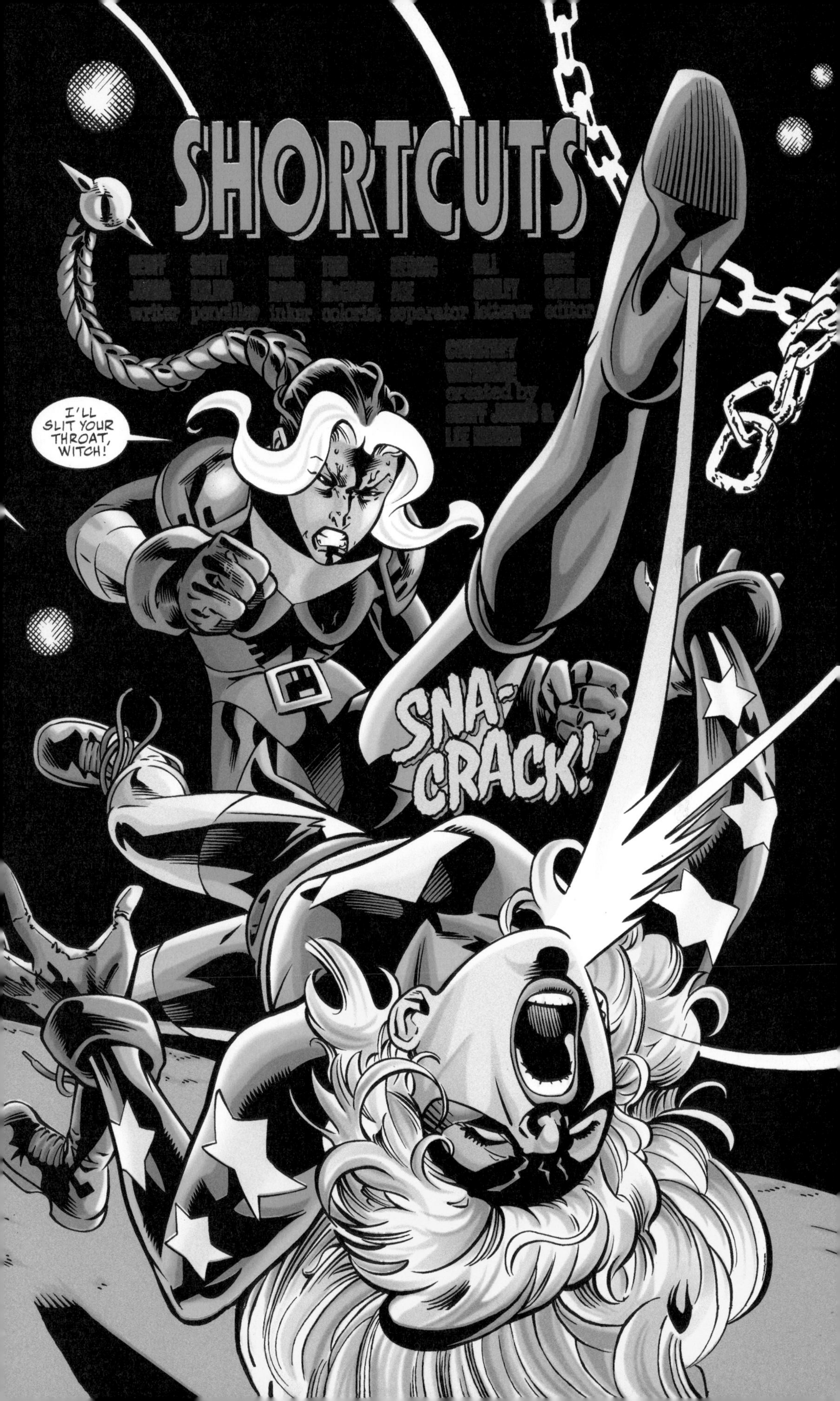
SHORTCUTS
writer penciller inker colorist seperator letterer editor
created by
I'LL SLIT YOUR THROAT, WITCH!
SNA-CRACK!

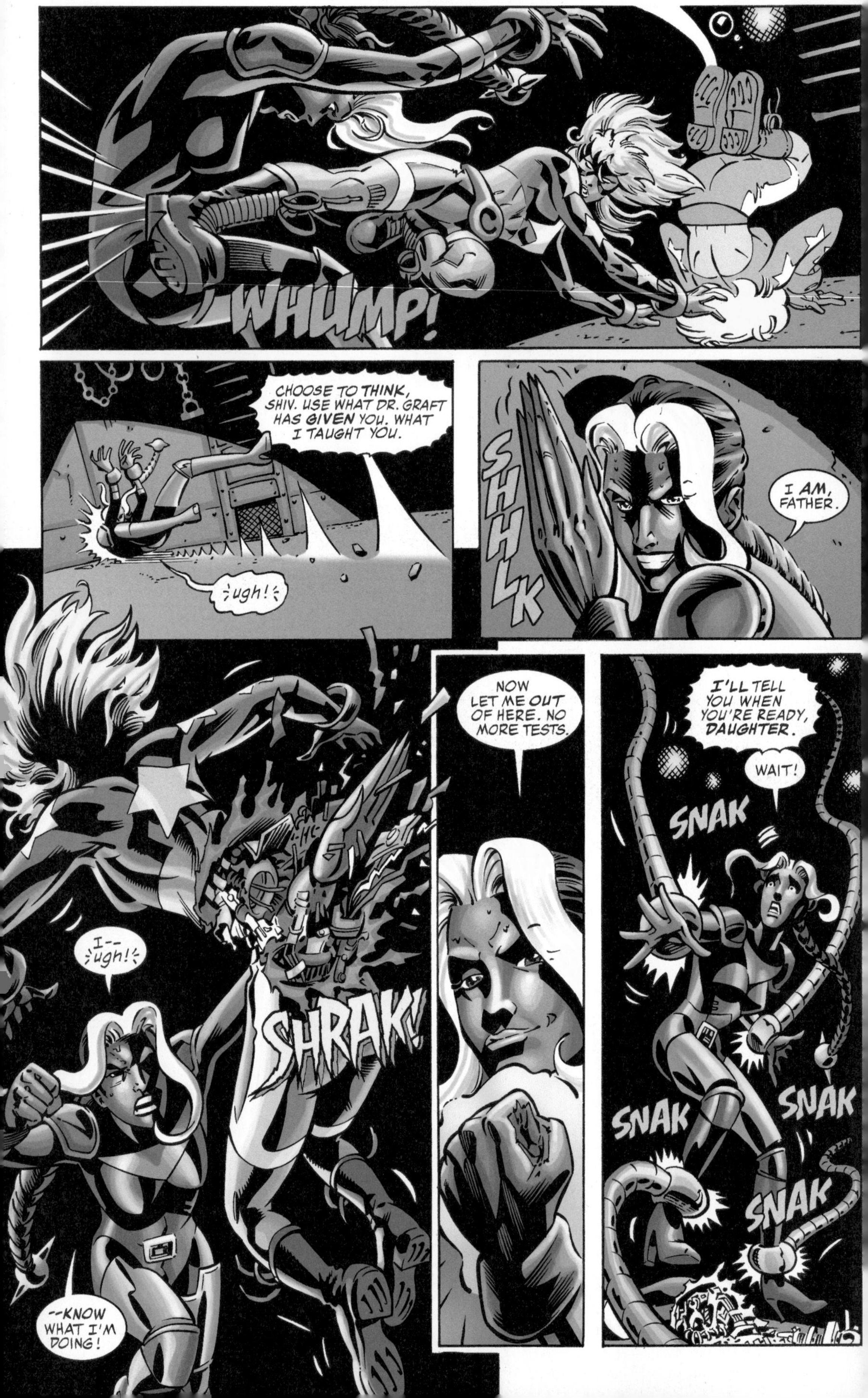
WHUMP!
CHOOSE TO THINK, SHIV. USE WHAT DR. GRAFT HAS GIVEN YOU. WHAT I TAUGHT YOU.
ugh!
SHHHLK
I AM, FATHER.
I-- ugh!
SHRAK!
--KNOW WHAT I'M DOING!
NOW LET ME OUT OF HERE. NO MORE TESTS.
I'LL TELL YOU WHEN YOU'RE READY, DAUGHTER.
WAIT!
SNAK
SNAK
SNAK
SNAK

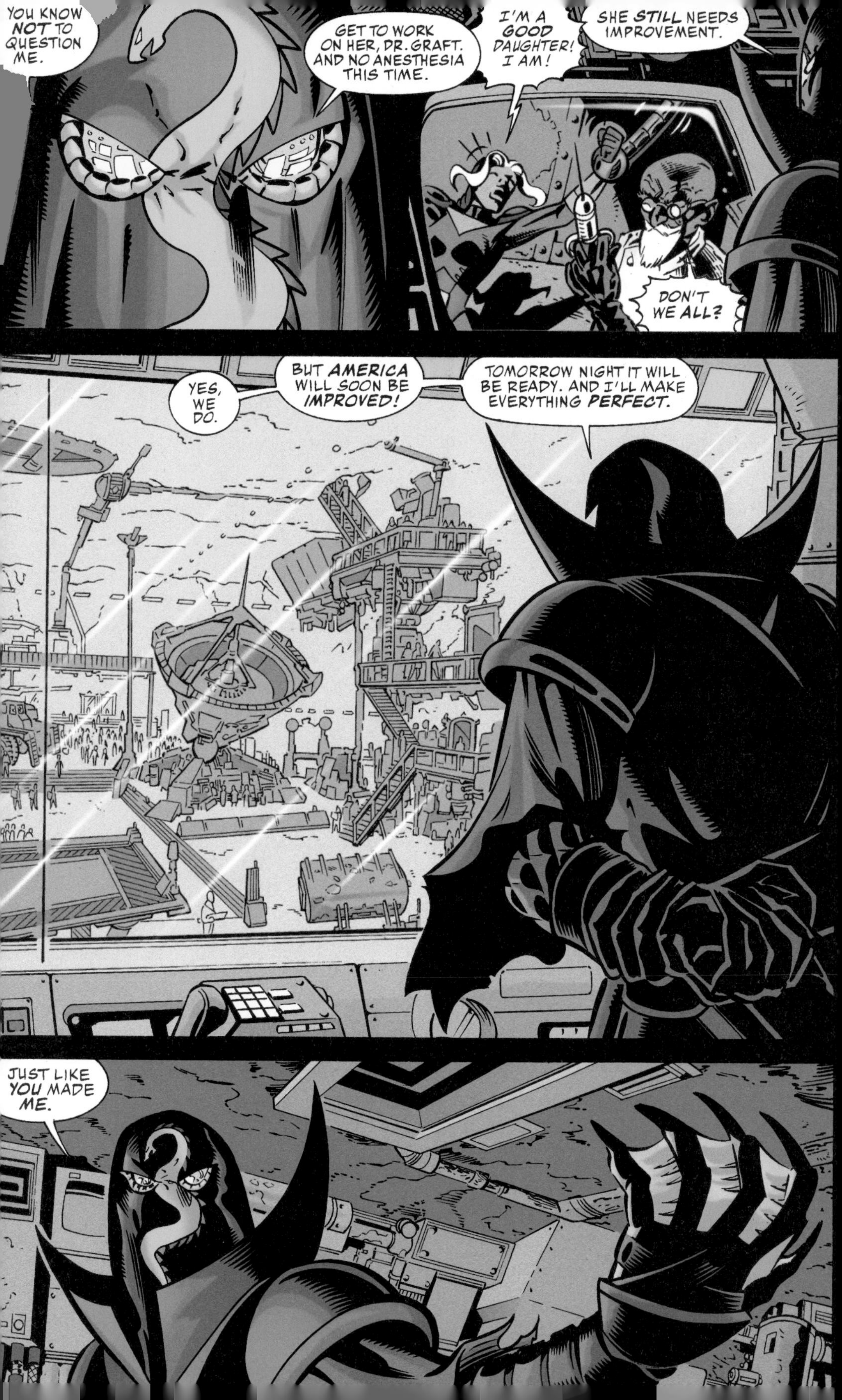
YOU KNOW NOT TO QUESTION ME.
GET TO WORK ON HER, DR. GRAFT. AND NO ANESTHESIA THIS TIME.
I'M A GOOD DAUGHTER! I AM!
SHE STILL NEEDS IMPROVEMENT.
DON'T WE ALL?
YES, WE DO.
BUT AMERICA WILL SOON BE IMPROVED!
TOMORROW NIGHT IT WILL BE READY. AND I'LL MAKE EVERYTHING PERFECT.
JUST LIKE YOU MADE ME.

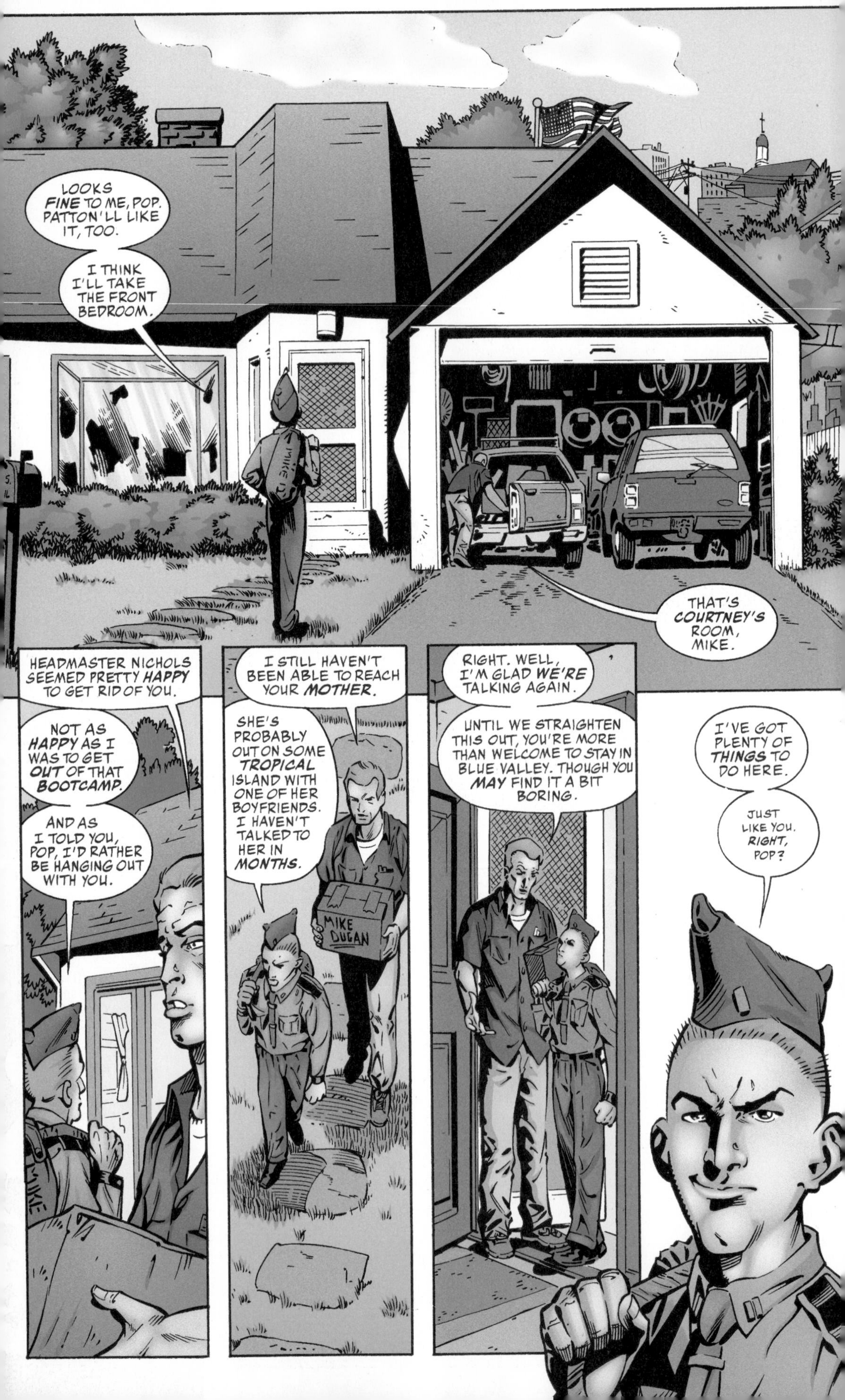
LOOKS FINE TO ME, POP. PATTON'LL LIKE IT, TOO.
I THINK I'LL TAKE THE FRONT BEDROOM.
THAT'S COURTNEY'S ROOM, MIKE.
MIKE
HEADMASTER NICHOLS SEEMED PRETTY HAPPY TO GET RID OF YOU.
NOT AS HAPPY AS I WAS TO GET OUT OF THAT BOOTCAMP.
AND AS I TOLD YOU, POP, I'D RATHER BE HANGING OUT WITH YOU.
I STILL HAVEN'T BEEN ABLE TO REACH YOUR MOTHER.
SHE'S PROBABLY OUT ON SOME TROPICAL ISLAND WITH ONE OF HER BOYFRIENDS. I HAVEN'T TALKED TO HER IN MONTHS.
MIKE DUGAN
RIGHT. WELL, I'M GLAD WE'RE TALKING AGAIN.
UNTIL WE STRAIGHTEN THIS OUT, YOU'RE MORE THAN WELCOME TO STAY IN BLUE VALLEY. THOUGH YOU MAY FIND IT A BIT BORING.
I'VE GOT PLENTY OF THINGS TO DO HERE.
JUST LIKE YOU. RIGHT, POP?

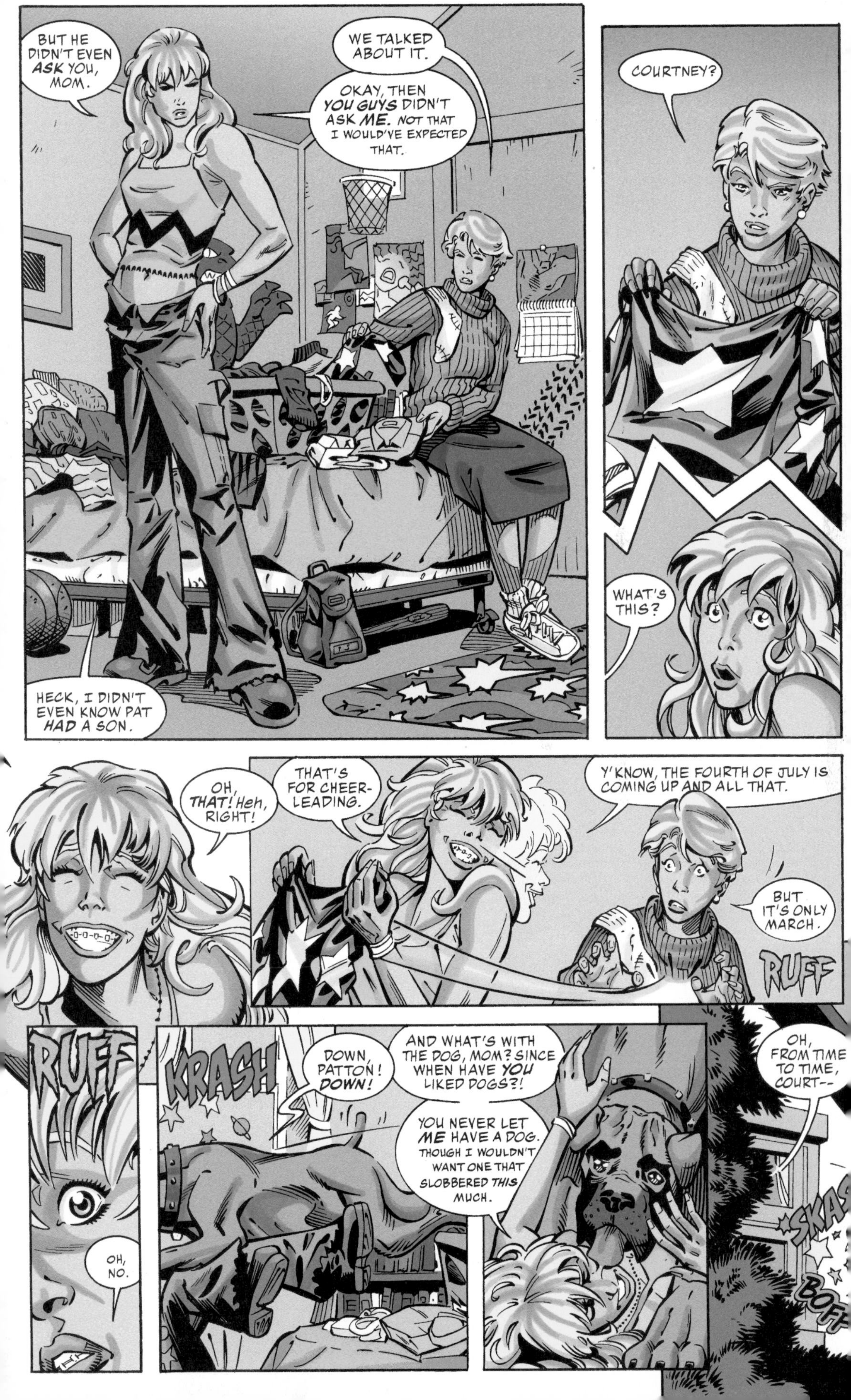

BUT HE DIDN'T EVEN ASK YOU, MOM.
WE TALKED ABOUT IT.
OKAY, THEN YOU GUYS DIDN'T ASK ME. NOT THAT I WOULD'VE EXPECTED THAT.
HECK, I DIDN'T EVEN KNOW PAT HAD A SON.
COURTNEY?
WHAT'S THIS?
OH, THAT! Heh, RIGHT!
THAT'S FOR CHEER-LEADING.
Y'KNOW, THE FOURTH OF JULY IS COMING UP AND ALL THAT.
BUT IT'S ONLY MARCH.
RUFF
RUFF
OH, NO.
KRASH
DOWN, PATTON! DOWN!
AND WHAT'S WITH THE DOG, MOM? SINCE WHEN HAVE YOU LIKED DOGS?!
YOU NEVER LET ME HAVE A DOG. THOUGH I WOULDN'T WANT ONE THAT SLOBBERED THIS MUCH.
OH, FROM TIME TO TIME, COURT--
BOFF

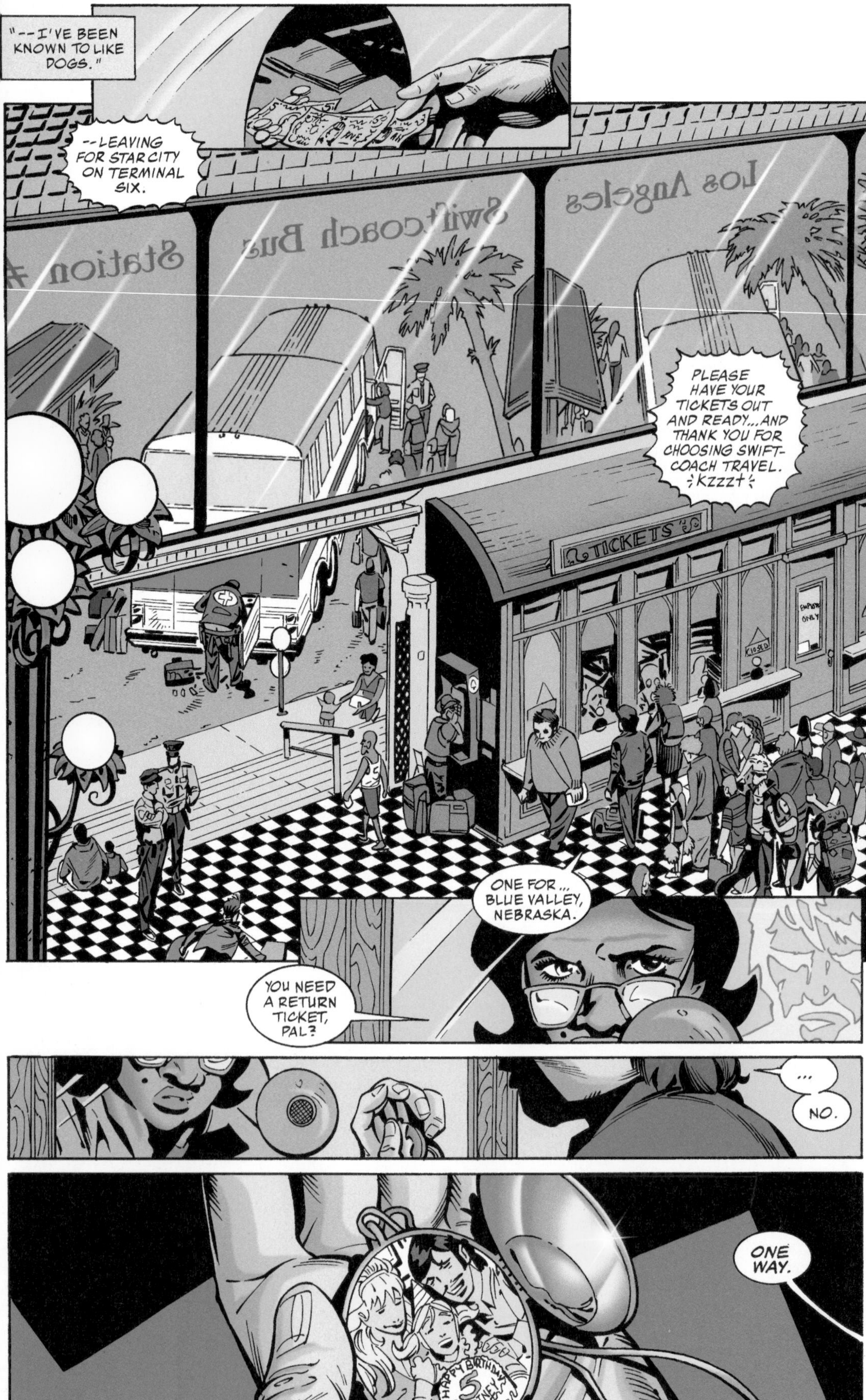
"--I'VE BEEN KNOWN TO LIKE DOGS."
--LEAVING FOR STAR CITY ON TERMINAL SIX.
Los Angeles Swiftcoach Bus Station #
PLEASE HAVE YOUR TICKETS OUT AND READY... AND THANK YOU FOR CHOOSING SWIFT-COACH TRAVEL. Kzzzt
TICKETS
EMPLOYEE ONLY
CLOSED
ONE FOR... BLUE VALLEY, NEBRASKA.
YOU NEED A RETURN TICKET, PAL?
...
NO.
ONE WAY.
HAPPY BIRTHDAY 5 COURTNEY

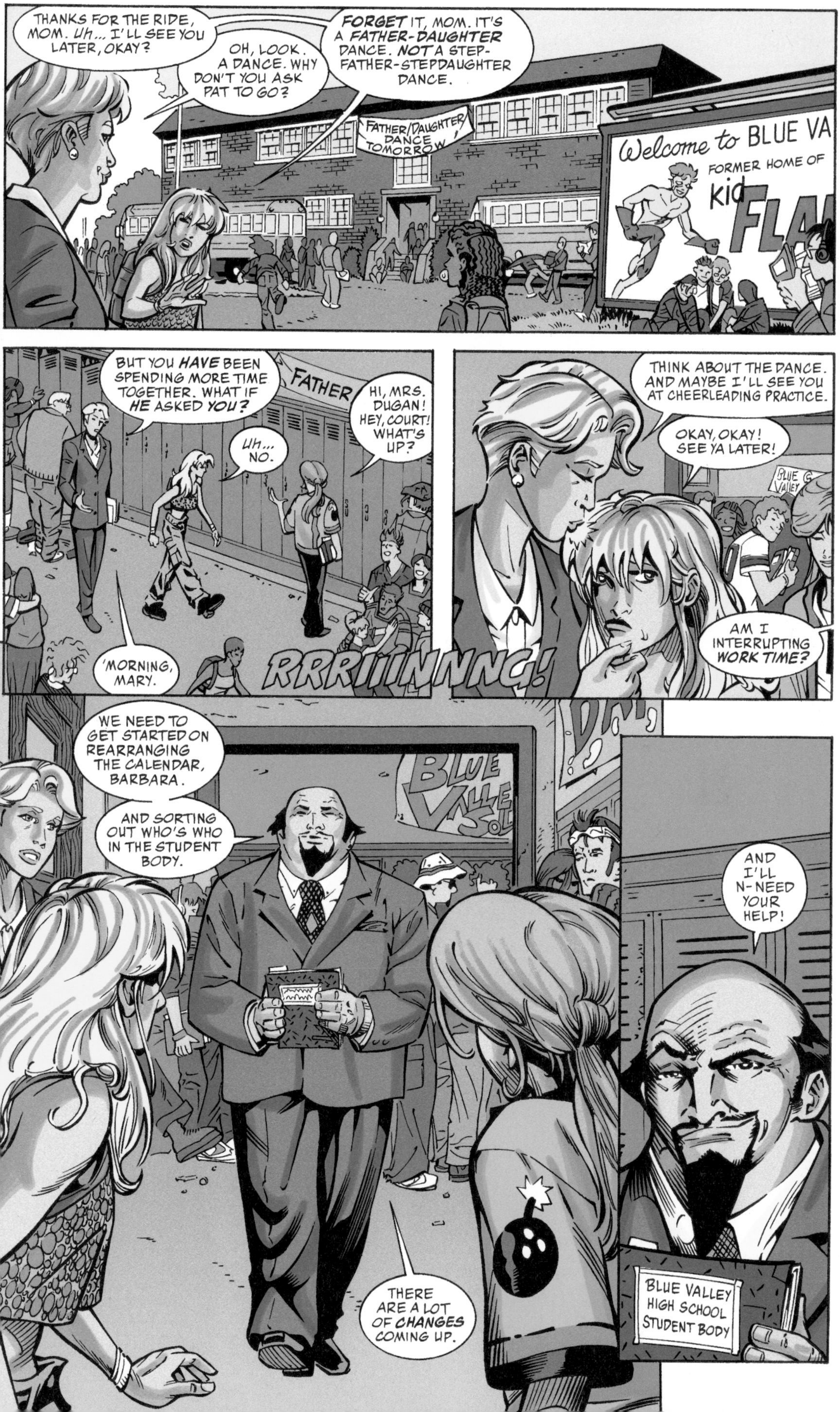
THANKS FOR THE RIDE, MOM. UH... I'LL SEE YOU LATER, OKAY?
OH, LOOK. A DANCE. WHY DON'T YOU ASK PAT TO GO?
FORGET IT, MOM. IT'S A FATHER-DAUGHTER DANCE. NOT A STEP-FATHER-STEPDAUGHTER DANCE.
FATHER/DAUGHTER DANCE TOMORROW
Welcome to BLUE VA
FORMER HOME OF
kid FLA
BUT YOU HAVE BEEN SPENDING MORE TIME TOGETHER. WHAT IF HE ASKED YOU?
FATHER
UH... NO.
HI, MRS. DUGAN! HEY, COURT! WHAT'S UP?
'MORNING, MARY.
RRRIIINNNG!
THINK ABOUT THE DANCE. AND MAYBE I'LL SEE YOU AT CHEERLEADING PRACTICE.
OKAY, OKAY! SEE YA LATER!
AM I INTERRUPTING WORK TIME?
WE NEED TO GET STARTED ON REARRANGING THE CALENDAR, BARBARA.
AND SORTING OUT WHO'S WHO IN THE STUDENT BODY.
THERE ARE A LOT OF CHANGES COMING UP.
AND I'LL N-NEED YOUR HELP!
BLUE VALLEY HIGH SCHOOL STUDENT BODY

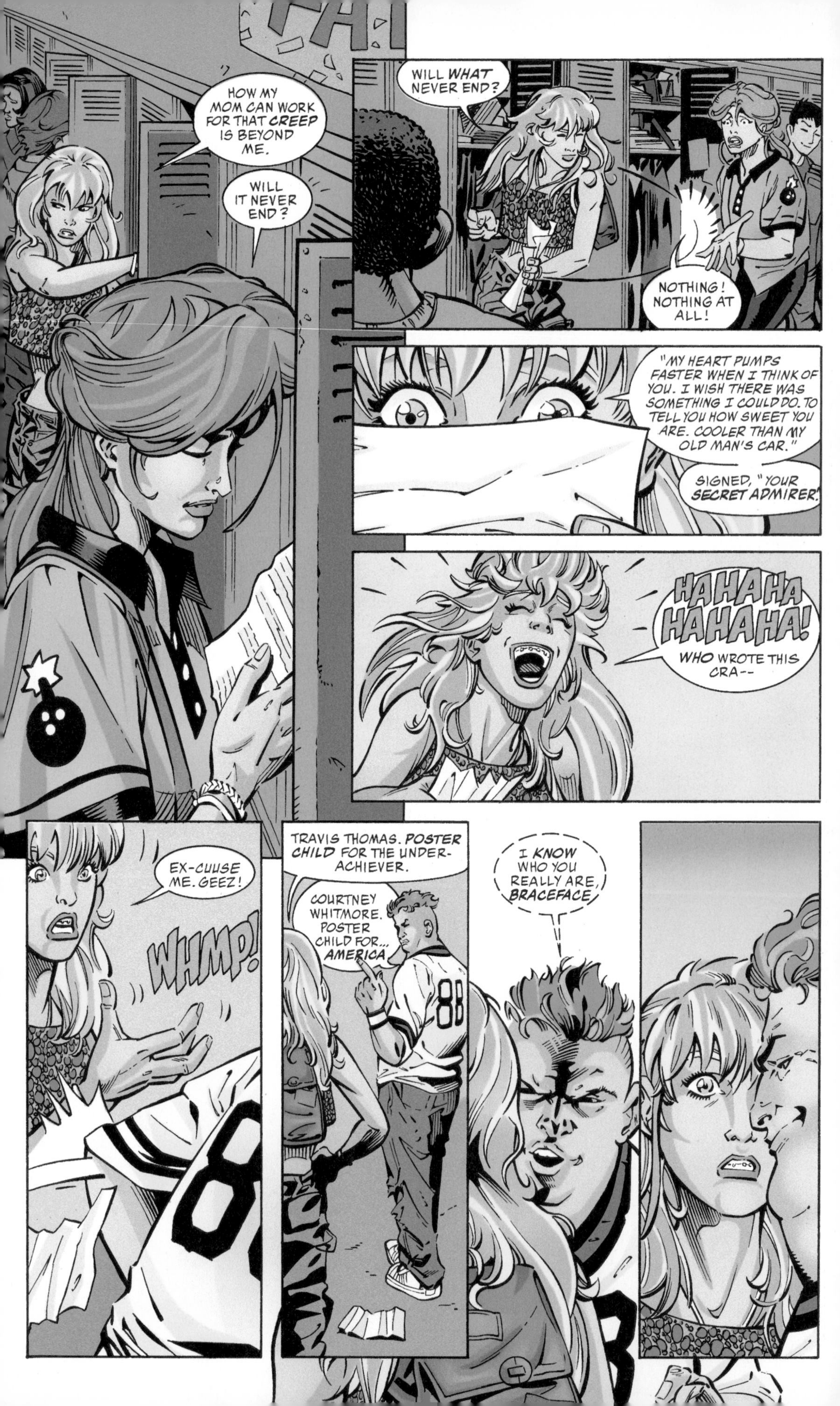

CH
HOW MY MOM CAN WORK FOR THAT CREEP IS BEYOND ME.
WILL IT NEVER END?
WILL WHAT NEVER END?
NOTHING! NOTHING AT ALL!
"MY HEART PUMPS FASTER WHEN I THINK OF YOU. I WISH THERE WAS SOMETHING I COULD DO. TO TELL YOU HOW SWEET YOU ARE. COOLER THAN MY OLD MAN'S CAR."
SIGNED, "YOUR SECRET ADMIRER."
HAHAHA HAHAHA!
WHO WROTE THIS CRA--
EX-CUUSE ME. GEEZ!
WHMP!
TRAVIS THOMAS. POSTER CHILD FOR THE UNDER-ACHIEVER.
COURTNEY WHITMORE. POSTER CHILD FOR... AMERICA.
88
I KNOW WHO YOU REALLY ARE, BRACEFACE.

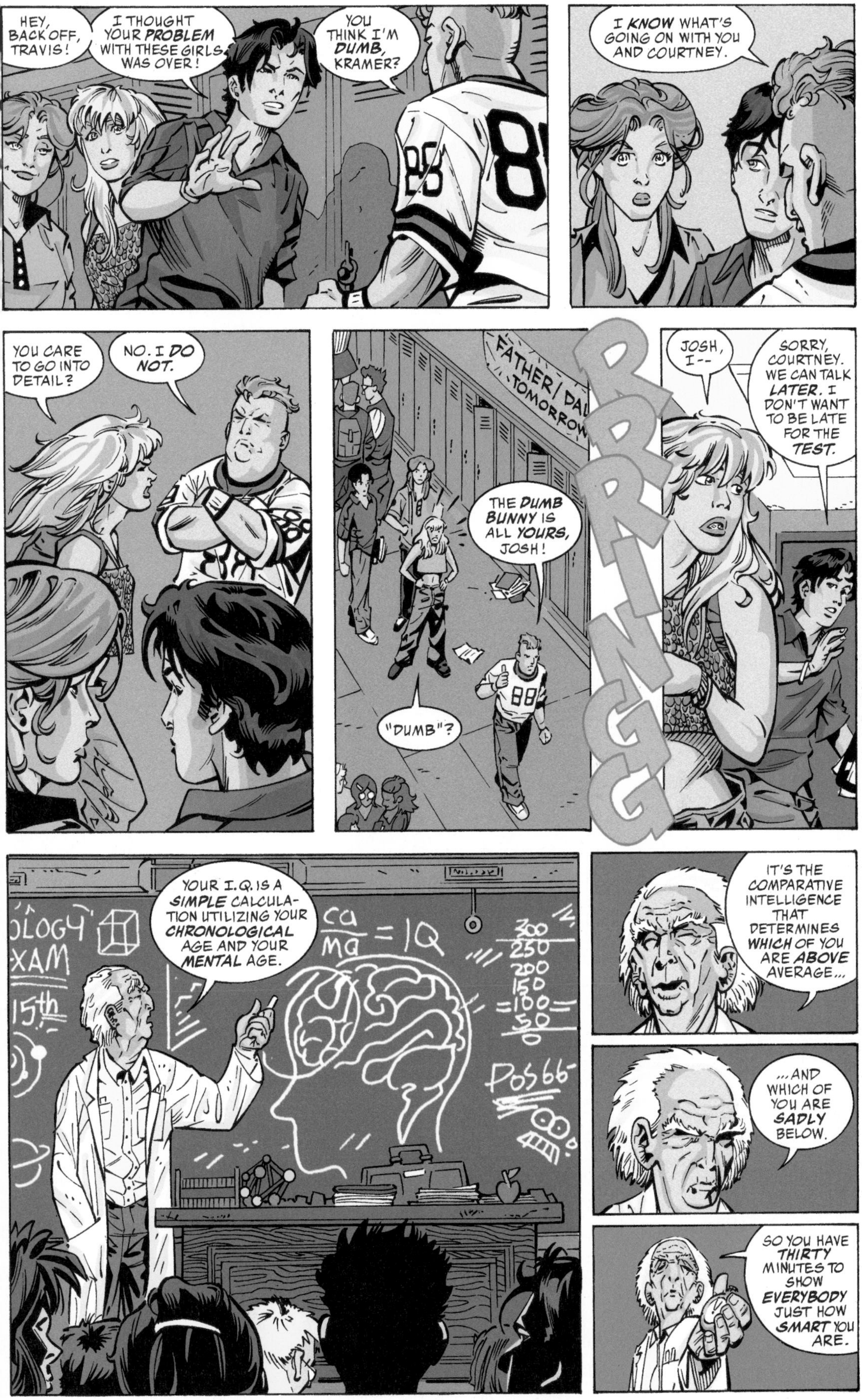
HEY, BACK OFF, TRAVIS!
I THOUGHT YOUR PROBLEM WITH THESE GIRLS WAS OVER!
YOU THINK I'M DUMB, KRAMER?
I KNOW WHAT'S GOING ON WITH YOU AND COURTNEY.
YOU CARE TO GO INTO DETAIL?
NO. I DO NOT.
FATHER/DAU TOMORROW
THE DUMB BUNNY IS ALL YOURS, JOSH!
"DUMB"?
RRRINGG
JOSH, I--
SORRY, COURTNEY. WE CAN TALK LATER. I DON'T WANT TO BE LATE FOR THE TEST.
YOUR I.Q. IS A SIMPLE CALCULATION UTILIZING YOUR CHRONOLOGICAL AGE AND YOUR MENTAL AGE.
IT'S THE COMPARATIVE INTELLIGENCE THAT DETERMINES WHICH OF YOU ARE ABOVE AVERAGE...
...AND WHICH OF YOU ARE SADLY BELOW.
SO YOU HAVE THIRTY MINUTES TO SHOW EVERYBODY JUST HOW SMART YOU ARE.

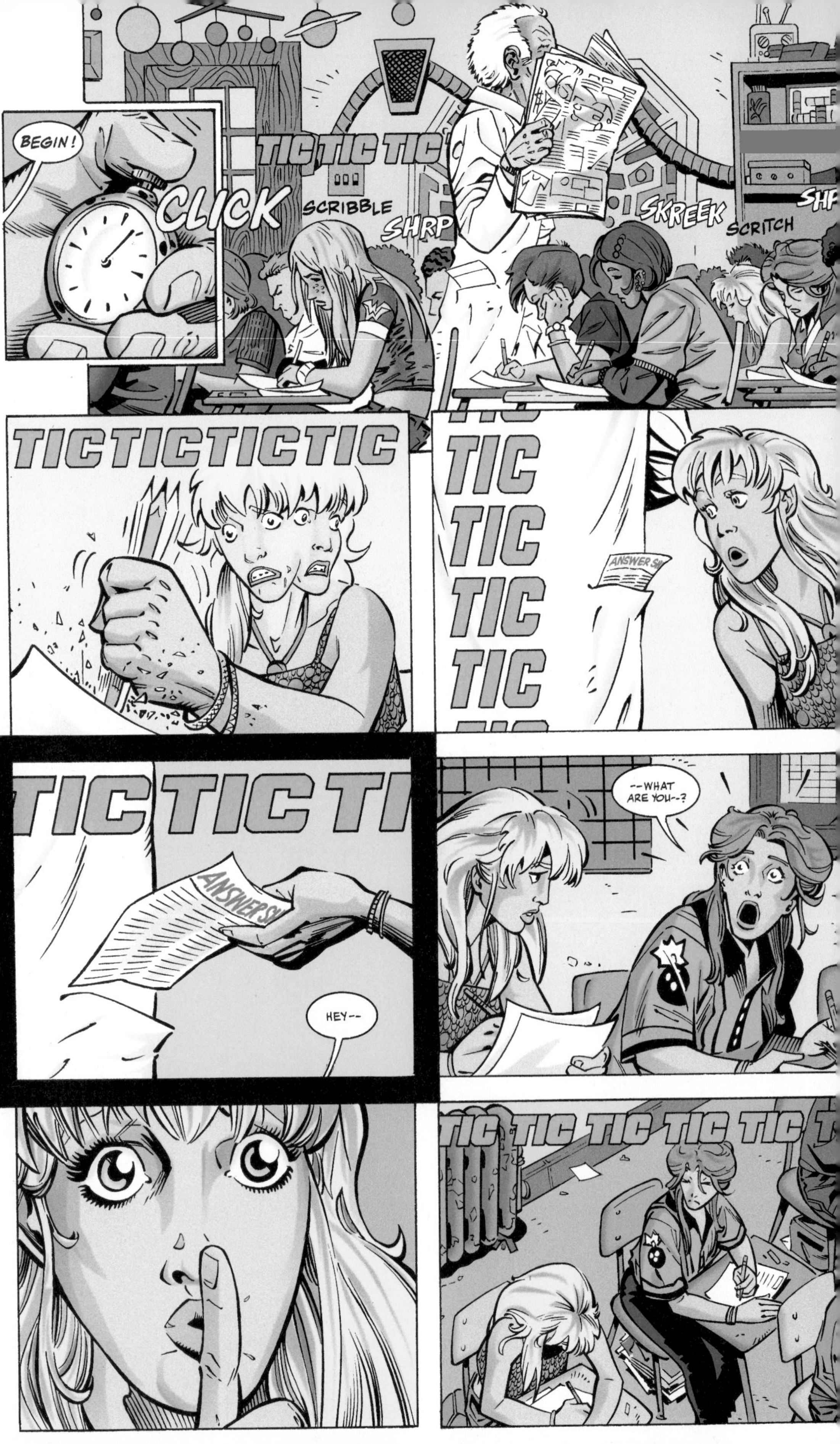

BEGIN!
CLICK
TIC TIC TIC
SCRIBBLE
SHRP
SKREEK
SCRITCH
TICTICTICTICTIC
TIC
TIC
TIC
TIC
ANSWER SH
TIC TIC TI
ANSWER SH
HEY--
--WHAT ARE YOU--?
TIC TIC TIC TIC TIC

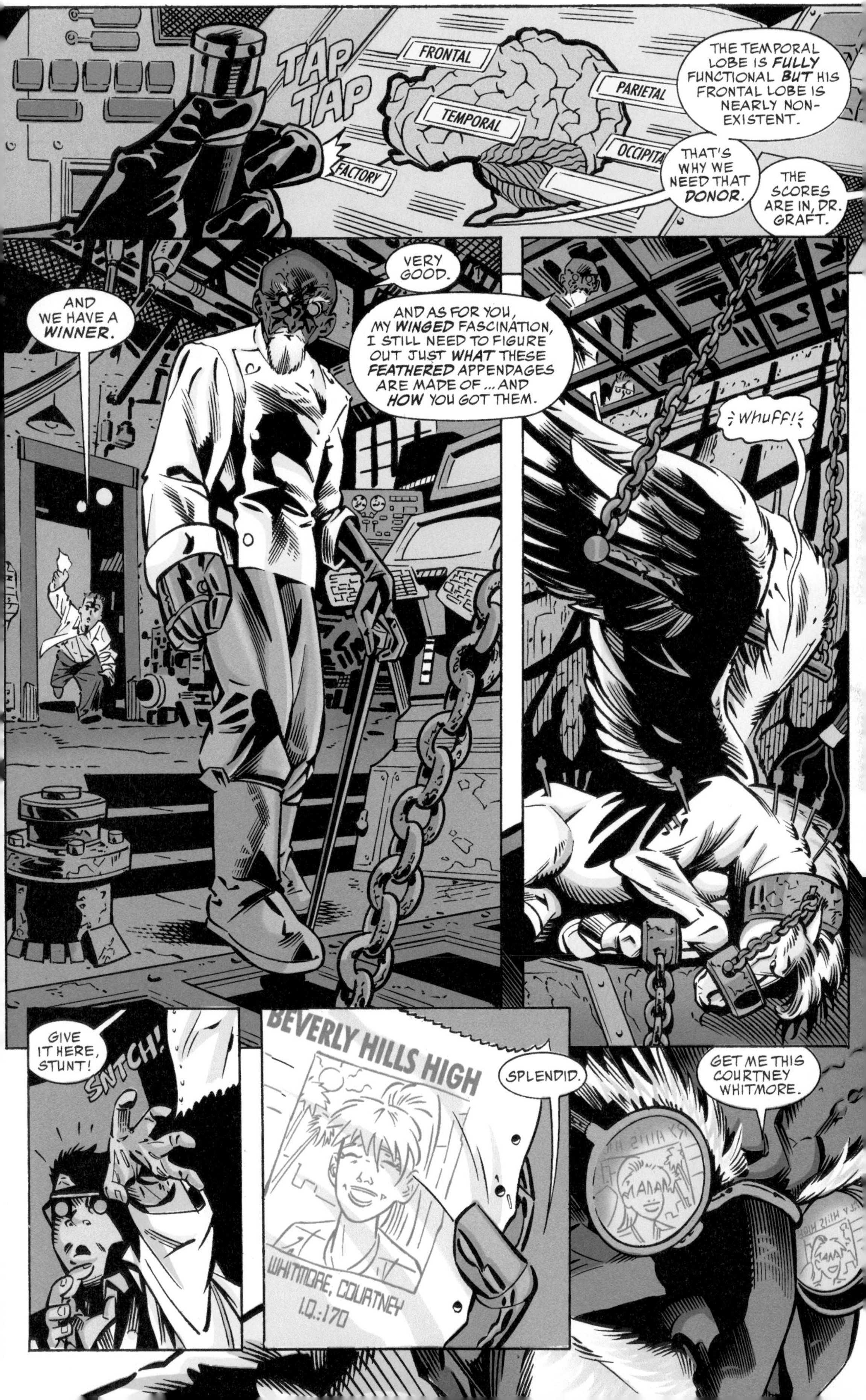

TAP TAP
FRONTAL
PARIETAL
TEMPORAL
OCCIPITA
FACTORY
THE TEMPORAL LOBE IS FULLY FUNCTIONAL BUT HIS FRONTAL LOBE IS NEARLY NON-EXISTENT.
THAT'S WHY WE NEED THAT DONOR.
THE SCORES ARE IN, DR. GRAFT.
AND WE HAVE A WINNER.
VERY GOOD.
AND AS FOR YOU, MY WINGED FASCINATION, I STILL NEED TO FIGURE OUT JUST WHAT THESE FEATHERED APPENDAGES ARE MADE OF ... AND HOW YOU GOT THEM.
WHUFF!
GIVE IT HERE, STUNT!
SNTCH!
BEVERLY HILLS HIGH
WHITMORE, COURTNEY
I.Q.:170
SPLENDID.
GET ME THIS COURTNEY WHITMORE.

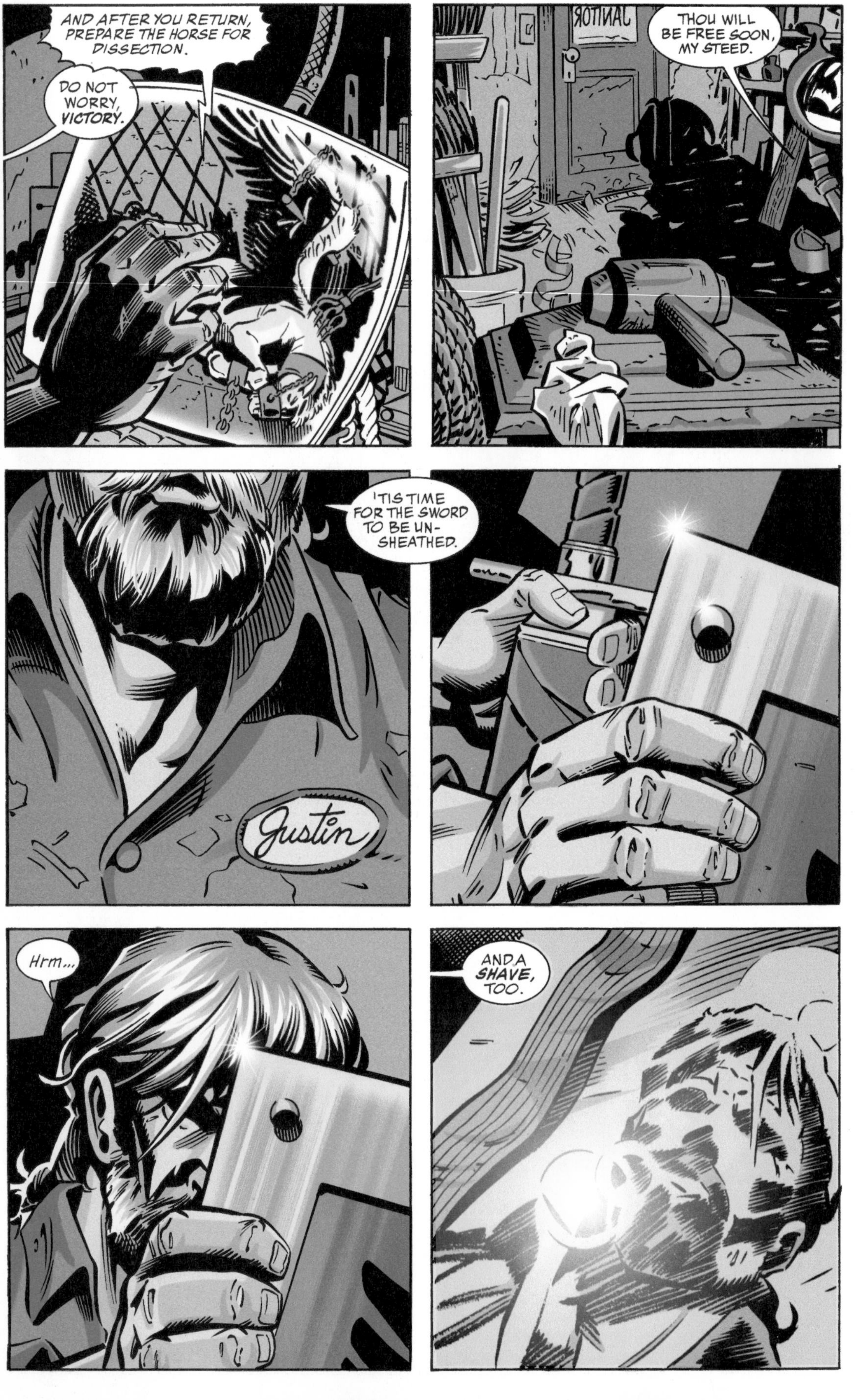
AND AFTER YOU RETURN, PREPARE THE HORSE FOR DISSECTION.
DO NOT WORRY, VICTORY.
JANITOR
THOU WILL BE FREE SOON, MY STEED.
'TIS TIME FOR THE SWORD TO BE UN-SHEATHED.
Justin
Hrm...
AND A SHAVE, TOO.

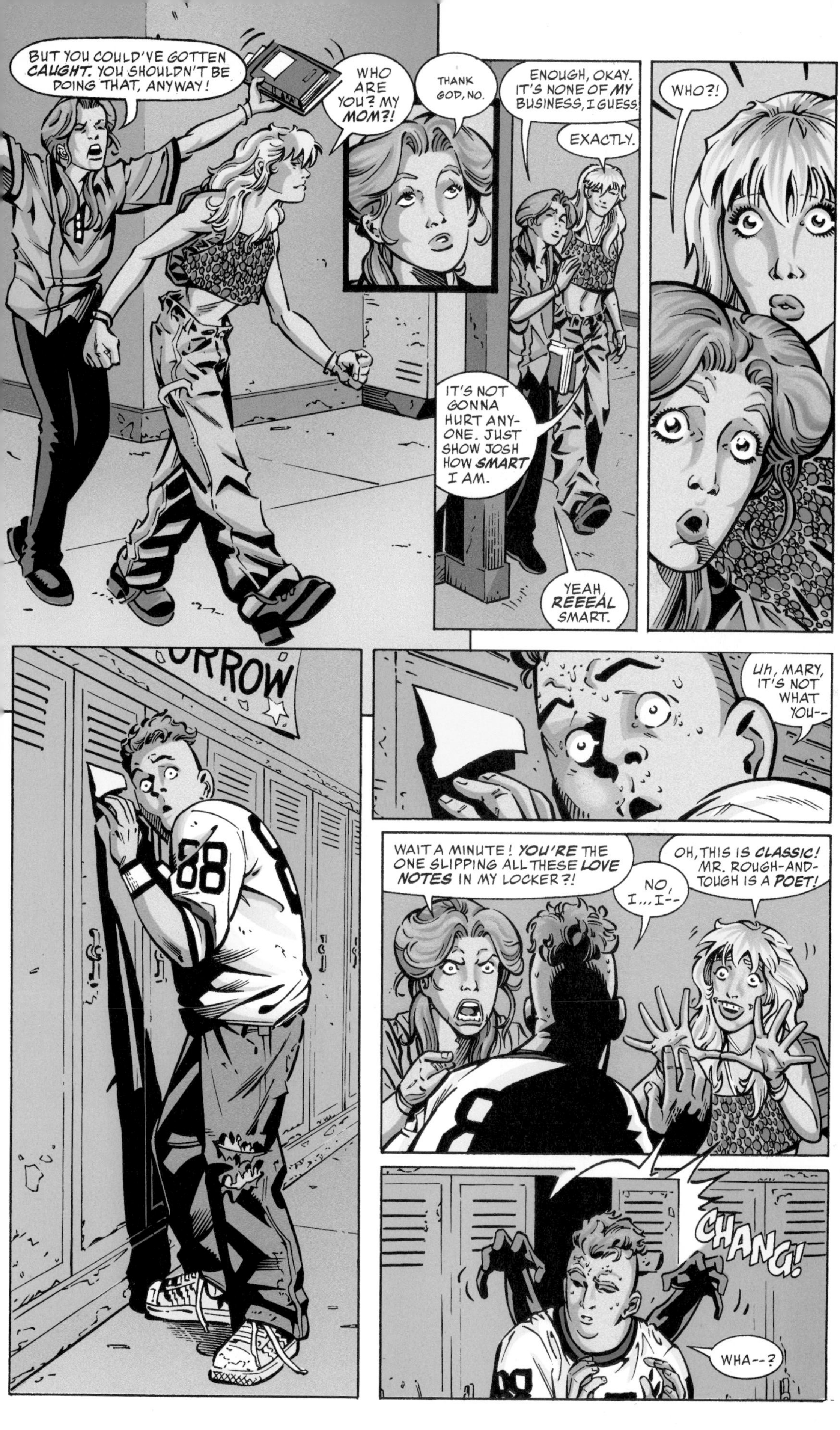

BUT YOU COULD'VE GOTTEN CAUGHT. YOU SHOULDN'T BE DOING THAT, ANYWAY!
WHO ARE YOU? MY MOM?!
THANK GOD, NO.
ENOUGH, OKAY. IT'S NONE OF MY BUSINESS, I GUESS.
EXACTLY.
IT'S NOT GONNA HURT ANY-ONE. JUST SHOW JOSH HOW SMART I AM.
YEAH, REEEAL SMART.
WHO?!
ORROW
UH, MARY, IT'S NOT WHAT YOU--
WAIT A MINUTE! YOU'RE THE ONE SLIPPING ALL THESE LOVE NOTES IN MY LOCKER?!
NO, I... I--
OH, THIS IS CLASSIC! MR. ROUGH-AND-TOUGH IS A POET!
CHANG!
WHA--?

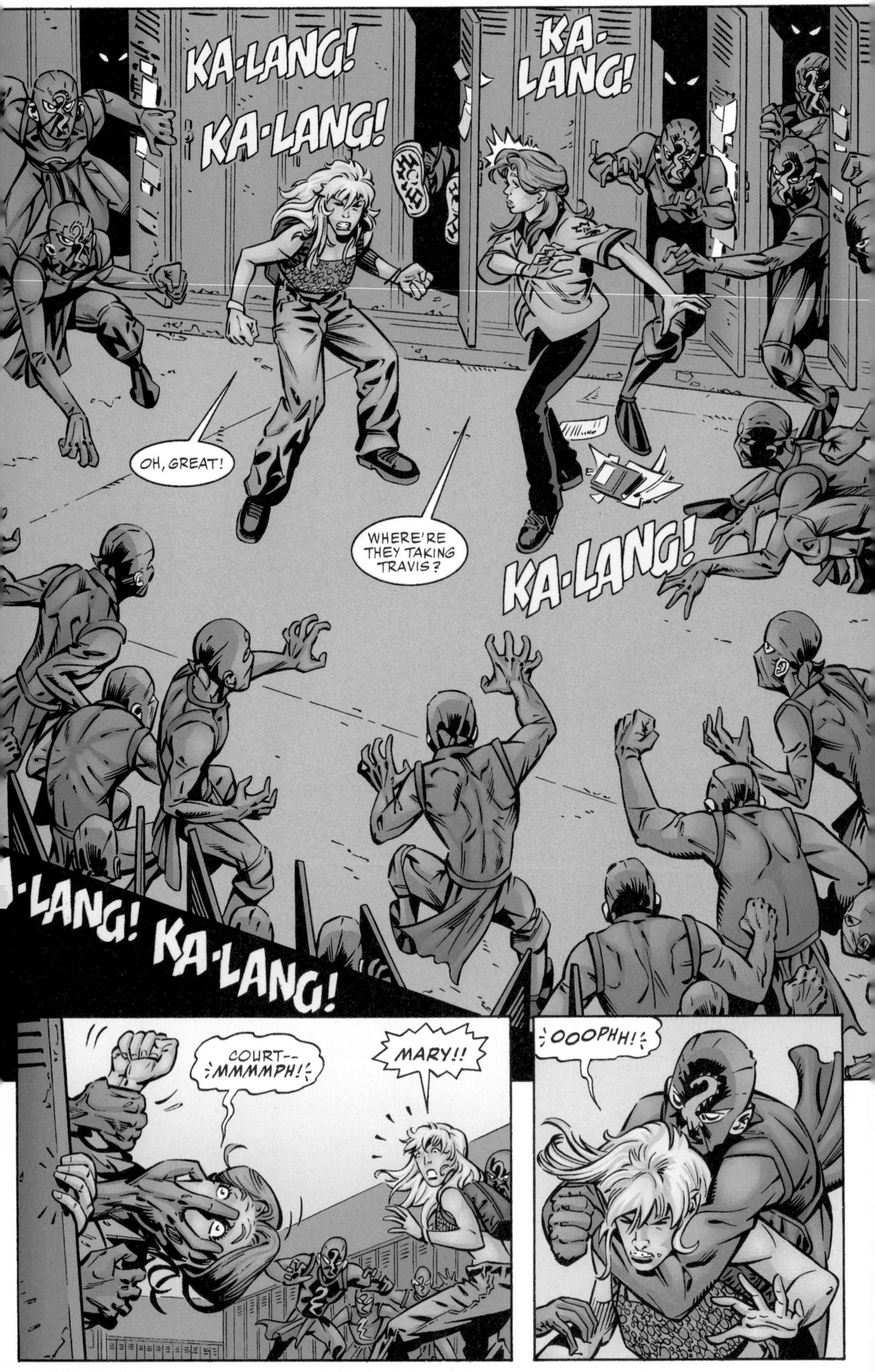
KA-LANG!
KA-LANG!
KA-LANG!
OH, GREAT!
WHERE'RE THEY TAKING TRAVIS?
KA-LANG!
-LANG! KA-LANG!
COURT-- MMMMPH!
MARY!!
OOOPHH!

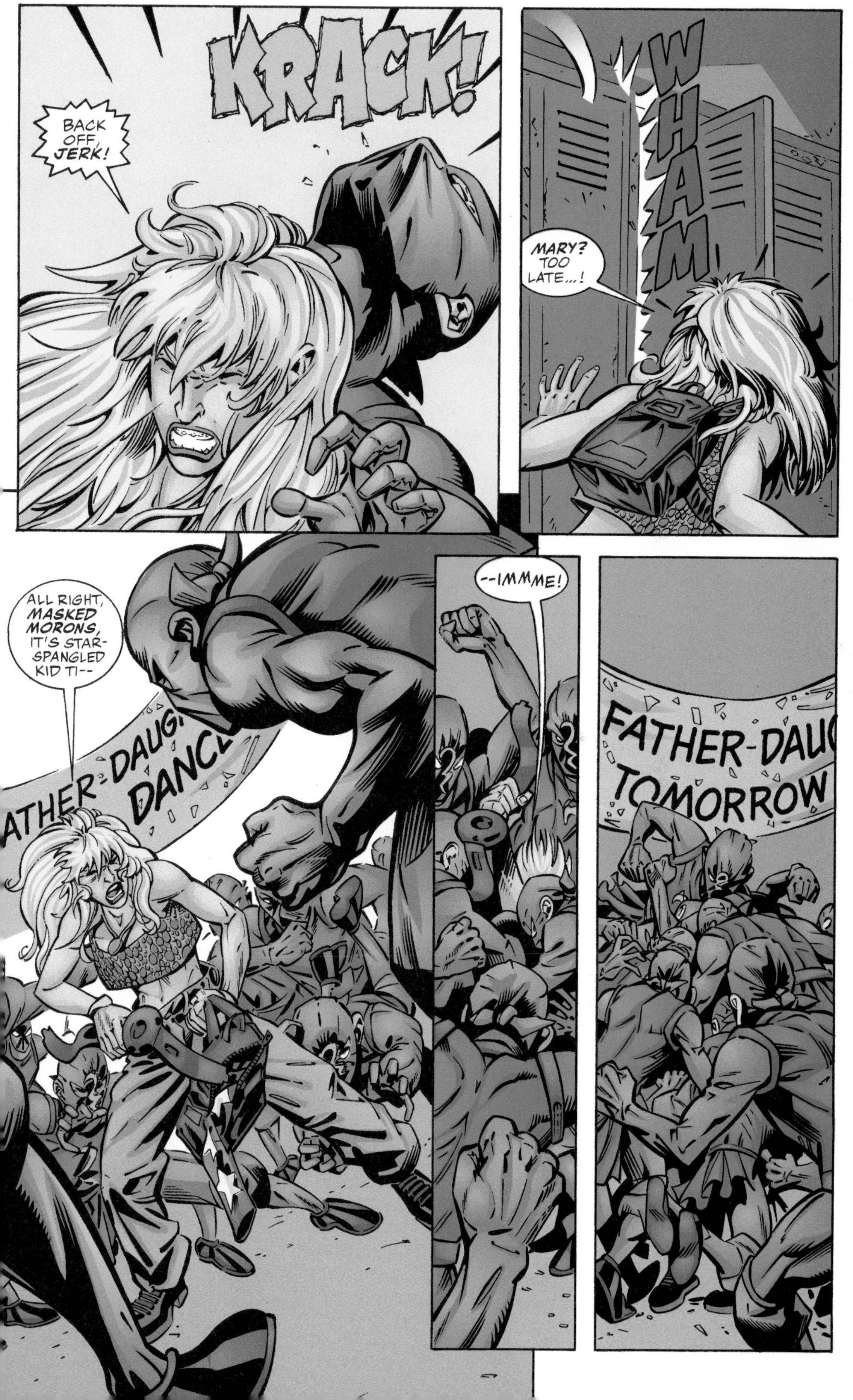
KRACK!
BACK OFF, JERK!
WHAM
MARY? TOO LATE...!
ALL RIGHT, MASKED MORONS, IT'S STAR-SPANGLED KID TI--
FATHER-DAUG
DANC
--IMMME!
FATHER-DAUG
TOMORROW

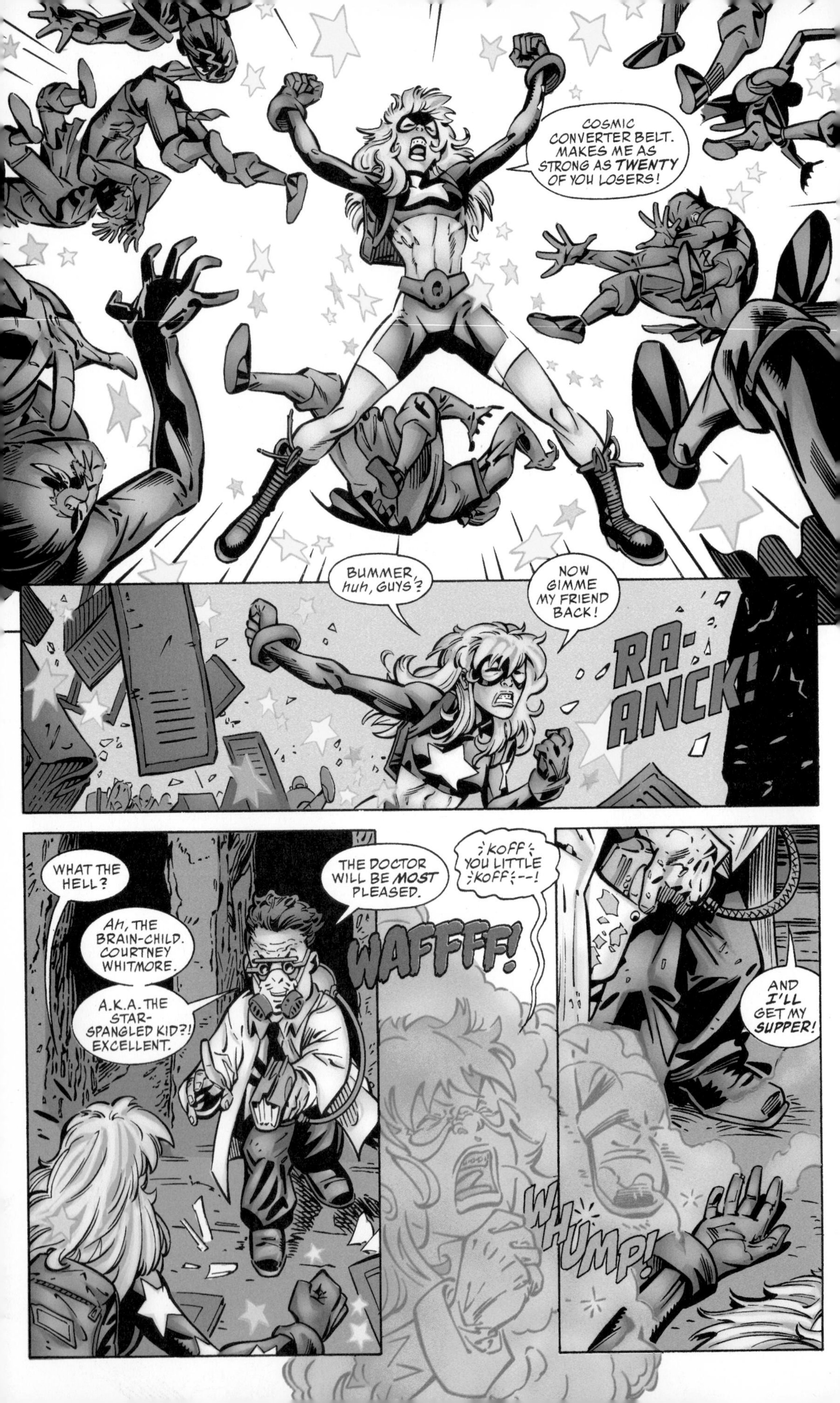
COSMIC CONVERTER BELT. MAKES ME AS STRONG AS TWENTY OF YOU LOSERS!
BUMMER, huh, GUYS?
NOW GIMME MY FRIEND BACK!
RA-ANCK!
WHAT THE HELL?
Ah, THE BRAIN-CHILD. COURTNEY WHITMORE.
A.K.A. THE STAR-SPANGLED KID?! EXCELLENT.
THE DOCTOR WILL BE MOST PLEASED.
WAFFFF!
KOFF YOU LITTLE KOFF--!
AND I'LL GET MY SUPPER!
WHUMP!

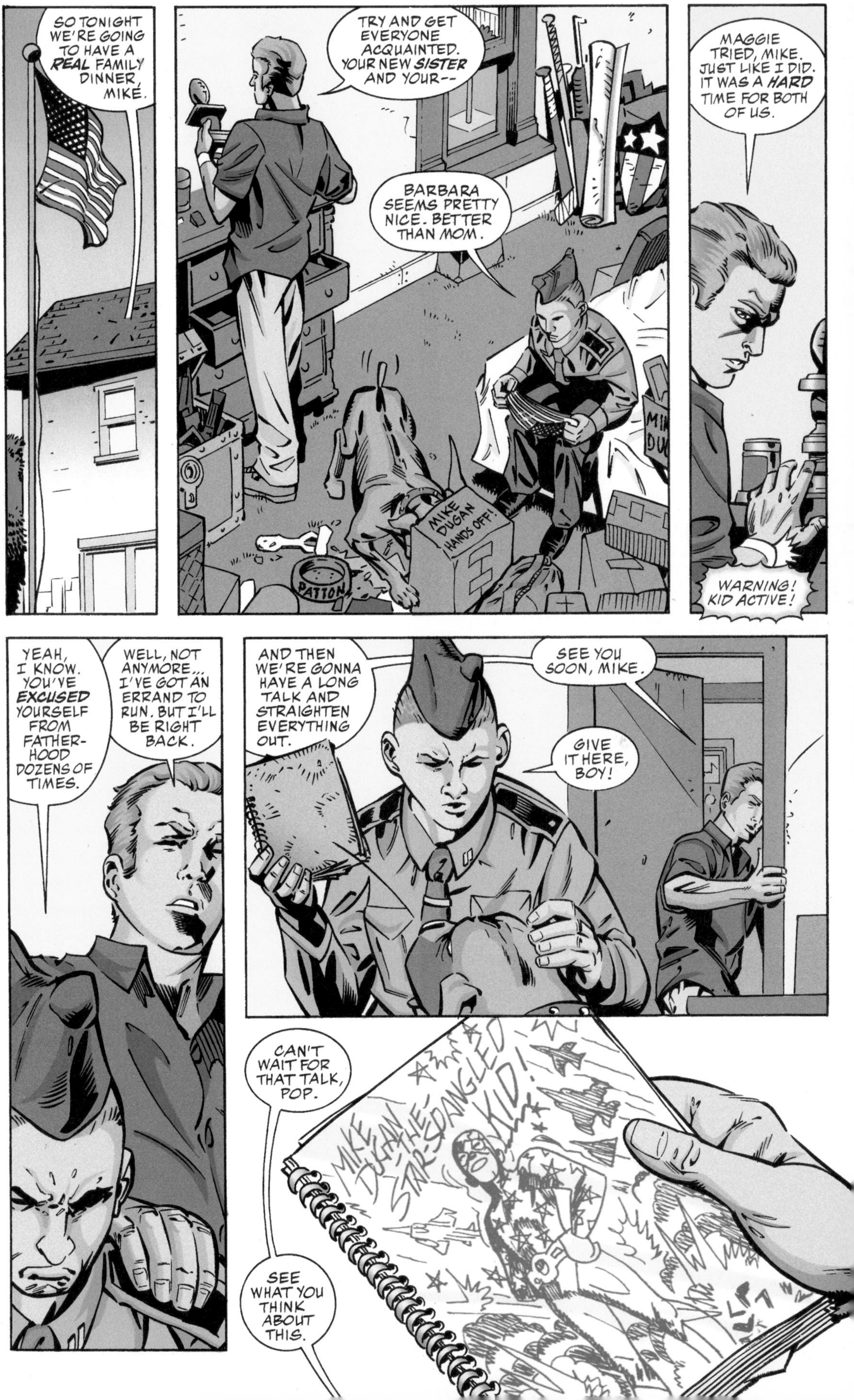
SO TONIGHT WE'RE GOING TO HAVE A REAL FAMILY DINNER, MIKE.
TRY AND GET EVERYONE ACQUAINTED. YOUR NEW SISTER AND YOUR--
BARBARA SEEMS PRETTY NICE. BETTER THAN MOM.
MIKE DUGAN HANDS OFF!
PATTON
MAGGIE TRIED, MIKE. JUST LIKE I DID. IT WAS A HARD TIME FOR BOTH OF US.
WARNING! KID ACTIVE!
YEAH, I KNOW. YOU'VE EXCUSED YOURSELF FROM FATHER-HOOD DOZENS OF TIMES.
WELL, NOT ANYMORE... I'VE GOT AN ERRAND TO RUN. BUT I'LL BE RIGHT BACK.
AND THEN WE'RE GONNA HAVE A LONG TALK AND STRAIGHTEN EVERYTHING OUT.
SEE YOU SOON, MIKE.
GIVE IT HERE, BOY!
CAN'T WAIT FOR THAT TALK, POP.
SEE WHAT YOU THINK ABOUT THIS.
MIKE DUGAN THE STAR-SPANGLED KID!

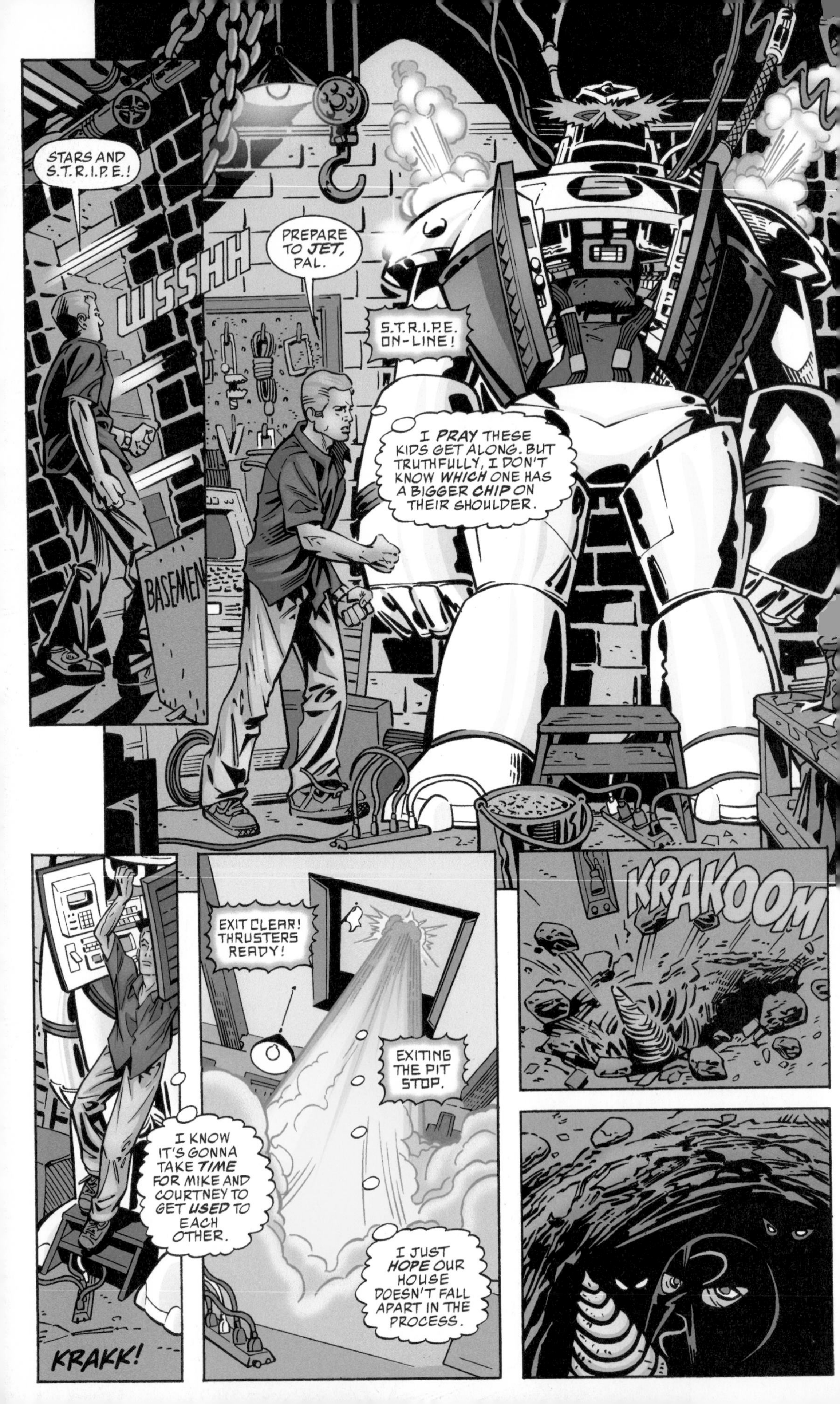
STARS AND S.T.R.I.P.E.!
WSSHH
BASEMEN
PREPARE TO JET, PAL.
S.T.R.I.P.E. ON-LINE!
I PRAY THESE KIDS GET ALONG. BUT TRUTHFULLY, I DON'T KNOW WHICH ONE HAS A BIGGER CHIP ON THEIR SHOULDER.
KRAKK!
I KNOW IT'S GONNA TAKE TIME FOR MIKE AND COURTNEY TO GET USED TO EACH OTHER.
EXIT CLEAR! THRUSTERS READY!
EXITING THE PIT STOP.
I JUST HOPE OUR HOUSE DOESN'T FALL APART IN THE PROCESS.
KRAKOOM

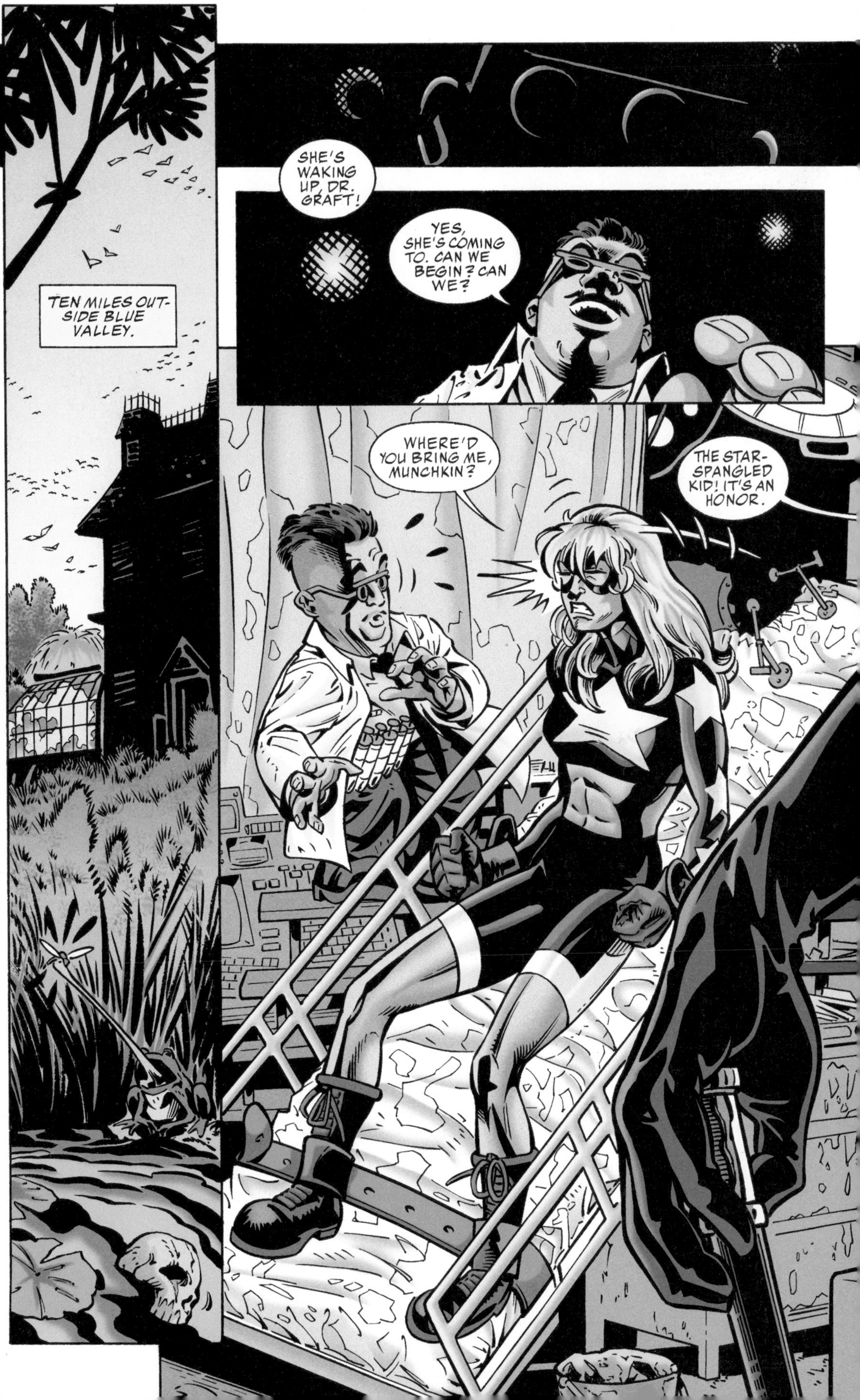
TEN MILES OUT-SIDE BLUE VALLEY.
SHE'S WAKING UP, DR. GRAFT!
YES, SHE'S COMING TO. CAN WE BEGIN? CAN WE?
WHERE'D YOU BRING ME, MUNCHKIN?
THE STAR-SPANGLED KID! IT'S AN HONOR.

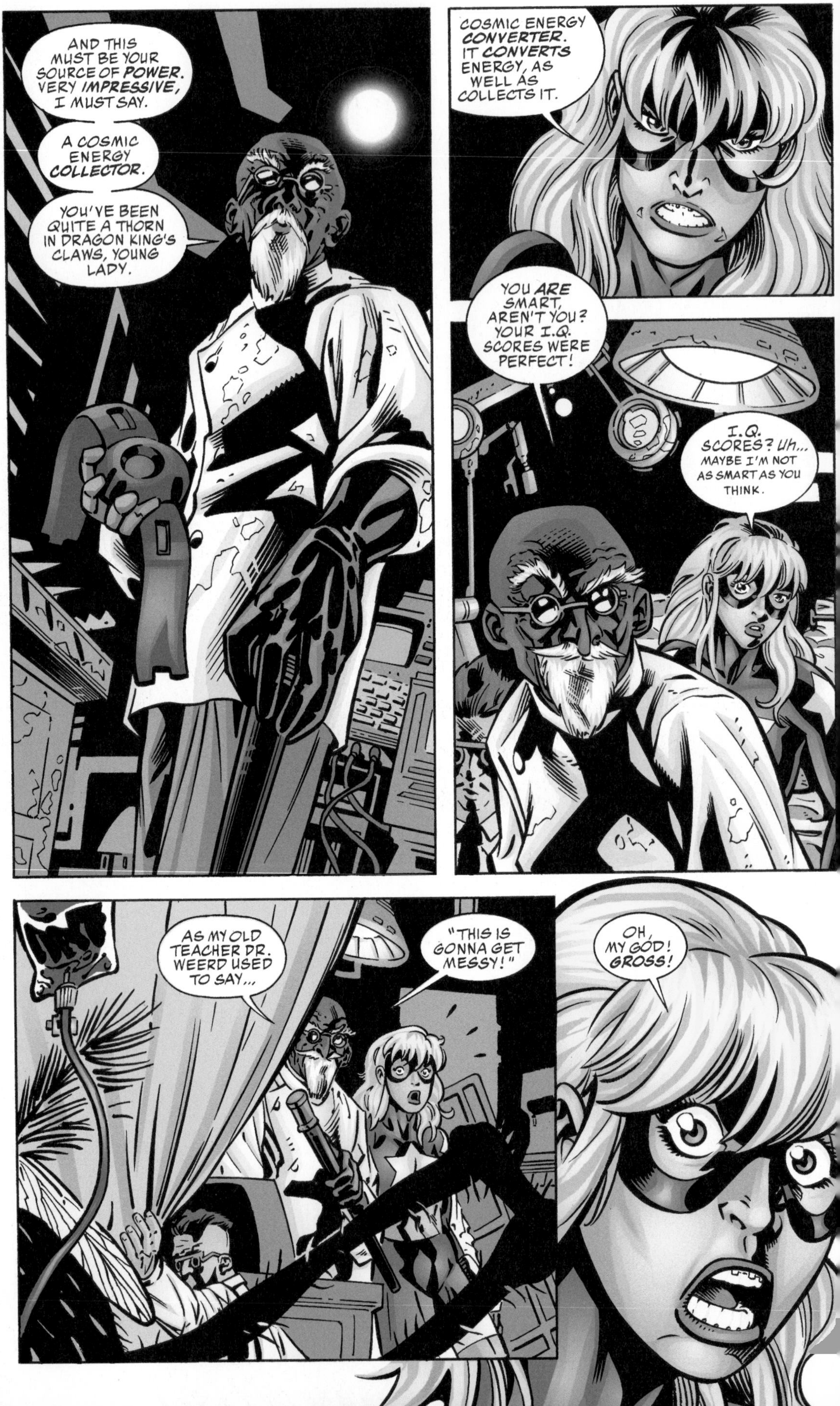
AND THIS MUST BE YOUR SOURCE OF POWER. VERY IMPRESSIVE, I MUST SAY.
A COSMIC ENERGY COLLECTOR.
YOU'VE BEEN QUITE A THORN IN DRAGON KING'S CLAWS, YOUNG LADY.
COSMIC ENERGY CONVERTER. IT CONVERTS ENERGY, AS WELL AS COLLECTS IT.
YOU ARE SMART, AREN'T YOU? YOUR I.Q. SCORES WERE PERFECT!
I.Q. SCORES? UH... MAYBE I'M NOT AS SMART AS YOU THINK.
AS MY OLD TEACHER DR. WEERD USED TO SAY...
"THIS IS GONNA GET MESSY!"
OH, MY GOD! GROSS!

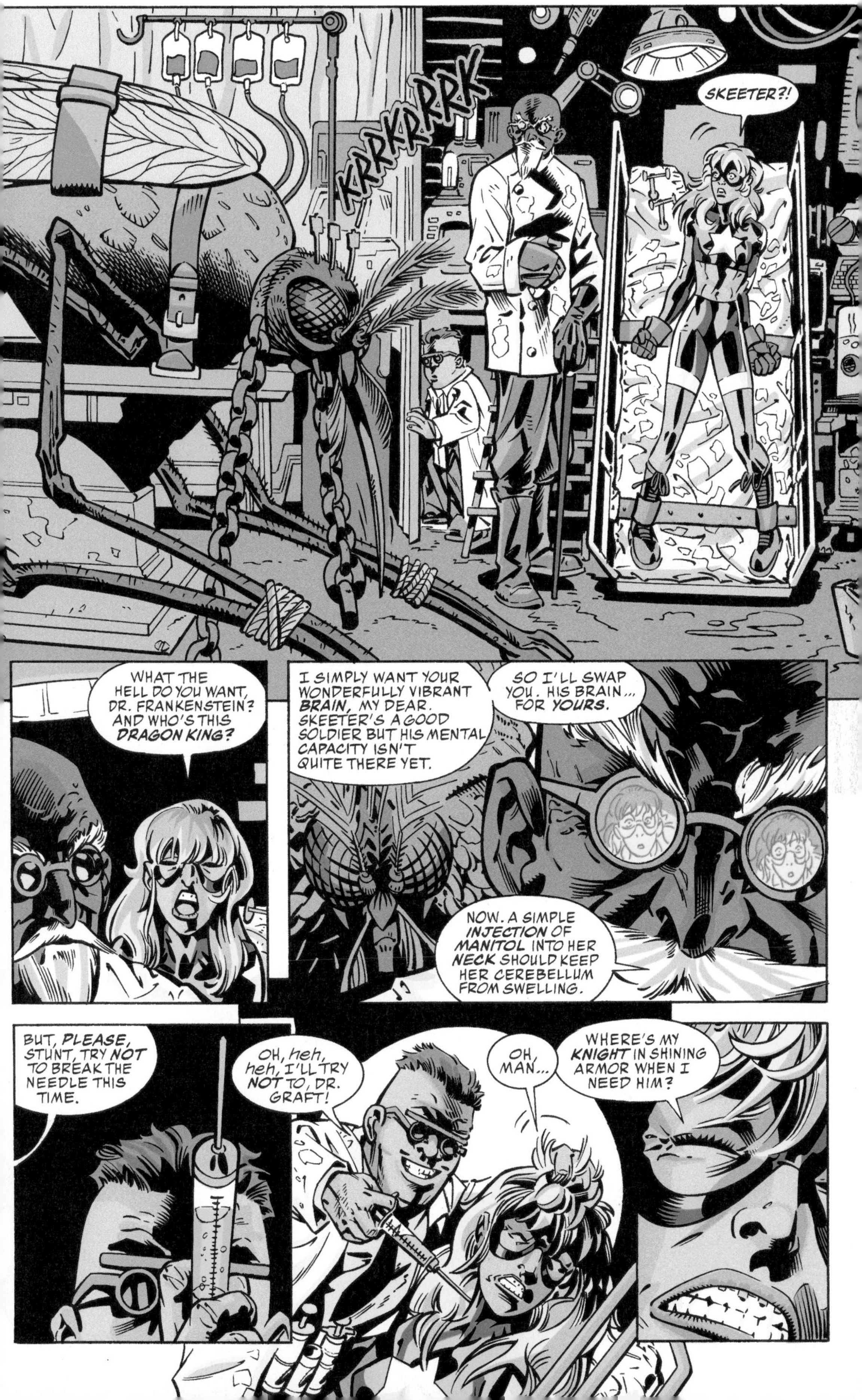
KRRKRRRK
SKEETER?!
WHAT THE HELL DO YOU WANT, DR. FRANKENSTEIN? AND WHO'S THIS DRAGON KING?
I SIMPLY WANT YOUR WONDERFULLY VIBRANT BRAIN, MY DEAR. SKEETER'S A GOOD SOLDIER BUT HIS MENTAL CAPACITY ISN'T QUITE THERE YET.
SO I'LL SWAP YOU. HIS BRAIN... FOR YOURS.
NOW. A SIMPLE INJECTION OF MANITOL INTO HER NECK SHOULD KEEP HER CEREBELLUM FROM SWELLING.
BUT, PLEASE, STUNT, TRY NOT TO BREAK THE NEEDLE THIS TIME.
OH, heh, heh, I'LL TRY NOT TO, DR. GRAFT!
OH, MAN...
WHERE'S MY KNIGHT IN SHINING ARMOR WHEN I NEED HIM?

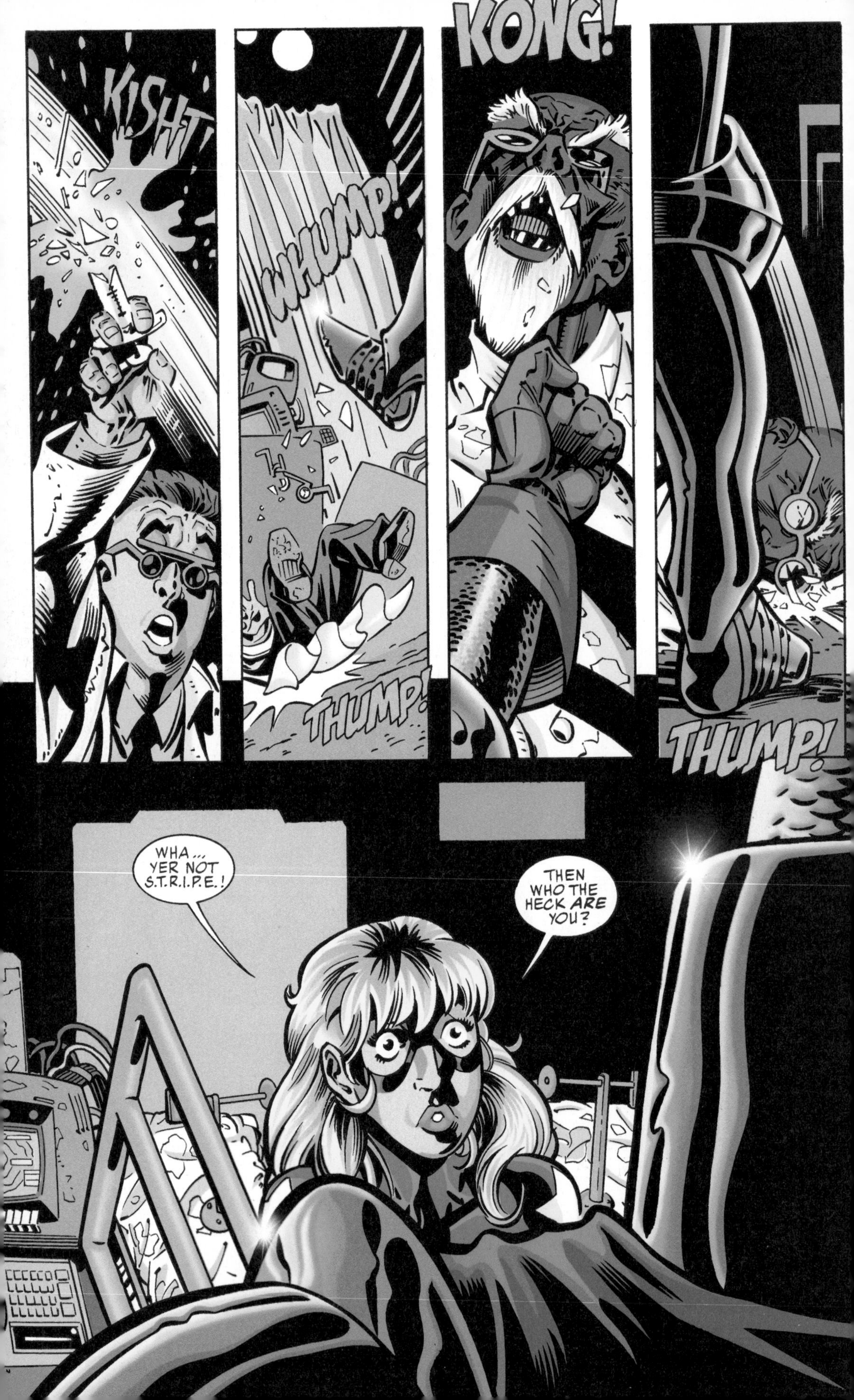
KISHT!
WHUMP!
THUMP!
KONG!
THUMP!
WHA... YER NOT S.T.R.I.P.E.!
THEN WHO THE HECK ARE YOU?

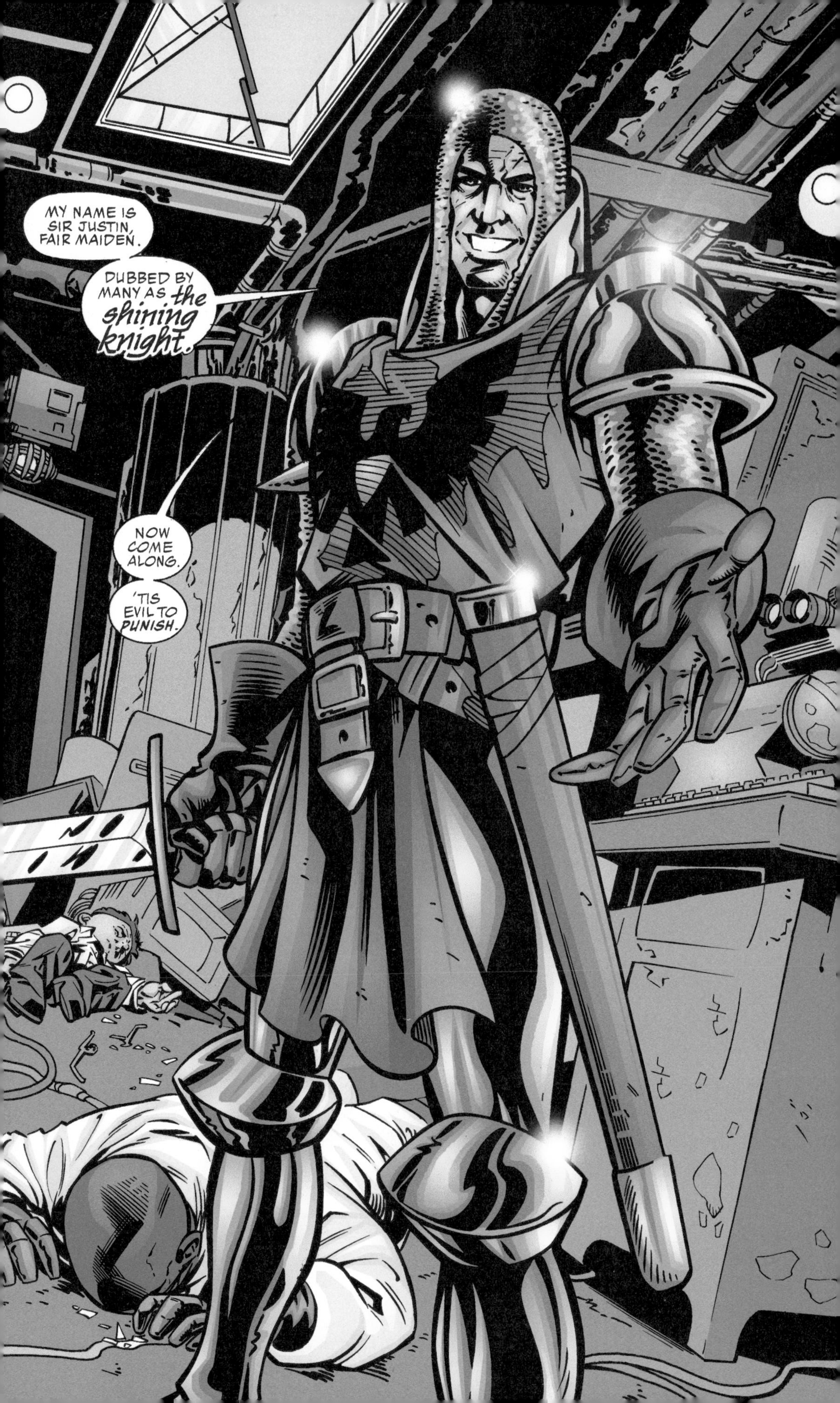
MY NAME IS SIR JUSTIN, FAIR MAIDEN.
DUBBED BY MANY AS the shining knight.
NOW COME ALONG.
'TIS EVIL TO PUNISH.

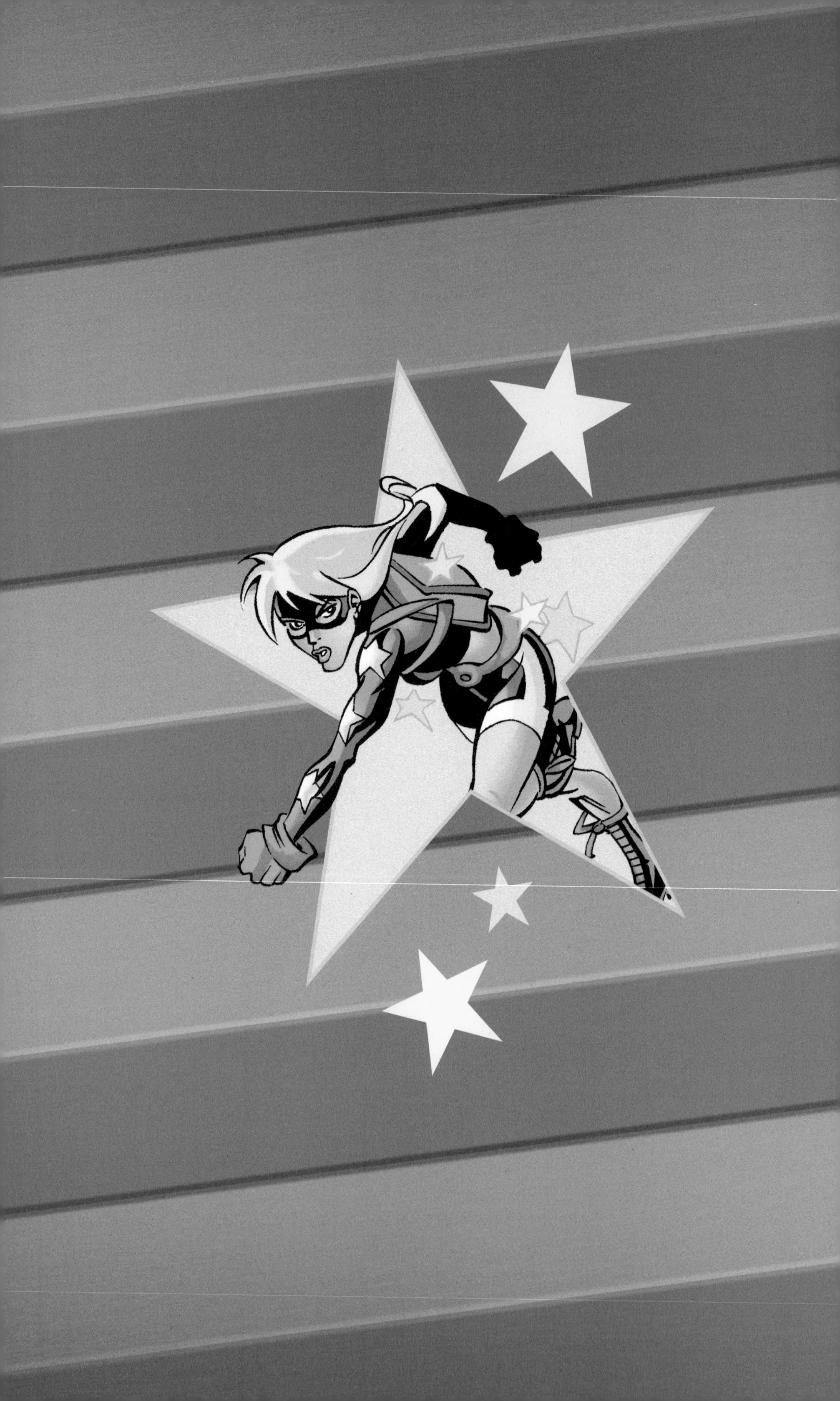

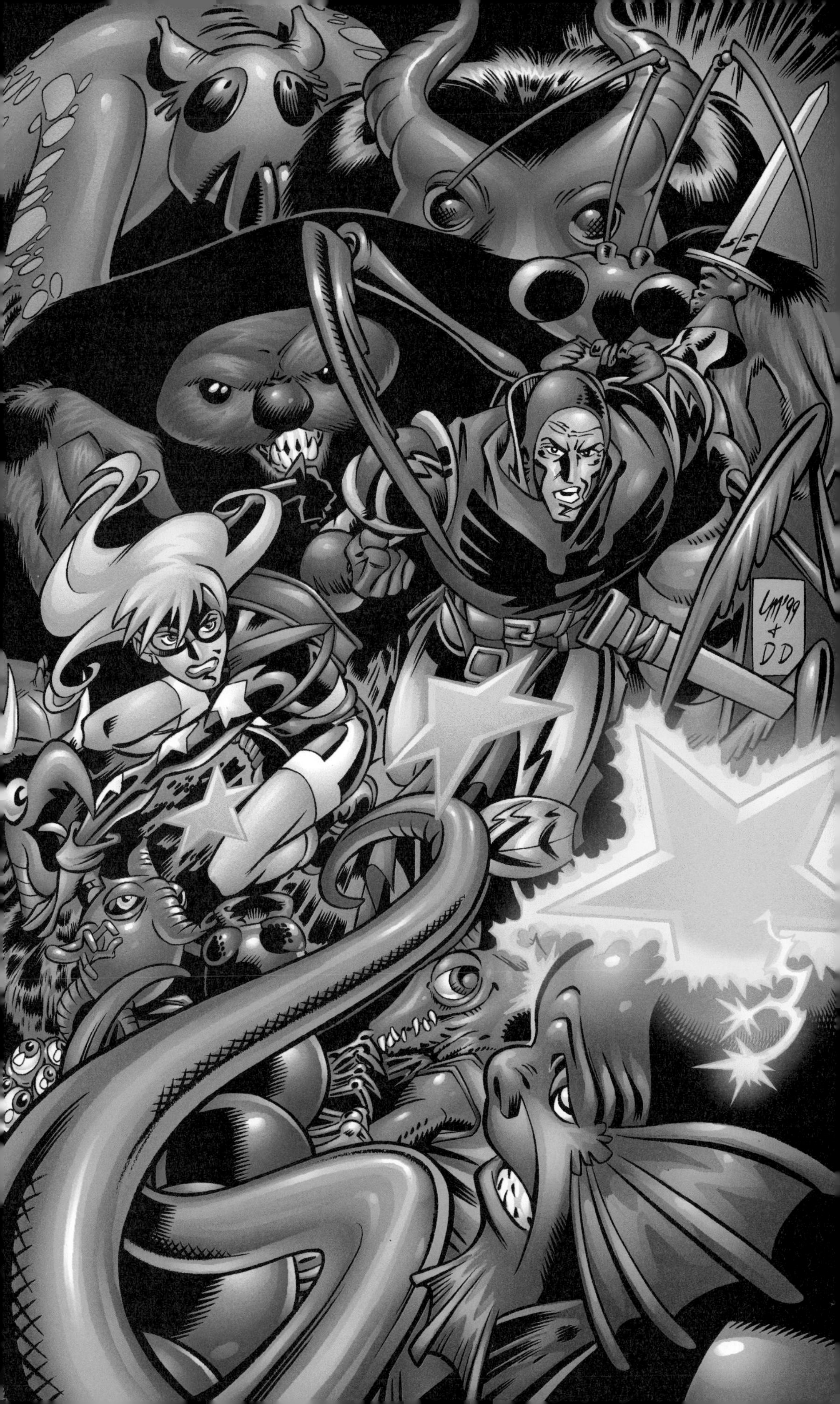

STARS AND S.T.R.I.P.E. #11
Written by GEOFF JOHNS
Pencils by SCOTT KOLINS
Inks by DAN DAVIS
Colors by TOM McCRAW
Letters by BILL OAKLEY
Cover art by LEE MODER and DAN DAVIS
Cover color by RICHARD & TANYA HORIE

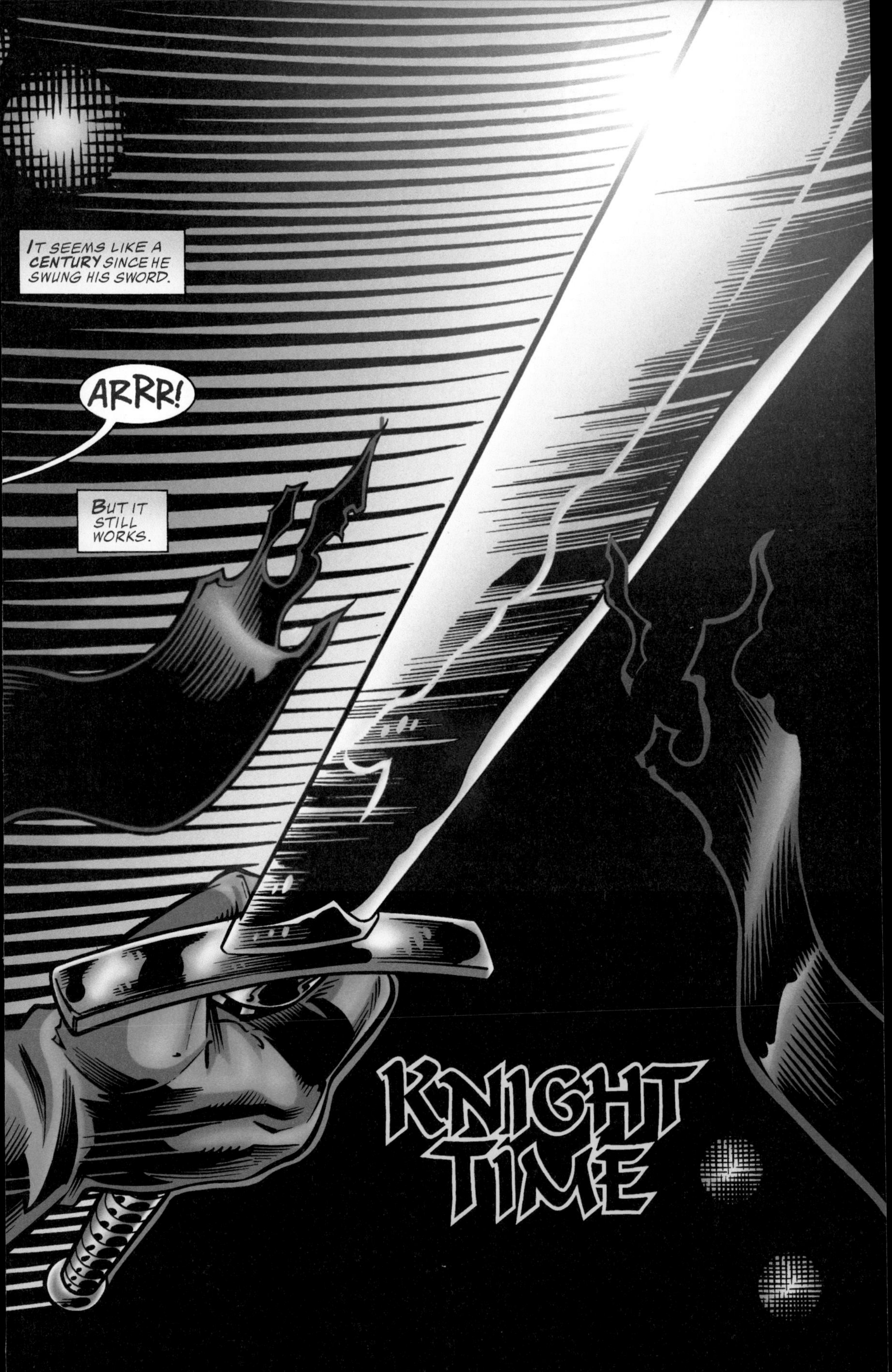
IT SEEMS LIKE A CENTURY SINCE HE SWUNG HIS SWORD.
ARRR!
BUT IT STILL WORKS.
KNIGHT TIME

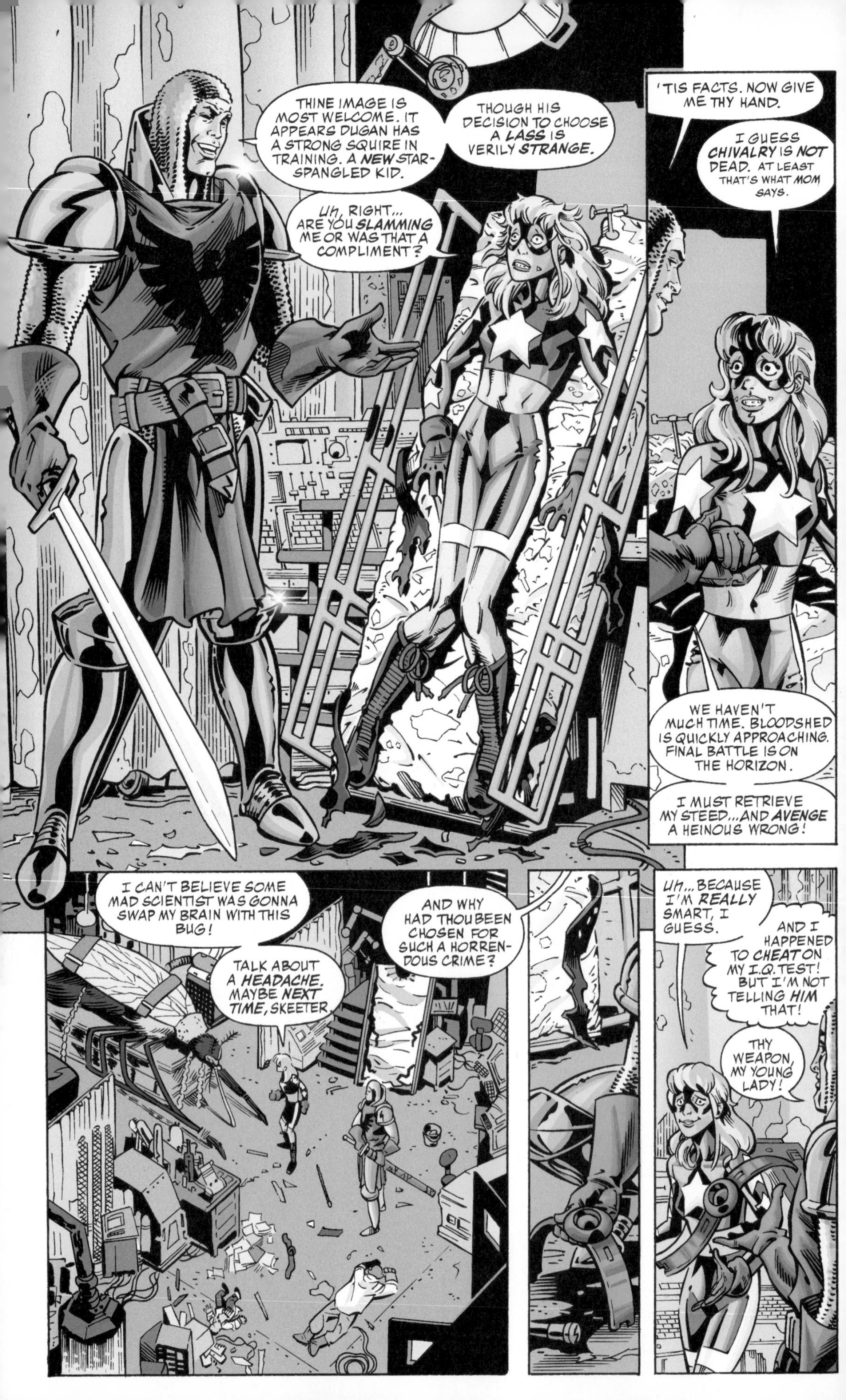

THINE IMAGE IS MOST WELCOME. IT APPEARS DUGAN HAS A STRONG SQUIRE IN TRAINING. A NEW STAR-SPANGLED KID.
THOUGH HIS DECISION TO CHOOSE A LASS IS VERILY STRANGE.
UH, RIGHT... ARE YOU SLAMMING ME OR WAS THAT A COMPLIMENT?
'TIS FACTS. NOW GIVE ME THY HAND.
I GUESS CHIVALRY IS NOT DEAD. AT LEAST THAT'S WHAT MOM SAYS.
WE HAVEN'T MUCH TIME. BLOODSHED IS QUICKLY APPROACHING. FINAL BATTLE IS ON THE HORIZON.
I MUST RETRIEVE MY STEED...AND AVENGE A HEINOUS WRONG!
I CAN'T BELIEVE SOME MAD SCIENTIST WAS GONNA SWAP MY BRAIN WITH THIS BUG!
TALK ABOUT A HEADACHE. MAYBE NEXT TIME, SKEETER.
AND WHY HAD THOU BEEN CHOSEN FOR SUCH A HORRENDOUS CRIME?
UH... BECAUSE I'M REALLY SMART, I GUESS.
AND I HAPPENED TO CHEAT ON MY I.Q. TEST! BUT I'M NOT TELLING HIM THAT!
THY WEAPON, MY YOUNG LADY!

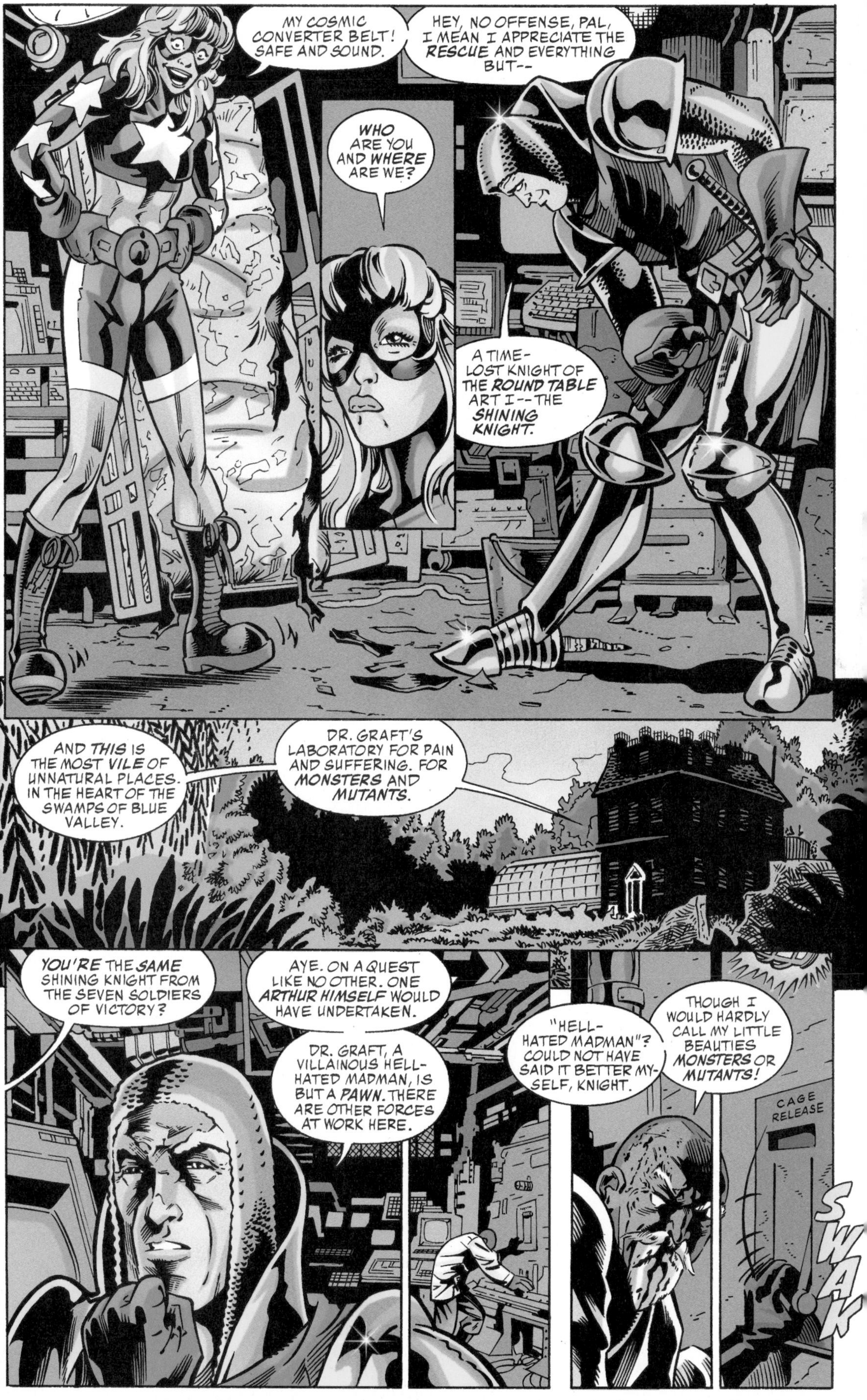
MY COSMIC CONVERTER BELT! SAFE AND SOUND.
HEY, NO OFFENSE, PAL, I MEAN I APPRECIATE THE RESCUE AND EVERYTHING BUT--
WHO ARE YOU AND WHERE ARE WE?
A TIME-LOST KNIGHT OF THE ROUND TABLE ART I--THE SHINING KNIGHT.
AND THIS IS THE MOST VILE OF UNNATURAL PLACES. IN THE HEART OF THE SWAMPS OF BLUE VALLEY.
DR. GRAFT'S LABORATORY FOR PAIN AND SUFFERING. FOR MONSTERS AND MUTANTS.
YOU'RE THE SAME SHINING KNIGHT FROM THE SEVEN SOLDIERS OF VICTORY?
AYE. ON A QUEST LIKE NO OTHER. ONE ARTHUR HIMSELF WOULD HAVE UNDERTAKEN.
DR. GRAFT, A VILLAINOUS HELL-HATED MADMAN, IS BUT A PAWN. THERE ARE OTHER FORCES AT WORK HERE.
"HELL-HATED MADMAN"? COULD NOT HAVE SAID IT BETTER MYSELF, KNIGHT.
THOUGH I WOULD HARDLY CALL MY LITTLE BEAUTIES MONSTERS OR MUTANTS!
CAGE RELEASE
SWAK

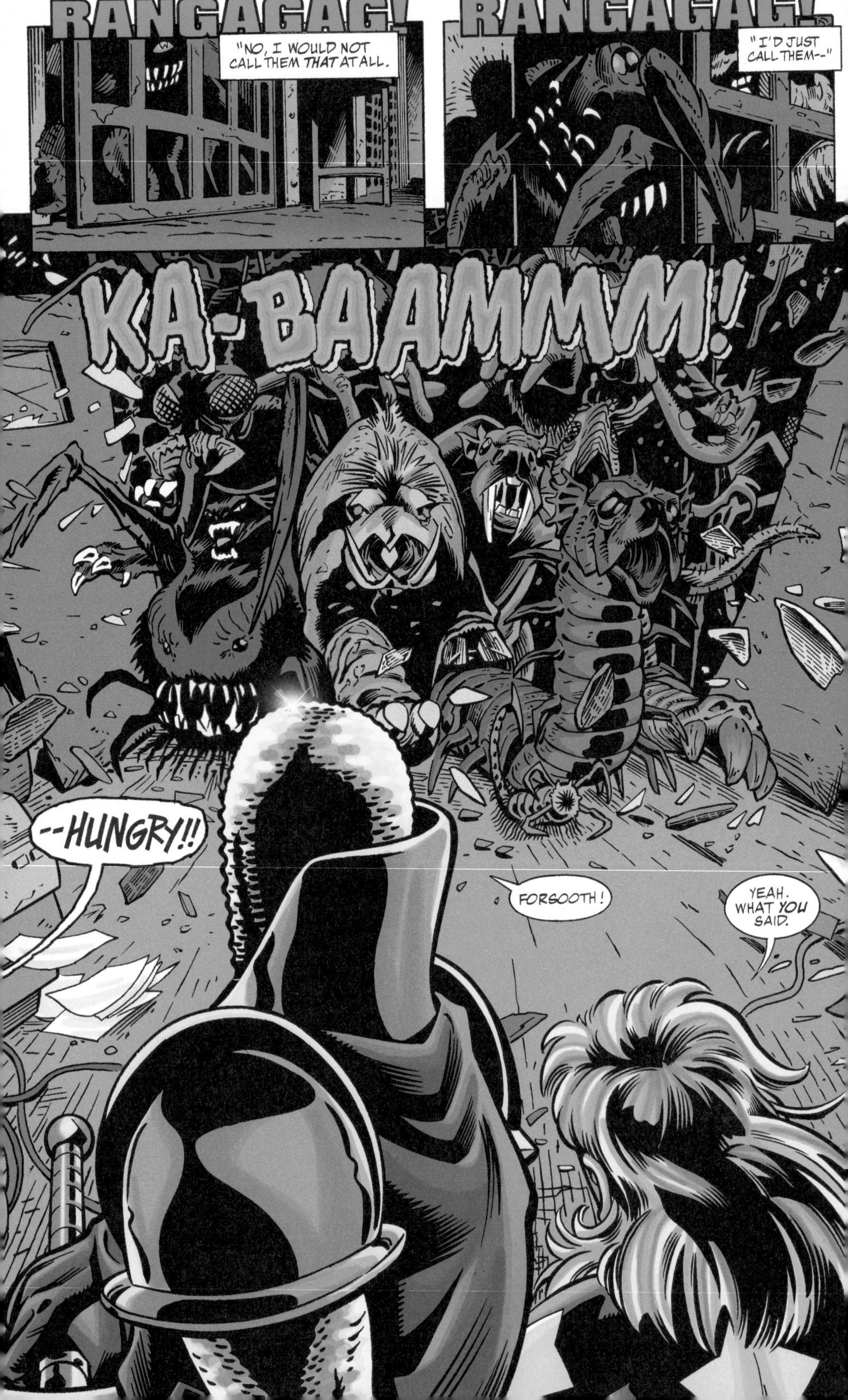
RANGAGAG!
"NO, I WOULD NOT CALL THEM THAT AT ALL.
RANGAGAG!
"I'D JUST CALL THEM--"
KA-BAAMMM!
--HUNGRY!!
FORSOOTH!
YEAH. WHAT YOU SAID.

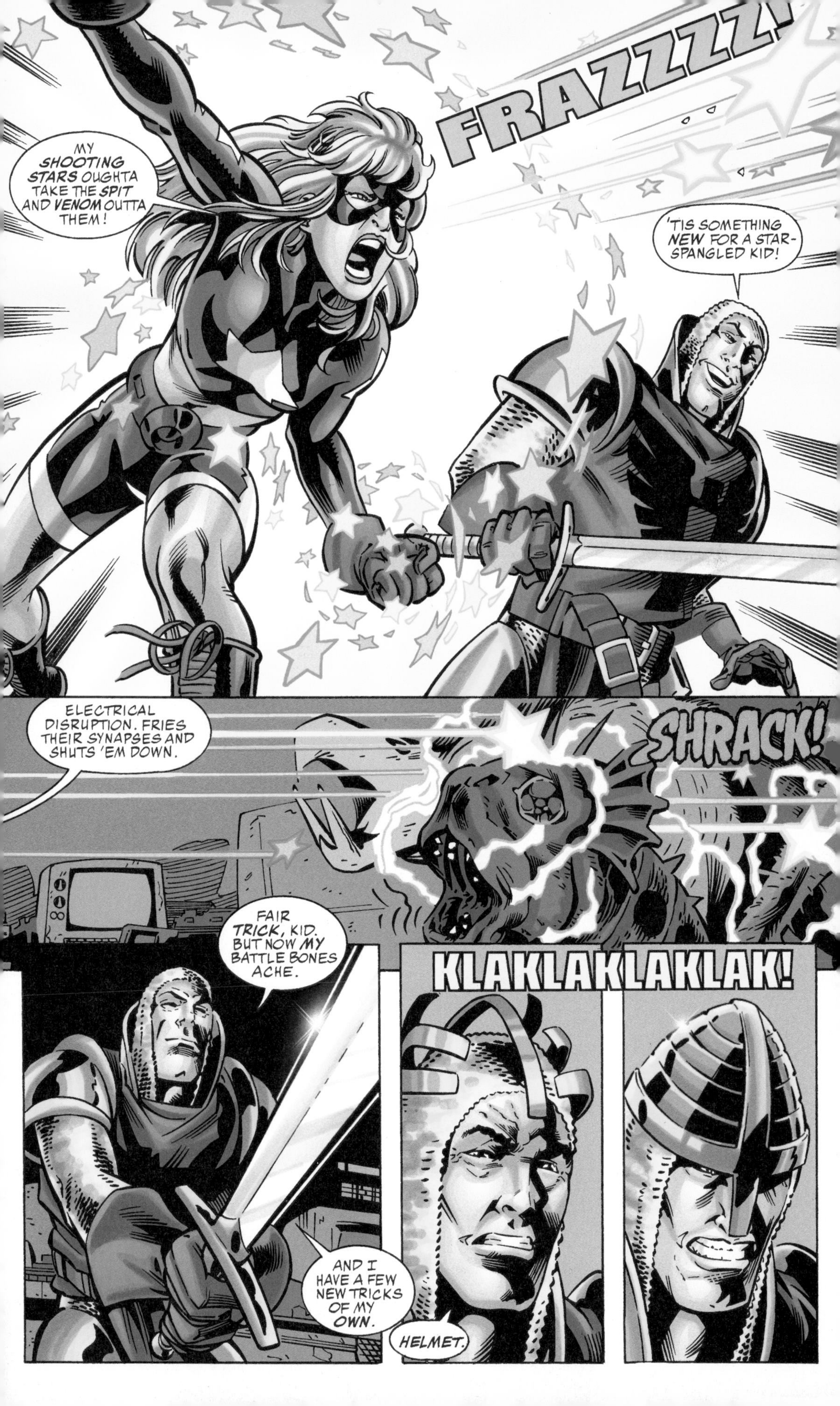

FRAZZZZZ!
MY SHOOTING STARS OUGHTA TAKE THE SPIT AND VENOM OUTTA THEM!
'TIS SOMETHING NEW FOR A STAR-SPANGLED KID!
ELECTRICAL DISRUPTION. FRIES THEIR SYNAPSES AND SHUTS 'EM DOWN.
SHRACK!
FAIR TRICK, KID. BUT NOW MY BATTLE BONES ACHE.
AND I HAVE A FEW NEW TRICKS OF MY OWN.
HELMET.
KLAKLAKLAKLAKLAK!

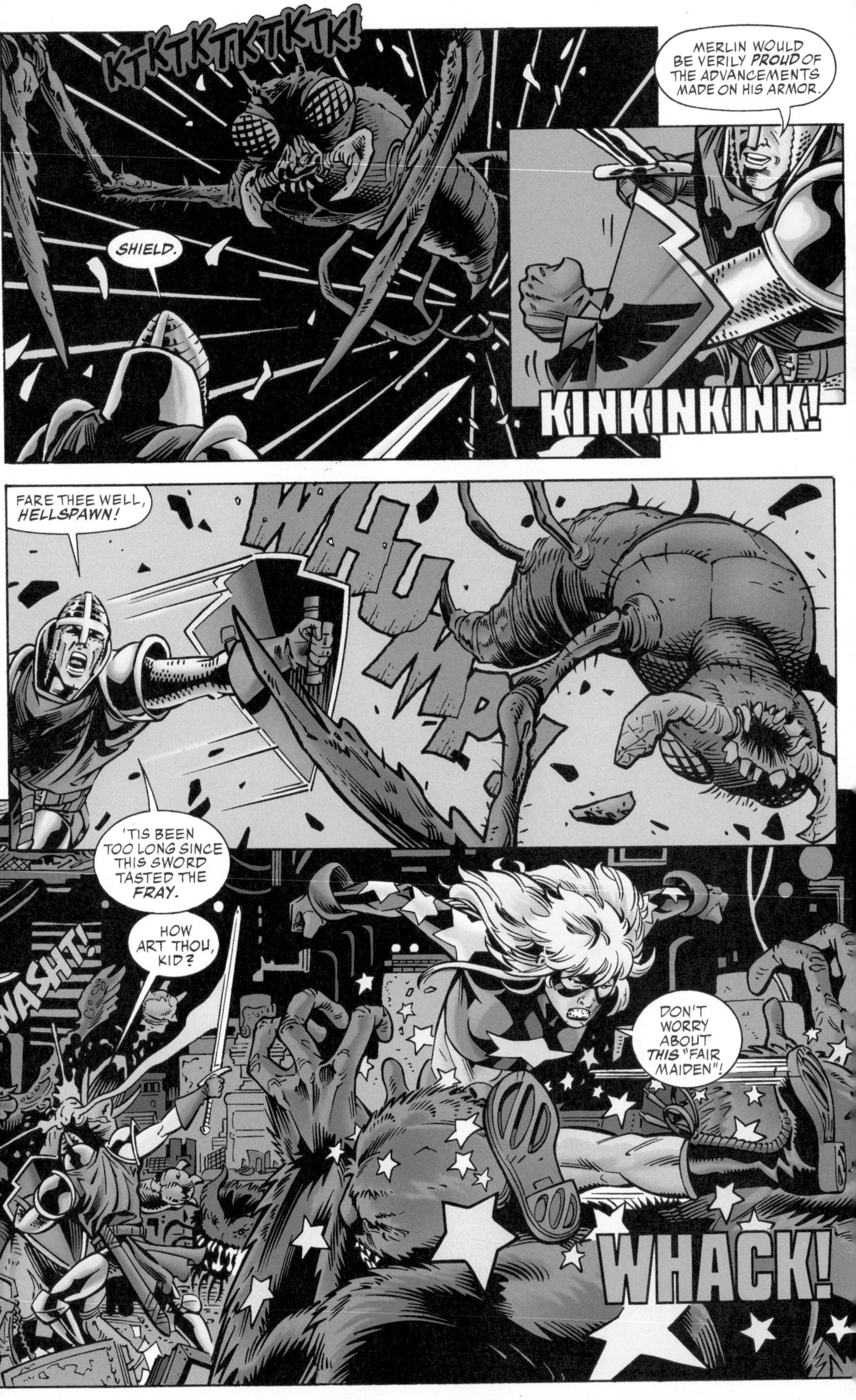
KTKTKTIKTIKTIK!
MERLIN WOULD BE VERILY PROUD OF THE ADVANCEMENTS MADE ON HIS ARMOR.
SHIELD.
KINKINKINK!
FARE THEE WELL, HELLSPAWN!
WHUMP!
'TIS BEEN TOO LONG SINCE THIS SWORD TASTED THE FRAY.
HOW ART THOU, KID?
WASHT!
DON'T WORRY ABOUT THIS "FAIR MAIDEN"!
WHACK!

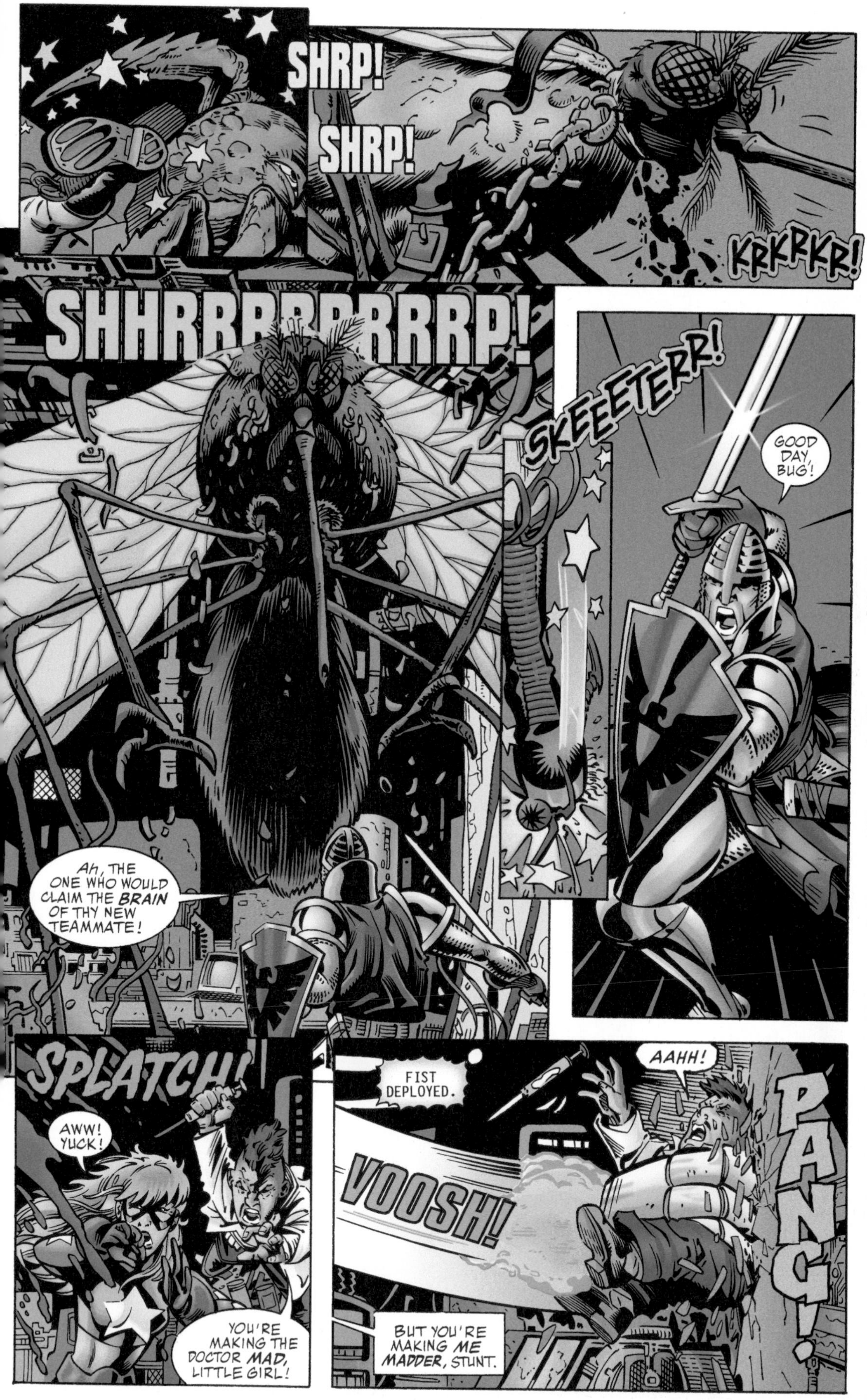
SHRP!
SHRP!
KRKRKR!
SHHRRRRRRRP!
SKEEETERR!
GOOD DAY, BUG!
Ah, THE ONE WHO WOULD CLAIM THE BRAIN OF THY NEW TEAMMATE!
SPLATCH!
AWW! YUCK!
YOU'RE MAKING THE DOCTOR MAD, LITTLE GIRL!
FIST DEPLOYED.
AAHH!
VOOSH!
PANG!
BUT YOU'RE MAKING ME MADDER, STUNT.

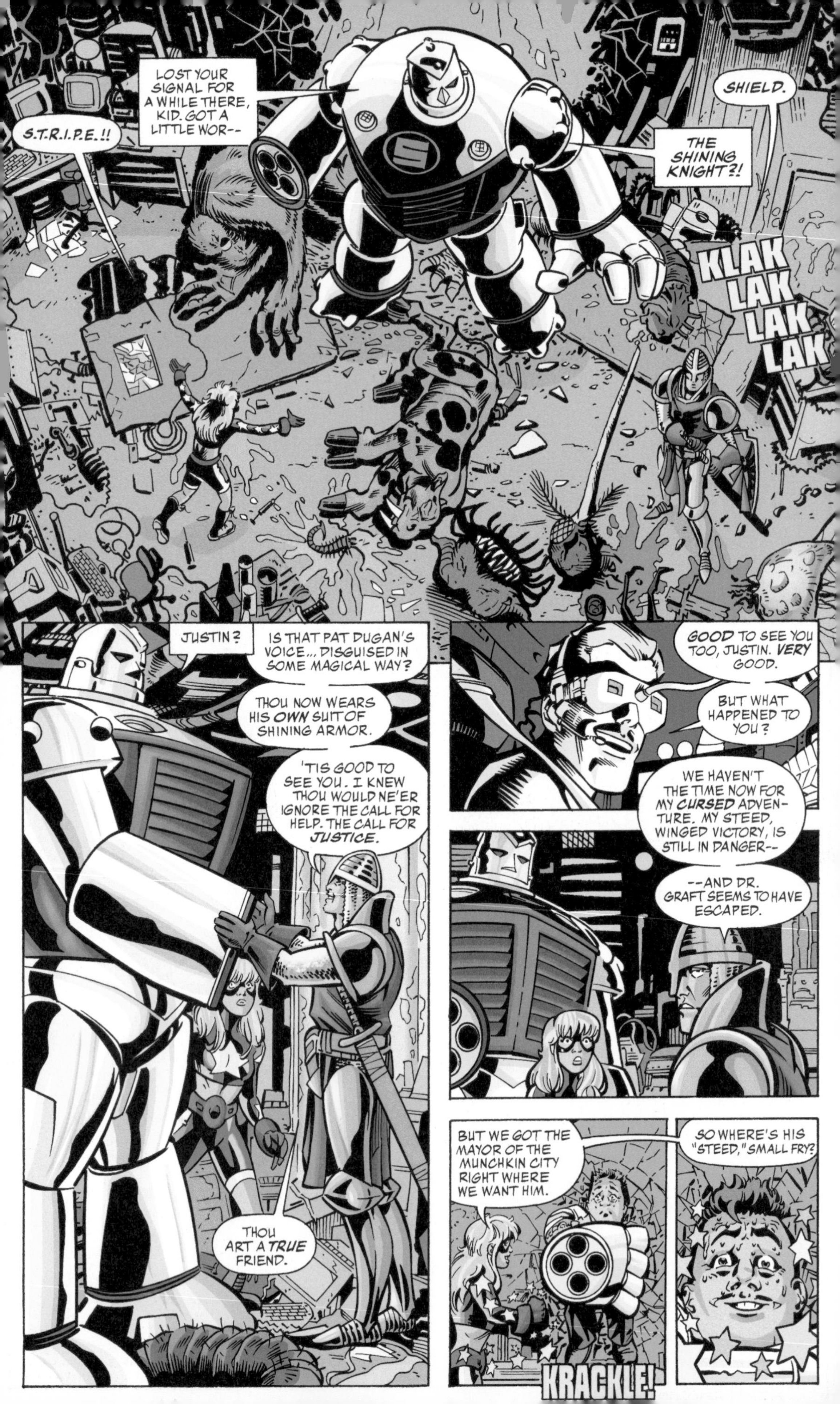

S.T.R.I.P.E.!!
LOST YOUR SIGNAL FOR A WHILE THERE, KID. GOT A LITTLE WOR--
SHIELD.
THE SHINING KNIGHT?!
KLAK LAK LAK LAK
JUSTIN?
IS THAT PAT DUGAN'S VOICE... DISGUISED IN SOME MAGICAL WAY?
THOU NOW WEARS HIS OWN SUIT OF SHINING ARMOR.
'TIS GOOD TO SEE YOU. I KNEW THOU WOULD NE'ER IGNORE THE CALL FOR HELP. THE CALL FOR JUSTICE.
THOU ART A TRUE FRIEND.
GOOD TO SEE YOU TOO, JUSTIN. VERY GOOD.
BUT WHAT HAPPENED TO YOU?
WE HAVEN'T THE TIME NOW FOR MY CURSED ADVENTURE. MY STEED, WINGED VICTORY, IS STILL IN DANGER--
--AND DR. GRAFT SEEMS TO HAVE ESCAPED.
BUT WE GOT THE MAYOR OF THE MUNCHKIN CITY RIGHT WHERE WE WANT HIM.
KRACKLE!
SO WHERE'S HIS "STEED," SMALL FRY?

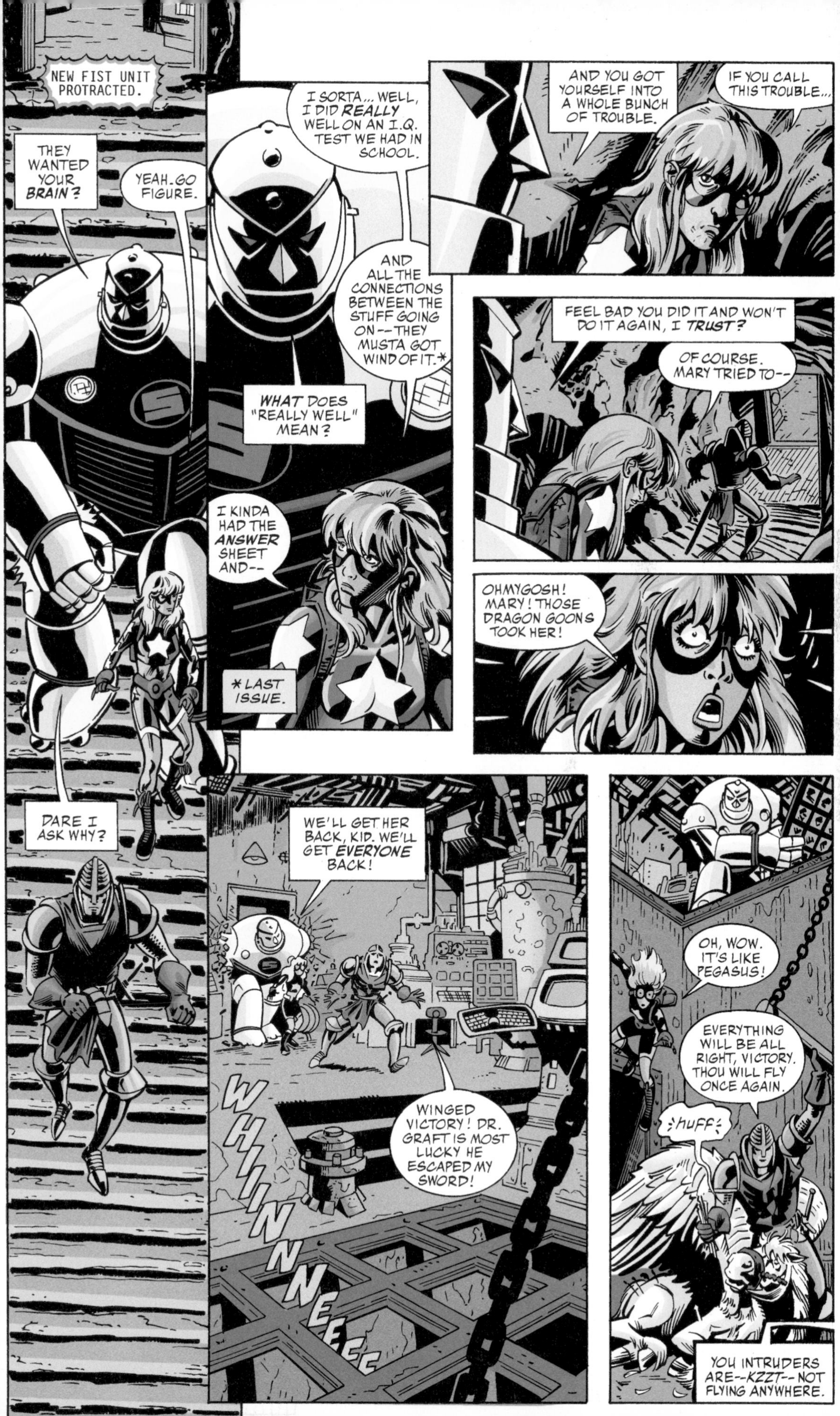
NEW FIST UNIT PROTRACTED.
THEY WANTED YOUR BRAIN?
YEAH. GO FIGURE.
DARE I ASK WHY?
I SORTA... WELL, I DID REALLY WELL ON AN I.Q. TEST WE HAD IN SCHOOL.
AND ALL THE CONNECTIONS BETWEEN THE STUFF GOING ON--THEY MUSTA GOT WIND OF IT.*
WHAT DOES "REALLY WELL" MEAN?
I KINDA HAD THE ANSWER SHEET AND--
*LAST ISSUE.
AND YOU GOT YOURSELF INTO A WHOLE BUNCH OF TROUBLE.
IF YOU CALL THIS TROUBLE...
FEEL BAD YOU DID IT AND WON'T DO IT AGAIN, I TRUST?
OF COURSE. MARY TRIED TO--
OHMYGOSH! MARY! THOSE DRAGON GOONS TOOK HER!
WE'LL GET HER BACK, KID. WE'LL GET EVERYONE BACK!
WINGED VICTORY! DR. GRAFT IS MOST LUCKY HE ESCAPED MY SWORD!
WHINNNEEEE
OH, WOW. IT'S LIKE PEGASUS!
EVERYTHING WILL BE ALL RIGHT, VICTORY. THOU WILL FLY ONCE AGAIN.
huff
YOU INTRUDERS ARE--KZZT--NOT FLYING ANYWHERE.

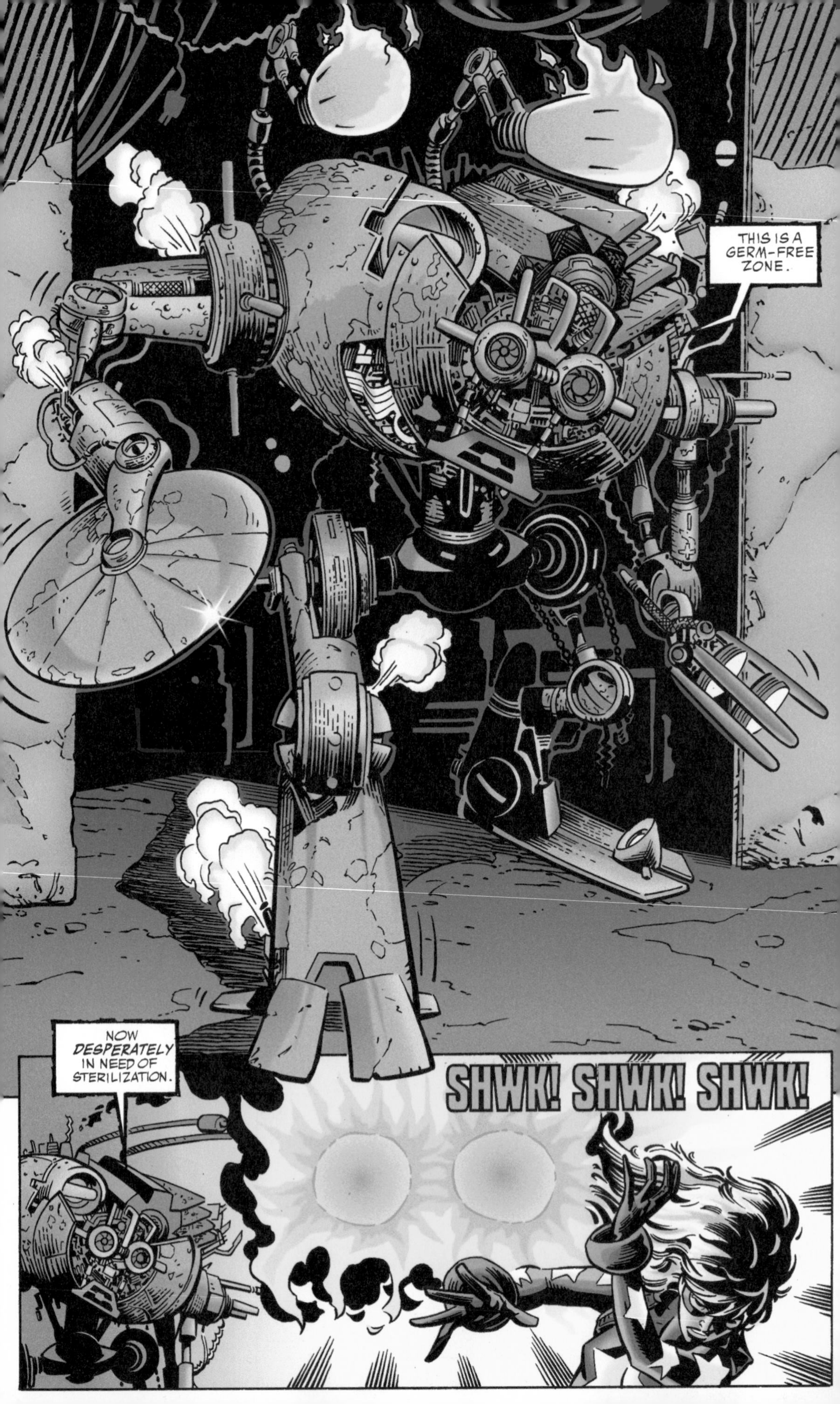
THIS IS A GERM-FREE ZONE.
NOW DESPERATELY IN NEED OF STERILIZATION.
SHWK! SHWK! SHWK!

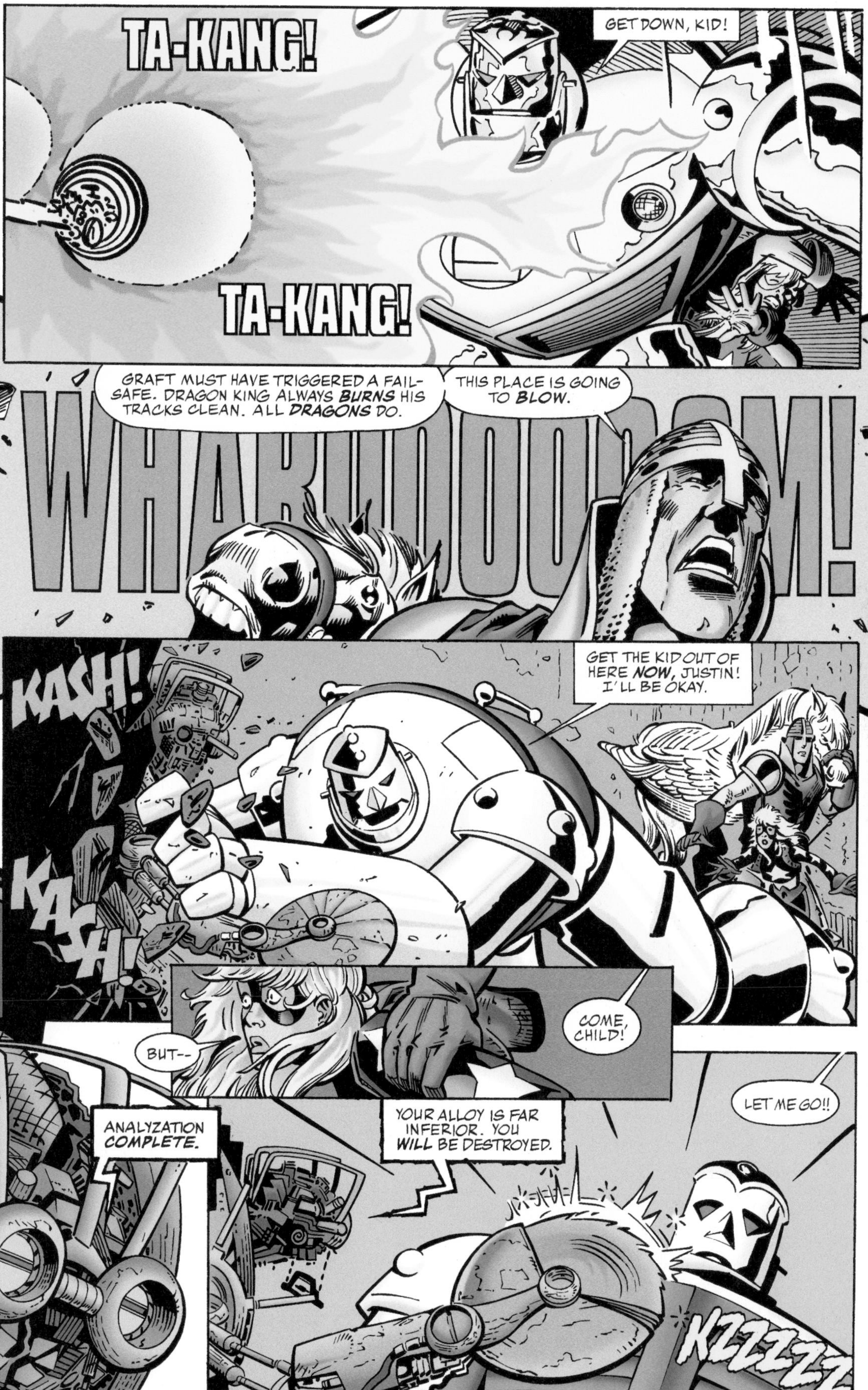
TA-KANG!
GET DOWN, KID!
TA-KANG!
GRAFT MUST HAVE TRIGGERED A FAIL-SAFE. DRAGON KING ALWAYS BURNS HIS TRACKS CLEAN. ALL DRAGONS DO.
THIS PLACE IS GOING TO BLOW.
KASH!
GET THE KID OUT OF HERE NOW, JUSTIN! I'LL BE OKAY.
KASH!
BUT--
COME, CHILD!
LET ME GO!!
ANALYZATION COMPLETE.
YOUR ALLOY IS FAR INFERIOR. YOU WILL BE DESTROYED.
KZZZZZ

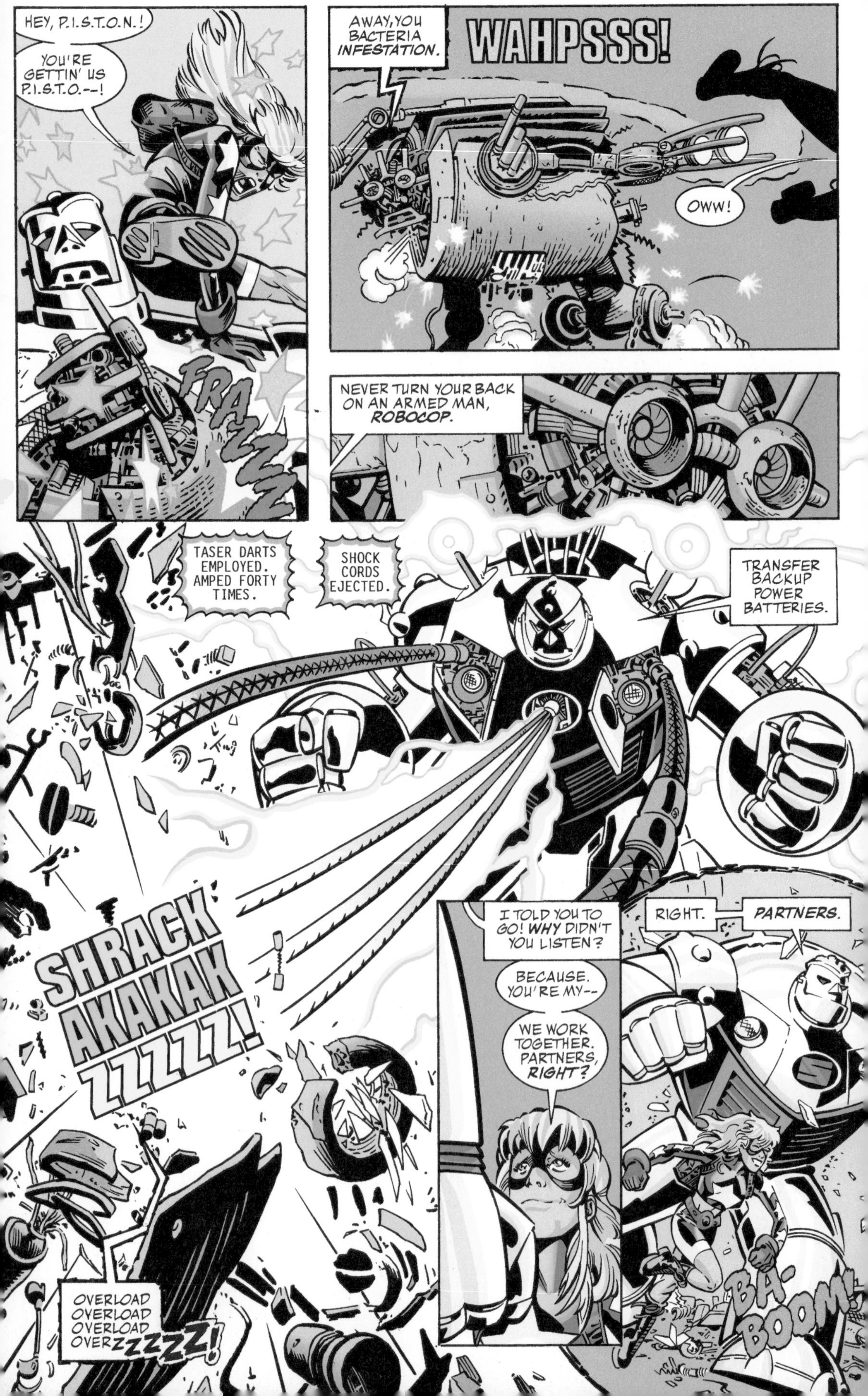
HEY, P.I.S.T.O.N.!
YOU'RE GETTIN' US P.I.S.T.O.--!
FRAZZZ
AWAY, YOU BACTERIA INFESTATION.
WAHPSSS!
OWW!
NEVER TURN YOUR BACK ON AN ARMED MAN, ROBOCOP.
TASER DARTS EMPLOYED. AMPED FORTY TIMES.
SHOCK CORDS EJECTED.
TRANSFER BACKUP POWER BATTERIES.
SHRACK AKAKAK ZZZZZ!
OVERLOAD OVERLOAD OVERLOAD OVERZZZZZ!
I TOLD YOU TO GO! WHY DIDN'T YOU LISTEN?
BECAUSE. YOU'RE MY--
WE WORK TOGETHER. PARTNERS, RIGHT?
RIGHT.
PARTNERS.
BA-BOOM!

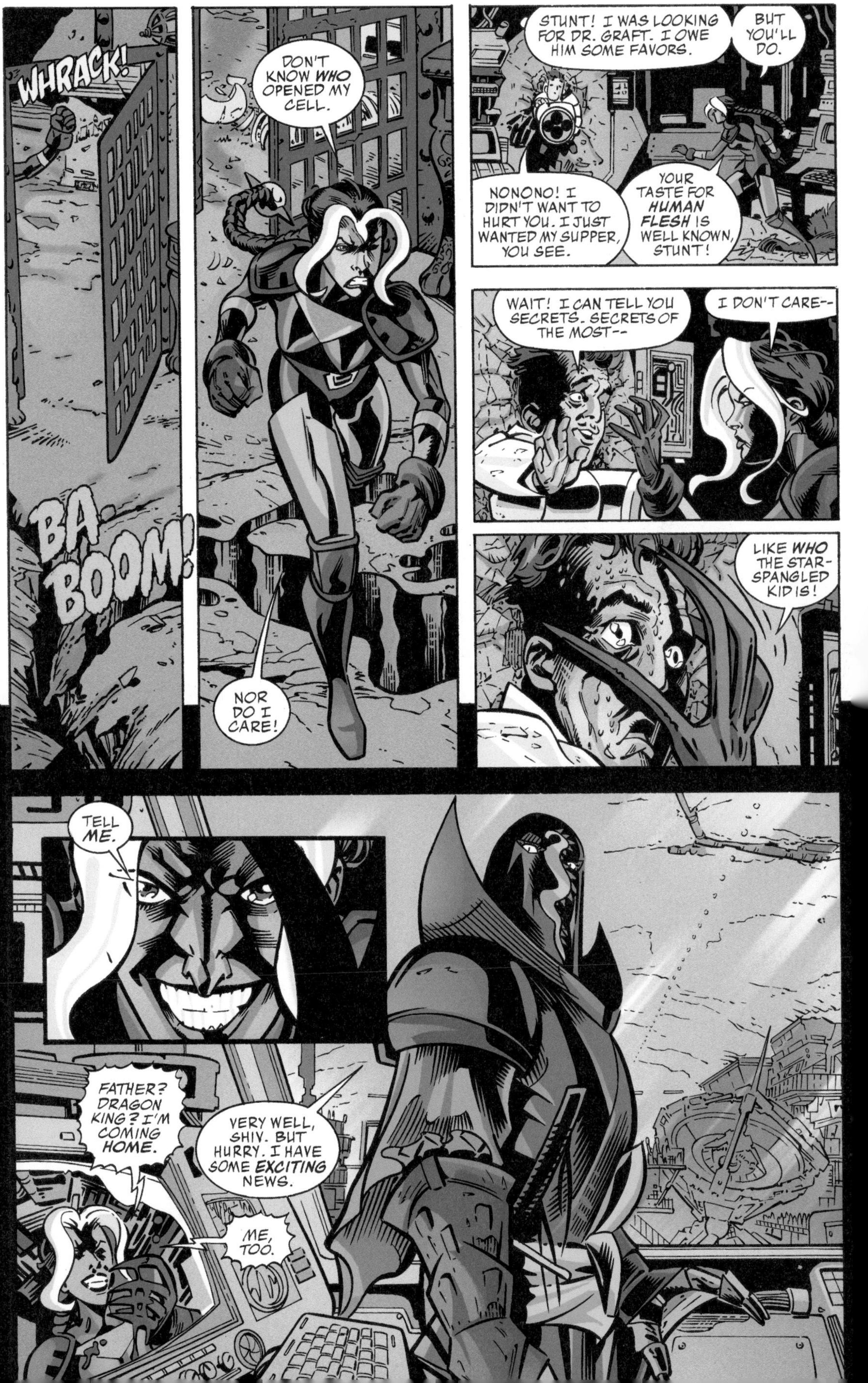
WHRACK!
BA BOOM!
DON'T KNOW WHO OPENED MY CELL.
NOR DO I CARE!
STUNT! I WAS LOOKING FOR DR. GRAFT. I OWE HIM SOME FAVORS.
BUT YOU'LL DO.
NONONO! I DIDN'T WANT TO HURT YOU. I JUST WANTED MY SUPPER, YOU SEE.
YOUR TASTE FOR HUMAN FLESH IS WELL KNOWN, STUNT!
WAIT! I CAN TELL YOU SECRETS. SECRETS OF THE MOST--
I DON'T CARE--
LIKE WHO THE STAR-SPANGLED KID IS!
TELL ME.
FATHER? DRAGON KING? I'M COMING HOME.
VERY WELL, SHIV. BUT HURRY. I HAVE SOME EXCITING NEWS.
ME, TOO.

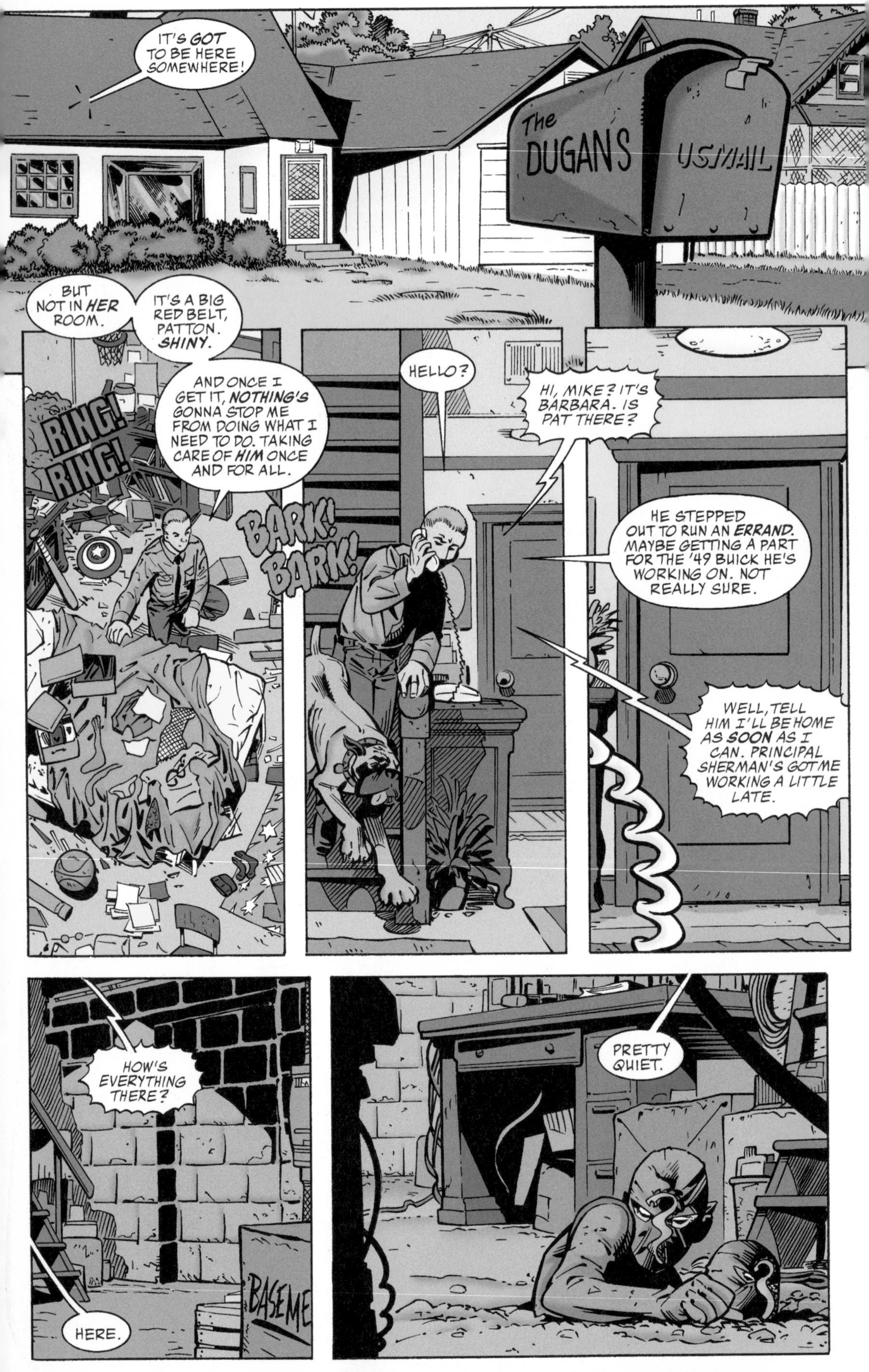
IT'S GOT TO BE HERE SOMEWHERE!
The DUGANS
U.S. MAIL
BUT NOT IN HER ROOM.
IT'S A BIG RED BELT, PATTON. SHINY.
AND ONCE I GET IT, NOTHING'S GONNA STOP ME FROM DOING WHAT I NEED TO DO. TAKING CARE OF HIM ONCE AND FOR ALL.
RING! RING!
BARK! BARK!
HELLO?
HI, MIKE? IT'S BARBARA. IS PAT THERE?
HE STEPPED OUT TO RUN AN ERRAND. MAYBE GETTING A PART FOR THE '49 BUICK HE'S WORKING ON. NOT REALLY SURE.
WELL, TELL HIM I'LL BE HOME AS SOON AS I CAN. PRINCIPAL SHERMAN'S GOT ME WORKING A LITTLE LATE.
HOW'S EVERYTHING THERE?
HERE.
BASEME
PRETTY QUIET.

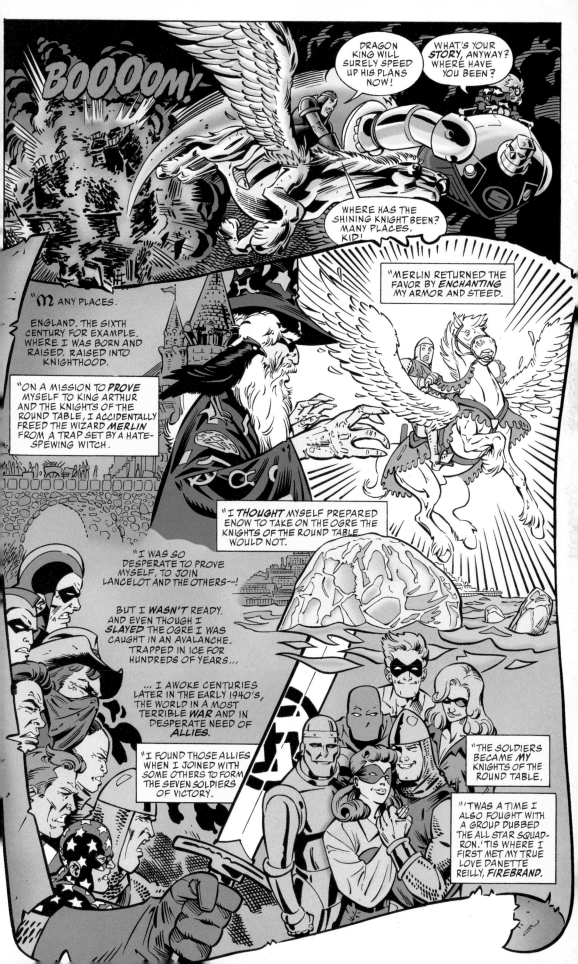

BOOOOM!

DRAGON KING WILL SURELY SPEED UP HIS PLANS NOW!

WHAT'S YOUR *STORY,* ANYWAY? WHERE HAVE YOU BEEN?

WHERE HAS THE SHINING KNIGHT BEEN? MANY PLACES, KID!

"MERLIN RETURNED THE FAVOR BY *ENCHANTING* MY ARMOR AND STEED."

"ᴹANY PLACES.

ENGLAND. THE SIXTH CENTURY FOR EXAMPLE. WHERE I WAS BORN AND RAISED. RAISED INTO KNIGHTHOOD.

"ON A MISSION TO *PROVE* MYSELF TO KING ARTHUR AND THE KNIGHTS OF THE ROUND TABLE, I ACCIDENTALLY FREED THE WIZARD *MERLIN* FROM A TRAP SET BY A HATE-SPEWING WITCH.

"I *THOUGHT* MYSELF PREPARED ENOW TO TAKE ON THE OGRE THE KNIGHTS OF THE ROUND TABLE WOULD NOT.

"I WAS SO DESPERATE TO PROVE MYSELF, TO JOIN LANCELOT AND THE OTHERS--!

BUT I *WASN'T* READY. AND EVEN THOUGH I *SLAYED* THE OGRE I WAS CAUGHT IN AN AVALANCHE. TRAPPED IN ICE FOR HUNDREDS OF YEARS...

... I AWOKE CENTURIES LATER IN THE EARLY 1940'S, THE WORLD IN A MOST TERRIBLE *WAR* AND IN DESPERATE NEED OF *ALLIES.*

"I FOUND THOSE ALLIES WHEN I JOINED WITH SOME OTHERS TO FORM THE SEVEN SOLDIERS OF VICTORY.

"THE SOLDIERS BECAME *MY* KNIGHTS OF THE ROUND TABLE.

"'TWAS A TIME I ALSO FOUGHT WITH A GROUP DUBBED THE ALL STAR SQUADRON. 'TIS WHERE I FIRST MET MY TRUE LOVE DANETTE REILLY, *FIREBRAND.*

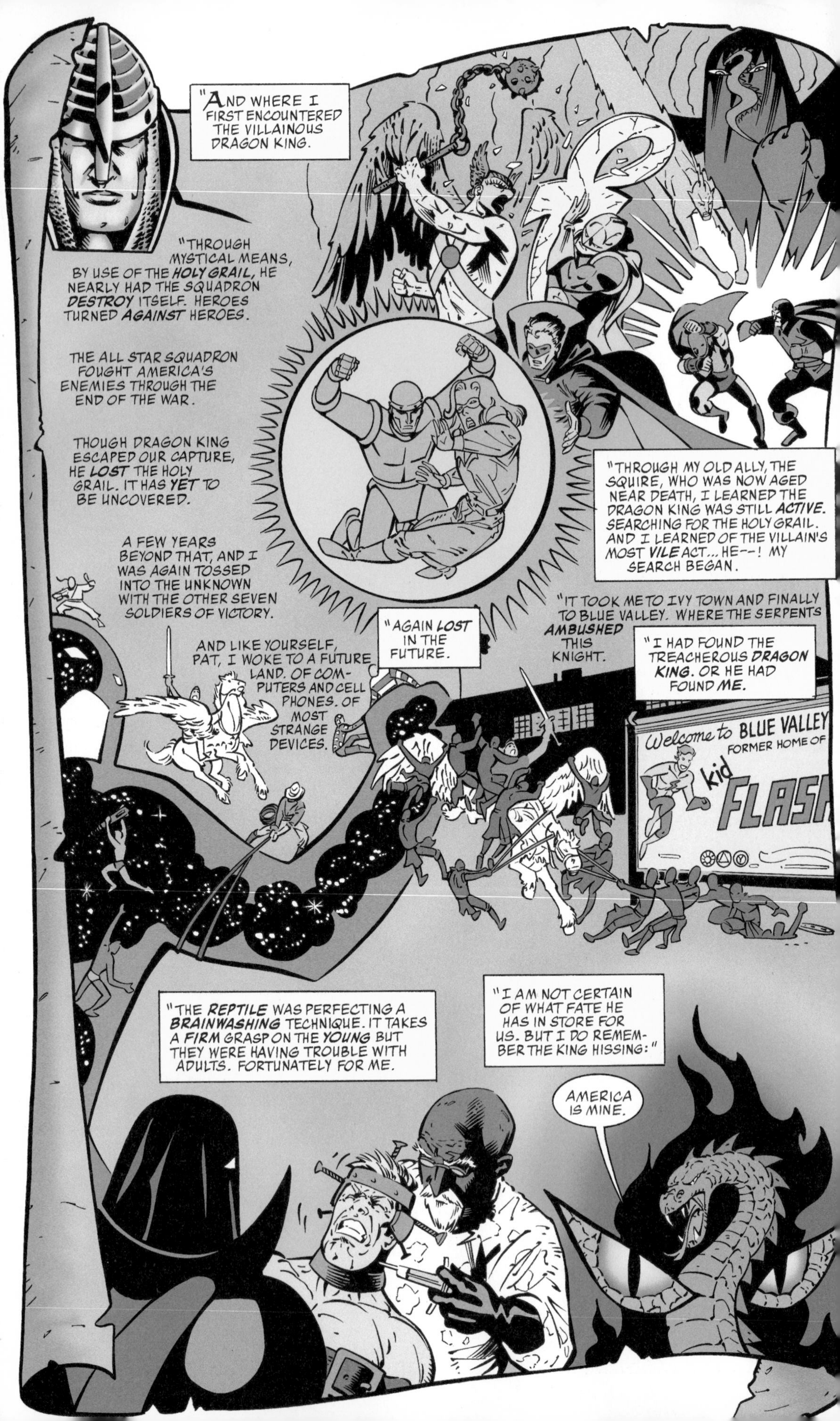
"AND WHERE I FIRST ENCOUNTERED THE VILLAINOUS DRAGON KING.
"THROUGH MYSTICAL MEANS, BY USE OF THE HOLY GRAIL, HE NEARLY HAD THE SQUADRON DESTROY ITSELF. HEROES TURNED AGAINST HEROES.
THE ALL STAR SQUADRON FOUGHT AMERICA'S ENEMIES THROUGH THE END OF THE WAR.
THOUGH DRAGON KING ESCAPED OUR CAPTURE, HE LOST THE HOLY GRAIL. IT HAS YET TO BE UNCOVERED.
A FEW YEARS BEYOND THAT, AND I WAS AGAIN TOSSED INTO THE UNKNOWN WITH THE OTHER SEVEN SOLDIERS OF VICTORY.
AND LIKE YOURSELF, PAT, I WOKE TO A FUTURE LAND. OF COMPUTERS AND CELL PHONES. OF MOST STRANGE DEVICES.
"AGAIN LOST IN THE FUTURE.
"THROUGH MY OLD ALLY, THE SQUIRE, WHO WAS NOW AGED NEAR DEATH, I LEARNED THE DRAGON KING WAS STILL ACTIVE. SEARCHING FOR THE HOLY GRAIL. AND I LEARNED OF THE VILLAIN'S MOST VILE ACT... HE--! MY SEARCH BEGAN.
"IT TOOK ME TO IVY TOWN AND FINALLY TO BLUE VALLEY. WHERE THE SERPENTS AMBUSHED THIS KNIGHT.
"I HAD FOUND THE TREACHEROUS DRAGON KING. OR HE HAD FOUND ME.
Welcome to BLUE VALLEY
FORMER HOME OF
kid FLASH
"THE REPTILE WAS PERFECTING A BRAINWASHING TECHNIQUE. IT TAKES A FIRM GRASP ON THE YOUNG BUT THEY WERE HAVING TROUBLE WITH ADULTS. FORTUNATELY FOR ME.
"I AM NOT CERTAIN OF WHAT FATE HE HAS IN STORE FOR US. BUT I DO REMEMBER THE KING HISSING:"
AMERICA IS MINE.

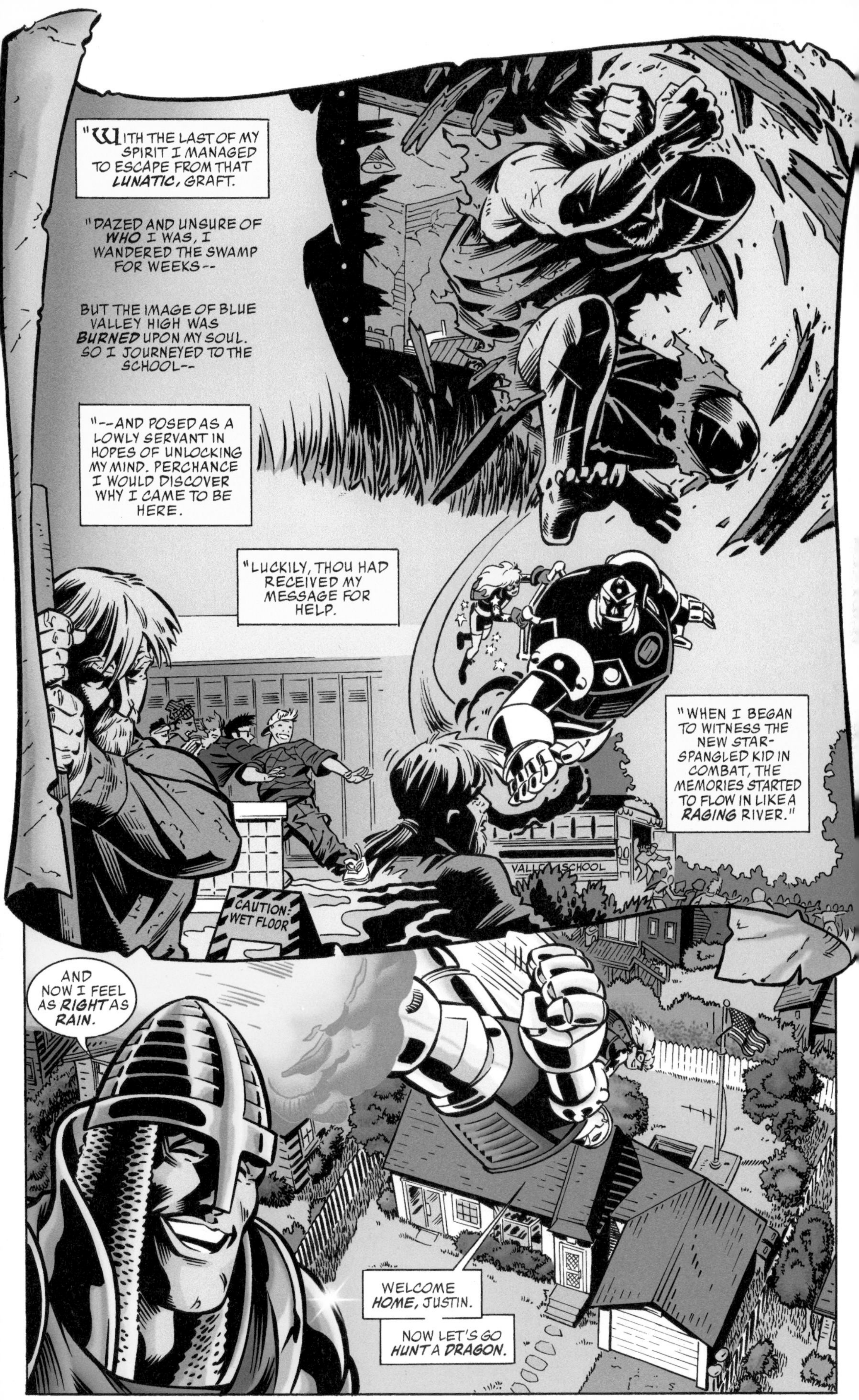
"WITH THE LAST OF MY SPIRIT I MANAGED TO ESCAPE FROM THAT LUNATIC, GRAFT.
"DAZED AND UNSURE OF WHO I WAS, I WANDERED THE SWAMP FOR WEEKS--
BUT THE IMAGE OF BLUE VALLEY HIGH WAS BURNED UPON MY SOUL. SO I JOURNEYED TO THE SCHOOL--
"--AND POSED AS A LOWLY SERVANT IN HOPES OF UNLOCKING MY MIND. PERCHANCE I WOULD DISCOVER WHY I CAME TO BE HERE.
"LUCKILY, THOU HAD RECEIVED MY MESSAGE FOR HELP.
"WHEN I BEGAN TO WITNESS THE NEW STAR-SPANGLED KID IN COMBAT, THE MEMORIES STARTED TO FLOW IN LIKE A RAGING RIVER."
CAUTION: WET FLOOR
AND NOW I FEEL AS RIGHT AS RAIN.
WELCOME HOME, JUSTIN.
NOW LET'S GO HUNT A DRAGON.

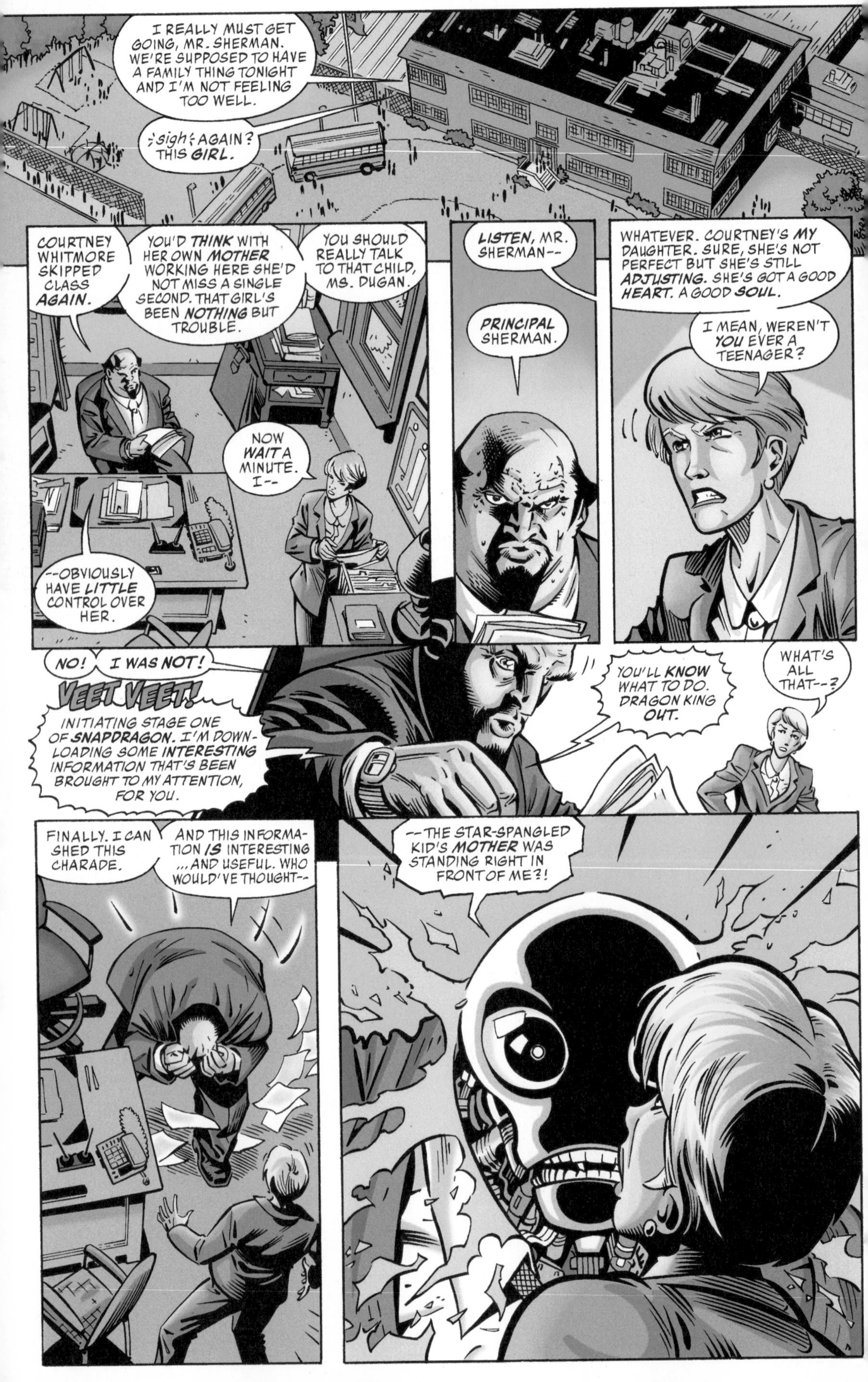
I REALLY MUST GET GOING, MR. SHERMAN. WE'RE SUPPOSED TO HAVE A FAMILY THING TONIGHT AND I'M NOT FEELING TOO WELL.
sigh AGAIN? THIS GIRL.
COURTNEY WHITMORE SKIPPED CLASS AGAIN.
YOU'D THINK WITH HER OWN MOTHER WORKING HERE SHE'D NOT MISS A SINGLE SECOND. THAT GIRL'S BEEN NOTHING BUT TROUBLE.
YOU SHOULD REALLY TALK TO THAT CHILD, MS. DUGAN.
NOW WAIT A MINUTE. I--
--OBVIOUSLY HAVE LITTLE CONTROL OVER HER.
LISTEN, MR. SHERMAN--
PRINCIPAL SHERMAN.
WHATEVER. COURTNEY'S MY DAUGHTER. SURE, SHE'S NOT PERFECT BUT SHE'S STILL ADJUSTING. SHE'S GOT A GOOD HEART. A GOOD SOUL.
I MEAN, WEREN'T YOU EVER A TEENAGER?
NO!
I WAS NOT!
VEET VEET!
INITIATING STAGE ONE OF SNAPDRAGON. I'M DOWNLOADING SOME INTERESTING INFORMATION THAT'S BEEN BROUGHT TO MY ATTENTION, FOR YOU.
YOU'LL KNOW WHAT TO DO. DRAGON KING OUT.
WHAT'S ALL THAT--?
FINALLY. I CAN SHED THIS CHARADE.
AND THIS INFORMATION IS INTERESTING ...AND USEFUL. WHO WOULD'VE THOUGHT--
--THE STAR-SPANGLED KID'S MOTHER WAS STANDING RIGHT IN FRONT OF ME?!

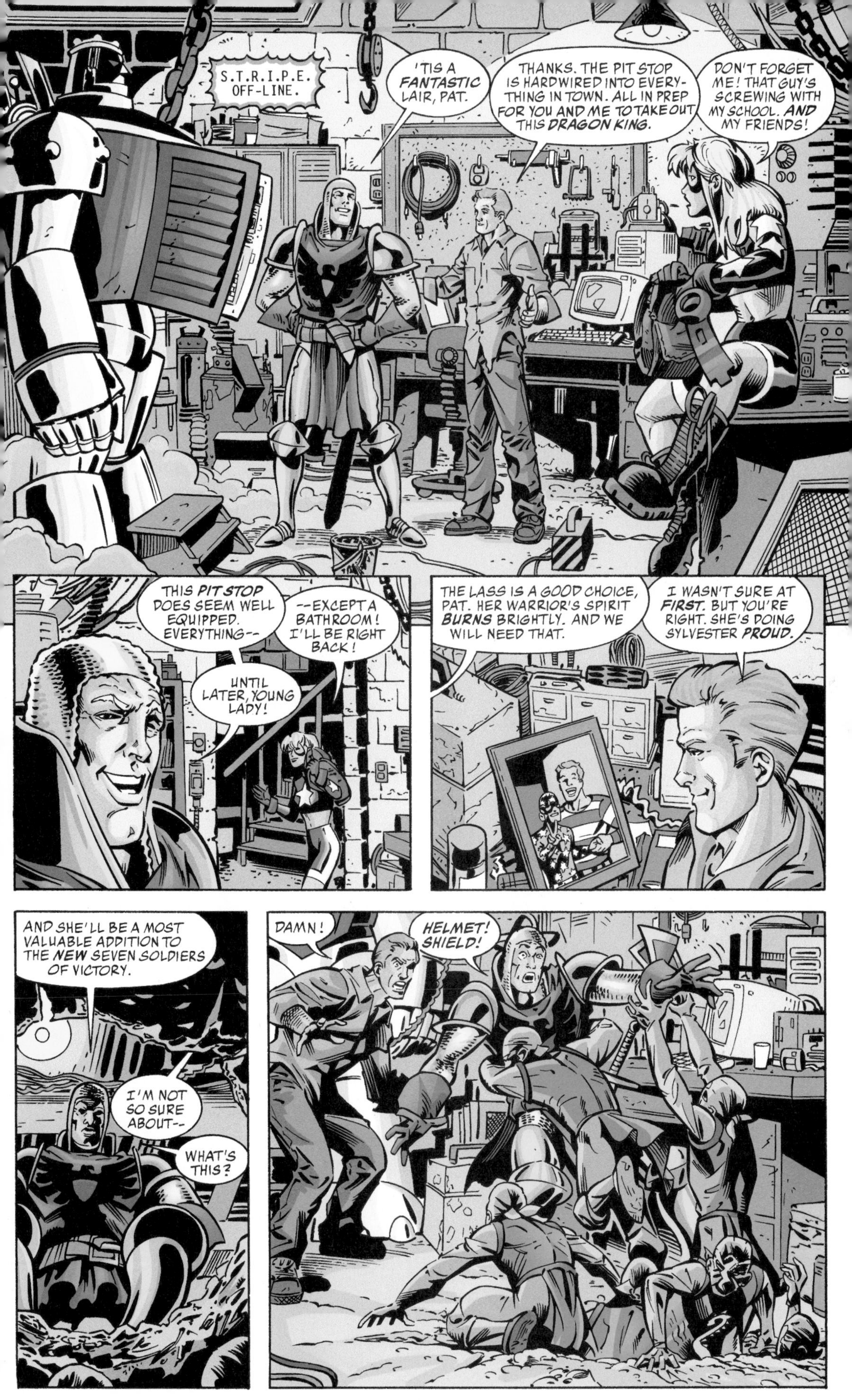
S.T.R.I.P.E. OFF-LINE.
'TIS A FANTASTIC LAIR, PAT.
THANKS. THE PIT STOP IS HARDWIRED INTO EVERYTHING IN TOWN. ALL IN PREP FOR YOU AND ME TO TAKE OUT THIS DRAGON KING.
DON'T FORGET ME! THAT GUY'S SCREWING WITH MY SCHOOL. AND MY FRIENDS!
THIS PIT STOP DOES SEEM WELL EQUIPPED. EVERYTHING--
--EXCEPT A BATHROOM! I'LL BE RIGHT BACK!
UNTIL LATER, YOUNG LADY!
THE LASS IS A GOOD CHOICE, PAT. HER WARRIOR'S SPIRIT BURNS BRIGHTLY. AND WE WILL NEED THAT.
I WASN'T SURE AT FIRST. BUT YOU'RE RIGHT. SHE'S DOING SYLVESTER PROUD.
AND SHE'LL BE A MOST VALUABLE ADDITION TO THE NEW SEVEN SOLDIERS OF VICTORY.
I'M NOT SO SURE ABOUT--
WHAT'S THIS?
DAMN!
HELMET! SHIELD!

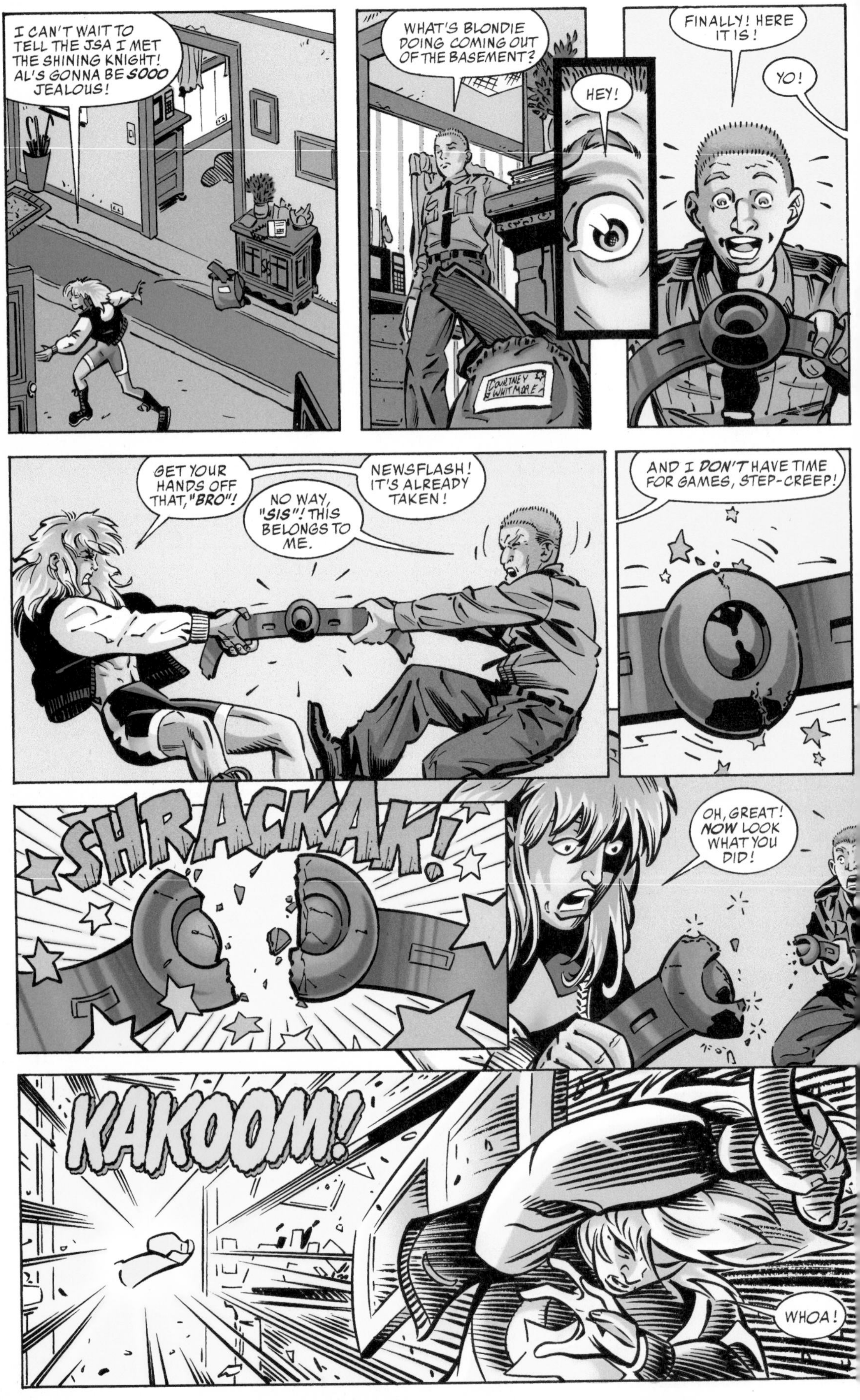
I CAN'T WAIT TO TELL THE JSA I MET THE SHINING KNIGHT! AL'S GONNA BE SOOO JEALOUS!
WHAT'S BLONDIE DOING COMING OUT OF THE BASEMENT?
COURTNEY WHITMORE
HEY!
FINALLY! HERE IT IS!
YO!
GET YOUR HANDS OFF THAT, "BRO"!
NO WAY, "SIS"! THIS BELONGS TO ME.
NEWSFLASH! IT'S ALREADY TAKEN!
AND I DON'T HAVE TIME FOR GAMES, STEP-CREEP!
SHRACKAK!
OH, GREAT! NOW LOOK WHAT YOU DID!
KAKOOM!
WHOA!

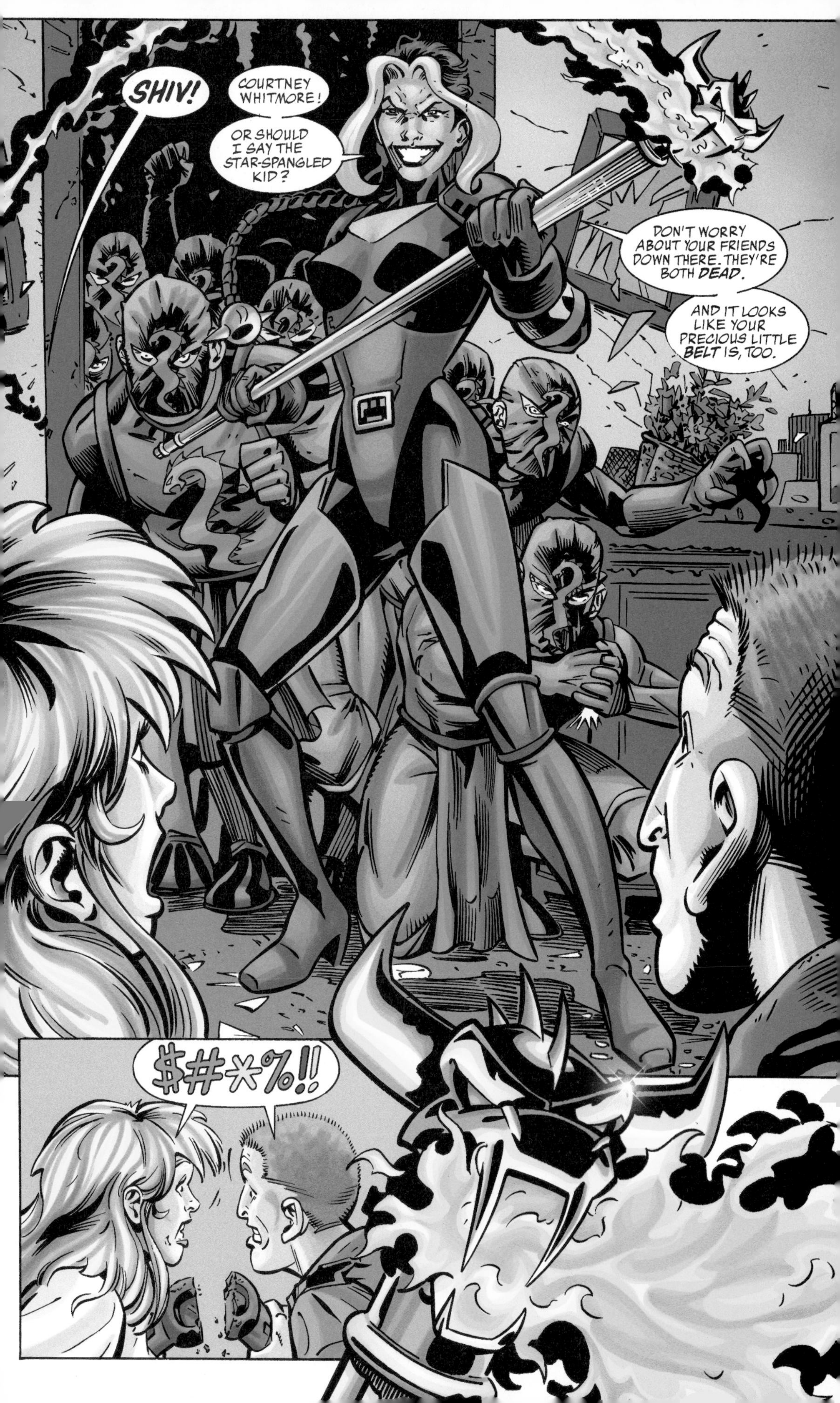
SHIV!
COURTNEY WHITMORE!
OR SHOULD I SAY THE STAR-SPANGLED KID?
DON'T WORRY ABOUT YOUR FRIENDS DOWN THERE. THEY'RE BOTH DEAD.
AND IT LOOKS LIKE YOUR PRECIOUS LITTLE BELT IS, TOO.
$#*%!!

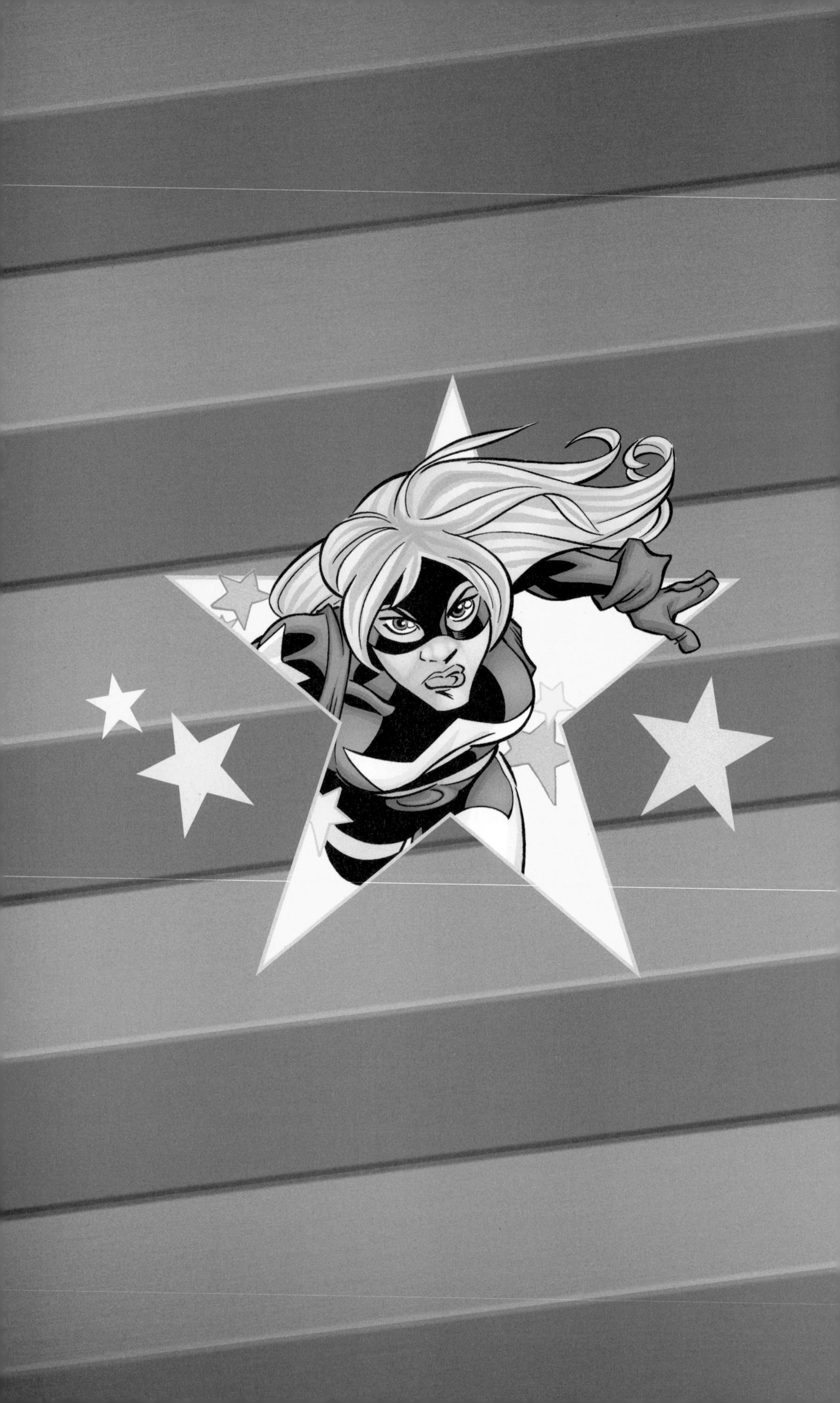

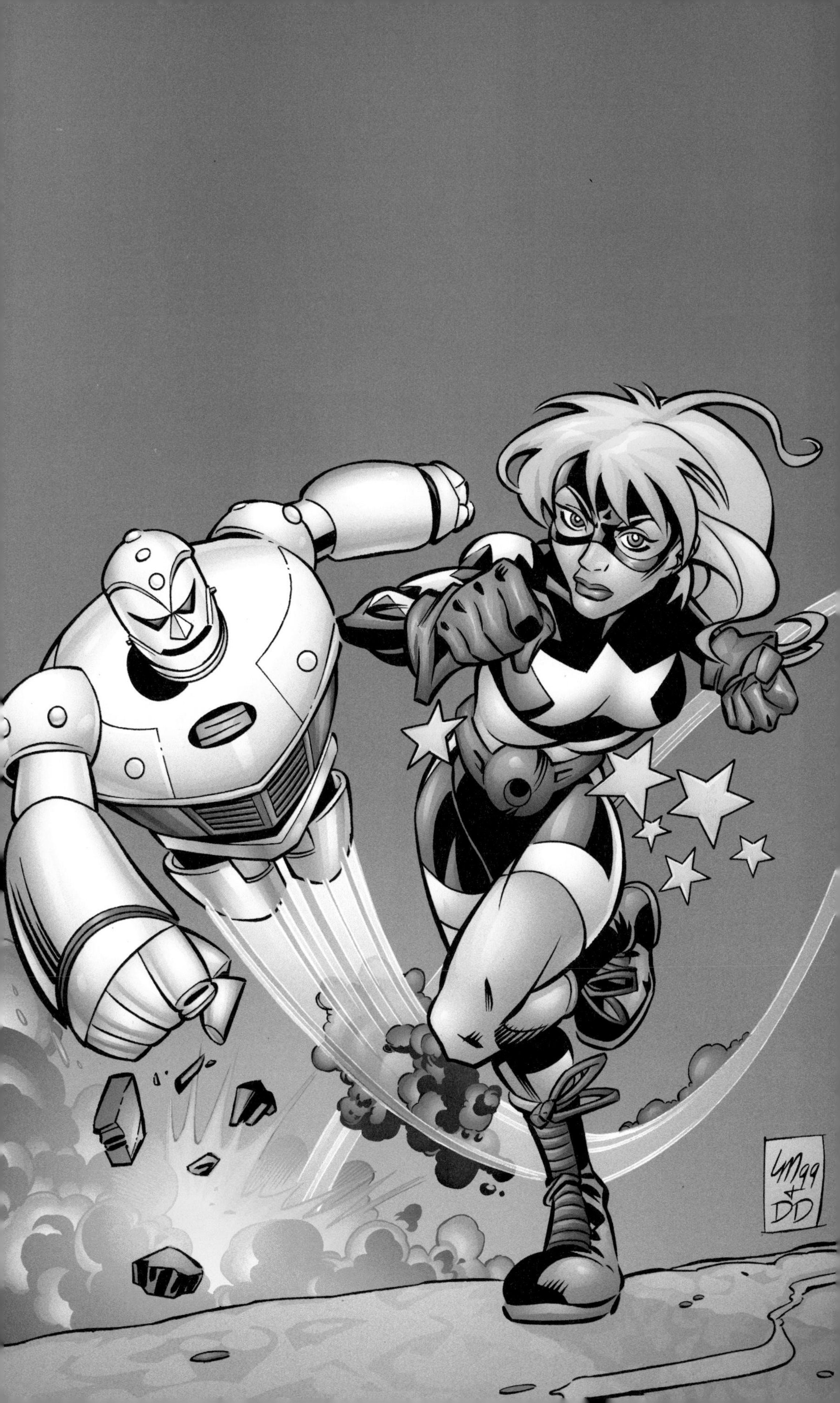

STARS AND S.T.R.I.P.E. #12

Written by GEOFF JOHNS
Pencils by LEE MODER
Inks by DAN DAVIS
Colors by TOM McCRAW
Letters by BILL OAKLEY
Cover art by LEE MODER and DAN DAVIS
Cover color by RICHARD & TANYA HORIE

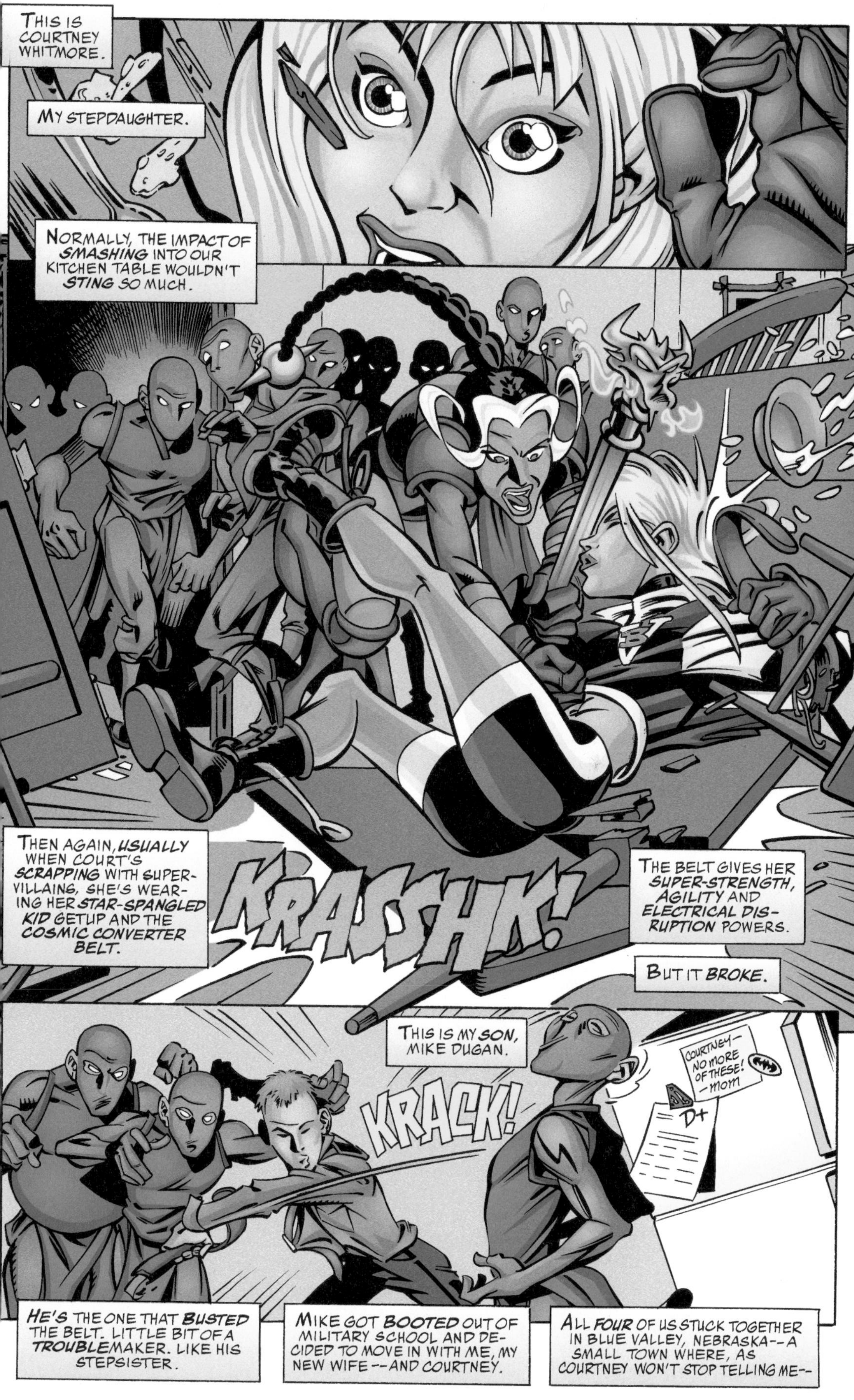

THIS IS COURTNEY WHITMORE.
MY STEPDAUGHTER.
NORMALLY, THE IMPACT OF SMASHING INTO OUR KITCHEN TABLE WOULDN'T STING SO MUCH.
THEN AGAIN, USUALLY WHEN COURT'S SCRAPPING WITH SUPER-VILLAINS, SHE'S WEARING HER STAR-SPANGLED KID GETUP AND THE COSMIC CONVERTER BELT.
KRASSHK!
THE BELT GIVES HER SUPER-STRENGTH, AGILITY AND ELECTRICAL DISRUPTION POWERS.
BUT IT BROKE.
THIS IS MY SON, MIKE DUGAN.
KRACK!
COURTNEY— NO MORE OF THESE! -MOM
D+
HE'S THE ONE THAT BUSTED THE BELT. LITTLE BIT OF A TROUBLEMAKER. LIKE HIS STEPSISTER.
MIKE GOT BOOTED OUT OF MILITARY SCHOOL AND DECIDED TO MOVE IN WITH ME, MY NEW WIFE -- AND COURTNEY.
ALL FOUR OF US STUCK TOGETHER IN BLUE VALLEY, NEBRASKA-- A SMALL TOWN WHERE, AS COURTNEY WON'T STOP TELLING ME--

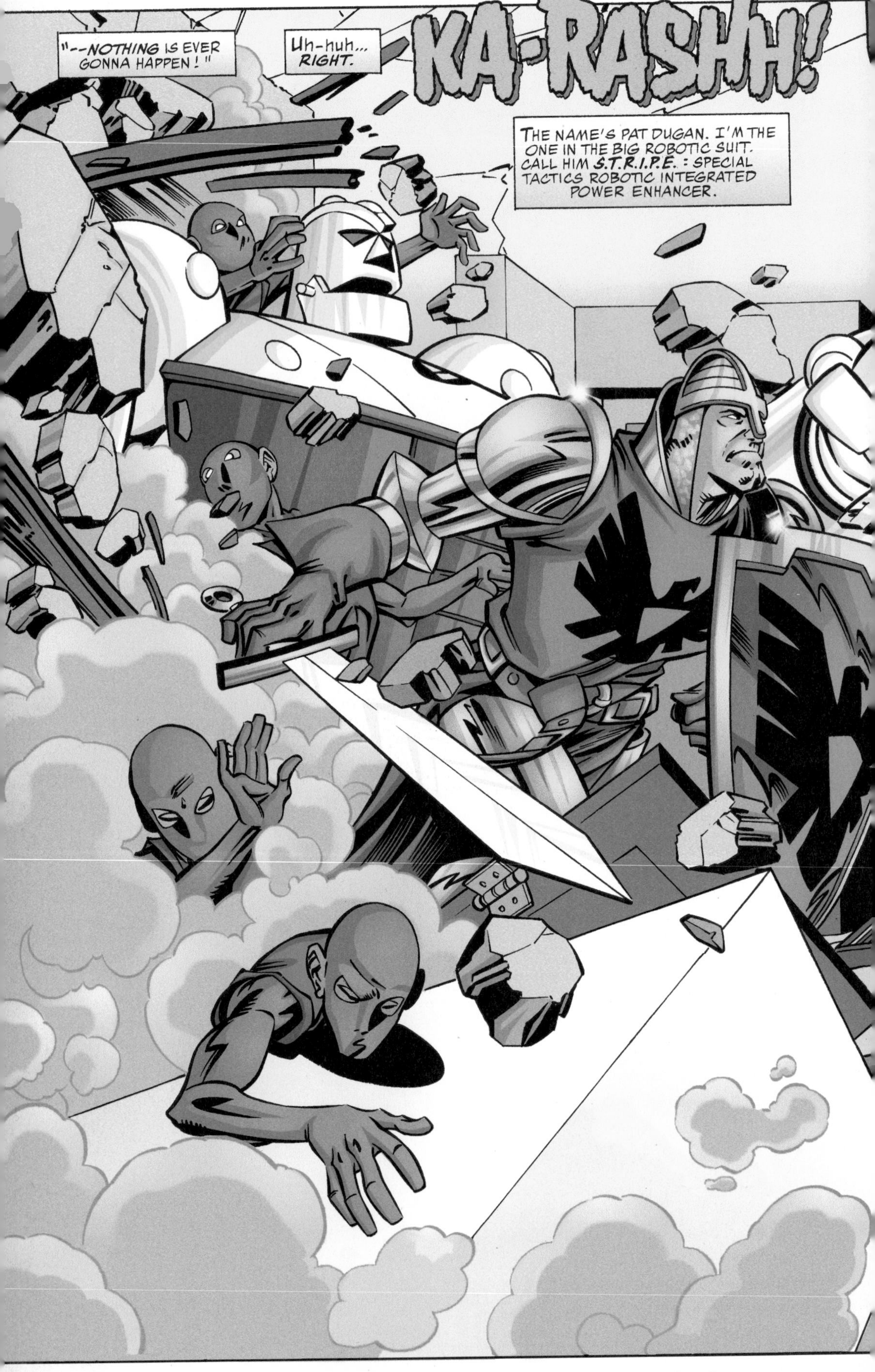
"--NOTHING IS EVER GONNA HAPPEN!"
Uh-huh... RIGHT.
KA-RASHH!
THE NAME'S PAT DUGAN. I'M THE ONE IN THE BIG ROBOTIC SUIT. CALL HIM S.T.R.I.P.E.: SPECIAL TACTICS ROBOTIC INTEGRATED POWER ENHANCER.

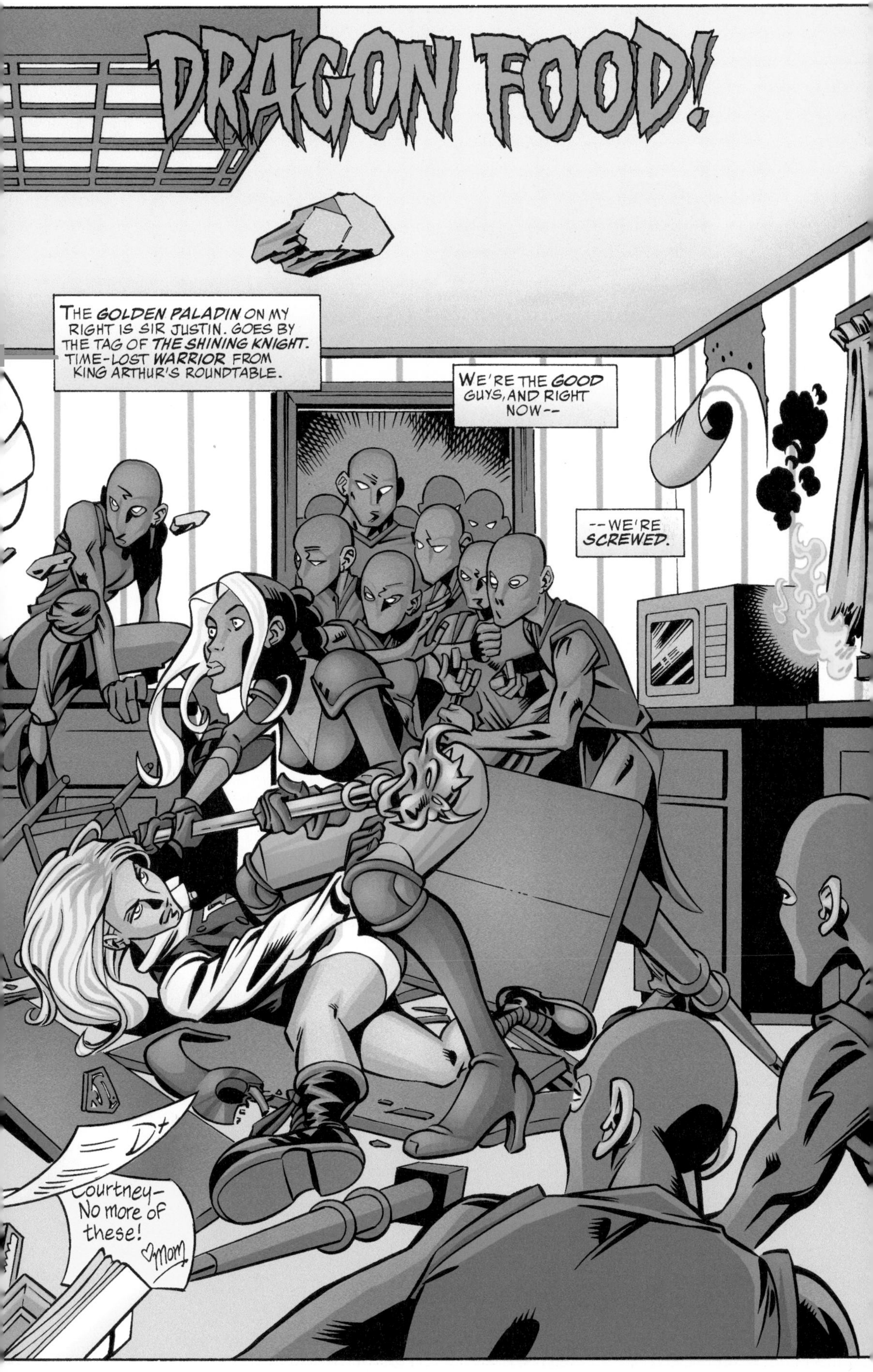
DRAGON FOOD!
THE GOLDEN PALADIN ON MY RIGHT IS SIR JUSTIN. GOES BY THE TAG OF THE SHINING KNIGHT. TIME-LOST WARRIOR FROM KING ARTHUR'S ROUNDTABLE.
WE'RE THE GOOD GUYS, AND RIGHT NOW--
--WE'RE SCREWED.
D+
Courtney-
No more of these!
♡Mom

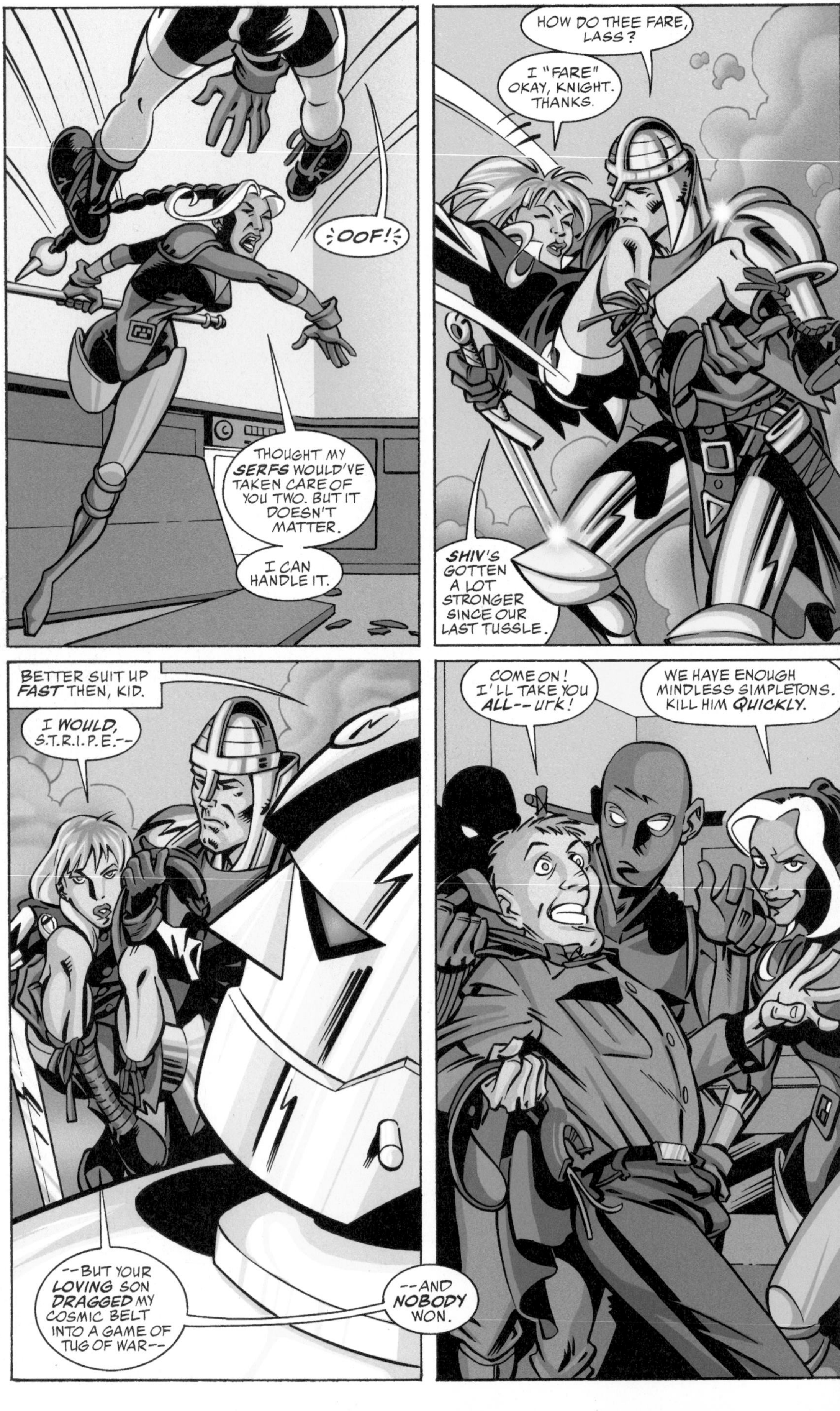

OOF!
THOUGHT MY SERFS WOULD'VE TAKEN CARE OF YOU TWO. BUT IT DOESN'T MATTER.
I CAN HANDLE IT.
HOW DO THEE FARE, LASS?
I "FARE" OKAY, KNIGHT. THANKS.
SHIV'S GOTTEN A LOT STRONGER SINCE OUR LAST TUSSLE.
BETTER SUIT UP FAST THEN, KID.
I WOULD, S.T.R.I.P.E.--
--BUT YOUR LOVING SON DRAGGED MY COSMIC BELT INTO A GAME OF TUG OF WAR--
--AND NOBODY WON.
COME ON! I'LL TAKE YOU ALL--urk!
WE HAVE ENOUGH MINDLESS SIMPLETONS. KILL HIM QUICKLY.

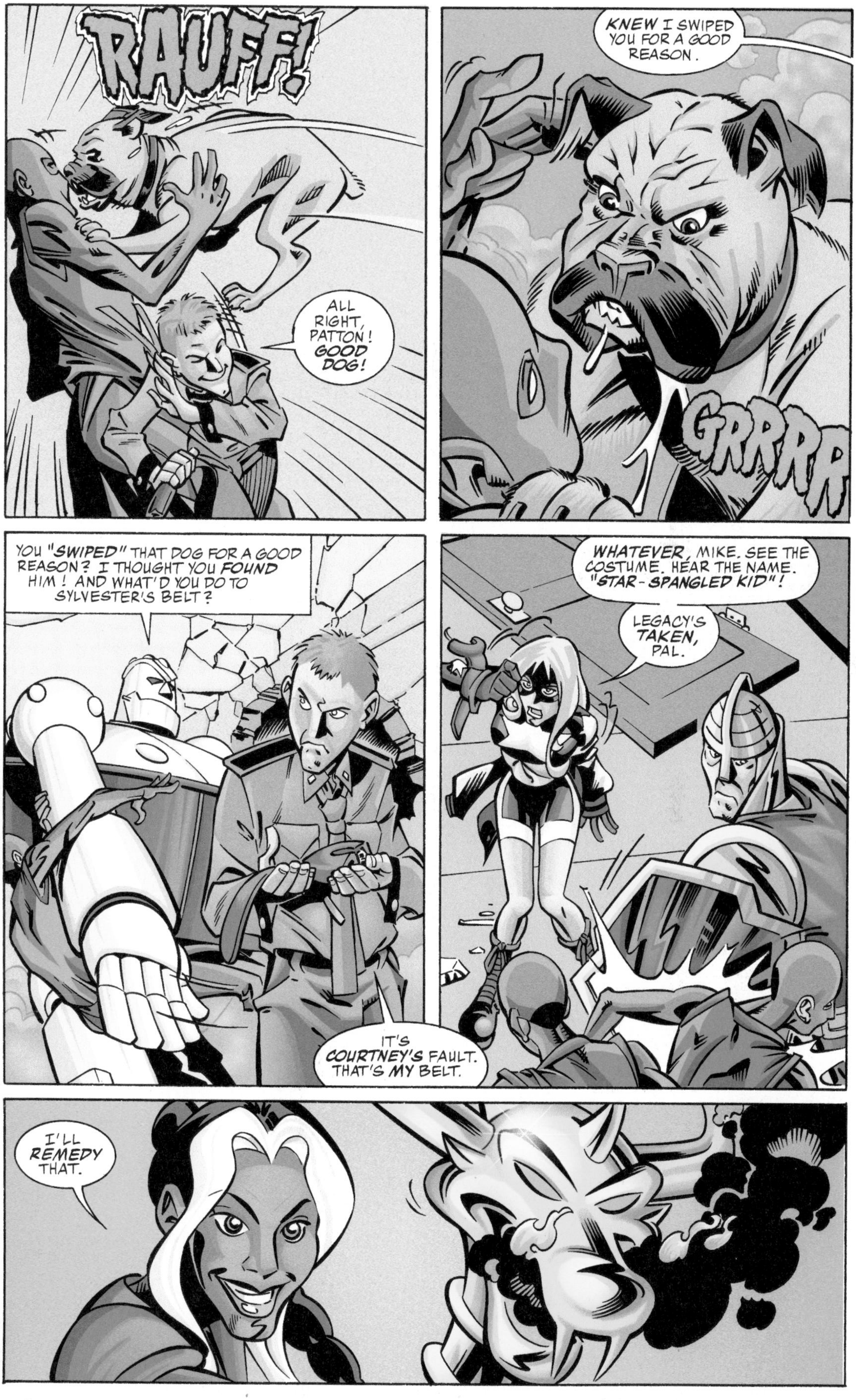
RAUFF!
ALL RIGHT, PATTON! GOOD DOG!
KNEW I SWIPED YOU FOR A GOOD REASON.
GRRRR
YOU "SWIPED" THAT DOG FOR A GOOD REASON? I THOUGHT YOU FOUND HIM! AND WHAT'D YOU DO TO SYLVESTER'S BELT?
IT'S COURTNEY'S FAULT. THAT'S MY BELT.
WHATEVER, MIKE. SEE THE COSTUME. HEAR THE NAME. "STAR-SPANGLED KID"!
LEGACY'S TAKEN, PAL.
I'LL REMEDY THAT.

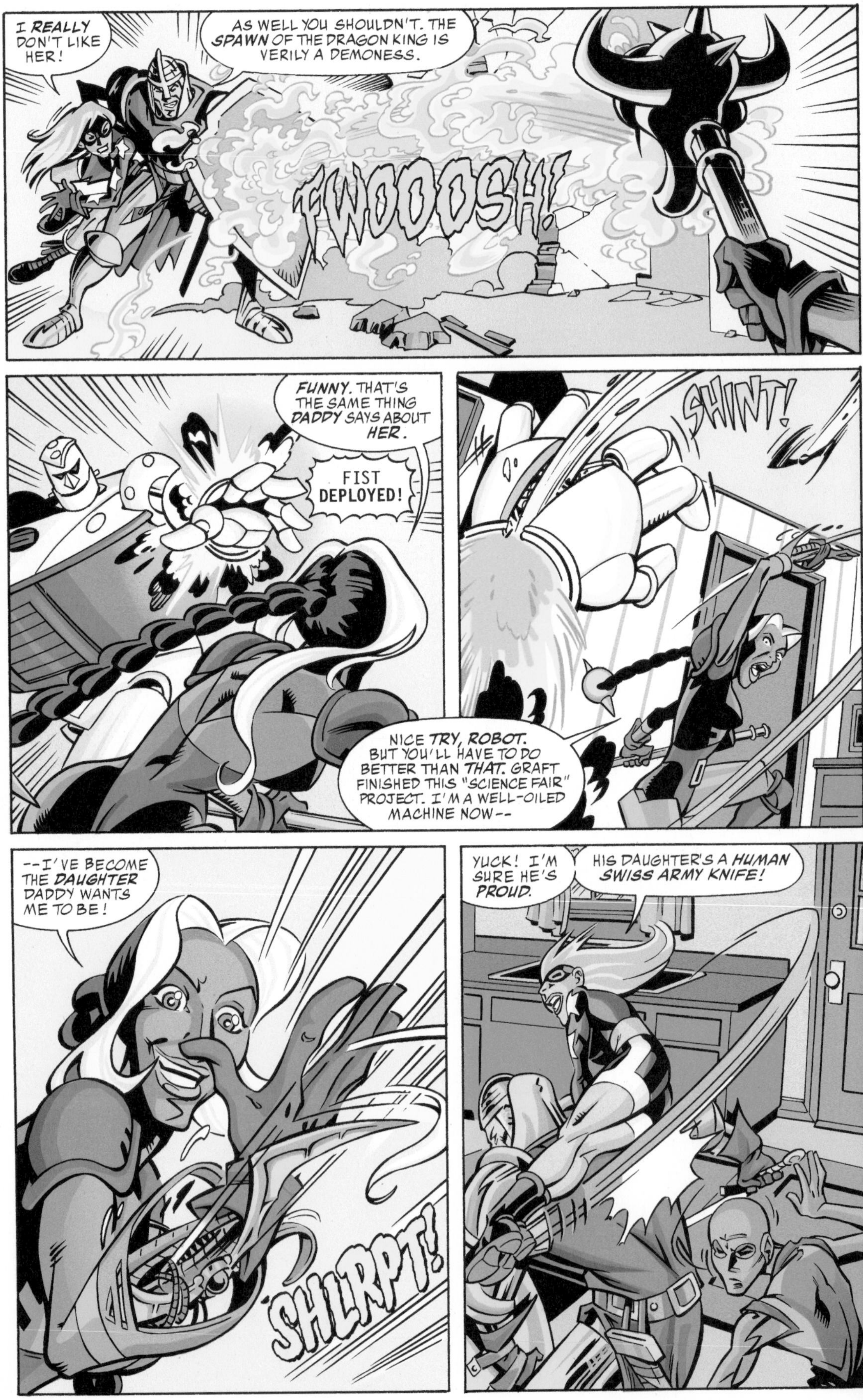

I REALLY DON'T LIKE HER!
AS WELL YOU SHOULDN'T. THE SPAWN OF THE DRAGON KING IS VERILY A DEMONESS.
FWOOOSH!
FUNNY. THAT'S THE SAME THING DADDY SAYS ABOUT HER.
FIST DEPLOYED!
SHINT!
NICE TRY, ROBOT. BUT YOU'LL HAVE TO DO BETTER THAN THAT. GRAFT FINISHED THIS "SCIENCE FAIR" PROJECT. I'M A WELL-OILED MACHINE NOW--
--I'VE BECOME THE DAUGHTER DADDY WANTS ME TO BE!
SHLRPT!
YUCK! I'M SURE HE'S PROUD.
HIS DAUGHTER'S A HUMAN SWISS ARMY KNIFE!

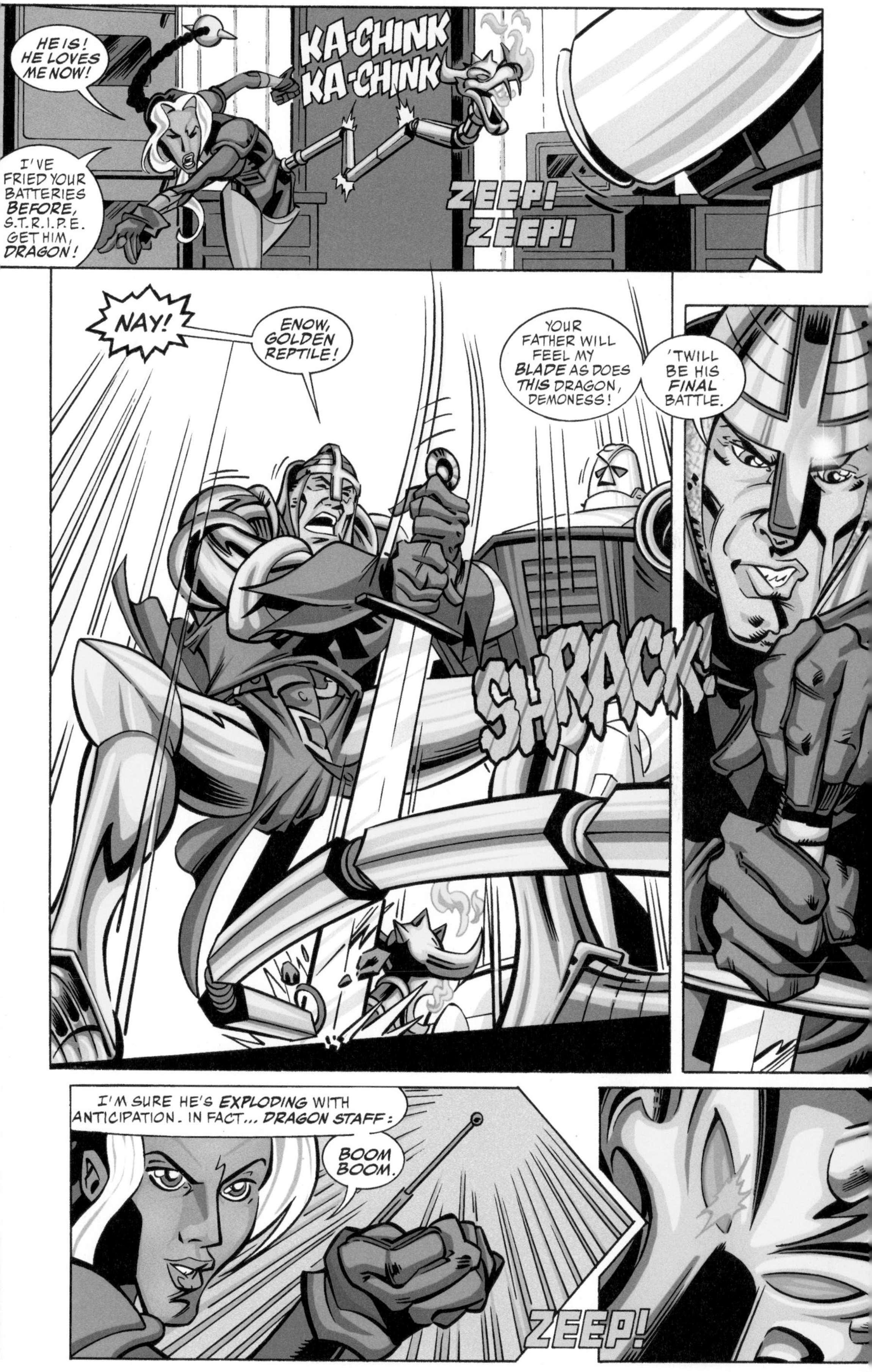
HE IS! HE LOVES ME NOW!
I'VE FRIED YOUR BATTERIES BEFORE, S.T.R.I.P.E. GET HIM, DRAGON!
KA-CHINK KA-CHINK
ZEEP! ZEEP!
NAY!
ENOW, GOLDEN REPTILE!
YOUR FATHER WILL FEEL MY BLADE AS DOES THIS DRAGON, DEMONESS!
'TWILL BE HIS FINAL BATTLE.
SHRACK!
I'M SURE HE'S EXPLODING WITH ANTICIPATION. IN FACT... DRAGON STAFF:
BOOM BOOM.
ZEEP!

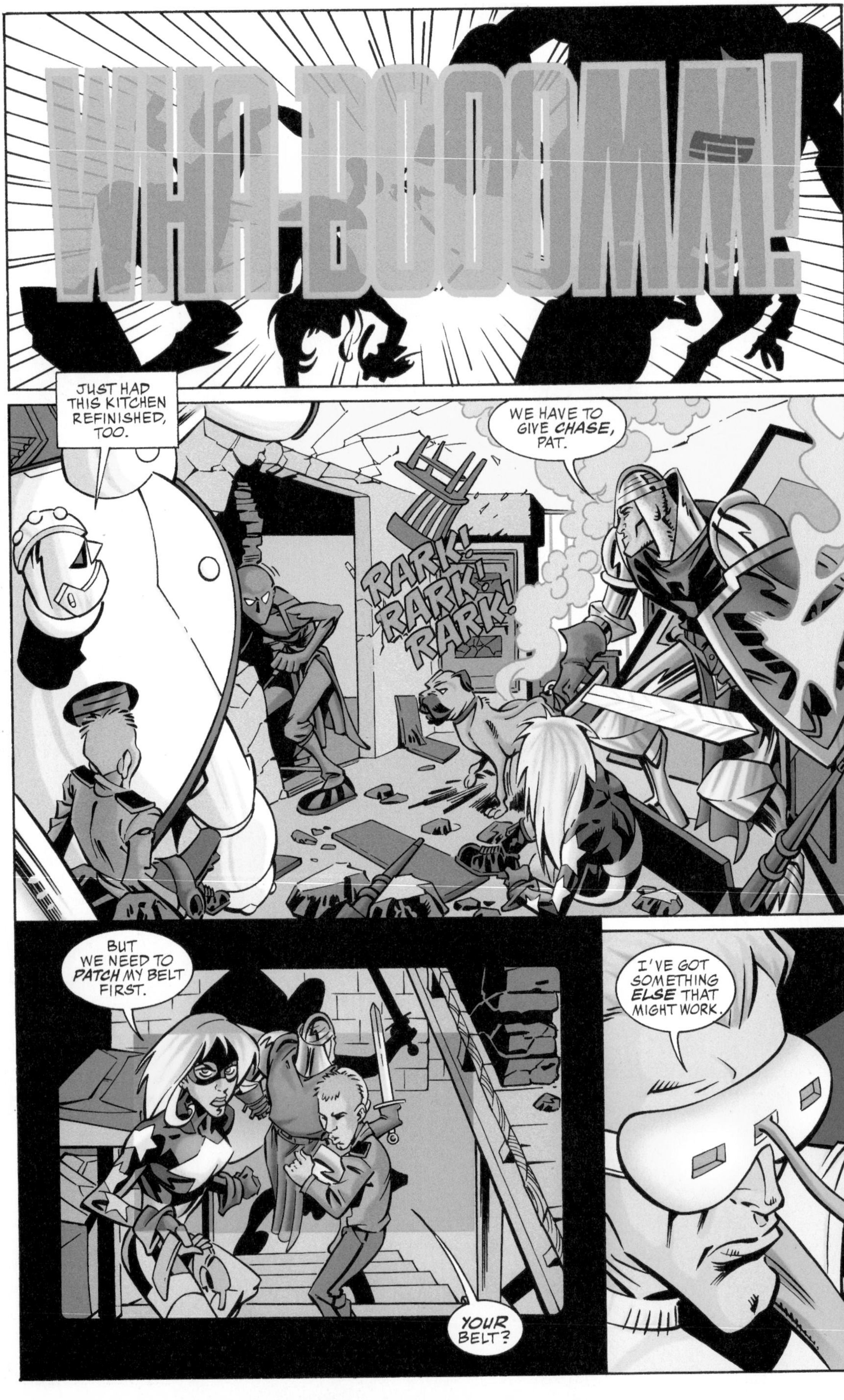
WHA-BOOOMM!
JUST HAD THIS KITCHEN REFINISHED, TOO.
WE HAVE TO GIVE CHASE, PAT.
RARK! RARK! RARK!
BUT WE NEED TO PATCH MY BELT FIRST.
YOUR BELT?
I'VE GOT SOMETHING ELSE THAT MIGHT WORK.

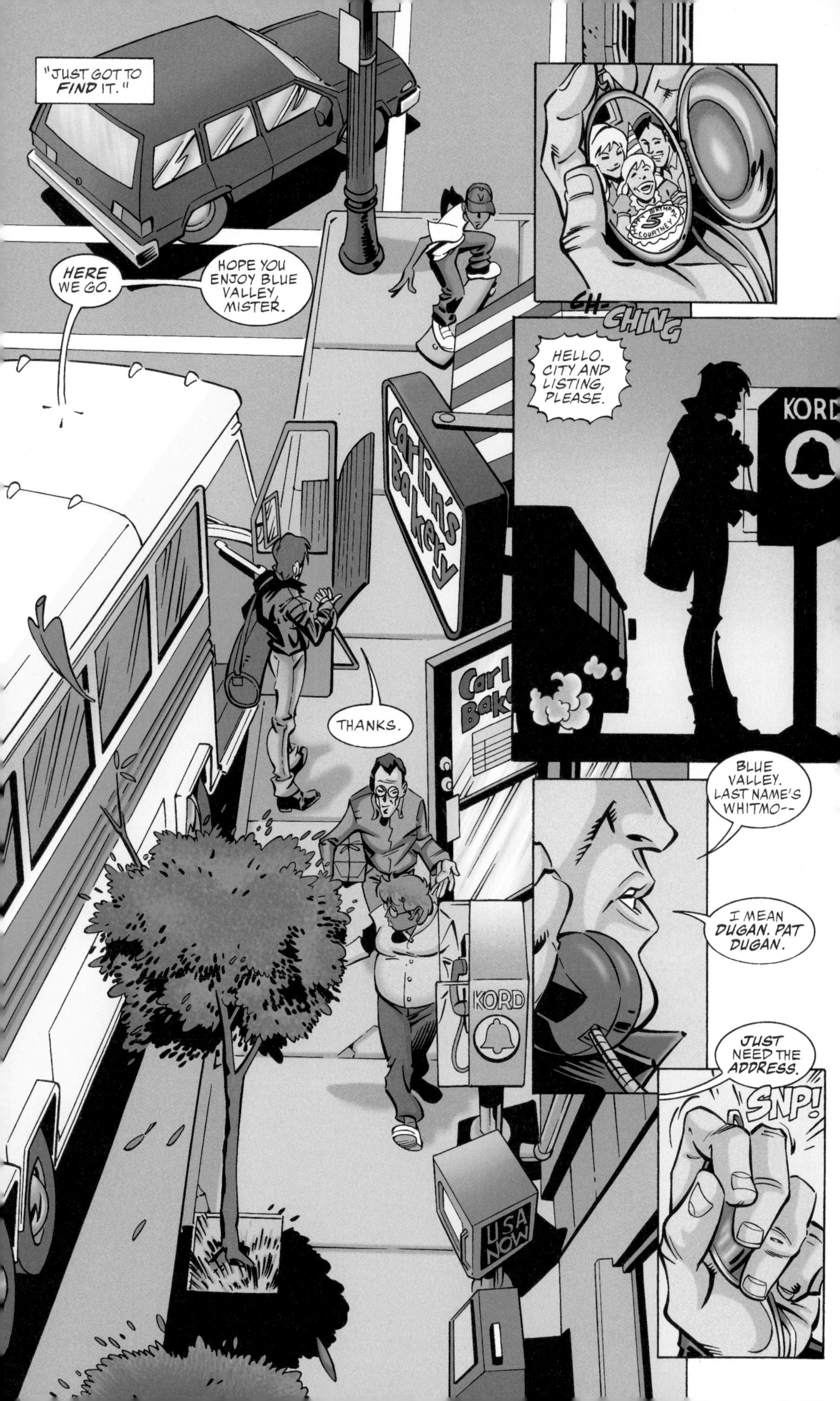

"JUST GOT TO FIND IT."
HERE WE GO.
HOPE YOU ENJOY BLUE VALLEY, MISTER.
THANKS.
HAPPY BIRTHDAY 5 COURTNEY
CH-CHING
HELLO. CITY AND LISTING, PLEASE.
KORD
BLUE VALLEY. LAST NAME'S WHITMO--
I MEAN DUGAN. PAT DUGAN.
JUST NEED THE ADDRESS.
SNP!
Carlin's Bakery
USA NOW

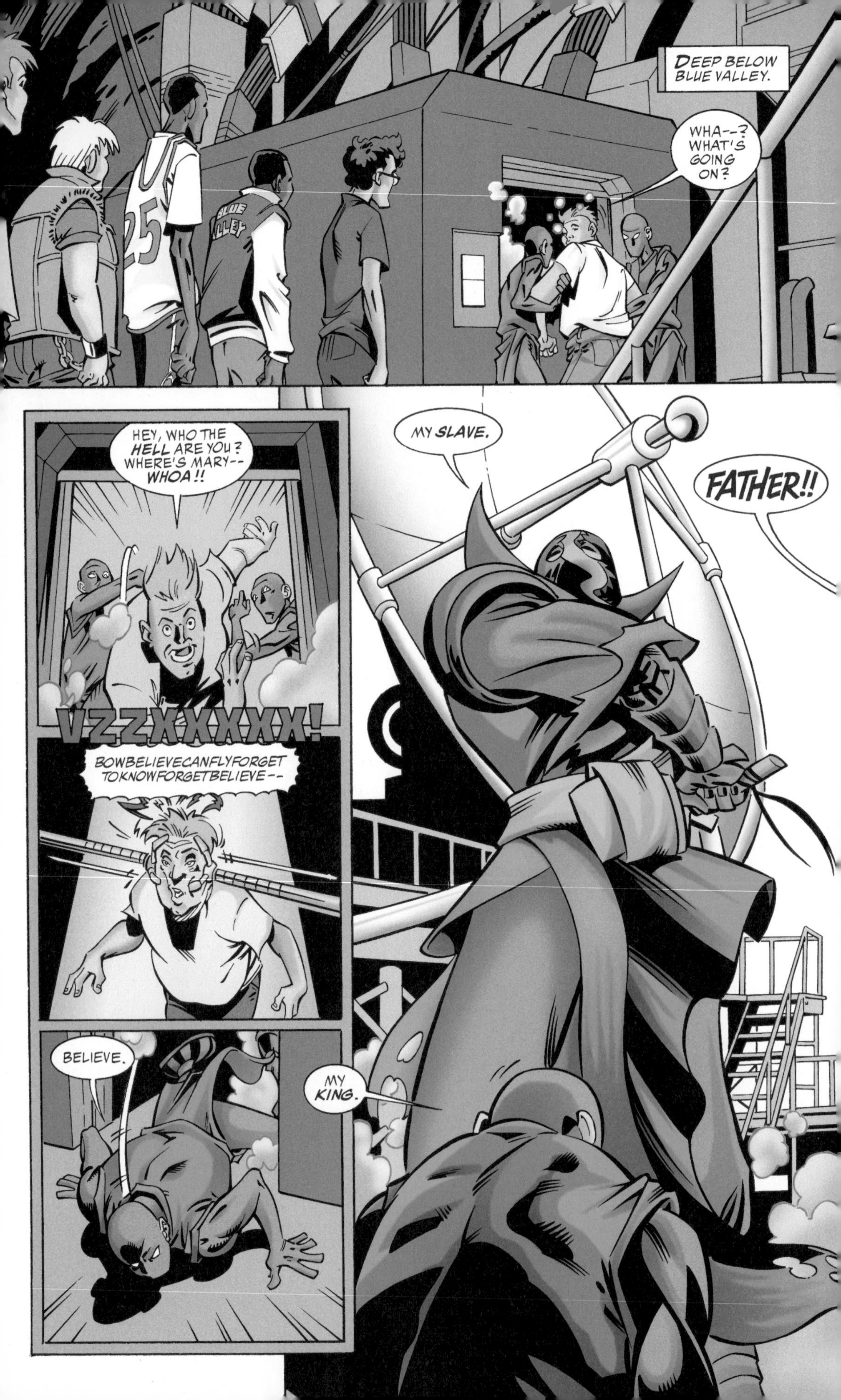
DEEP BELOW BLUE VALLEY.
WHA--? WHAT'S GOING ON?
25
BLUE VALLEY
HEY, WHO THE HELL ARE YOU? WHERE'S MARY-- WHOA!!
VZZXXXXXX!
BOWBELIEVECANFLYFORGET TOKNOWFORGETBELIEVE--
BELIEVE.
MY SLAVE.
FATHER!!
MY KING.

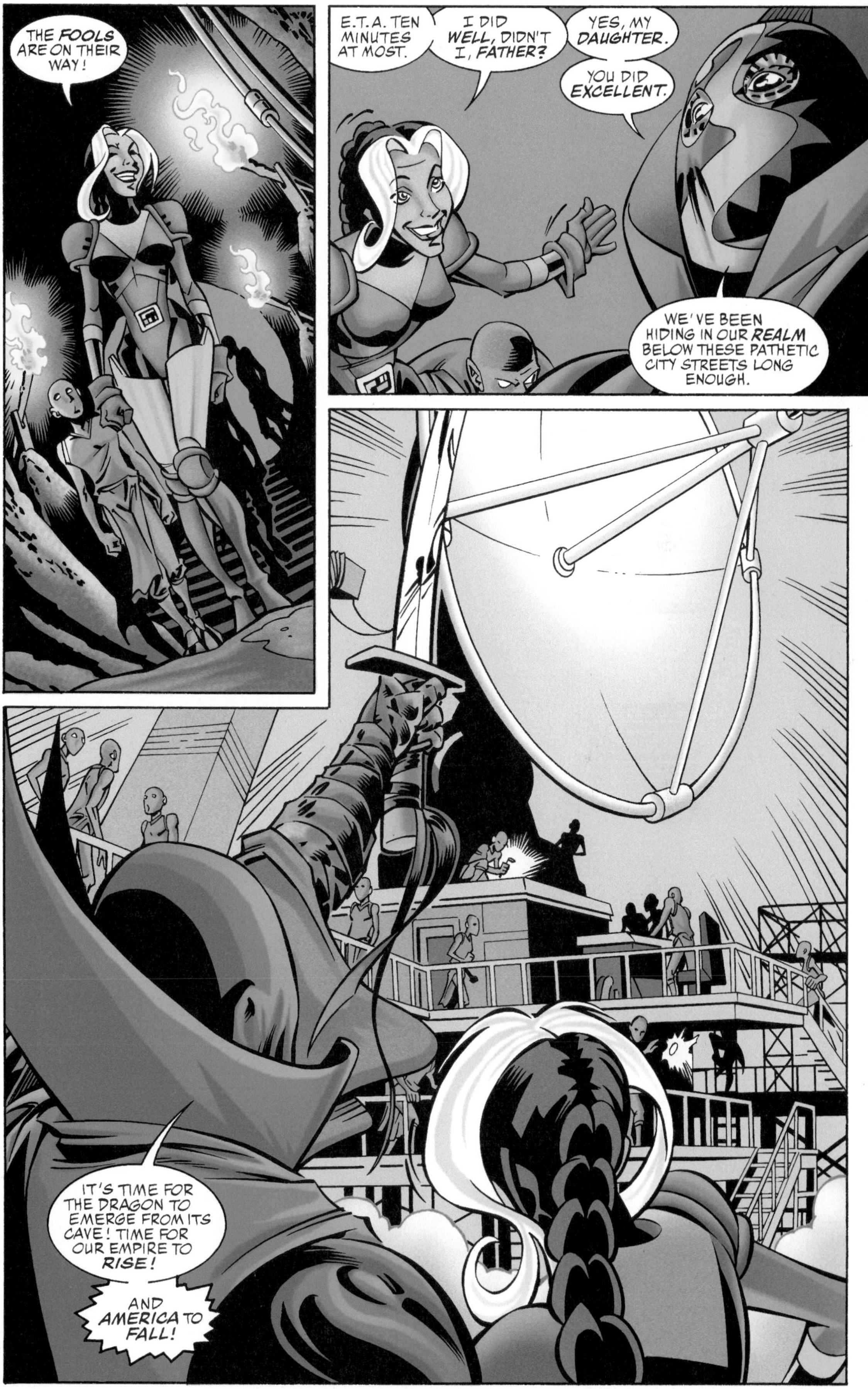
THE FOOLS ARE ON THEIR WAY!
E.T.A. TEN MINUTES AT MOST.
I DID WELL, DIDN'T I, FATHER?
YES, MY DAUGHTER.
YOU DID EXCELLENT.
WE'VE BEEN HIDING IN OUR REALM BELOW THESE PATHETIC CITY STREETS LONG ENOUGH.
IT'S TIME FOR THE DRAGON TO EMERGE FROM ITS CAVE! TIME FOR OUR EMPIRE TO RISE!
AND AMERICA TO FALL!

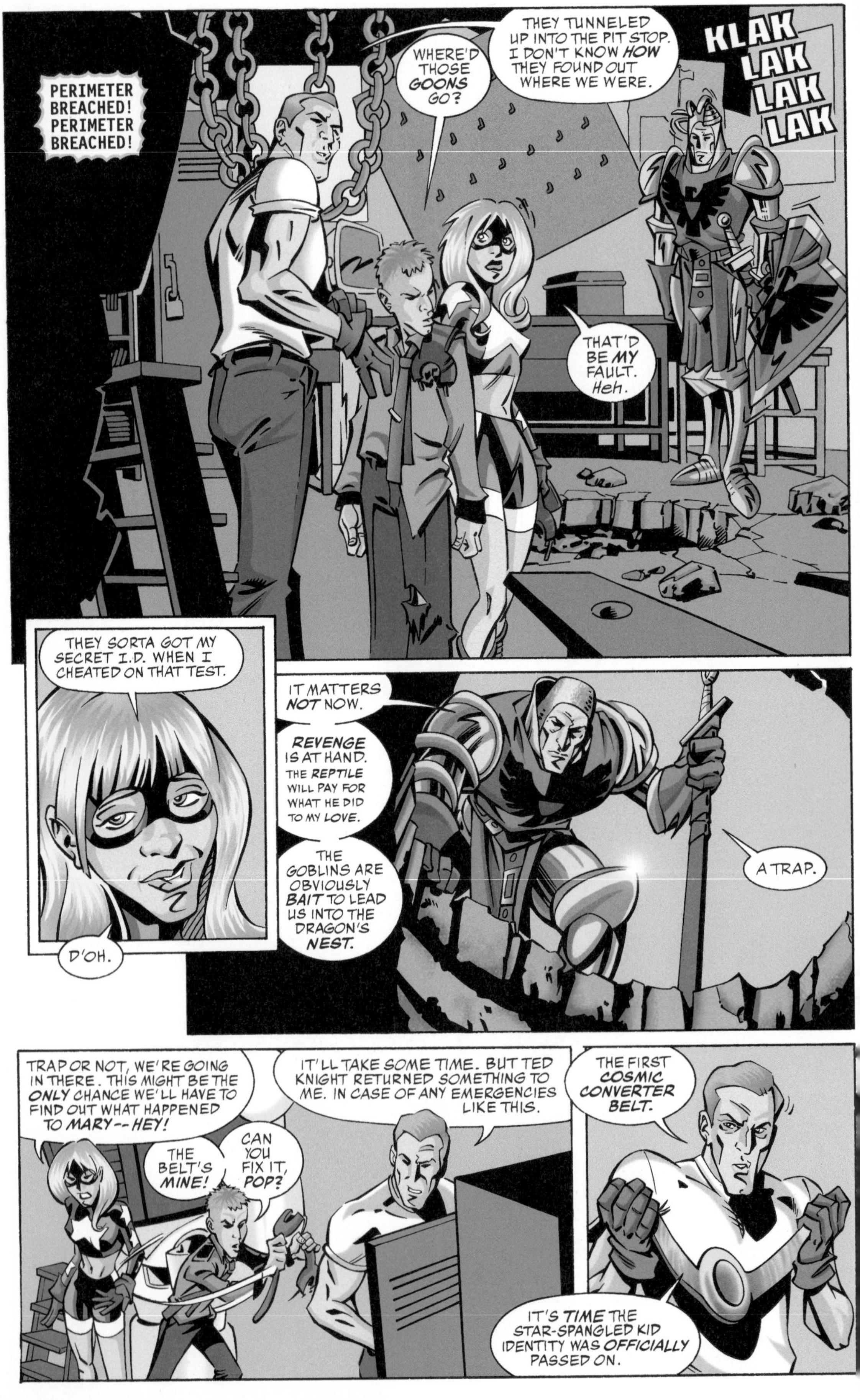

PERIMETER BREACHED! PERIMETER BREACHED!
WHERE'D THOSE GOONS GO?
THEY TUNNELED UP INTO THE PIT STOP. I DON'T KNOW HOW THEY FOUND OUT WHERE WE WERE.
KLAK LAK LAK LAK
THAT'D BE MY FAULT. Heh.
THEY SORTA GOT MY SECRET I.D. WHEN I CHEATED ON THAT TEST.
D'OH.
IT MATTERS NOT NOW.
REVENGE IS AT HAND. THE REPTILE WILL PAY FOR WHAT HE DID TO MY LOVE.
THE GOBLINS ARE OBVIOUSLY BAIT TO LEAD US INTO THE DRAGON'S NEST.
A TRAP.
TRAP OR NOT, WE'RE GOING IN THERE. THIS MIGHT BE THE ONLY CHANCE WE'LL HAVE TO FIND OUT WHAT HAPPENED TO MARY-- HEY!
THE BELT'S MINE!
CAN YOU FIX IT, POP?
IT'LL TAKE SOME TIME. BUT TED KNIGHT RETURNED SOMETHING TO ME. IN CASE OF ANY EMERGENCIES LIKE THIS.
THE FIRST COSMIC CONVERTER BELT.
IT'S TIME THE STAR-SPANGLED KID IDENTITY WAS OFFICIALLY PASSED ON.

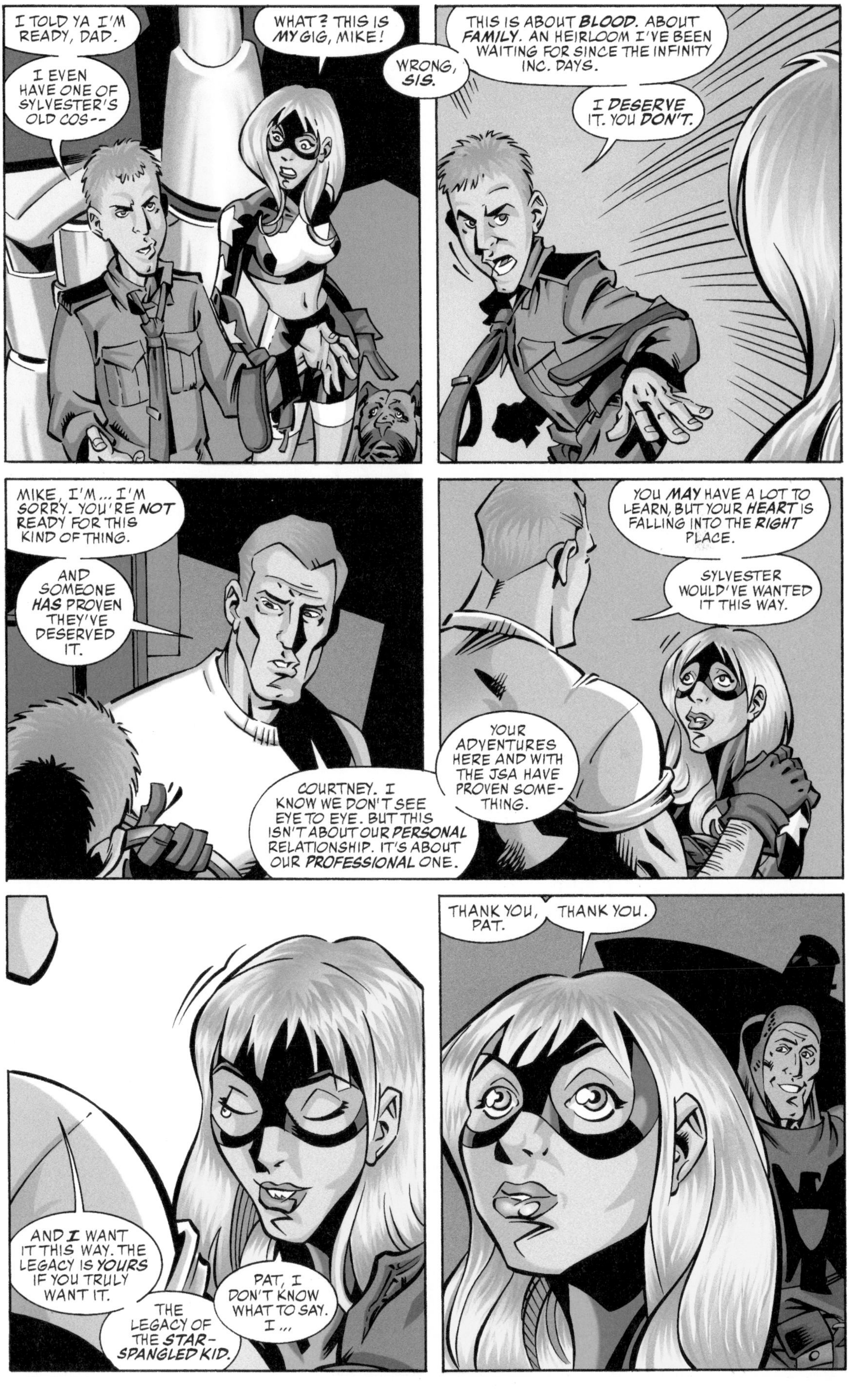

I TOLD YA I'M READY, DAD.
I EVEN HAVE ONE OF SYLVESTER'S OLD COS--
WHAT? THIS IS MY GIG, MIKE!
WRONG, SIS.
THIS IS ABOUT BLOOD. ABOUT FAMILY. AN HEIRLOOM I'VE BEEN WAITING FOR SINCE THE INFINITY INC. DAYS.
I DESERVE IT. YOU DON'T.
MIKE, I'M... I'M SORRY. YOU'RE NOT READY FOR THIS KIND OF THING.
AND SOMEONE HAS PROVEN THEY'VE DESERVED IT.
COURTNEY. I KNOW WE DON'T SEE EYE TO EYE. BUT THIS ISN'T ABOUT OUR PERSONAL RELATIONSHIP. IT'S ABOUT OUR PROFESSIONAL ONE.
YOUR ADVENTURES HERE AND WITH THE JSA HAVE PROVEN SOMETHING.
YOU MAY HAVE A LOT TO LEARN, BUT YOUR HEART IS FALLING INTO THE RIGHT PLACE.
SYLVESTER WOULD'VE WANTED IT THIS WAY.
AND I WANT IT THIS WAY. THE LEGACY IS YOURS IF YOU TRULY WANT IT.
THE LEGACY OF THE STAR-SPANGLED KID.
PAT, I DON'T KNOW WHAT TO SAY. I...
THANK YOU, PAT.
THANK YOU.

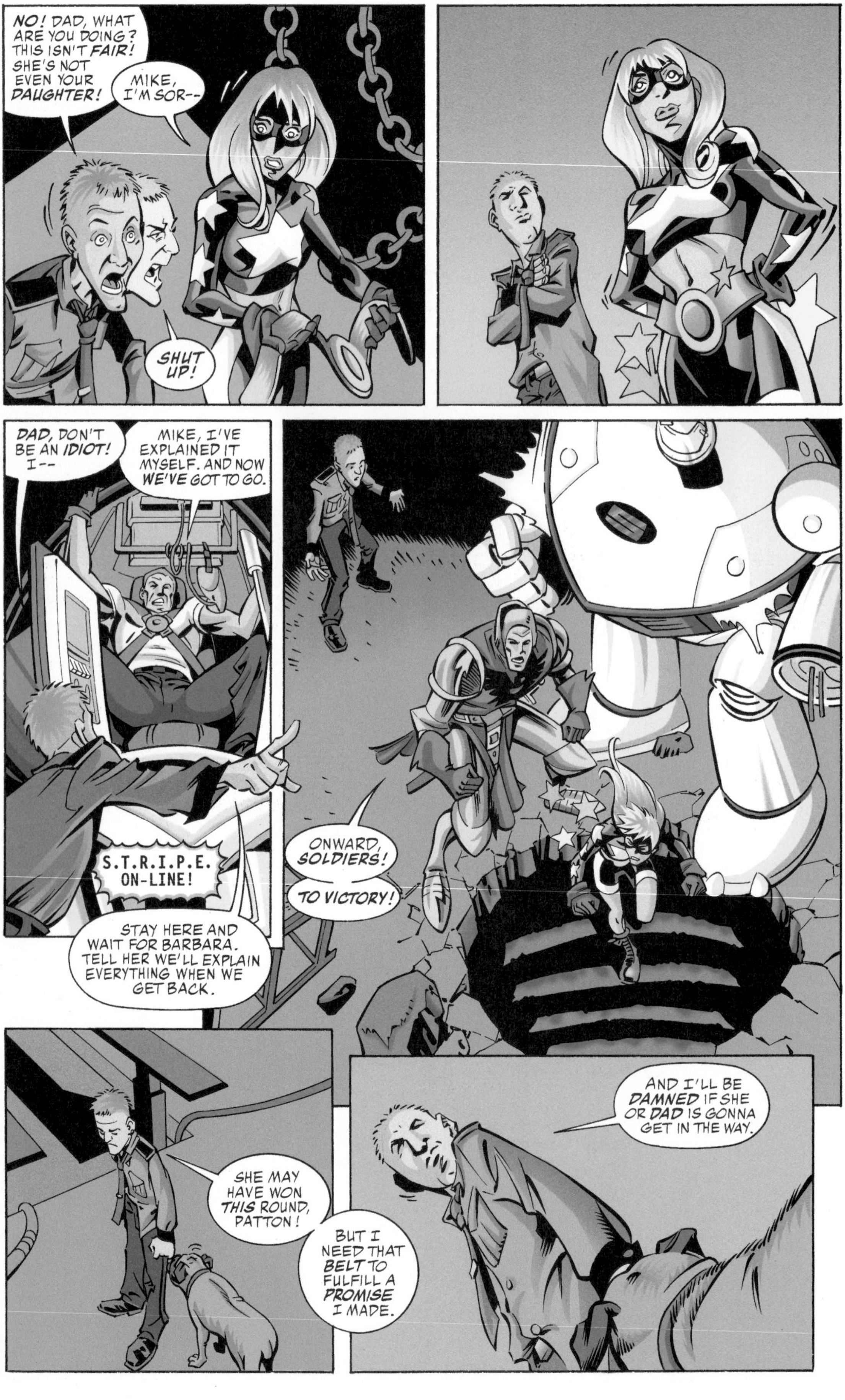

NO! DAD, WHAT ARE YOU DOING? THIS ISN'T FAIR! SHE'S NOT EVEN YOUR DAUGHTER!
MIKE, I'M SOR--
SHUT UP!
DAD, DON'T BE AN IDIOT! I--
MIKE, I'VE EXPLAINED IT MYSELF. AND NOW WE'VE GOT TO GO.
S.T.R.I.P.E. ON-LINE!
STAY HERE AND WAIT FOR BARBARA. TELL HER WE'LL EXPLAIN EVERYTHING WHEN WE GET BACK.
ONWARD, SOLDIERS!
TO VICTORY!
SHE MAY HAVE WON THIS ROUND, PATTON!
BUT I NEED THAT BELT TO FULFILL A PROMISE I MADE.
AND I'LL BE DAMNED IF SHE OR DAD IS GONNA GET IN THE WAY.

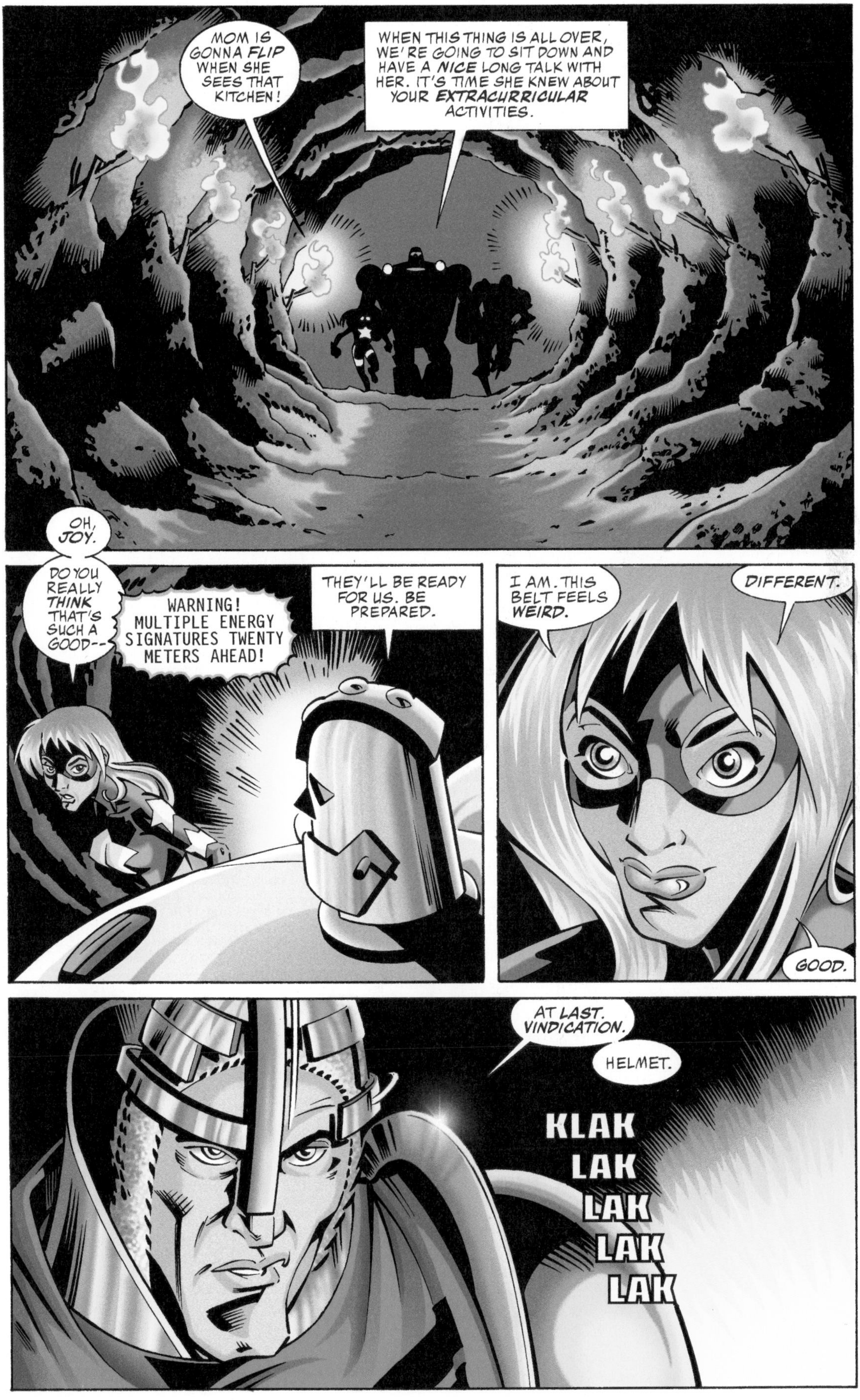
MOM IS GONNA FLIP WHEN SHE SEES THAT KITCHEN!
WHEN THIS THING IS ALL OVER, WE'RE GOING TO SIT DOWN AND HAVE A NICE LONG TALK WITH HER. IT'S TIME SHE KNEW ABOUT YOUR EXTRACURRICULAR ACTIVITIES.
OH, JOY.
DO YOU REALLY THINK THAT'S SUCH A GOOD--
WARNING! MULTIPLE ENERGY SIGNATURES TWENTY METERS AHEAD!
THEY'LL BE READY FOR US. BE PREPARED.
I AM. THIS BELT FEELS WEIRD.
DIFFERENT.
GOOD.
AT LAST. VINDICATION.
HELMET.
KLAK
LAK
LAK
LAK
LAK

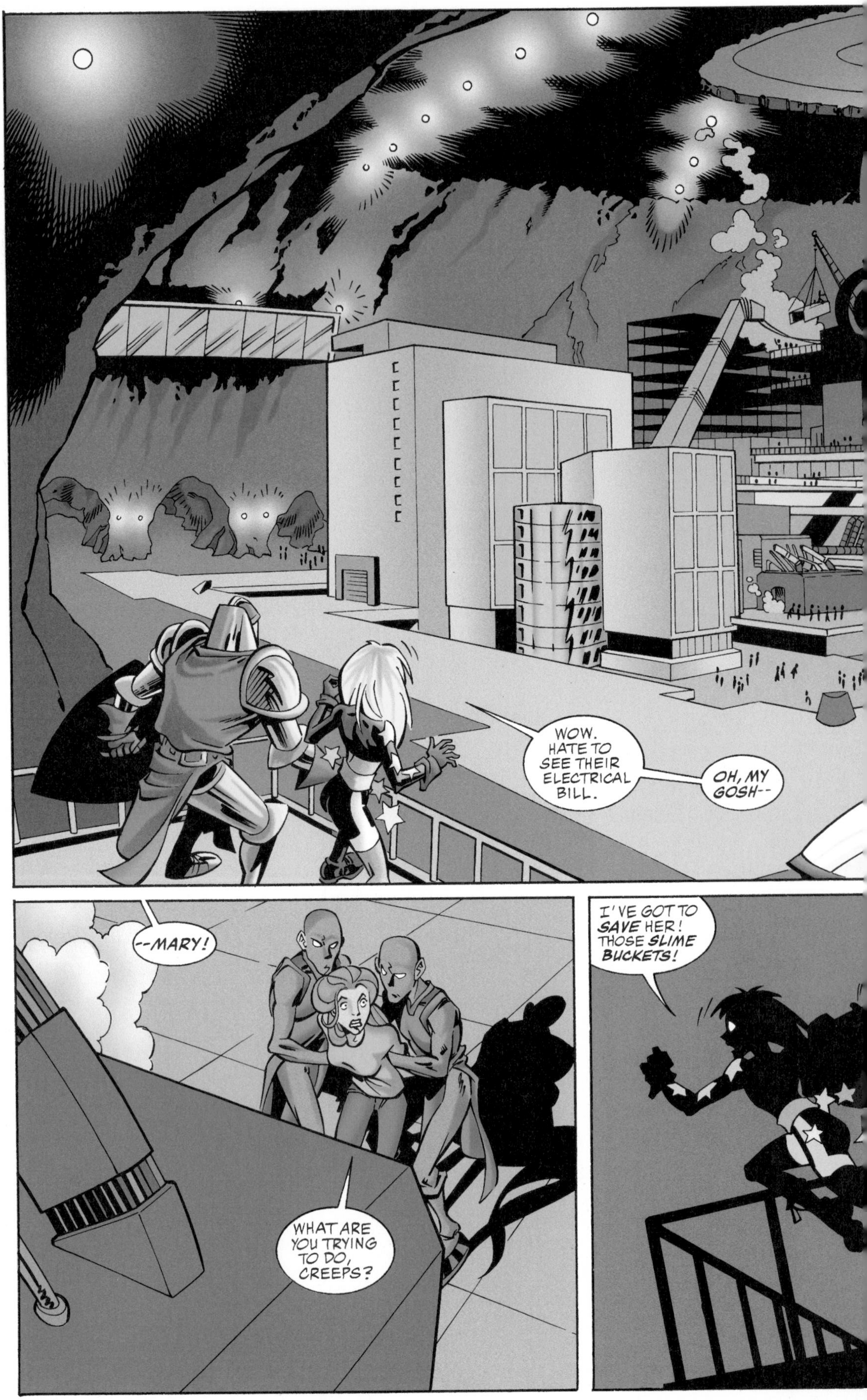
WOW. HATE TO SEE THEIR ELECTRICAL BILL.
OH, MY GOSH--
--MARY!
WHAT ARE YOU TRYING TO DO, CREEPS?
I'VE GOT TO SAVE HER! THOSE SLIME BUCKETS!

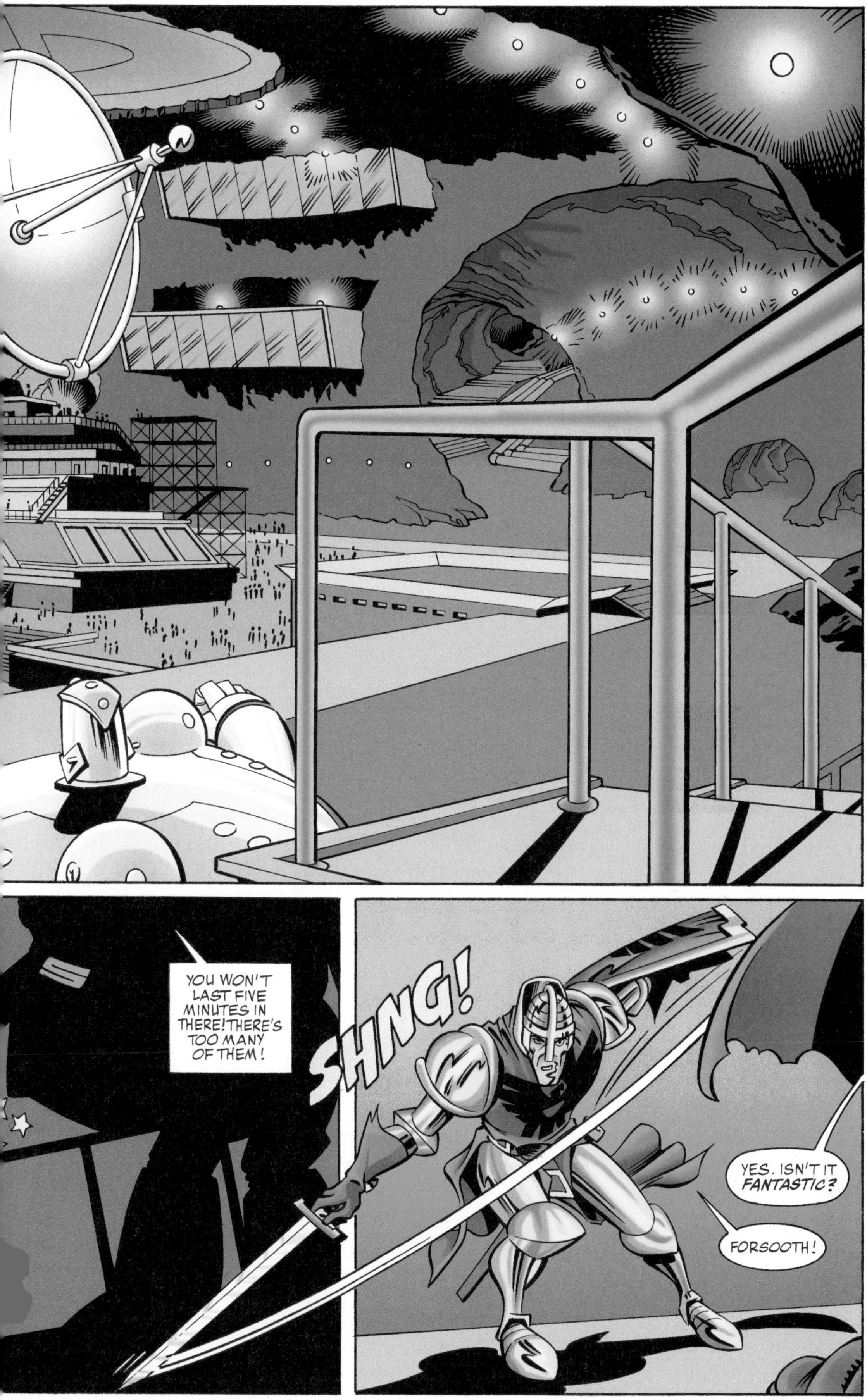
YOU WON'T LAST FIVE MINUTES IN THERE! THERE'S TOO MANY OF THEM!
SHNG!
YES. ISN'T IT FANTASTIC?
FORSOOTH!

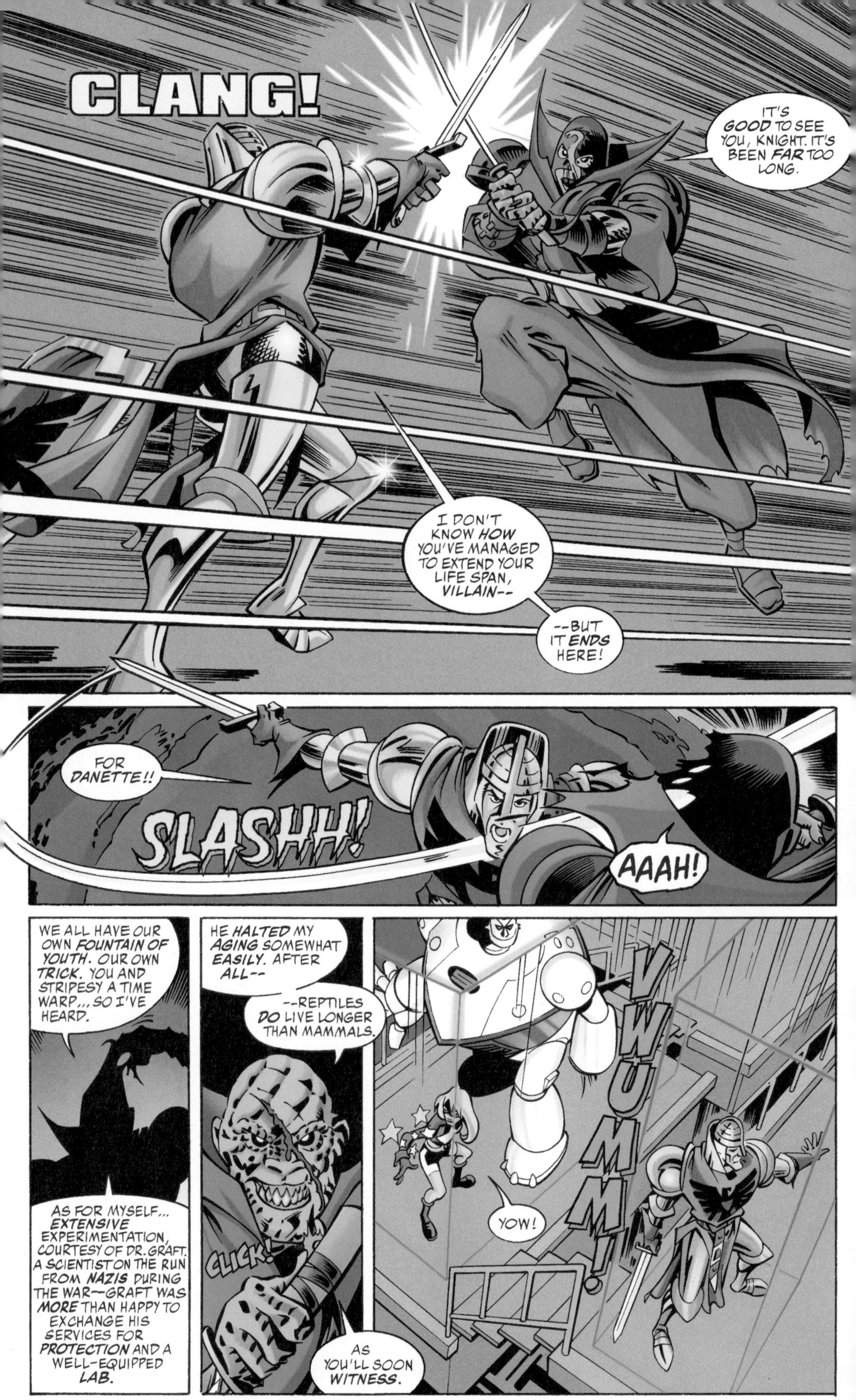
CLANG!
IT'S GOOD TO SEE YOU, KNIGHT. IT'S BEEN FAR TOO LONG.
I DON'T KNOW HOW YOU'VE MANAGED TO EXTEND YOUR LIFE SPAN, VILLAIN--
--BUT IT ENDS HERE!
FOR DANETTE!!
SLASHH!
AAAH!
WE ALL HAVE OUR OWN FOUNTAIN OF YOUTH. OUR OWN TRICK. YOU AND STRIPESY A TIME WARP... SO I'VE HEARD.
AS FOR MYSELF... EXTENSIVE EXPERIMENTATION, COURTESY OF DR. GRAFT. A SCIENTIST ON THE RUN FROM NAZIS DURING THE WAR--GRAFT WAS MORE THAN HAPPY TO EXCHANGE HIS SERVICES FOR PROTECTION AND A WELL-EQUIPPED LAB.
HE HALTED MY AGING SOMEWHAT EASILY. AFTER ALL--
--REPTILES DO LIVE LONGER THAN MAMMALS.
CLICK!
AS YOU'LL SOON WITNESS.
VWUMMM!
YOW!

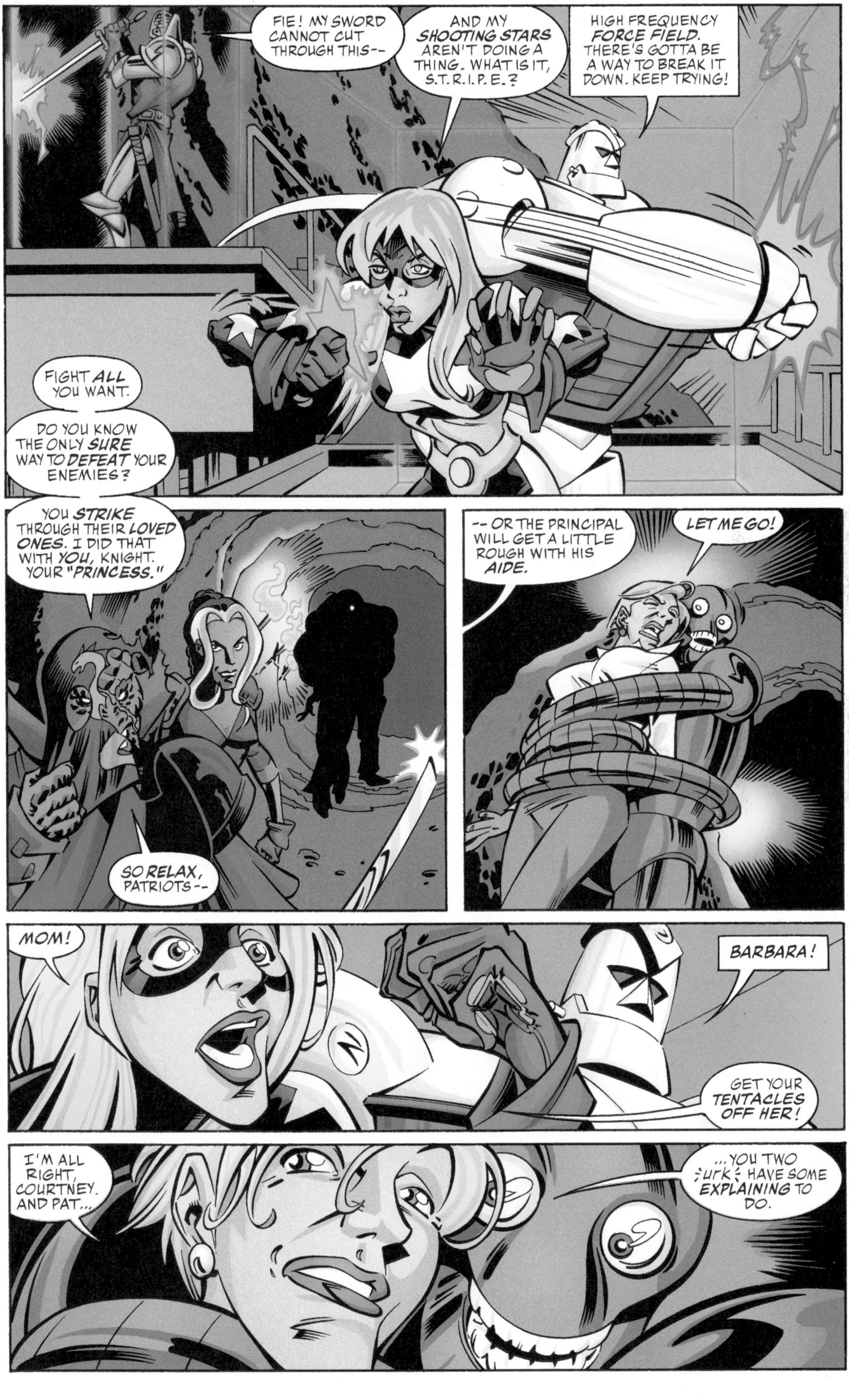

FIE! MY SWORD CANNOT CUT THROUGH THIS--
AND MY SHOOTING STARS AREN'T DOING A THING. WHAT IS IT, S.T.R.I.P.E.?
HIGH FREQUENCY FORCE FIELD. THERE'S GOTTA BE A WAY TO BREAK IT DOWN. KEEP TRYING!
FIGHT ALL YOU WANT.
DO YOU KNOW THE ONLY SURE WAY TO DEFEAT YOUR ENEMIES?
YOU STRIKE THROUGH THEIR LOVED ONES. I DID THAT WITH YOU, KNIGHT. YOUR "PRINCESS."
SO RELAX, PATRIOTS--
--OR THE PRINCIPAL WILL GET A LITTLE ROUGH WITH HIS AIDE.
LET ME GO!
MOM!
BARBARA!
GET YOUR TENTACLES OFF HER!
I'M ALL RIGHT, COURTNEY. AND PAT...
...YOU TWO *urk* HAVE SOME EXPLAINING TO DO.

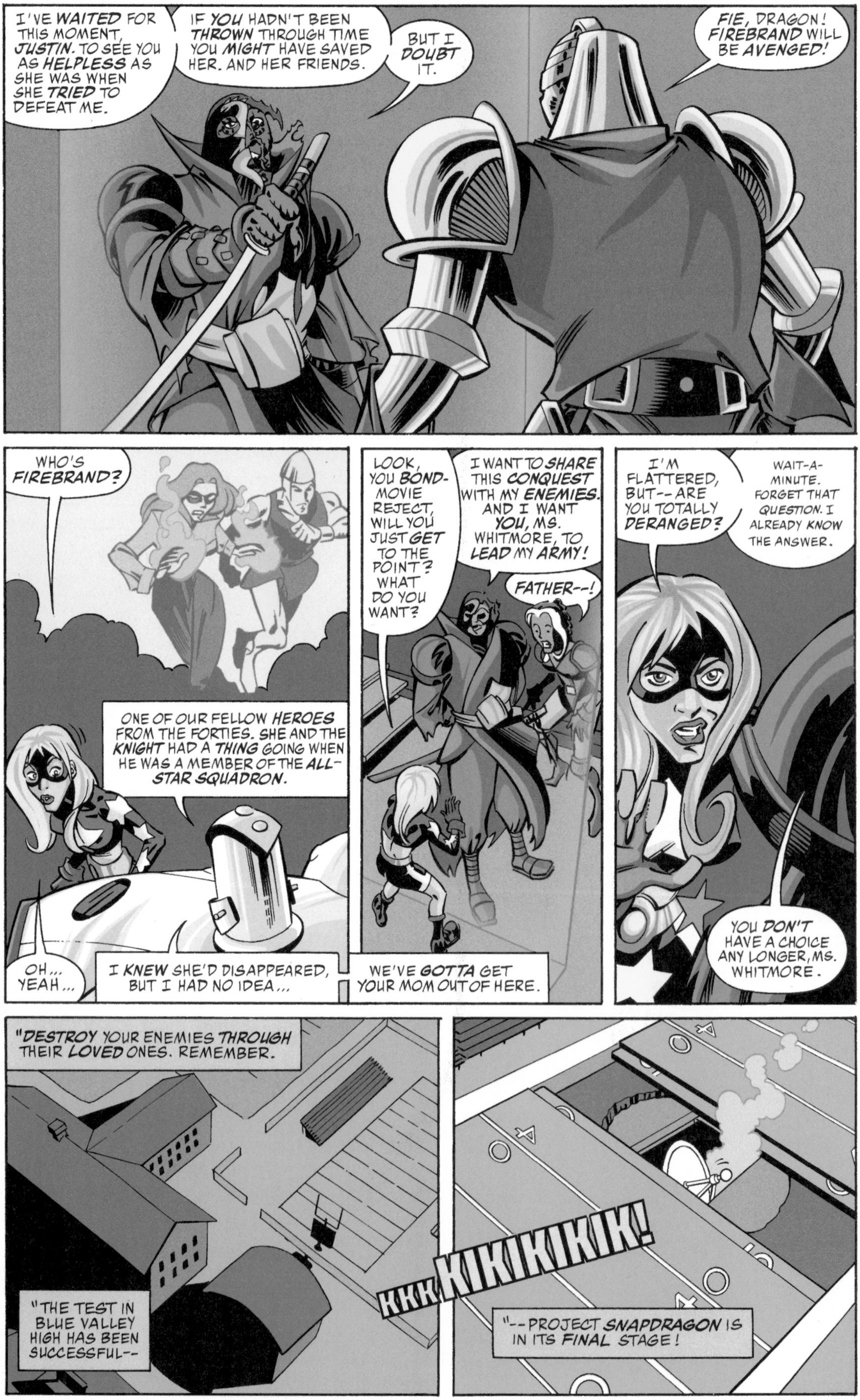
I'VE WAITED FOR THIS MOMENT, JUSTIN. TO SEE YOU AS HELPLESS AS SHE WAS WHEN SHE TRIED TO DEFEAT ME.
IF YOU HADN'T BEEN THROWN THROUGH TIME YOU MIGHT HAVE SAVED HER. AND HER FRIENDS.
BUT I DOUBT IT.
FIE, DRAGON! FIREBRAND WILL BE AVENGED!
WHO'S FIREBRAND?
ONE OF OUR FELLOW HEROES FROM THE FORTIES. SHE AND THE KNIGHT HAD A THING GOING WHEN HE WAS A MEMBER OF THE ALL-STAR SQUADRON.
OH... YEAH...
I KNEW SHE'D DISAPPEARED, BUT I HAD NO IDEA...
LOOK, YOU BOND-MOVIE REJECT, WILL YOU JUST GET TO THE POINT? WHAT DO YOU WANT?
I WANT TO SHARE THIS CONQUEST WITH MY ENEMIES. AND I WANT YOU, MS. WHITMORE, TO LEAD MY ARMY!
FATHER--!
WE'VE GOTTA GET YOUR MOM OUT OF HERE.
I'M FLATTERED, BUT--ARE YOU TOTALLY DERANGED?
WAIT-A-MINUTE. FORGET THAT QUESTION. I ALREADY KNOW THE ANSWER.
YOU DON'T HAVE A CHOICE ANY LONGER, MS. WHITMORE.
"DESTROY YOUR ENEMIES THROUGH THEIR LOVED ONES. REMEMBER.
"THE TEST IN BLUE VALLEY HIGH HAS BEEN SUCCESSFUL--
KKKKIKIKIKIKIK!
"--PROJECT SNAPDRAGON IS IN ITS FINAL STAGE!

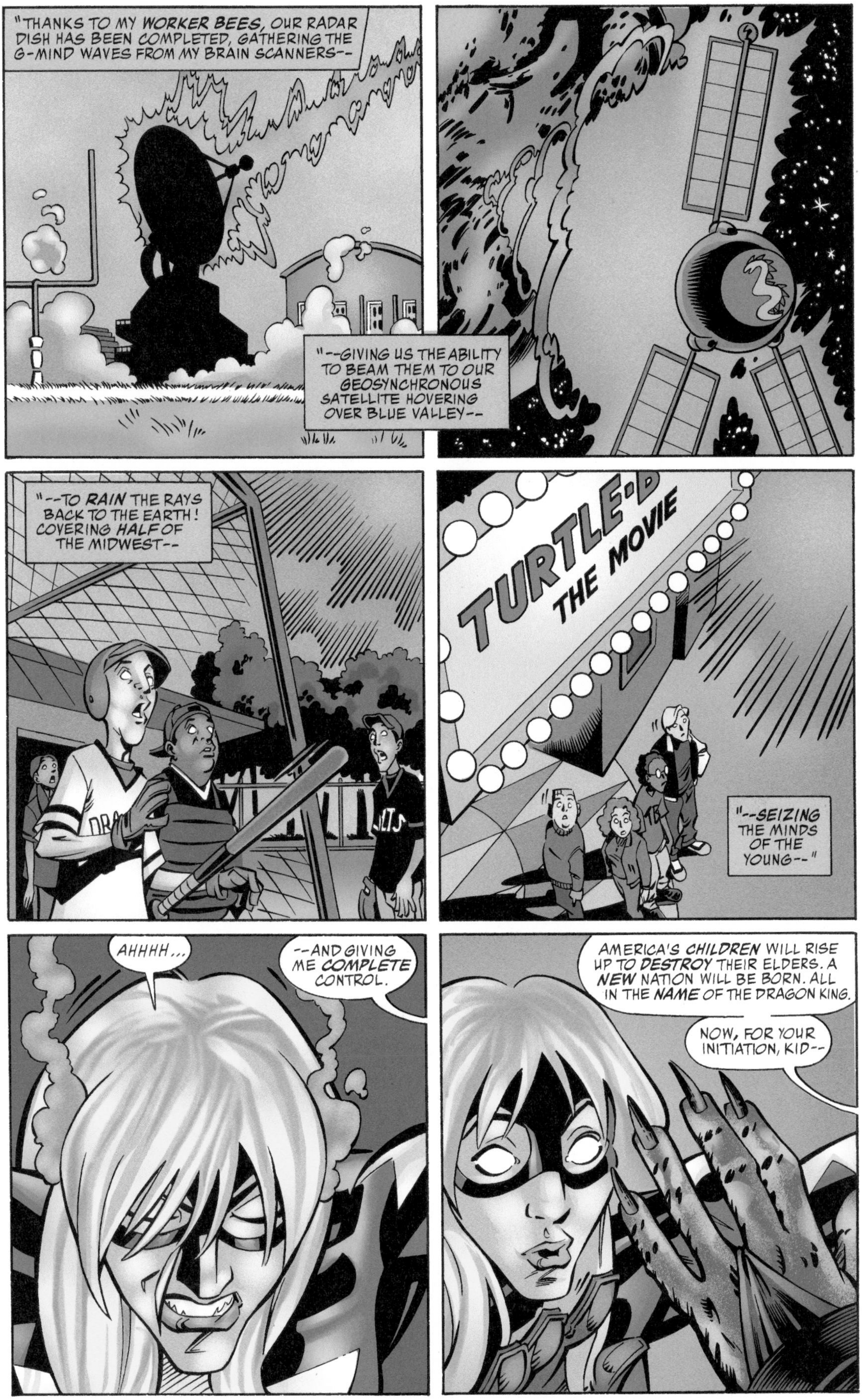
"THANKS TO MY WORKER BEES, OUR RADAR DISH HAS BEEN COMPLETED, GATHERING THE G-MIND WAVES FROM MY BRAIN SCANNERS--
"--GIVING US THE ABILITY TO BEAM THEM TO OUR GEOSYNCHRONOUS SATELLITE HOVERING OVER BLUE VALLEY--
"--TO RAIN THE RAYS BACK TO THE EARTH! COVERING HALF OF THE MIDWEST--
TURTLE-D THE MOVIE
"--SEIZING THE MINDS OF THE YOUNG--"
AHHHH...
--AND GIVING ME COMPLETE CONTROL.
AMERICA'S CHILDREN WILL RISE UP TO DESTROY THEIR ELDERS. A NEW NATION WILL BE BORN. ALL IN THE NAME OF THE DRAGON KING.
NOW, FOR YOUR INITIATION, KID--

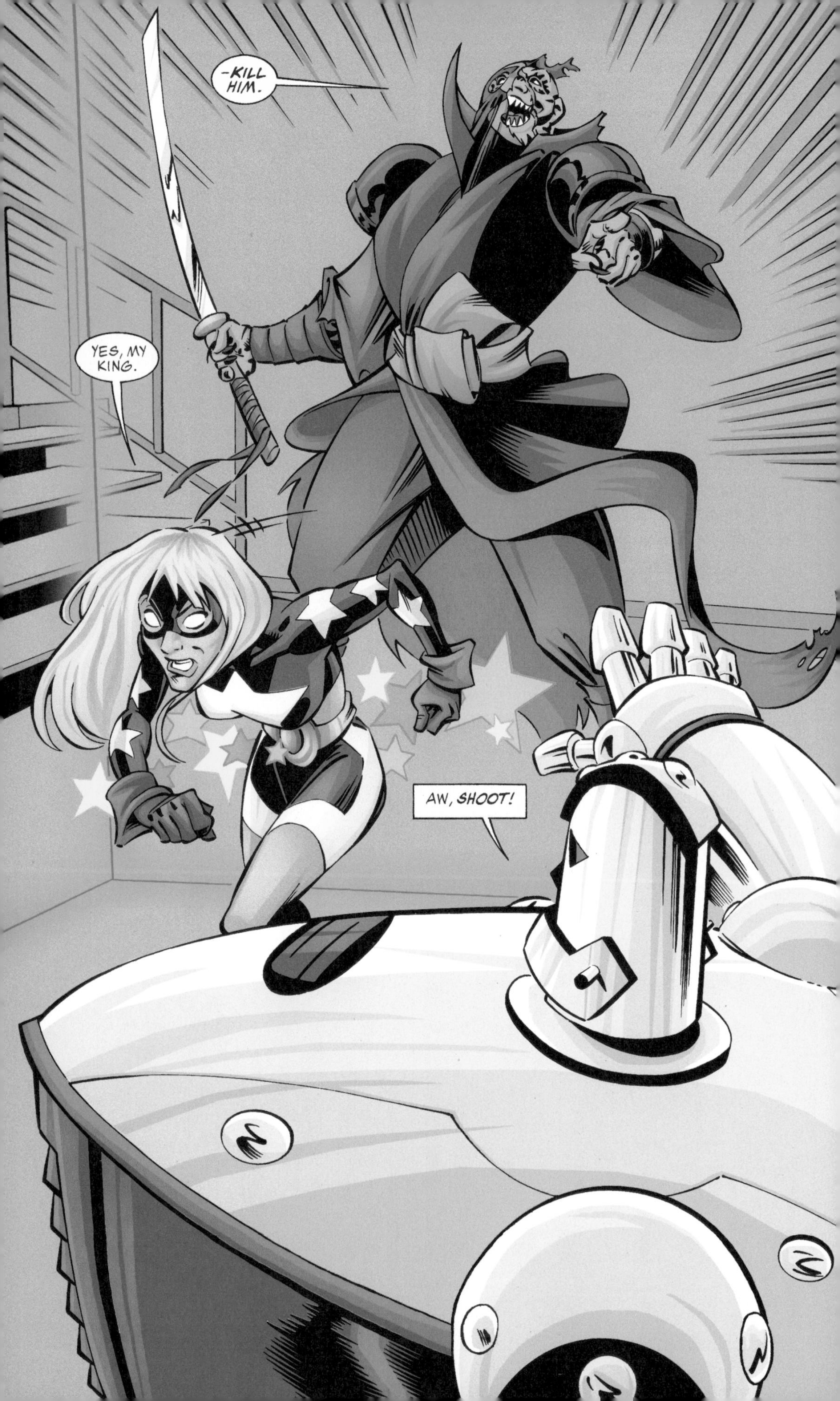
-KILL HIM.
YES, MY KING.
AW, SHOOT!

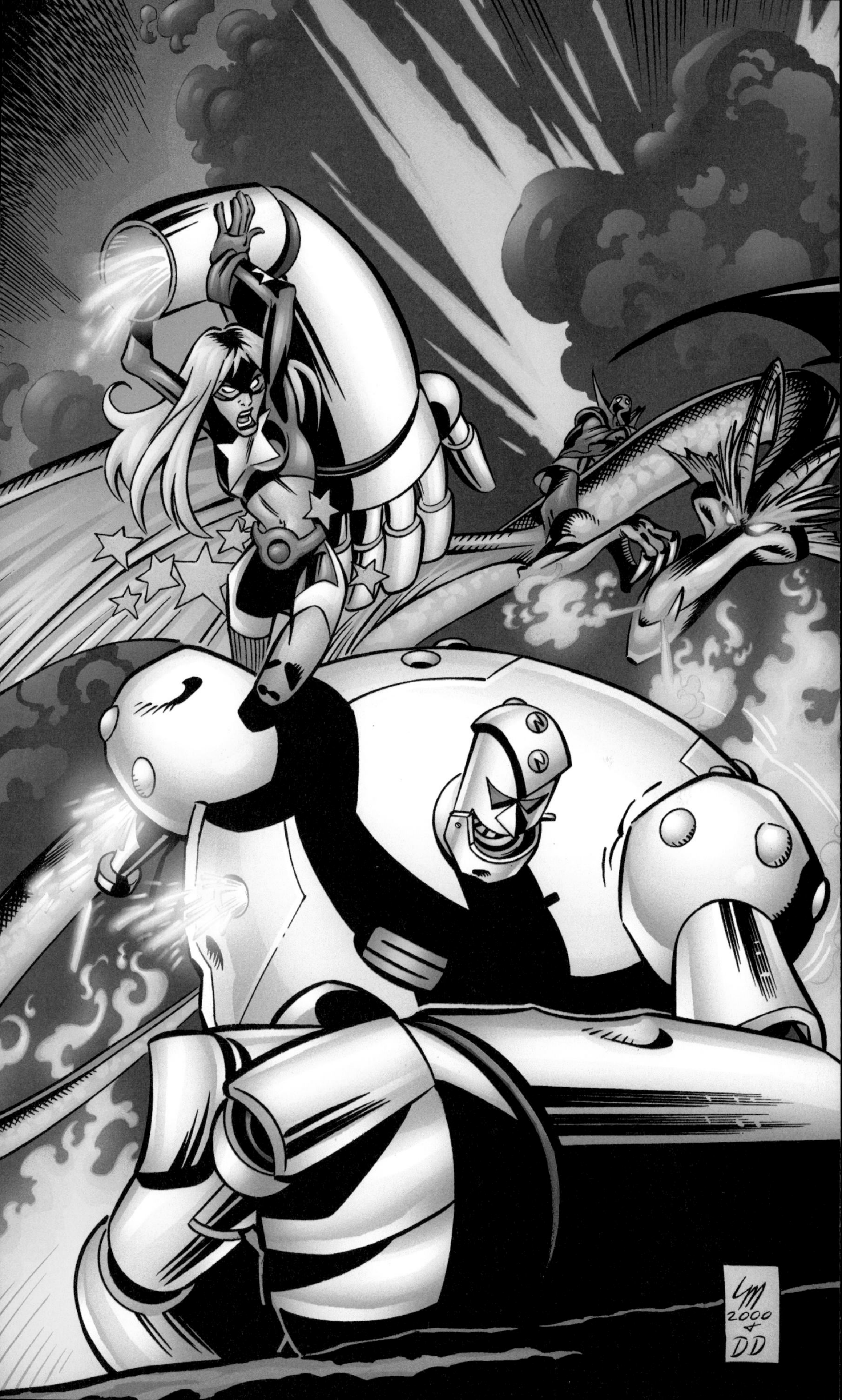

2000
DD

STARS AND S.T.R.I.P.E. #13

Written by GEOFF JOHNS
Pencils by LEE MODER
Inks by DAN DAVIS
Colors by TOM McCRAW
Letters by BILL OAKLEY
Cover art by LEE MODER and DAN DAVIS
Cover color by RICHARD & TANYA HORIE

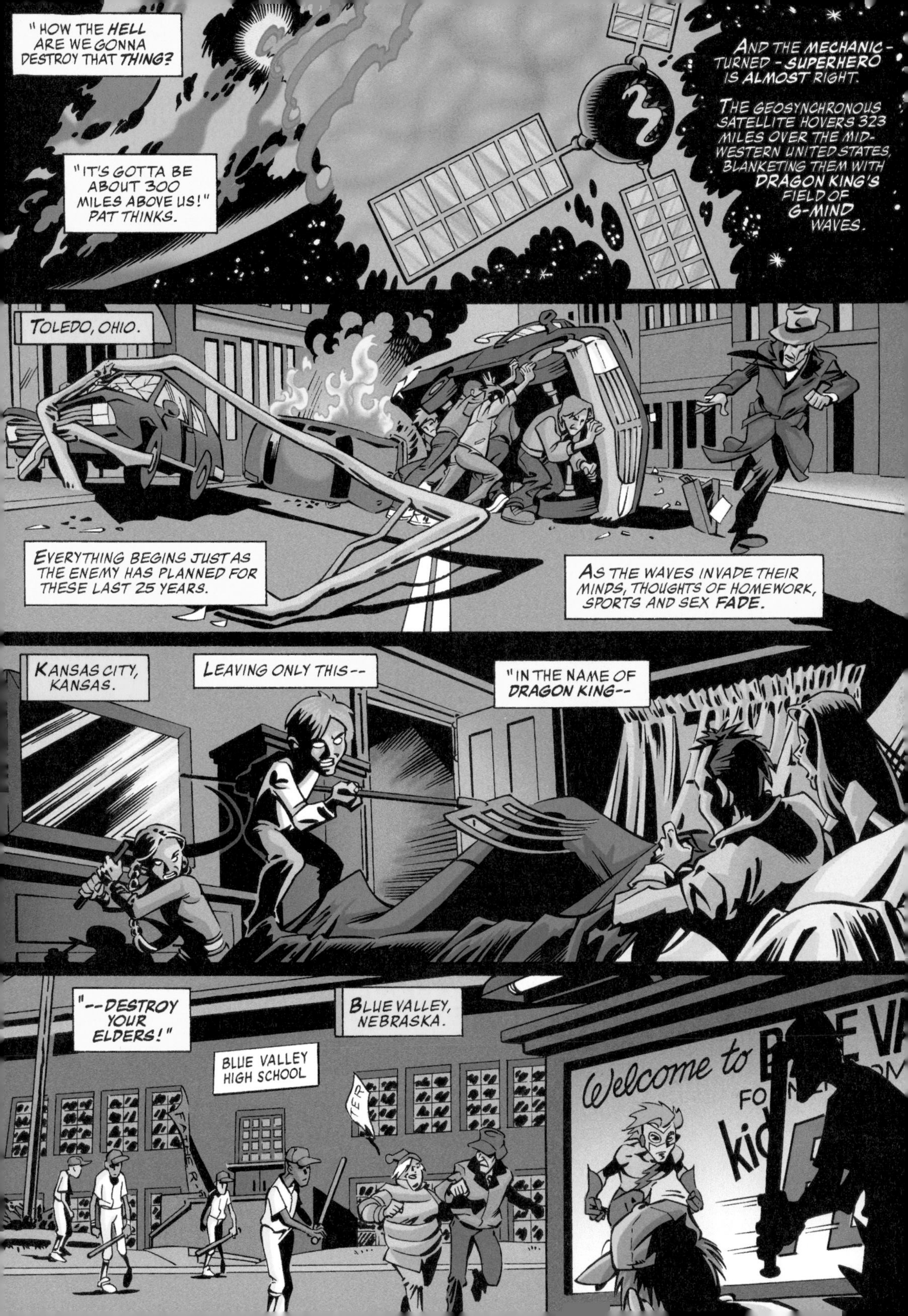
"HOW THE HELL ARE WE GONNA DESTROY THAT THING?
AND THE MECHANIC-TURNED-SUPERHERO IS ALMOST RIGHT.
THE GEOSYNCHRONOUS SATELLITE HOVERS 323 MILES OVER THE MID-WESTERN UNITED STATES, BLANKETING THEM WITH DRAGON KING'S FIELD OF G-MIND WAVES.
"IT'S GOTTA BE ABOUT 300 MILES ABOVE US!" PAT THINKS.
TOLEDO, OHIO.
EVERYTHING BEGINS JUST AS THE ENEMY HAS PLANNED FOR THESE LAST 25 YEARS.
AS THE WAVES INVADE THEIR MINDS, THOUGHTS OF HOMEWORK, SPORTS AND SEX FADE.
KANSAS CITY, KANSAS.
LEAVING ONLY THIS--
"IN THE NAME OF DRAGON KING--
"--DESTROY YOUR ELDERS!"
BLUE VALLEY, NEBRASKA.
BLUE VALLEY HIGH SCHOOL
Welcome to

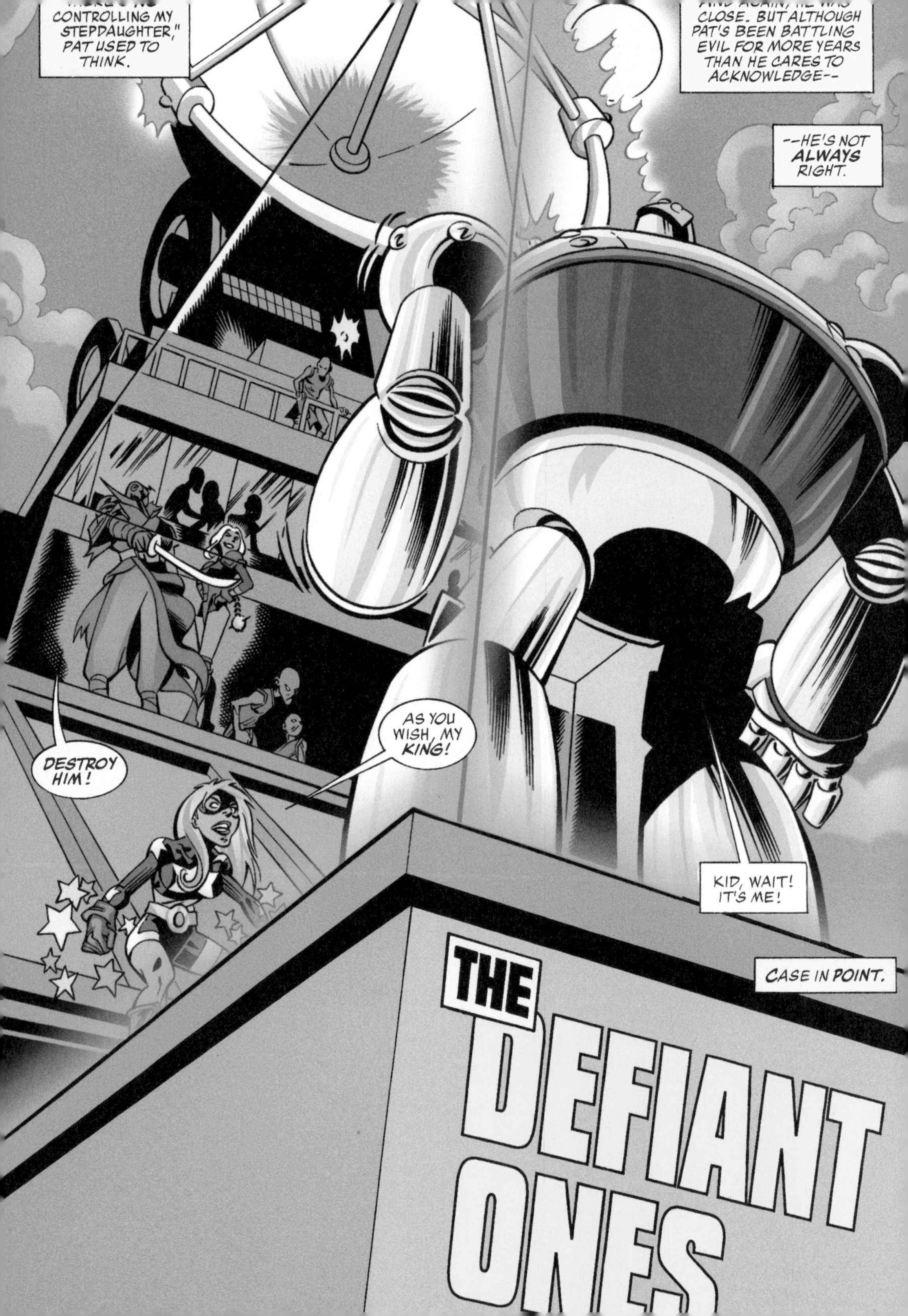
CONTROLLING MY STEPDAUGHTER," PAT USED TO THINK.
CLOSE. BUT ALTHOUGH PAT'S BEEN BATTLING EVIL FOR MORE YEARS THAN HE CARES TO ACKNOWLEDGE--
--HE'S NOT ALWAYS RIGHT.
DESTROY HIM!
AS YOU WISH, MY KING!
KID, WAIT! IT'S ME!
CASE IN POINT.
THE DEFIANT ONES

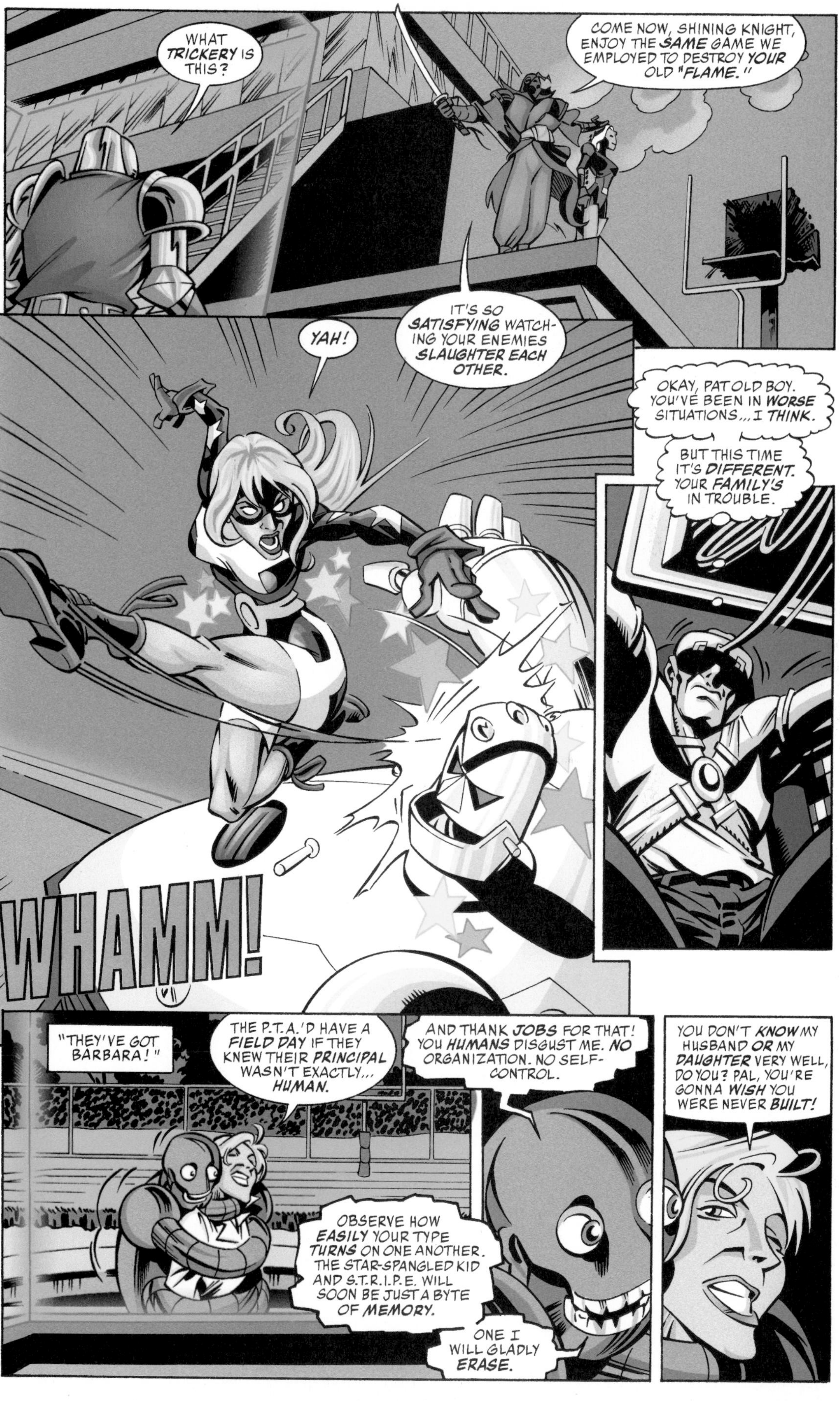
WHAT TRICKERY IS THIS?
COME NOW, SHINING KNIGHT, ENJOY THE SAME GAME WE EMPLOYED TO DESTROY YOUR OLD "FLAME."
IT'S SO SATISFYING WATCHING YOUR ENEMIES SLAUGHTER EACH OTHER.
YAH!
OKAY, PAT OLD BOY. YOU'VE BEEN IN WORSE SITUATIONS... I THINK.
BUT THIS TIME IT'S DIFFERENT. YOUR FAMILY'S IN TROUBLE.
WHAMM!
"THEY'VE GOT BARBARA!"
THE P.T.A.'D HAVE A FIELD DAY IF THEY KNEW THEIR PRINCIPAL WASN'T EXACTLY... HUMAN.
OBSERVE HOW EASILY YOUR TYPE TURNS ON ONE ANOTHER. THE STAR-SPANGLED KID AND S.T.R.I.P.E. WILL SOON BE JUST A BYTE OF MEMORY.
ONE I WILL GLADLY ERASE.
AND THANK JOBS FOR THAT! YOU HUMANS DISGUST ME. NO ORGANIZATION. NO SELF-CONTROL.
YOU DON'T KNOW MY HUSBAND OR MY DAUGHTER VERY WELL, DO YOU? PAL, YOU'RE GONNA WISH YOU WERE NEVER BUILT!

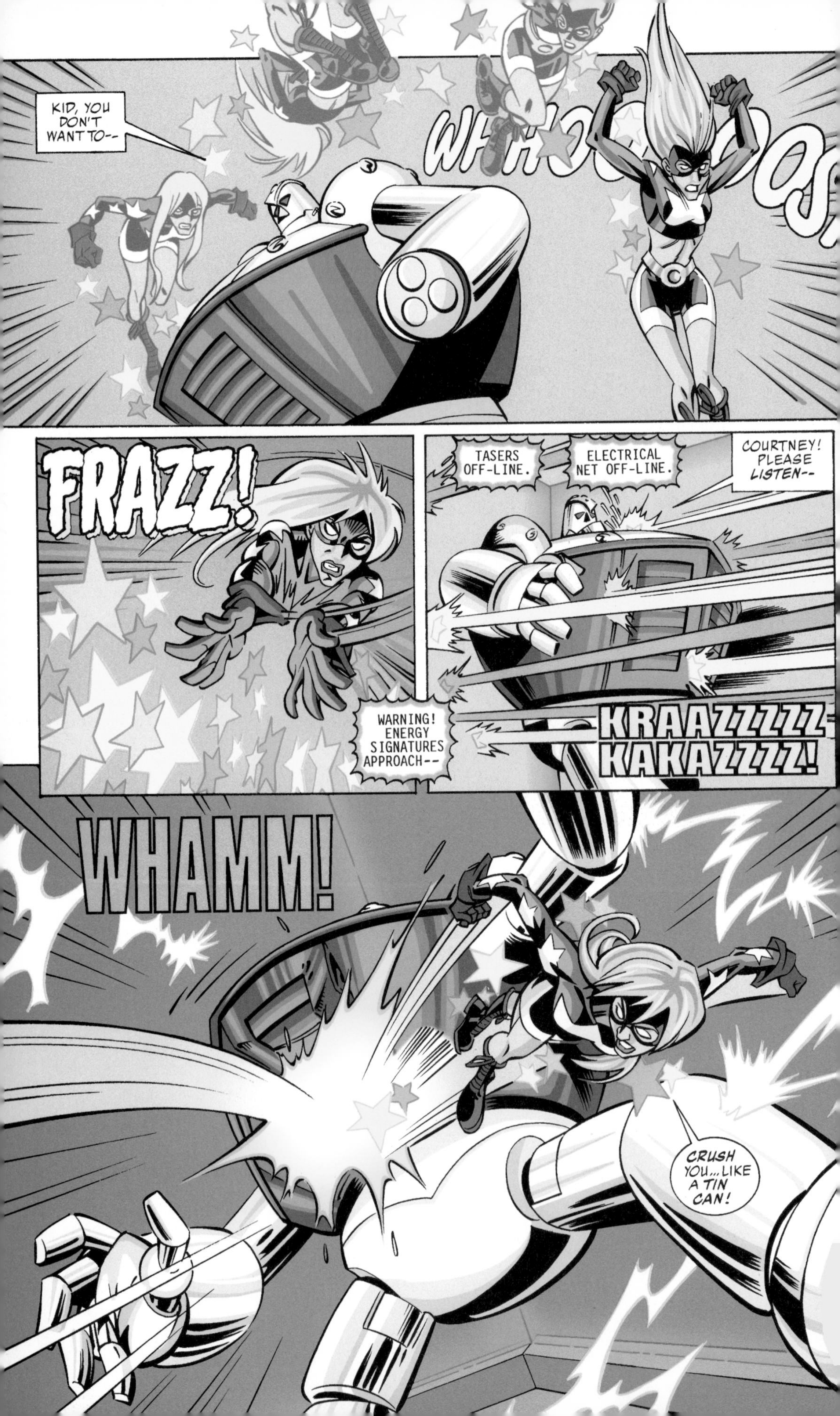
KID, YOU DON'T WANT TO--
WHHOOOOOSH
FRAZZ!
TASERS OFF-LINE.
ELECTRICAL NET OFF-LINE.
COURTNEY! PLEASE LISTEN--
WARNING! ENERGY SIGNATURES APPROACH--
KRAAZZZZZ-
KAKAZZZZZ!
WHAMM!
CRUSH YOU... LIKE A TIN CAN!

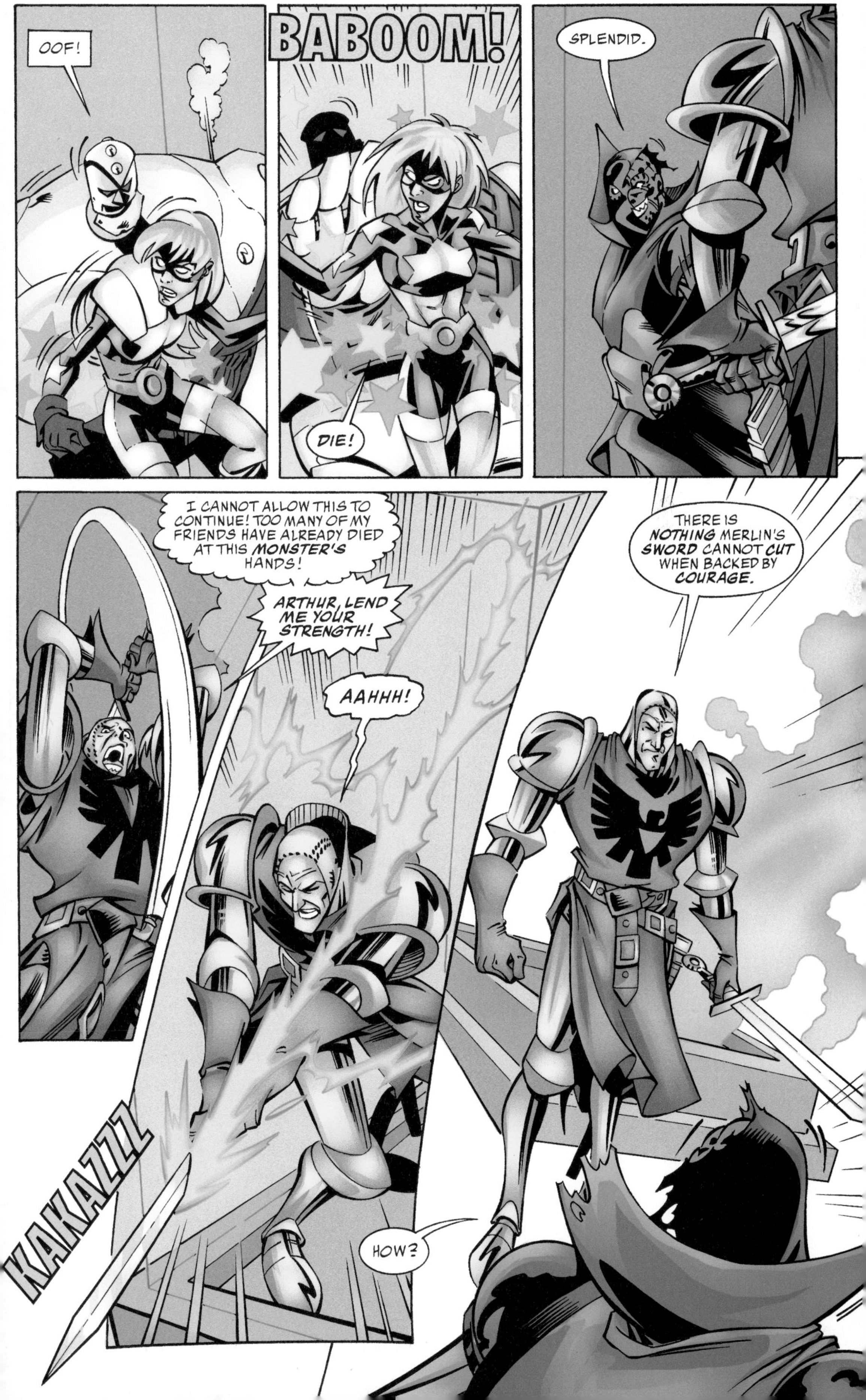

OOF!
BABOOM!
DIE!
SPLENDID.
I CANNOT ALLOW THIS TO CONTINUE! TOO MANY OF MY FRIENDS HAVE ALREADY DIED AT THIS MONSTER'S HANDS!
ARTHUR, LEND ME YOUR STRENGTH!
AAHHH!
KAKAZZZ
THERE IS NOTHING MERLIN'S SWORD CANNOT CUT WHEN BACKED BY COURAGE.
HOW?

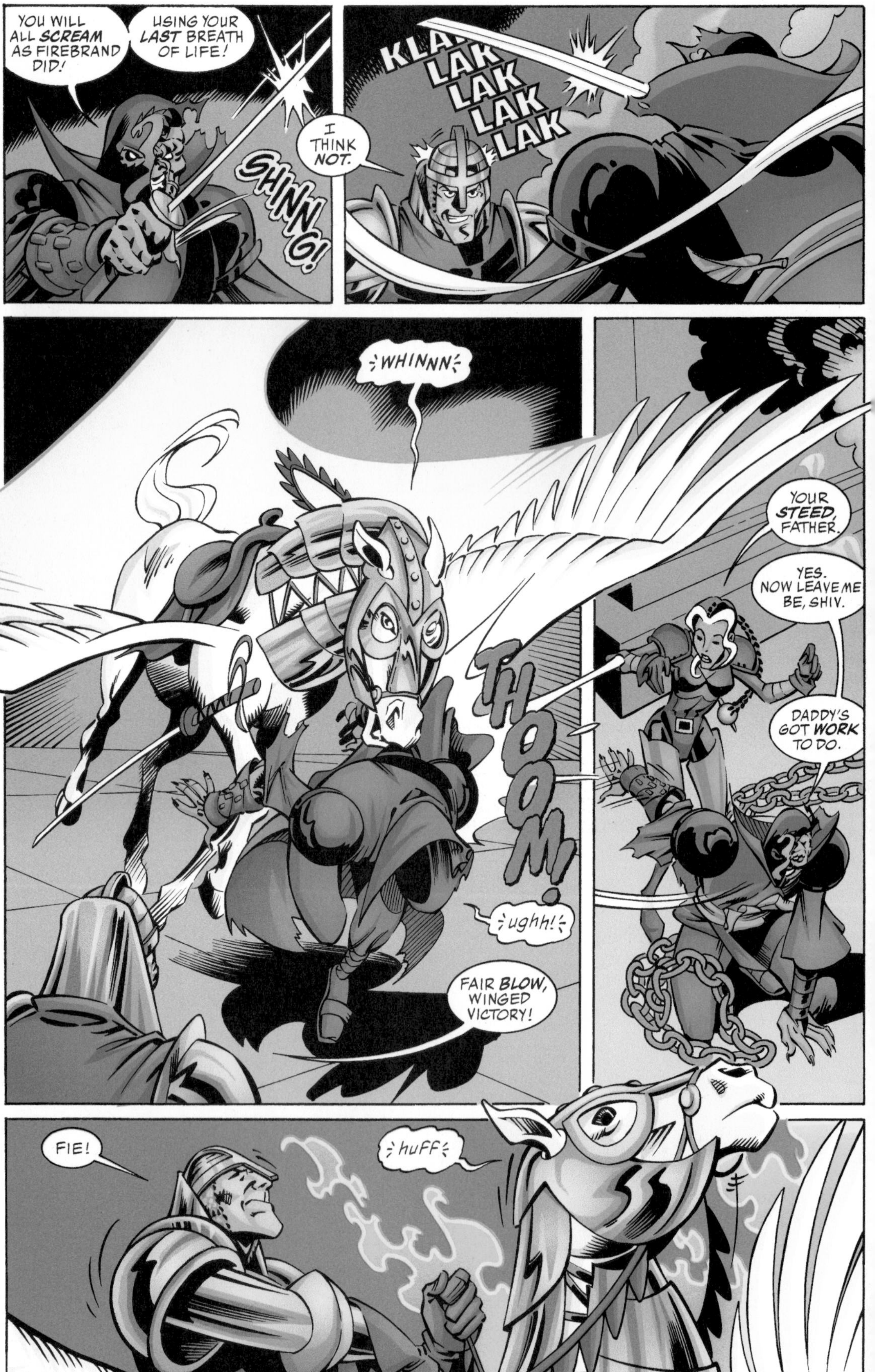
YOU WILL ALL SCREAM AS FIREBRAND DID!
USING YOUR LAST BREATH OF LIFE!
SHINNG!
KLAK LAK LAK LAK LAK
I THINK NOT.
WHINNN
YOUR STEED, FATHER.
YES. NOW LEAVE ME BE, SHIV.
DADDY'S GOT WORK TO DO.
THOOM!
ughh!
FAIR BLOW, WINGED VICTORY!
FIE!
huff

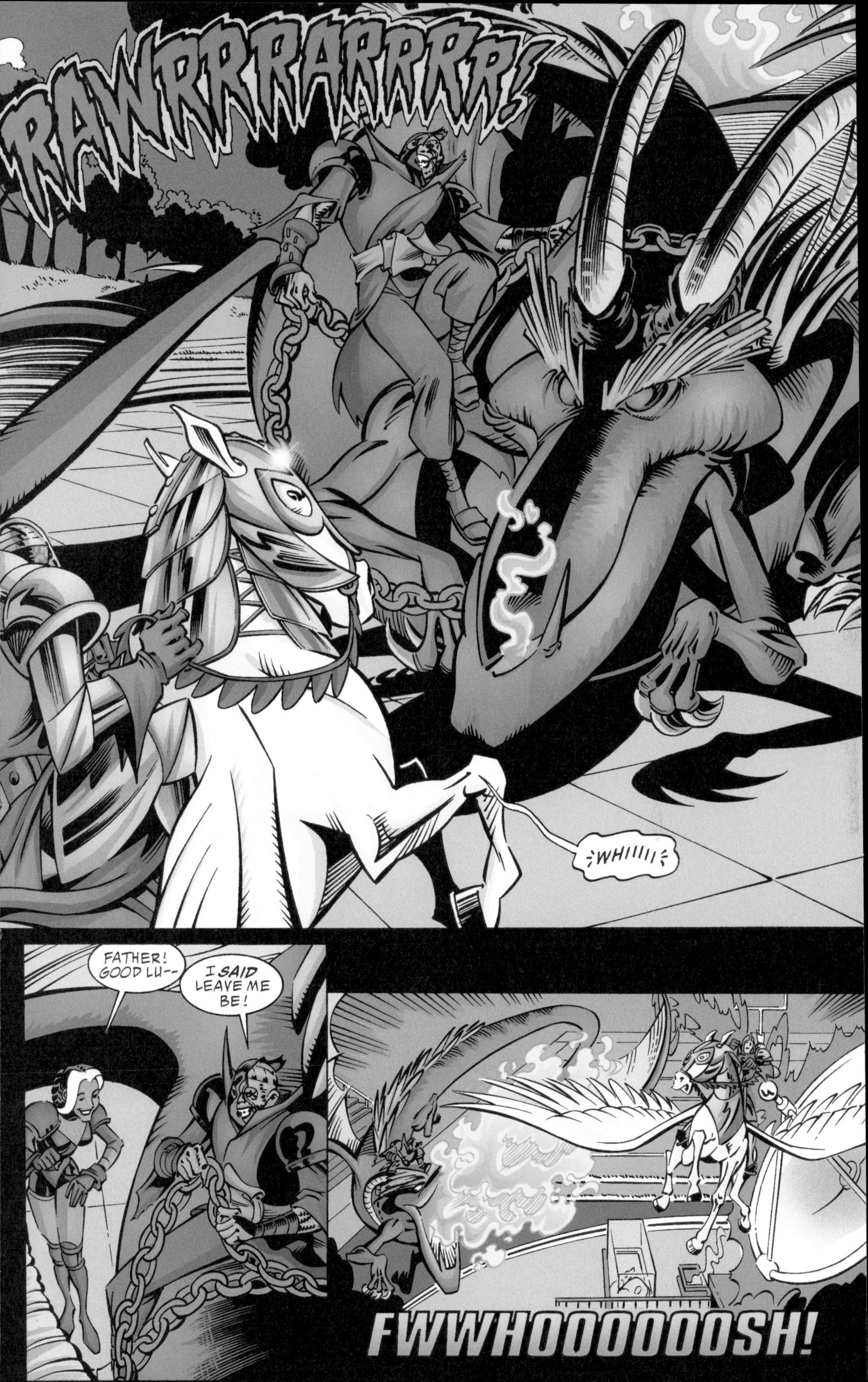
RAWRRRARRRR!
WHIIIII
FATHER! GOOD LU--
I SAID LEAVE ME BE!
FWWHOOOOOOOSH!

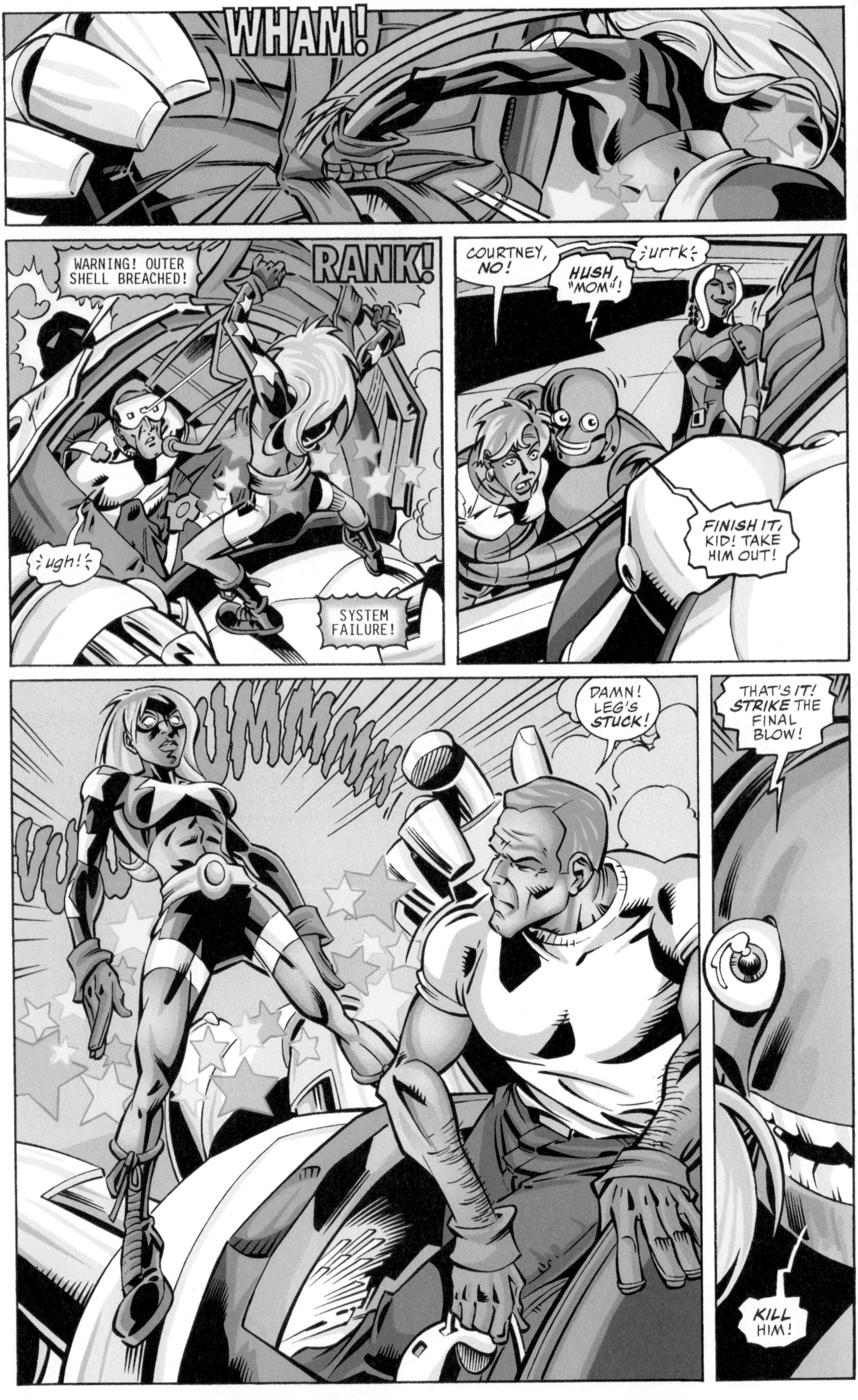
WHAM!
WARNING! OUTER SHELL BREACHED!
RANK!
ugh!
SYSTEM FAILURE!
COURTNEY, NO!
HUSH, "MOM"!
urrk
FINISH IT, KID! TAKE HIM OUT!
VUMMMMMM
DAMN! LEG'S STUCK!
THAT'S IT! STRIKE THE FINAL BLOW!
KILL HIM!

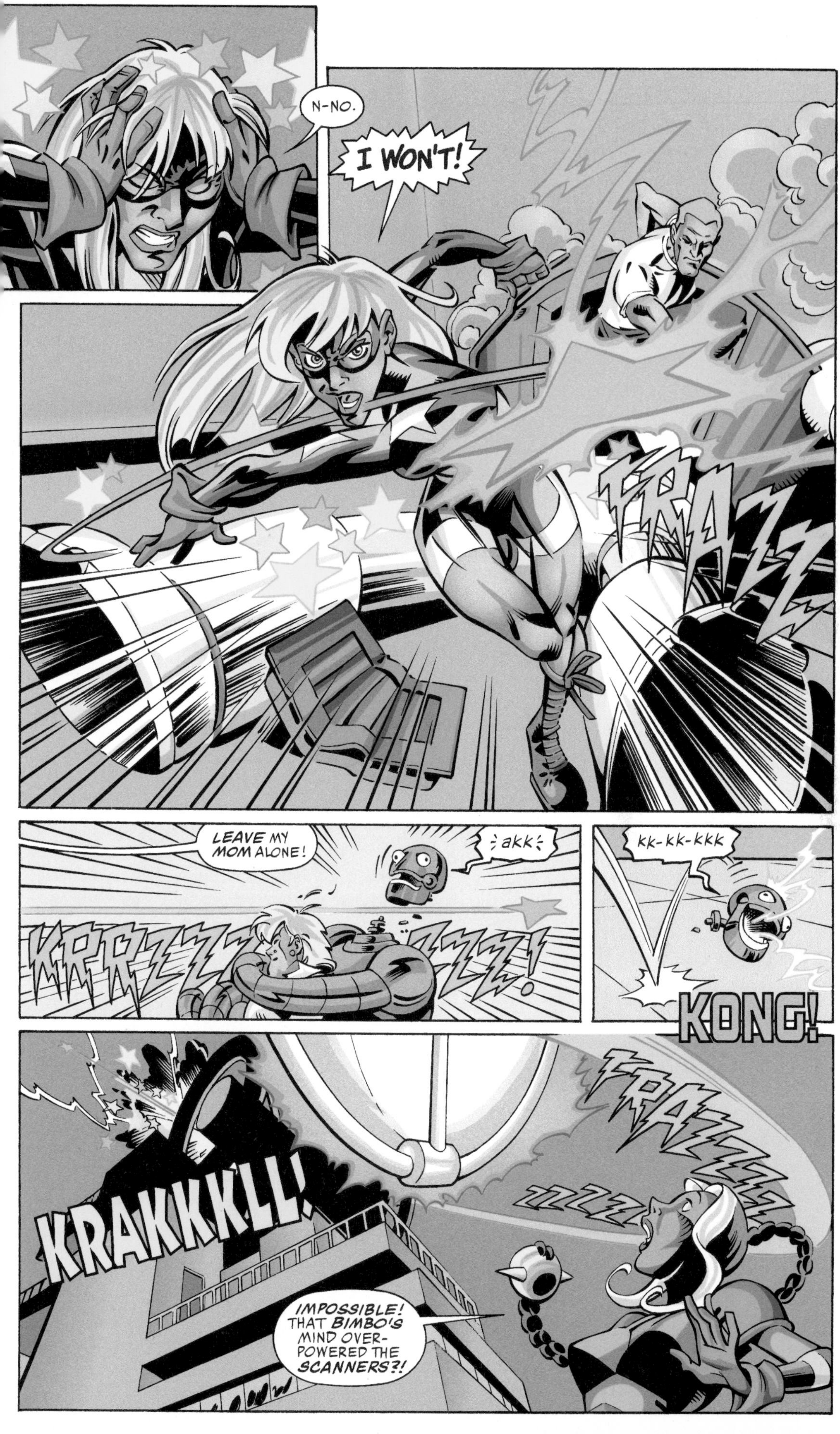

N-NO.
I WON'T!
FRAZZ
LEAVE MY MOM ALONE!
akk
KRRZZZZZZZZZ!
kk-kk-kkk
KONG!
KRAKKKLL!
FRAZZZZZZZZZZ
IMPOSSIBLE! THAT BIMBO'S MIND OVER-POWERED THE SCANNERS?!

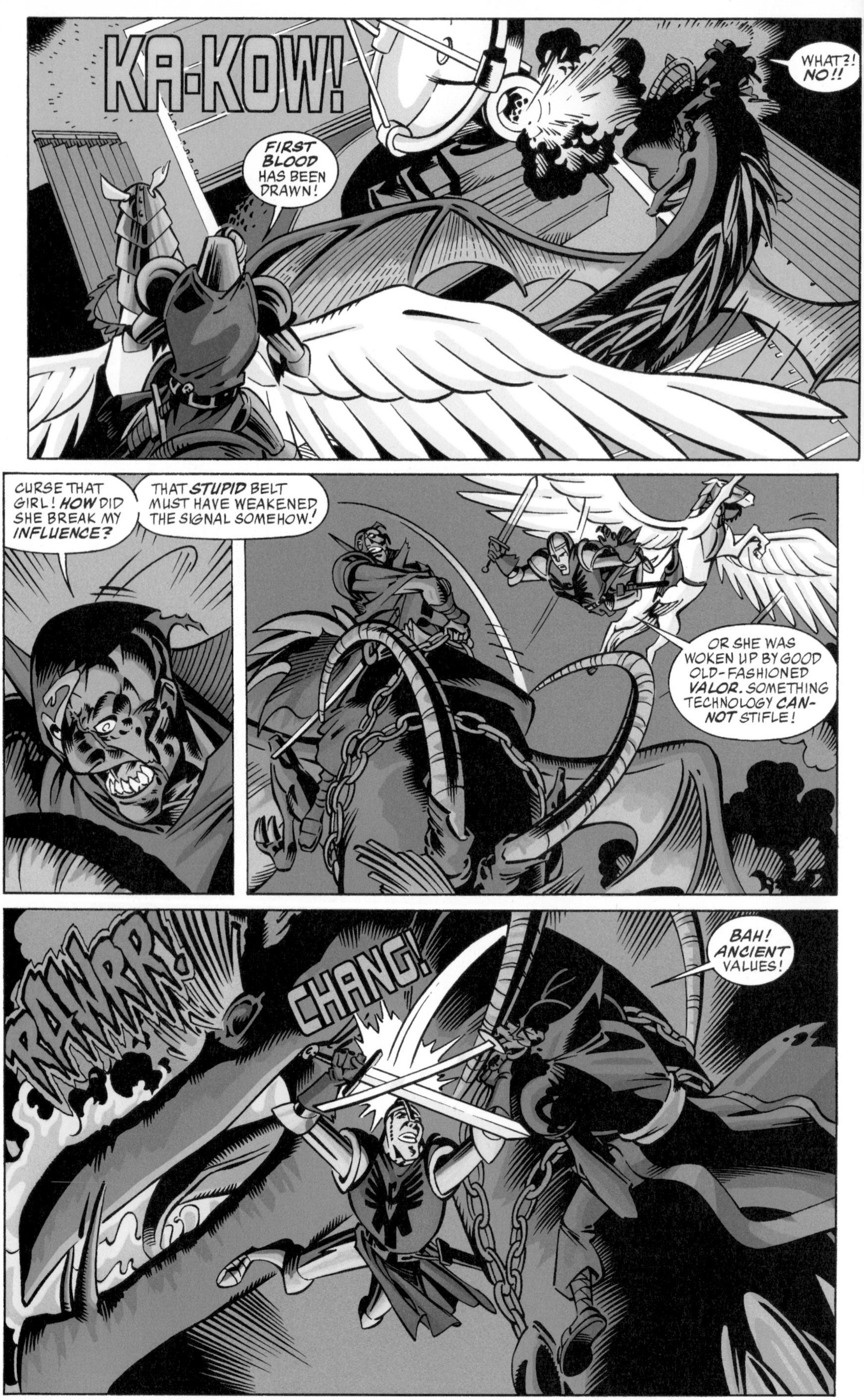
KA-KOW!
FIRST BLOOD HAS BEEN DRAWN!
WHAT?! NO!!
CURSE THAT GIRL! HOW DID SHE BREAK MY INFLUENCE?
THAT STUPID BELT MUST HAVE WEAKENED THE SIGNAL SOMEHOW!
OR SHE WAS WOKEN UP BY GOOD OLD-FASHIONED VALOR. SOMETHING TECHNOLOGY CAN-NOT STIFLE!
RAWRR!
CHANG!
BAH! ANCIENT VALUES!

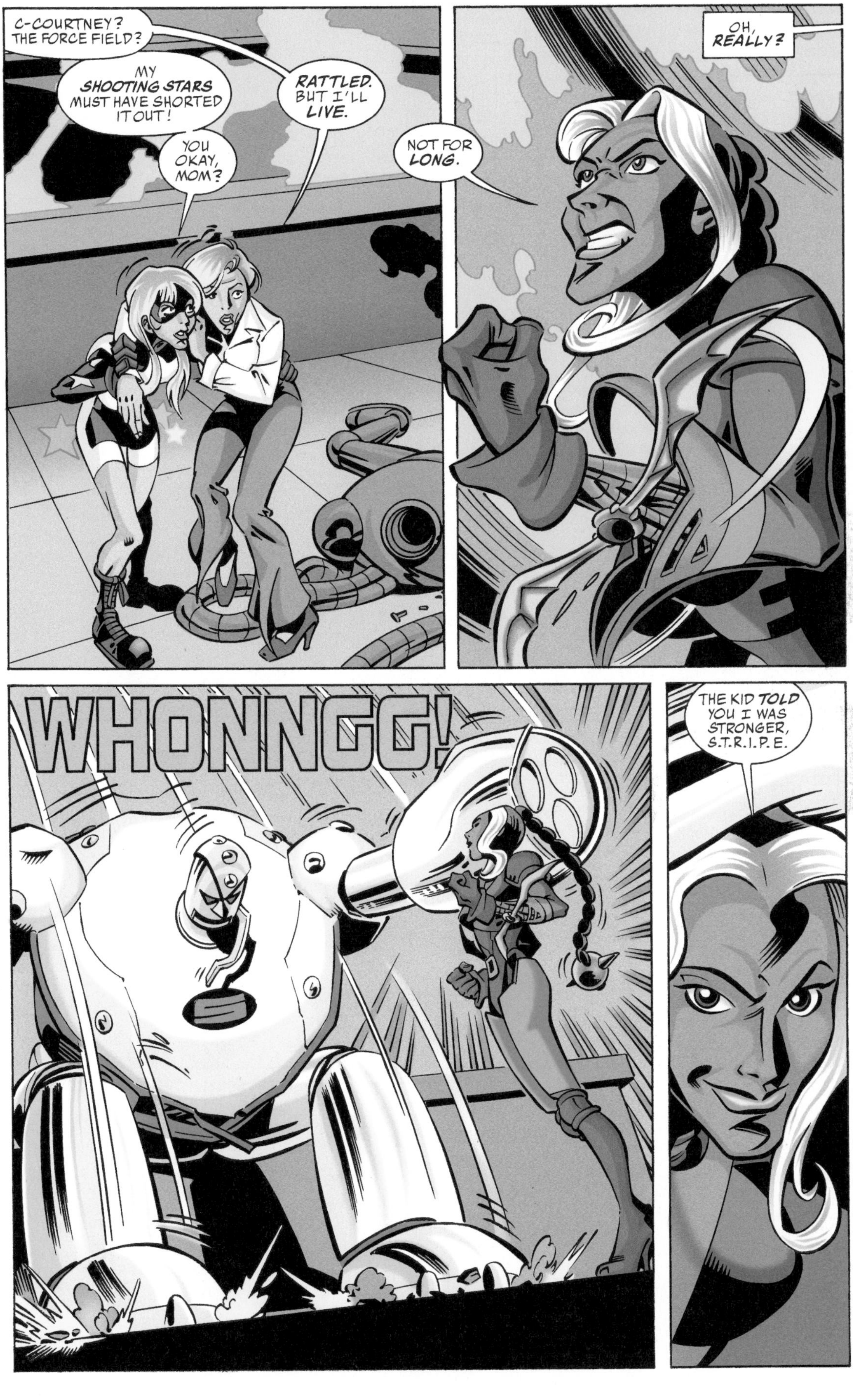
C-COURTNEY? THE FORCE FIELD?
MY SHOOTING STARS MUST HAVE SHORTED IT OUT!
YOU OKAY, MOM?
RATTLED. BUT I'LL LIVE.
NOT FOR LONG.
OH, REALLY?
WHONNGG!
THE KID TOLD YOU I WAS STRONGER, S.T.R.I.P.E.

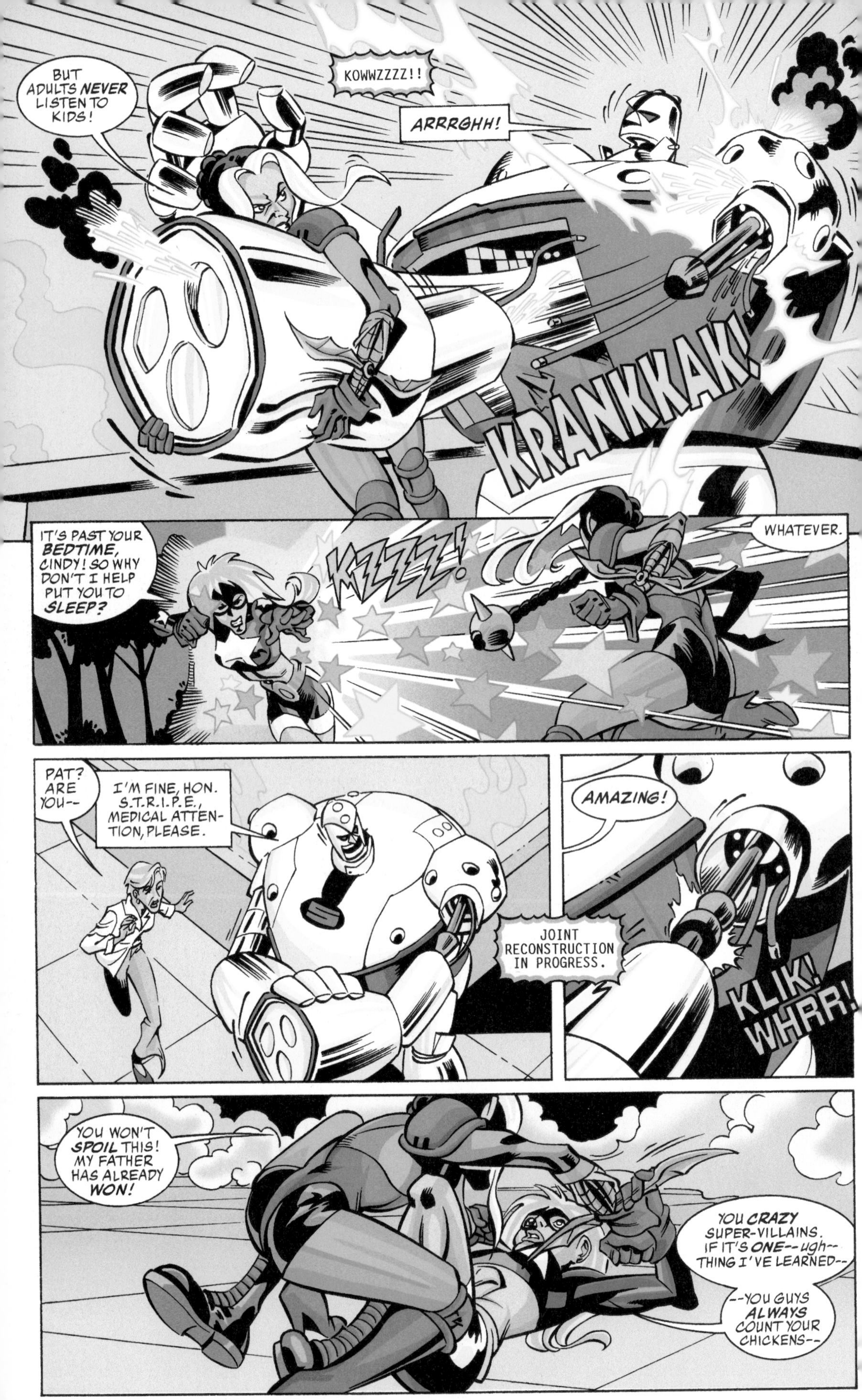
BUT ADULTS NEVER LISTEN TO KIDS!
KOWWZZZZ!!
ARRRGHH!
KRANKKAK!
IT'S PAST YOUR BEDTIME, CINDY! SO WHY DON'T I HELP PUT YOU TO SLEEP?
KZZZZ!
WHATEVER.
PAT? ARE YOU--
I'M FINE, HON. S.T.R.I.P.E., MEDICAL ATTENTION, PLEASE.
JOINT RECONSTRUCTION IN PROGRESS.
AMAZING!
KLIK! WHRR!
YOU WON'T SPOIL THIS! MY FATHER HAS ALREADY WON!
YOU CRAZY SUPER-VILLAINS. IF IT'S ONE--ugh--THING I'VE LEARNED--
--YOU GUYS ALWAYS COUNT YOUR CHICKENS--

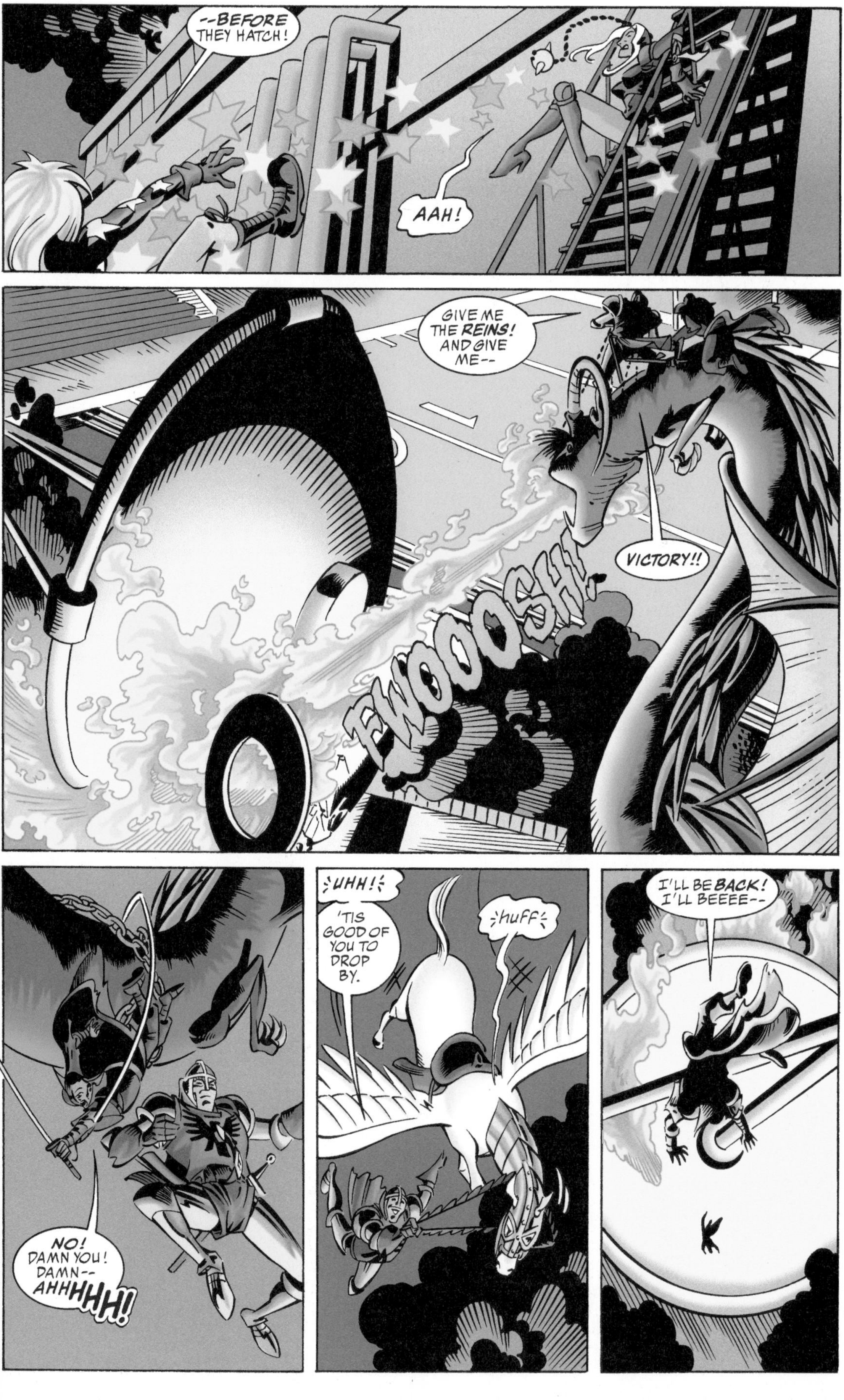
--BEFORE THEY HATCH!
AAH!
GIVE ME THE REINS! AND GIVE ME--
VICTORY!!
FWOOOSH!
NO! DAMN YOU! DAMN-- AHHHHH!
UHH!
'TIS GOOD OF YOU TO DROP BY.
huff
I'LL BE BACK! I'LL BEEEE--

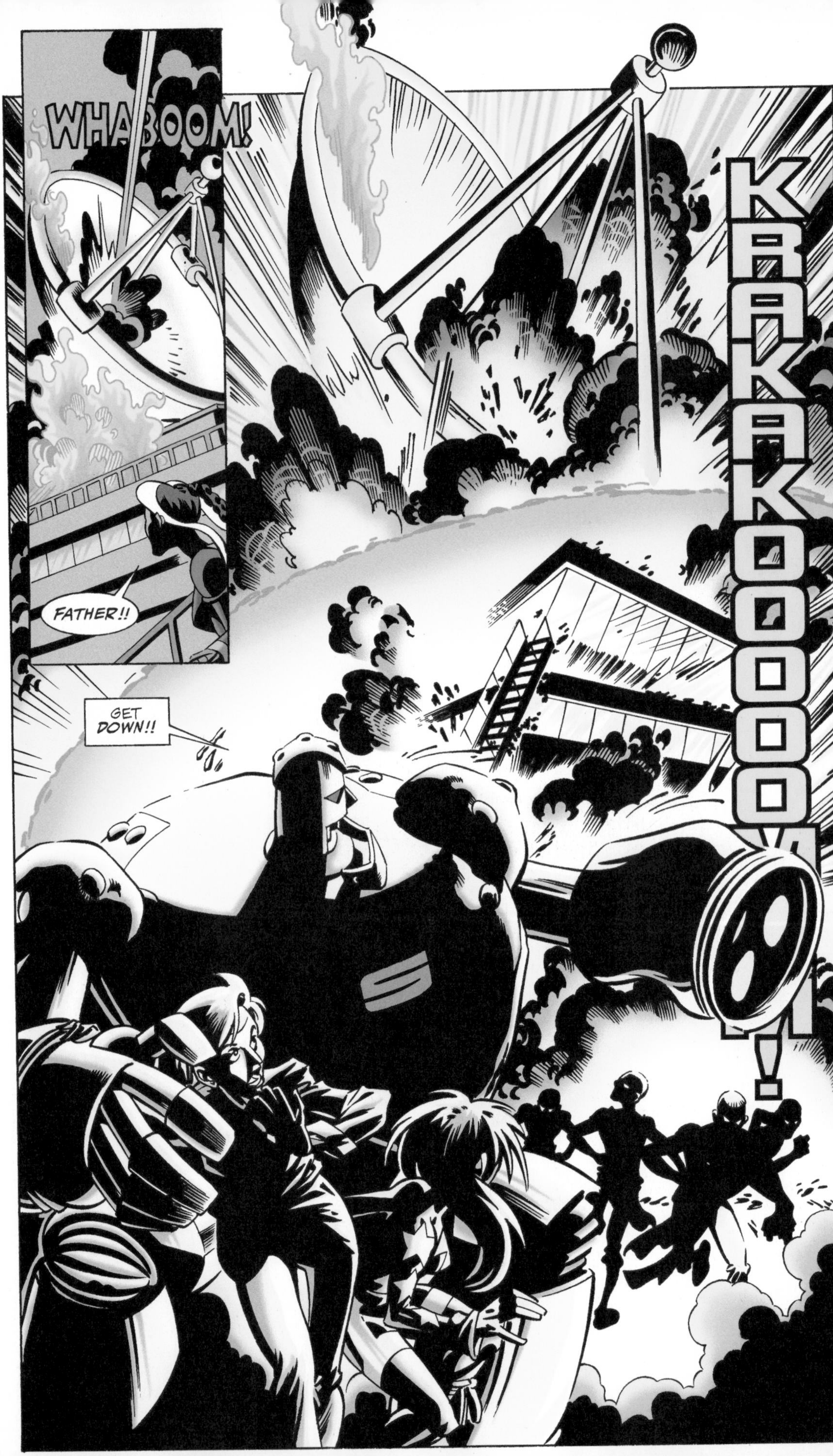

WHABOOM!
FATHER!!
KRAKAKOOOOOOM!
GET DOWN!!

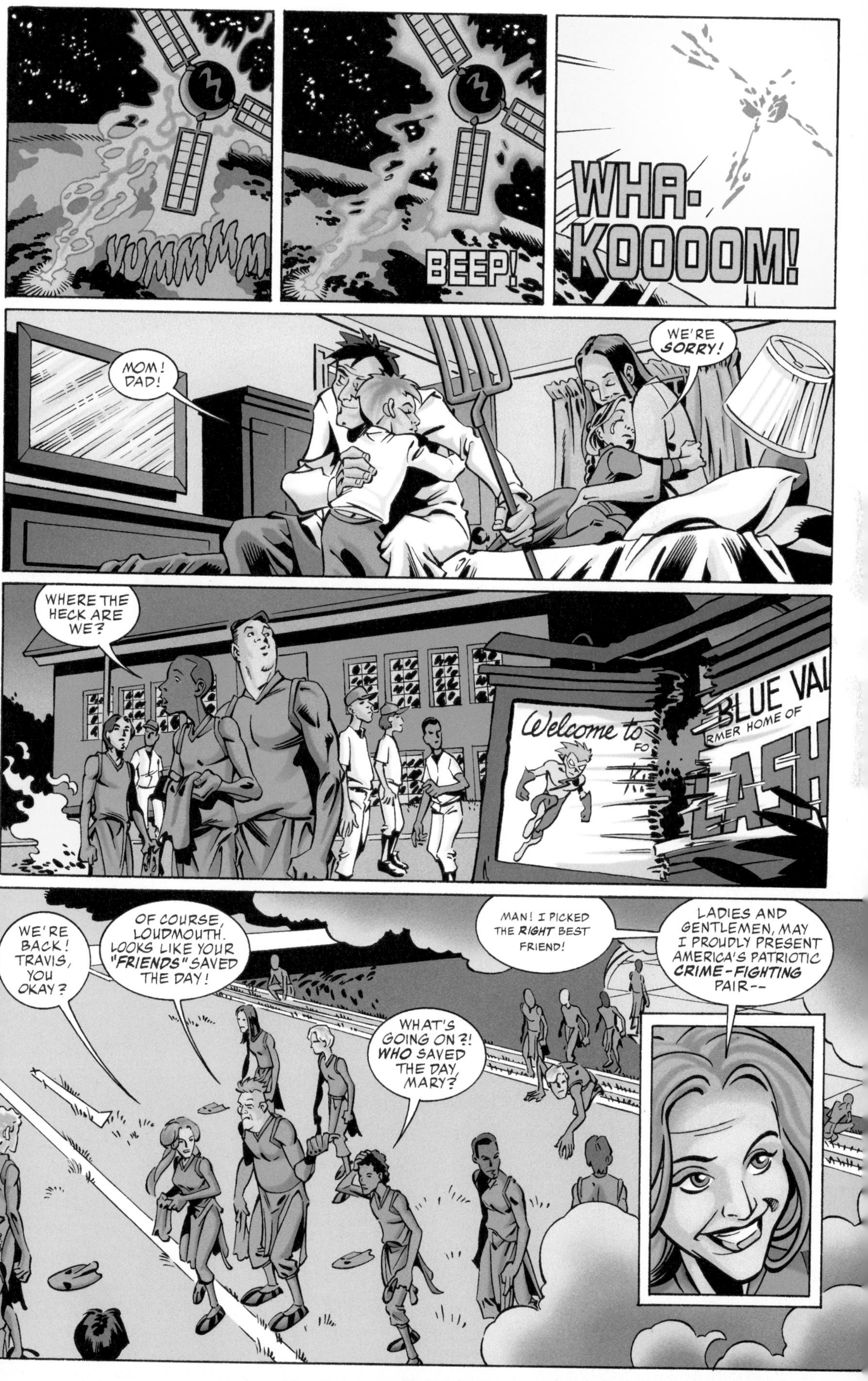
VUMMMM
BEEP!
WHA-KOOOOM!
MOM! DAD!
WE'RE SORRY!
WHERE THE HECK ARE WE?
BLUE VAL
Welcome to
RMER HOME OF
LASH
WE'RE BACK! TRAVIS, YOU OKAY?
OF COURSE, LOUDMOUTH. LOOKS LIKE YOUR "FRIENDS" SAVED THE DAY!
WHAT'S GOING ON?! WHO SAVED THE DAY, MARY?
MAN! I PICKED THE RIGHT BEST FRIEND!
LADIES AND GENTLEMEN, MAY I PROUDLY PRESENT AMERICA'S PATRIOTIC CRIME-FIGHTING PAIR--

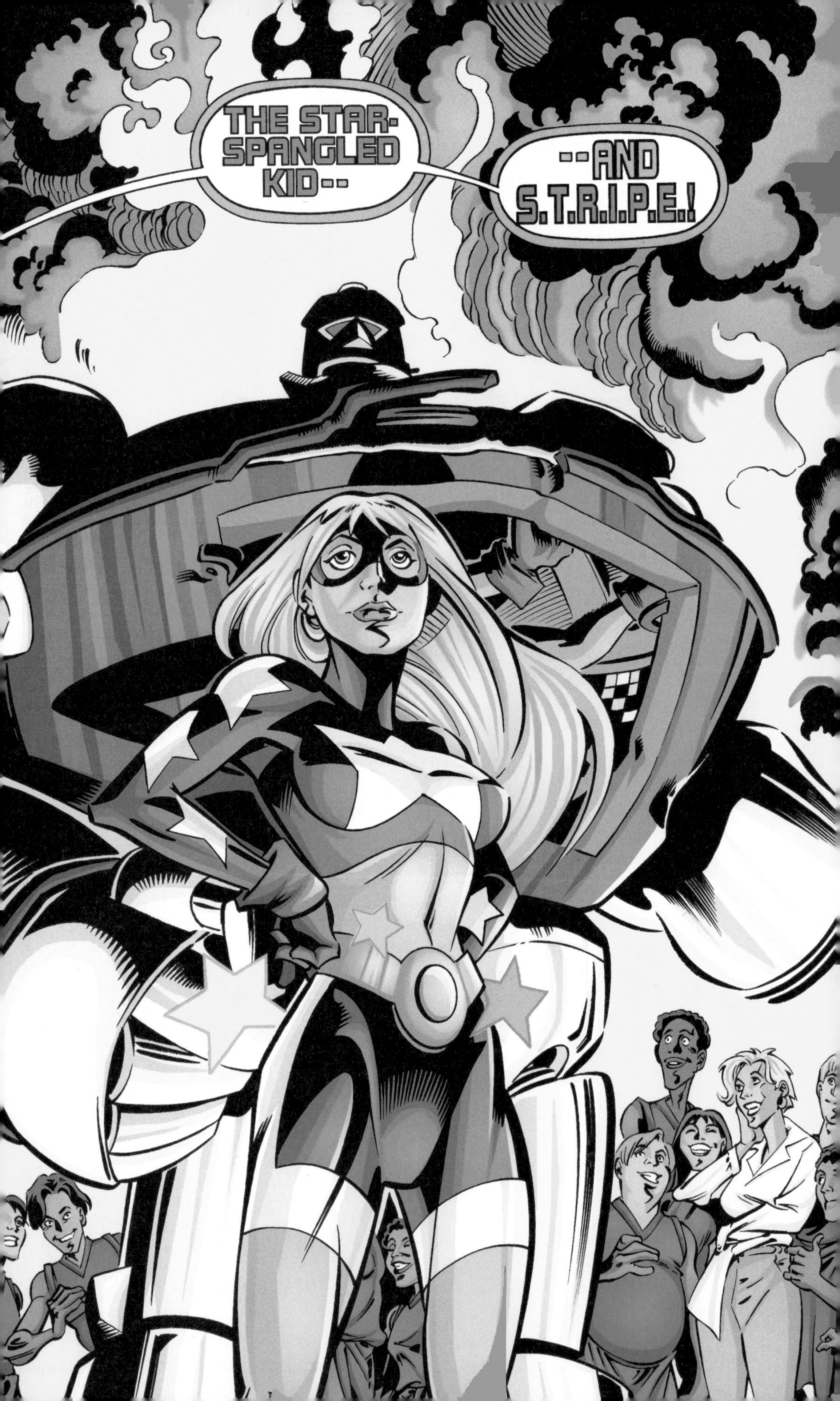
THE STAR-SPANGLED KID--
--AND S.T.R.I.P.E.!

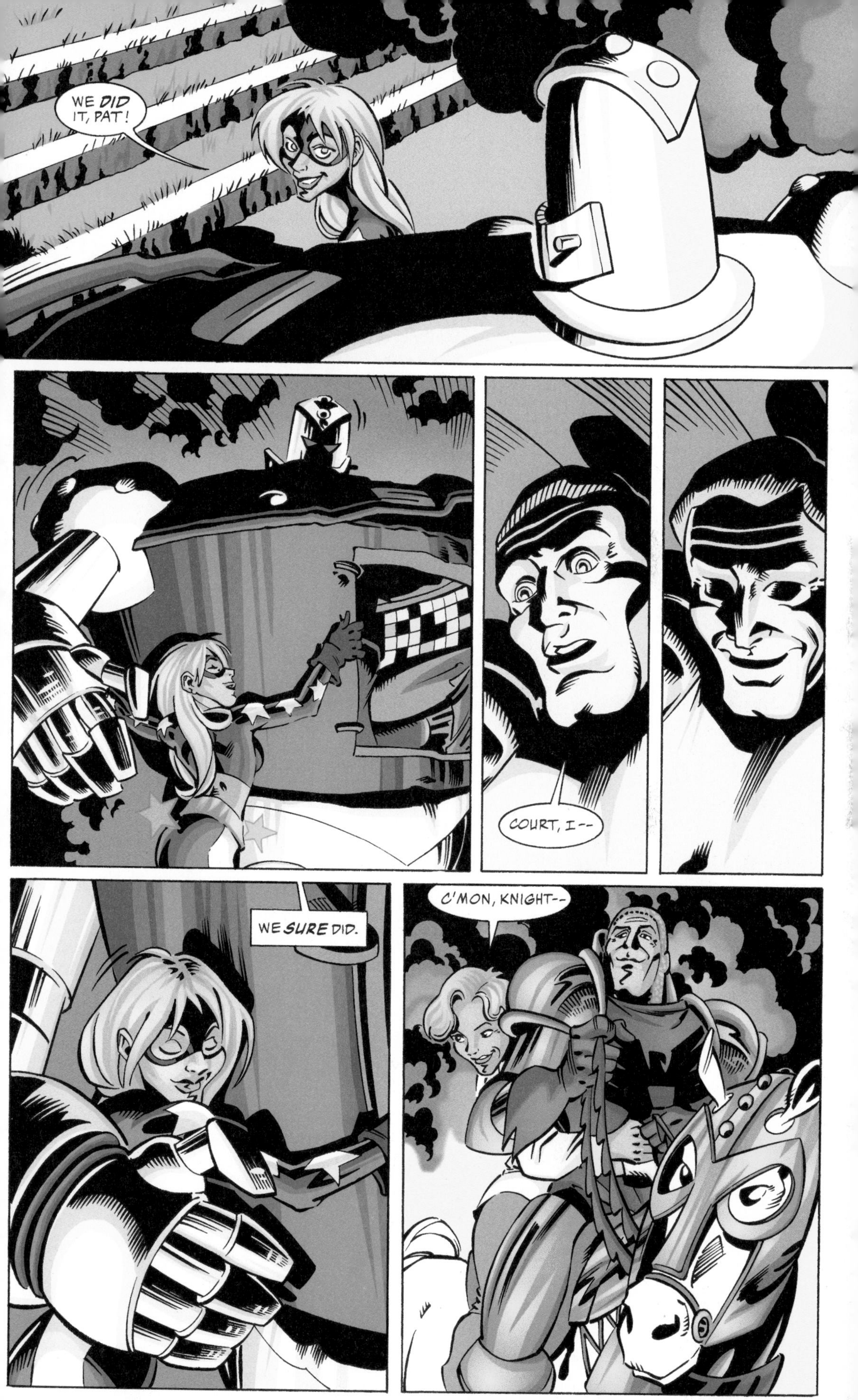
WE DID IT, PAT!
COURT, I--
WE SURE DID.
C'MON, KNIGHT--

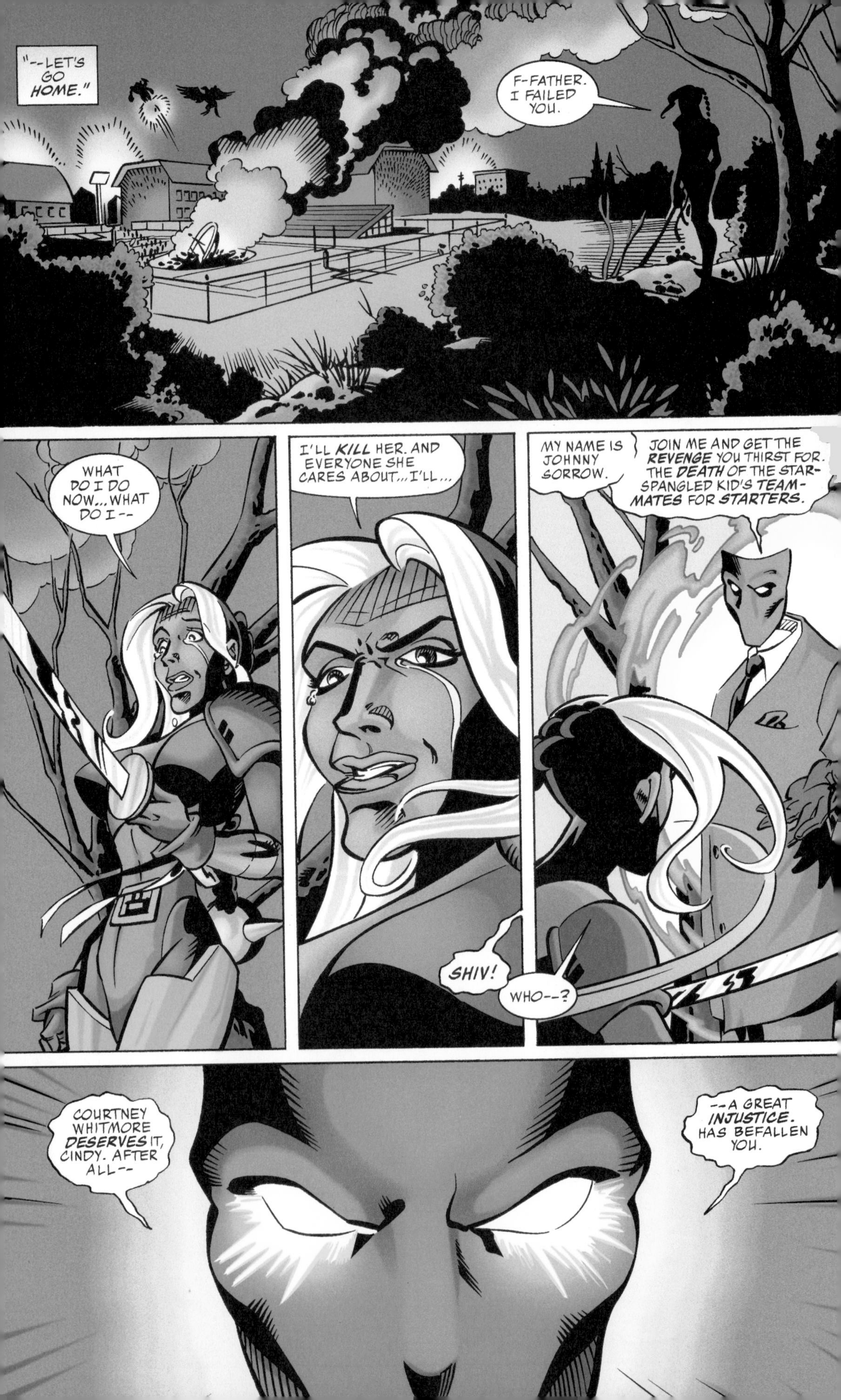
"--LET'S GO HOME."
F-FATHER. I FAILED YOU.
WHAT DO I DO NOW... WHAT DO I--
I'LL KILL HER. AND EVERYONE SHE CARES ABOUT... I'LL...
MY NAME IS JOHNNY SORROW.
JOIN ME AND GET THE REVENGE YOU THIRST FOR. THE DEATH OF THE STAR-SPANGLED KID'S TEAMMATES FOR STARTERS.
SHIV!
WHO--?
COURTNEY WHITMORE DESERVES IT, CINDY. AFTER ALL--
--A GREAT INJUSTICE. HAS BEFALLEN YOU.

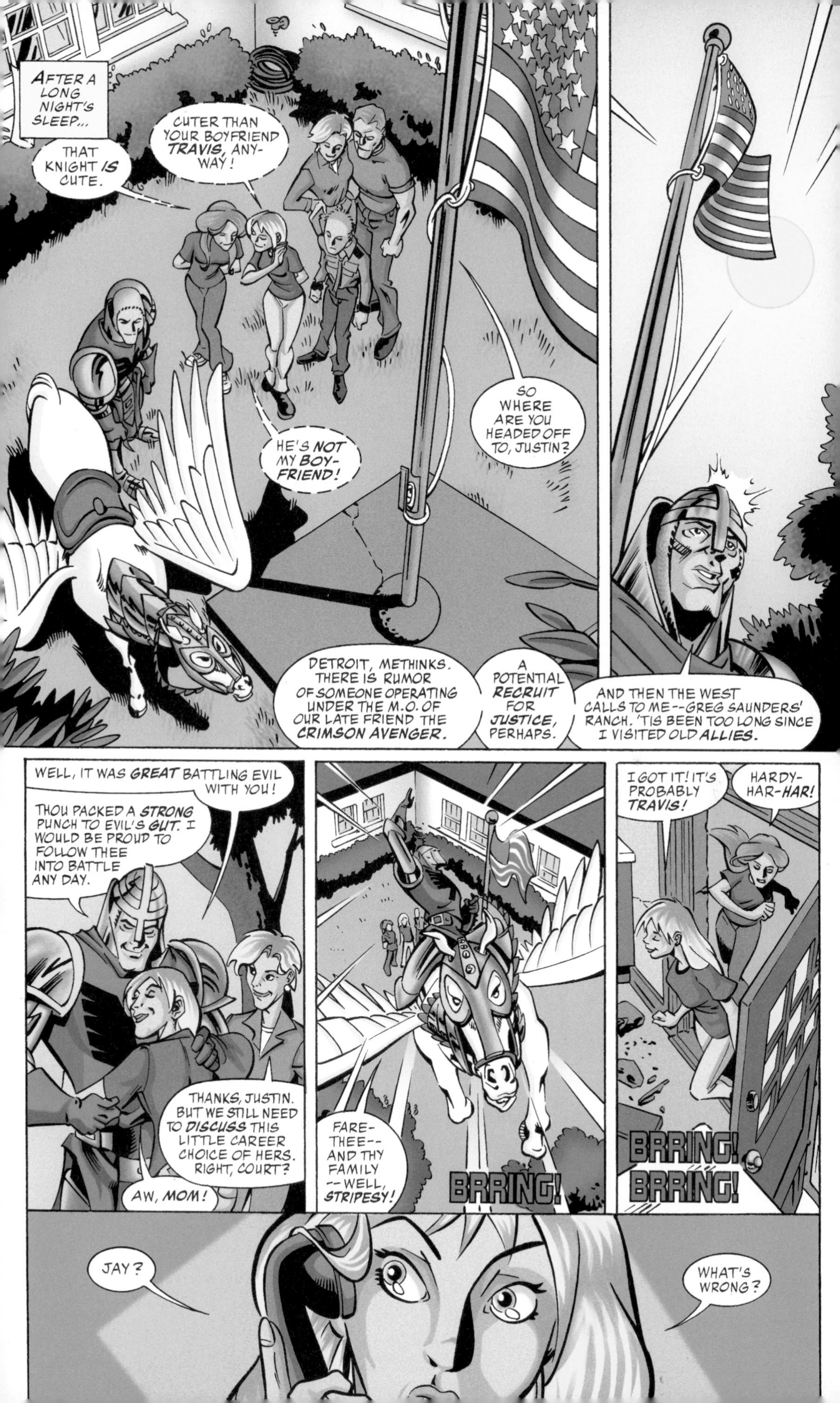

AFTER A LONG NIGHT'S SLEEP...
THAT KNIGHT IS CUTE.
CUTER THAN YOUR BOYFRIEND TRAVIS, ANYWAY!
HE'S NOT MY BOYFRIEND!
SO WHERE ARE YOU HEADED OFF TO, JUSTIN?
DETROIT, METHINKS. THERE IS RUMOR OF SOMEONE OPERATING UNDER THE M.O. OF OUR LATE FRIEND THE CRIMSON AVENGER.
A POTENTIAL RECRUIT FOR JUSTICE, PERHAPS.
AND THEN THE WEST CALLS TO ME--GREG SAUNDERS' RANCH. 'TIS BEEN TOO LONG SINCE I VISITED OLD ALLIES.
WELL, IT WAS GREAT BATTLING EVIL WITH YOU!
THOU PACKED A STRONG PUNCH TO EVIL'S GUT. I WOULD BE PROUD TO FOLLOW THEE INTO BATTLE ANY DAY.
THANKS, JUSTIN. BUT WE STILL NEED TO DISCUSS THIS LITTLE CAREER CHOICE OF HERS. RIGHT, COURT?
AW, MOM!
FARE-THEE--AND THY FAMILY--WELL, STRIPESY!
BRRING!
I GOT IT! IT'S PROBABLY TRAVIS!
HARDY-HAR-HAR!
BRRING! BRRING!
JAY?
WHAT'S WRONG?

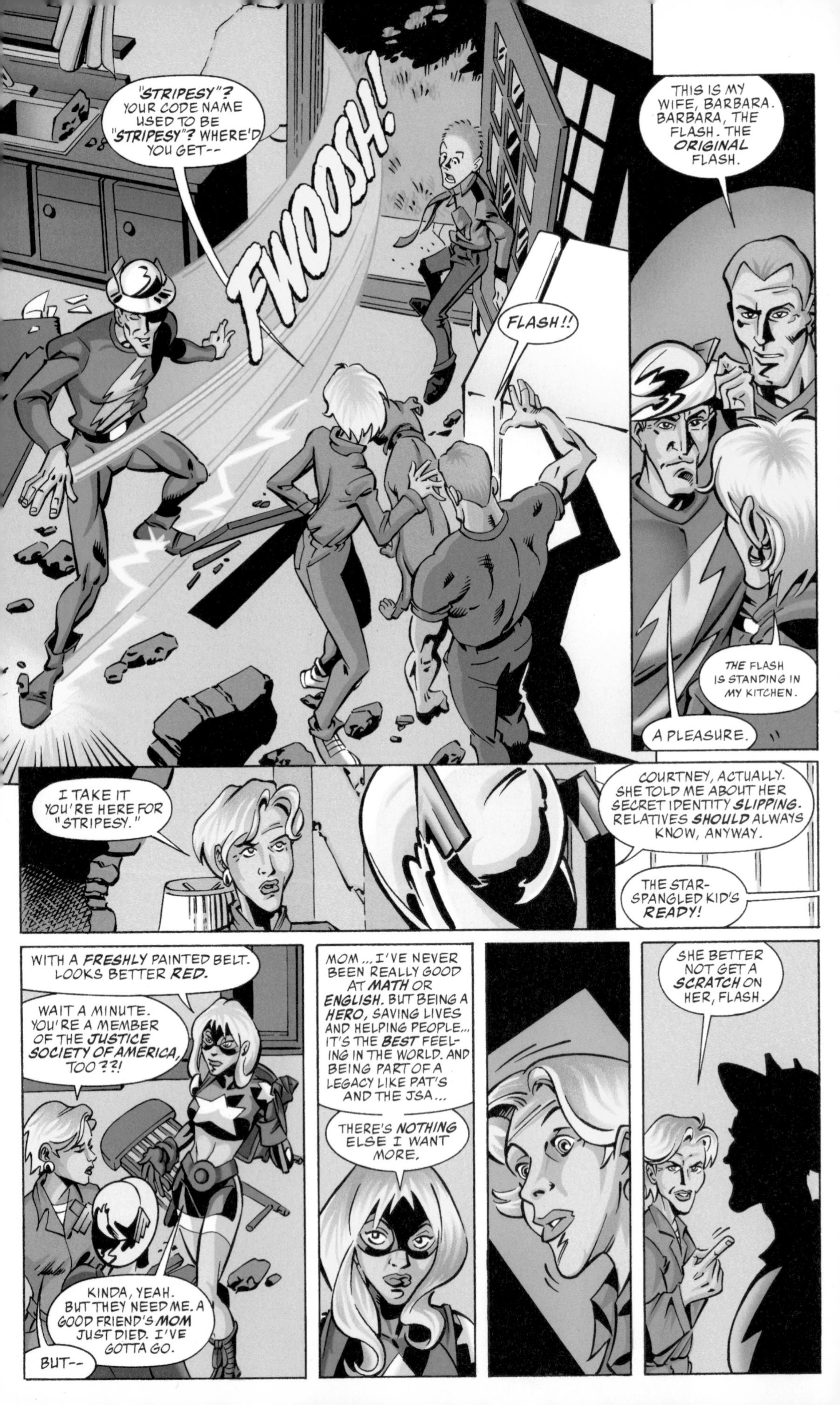
"STRIPESY"? YOUR CODE NAME USED TO BE "STRIPESY"? WHERE'D YOU GET--
FWOOSH!
FLASH!!
THIS IS MY WIFE, BARBARA. BARBARA, THE FLASH. THE ORIGINAL FLASH.
THE FLASH IS STANDING IN MY KITCHEN.
A PLEASURE.
I TAKE IT YOU'RE HERE FOR "STRIPESY."
COURTNEY, ACTUALLY. SHE TOLD ME ABOUT HER SECRET IDENTITY SLIPPING. RELATIVES SHOULD ALWAYS KNOW, ANYWAY.
THE STAR-SPANGLED KID'S READY!
WITH A FRESHLY PAINTED BELT. LOOKS BETTER RED.
WAIT A MINUTE. YOU'RE A MEMBER OF THE JUSTICE SOCIETY OF AMERICA, TOO??!
KINDA, YEAH. BUT THEY NEED ME. A GOOD FRIEND'S MOM JUST DIED. I'VE GOTTA GO.
BUT--
MOM... I'VE NEVER BEEN REALLY GOOD AT MATH OR ENGLISH. BUT BEING A HERO, SAVING LIVES AND HELPING PEOPLE... IT'S THE BEST FEELING IN THE WORLD. AND BEING PART OF A LEGACY LIKE PAT'S AND THE JSA...
THERE'S NOTHING ELSE I WANT MORE.
SHE BETTER NOT GET A SCRATCH ON HER, FLASH.

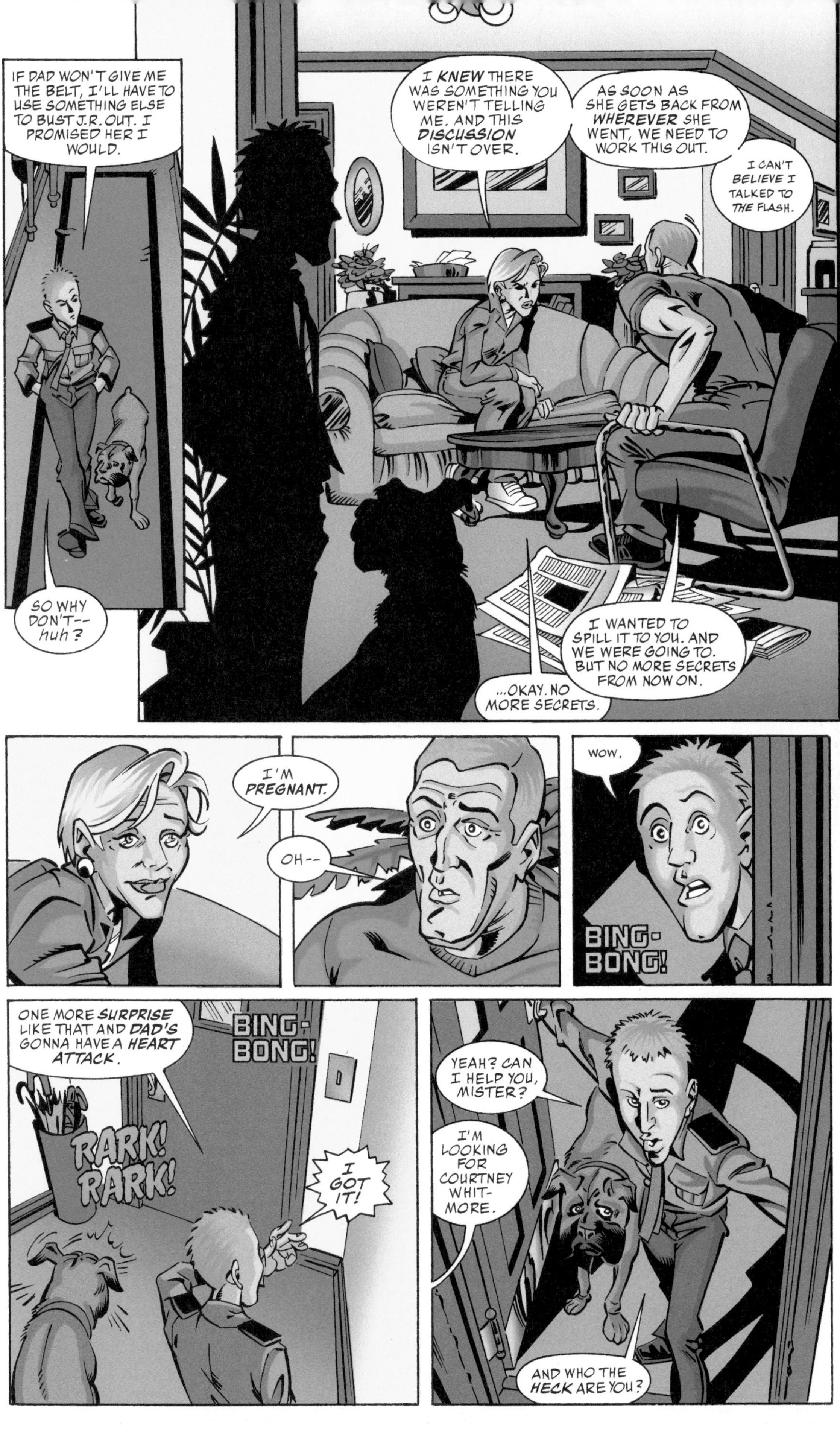
IF DAD WON'T GIVE ME THE BELT, I'LL HAVE TO USE SOMETHING ELSE TO BUST J.R. OUT. I PROMISED HER I WOULD.
SO WHY DON'T-- huh?
I KNEW THERE WAS SOMETHING YOU WEREN'T TELLING ME. AND THIS DISCUSSION ISN'T OVER.
AS SOON AS SHE GETS BACK FROM WHEREVER SHE WENT, WE NEED TO WORK THIS OUT.
I CAN'T BELIEVE I TALKED TO THE FLASH.
I WANTED TO SPILL IT TO YOU. AND WE WERE GOING TO. BUT NO MORE SECRETS FROM NOW ON.
...OKAY. NO MORE SECRETS.
I'M PREGNANT.
OH--
WOW.
BING-BONG!
ONE MORE SURPRISE LIKE THAT AND DAD'S GONNA HAVE A HEART ATTACK.
BING-BONG!
RARK! RARK!
I GOT IT!
YEAH? CAN I HELP YOU, MISTER?
I'M LOOKING FOR COURTNEY WHIT-MORE.
AND WHO THE HECK ARE YOU?

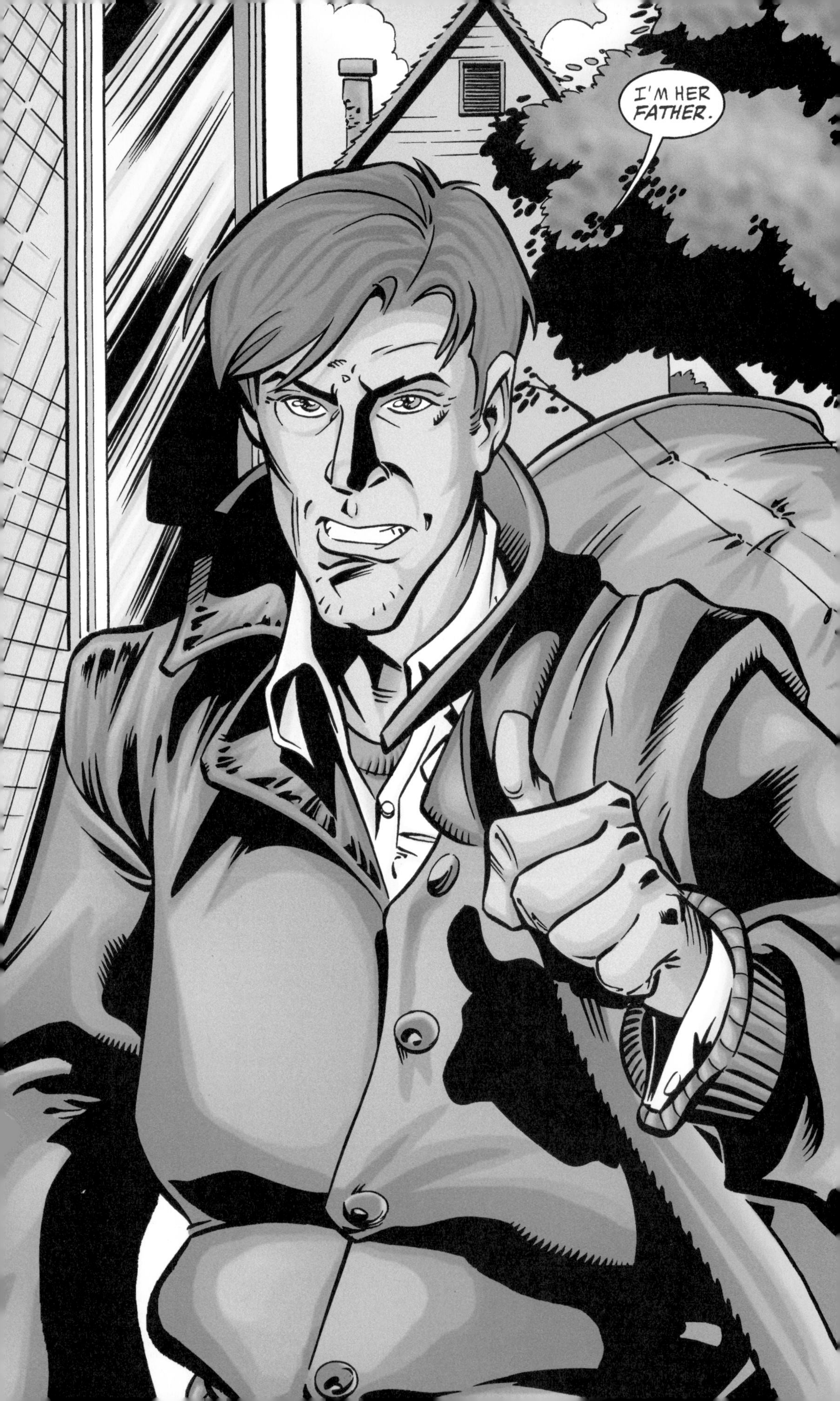
I'M HER FATHER.

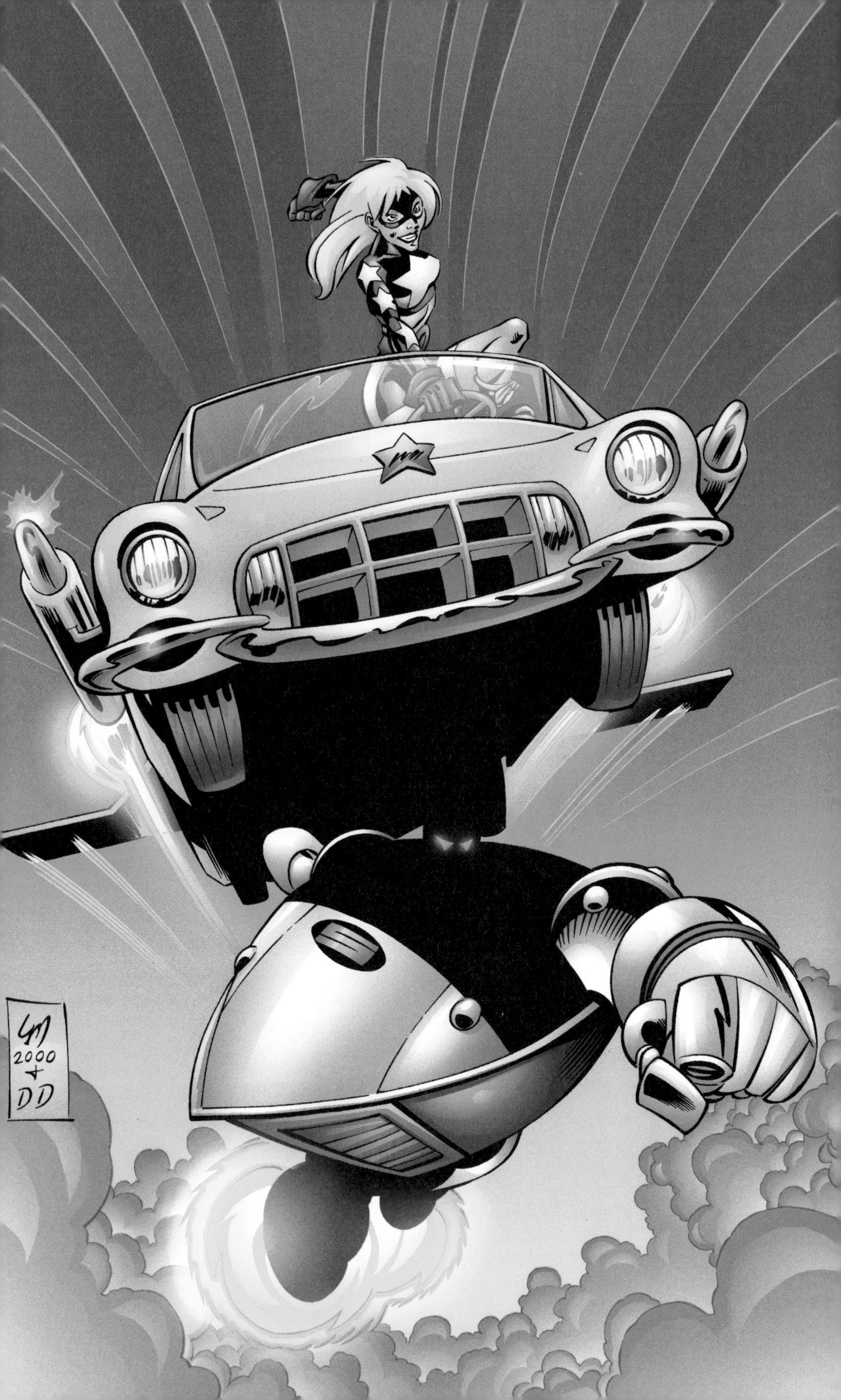
2000
+
DD

STARS AND S.T.R.I.P.E. #14
Written by GEOFF JOHNS
Pencils by LEE MODER
Inks by DAN DAVIS
Colors by TOM McCRAW
Letters by BILL OAKLEY
Cover art by LEE MODER and DAN DAVIS
Cover color by RICHARD & TANYA HORIE

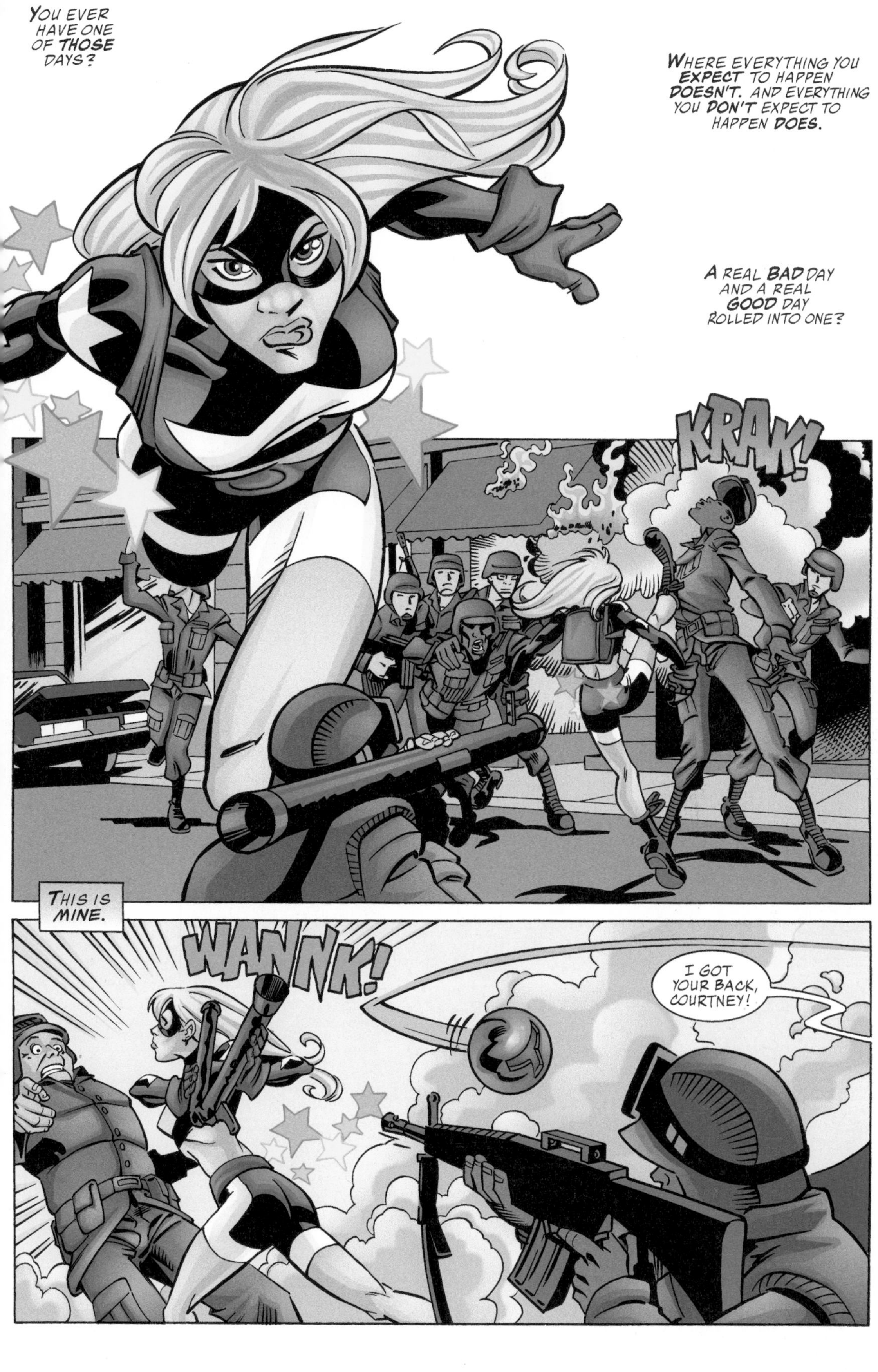
YOU EVER HAVE ONE OF THOSE DAYS?
WHERE EVERYTHING YOU EXPECT TO HAPPEN DOESN'T. AND EVERYTHING YOU DON'T EXPECT TO HAPPEN DOES.
A REAL BAD DAY AND A REAL GOOD DAY ROLLED INTO ONE?
KRAK!
THIS IS MINE.
WANNK!
I GOT YOUR BACK, COURTNEY!

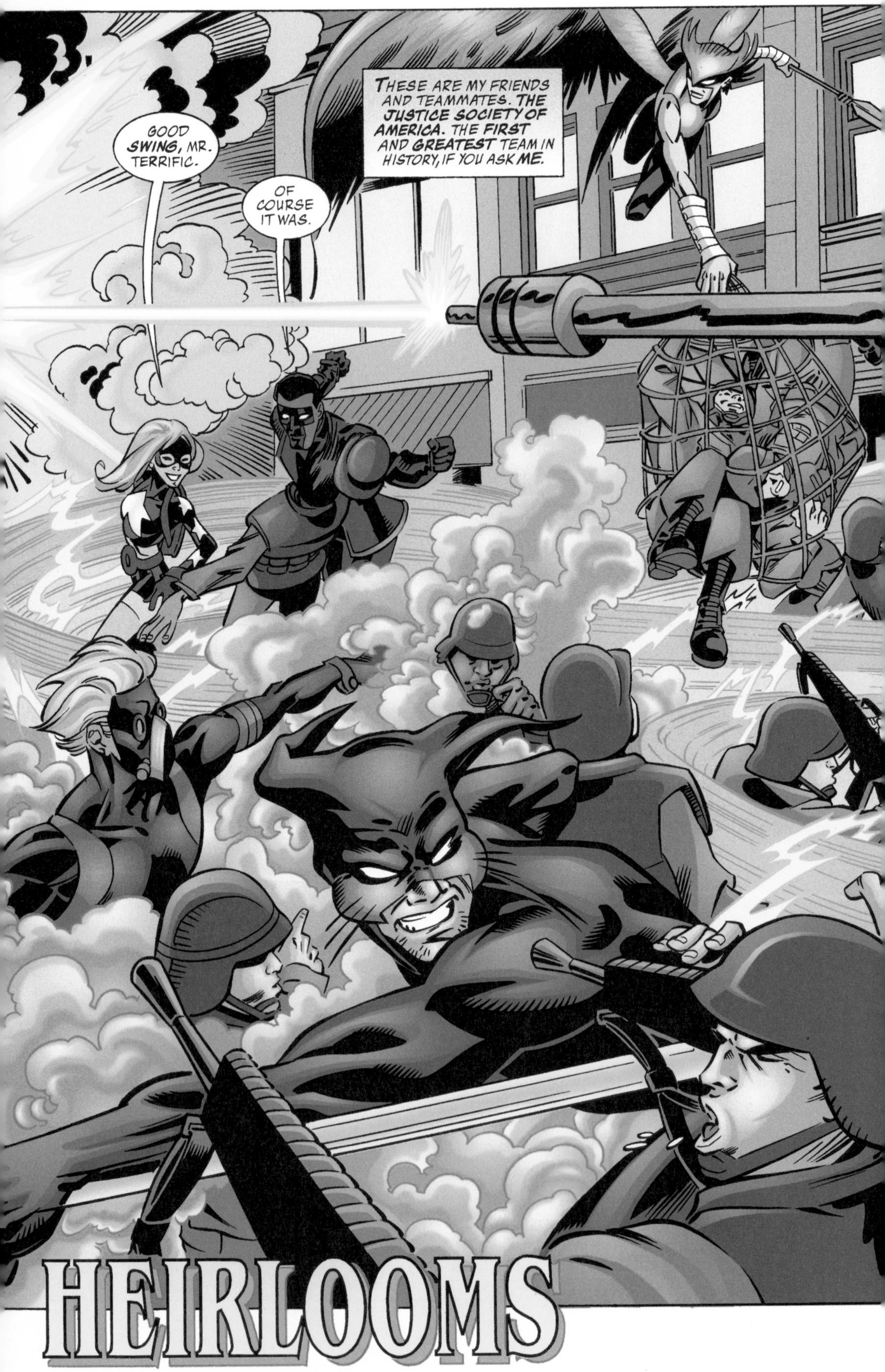

THESE ARE MY FRIENDS AND TEAMMATES. THE JUSTICE SOCIETY OF AMERICA. THE FIRST AND GREATEST TEAM IN HISTORY, IF YOU ASK ME.
GOOD SWING, MR. TERRIFIC.
OF COURSE IT WAS.
HEIRLOOMS

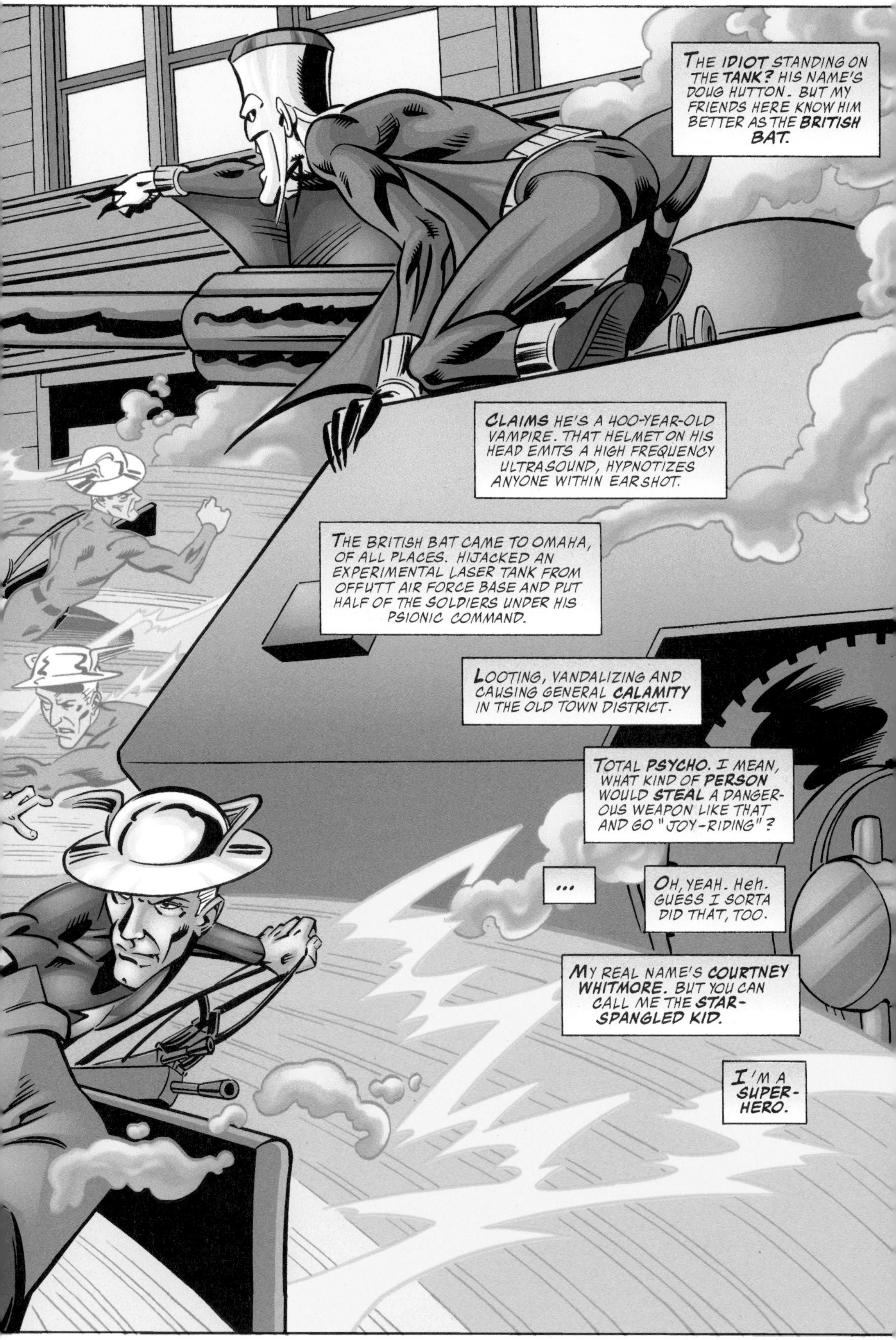
THE IDIOT STANDING ON THE TANK? HIS NAME'S DOUG HUTTON. BUT MY FRIENDS HERE KNOW HIM BETTER AS THE BRITISH BAT.
CLAIMS HE'S A 400-YEAR-OLD VAMPIRE. THAT HELMET ON HIS HEAD EMITS A HIGH FREQUENCY ULTRASOUND, HYPNOTIZES ANYONE WITHIN EARSHOT.
THE BRITISH BAT CAME TO OMAHA, OF ALL PLACES. HIJACKED AN EXPERIMENTAL LASER TANK FROM OFFUTT AIR FORCE BASE AND PUT HALF OF THE SOLDIERS UNDER HIS PSIONIC COMMAND.
LOOTING, VANDALIZING AND CAUSING GENERAL CALAMITY IN THE OLD TOWN DISTRICT.
TOTAL PSYCHO. I MEAN, WHAT KIND OF PERSON WOULD STEAL A DANGEROUS WEAPON LIKE THAT AND GO "JOY-RIDING"?
...
OH, YEAH. Heh. GUESS I SORTA DID THAT, TOO.
MY REAL NAME'S COURTNEY WHITMORE. BUT YOU CAN CALL ME THE STAR-SPANGLED KID.
I'M A SUPER-HERO.

YOUR SPECIAL EAR-PLUGS STILL IN THERE TIGHT, KID?

SAFE AND SOUND.

NO ONE'S CONTROLLING ME AGAIN.

SHRAKA!

THE JSA! SO NICE OF YOU TO JOIN US. SO VERY NICE.

FINALLY BROKE OUT OF THAT D.E.O. PRISON YOU THREW ME IN. TIME TO GET SOME REVENGE. THESE SOLDIERS WILL SPILL YOUR BLOOD.

I'LL DRINK IT.

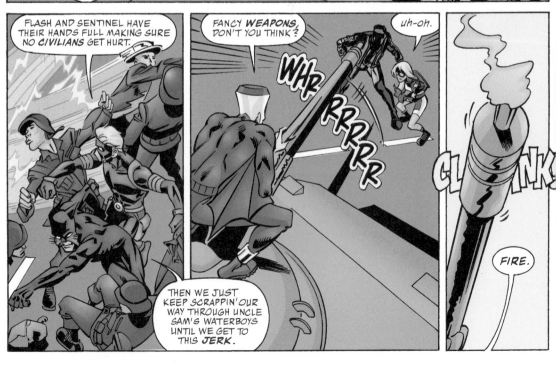

FLASH AND SENTINEL HAVE THEIR HANDS FULL MAKING SURE NO CIVILIANS GET HURT.

FANCY WEAPONS, DON'T YOU THINK?

uh-oh.

WHRRRRRR

CLANK

FIRE.

THEN WE JUST KEEP SCRAPPIN' OUR WAY THROUGH UNCLE SAM'S WATERBOYS UNTIL WE GET TO THIS JERK.

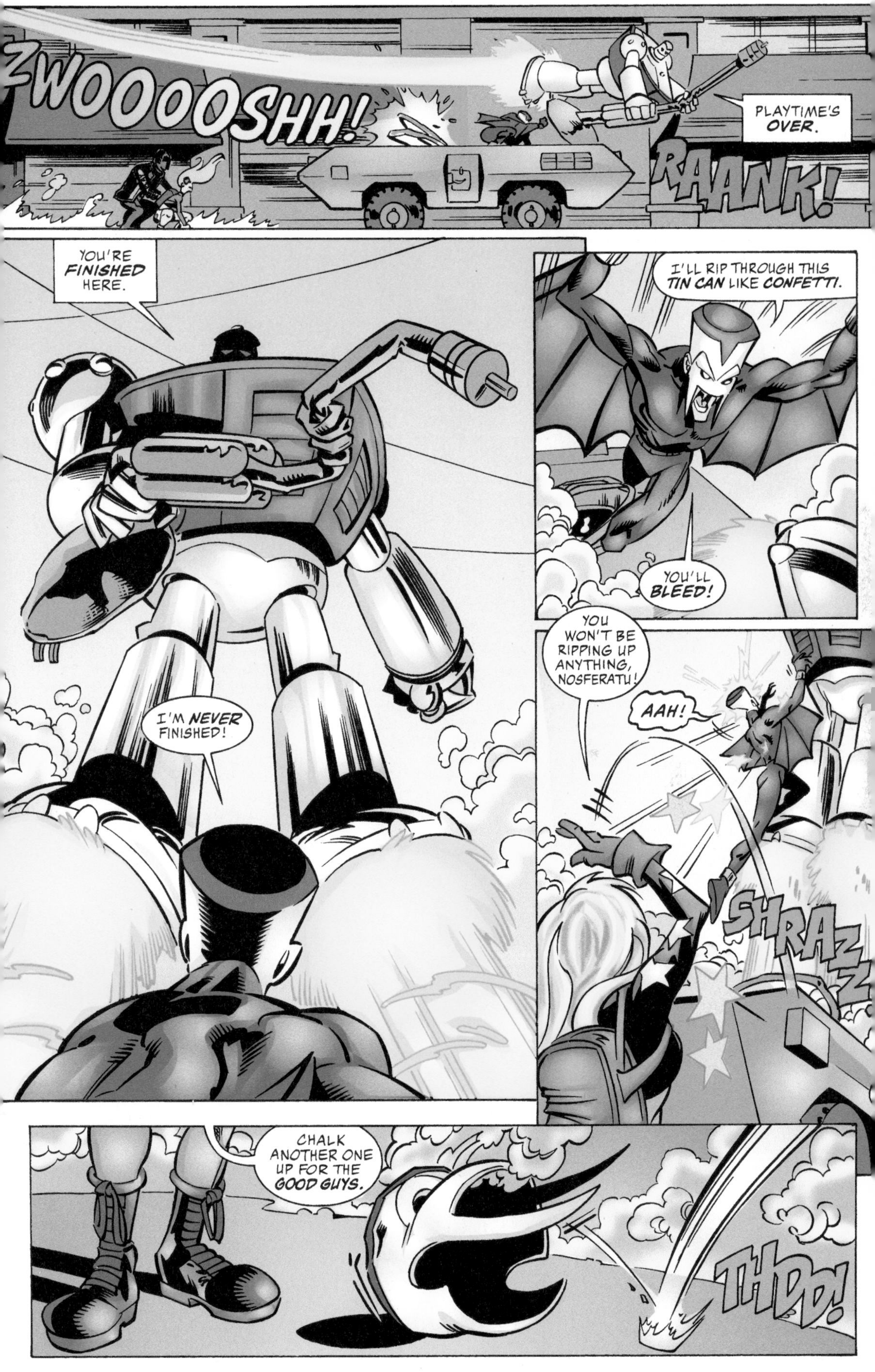
ZWOOOOSHH!
PLAYTIME'S OVER.
RAANK!
YOU'RE FINISHED HERE.
I'LL RIP THROUGH THIS TIN CAN LIKE CONFETTI.
YOU'LL BLEED!
I'M NEVER FINISHED!
YOU WON'T BE RIPPING UP ANYTHING, NOSFERATU!
AAH!
SHRAZZ
CHALK ANOTHER ONE UP FOR THE GOOD GUYS.
THDD!

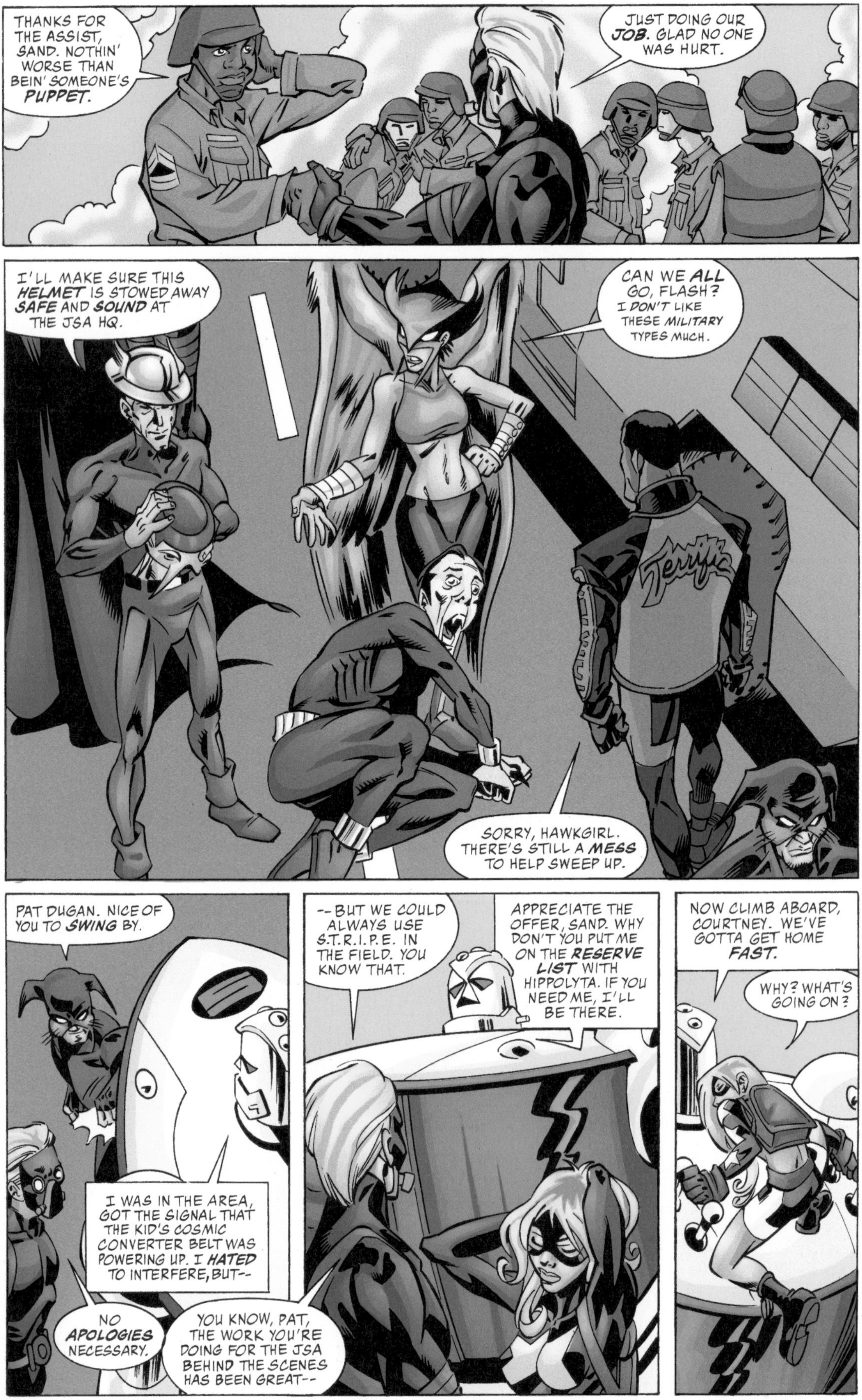
THANKS FOR THE ASSIST, SAND. NOTHIN' WORSE THAN BEIN' SOMEONE'S PUPPET.
JUST DOING OUR JOB. GLAD NO ONE WAS HURT.
I'LL MAKE SURE THIS HELMET IS STOWED AWAY SAFE AND SOUND AT THE JSA HQ.
CAN WE ALL GO, FLASH? I DON'T LIKE THESE MILITARY TYPES MUCH.
SORRY, HAWKGIRL. THERE'S STILL A MESS TO HELP SWEEP UP.
PAT DUGAN. NICE OF YOU TO SWING BY.
I WAS IN THE AREA, GOT THE SIGNAL THAT THE KID'S COSMIC CONVERTER BELT WAS POWERING UP. I HATED TO INTERFERE, BUT--
NO APOLOGIES NECESSARY.
YOU KNOW, PAT, THE WORK YOU'RE DOING FOR THE JSA BEHIND THE SCENES HAS BEEN GREAT--
--BUT WE COULD ALWAYS USE S.T.R.I.P.E. IN THE FIELD. YOU KNOW THAT.
APPRECIATE THE OFFER, SAND. WHY DON'T YOU PUT ME ON THE RESERVE LIST WITH HIPPOLYTA. IF YOU NEED ME, I'LL BE THERE.
NOW CLIMB ABOARD, COURTNEY. WE'VE GOTTA GET HOME FAST.
WHY? WHAT'S GOING ON?

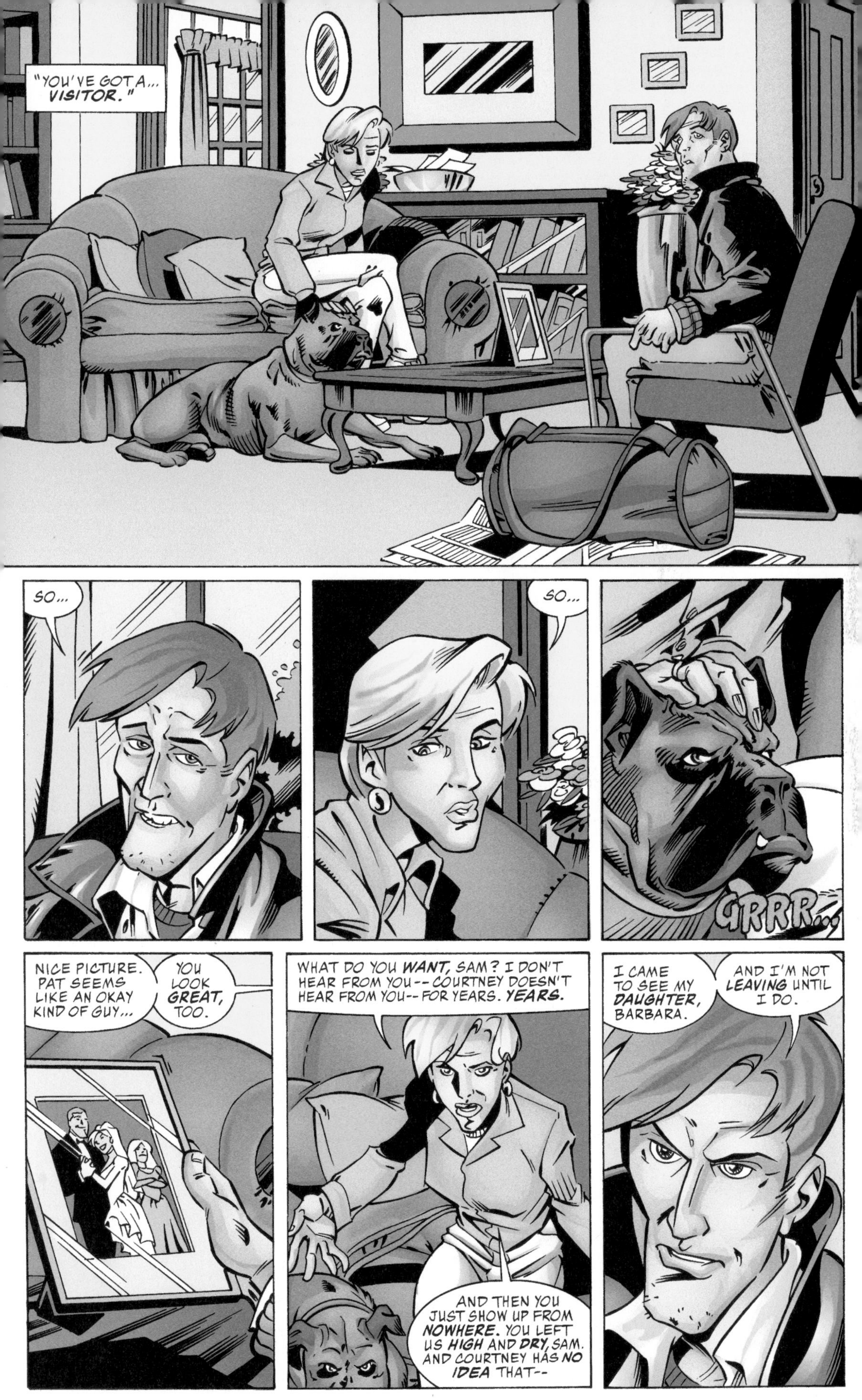
"YOU'VE GOT A... VISITOR."
SO...
SO...
GRRR...
NICE PICTURE. PAT SEEMS LIKE AN OKAY KIND OF GUY...
YOU LOOK GREAT, TOO.
WHAT DO YOU WANT, SAM? I DON'T HEAR FROM YOU-- COURTNEY DOESN'T HEAR FROM YOU-- FOR YEARS. YEARS.
AND THEN YOU JUST SHOW UP FROM NOWHERE. YOU LEFT US HIGH AND DRY, SAM. AND COURTNEY HAS NO IDEA THAT--
I CAME TO SEE MY DAUGHTER, BARBARA.
AND I'M NOT LEAVING UNTIL I DO.

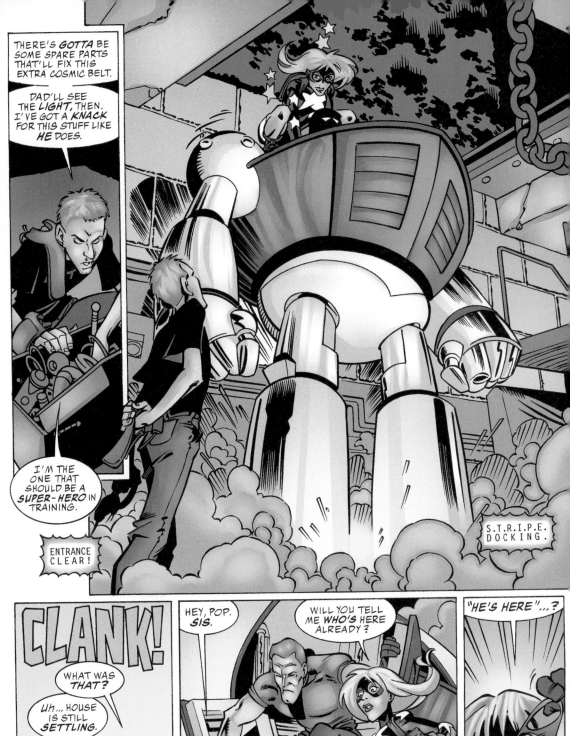

THERE'S *GOTTA* BE SOME SPARE PARTS THAT'LL FIX THIS EXTRA COSMIC BELT.

DAD'LL SEE THE *LIGHT*, THEN. I'VE GOT A *KNACK* FOR THIS STUFF LIKE *HE* DOES.

I'M THE ONE THAT SHOULD BE A *SUPER-HERO* IN TRAINING.

ENTRANCE CLEAR!

S.T.R.I.P.E. DOCKING.

CLANK!

WHAT WAS *THAT*?

UH... HOUSE IS STILL *SETTLING*.

HEY, POP. *SIS*.

WILL YOU TELL ME *WHO'S* HERE ALREADY?

DAD, YOU *DIDN'T* TELL HER *HE'S* HERE?

"HE'S HERE"...?

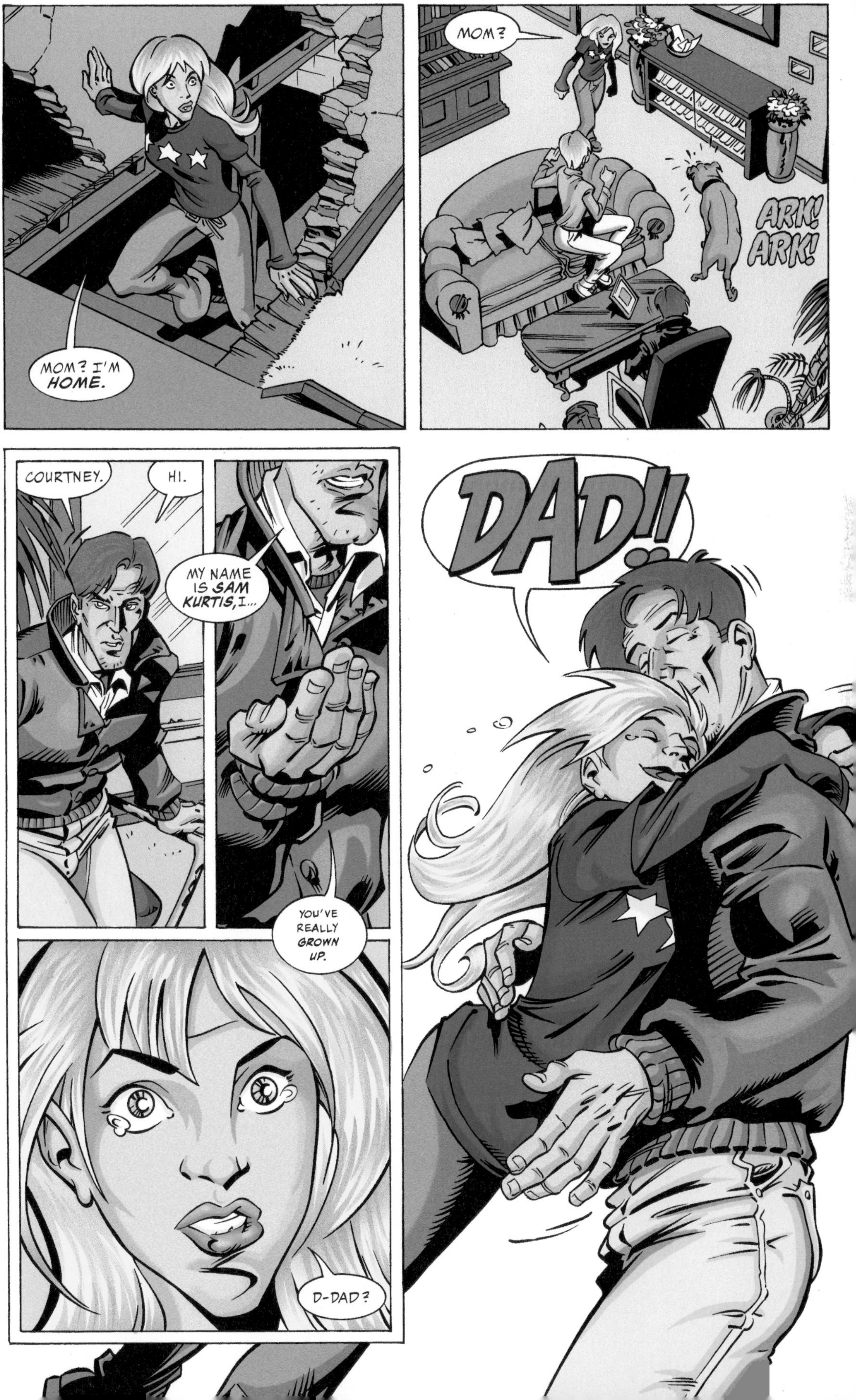
MOM? I'M HOME.
MOM?
ARK! ARK!
COURTNEY.
HI.
MY NAME IS SAM KURTIS, I...
YOU'VE REALLY GROWN UP.
D-DAD?
DAD!!

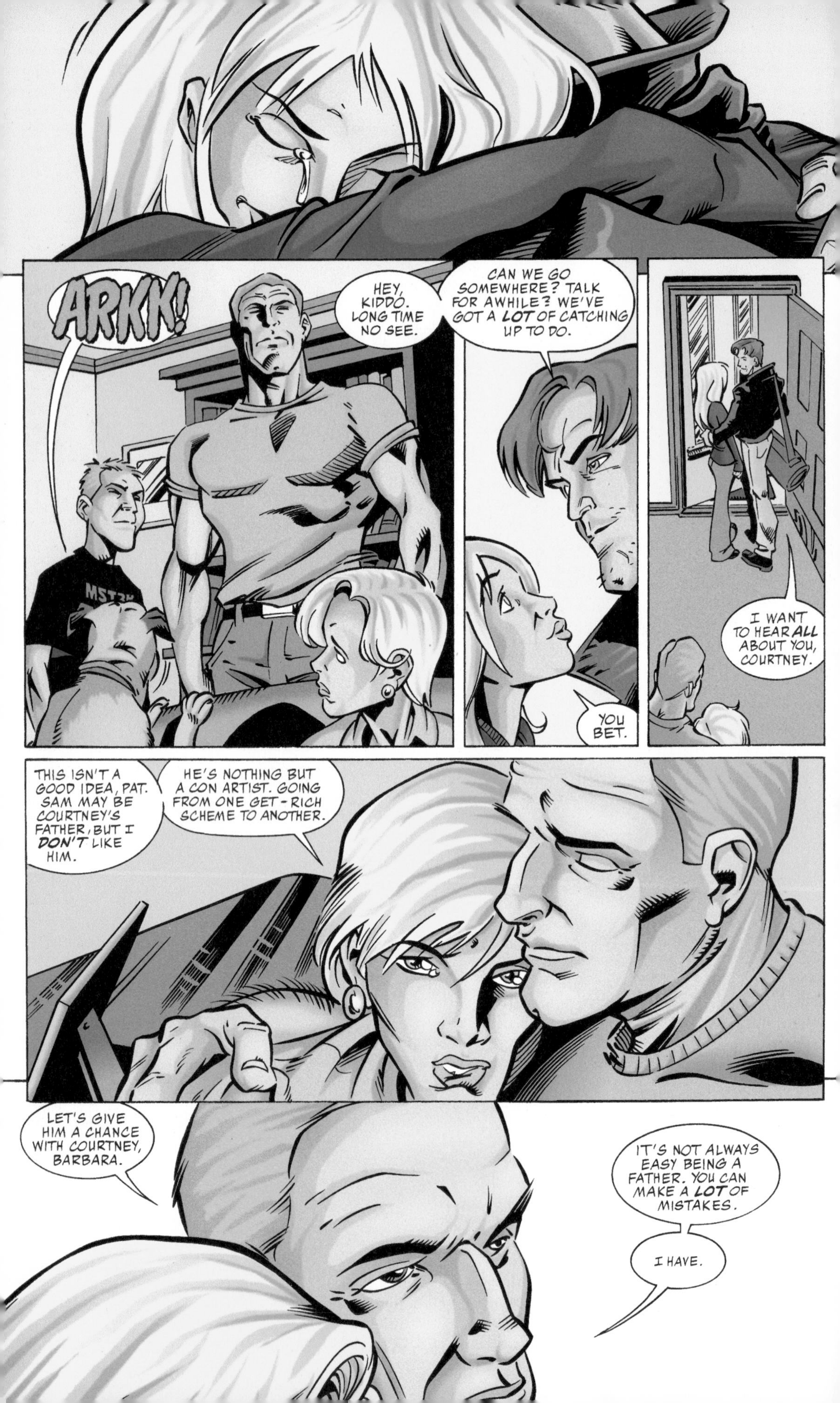
ARKK!
HEY, KIDDO. LONG TIME NO SEE.
CAN WE GO SOMEWHERE? TALK FOR AWHILE? WE'VE GOT A LOT OF CATCHING UP TO DO.
YOU BET.
I WANT TO HEAR ALL ABOUT YOU, COURTNEY.
THIS ISN'T A GOOD IDEA, PAT. SAM MAY BE COURTNEY'S FATHER, BUT I DON'T LIKE HIM.
HE'S NOTHING BUT A CON ARTIST. GOING FROM ONE GET-RICH SCHEME TO ANOTHER.
LET'S GIVE HIM A CHANCE WITH COURTNEY, BARBARA.
IT'S NOT ALWAYS EASY BEING A FATHER. YOU CAN MAKE A LOT OF MISTAKES.
I HAVE.

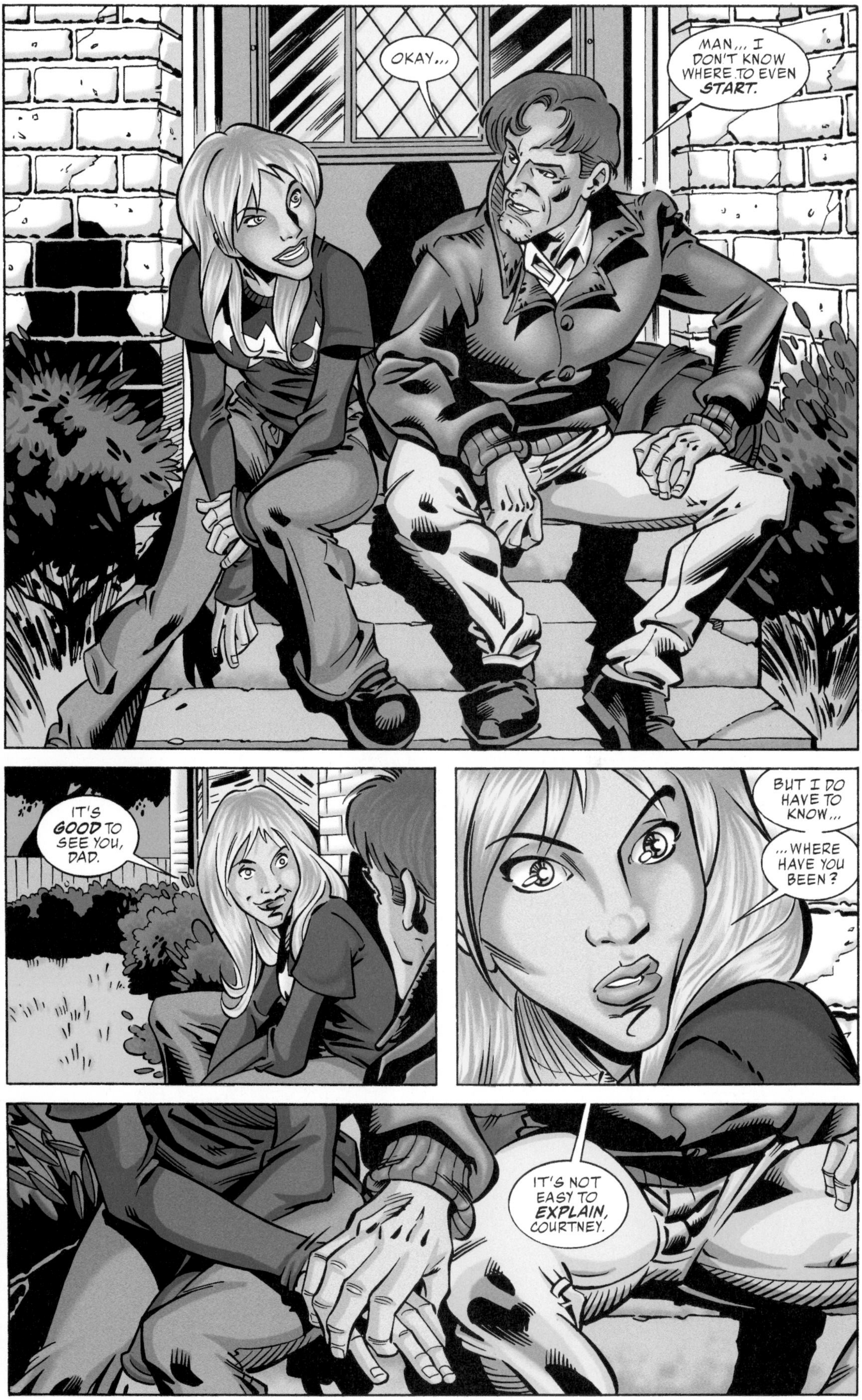
OKAY...
MAN... I DON'T KNOW WHERE TO EVEN START.
IT'S GOOD TO SEE YOU, DAD.
BUT I DO HAVE TO KNOW...
...WHERE HAVE YOU BEEN?
IT'S NOT EASY TO EXPLAIN, COURTNEY.

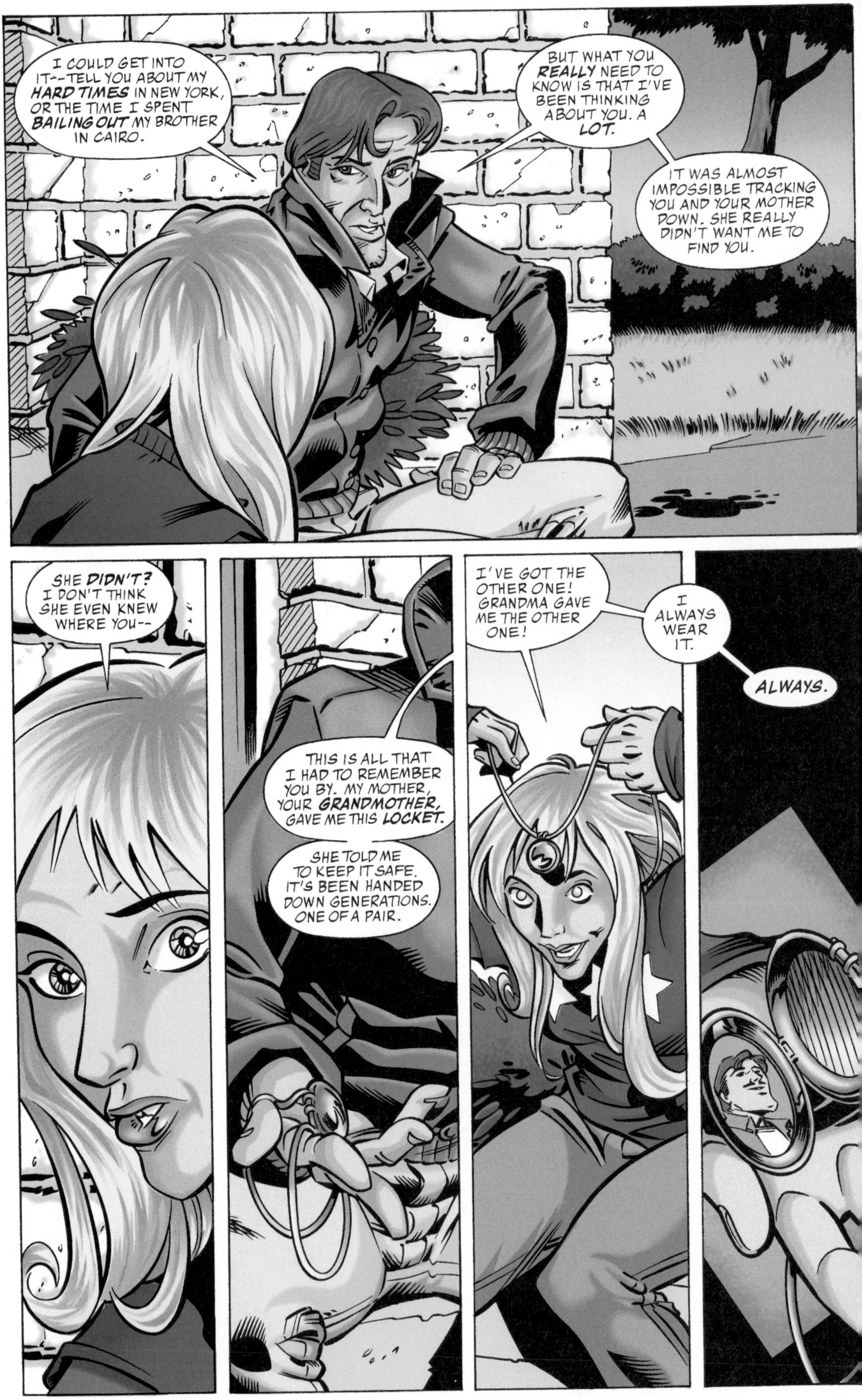
I COULD GET INTO IT--TELL YOU ABOUT MY HARD TIMES IN NEW YORK, OR THE TIME I SPENT BAILING OUT MY BROTHER IN CAIRO.
BUT WHAT YOU REALLY NEED TO KNOW IS THAT I'VE BEEN THINKING ABOUT YOU. A LOT.
IT WAS ALMOST IMPOSSIBLE TRACKING YOU AND YOUR MOTHER DOWN. SHE REALLY DIDN'T WANT ME TO FIND YOU.
SHE DIDN'T? I DON'T THINK SHE EVEN KNEW WHERE YOU--
THIS IS ALL THAT I HAD TO REMEMBER YOU BY. MY MOTHER, YOUR GRANDMOTHER, GAVE ME THIS LOCKET.
SHE TOLD ME TO KEEP IT SAFE. IT'S BEEN HANDED DOWN GENERATIONS. ONE OF A PAIR.
I'VE GOT THE OTHER ONE! GRANDMA GAVE ME THE OTHER ONE!
I ALWAYS WEAR IT.
ALWAYS.

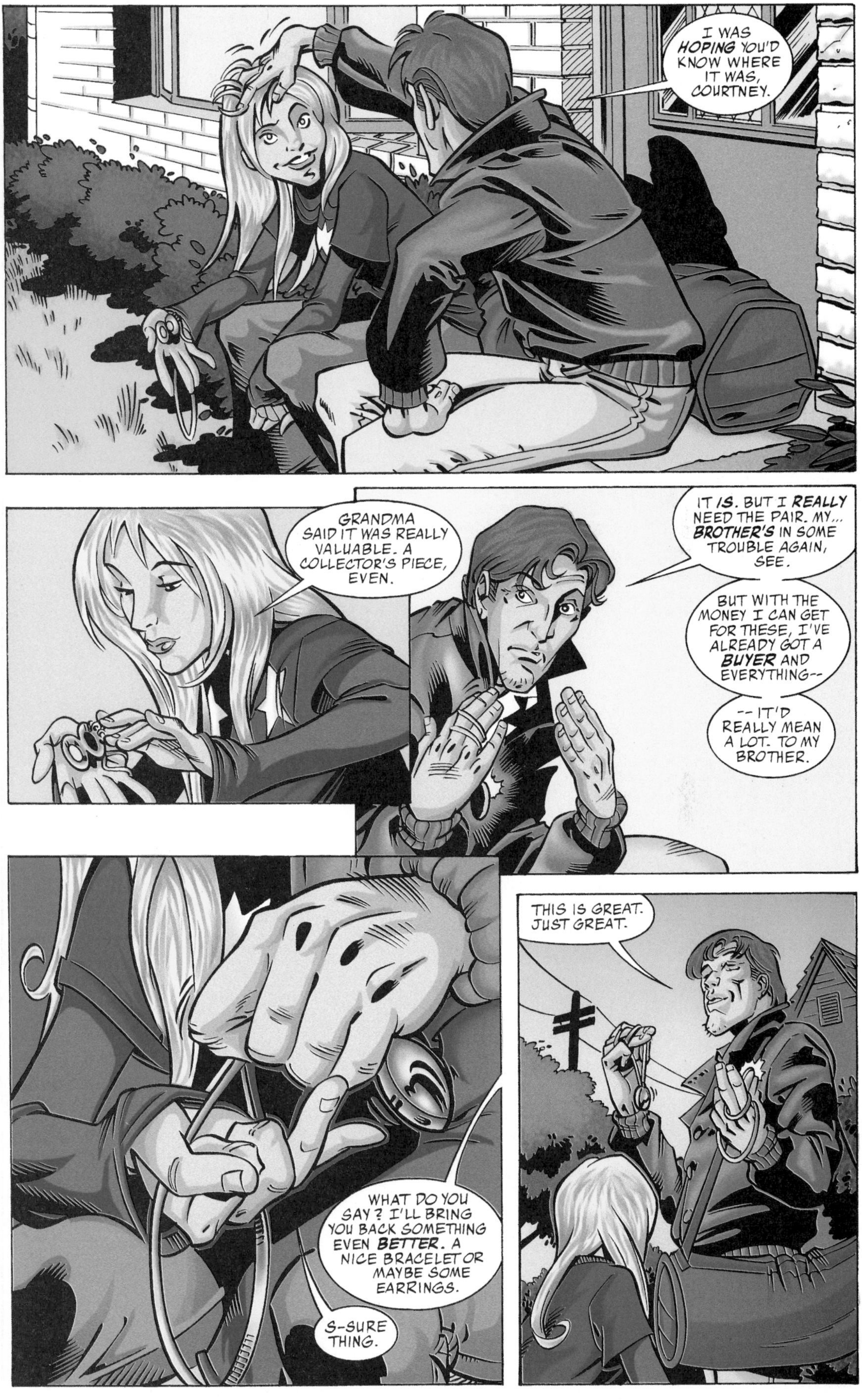

I WAS HOPING YOU'D KNOW WHERE IT WAS, COURTNEY.
GRANDMA SAID IT WAS REALLY VALUABLE. A COLLECTOR'S PIECE, EVEN.
IT IS. BUT I REALLY NEED THE PAIR. MY... BROTHER'S IN SOME TROUBLE AGAIN, SEE.
BUT WITH THE MONEY I CAN GET FOR THESE, I'VE ALREADY GOT A BUYER AND EVERYTHING--
-- IT'D REALLY MEAN A LOT. TO MY BROTHER.
WHAT DO YOU SAY? I'LL BRING YOU BACK SOMETHING EVEN BETTER. A NICE BRACELET OR MAYBE SOME EARRINGS.
S-SURE THING.
THIS IS GREAT. JUST GREAT.

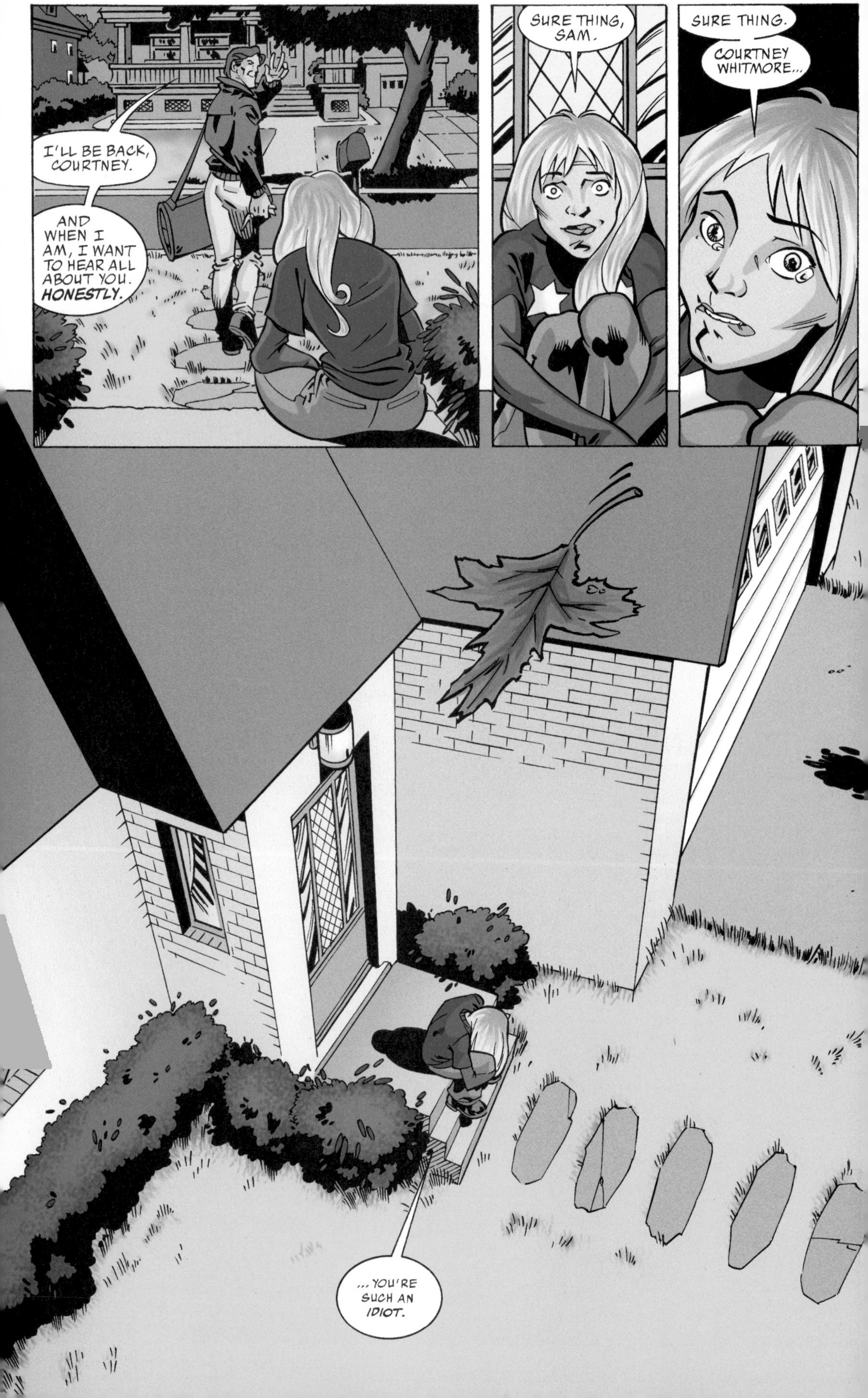
I'LL BE BACK, COURTNEY.
AND WHEN I AM, I WANT TO HEAR ALL ABOUT YOU. **HONESTLY**.
SURE THING, SAM.
SURE THING.
COURTNEY WHITMORE...
...YOU'RE SUCH AN *IDIOT*.

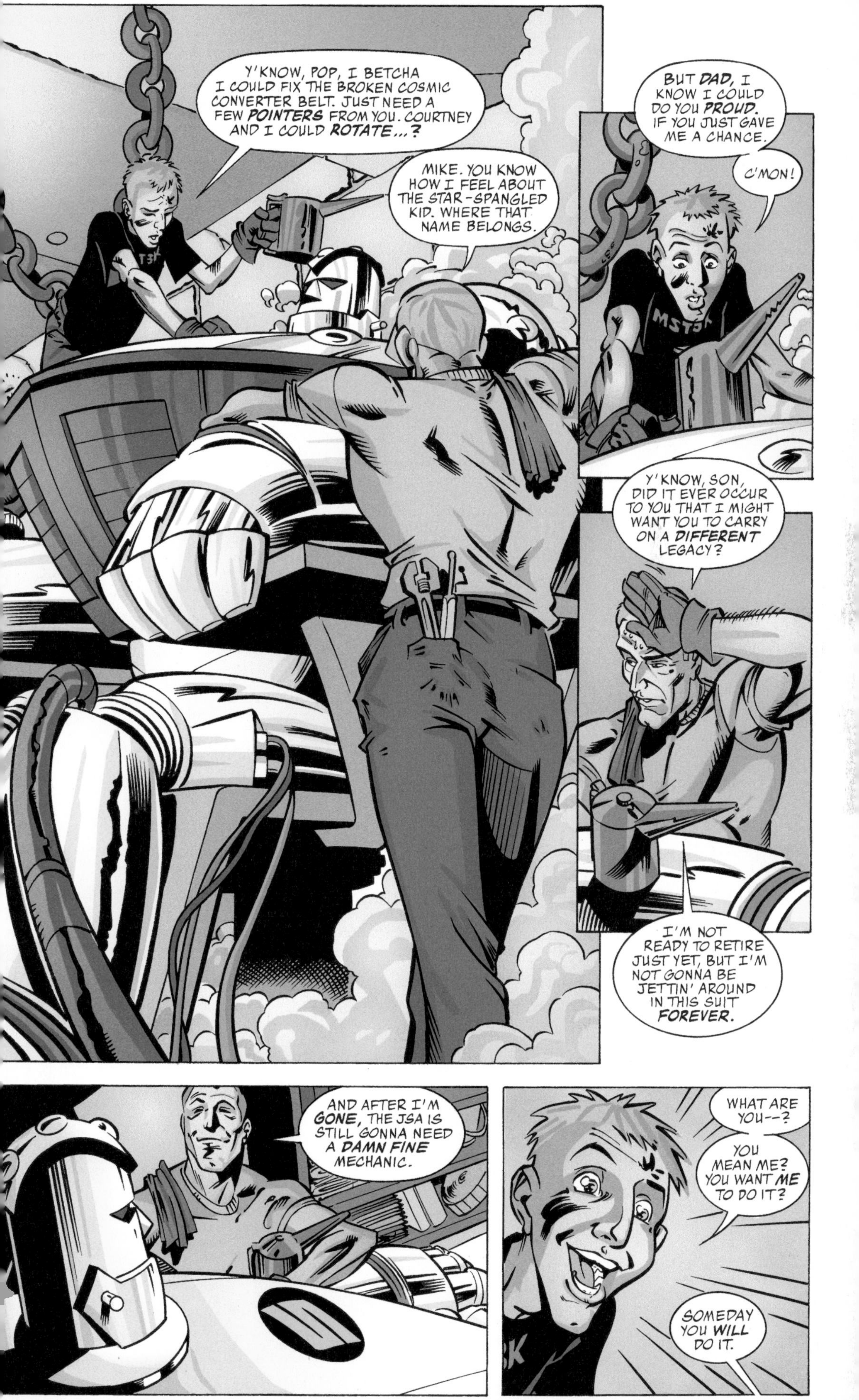

Y'KNOW, POP, I BETCHA I COULD FIX THE BROKEN COSMIC CONVERTER BELT. JUST NEED A FEW POINTERS FROM YOU. COURTNEY AND I COULD ROTATE...?
MIKE. YOU KNOW HOW I FEEL ABOUT THE STAR-SPANGLED KID. WHERE THAT NAME BELONGS.
BUT DAD, I KNOW I COULD DO YOU PROUD. IF YOU JUST GAVE ME A CHANCE.
C'MON!
Y'KNOW, SON, DID IT EVER OCCUR TO YOU THAT I MIGHT WANT YOU TO CARRY ON A DIFFERENT LEGACY?
I'M NOT READY TO RETIRE JUST YET, BUT I'M NOT GONNA BE JETTIN' AROUND IN THIS SUIT FOREVER.
AND AFTER I'M GONE, THE JSA IS STILL GONNA NEED A DAMN FINE MECHANIC.
WHAT ARE YOU--?
YOU MEAN ME? YOU WANT ME TO DO IT?
SOMEDAY YOU WILL DO IT.

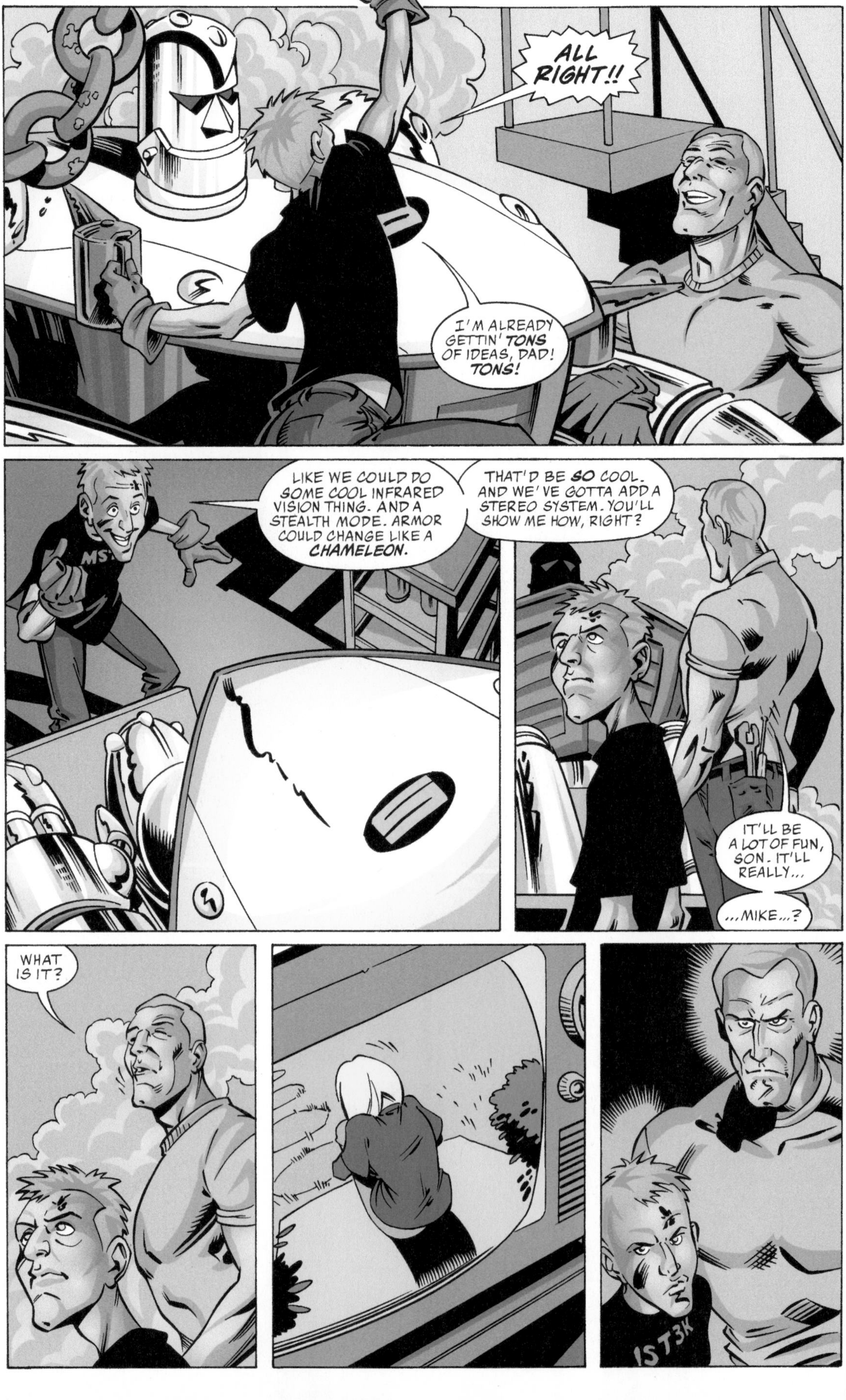
ALL RIGHT!!
I'M ALREADY GETTIN' TONS OF IDEAS, DAD! TONS!
LIKE WE COULD DO SOME COOL INFRARED VISION THING. AND A STEALTH MODE. ARMOR COULD CHANGE LIKE A CHAMELEON.
THAT'D BE SO COOL. AND WE'VE GOTTA ADD A STEREO SYSTEM. YOU'LL SHOW ME HOW, RIGHT?
IT'LL BE A LOT OF FUN, SON. IT'LL REALLY...
...MIKE...?
WHAT IS IT?

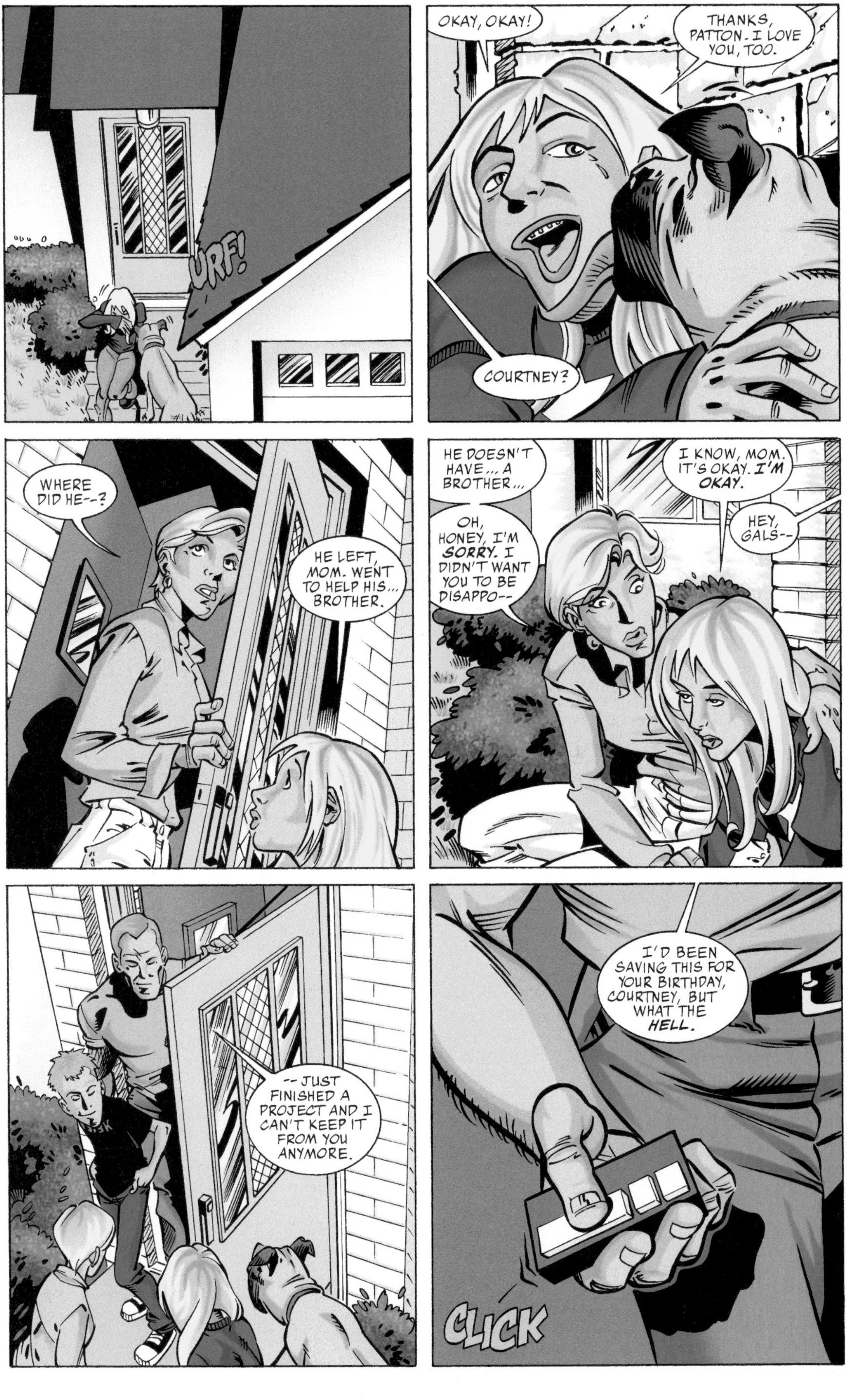
URF!
OKAY, OKAY!
THANKS, PATTON. I LOVE YOU, TOO.
COURTNEY?
WHERE DID HE--?
HE LEFT, MOM. WENT TO HELP HIS... BROTHER.
HE DOESN'T HAVE... A BROTHER...
OH, HONEY, I'M SORRY. I DIDN'T WANT YOU TO BE DISAPPO--
I KNOW, MOM. IT'S OKAY. I'M OKAY.
HEY, GALS--
--JUST FINISHED A PROJECT AND I CAN'T KEEP IT FROM YOU ANYMORE.
I'D BEEN SAVING THIS FOR YOUR BIRTHDAY, COURTNEY, BUT WHAT THE HELL.
CLICK

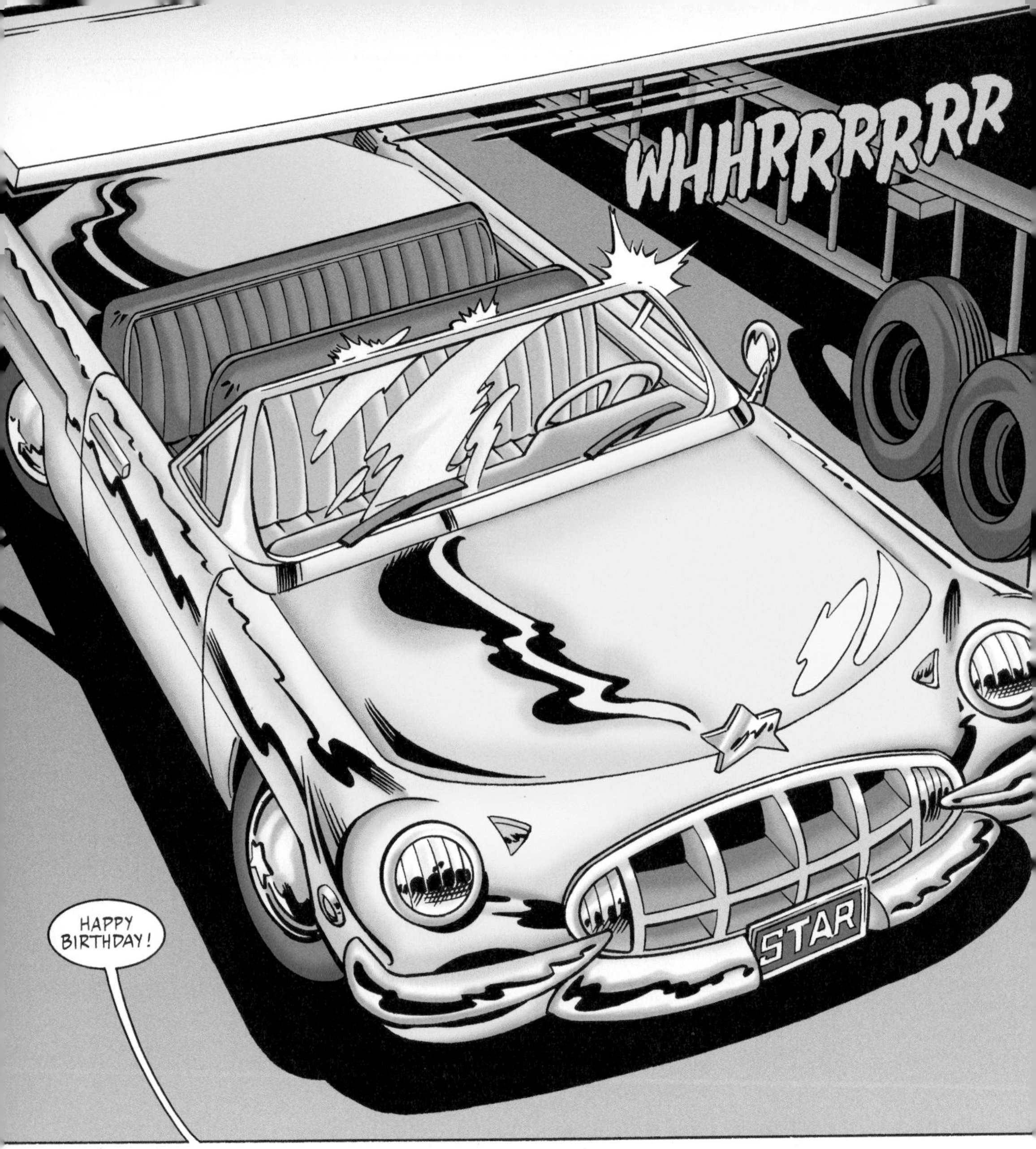
WHHRRRRRR
HAPPY BIRTHDAY!
STAR

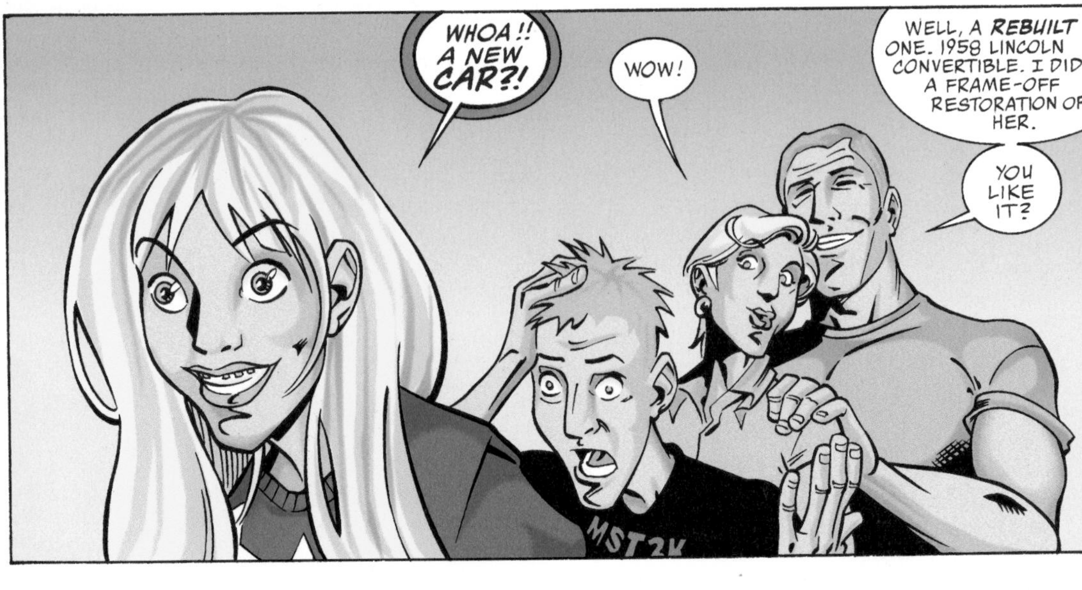
WHOA!! A NEW CAR?!
WOW!
WELL, A REBUILT ONE. 1958 LINCOLN CONVERTIBLE. I DID A FRAME-OFF RESTORATION OF HER.
YOU LIKE IT?
MST 2K

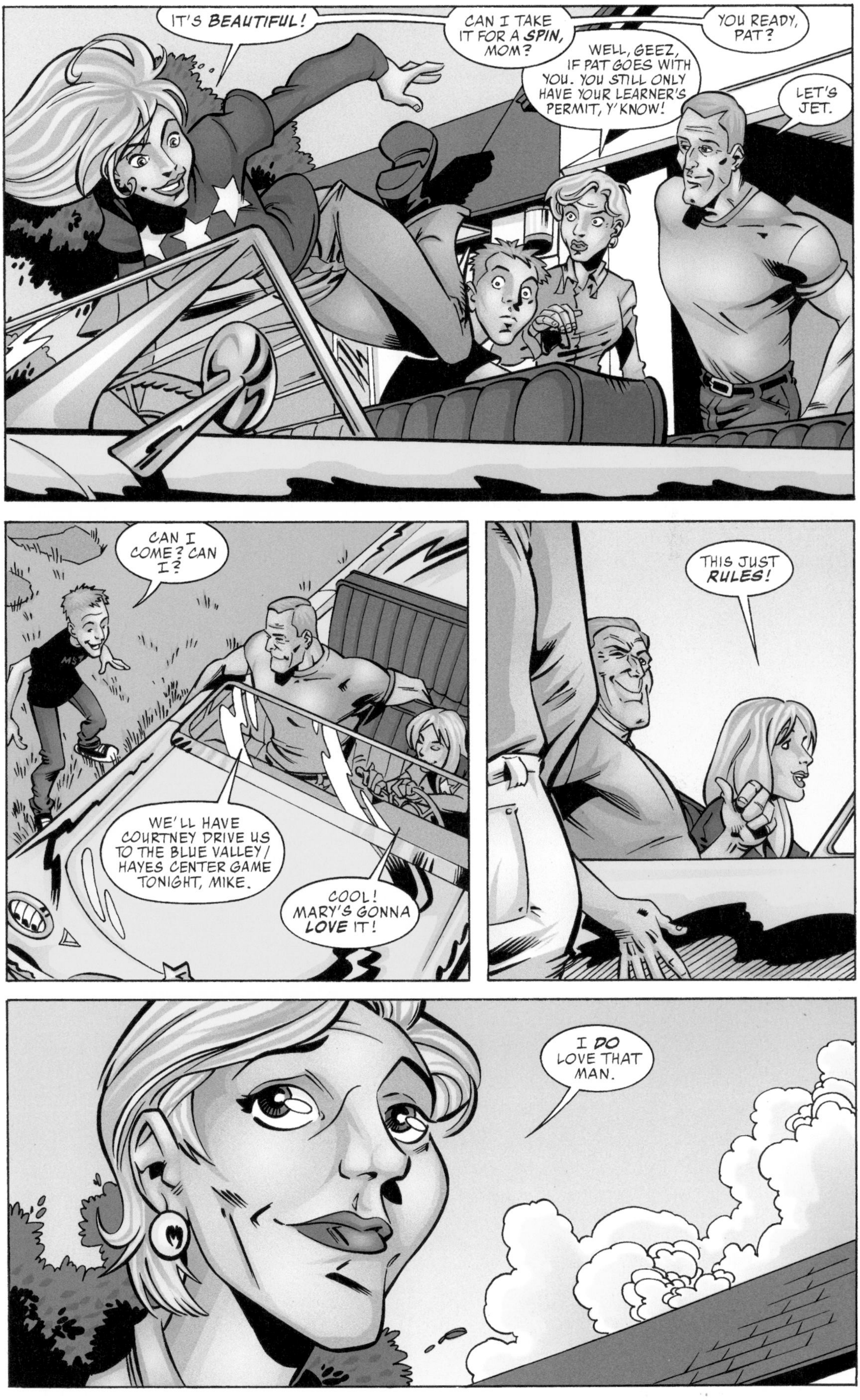
IT'S BEAUTIFUL!
CAN I TAKE IT FOR A SPIN, MOM?
WELL, GEEZ, IF PAT GOES WITH YOU. YOU STILL ONLY HAVE YOUR LEARNER'S PERMIT, Y'KNOW!
YOU READY, PAT?
LET'S JET.
CAN I COME? CAN I?
WE'LL HAVE COURTNEY DRIVE US TO THE BLUE VALLEY/ HAYES CENTER GAME TONIGHT, MIKE.
COOL! MARY'S GONNA LOVE IT!
THIS JUST RULES!
I DO LOVE THAT MAN.

DON'T HIT THE **BRAKES** TOO HARD.

AND DON'T FORGET TO SIGNAL.

I KNOW! I KNOW!

WHAT'S **THIS** DO?

YOU DON'T WANT TO PUSH **THAT**, KID. NOT YET. WE'LL GET TO IT **EVENTUALLY.**

HOW'S SHE DRIVE?

STAR ROCKET RACER

JUST **GREAT.** THIS IS **SO** TOTALLY COOL!

THANKS A LOT, **DAD.** I--

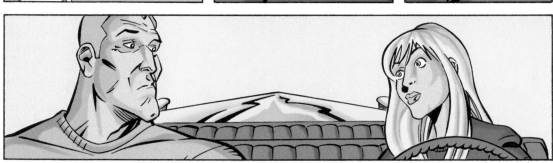

I MEANT, *uh,* **DUDE.** SORRY, I DIDN'T MEAN ... I MEAN ...

HEY, COURTNEY.

YEAH?

ANYTIME.

YO!!

WHAT THE--?

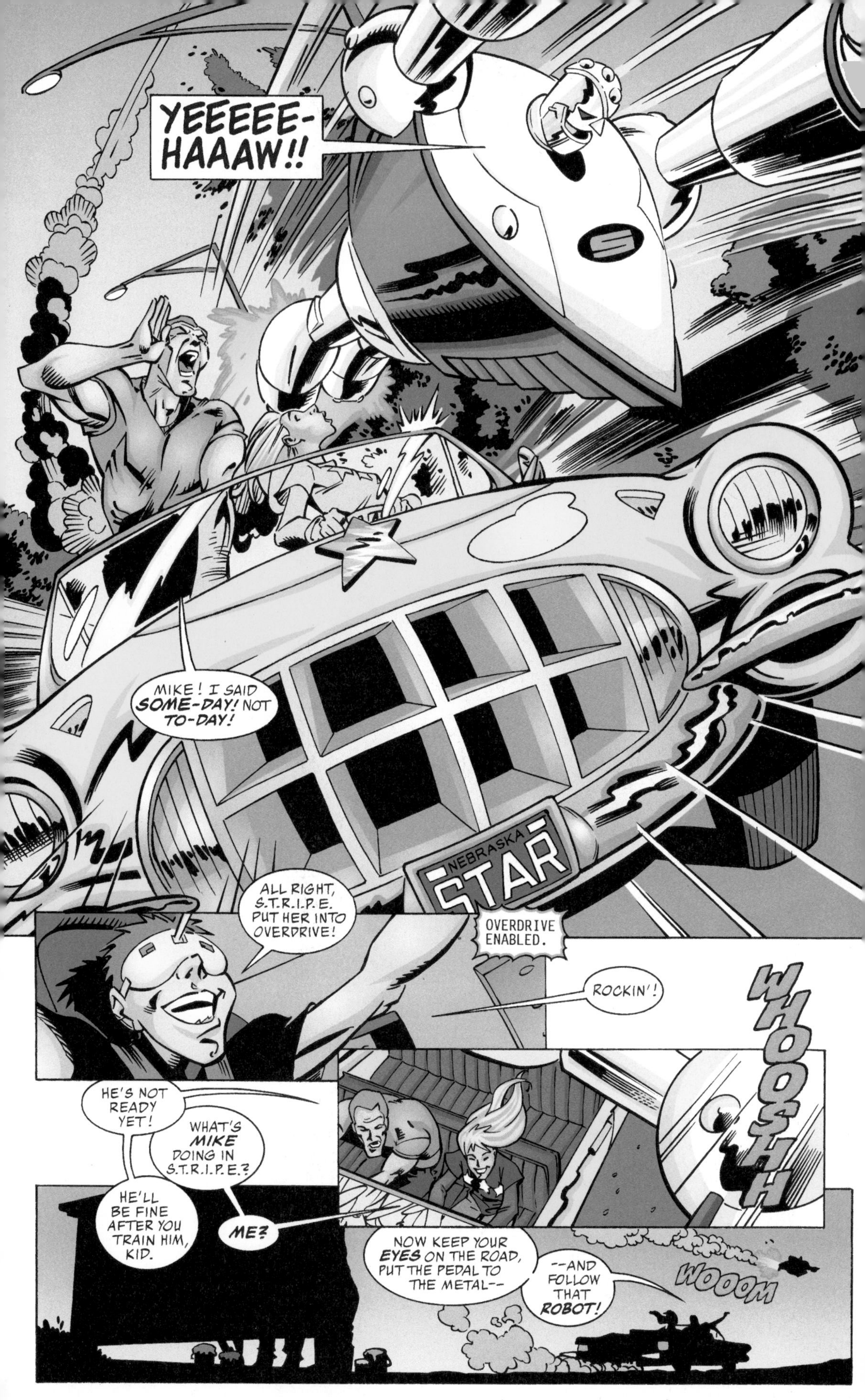
YEEEEE-HAAAW!!
MIKE! I SAID SOME-DAY! NOT TO-DAY!
NEBRASKA STAR
ALL RIGHT, S.T.R.I.P.E. PUT HER INTO OVERDRIVE!
OVERDRIVE ENABLED.
ROCKIN'!
WHOOOSHH
HE'S NOT READY YET!
WHAT'S MIKE DOING IN S.T.R.I.P.E.?
HE'LL BE FINE AFTER YOU TRAIN HIM, KID.
ME?
NOW KEEP YOUR EYES ON THE ROAD, PUT THE PEDAL TO THE METAL--
--AND FOLLOW THAT ROBOT!
WOOOM

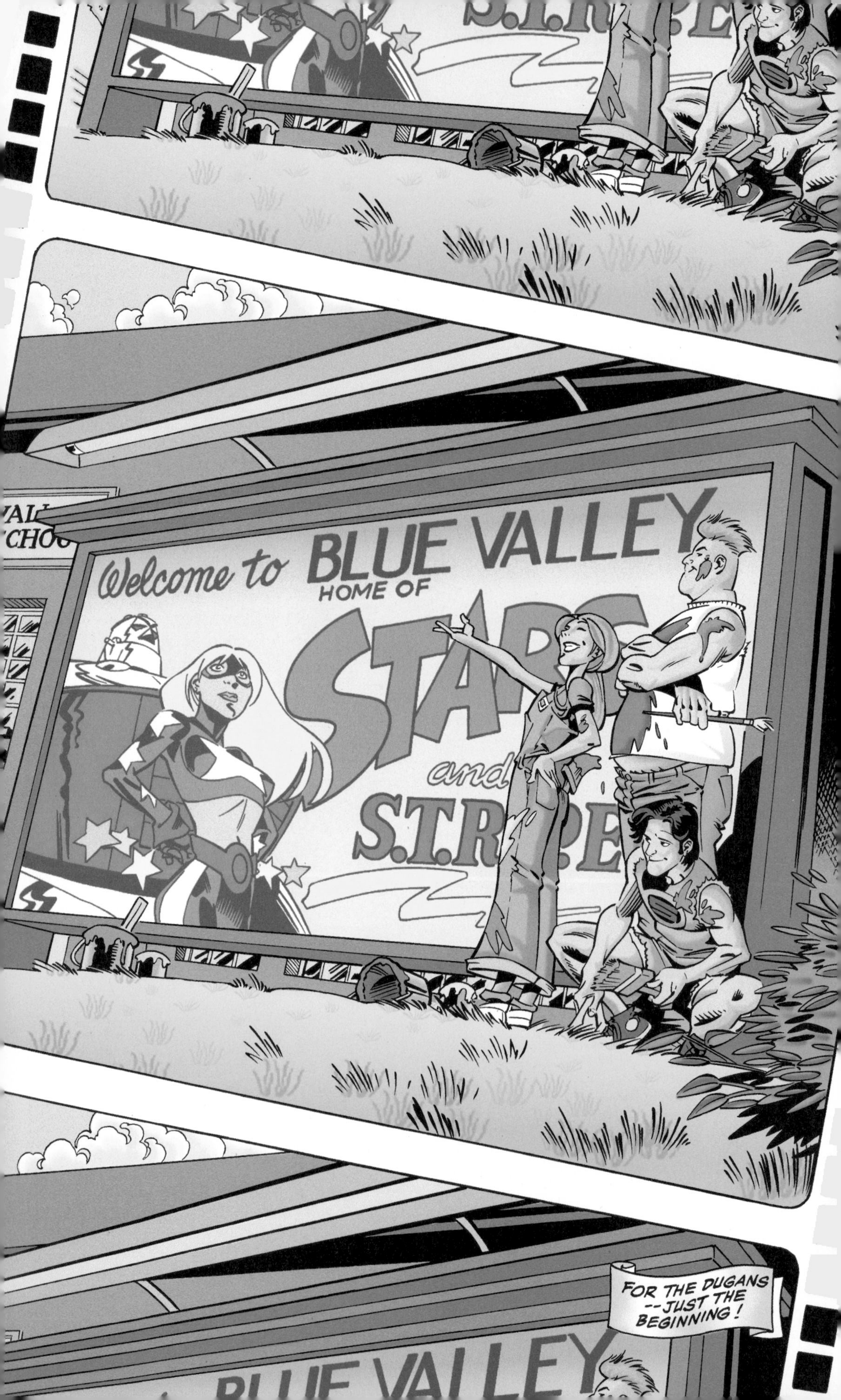
Welcome to BLUE VALLEY
HOME OF
STARS
and
S.T.R.I.P.E.
FOR THE DUGANS --JUST THE BEGINNING!

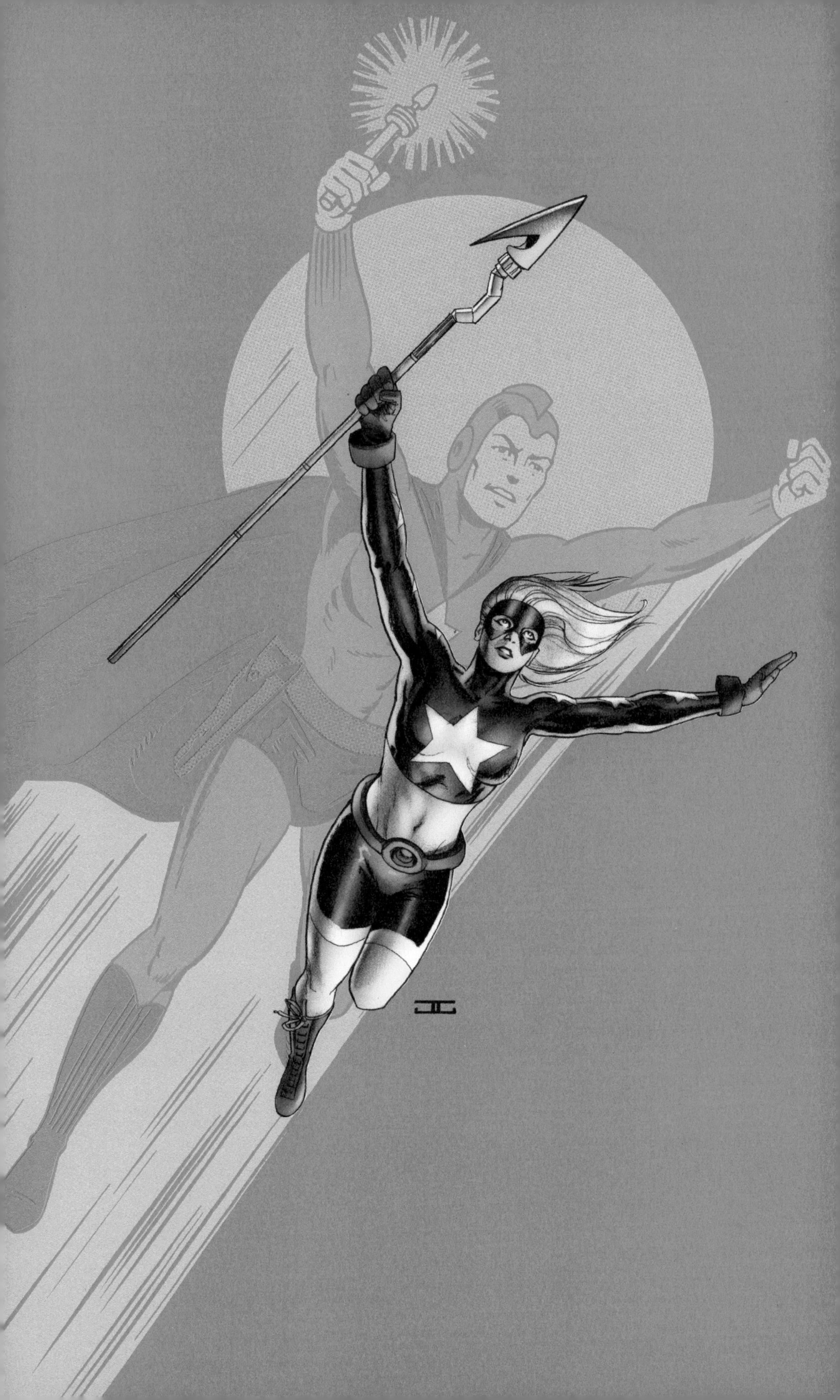

JSA ALL STARS #4

Written by GEOFF JOHNS and DAVID S. GOYER
Pencils by MIKE McKONE
Inks by WAYNE FAUCHER
Colors by JOHN KALISZ
Letters by KURT HATHAWAY
Cover art by JOHN CASSADAY and MARK LEWIS
Cover color by DAVID BARON

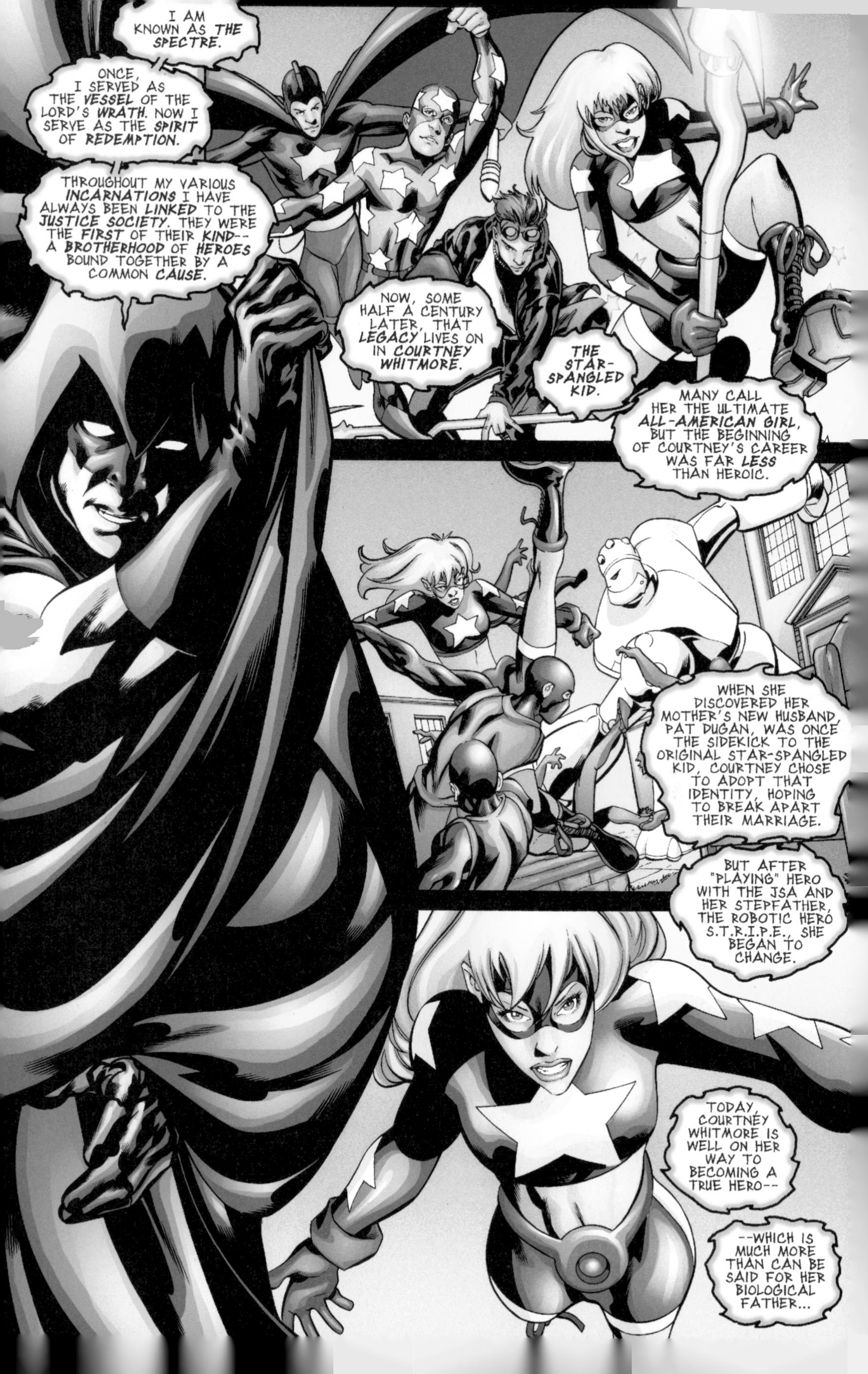
I AM KNOWN AS THE SPECTRE.
ONCE, I SERVED AS THE VESSEL OF THE LORD'S WRATH. NOW I SERVE AS THE SPIRIT OF REDEMPTION.
THROUGHOUT MY VARIOUS INCARNATIONS I HAVE ALWAYS BEEN LINKED TO THE JUSTICE SOCIETY. THEY WERE THE FIRST OF THEIR KIND-- A BROTHERHOOD OF HEROES BOUND TOGETHER BY A COMMON CAUSE.
NOW, SOME HALF A CENTURY LATER, THAT LEGACY LIVES ON IN COURTNEY WHITMORE.
THE STAR-SPANGLED KID.
MANY CALL HER THE ULTIMATE ALL-AMERICAN GIRL, BUT THE BEGINNING OF COURTNEY'S CAREER WAS FAR LESS THAN HEROIC.
WHEN SHE DISCOVERED HER MOTHER'S NEW HUSBAND, PAT DUGAN, WAS ONCE THE SIDEKICK TO THE ORIGINAL STAR-SPANGLED KID, COURTNEY CHOSE TO ADOPT THAT IDENTITY, HOPING TO BREAK APART THEIR MARRIAGE.
BUT AFTER "PLAYING" HERO WITH THE JSA AND HER STEPFATHER, THE ROBOTIC HERO S.T.R.I.P.E., SHE BEGAN TO CHANGE.
TODAY, COURTNEY WHITMORE IS WELL ON HER WAY TO BECOMING A TRUE HERO--
--WHICH IS MUCH MORE THAN CAN BE SAID FOR HER BIOLOGICAL FATHER...

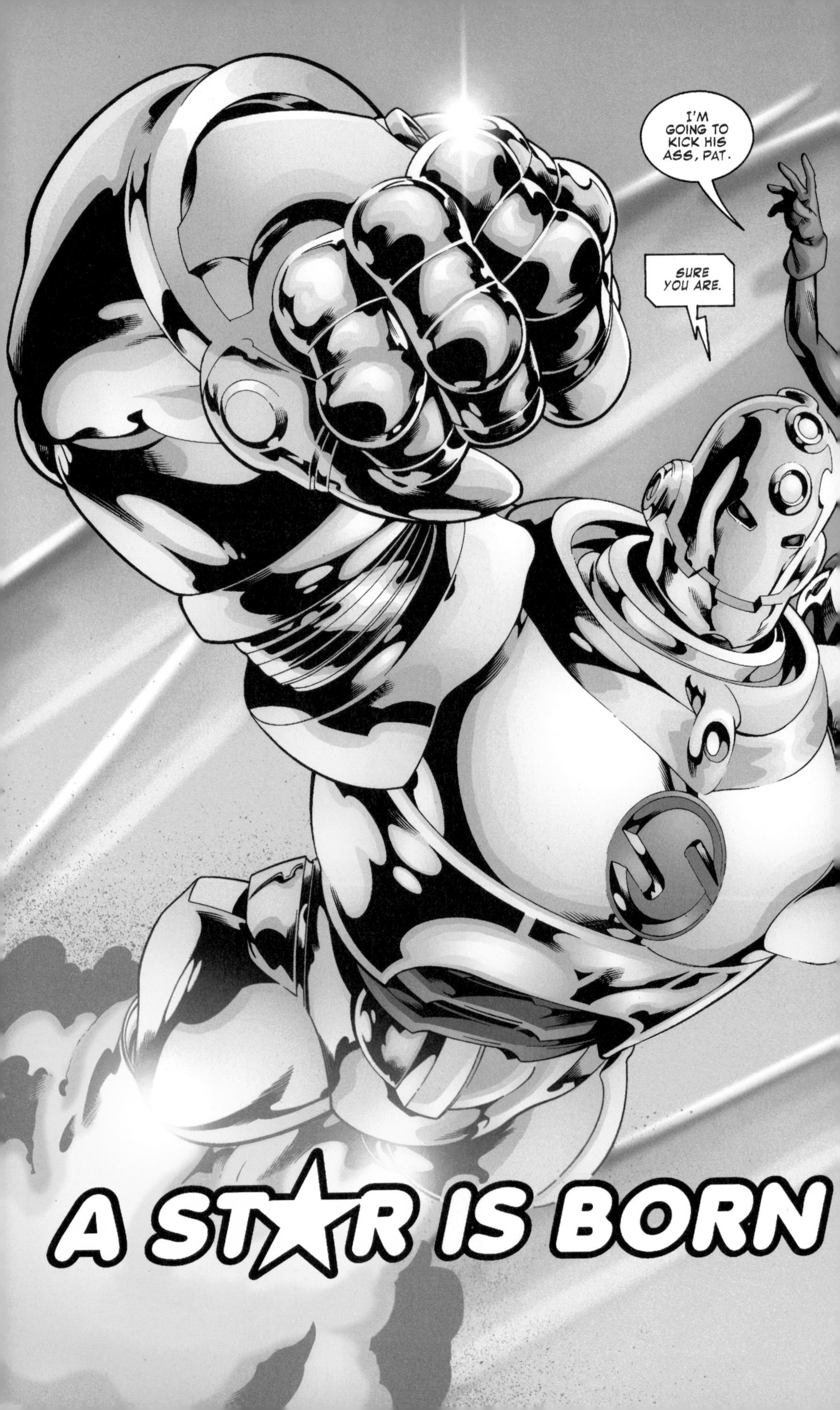
I'M GOING TO KICK HIS ASS, PAT.
SURE YOU ARE.
A STAR IS BORN

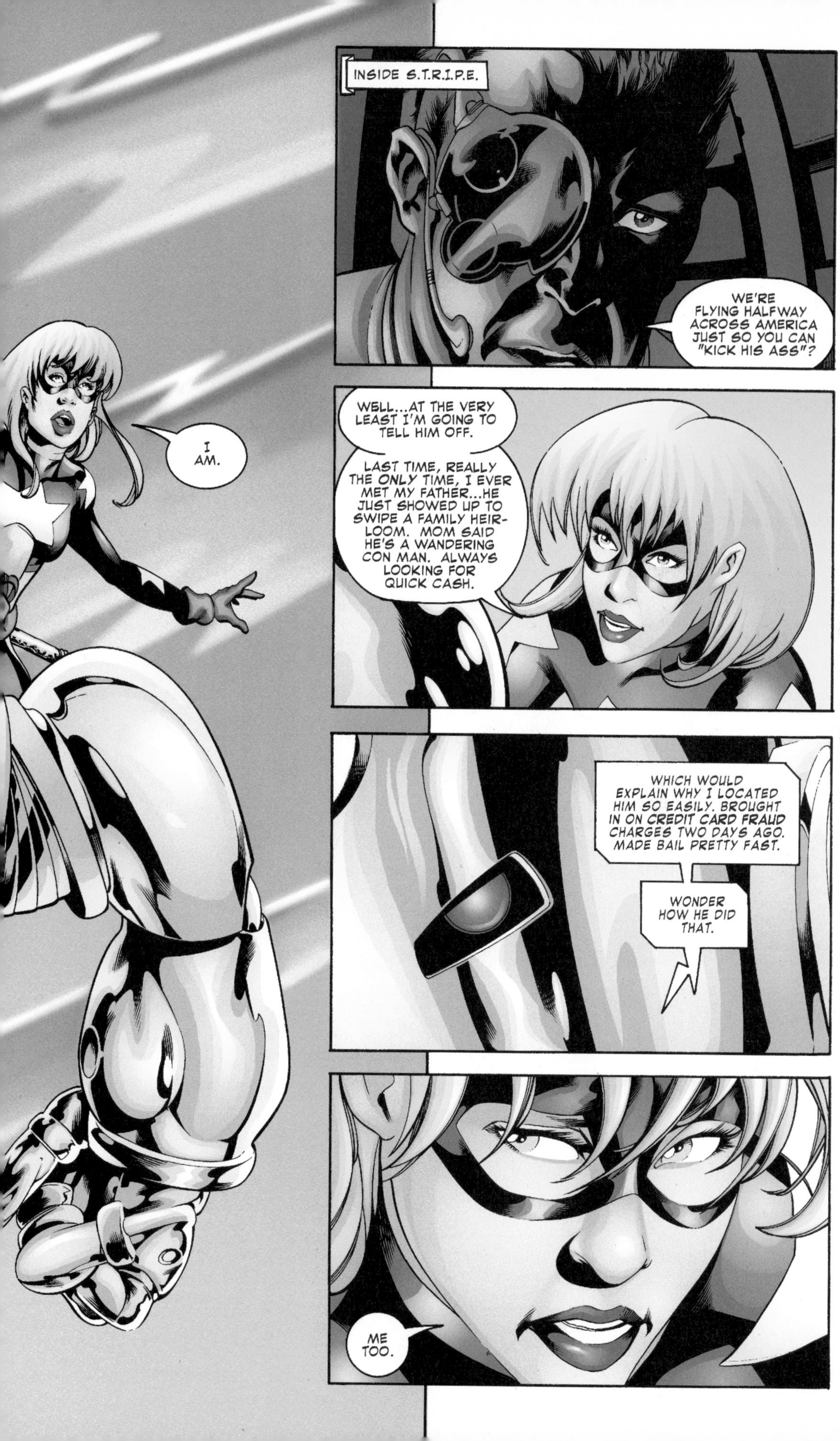

I AM.
INSIDE S.T.R.I.P.E.
WE'RE FLYING HALFWAY ACROSS AMERICA JUST SO YOU CAN "KICK HIS ASS"?
WELL...AT THE VERY LEAST I'M GOING TO TELL HIM OFF.
LAST TIME, REALLY THE ONLY TIME, I EVER MET MY FATHER...HE JUST SHOWED UP TO SWIPE A FAMILY HEIR-LOOM. MOM SAID HE'S A WANDERING CON MAN. ALWAYS LOOKING FOR QUICK CASH.
WHICH WOULD EXPLAIN WHY I LOCATED HIM SO EASILY. BROUGHT IN ON CREDIT CARD FRAUD CHARGES TWO DAYS AGO. MADE BAIL PRETTY FAST.
WONDER HOW HE DID THAT.
ME TOO.

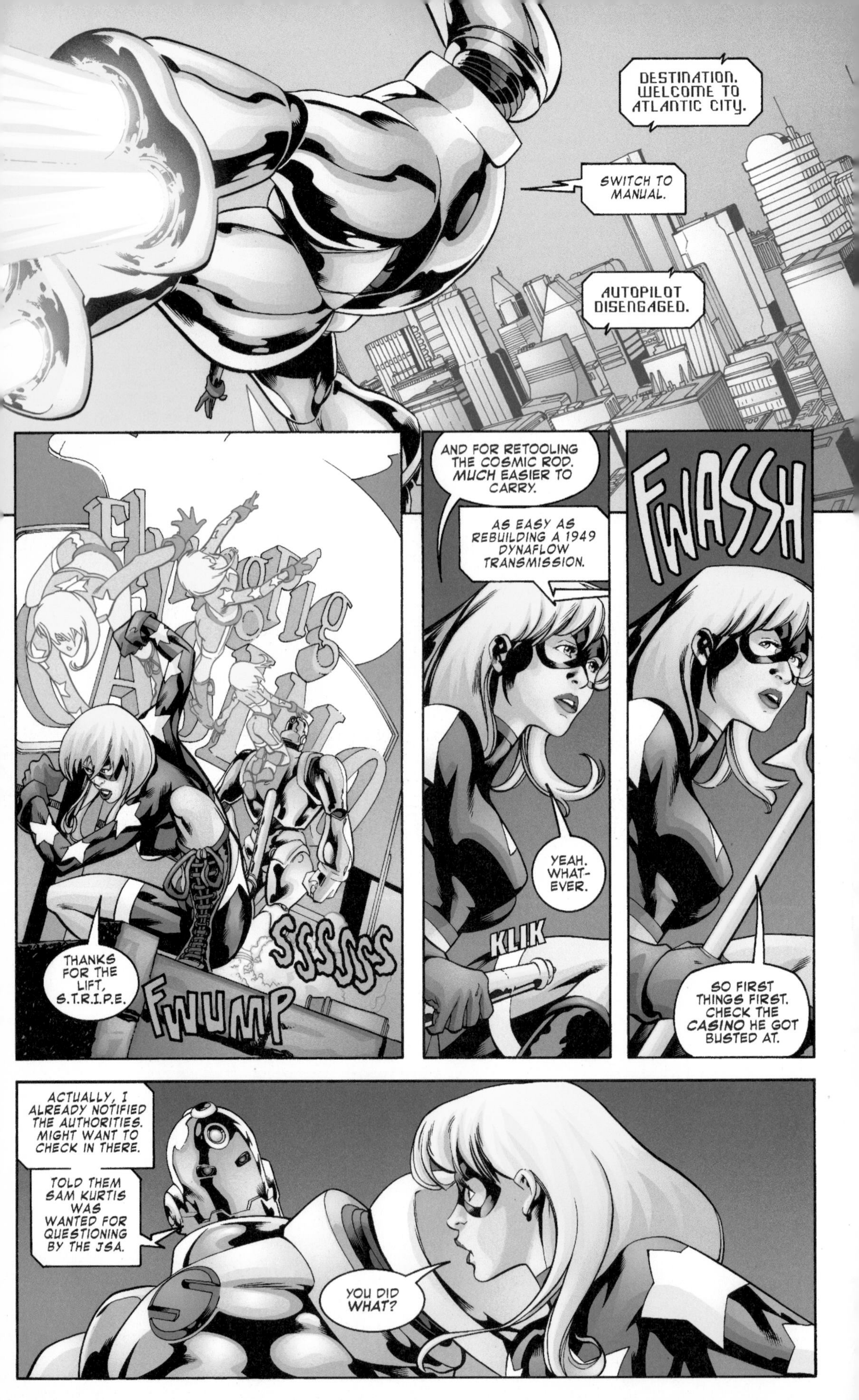
DESTINATION. WELCOME TO ATLANTIC CITY.
SWITCH TO MANUAL.
AUTOPILOT DISENGAGED.
THANKS FOR THE LIFT, S.T.R.I.P.E.
SSSSSS
FWUMP
AND FOR RETOOLING THE COSMIC ROD. MUCH EASIER TO CARRY.
AS EASY AS REBUILDING A 1949 DYNAFLOW TRANSMISSION.
YEAH. WHAT-EVER.
KLIK
FWASSH
SO FIRST THINGS FIRST. CHECK THE CASINO HE GOT BUSTED AT.
ACTUALLY, I ALREADY NOTIFIED THE AUTHORITIES. MIGHT WANT TO CHECK IN THERE.
TOLD THEM SAM KURTIS WAS WANTED FOR QUESTIONING BY THE JSA.
YOU DID WHAT?

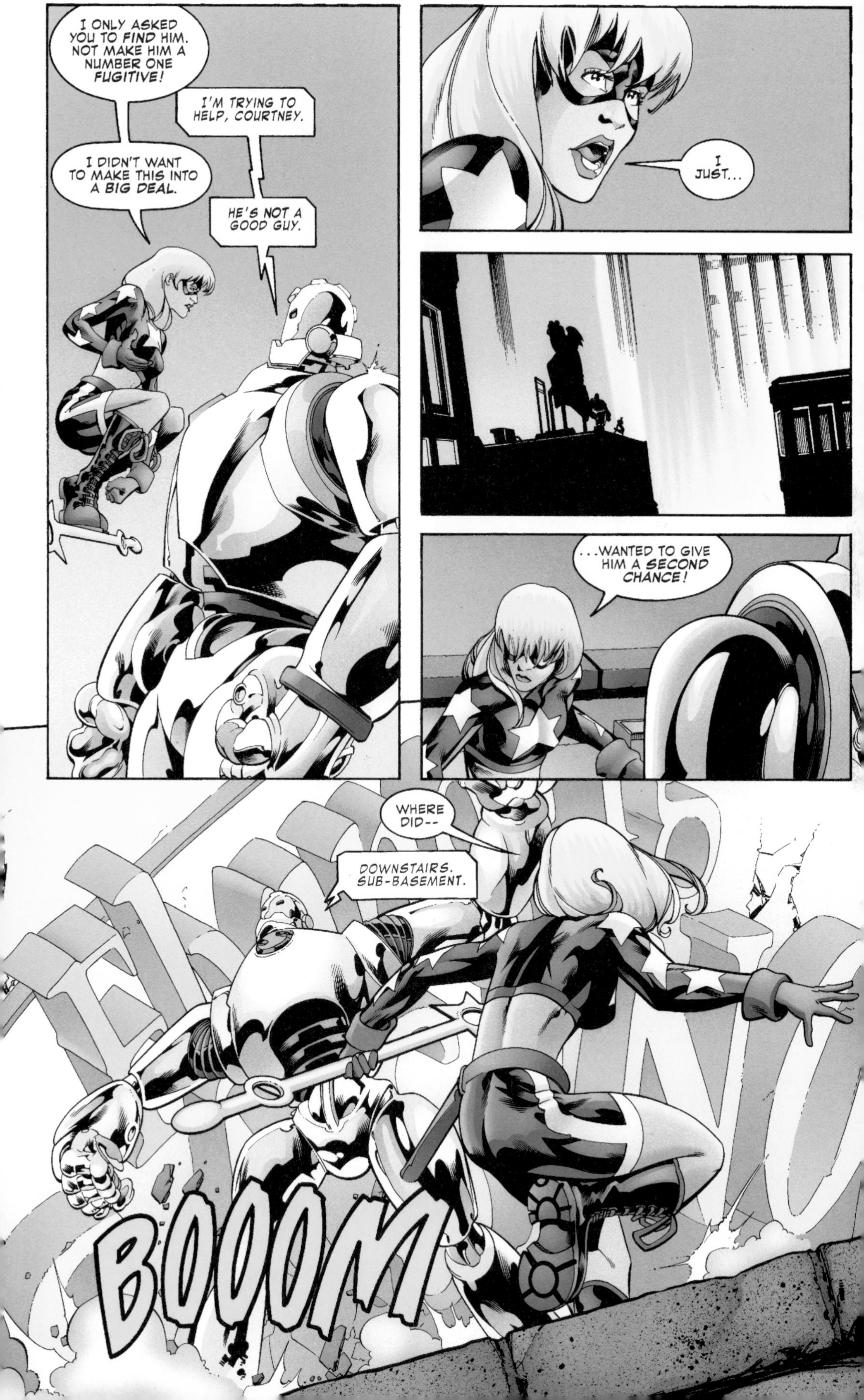
I ONLY ASKED YOU TO FIND HIM. NOT MAKE HIM A NUMBER ONE FUGITIVE!
I'M TRYING TO HELP, COURTNEY.
I DIDN'T WANT TO MAKE THIS INTO A BIG DEAL.
HE'S NOT A GOOD GUY.
I JUST...
...WANTED TO GIVE HIM A SECOND CHANCE!
WHERE DID--
DOWNSTAIRS. SUB-BASEMENT.
BOOOM

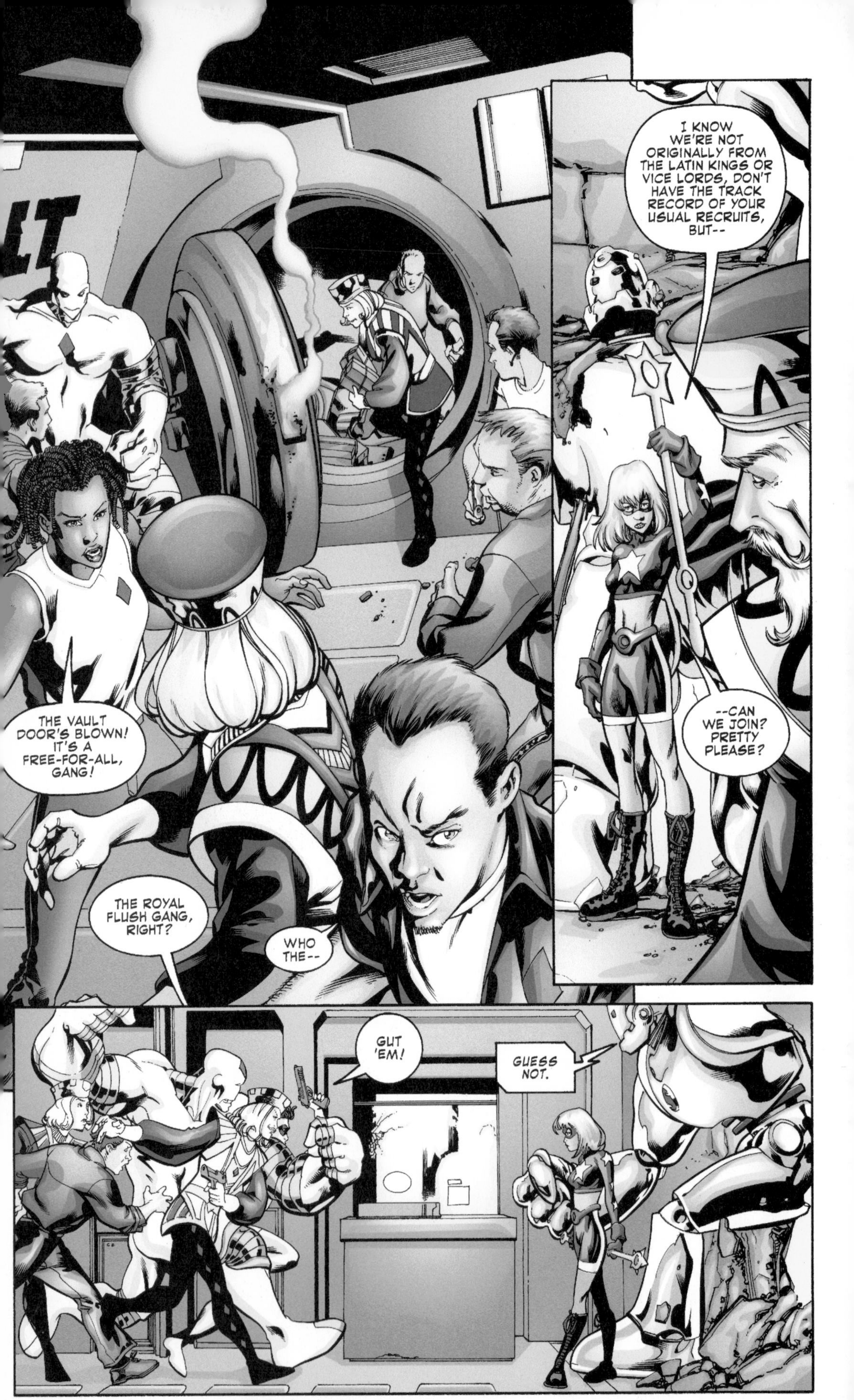
THE VAULT DOOR'S BLOWN! IT'S A FREE-FOR-ALL, GANG!
THE ROYAL FLUSH GANG, RIGHT?
WHO THE--
I KNOW WE'RE NOT ORIGINALLY FROM THE LATIN KINGS OR VICE LORDS, DON'T HAVE THE TRACK RECORD OF YOUR USUAL RECRUITS, BUT--
--CAN WE JOIN? PRETTY PLEASE?
GUT 'EM!
GUESS NOT.

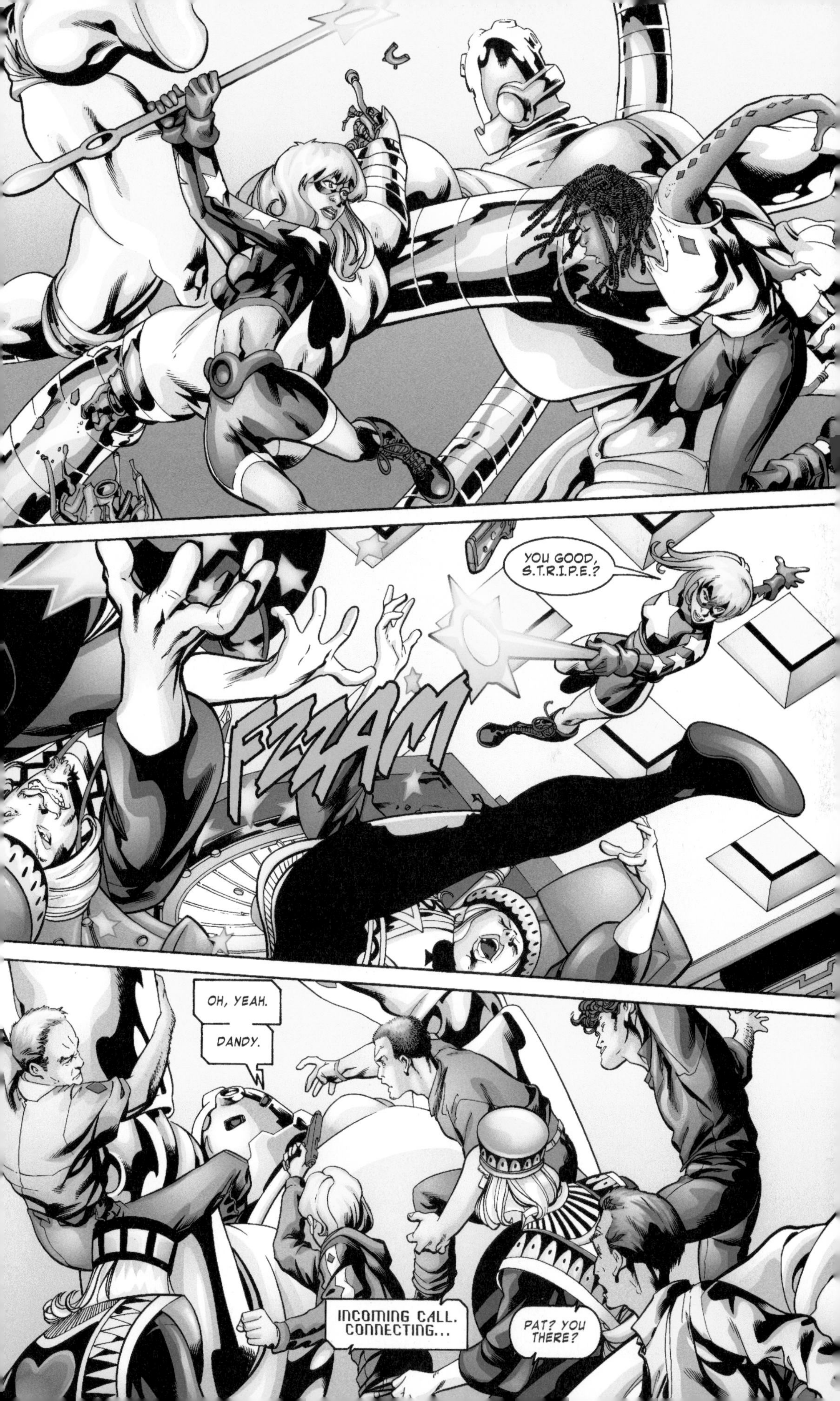

YOU GOOD, S.T.R.I.P.E.?
FZZAM
OH, YEAH.
DANDY.
INCOMING CALL. CONNECTING...
PAT? YOU THERE?

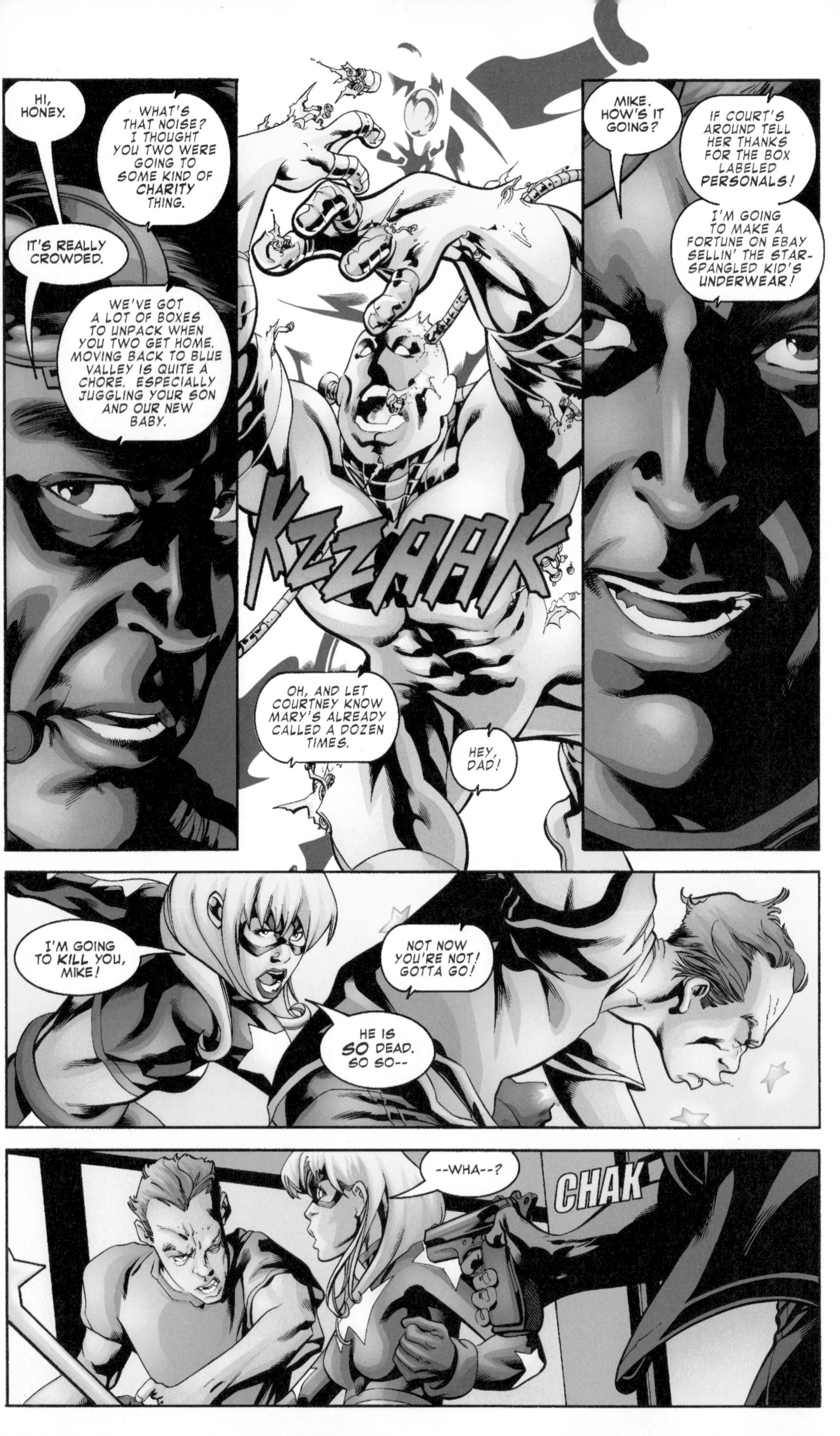
HI, HONEY.
WHAT'S THAT NOISE? I THOUGHT YOU TWO WERE GOING TO SOME KIND OF CHARITY THING.
IT'S REALLY CROWDED.
WE'VE GOT A LOT OF BOXES TO UNPACK WHEN YOU TWO GET HOME. MOVING BACK TO BLUE VALLEY IS QUITE A CHORE. ESPECIALLY JUGGLING YOUR SON AND OUR NEW BABY.
KZZAAK
OH, AND LET COURTNEY KNOW MARY'S ALREADY CALLED A DOZEN TIMES.
HEY, DAD!
MIKE. HOW'S IT GOING?
IF COURT'S AROUND TELL HER THANKS FOR THE BOX LABELED PERSONALS!
I'M GOING TO MAKE A FORTUNE ON EBAY SELLIN' THE STAR-SPANGLED KID'S UNDERWEAR!
I'M GOING TO KILL YOU, MIKE!
NOT NOW YOU'RE NOT! GOTTA GO!
HE IS SO DEAD. SO SO--
--WHA--?
CHAK

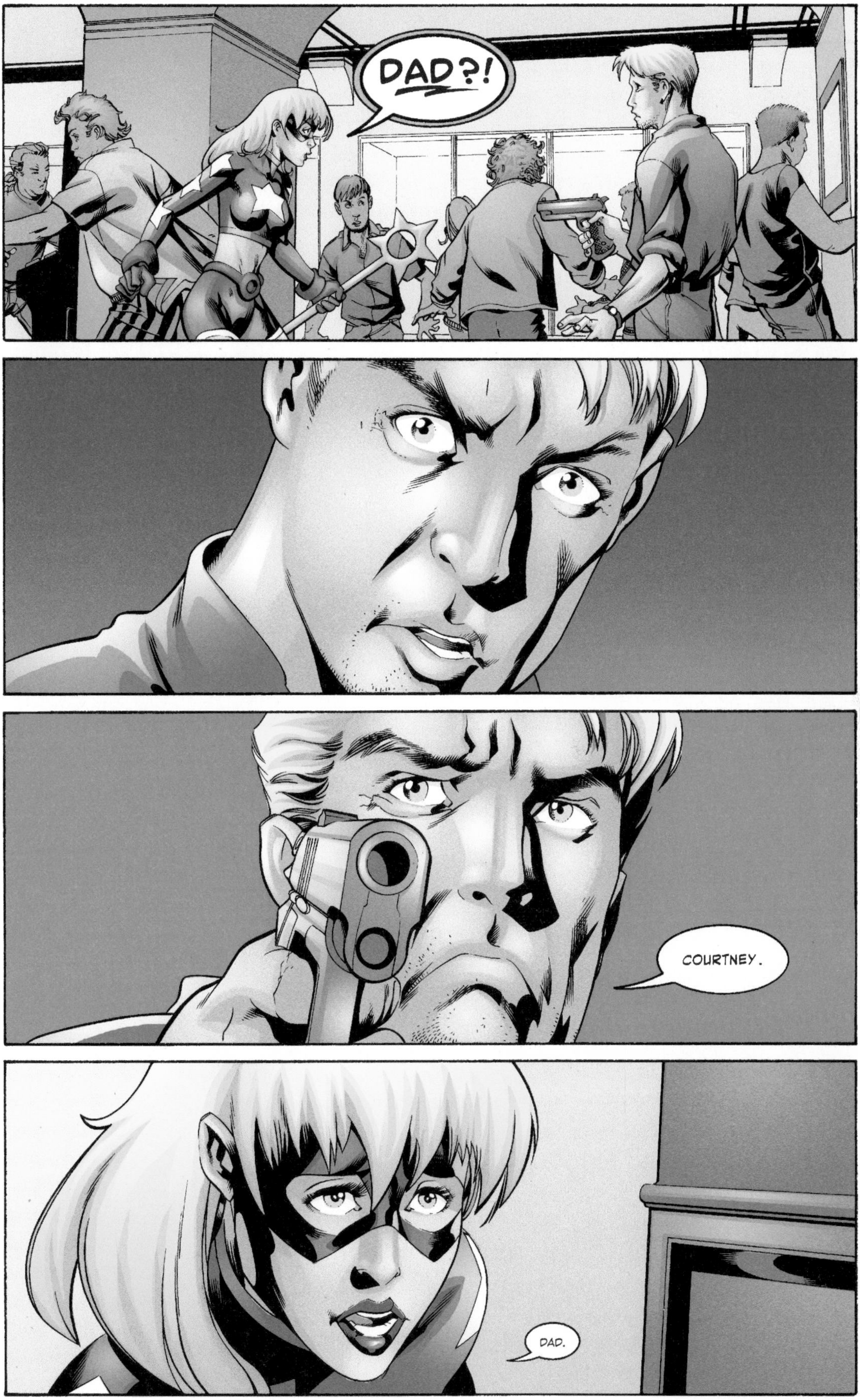
DAD?!
COURTNEY.
DAD.

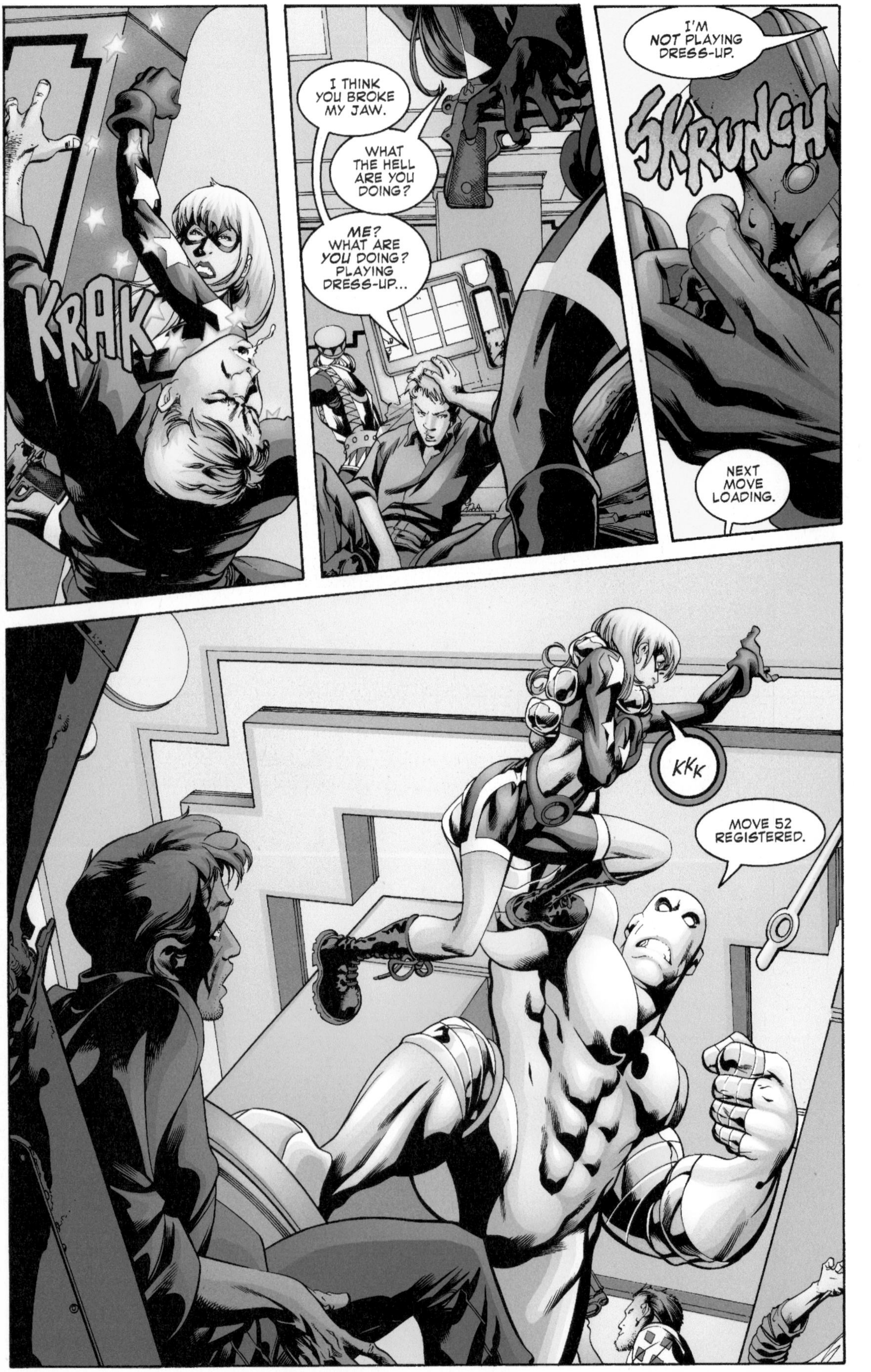
KRAK
I THINK YOU BROKE MY JAW.
WHAT THE HELL ARE YOU DOING?
ME? WHAT ARE YOU DOING? PLAYING DRESS-UP...
I'M NOT PLAYING DRESS-UP.
SKRUNCH
NEXT MOVE LOADING.
KKK
MOVE 52 REGISTERED.

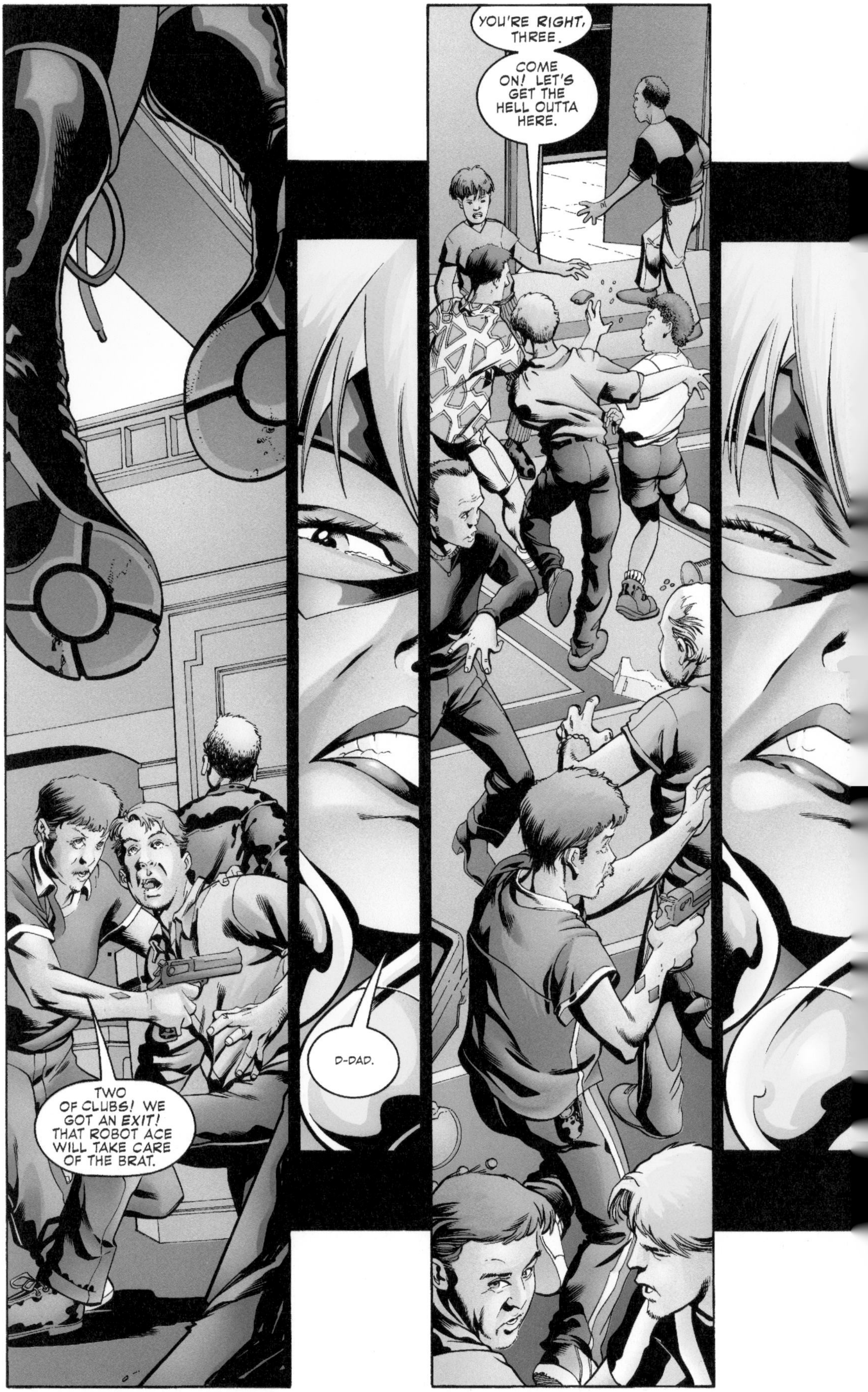
TWO OF CLUBS! WE GOT AN EXIT! THAT ROBOT ACE WILL TAKE CARE OF THE BRAT.
D-DAD.
YOU'RE RIGHT, THREE.
COME ON! LET'S GET THE HELL OUTTA HERE.

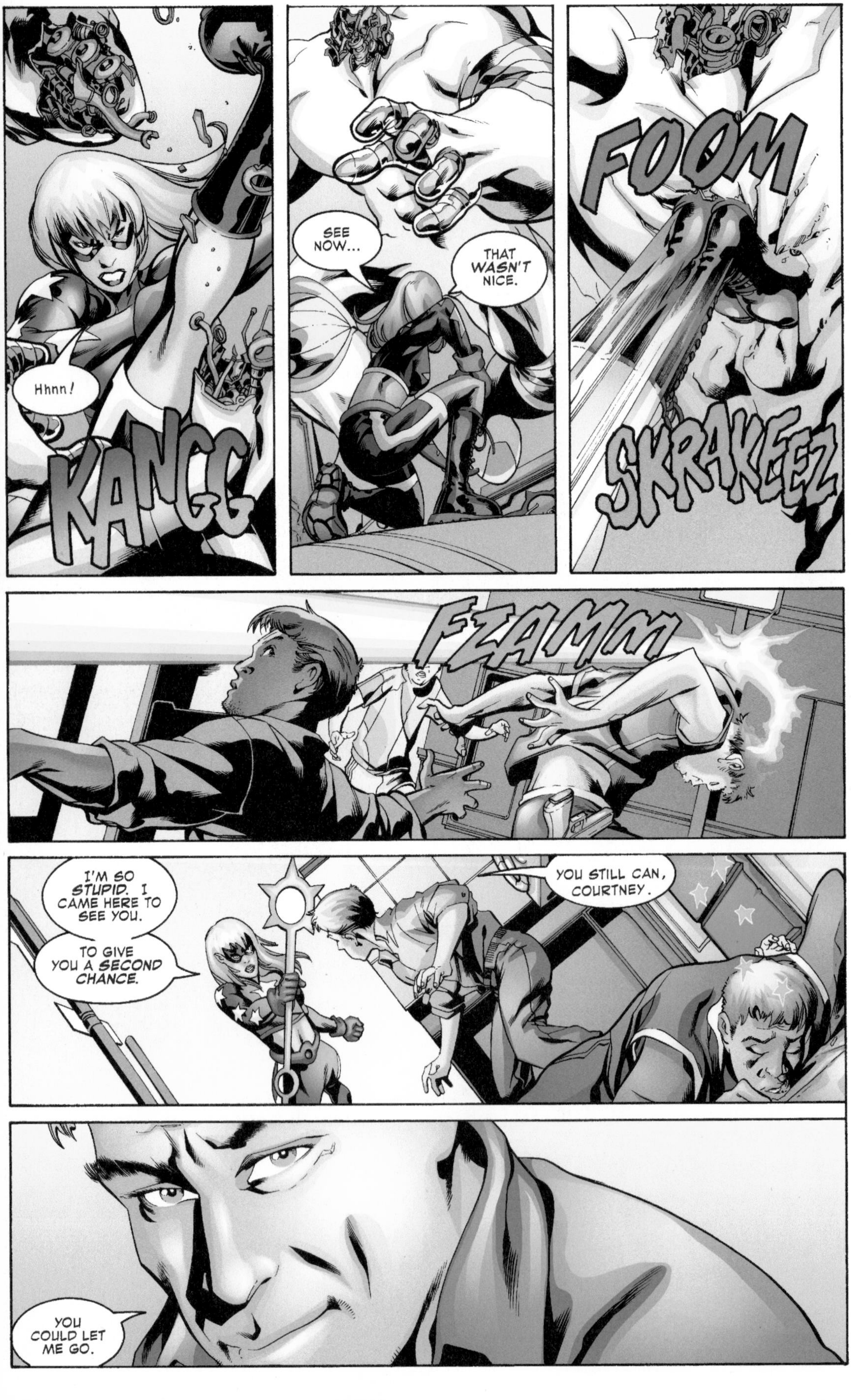
Hhnn!
KANGG
SEE NOW...
THAT WASN'T NICE.
FOOM
SKRAKEEZ
FZAMM
I'M SO STUPID. I CAME HERE TO SEE YOU.
TO GIVE YOU A SECOND CHANCE.
YOU STILL CAN, COURTNEY.
YOU COULD LET ME GO.

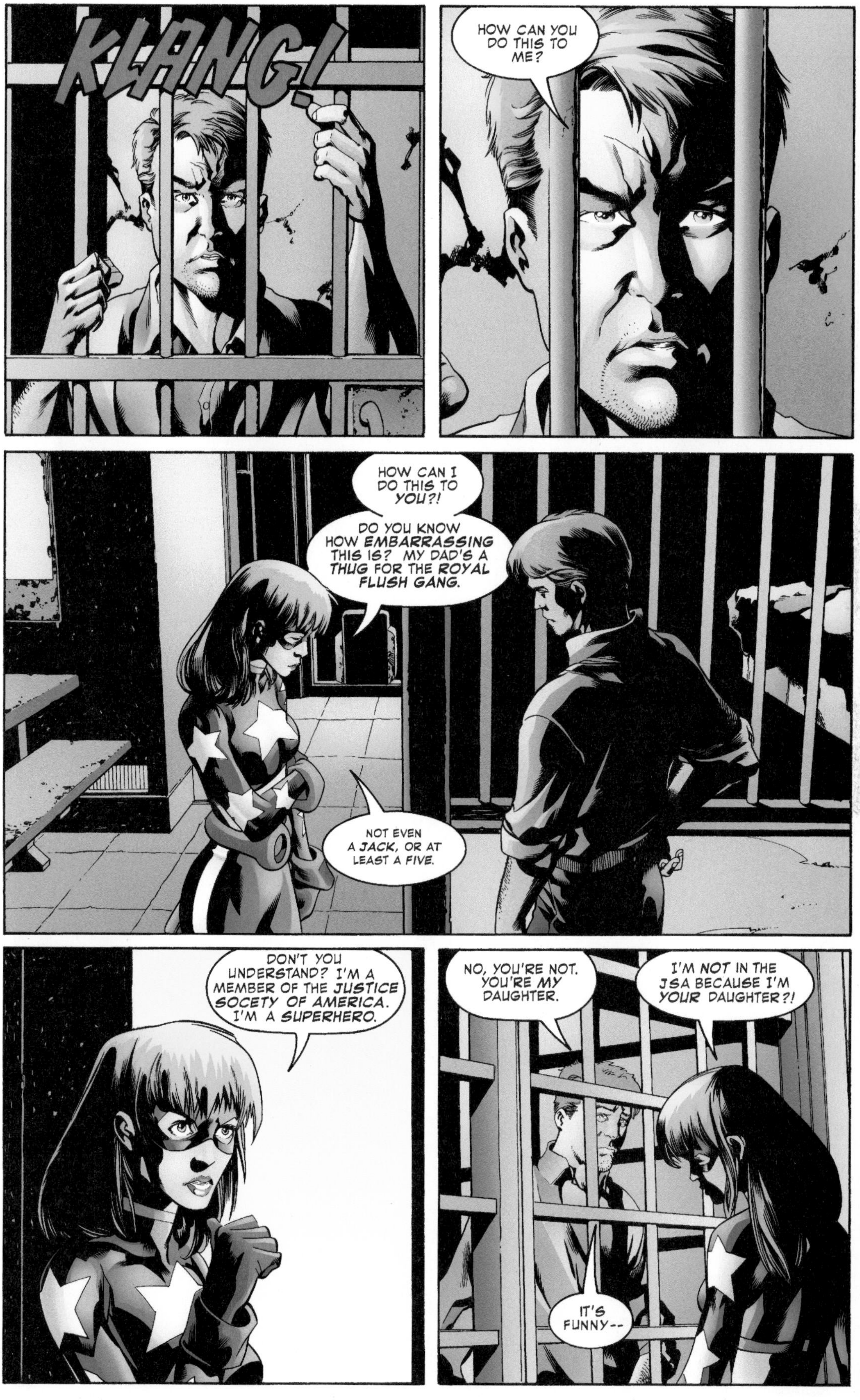
KLANG!
HOW CAN YOU DO THIS TO ME?
HOW CAN I DO THIS TO YOU?!
DO YOU KNOW HOW EMBARRASSING THIS IS? MY DAD'S A THUG FOR THE ROYAL FLUSH GANG.
NOT EVEN A JACK, OR AT LEAST A FIVE.
DON'T YOU UNDERSTAND? I'M A MEMBER OF THE JUSTICE SOCETY OF AMERICA. I'M A SUPERHERO.
NO, YOU'RE NOT. YOU'RE MY DAUGHTER.
I'M NOT IN THE JSA BECAUSE I'M YOUR DAUGHTER?!
IT'S FUNNY--

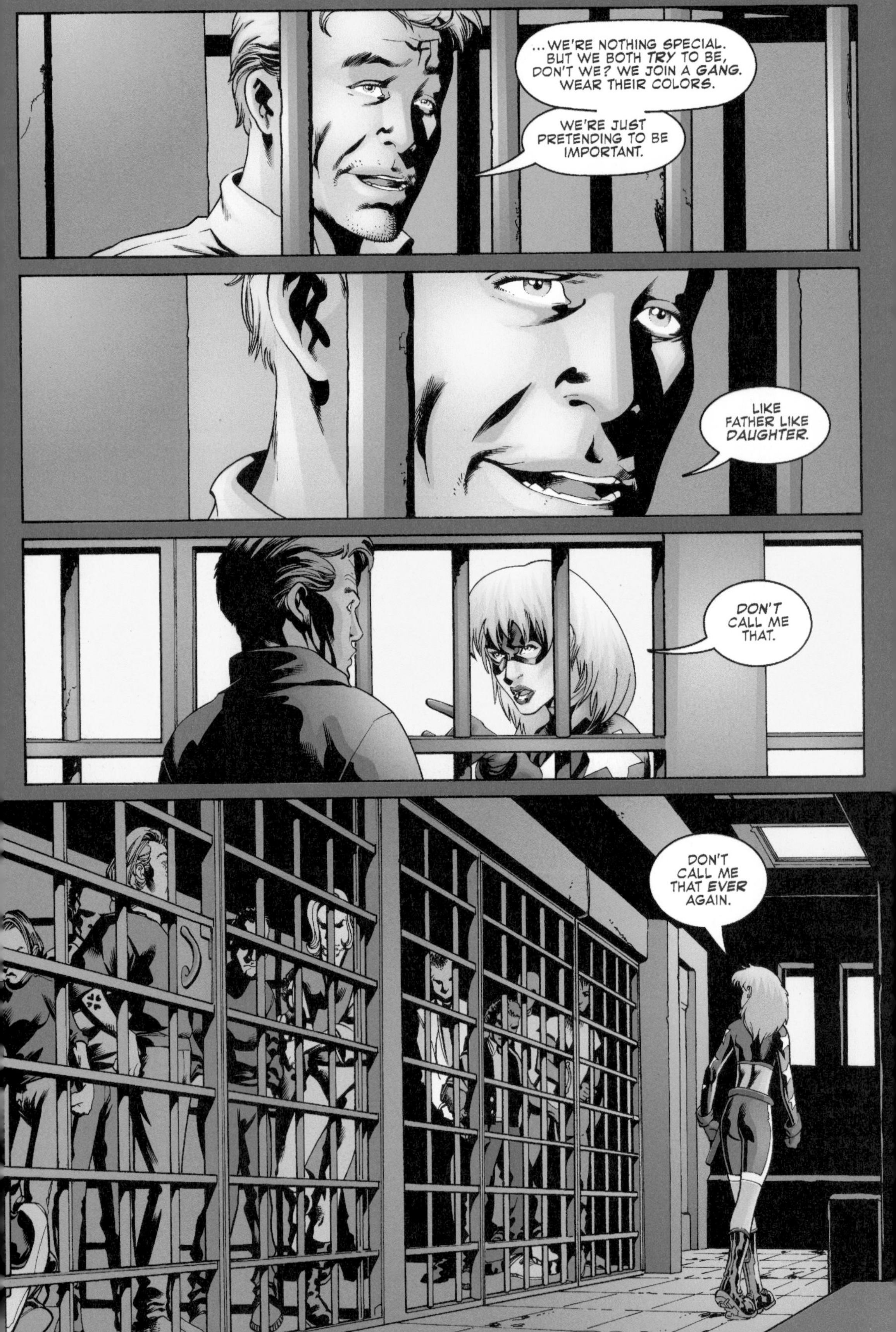
...WE'RE NOTHING SPECIAL. BUT WE BOTH *TRY* TO BE, DON'T WE? WE JOIN A *GANG*. WEAR THEIR COLORS.
WE'RE JUST PRETENDING TO BE IMPORTANT.
LIKE FATHER LIKE *DAUGHTER*.
DON'T CALL ME THAT.
DON'T CALL ME THAT *EVER* AGAIN.

YOU'VE BEEN QUIET EVER SINCE WE LEFT THE PRECINCT.

YOU OKAY?

I GUESS.

I DON'T KNOW...MAYBE HE'S RIGHT.

MAYBE I'M JUST PRETENDING TO BE A PART OF THE JSA.

YOU'RE WHAT THE JUSTICE SOCIETY IS ALL ABOUT. A HERO IN TRAINING. AND YOU'RE DOING SOMETHING NO ONE ELSE ON THAT TEAM IS DOING.

WHAT'S THAT?

YOU'RE CARRYING ON TWO LEGACIES...

...FOR MY OLD PARTNER, SYLVESTER PEMBERTON. THE ORIGINAL STAR-SPANGLED KID.

AND FOR TED AND JACK KNIGHT. BOTH KNOWN AS STARMAN BEFORE YOU WERE GIVEN THE COSMIC ROD.

SO FAR, SO GOOD, KID.

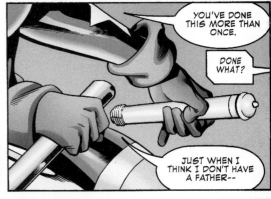

YOU'VE DONE THIS MORE THAN ONCE.

DONE WHAT?

JUST WHEN I THINK I DON'T HAVE A FATHER--

--YOU REMIND ME I DO.

FWASHT

BUT DON'T CALL ME KID. I'M CARRYING ON TWO LEGACIES.

SO I'M NOT JUST THE STAR-SPANGLED KID--

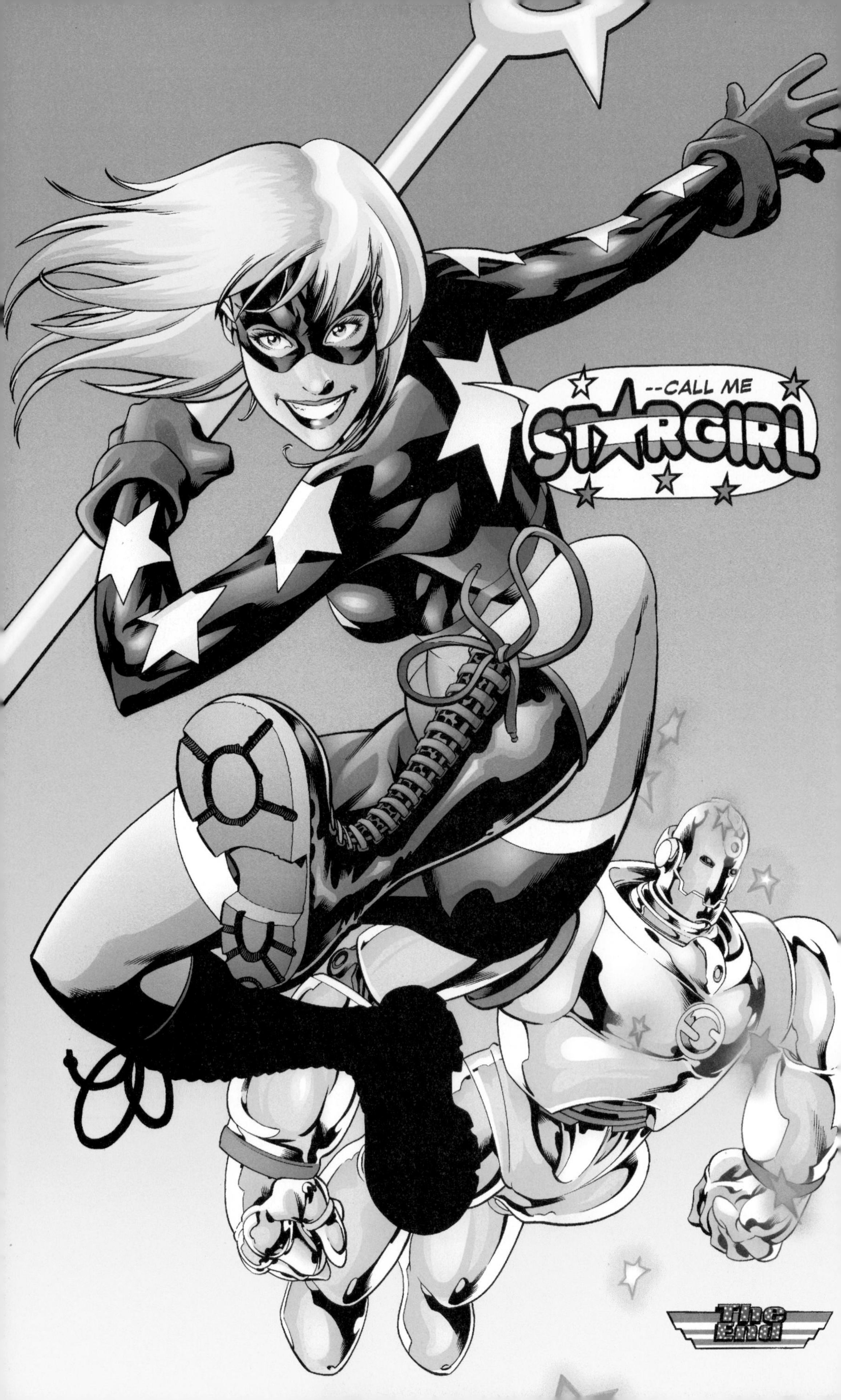
--CALL ME
STARGIRL
The End

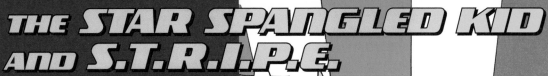

THE STAR SPANGLED KID AND S.T.R.I.P.E.

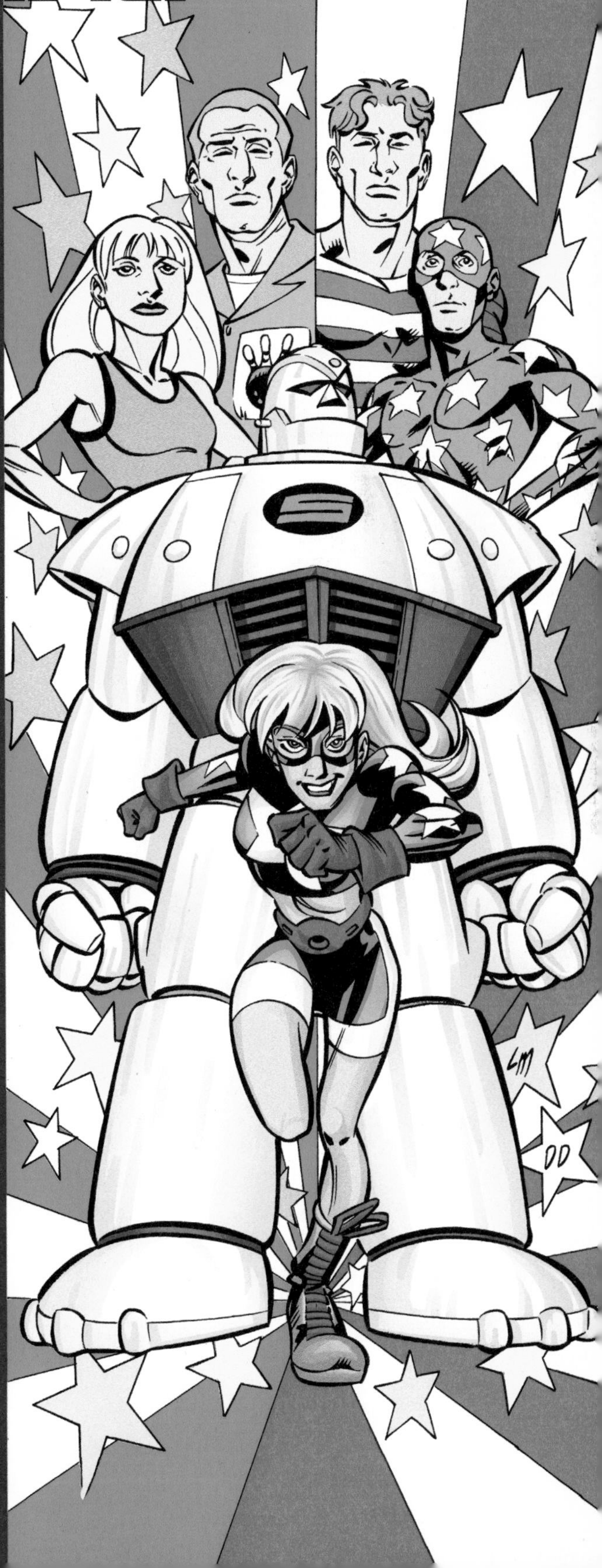

Real Name: ***Courtney Whitmore / Pat Dugan***
Occupation: ***Student / Mechanic***
Base of Operations: ***Blue Valley, Nebraska / ditto***
Marital Status: ***Single / Married***
Ht: ***5' 5"/6'10"***
Wt: ***110 lbs. / 195 lbs.***
Eyes: ***Blue / Blue***
Hair: ***Blonde / Red***
First Appearance: ***Stars and S.T.R.I.P.E. #1 (1999) / Action Comics #40 September, 1941)***

Courtney Whitmore was enjoying a great social career at Beverly Hills High when her mother married "some guy" named Pat Dugan. To Courtney's dismay, her mom and Pat then decided to escape the pressures of city life and move to Blue Valley, Nebraska. Stuck in a small town without much to do, Courtney decided to focus her energy on something more productive — making her stepfather's life miserable.

When Courtney stumbled upon an old box of Pat's memorabilia, she discovered he was once a hero named Stripesy, sidekick to the original Star Spangled Kid. So she did what she thought would tick him off the most. Courtney took the original Kid's cosmic converter belt and posed as the all-new Star Spangled Kid. Pat retaliated by creating an eight-foot robotic suit — S.T.R.I.P.E. — programmed to follow her around and keep her out of trouble — something he rarely succeeds in doing.

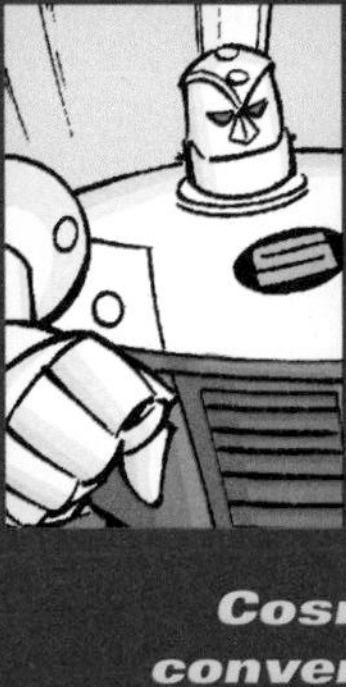

Besides great strength and flight, S.T.R.I.P.E. has a fridge and satellite TV.

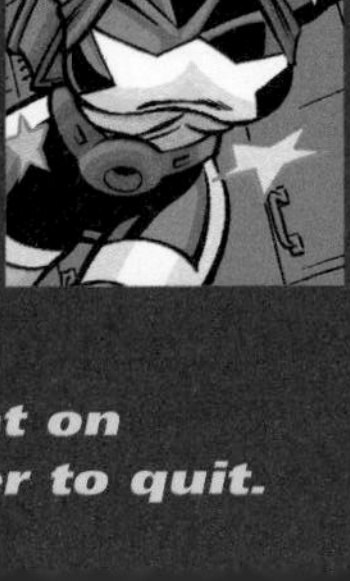

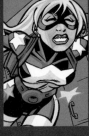

Cosmic converter belt gives the Kid strength, agility...and something more.

Each one is bent on getting the other to quit.

SHIV

Real Name: ***Cindy Burman***

Occupation: ***Student***

Base of Operations: ***Blue Valley, Nebraska***

Marital Status: ***Single***

Ht: ***5′ 7″***

Wt: ***115 lbs.***

Eyes: ***Green***

Hair: ***Black***

First Appearance: ***(as Cindy) Stars and S.T.R.I.P.E #1 (August, 1999), (as Shiv) Stars and S.T.R.I.P.E #1 (November, 1999)***

Cindy Burman studied in several highbrow schools abroad, acquiring a fantastic amount of skill and knowledge before attending mundane Blue Valley High. She quickly became head cheerleader, homecoming queen, debate team captain and class vice-president. Cindy has never really had to work hard for anything — something she takes pride in. Although she walks down the halls with her nose in the air, she is a favorite among the faculty and students alike. Whether this is because they fear her or respect her remains to be seen.

When the class president mysteriously disappears, Cindy moves up the political ladder and takes on the leadership of her school's student council. This pleases her father, the villainous Dragon King, very much. As Cindy blossoms into Shiv, the super-villain her daddy would be proud of, Courtney Whitmore — the new Star-Spangled Kid — finds her little high school rivalry taking on a frightening new dimension.

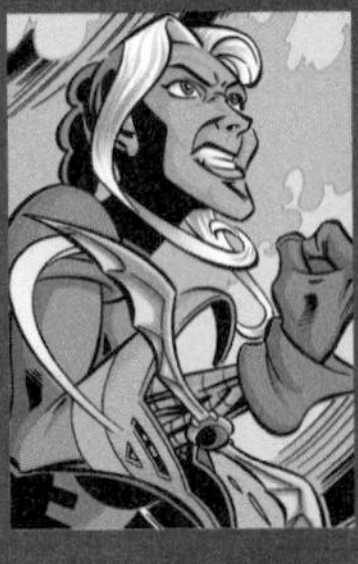

An Arsenal of hidden weaponry and blades is contained in her costume.

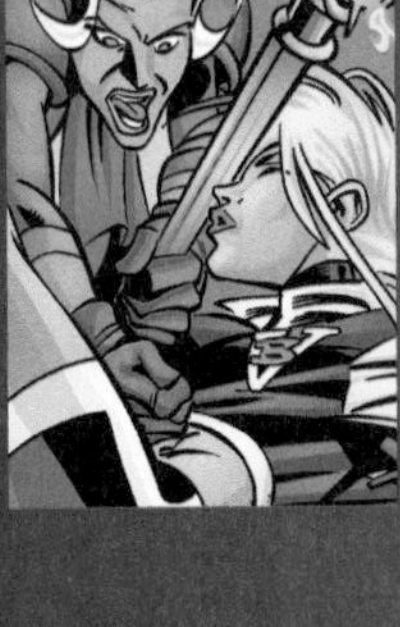

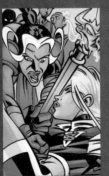

Her "Golden Dragon" staff not only spews fire, but also acts as a robotic boa constrictor, able to squeeze the life out of its victims.

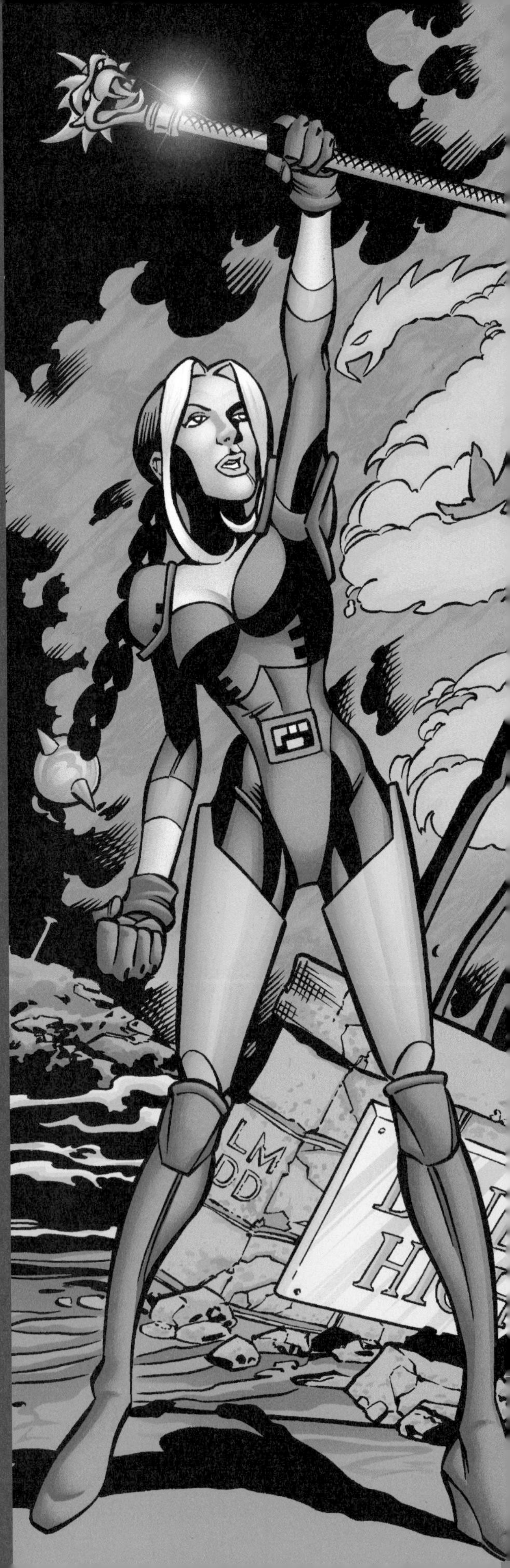

STARGIRL SKETCHBOOK
By Lee Moder

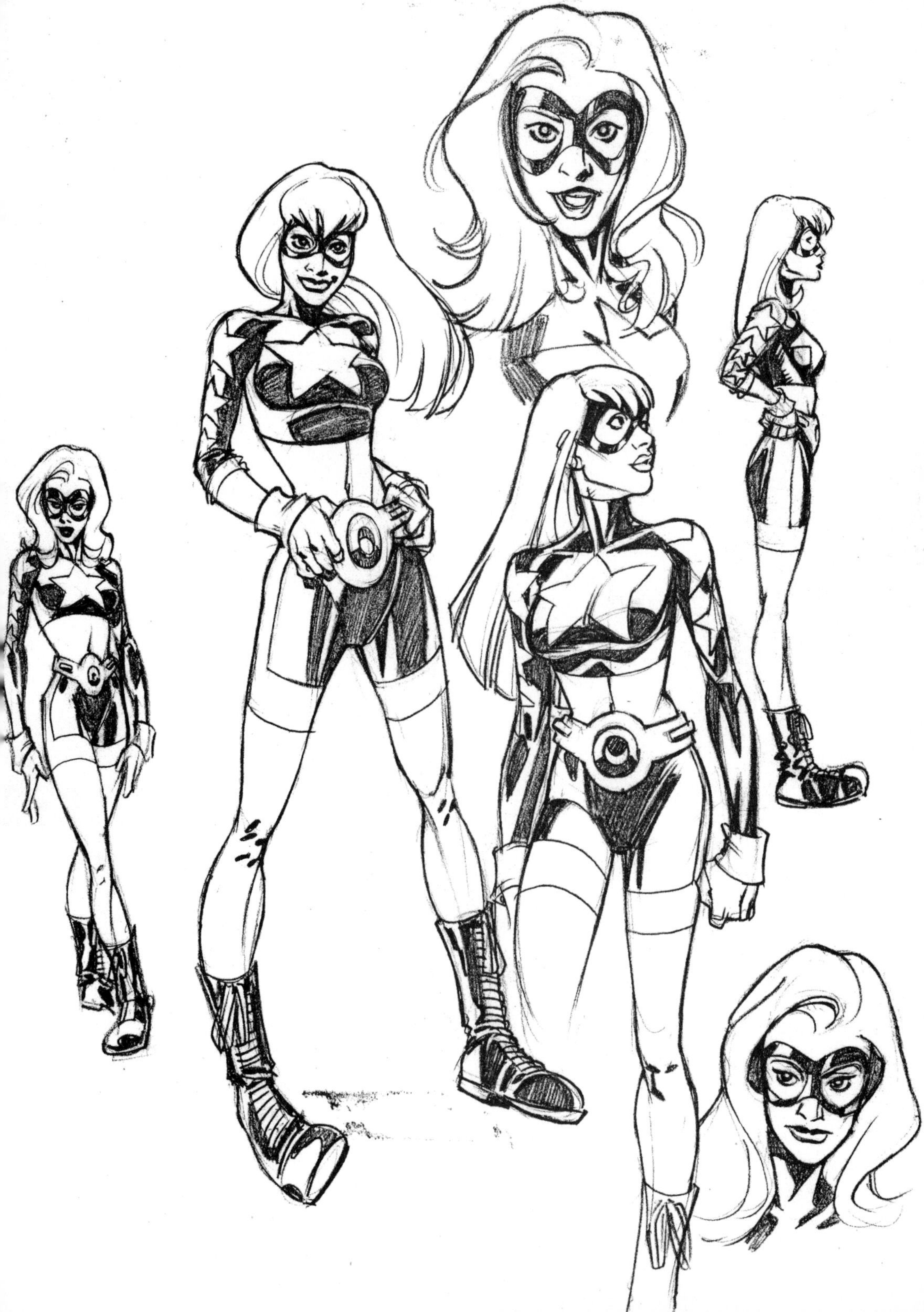

STARGIRL SKETCHBOOK

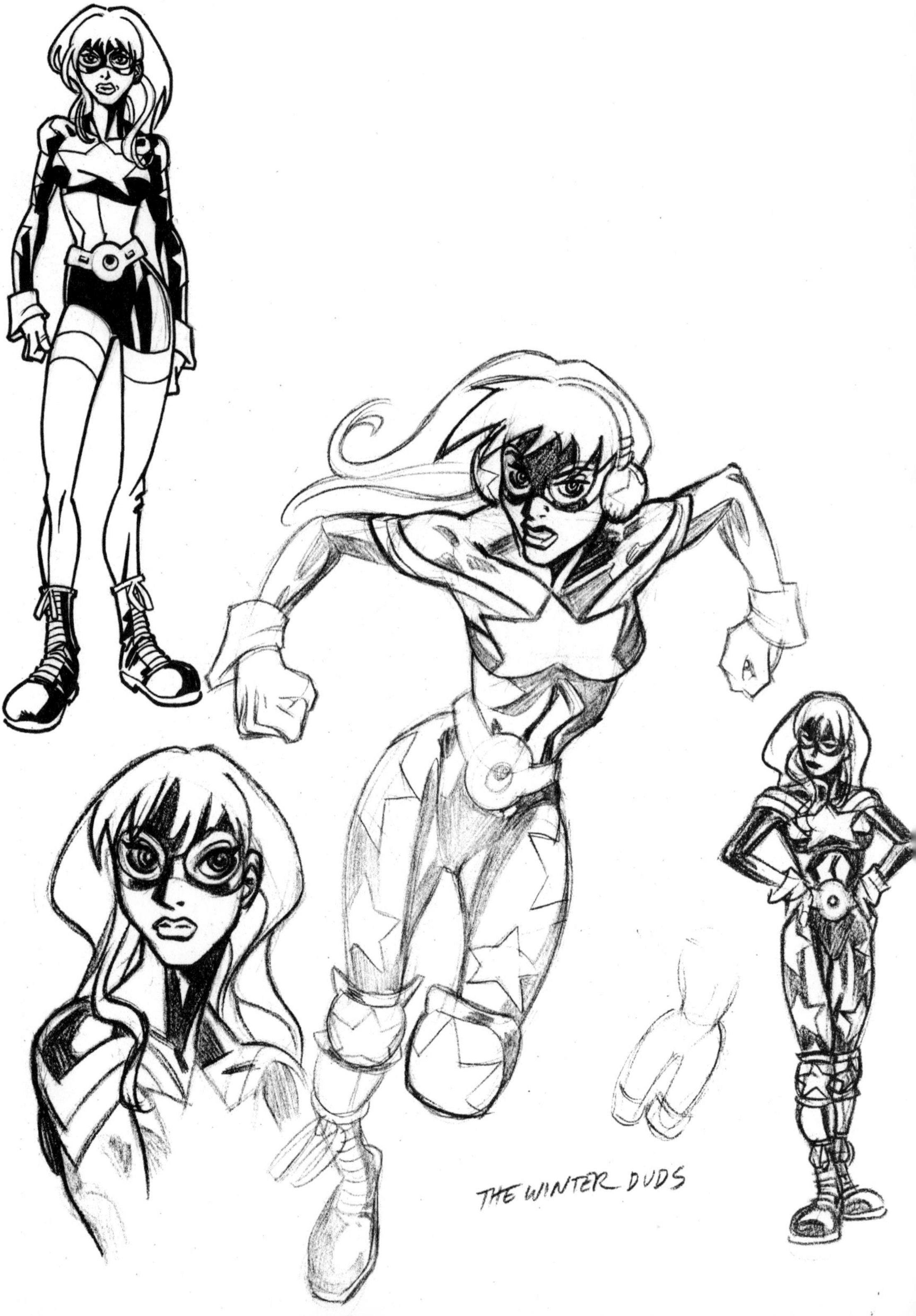
THE WINTER DUDS

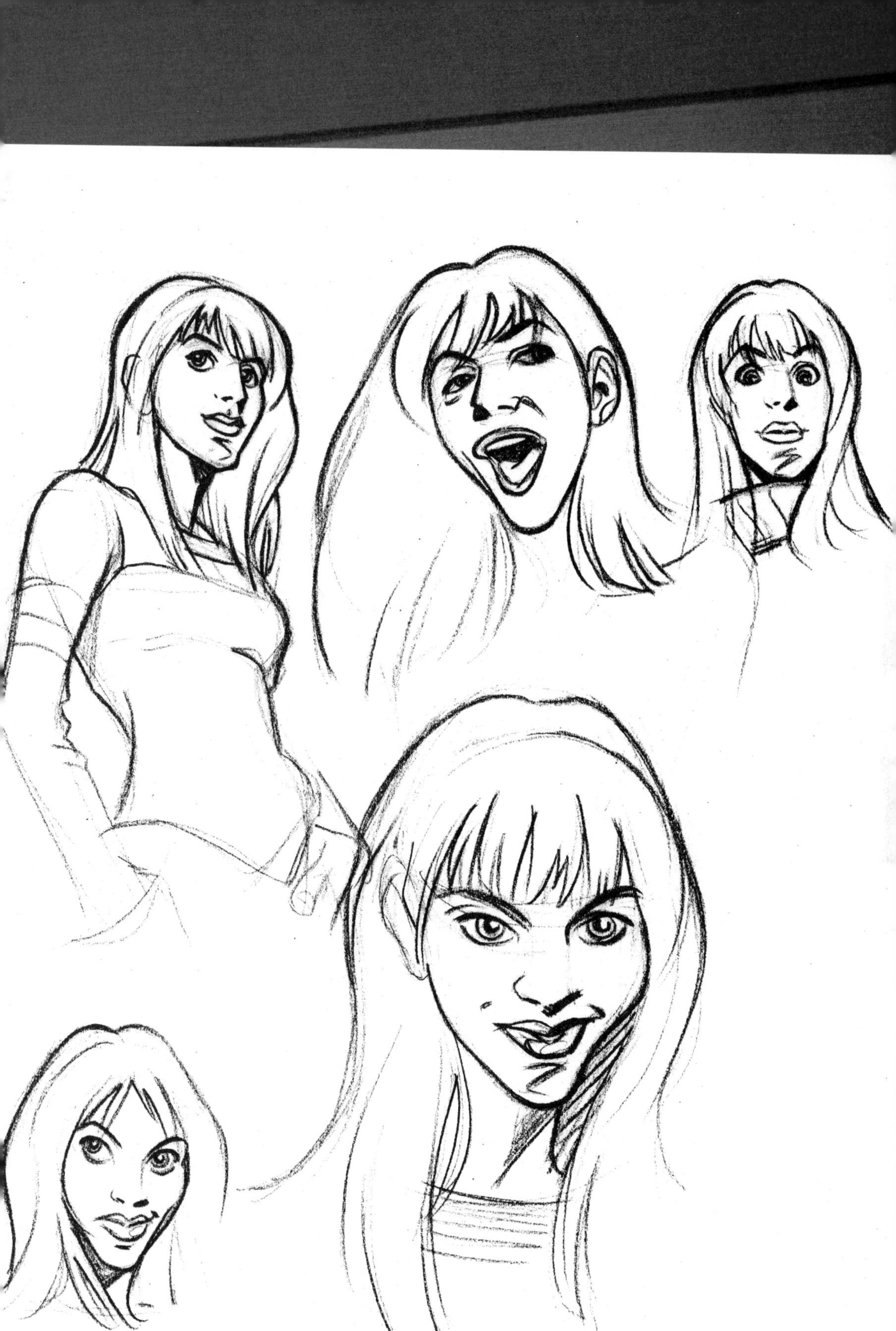

STARGIRL SKETCHBOOK

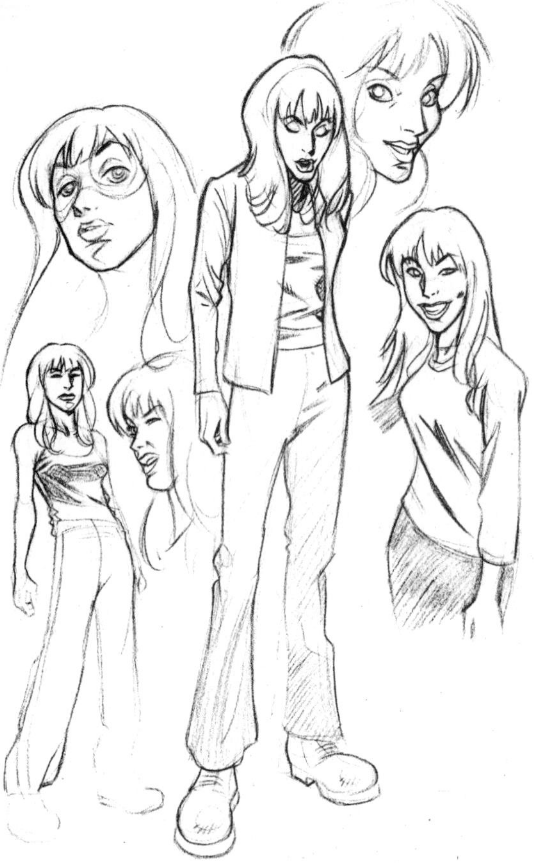

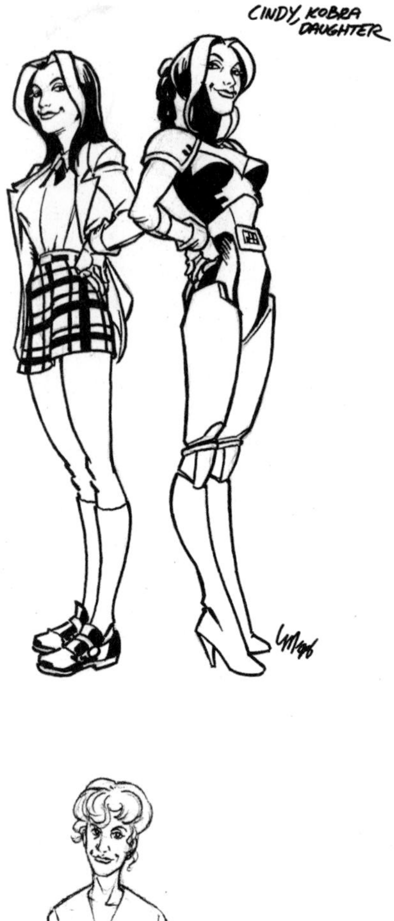
CINDY, KOBRA DAUGHTER

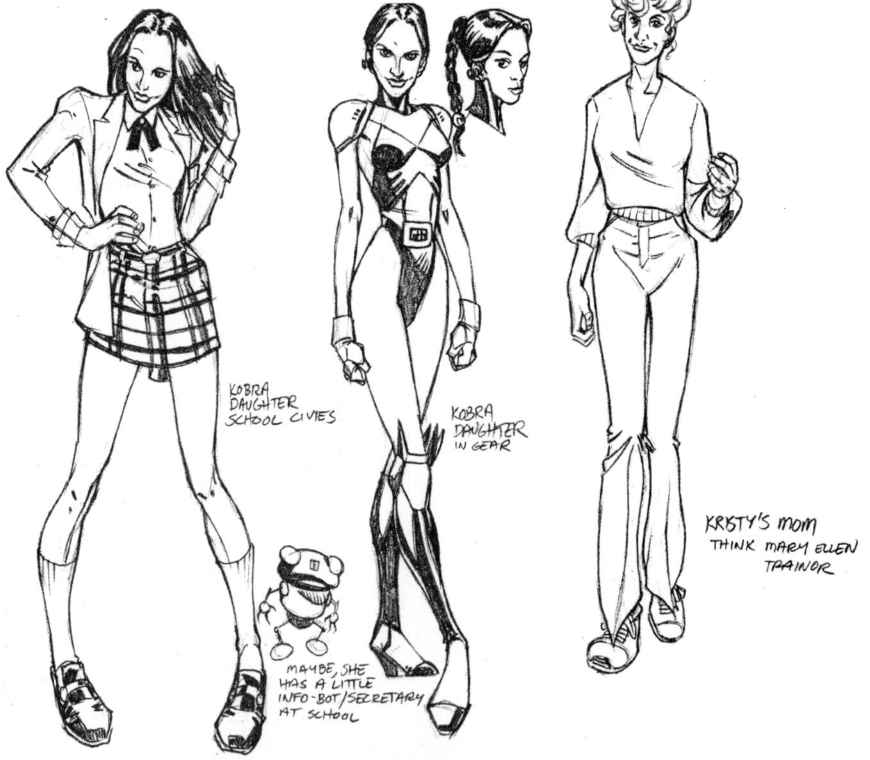
KOBRA DAUGHTER SCHOOL CIVIES
KOBRA DAUGHTER IN GEAR
MAYBE, SHE HAS A LITTLE INFO-BOT/SECRETARY AT SCHOOL
KRISTY'S mom
THINK mary ellen TRAINOR

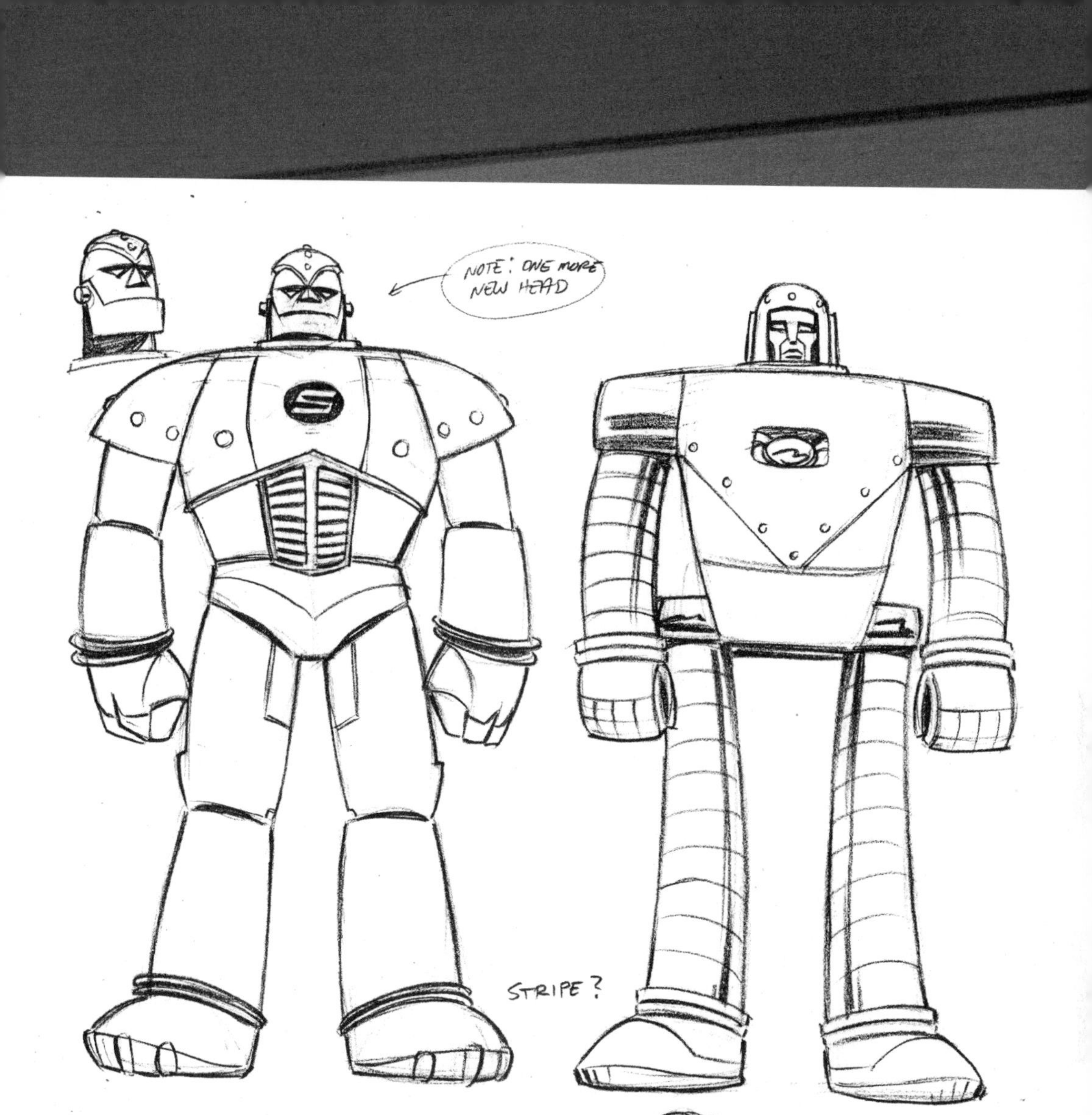
NOTE: ONE MORE NEW HEAD
STRIPE?

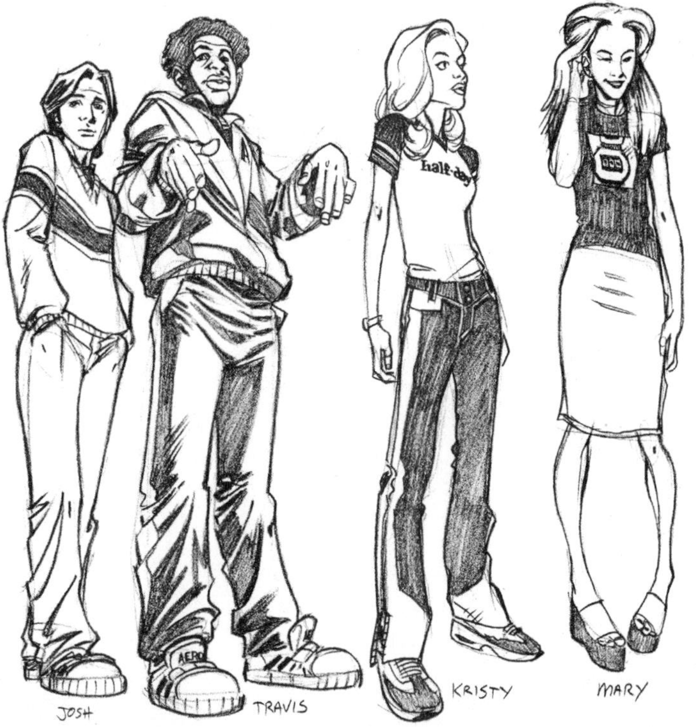
half-day
AERO
JOSH
TRAVIS
KRISTY
MARY

STARGIRL SKETCHBOOK

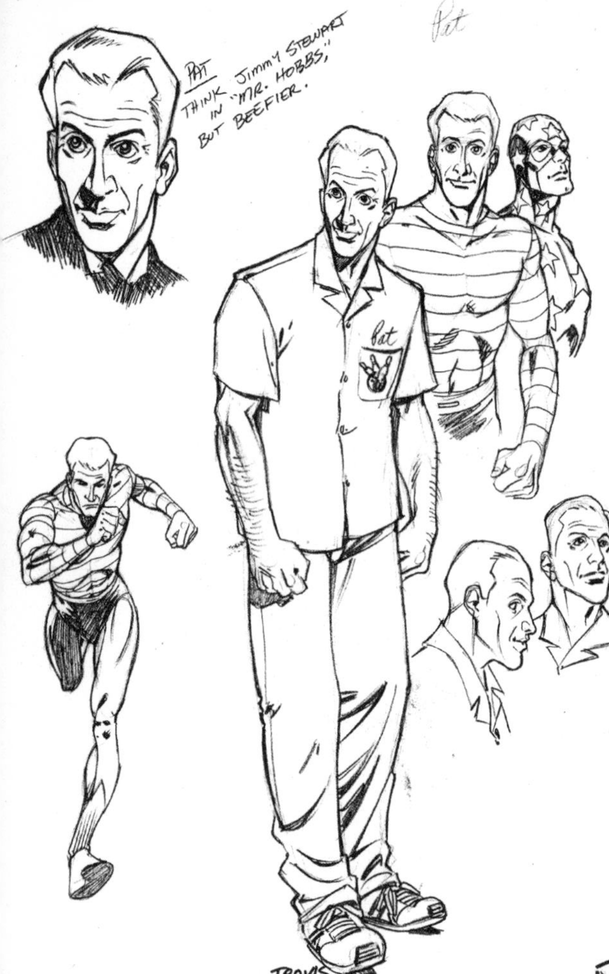
Pat
PAT
THINK JIMMY STEWART IN "MR. HOBBS," BUT BEEFIER.
Pat
TRAVIS

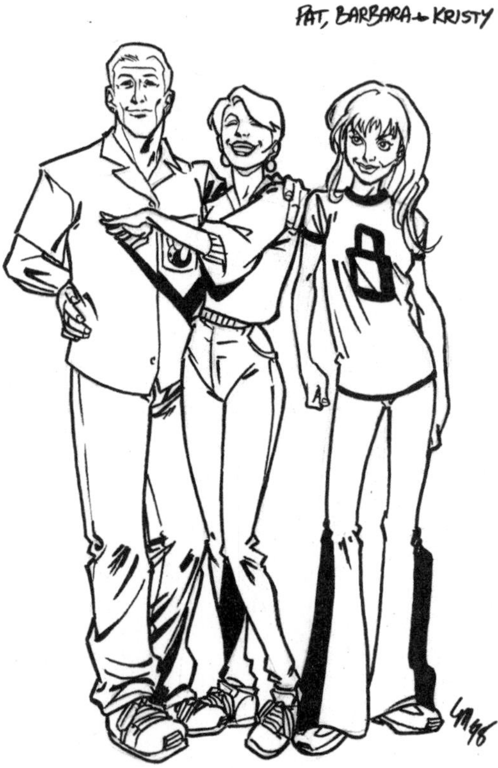
PAT, BARBARA & KRISTY

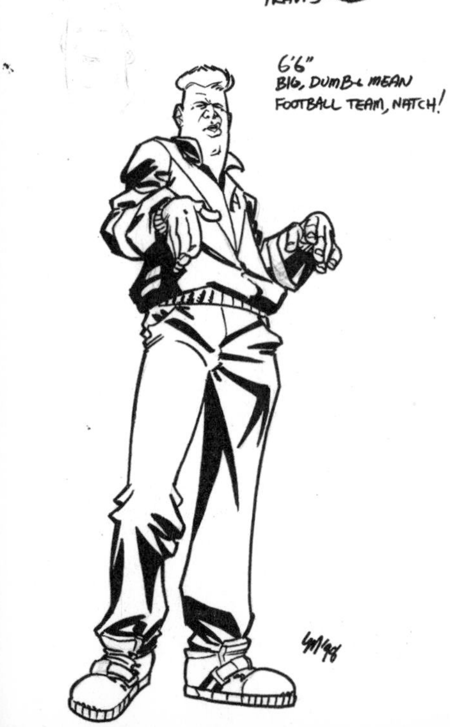
6'6"
BIG, DUMB & MEAN
FOOTBALL TEAM, NATCH!

THE NEW DRAGON KING

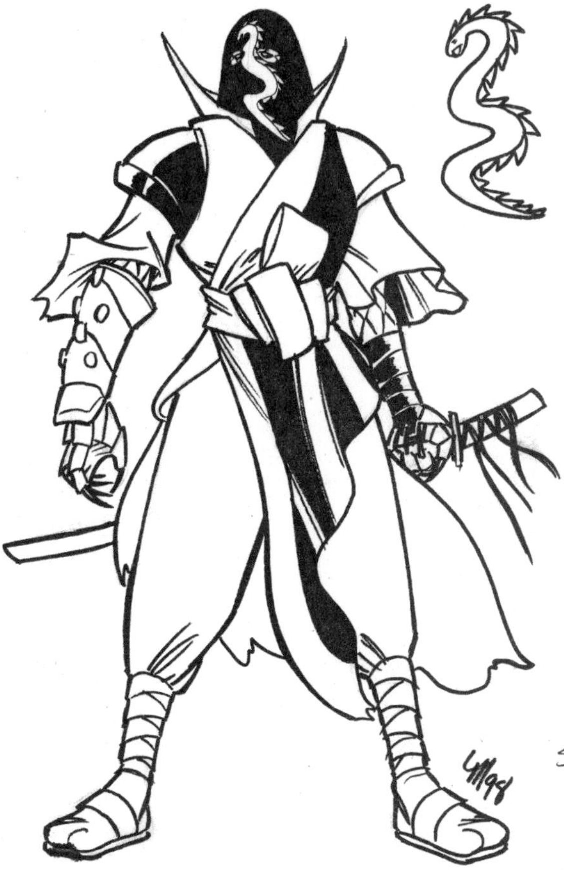

SHERMAN

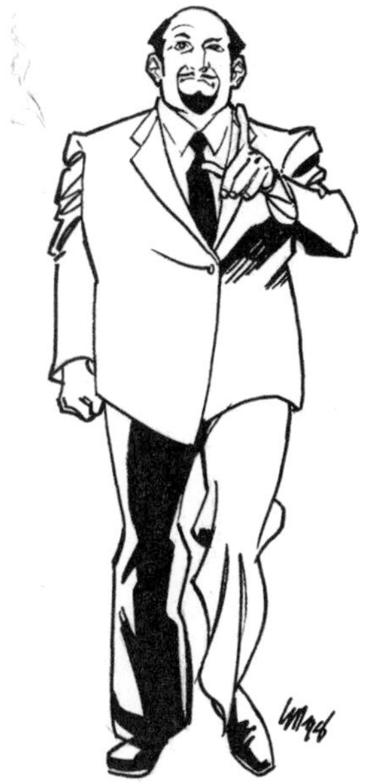

SKEETER

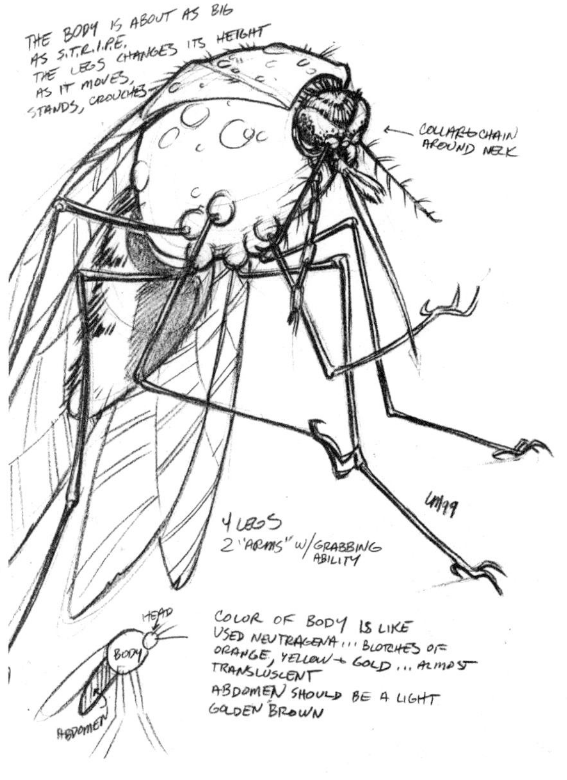
NOTE: ONLY FEMALE MOSQUITOES DRINK BLOOD
THE BODY IS ABOUT AS BIG AS S.T.R.I.P.E. THE LEGS CHANGES ITS HEIGHT AS IT MOVES, STANDS, CROUCHES
COLLAR&CHAIN AROUND NECK
4 LEGS
2 "ARMS" W/GRABBING ABILITY
HEAD
BODY
ABDOMEN
COLOR OF BODY IS LIKE USED NEUTRAGENA... BLOTCHES OF ORANGE, YELLOW + GOLD... ALMOST TRANSLUSCENT
ABDOMEN SHOULD BE A LIGHT GOLDEN BROWN

STUNT

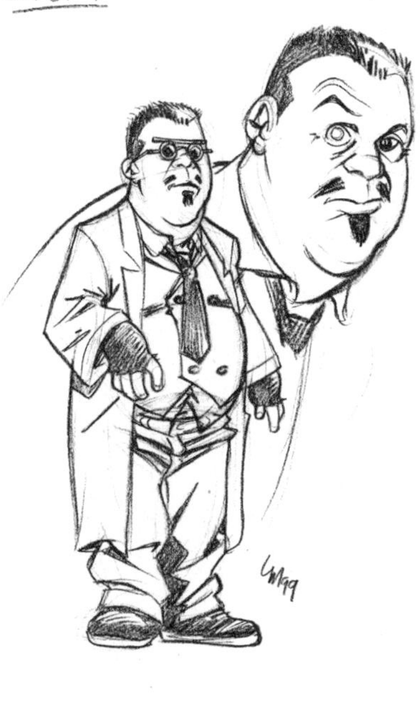

STARGIRL SKETCHBOOK

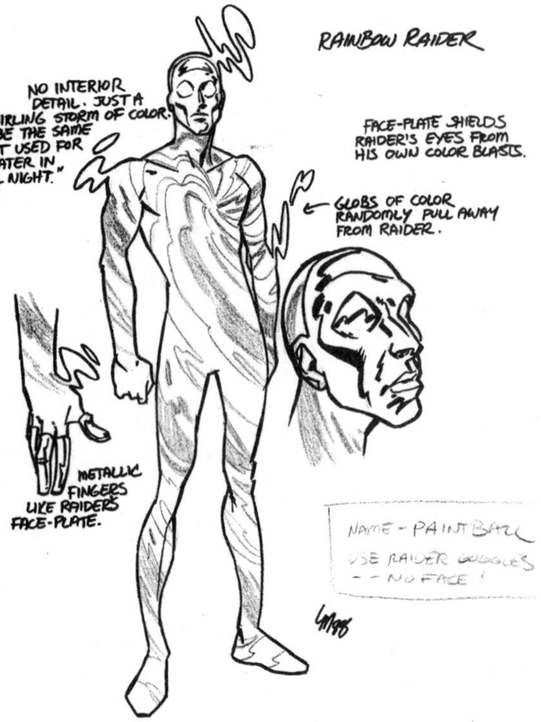
RAINBOW RAIDER
NO INTERIOR DETAIL. JUST A SWIRLING STORM OF COLOR. MAYBE THE SAME EFFECT USED FOR SUN-EATER IN "FINAL NIGHT."
FACE-PLATE SHIELDS RAIDER'S EYES FROM HIS OWN COLOR BLASTS.
GLOBS OF COLOR RANDOMLY PULL AWAY FROM RAIDER.
METALLIC FINGERS LIKE RAIDERS FACE-PLATE.
NAME - PAINTBALL
USE RAIDER GOGGLES
- - NO FACE!

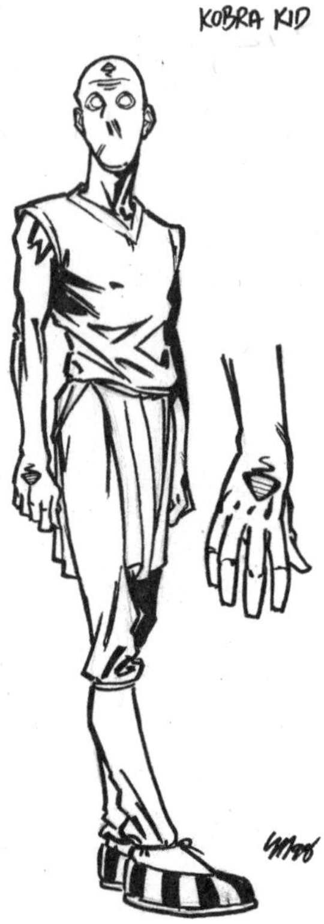
KOBRA KID

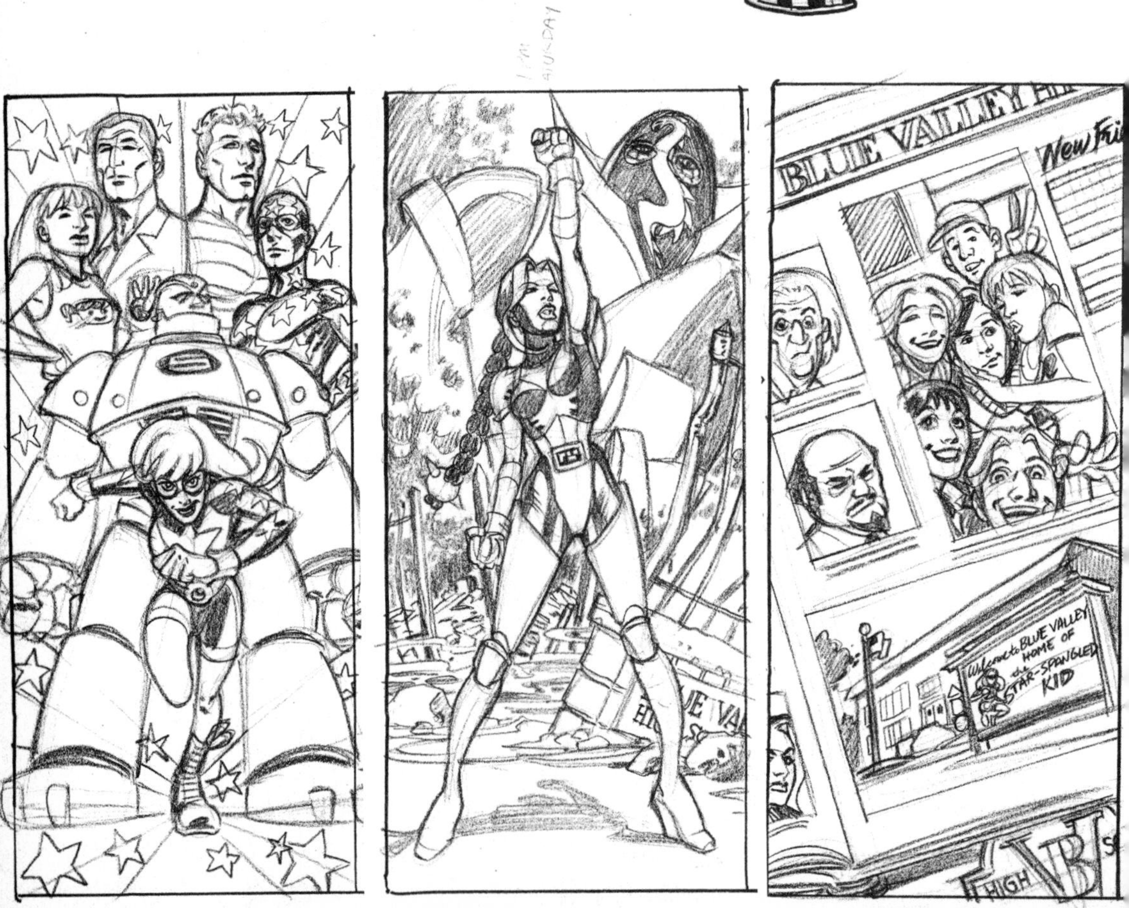
BLUE VALLEY
Welcome to BLUE VALLEY the HOME OF STAR-SPANGLED KID
HIGH

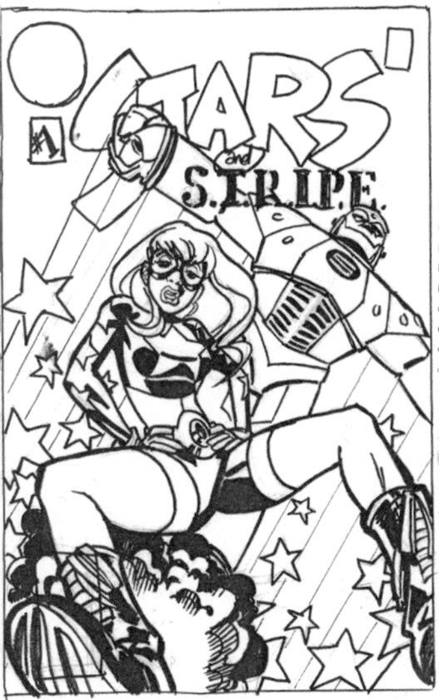
#1
STARS
and
S.T.R.I.P.E.

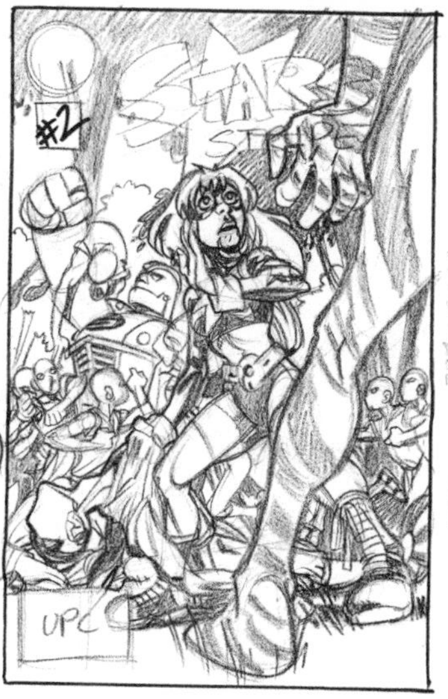
#2
STARS
UPC

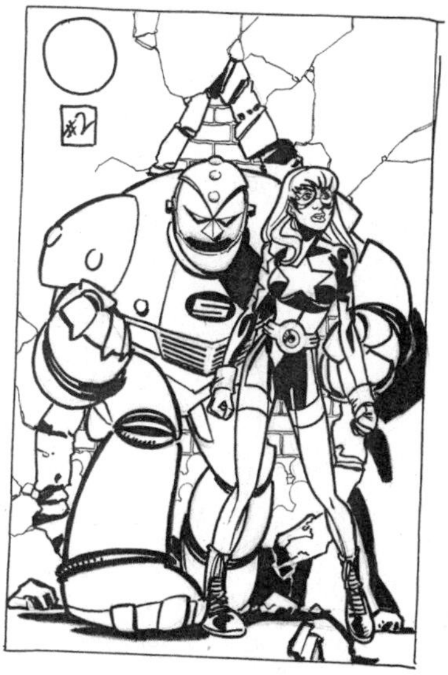
#2

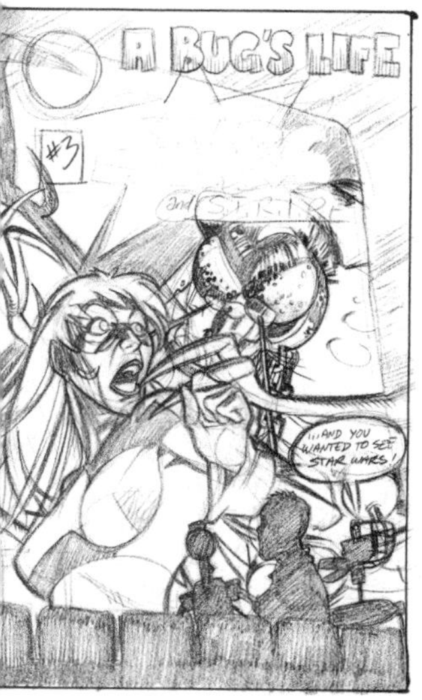
A BUG'S LIFE
#3
...AND YOU WANTED TO SEE STAR WARS!

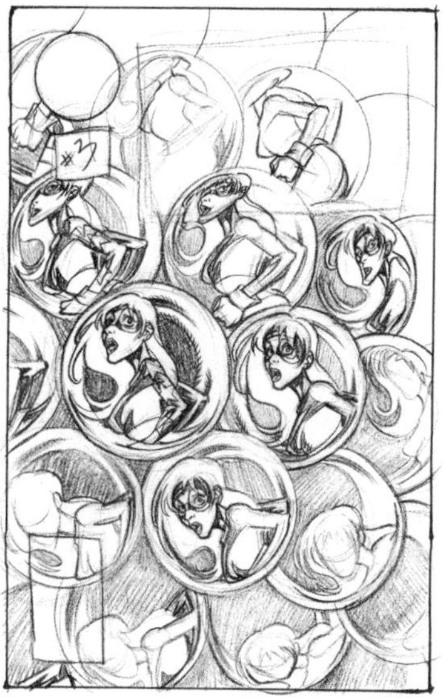
#3

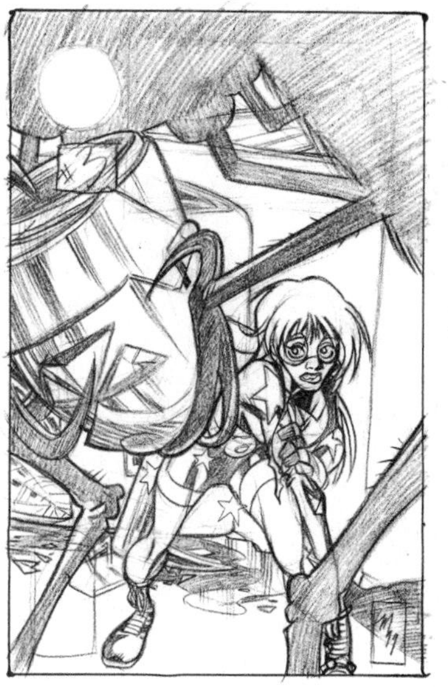

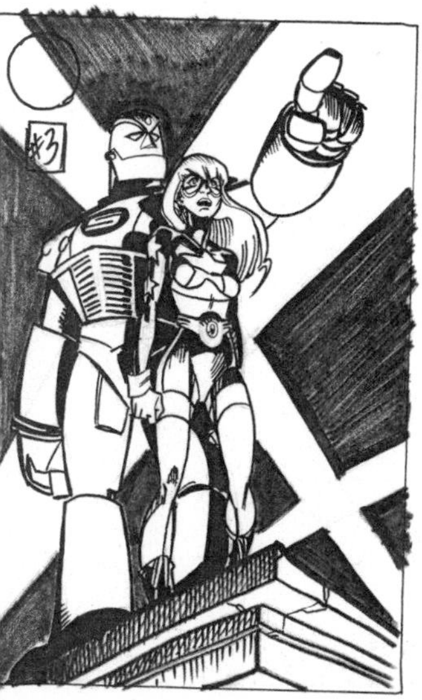
#3

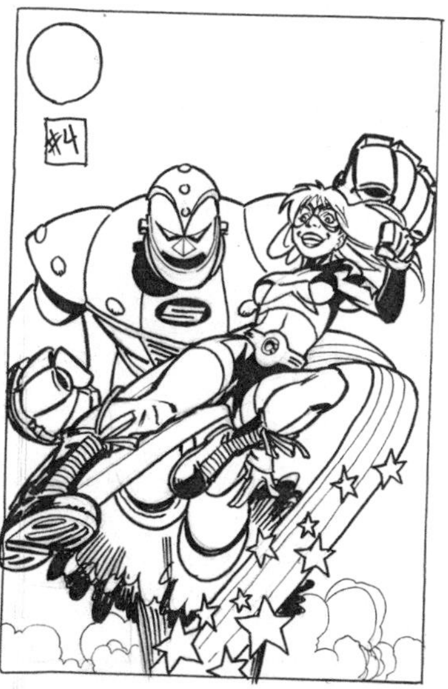
#4

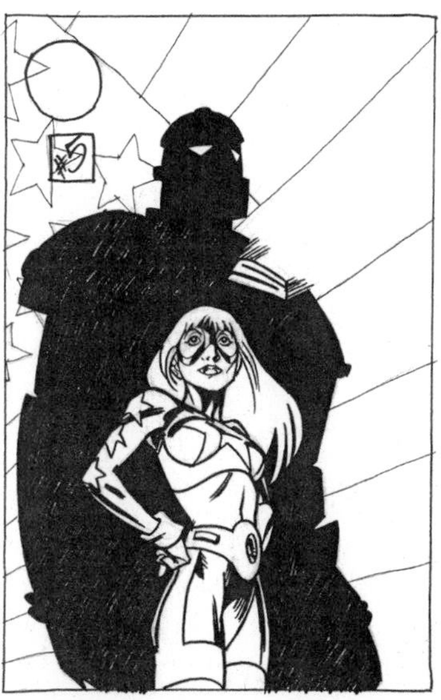
#5

STARGIRL SKETCHBOOK

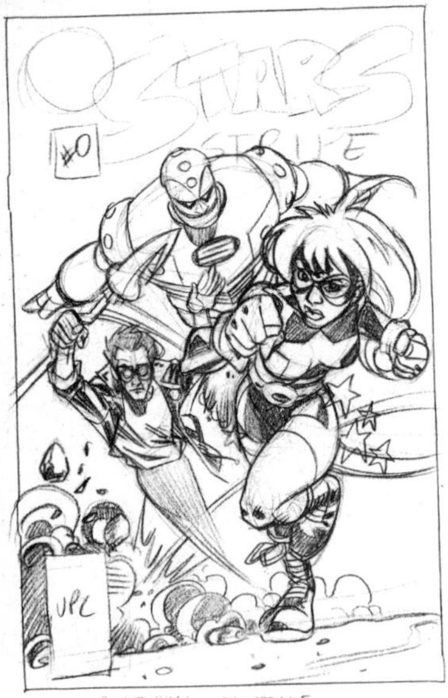
STARS
#0
UPC

PRIVATE RYAN _ THIN RED LINE

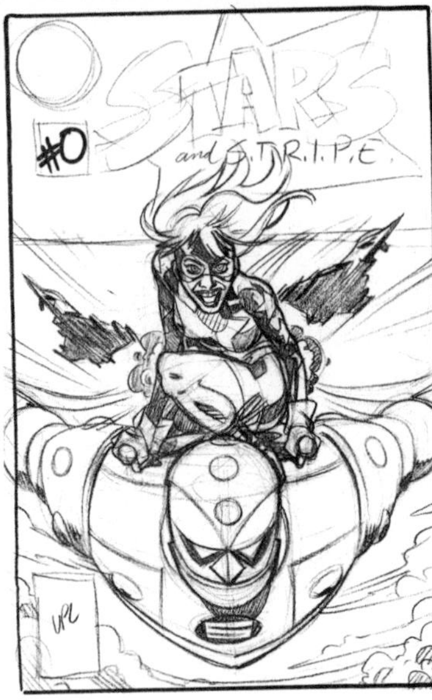
STARS
and S.T.R.I.P.E.
#0
UPC

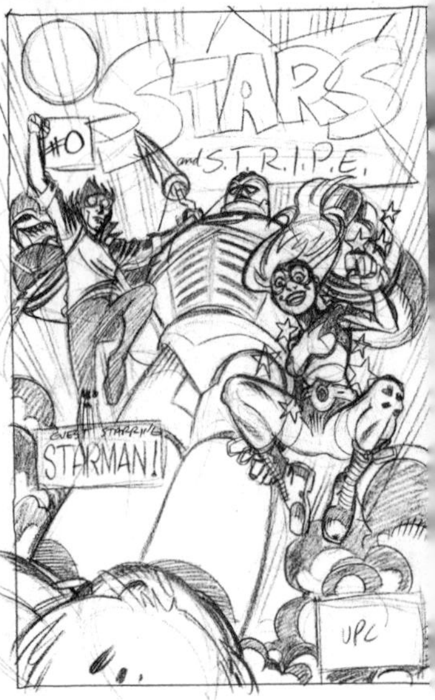
STARS
and S.T.R.I.P.E.
#0
GUEST STARRING
STARMAN!!
UPC

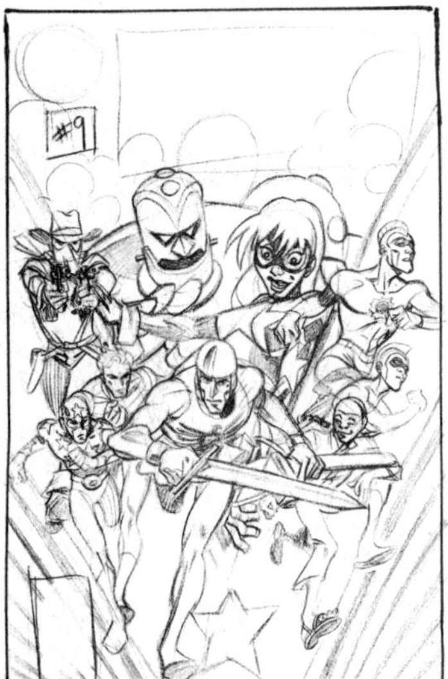
#9

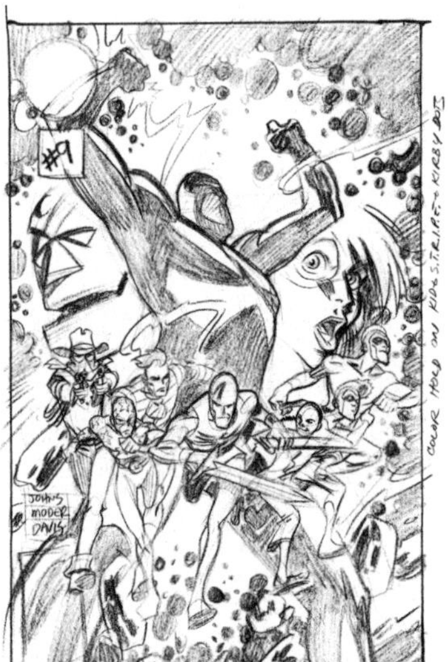
#9
JOHNS
MODER
DAVIS

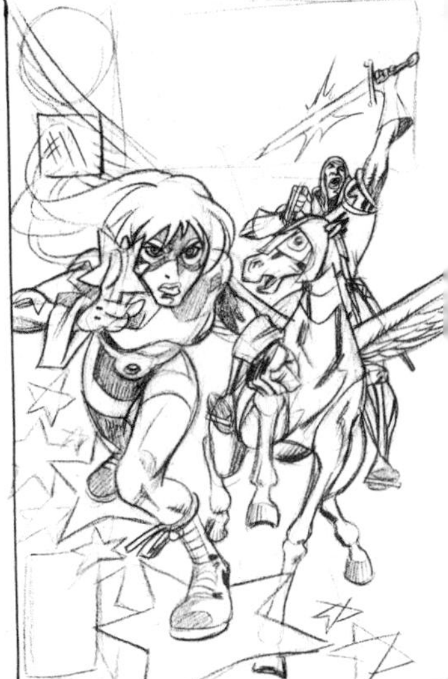
#11

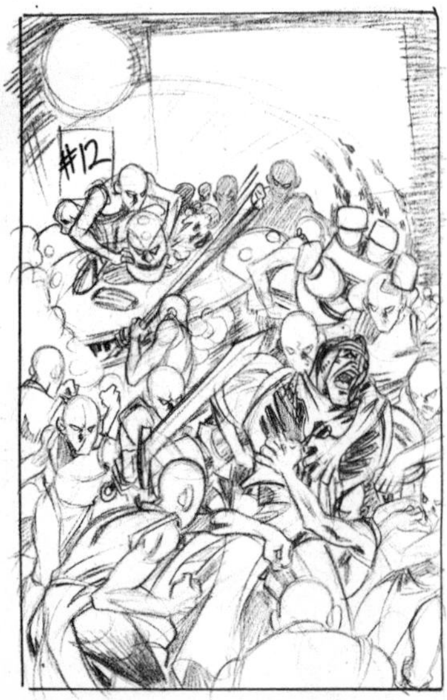
#12

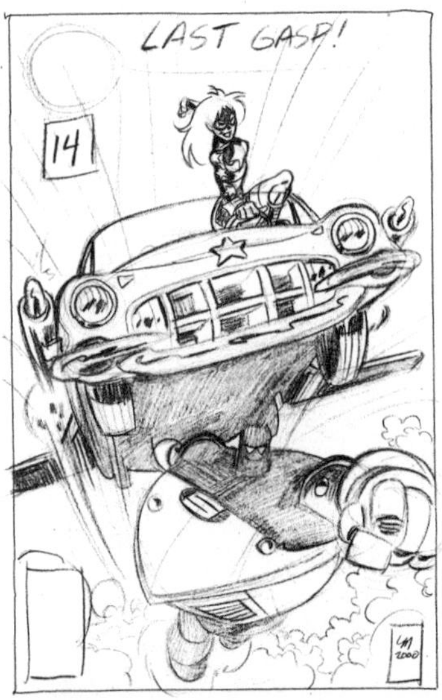
LAST GASP!
14

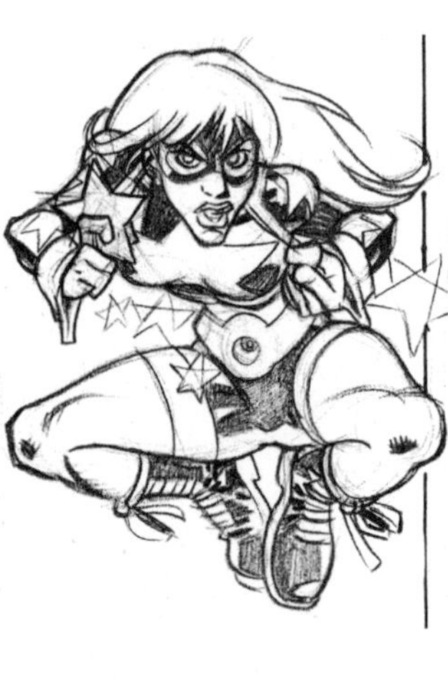